A CHECKLIST OF AMERICAN IMPRINTS for 1831

Items 5610 - 10775

compiled by

SCOTT BRUNTJEN

and

CAROL BRUNTJEN

The Scarecrow Press, Inc.

Metuchen, N.J. 1975

Printed in the United States of America

Library of Congress Card Catalog No. 64-11784

ISBN 0-8108-0828-5

PREFACE TO 1831

Unless a worker considers the philosophy and history of a tool's construction and design, his use of the tool will not only be difficult but may well be misguided. The novice bibliographer, upon discovering an 1831 pamphlet, for example, might be tempted to make a statement about it in the Evans' tradition: "Only one copy located by American Imprints!" This announcement might lend credence to the unknowing about the supposed scarcity of the publication in hand. Unfortunately, the design and purpose of American Imprints does not make such a comment legitimate.

A history of the present set can be pieced together from the prefaces of the 1820, the 1824, and the 1826 volumes. While the "preliminary" nature of the current work is stressed and while the reliance of the publication on somewhat sketchy and uneven intermediate sources is intimated, the user can not fully grasp the limitations and strengths of the work from these short paragraphs. The strength of the work is obvious. As Winchell notes, American Imprints probably lists eight times as many titles as Roorbach for the period covered. Experience leads the current compilers to feel that the work also significantly increases the scope of known American publishing currently reflected by the National Union Catalog; Pre-1956 Imprints. The presentation of one year of American publishing per volume undoubtedly does provide a first beginning for an examination of the publishing history of this nation as a whole. The basic reason for the bibliography, however, is to present a preliminary checklist of items published in America. Selected locations, which are provided from the WPA files, are intended to give a geographic spread. However, the holdings of these libraries, which were valid in the 1930's, have not been rechecked by the current compilers. The limitations of the work come, for the most part, from the resources searched. This checklist is a combination of work done by the WPA's

American Imprint Inventory cross-checked with the National Union Catalog, theses of the Catholic University, a variety of published bibliographies, and, to some extent, with the catalogue of the American Antiquarian Society. All of this comparison has the built-in limitation that it often returns to the same secondary source: the WPA. With the exception of the "United States" entries, few of the items entered have been personally examined by the compilers.

The work of the WPA varied in quality but most connected with the project seemed conscientious about their work. In an attempt to find a personal author for every work, one WPA cataloguer attributed several works to "Freeholder, A." A cross reference in the file noted that Crumbs from the Master's Table were to be found under the American Tract Society while the most tenuous location reported was for a copy of Horne's Introduction to the Critical Study and Knowledge of the Holy Scriptures. This work was located as follows: NCas (Not catalog--barn, second floor). Confidence in the WPA efforts, however, was increased after some supposed bibliographic puzzles were examined first hand at the American Antiquarian Society and at the State Library of Massachusetts. After two years of work on the 100,000 plus WPA slips for 1831, the compilers came to the dual conclusion that the work as presented was imperfect but needed.

There is no question that a volume of corrections and additions will be necessary to supplement the decade of the 1830's. The compilers request that reader's suggestions be forwarded to them at Box 502, Shippensburg State College, Shippensburg, Pennsylvania 17257. There is little doubt, however, that the present volume, like the several before it, will come to have solved many more problems than it has created. For this opportunity the compilers would like to express appreciation for the support of a Faculty Summer Research Grant from Shippensburg State College which provided the impetus to properly begin this project.

Scott Bruntjen
Carol Bruntjen

Shippensburg, Pennsylvania
January 1975

1831

A

Abbot, Abiel, 1770-1828.
Sermons, by the late Rev. Abiel Abbot... With a memoir of his life, by S. Everett. Boston, Pr. by John Putnam for Wait, Greene & Co., 1831. 297 p. DLC; ICMe; MB; MH; MeB. 5610

Abbot, John S.
An address delivered at the reorganization of the Temperance Society of Temple, December 1, 1831. Portland, Pr. by A. Shirley, 1831. 23 p. MBC; MeLewB; MH-AH 5611

[Abbott, Gorham D.] 1807-1874.
Memoir of Nathan W. Dickermen, Who Died at Boston, January 2, 1830, In the Eighth Year of His Age. By Gorham D. Abbott. Boston, Peirce & Parker, 1831. 184 p. CtHWatk; ICU; MAbD; MBAt; MeB. 5612

[----] ---- 2d ed. Boston, 1831. 140 p. MWA. 5613

[----] ---- 3d ed. Boston, Peirce, & Parker, 1831. 184 p. ICU; MB; MWA; NNUT. 5614

Abbott, Jacob, 1803-1879.
Early piety. Two sermons. 1 Sam. 3.19. New York, 1831. 15 p. MH-AH. 5615

[----] A lecture on moral education, delivered in Boston, before the American institute of instruction, Aug. 26, 1831. By Jacob Abbot. Boston, Hilliard, Gray, Little and Wilkins, 1831. 22 p. CBPSR; MB; MBC; MH-AH; MWA; WU. 5616

[----] The little philosopher; or, The infant school at home. No. III. By Erodore. Boston, Carter Hendee & Babcock, 1831. 34 p. NNC. 5617

Abercrombie, John, 1780-1844.
Pathological and practical researches on diseases of the brain and the spinal cord. By John Abercrombie... 1st American from the 2d Edinburgh ed., enl. Philadelphia, Carey & Lea, 1831. 464 p. ArU-M; CtY; DLC; ICJ; MH. 5618

Abert, John James, 1788-1863.
Report of Col. John J. Abert and Col. James Kearney, of the United States topographical engineers, upon an examination of the Chesapeake and Ohio canal from Washington City to the "Point of Rocks"; made by order of the secretary of war, at the request of the president and directors of the Chesapeake and Ohio canal company. Printed by order of the stockholders of the Chesapeake and Ohio canal company. Washington, Pr. by Gales and Seaton, 1831. 24 p. DLC; MdBJ; MdHi; NN. 5619

Abrams, Isaac
Trial of Isaac Abrams... for preaching in the public highways, Sunday morning April 17th, 1831; to which is added part of the trial of William Penn, & William

Mead, for preaching in the streets of London. Philadelphia, 1831. 20 p. MH; MH-L; PU. 5620

[----] The truth's come out at last. A true history of the Wild Methodist; (or odd man's experience)... Philadelphia, 1831. 36 p. MdHi; PHi. 5621

Abrantes, Laure Saint-Martin (Permon) Junot, (duchess d') 1784-1838.

Memoirs of the duchesse d'-Abrantes, (Madame Junot). New York, 1831-32. 2 vols. PPL; PPL-R. 5622

Academy of Natural Sciences. Philadelphia. See Philadelphia. Academy of Natural Sciences.

Adam, Alexander, 1741-1809.

Adam's Latin grammer, with some improvements, and the following additions: rules for the right pronunciation of the Latin language; a metrical key to the odes of Horace; a list of Latin authors arranged according to the different ages of Roman literature, tables showing the value of different coins, weights, and measures, used among Romans. By Benjamin A. Gould... Boston, Hilliard, Gray, Little, and Wilkins [etc.] 1831. 299 p. DLC; ICU; MH; NNC; PPM. 5623

---- Latin Grammar, with the following additions: the ancient and modern pronunciation of the Latin language; observations on the cellinable parts of speech, rules for the government of the subjunctive mood, and with various improvements. By David Patterson. New York, Collins, 1831. 276 p. InCW; MoS; OO; OrU. 5624

---- Rudiments of Latin and English grammar... By James D. Johnson... Philadelphia, Key & Mielke, 1831. DLC; MH; PPL. 5625

Adams, Daniel, 1773-1864.

Answer of Daniel Adams to the reply of Roswell C. Smith (relating to a charge of plagiarism). [Mt. Vernon, N.H. ? 1831?] 18 p. MiU; MWA; NhDo. 5626

---- Geography; or a description of the world. ...accompanied with an atlas. ...By Daniel Adams. 13th ed. Boston, Lincoln & Edmonds, 1831. 336 p. InSbNHi; InU; MH. 5627

Adams, Elisha, defendant.

The Masonic trials. Lockport, Feb. 28, 1831. Special circuit--Niagara county. The people vs. Elisha Adams. Judge Nelson presiding. [Ann Arbor? 1831?] 16 p. CSmH. 5628

Adams, John.

The flowers of celebrated travellers; being a selection from the most elegant, entertaining and instructive travels. Baltimore, Pr. by J. Matchett, 1831. 473 p. MdW; NSYU. 5629

Adams, John Quincy, 6th pres. U.S., 1767-1848.

An eulogy, on the life and character of James Monroe, fifth president of the United States. Delivered at the request of the corporation of the city of Boston, on the 25th of August, 1831. By John Quincy Adams... Boston, J. H. Eastburn, city printer, 1831. 96 p. CU; MB; MeB; O; VtU. 5630

---- An oration addressed to the citizens of the town of Quincy, on the fourth of July, 1831, the fifty-fifth anniversary of the independence of the United States of America. By John Quincy Adams. Boston, Richardson, Lord and

Holbrook, 1831. 40 p. CoU; DLC; ICU; MH; ScCC. 5631

Adams Female Academy. Derry, N. H.
A General View of the Plan of Education pursued at The Adams Female Academy. Exeter, N. H., Pr. by S. Adams, 1831. 12 p. MB; MeB; MH; Nh-Hi. 5632

Addicks, Barbara O'Sullivan.
Essay on education; in which the subject is treated as a natural science: in a series of short familiar lectures. Published periodically. By Mrs. Barbara O'-Sullivan Addicks. Philadelphia, Pr. by Martin & Boden, for the Author, 1831. 29 p. DLC; MBAt; MdHi; PHi; PPM. 5633

Address to the Calvinistic Society in Springfield. Springfield, from the press of S. Bowles, July 1831. 15 p. NN. 5634

An address to the churches on the subjects of slavery. Georgetown, Ohio, D. Ammen & Co., Printers, August 5, 1831. OClWHi. 5635

An address to the freemen of Rhode Island. By a land holder. Providence, Pr. at the Herald office, 1831. 16 p. NN. 5636

Address to the Friends of domestic industry assembled in Convention, at New York, October 26, 1831... Baltimore, 1831. DLC. 5637

An address to the friends of the railroad from Philadelphia to Reading, proposed to be located on the west side of the river Schuylkill. Pub. by direction of the meeting at the "Bull Tavern," held 9th of the 5th mo. (May) 1831--for the use of the committees. Philadelphia, Pr. by W. Brown, 1831. 8 p. ICJ; NN; PHi; PPGi. 5638

An address to the leaders of the abstinence enterprise. By a friend of temperance... 2d ed. with additions and corrections. Pr. for the author, 1831. 11 p. CtY. 5639

Address to the youth of the Society of Friends. New York, 1831. 8 p. PHi; PPULC. 5640

The adventures of a Yankee; or The Singular life of John Ledyard; with an account of his voyage round the world with the celebrated Captain Cooke. Designed for a youth. By a Yankee. Boston, Carter, Hendee, and Babcock, 1831. 90 p. CtY; DLC; ICBB; PHi; PPULC. 5641

Aesopus, 570 B.C.
Fables of Aesop, and others, translated into English, with instructive Applications and a print before each fable. By Samuel Croxall, D.D. Late Archdeacon of Hereford. New-York, Pr. by W. E. Dean, 1831. 276 p. CtMW; MBU-E; MH. 5642

---- ---- Philadelphia, Simon Probasco, 1831. 358 p. DLC; LNH; MH; NjP; PU. 5643

The Affecting History of the Children in the woods. see Children in the woods.

Affecting Scenes: Being Passages from the Diary of a Physician. New York, J. and J. Harper, 1831. 352 p. CtY-M; DLC; MH; NcD; PPL. 5644

...The affectionate daughter. New York, Pub. by the American Tract Society, 183-? 16 p. NN. 5645

Affection's gift; or Religious Conversations. Boston, N.S. & S. G. Simpkins, 1831. 62 p. MB; NN; PP. 5646

Aikin, Jesse.
The citizen's tutor, containing a variety of valuable receipts, for the cure of different diseases of man & beast: also for colouring wool, cotton, and hats... Mountpleasant, [Ohio] 1831. 106 p. DNLM. 5647

Aiken, John, 1747-1822.
Evenings at Home; or The Juvenile Budget opened; consisting of a variety of Miscellaneous pieces, for the instruction and amusement of Young Persons. New ed. Illustrated by 100 engravings. Philadelphia, T. Desilver; Pittsburg, John I. Kay & Co., 1831. 2 vols. 291 p. ICBB; MtUrAc; NNS; OO; ScCMu. 5648

Ainsworth, Robert, 1660-1743.
An abridgment of Ainsworth's dictionary, English and Latin, designed for the use of schools. By Thomas Morell, D.D. carefully corrected and improved from the last London quarto edition by John Carey, LL.D. Philadelphia, Uriah Hunt; New-York, J. & J. Harper, and Collins & Hannay; Boston, Richardson & Lord, and Hilliard, Gray, & co. 1831. 1028 p. CoU; DLC; MB; MiU; PPA; PPULC; PU. 5649

---- A new abridgement of Ainsworth's dictionary. English and Latin, for the use of grammar schools. Into this edition are introduced several alterations and improvements...by John Dymock, LL.D. 1st American ed., with corrections and improvements, by Charles Anthon. New York, Sleight, 1831. 405 p. Ia; MB; NN; OO. 5650

---- ---- Philadelphia, Hunt, 1831. 405 p. NcBe; ODaJ; PPCP. 5651

Alabama.
Acts passed at the twelfth annual session of the general assembly of the state of Alabama, begun and held in the town of Tuscaloosa, on the third Monday in November, one thousand eight hundred and thirty. Gabriel Moore, governor. Samuel B. Moore, president of the senate. James Penn, speaker of the house of representatives. Tuscaloosa, Pr. by Wiley, M'Guire, & Henry, state printers, 1831. 80 p. AU-L; DLC; ICLow; In-SC; MH-L; NNB; NNLI; RPL; PU-L; BrMus. 5652

---- Journal of the House of Representatives, of the State of Alabama. Begun and held at the Town of Tuscaloosa, on the Third Monday in November, 1830. Being the twelfth annual session, of the General Assembly of said State. Tuscaloosa, Pr. by Wiley, McGuire and Henry, 1831. 274 p. A-SC. 5653

---- Journal of the Senate of the state of Alabama. Begun and held at the town of Tuscaloosa, on the third Monday in November, 1830. Being the twelfth annual session of the General Assembly of said State. Tuscaloosa, Pr. by Wiley, McGuire and Henry, 1831. 198 p. A-SC; BrMus. 5654

Alabama. University.
Annual catalog of University of Alabama. 1831. AU. 5655

---- Ordinances and resolutions of the board of trustees, of the University of Alabama, which are of a general and public nature, passed since the session of 1826,---and some previous to that period---up to the close of the session, on the 15th of January, 1831. Together with a list of the trustees and professors of the University. Tuscaloosa, Pr. by Jno. R. Hampton, 1831. 30 p. AU; DLC. 5656

Albany Academy.
The Statutes. ...Albany, Pr. by Webster and Skinners, 1831. 33 p. NN. 5657

[Albany and Schenectady Turnpike Company]
Remonstrance against the application of Mohawk and Hudson Rail-Road Company. 1831. Broadside. NN. 5658

---- Report, made to the president and directors of the Albany and Schenectady turnpike company, upon laying a railroad upon their turnpike, made August 1831, by William M. Cushman, engineer. [Albany? 1831] 15 p. CSt; MB; NN. 5659

The Albany directory and city register... Compiled by E. B. Child & W. H. Shiffer. Albany, Pr. by E. B. Child, 1831. MiD-B. 5660

Albany. Society for the relief of Orphan and destitute children.
The constitution and by-laws of the Society for the Relief of Orphan and Destitute Children, in the city of Albany; together with the report of the managers, to which is added An address, delivered by the Rev. E. N. Kirk, at the anniversary of the society, held at St. Peter's Church, January 13, 1831. Albany, J. B. Van Steenbergh, 1831. 51 p. MB; MH-AH; NN; NbU. 5661

The Album, or Panacea for Ennui. Fitchburg, Pub. by the editor, 1831. 168 p. MFiHi; RPB. 5662

Alexander, Archibald, 1772-1831.
Evidences of the authenticity, inspiration, and canonical authority of the Holy Scriptures. By the Rev. Archibald Alexander... Philadelphia, Presbyterian board of publication [183-?] 308 p. DLC; MB; NjP; WaWW. 5663

---- A pocket dictionary of the Holy Bible. Containing, a historical and geographical account of the persons and places mentioned in the Old and New Testaments... Prepared for the American S. S. union, and adapted to general use. By Archibald Alexander... Rev. by the committee of publications... 7th ed. Philadelphia, American Sunday school union, 1831. 546 p. CU; ICB; MB; NjR; PLT; ViRU. 5664

---- A Selection of Hymns, Adapted to the devotions of the closet, the family, the social circle; and containing subjects appropriate to the monthly concerts of prayer for the success of missions and Sunday schools; and other special occasions. By Archibald Alexander. New-York, Pub. by Jonathan Leavitt; Boston, Crocker & Brewster; Stereotyped by James Conner, 1831. 624 p. DLC; NjPT; PPPrHi; ViRut. 5665

Alexander, James Waddell, 1804-1859.
Suggestions in vindication of the temperance society; originally published in "Biblical repertory and theological review." Philadelphia, Russel & Martier, 1831. 18 p. MH-AH; NjPT; NjP; PPL; PPPrHi. 5666

Alger, Israel, Jr.
The orthoepical guide to the English tongue, being Perry's spelling book revised and

corrected... Boston, Richardson, Lord & Holbrook, 1831. 168 p. MLy. 5667

Alighieri, Dante.
Inferno, translated from the original...by the Rev. Henry Francis Cary and illustrated by Gustave Dore. By Dante Alighieri. Edited by Henry C. Walsh. Philadelphia, H. Altemus [1831?] 163 p. MS. 5668

Allcott, William W.
Allcott's produce tables showing the value of any quantity of grain estimated at sixty pounds to the bushel.... Rochester, Pr. by Marshall & Dean, 1831. 128 p. DLC; NRHi. 5669

Allen, Ethan.
A sermon preached at the convention of the Protestant Episcopal church in Ohio, Gambier, September 9, 1831, by Rev. Ethan Allen. Pub. by request of Rt. Rev. Bishop Philander Chase, D.D. [Ohio? 1831?] 12 p. MdBD; MdBP; MdHi. 5670

Allen, Joseph, 1790-1873.
Questions on select portions of the four evangelists. Part second, comprising the principal discourses and parables of Our Lord, Designed for the higher classes in Sunday schools. By Joseph Allen... Boston, Gray and Bowen, 1831. 124 p. DLC; IEG; MB; MNee. 5671

Allen, Joseph W.
Address delivered before the North Kingstown Temperance Society at their annual meeting... in Wickford on Saturday, May 25, 1831. Wickford, R.I., Pr. by J. J. Brenton, 1831. 15 p. RP. 5672

Allen, William, 1770-1843.
Brief remarks upon the carnal and spiritual state of man... Mountpleasant, 1831. 23 p. OClWHi; WRHist. 5673

Allen, William, 1784-1868.
Account of Arnold's expedition. In collection of the Maine Historical Society. Portland, Day, Frazer and Company, 1831. DLC; MN; OCl; OFH; OO. 5674

Allyn, Avery
Allyn's Anti-Masonic Almanac for the year 1832...the fifth after the Murder of Morgan. Philadelphia, Clarke [1831] 24 p. DLC; MB; MWA. 5675

----The book of oaths and penalties of the regular, honorary and ineffable degrees of symbolic and Knighthood masonry. Philadelphia, John Clarke, 1831. 96 p. IaCrM; MB; NN; PHi; PPFM. 5676

---- A ritual of freemasonry, illustrated by numerous engravings; with notes and remarks. To which is added a key to the Phi Beta Kappa. By Avery Allyn... Boston, John Marsh and co., 1831. 302 p. CtY; IaCrM; MB; MH; NN; PCC; PPFM. 5677

---- ---- Philadelphia, John Clarke, 1831. 269 p. DLC; MdBE; NN; OMC. 5678

Alvari, Emmanuelis.
Emmanuelis Alvari e Societate Jesu prosodia sive institutionum linguae Larinae liber quartus. In usum Studiosorum Societatis Jesu. Premissu superiorum. Geortiopoli, D. C., Typis Samuelis S. Rind, 1831. 73 p. DWP; NjMD. 5679

---- Prosodia linguae Latinae, by Emmanuel Alvari. Georgetown, D.C., n.p., 1831. NjMD. 5680

Amendment; or, Charles Grant & his Sister... New York, J. A.

Clussman, 1831. 36 p. N; PP. 5681

American Academy of the Fine Arts. See New York. American Academy of the Fine Arts

The American advertising directory for manufacturers and dealers. New York, Jocelyn, Darling & Co., 1831-32. Ct; MB; MWHi; NBj; PHi; WHi. 5682

The American almanac and repository of useful knowledge, for the year 1832. Boston, Gray and Bowen, and Carter and Hendee, 1831. 312 p. C; NNA; PMA; WM. 5683

American Annals of education and instruction; being a continuation of The American Journal of Education. Boston, Carter & Hendee, 1831-1839. InCW; MBAt; MH; MNBedf; MoSW; NjR; OO. 5684

The American annual register for the year 1829-30 or the 54th year of American Independence. Boston, Gray & Bowen; New York, L. & G. Blunt, 1831. 875 p. NNLI; NSchHi; NPV; NUtHi; PHi. 5685

American antiquarian society, Worcester, Mass.

By-laws of the American antiquarian society. 24th October, 1831. [Worcester? 1831] 7 p. CSmH; MH-AH; MnHi; WHi. 5686

American Baptist Foreign Mission Society.

Report of the Baptist Board of Foreign Missions, at its annual meeting, Providence [R.I.] 32 p. NRAB; PCA 5687

American Board of Commissioners for Foreign Missions.

Condition and character of females in pagan and Mohammedan countries. [Boston, 183-?] 16 p. MB. 5688

---- Containing the proceedings at large of the American Board of Commissioners for Foreign Missions; with a general view of other benevolent operations. For the year 1831. ...Boston, Pr. by Crocker & Brewster [1831] 400 p. ICP. 5689

---- Missionary Paper, No. XVII. On deciding early to become a Missionary to the heathen. 2d ed. 1831. Boston, Pr. by Crocker & Brewster [1831] 16 p. MiD-B. 5690

---- Missions will not impoverish in the country. By D. P. Kimball & L. Beecher. Boston, (n.p. n. pub.) 1831. 12 p. NjPT. 5691

---- Report of the American Board of Commissioners for Foreign Missions, read at the twenty-second annual meeting, which was held in the City of New Haven, Conn., Oct. 5, 6, and 7, 1831. Boston, Pr. for the board by Crocker and Brewster, 1831. 119 p. MA. 5692

---- Statements respecting the necessities and claims of the Missions and Missionaries, under the direction of the American board of commissioners for foreign Missions. April 1831. Ed. 2. New York [Pr. by Sleight and Robinson] 1831. 23 p. MB; MH-AH; NNMr; WHi. 5693

The American Christian Expositor, designed to promote the influence of sound principles and social order. Monthly periodical...Conducted by Alexander McLeod, D.D. New York, H. C. Sleight, 1831. DLC; GDecCT; MoWgT; NjP; PPPrHi. 5694

The American citizen. Two sermons on the State fast. Boston, 1831. PPL. 5695

American Colonization Society.
A few facts respecting the American Colonization Society & the Colony at Liberia. Boston, 1831. 16 p. PHi. 5696

---- Report made at an adjourned meeting of the friends of the American colonization society, in Worcester County, held in Worcester, Dec. 8, 1830, by a committee appointed for that purpose, with the proceedings of the meeting, etc. Worcester, Pr. by S. H. Colton and co., 1831. 20 p. M; MA; N; PHi; RP. 5697

---- Board of Managers.
Address of the Board of managers of the American colonization society to its auxiliary societies. Washington, Pr. by Gales and Seaton, 1831. 11 p. CtY; DLC; MA; MdHi; N. 5698

The American comic almanac, for 1832. With Whims... Boston, Charles Ellms [1831] 36 p. Ct; ICN; MBAt; MH; NcD. 5699

---- Philadelphia, John Grigg [1831] MWA. 5700

American Education Society.
Report of the American Education Society. Fifteenth Annual Report. 1831. Boston, Pr. by Perkins & Marvin, 1831. 63 p. CSt; Ct; MeB. 5701

The American Farmers' Almanack, being Leap Year, and the 56th of the Independence of the United States. Carefully calculated for the Horizon of Maryland, Pennsylvania and Virginia but will serve for the adjacent states, without material variation. By Charles F. Egelmann. Hagerstown, Md., Pr. and sold by J. Gruber, 1831. 24 p. IaHA; MdBSHG; MH; MWA. 5702

American Institute of Instruction.
The Act of incorporation, constitution and by-laws of the American Institute of instruction. Boston, Classic press, I. R. Butts [1831] 11 p. DLC; MBC; MH; MHi; PPAmP; PPL. 5703

---- Annual meetings of the American institute of instruction... Proceedings, constitution, list of active members, and addresses. Pub. by order of the Board of directors. Boston, Hilliard, Gray, Little and Wilkins & Carter, Hendee and Co., 1831-. CSt; CU; InCW; NjR; PPL. 5704

---- The lectures delivered before the... Institute see its Annual meeting.

The American Lancet.
Report of the trial on indictment for libel, in "The American Lancet," containing the whole evidence,...accusers in behalf of the state, Drs. J. B. Beck, E. G. Ludlow, and divers others, against Dr. J. G. Vought, editor and proprietor of the American Lancet, Dr. Wm. Anderson, asst. ed. & Dr. Samuel Osborn, one of the contributors. New-York, January 28, 1831. 48 p. DLC; NNNAM; PPPH. 5705

American library of useful knowledge. Published by authority of The Boston Society for the diffusion of useful knowledge. Boston, Stimpson & Clapp, 1831. CtY; IaHi; MH; MiU; NjP. 5706

American Lyceum, with the proceedings of the Convention held in New York May 4, 1831, to organize the National Department of the Institution. Boston, Pr. by Hiram Tupper, 1831. 31 p. KyDC; MB; MdBD; MnU; OClW; ScC. 5707

The American naval and patriotic songster. As sung at various places of amusement, in honor of Hull, Jones, Decatur, Perry, Bainbridge, Lawrence, &c, &c. &c. ...Baltimore, Pr. by Wm. Wooddy, for G. M'Dowell & son, 1831. 256 p. CSmH; MdHi; RPB; WHi. 5708

American naval battles: being a complete history of the battles fought by the navy of the United States from its establishment in 1794 to the present time, including the war with France, and with Tripoli, the late war with Great Britain, and with Algiers: with an account of the attack on Baltimore, and of the battle of New Orleans. With twenty-one elegant engravings, representing battles, etc. Boston, J. J. Smith, Jr., 1831. 278 p. CLU; ICHi; MH; PHi. 5709

American Philosophical Society, Philadelphia.

Letter to General Lafayette; dated Philadelphia, Feb. 7, 1831; encloses a letter announcing election to membership in the American philosophical society to be presented to his illustrious monarch Louis Philippe [1831] 1 p. PPAmP; PPULC. 5710

---- Letter to Louis Philippe, the first, King of the French; dated Philadelphia, February 7, 1831; announces his election to membership in the Society. 2 p. PPAmP; PPULC. 5711

---- Committee on astronomical observations.

Report on astronomical observations in different parts of the U.S. on the solar eclipse of Feb. 12, 1831. A.D. Bache, Jos. Roberts, jr. Isaiah Lukens, Committee of the Society. Phys. Sci. T. v. 1. [1831] PPAn. 5712

An American Physician, five thousand receipts in all useful... See MacKenzie, Colin.

American pioneer and military chronicle, Mar. 5, 1831-February 25, 1832. Philadelphia, 1831-32. PPL; PHi; PPUCC. 5713

American practical catechism, for use of schools, compiled by the aid of persons of various denominations; to which are annexed instructive lessons for youth. 4th ed. New York, Day, 1831. 35 p. PU. 5714

The American pulpit; a series of Original Sermons, by clergymen of the Protestant Episcopal Church. Published Monthly. Boston, Putnam & Hunt; Philadelphia, E. Little, 1831. Paging varied. MBD; MdBD; MHi; INID. 5715

The American rail-road journal. New York, D. K. Minor, 1831. ICLaw; NjR. 5716

The American repertory of arts, sciences, and useful literature. By M. T. C. Gould. Philadelphia, M. T. C. Gould, 1831. OrU. 5717

American Seamen's Friend Society.

Third annual report of the American seamen's friend society . ...New-York, Pr. by J. Seymour, 1831. 32 p. MeBaT; NNG. 5718

American Society for Educating Pious Youth for the Gospel Ministry. See American Education Society.

[American society for encouraging a settlement of the Oregon territory]
...Book of stock, subscriptions, &c....[Boston, Pr. by S. N. Dickinson, 1831] DLC. 5719

American Society for Encouraging a Settlement of the Oregon Territory.
[Certificate no. 26 of stock, signed by the president and secretary of the society; with the society's seal, dated 1831; the blanks not filled in. Boston, S. N. Dickinson, 1831-?] pp. (2). Attached is the stub for certificate no. 25, signed by C. C. Smith. 5720

---- An extract of the committee's report. 1831. 3 p. PPULC; PPAmP. 5721

----A general circular to all persons of good character who wish to emigrate to the Oregon territory, embracing some account of the character and advantages of the country, the right and the means and operations by which it is to be settled;--and all necessary directions for becoming an emigrant...Charlestown, W. W. Wheildon, 1831. 28 p. MH; NN; PHi; PPL. OrHi. 5722

---- The Oregon country; a circular to the citizens of the U. States. [n.p., 1831?] Broadside. CtY. 5723

American Society of Free Persons of Colour, for Improving Their Condition.
...Constitution of the society, also the proceedings of the convention, with their address to the free persons of colour in the U.S. Philadelphia, 1831. 12 p. CtY; PPL; PPULC. 5724

American Sunday-School Union.
The bow in the cloud. Written for the American Sunday School Union & revised by the Committee of publication. Philadelphia, American Sunday School Union [c1831] 24 p. NNU-W. 5725

---- Busy bee, revised by the committee of publication of the American Sunday School Union. Philadelphia, American Sunday School Union, c1831. 24 p. MWal; NUt; PU. 5726

---- Constitution of the American Sunday School Union; with the by-laws of the board, list of officers, Managers, and committees, 1831-32. Philadelphia, American Sunday School Union, 1831. 8 p. MBAt; NjPT; PPPAmP; PPULC; PPWa. 5727

---- Ellen: or the Disinterested Girl. Philadelphia (Pub. by the American Sunday School Union) 1831. 36 p. IaU; TU. 5728

---- Helen and her cousin. Written for the American Sunday School Union. Revised by the Committee of publication. Philadelphia, New York [etc.] American Sunday-School Union [c1831] 71 p. PSt; PPULC; WHi. 5729

---- A Help to the Acts of the Apostles adapted to the lesson system of reading and teaching the Scriptures and embodying the "Excercises on the Acts," used by children in learning that book. New-York, J. Leavitt, etc., 1831. 284 p. CtHC; GDecCT; MB; MBC; MH. 5730

---- Hints to aid the Organization and Support of Sabbath Schools in the Country. 6th ed. Philadelphia, 1831. 10 p. CtY; IU; MBC; MH. 5731

---- Memoirs of Augustus

Hermann Francke. Prepared for the American Sunday school union, and revised by the Committee of Publication. Philadelphia, American Sunday school union, 1831. 180 p. CSmH; ICU; MdBD; OClW; PU; ScNC. 5732

---- Nursery lessons,...revised by the committee of publication of the American Sunday-school union. American Sunday-school union. Philadelphia, 1831. 16 p. NNC. 5733

---- The patient pastor. Revised by the Committee of publication of the American Sunday school union. Philadelphia, American Sunday school union, 1831. 16 p. NNC 5734

---- Prayers suitable for children and Sunday schools... Philadelphia, American Sunday-school union, 1831. 86 p. NNU. 5735

---- Proceedings at the seventh Anniversary of the American Sunday school union with the addresses of Messrs. Reese, Cookman and Tappan. Philadelphia, American Sunday school Union, 1831. 32 p. DLC; ICU; OMC; PPWa; WHi. 5736

---- Proceedings of the public meeting held in Boston, to aid the American Sunday School Union, in their efforts to establish sunday schools throughout the Valley of the Mississippi. Philadelphia, American Sunday School Union, 1831. 23 p. DLC; ICP; MBC; NNUT; PP; WHi. 5737

---- Review of the annual report of the St. Louis, (Mo.) Sunday School Union of the Methodist Episcopal Church. Philadelphia, American Sunday School Union, 1831. 22 p. MB; MH; NjPT; WHi. 5738

---- Seventh report of the American Sunday School Union, May 24, 1831. 2nd ed. Philadelphia, American Sunday School Union, 1831. 42 p. IaCec; ICP; MA; OSW; PCA. 5739

----Short discourses, illustrating several interesting questions in the Bible. Philadelphia, American Sunday School Union, 1831. 2 vols. ICBB; NNU-W; OCl. 5740

---- The Sunday School children ... Philadelphia, American Sunday School Union [1831?] 36 p. NNU-W. 5741

---- The Sunday School Hymn Book... Philadelphia, American Sunday School Union, 1831. 128 p. AmSSchU; IU; ICU; NjPT; PHi. 5742

---- Third Reading book. Rev. by the Committee of publication of the American Sunday School Union. Philadelphia, American Sunday School Union, 1831. 36 p. ICU. 5743

---- Union questions, on select portions of Scripture. Philadelphia, American Sunday School Union, 1831. 156 p. MH; NPalK. 5744

American Temperance Society. Permanent Temperance Documents. Boston, S. Bliss, 1831-1835. 8 vols. DLC; GU; PMA; TxDam. 5745

American Tract Society. Family hymns. New York, Pr. by Fanshaw, for The American Tract Society, 1831. 216 p. GDecCT; MH-AH; NNUT; RPB. 5746

---- The history of Peter Thomson. In two parts. New York. [183-?] 34 p. RPB 5747

---- Narratives of the spoiled child; David Baldwin; and the generals widow. New York, American Tract Society [183-?] 117 p. NN; NjP; Vi; ViU. 5748

---- Sketch of the origin and character of the principal series of tracts. New York, 1831. MH-AH. 5749

---- Twenty-two plain reasons for not being a Roman Catholic. New York, American Tract Society [1831] 28 p. WHi. 5750

American Unitarian Association.
The divinity of Jesus Christ. 3d ed. Boston, Gray and Bowen, 1831. 28 p. MB-FA; MnU. 5751

---- An explanation of the words, by native children of wrath... Boston, 1831. PPL; PPULC. 5752

---- A letter on The Principles of The Missionary Enterprise. 3d ed., 1st series, No. 6. Pr. for the American Unitarian Association. Boston, Pr. by I. R. Butts, 1831. 39 p. MeB. 5753

---- The Reports of the American Unitarian Association prepared for the Sixth Anniversary. 1831. Boston, Gray & Bowen, 1831. 44 p. ICMe; MHi; MNF; MeB; MeBat. 5754

Americanischer Stadt und Land Calender auf das 1832ste Jahr Christi... Philadelphia, Gedruckt und zu haben bey Conrad Zentler...[1831] 32 p. MWA; PReaHi. 5755

Der Amerikanisch-Deutsche Hausfreund und Baltimore Calendar for 1832. Baltimore, Md., Johann T. Hanzsche [1831] CtY; DLC; PHi; PPG; MWA. 5756

The Amethyst; an annual of literature; ed. and pub. by H. C. Brooks. Baltimore, Pr. by W. A. Francis, 1831. 290 p. CoU; DLC; InU; MBAt; NN; PPL. 5757

Amherst Academy.
Catalogue of the trustees, instructors and students; during the year, ending, August 23, 1831. Amherst, Pr. by J. S. and C. Adams, 1831. 7 p. MA; MAJ; MH. 5758

Amherst College.
Catalogue of the corporation, faculty, and students. 1831. Amherst, Pr. by J. S. & C. Adams, 1831. KHi; MeB; MH; PU. 5759

----Catalogus eorum, qui munera et officia gesserunt quique alicujust gradus laurea donati sunt, in Collegio Amherstiense, Amherstiae, in Republica Massachusettensi. Amherstiae, J. S. et C. Adams, typographia. 1831. Rerumpublicarum foederatarum Americae Summae potestatis anno LVl. 14 p. CSmH; ICN; KHi; MA; NN. 5760

---- Order of exercises at commencement, August 24. Amherst, Pr. by J. S. and C. Adams [1831]. 4 p. MA; MBC; MH. 5761

---- Statement of a committee of the trustees respecting their late petition, and appeal to its friends and patrons. 1831. 16 p. MBC. 5762

Amherst. Mount Pleasant Classical Institute. See Mount Pleasant Institute.

Amherst. Mount Pleasant Institute. See Mount Pleasant Institute.

The amusing companion; or, Interesting story teller. Being a collection of marvellous, wonderful, moral, sentimental, humorous, and instructive tales... New York, C. P. Fessenden, 1831.

DLC; IU; MNU; NcD; NjP. 5763

Anderson, Rufus.
Memoir of Catherine Brown, a Christian Indian of the Cherokee nation, prepared for the American Sunday School Union by Rev. Rufus Anderson and revised by the Committee of Publication. Philadelphia, American Sunday School Union, 1831. 138 p. MA; MeB; MoSM; NjP; OMC; PP; ScCliTO. 5764

[Anderson, Thomas]
Superstition detected, by a Connecticut brickmaker, to which is added The downfall of despotism by [Charles Mead]. Philadelphia, 1831. 24 p. MB; RPB. 5765

Anderson, Thomas A.
The practical monitor, for the preservations of health, and the prevention of diseases. 1st ed. Pub. and sold by Z. Jayne, of Philadelphia, Monroe County, Tennessee. Knoxville, T[enn.] F. S. Heiskell, 1831. 253 p. CtY-M; DLC; DNLM; NcD; TU. 5766

Andover Theological Seminary, Cambridge, Mass.
Catalogue of the officers and students of the Theological Seminary, Andover, Mass. Jan. 1831. Andover, Pr. by Flagg and Gould, 1831. 12 p. CoU; MAnP; NN; NNG. 5767

---- Laws of the library of the Theological Seminary, Andover. As established by the trustees, Sept. 1831. Andover, Pr. by Flagg and Gould, 1831. 8 p. MAnP. 5768

Andrews, Charles C.
Geographical exercises for infant schools, accompanied by a hydro-geographic map... By Charles C. Andrews... New York, Pr. by B. J. Jansen, 1831. 16 p. DLC. 5769

Andrews, Josiah.
An oration delivered at Perry Village, N.Y. July 4th, 1831. By Josiah Andrews. Warsaw, Pr. by A. W. Young, 1831. 21 p. 5770

Andrews, Lewis F. W.
Faith and unbelief. A discourse delivered in the First Universalist Church. Hartford, Conn. ...By Lewis F. W. Andrews. Hartford, Pr. by G. W. Kappel, 1831. 8 p. MBUPH; MMeT-Hi. 5771

Andros, T.
Strictures on a Recent Publication (entitled, Proceedings of two Ecclesiastical Councils in the town of Berkley.) Pr. by B. Earl, (n.p., 1831). 36 p. CSmH; MB. 5772

Angell, Oliver, 1787-1858.
The union, No. IV. containing lessons for reading and spelling, arithmetical tables and exercises; mental arithmetic, orthography and being the fourth of a series of spelling and reading books in six numbers. By Oliver Angell, Baltimore, Joseph Lewis, etc., 1831. 252 p. DLC; MHod. 5773

---- ...The union, no. V. Containing lessons for reading and spelling, with exercises in mental arithmetic, abbreviations, definitions, &c. Being the fifth of a series of spelling and reading books, in six numbers. By Oliver Angel... Providence, Cory and Brown; Boston, Carter, Hendee and Babcock; [etc., etc.,] 1831. 296 p. DLC; RPB. 5774

Annapolis, Maryland. Mayor.
Message from the mayor of Annapolis to the aldermen and common councilmen. Transmitting the report of the treasurer for the year eighteen-hundred and thirty. Annapolis, Pr. by W.

Neir, 1831. 12 p. MdHi. 5775

Annie Moore. By her mother. Boston, Perkins & Marvin, 1831. 78 p. MHingHi. 5776

The Annual retrospect of public affairs for 1831. Boston, Stimpson and Clapp, 1831. 2 v. CU; DLC; MH; MNe; MWA; OO; P. 5777

Anthon, Henry, 1795-1861.
The Wise and Faithful Steward. A sermon preached in New York, Sept. 19, 1830, being the Sunday after the decease of Bishop Hobart. New York, 1831. 19 p. MH. 5778

Anthony, Joseph, Jr.
The western minstrel, or Ohio melodist; containing a choice collection of moral, patriotice and sentimental songs, with the appropriate music for each piece in patent notes, carefully selected and affixed thereto; together with instructions for learners. Being well calculated to give a correct knowledge of vocal music: and also designed to assist learners of the instrumental branch of that science. By Joseph Anthony, Jr. Cincinnati, Pr. at the Cincinnati Journal Office for E. H. Flint, 1831. 159 p. OClWHi; RPB. 5779

Anti-conspirator. see Infidelity Unmasked.

Anti-Guillotine, (pseud.)
Five letters to Governor Hamilton, by Anti-Guillotine. First publ. in the Charleston Courier. Charleston, Pr. by J. S. Burges, 1831. 32 p. ICU; MBA; MH; MHi. 5780

Anti-Masonic Almanac for 1832. Calculations by William Collom. Philadelphia, Pa., J. Clarke [1831] MWA. 5781

Anti-masonic almanac for the year 1832 by Edward Giddins. Utica, William Williams [1831] DLC; IaCrM; OClWHi; PPL; NN. 5782

Anti-masonic Convention, Baltimore, 1831. See U.S. anti masonic convention, Baltimore, 1831.

Anti-Masonic Republican Convention of the County of Saratoga.
Proceedings, at a convention of Republican antimasonic delegates from...towns in the county of Saratoga, convened at...Ballston Spa on 8th...of October 1831 and the address of the central committee; to which is added an address delivered before the convention by the honorable John W. Taylor... Balston Spa [N.Y.] 1831. 16 p. MB; MHi. 5783

Anti-masonic State Convention. Massachusetts.
An abstract of the proceedings of the Antimasonic state convention of Massachusetts. Held in Faneuil Hall, Boston, May 19 & 20, 1831. Boston, Pr. at the office of the Boston press, for the Publishing committee, 1831. 78 p. IaCrM; MHi; MWA; MeB; NjP; PHi. 5784

---- Ohio.
The proceedings of the Ohio antimasonic state convention held at Columbus Ohio, on the 11th, 12th, and 13th days of January, 1831... Milan, Ohio, Warren Jenkins, n.d. 32 p. OClWHi. 5785

---- Pennsylvania.
Proceedings of the Anti-Masonic state convention, held at Harrisburg, on the 25th of May, 1831. 19 p. DLC; MB; WHi. 5786

---- Rhode Island.
Proceedings. September 14, 1831. Providence, Daily

Advertiser Office, 1831. 28 p. MB. 5787

---- Vermont.
Proceedings... Montpelier, June 15 and 16, 1831. With reports, addresses, etc. Montpelier, Pr. by Gamaliel Small, by order of the convention, 1831. 23 p. DLC; VtHi. 5788

Anti-Tariff Meeting, Boston, Mass.
Preamble and resolutions, adopted at a meeting held at the exchange coffee house, on Thursday evening, August 16, for the purpose of choosing delegates to the anti-tariff convention. Boston, Pr. by Beals and Homer, 1831. 12 p. IU; MH; MHi; NNS; PPAmP. 5789

Apes, William, b. 1798.
The increase of the Kingdom of Christ, a sermon. By William Apes, a Missionary of the Pequod Tribe of Indians. New-York, Pr. by G. F. Bunce, for the author, 1831. 24 p. MBAt; MH; MWA; NNUT; WHi. 5790

---- A son of the forest: The experience of William Apes, a native of the forest. Written by himself. 2d. ed. rev. and corr. New York, Pr. by G. F. Bunce, for the author, 1831. 114 p. CSmH; ICN; MWA; MnHi; NhD; OC; PPM; PU; WHi. 5791

Appeal to the people of the United States, by a freeholder. [On indemnity under treaty of 1800.] Boston, Hilliard, Gray, Little & Wilkin, 1831. 88 p. DLC; MB; PHi; PPL; RPB; WHi. 5792

[Appleton, Nathan] 1779-1861.
An examination of the banking system of Massachusetts, in reference to the renewal of the bank charters. Boston, Stimpson and Clapp, 1831. 48 p. C; CtY; DLC; IU; MB; MH; MWA; NIC; NN; NhD. 5793

---- Reply to "An examination of the banking system of Massachusetts." Boston, Cottons and Barnard, 1831. 24 p. CtY; DLC; ICU; MH. 5794

Arkansas.
Acts passed by the General Assembly at the 7th Session... held in Little Rock from Oct. 3-Nov. 1, 1831. 102 p. ArL; DLC. 5795

Armstrong, John.
[Key] to the Western calculator, containing the solution of all the examples and questions for exercise, with reference to the pages where they stand. To which is added, some useful rules. Designed chiefly to facilitate the labour of teachers; and assist such as have not the opportunity of a tutor's aid. By John Armstrong. 3d ed., rev. and corrected. Pittsburgh, Johnston & Stockton, 1831. 139 p. CU. 5796

Armstrong, Lebbeus, 1775-1860.
Masonry proved to be a work of darkness repugnant to the Christian Religions inimical to a Repub. Government. 4th ed. New York, 1831. 24 p. PHi. 5797

---- ...William Morgan, abducted and murdered by masons, in conformity with masonic obligations; and masonic measures, to conceal that outrage against the laws; a practical comment on the sin of Cain. Illustrated and proved in a sermon, by Lebbeus Armstrong...delivered in Edinburgh, Saratoga County, Sept. 12, 1831... New York, Pr. by L. D. Dewey & co., 1831. 32 p. DLC; IaCrM; MB; NIC: NNUT. 5798

Arnold, Benedict.
Arnold the traitor, Andre the spy and Champe the patriot. New Haven, 1831. MH. 5799

Arnold [Lemuel Hastings]
Attempted Speculation of Lemuel H. Arnold and James F. Simmons, upon the funds of the State, while they were members of the General Assembly. Providence, Herald Office, 1831. 23 p. CSmH; MH; RHi; RP. 5800

Arnott, Neil, 1788-1874.
Elements of physics, or natural philosophy, general and medical, explained independently of technical mathematics, and containing new disquisitions and practical suggestions. In two volumes. Vol. I. By Neil Arnott, M.D., 2d American from the 4th London ed. With additions by Isaac Hays, A. M., M.D., &c. Philadelphia, Carey & Lea, 1831. 2 v. IaHi; MoU; NjP; TxH. 5801

Ashbridge, Elizabeth (Sampson), 1713-1755.
Some account of the early part of the life of Elizabeth Ashbridge ... Providence, 1831. 60 p. DLC; MBBC; MWA; NN; PHC; RPB. 5802

Ashmun, Jehudi, 1794-1828.
Map of the West Coast of Africa, from Sierra Leone to Cape Palmas: Including the Colony of Liberia: Compiled chiefly from the surveys and observations of the late Dr. J. Ashmun. Philadelphia, A. Finley, 1831. MF. 5803

The aspect of the times: a political poem, and other pieces. By a native of Newark. Newark, Pr. by Hull & Bartlett, for the author, 1831. 73 p. DLC; OClWHi; Sabin. 5804

Associate Reformed Church. New York.
Extracts from the Minutes of the Acts and Proceedings the Associate Reformed Synod of New-York: Met at Kortright, September 2, 1831 and continued by adjournments. Published by order of Synod. Schenectady, Pr. by S. S. Riggs, 1831. 35 p. NcMHi. 5805

---- ---- Rules for the transaction of business in the judicatories of the Associate Reformed church. Pr. at the Religious Examiner office, 1831. 8 p. OClWHi; PPPrHi; PPULC. 5806

---- ---- A testimony and solemn warning against prevailing errors, upon the doctrines of original sin--of the atonement--and the manner of a sinner's justification. Adopted by the Associate Reformed Synod of New York, at their meeting in Kortright, Sept. 1831. Published by order of Synod. Schenectady, Pr. by S. S. Riggs, 1831. 32 p. MH-AH; NAuT; NN; NSchHi; NbOP; PPPrHi. 5807

---- Synod of the West.
Extracts from the Minutes of the Proceedings of the Associate Reformed Synod of the West; which met in Pittsburgh, October 19th, A.D. 1831. Washington, Ohio, Office of the Religious Examiner, 1831. 32 p. CSmH; NcMHi; NjPT; PPiXT. 5808

Association for the Relief of Respectable Aged Indigent Females, New York.
The eighteenth annual report of the Association for the relief of respectable aged indigent females, established in New-York, Feb. 7, 1814, presented at the annual meeting of the society, November 24, 1831. New-York, Pr. by J. Seymour, 1831.

20 p. NNG. 5809

An Astronomical Diary for 1832. The Yankee. The Farmer's Almanack, for the year of our Lord and Saviour, 1832. Boston, [1831] NRivHi; NjR. 5810

Asylum for Indigent Boys, Boston.
An account of the Boston Asylum for Indigent boys. Boston, N. Hale, 1831. MB-FA; MH. 5811

Atherton, Charles Humphrey, 1773-1853.
An address delivered at Concord, before the New-Hampshire Historical Society, at their annual meeting, June 8, 1831. By Charles H. Atherton, a member of the society. Concord, Pr. by Jacob B. Moore, 1831. 29 p. CtY; DLC; MB; MH; MWA; NjP. 5812

[Atkins, Sarah]
Leben und witken des Johann Friedrich Oberlin, predigers zu Waldbach, in dem bezirke de La Roche... Aus dem englischen ubersetze von D. Christian Lehmus, mit einem vorwort an den deutschen leser verschen von S. S. Schunucker... 1. americanische aufl. Pittsburgh, Hrsg. von L. Loomis and comp., 1831. 218 p. DLC; OO; PHi; PLFM; PPi. 5813

Atkinson, Thomas, 1807-1881.
Progress of the Anglican church; a sermon preached in St. Peter's church, Baltimore, on the first Sunday after Trinity, June 22, 1831, in commemoration of the 150th anniversary of the Society for the propagation of the gospel in foreign parts. Baltimore, Brunner, 1831. 14 p. CSmH; NcU. 5814

The Atlantic Souvenir for 1831. Philadelphia, Pr. by James Kay, Jr., & Company, for Carey & Lea, 1831. 328 p. LNH; MdHi; MeB; Mi; NjR; RNR; TxU. 5815

Attempted speculation of Lemuel H. Arnold and James F. Simmons, upon the funds of the state, while they were members of the General Assembly. Providence, Pr. at the Herald Office, 1831. 23 p. CSmH; MH; RHi; RP. 5816

Atwater, Caleb, 1778-1867.
The Indians of the Northwest, their maners[!], customs, &c., &c., or Remarks made on a tour to Prairie du Chien and thence to Washington city in 1829... Columbus [O., 1831] 296 p. CSmH; CU; MB; MdBE; OHi; OMC. 5817

---- The Ohio Pocket lawyer. See under title.

---- Remarks made on a tour to Prairie du Chien; thence to Washington city, in 1829. By Caleb Atwater. Columbus [O.], Pr. by Jenkins and Grover, for Isaac N. Whiting, 1831. 296 p. CtY; DLC; IaHi; MnHi; PPiU. 5818

Atwood, Mose G.
The American definition spelling-book. Carefully revised and adapted to Walker's Principles of English orthoepy... Boston, B. B. Mussey, 1831. 180 p. MH; VtU. 5819

---- ---- Concord, N.H., Hoag and Atwood, 1831. 180 p. MH; OClWHi; VtU. 5820

Auber, Daniel François Eugène.
La muette... (Eng. libretto; orig. French) by Scribe and Delavigne...transl. by G. B. C. Baltimore, E. J. Coale, 1831. 46 p. CtY; PU. 5821

Auburn Theological Seminary,

Auburn, New York.
General catalogue of the Theological Seminary. Auburn, New York, 1831. 16 p. MBC; NAuT. 5822

---- Order of commencement in the Theological Seminary, Auburn, Pr. by Richard Oliphant, August 17, 1831. Broadside. NAuT. 5823

---- Theological Seminary, Auburn. Scheme of exercises, on Thursday evening. Auburn, Pr. by Richard Oliphant, August 16, 1831. [2] p. NAuT. 5824

Audubon, John James, 1780-1851.
Ornithological biography, or An account of the habits of the birds of the United States of America; accompanied by descriptions of the objects represented in the work entitled The birds of America, and interspersed with delineations of American scenery and manners. By John James Audubon... Philadelphia, J. Dobson [etc.] 1831-39. 5 vols. CSmH; KyDC; MH; OCY; PHC. 5825

The Aurora Borealis, or Flashes of wit;...With original etchings, designed and executed by D. C. Johnston. Boston, Pub. by the editors of the Galaxy of wit, 1831. 216 p. DLC; IaU; IU; MB; MnU; NSchU; PU; TU. 5826

Austin, James T[recothick], 1784-1870.
The duties of educated men. An oration ... before the Society of BK at Cambridge on Thursday 1st September 1831. 53 l. MH; MH-L. 5827

The authenticity of the Scriptures, and fundamental doctrines of Quaker Christianity, according to the Berean, and the investigation of Benjamin Webb's case before a committee from the quarterly meeting of Concord. Wilmington, Del., W. M. Naudain, 1831. 94 p. PHC. 5828

Auxiliary Bible Society of Bristol County, Mass.
Constitution... as amended at the annual meeting in September, 1818. Together with the report of the board, etc., September 15, 1830. Taunton, Pr. by Edmund Anthony, for Columbian Reporter Press, 1831. 12 p. MTaHi. 5829

Auxiliary Foreign Missionary Society. County of New Haven (West).
The eleventh annual report of the Auxiliary Foreign Missionary Society of New Haven County (West) at a meeting held at Humphreysville, (Derby), October 11, 1831. New Haven, Pr. by Hezekiah Howe, 1831. 23 p. Ct. 5830

---- County of Norfolk.
Addresses delivered at the Annual Meeting of the Auxiliary Foreign Missionary Society, in the County of Norfolk, in Wrentham, Sept. 14, 1831. Boston, Pr. by Peirce and Parker, 1831. 24 p. MB; MiD-B; MWA; NjR; RPB. 5831

Aydelott, B[enjamin] P[arham], 1795-1880.
The duties of parents, a discourse preached in Christ's Church, Cincinnati; January 17, 1831. Cincinnati, Pr. by Williamson and Wood, 1831. 16 p. MH; MH-Ed; MH-L; MdBD; OMC. 5832

---- The medical student's danger and means of safety; A discourse preached in Christ church, Cincinnati, January 9, 1831. By the Rev. B. P. Aydelott, M.D. Cincinnati, Pr. by J. Whetstone, jr., 1831. 12 p. IEG; MBAt;

MdBD; NNNAM; OClWHi; OMC; ScCC. 5833

---- A plea for Sunday-Schools. A discourse, preached and published by request of the Cincinnati Sunday-School Union. 1830. by Rev. B. P. Aydelott... Cincinnati, Cincinnati Journal Office, 1831. 23 p. MdBD. 5834

---- Statement of the Case of Bishop Provost, with remarks on the resignation of Diocesan jurisdiction. by Dr. Aydelott from the Episcopal Recorder. Philadelphia, 1831. 12 p. MdBD. 5835

B

Babcock, Sidney, comp.
Birthday present. From an affectionate friend. New Haven, Sidney's press, 1831. 17 p. MHi. 5836

---- The Girls Own Book. Full of Short Stories. By S. Babcock. New Haven, Pr. by Sidney's Press, 1831. 17 p. CtY; MHi. 5837

---- The Picture Book,... or a gift for Charles... New Haven, Sidney's Press, 1831. 17 p. MHi. 5838

---- Stories for little boys; or a present from father. New Haven, Sidney's press, 1831. 23 p. CtY; MHi. 5839

---- Stories for little girls; or a present from mother. New Haven, Sidney's press, 1831. 22 p. (Binder's title; A present from sister.) CtY; MHi. 5840

Babington, Thomas.
A practical view of Christian education... By T. Babington... With a preliminary essay. By Rev. T. H. Gallandet. 4th Amer. ed. Hartford, Cooke & Co., 1831. 212 p. CtMW; DLC; MeB; NjPT; PU. 5841

Bache, Alexander Dallas, 1806-1867.
Safety apparatus for steam boats, being a combination of the fusible metal disk with the common safety valve. By A. D. Bache... [Philadelphia, 1831] 4 p. DLC. 5842

Bacheler, Origen.
Discussion on the authenticity of the Bible. by Origen Bacheler & R. D. Owen. New York, n.p., 1831. CSmH; OC. 5843

Bachi, Pietro, 1787-1853.
A comparative view of the Spanish and Portuguese languages; or, An easy method of learning the Portuguese tongue for those who are already acquainted with the Spanish. By Pietro Bachi... Cambridge (Mass.), Hilliard and Brown, 1831. 104 p. CSt; CtY; DLC; MeB; MH; NN; PPM; VIU. 5844

---- A grammar of the Italian language. By Pietro Bachi. Boston, Little and Brown, 1831. 568 p. NjMD. 5845

Bachman, John, 1790-1874.
Funeral discourse of Rev. John G. Schwartz, Sept. 11, 1831. Charleston, James S. Burgess, 1831. 23 p. MWA; NcD; GEU; RPB; ScCC; TxU. 5846

Backus, Henry T.
An oration, delivered before the Republican citizens assembled in the First Congregational church. Norwich, 4th July, 1831... Norwich, Conn., Pr. by Wm. Faulkner, 1831. 14 p. CSmH; CtY; ICT; MBAt; NN; RPB. 5847

[Bacon, Delia Salter], 1811-1859.
Tales of the Puritans. The

regicides. --The fair Pilgrim. --Castine. New Haven, A. H. Maltby; New York, G. and C. Carvill, and J. Leavitt; [etc. etc.] 1831. 300 p. MB; MH; NN; PU; RPB. 5848

Bacon, Francis.
Essays, moral, economical, and political. By Francis Bacon. Boston, C. D. Strong, 1831. 218 p. CtMW; KyOw; MH. 5849

Bacon, [Samuel], 1781-1820.
Memoir of Rev. Samuel Bacon, an early advocate of Sunday Schools, and principal Agent of the American Government on the coast of Africa, etc. Philadelphia, American Sunday School Union, 1831. 126 p. MBAt. 5850

Badcock, John, fl. 1816-1830.
The grooms' oracle, and pocket stable directory, in which the management of horses generally, as to health, dieting, and exercise, are considered, in a series of familiar dialogues, between two grooms engaged in training horses to their work. By John Hinds (pseud.) From the 2d London ed. with notes and an appendix, including extracts from the receipt book of the author. Philadelphia, E. L. Carey and A. Hart, 1831. 228 p. MWA; NjP; P; ViWI. 5851

Baddeley, T.
A sure way to find out the true religion in a conversation between father and son... Boston, Smith, 1831. 126 p. MdBLC. 5852

Badell [G. L.]
"Pay Thy Vows" a Pastoral Address Subsequent to Confirmations. Philadelphia, 1831. OCHP. 5853

Bailey, Ebenezer, 1795-1839.
The young ladies' class book; a selection of lessons for reading, in prose and verse. By Ebenezer Bailey... Boston, Lincoln & Edmands; New York, Collins and Hannay [etc., etc.] 1831. 408 p. CtMWatk; MB; MBAt; MH; OFH; TxU-T. 5854

Bailey, Luther.
Sermon on the death of Abijah R. Thayer and Asa C. Thayer. Boston, 1831. 19 p. MBC; RPB. 5855

---- Sermon preached on Oct. 17, 1830, occasioned by the death of Miss Betsey Adams, daughter of Mr. Moses Adams, aged 25. Boston, Freeman & Bailes, 1831. 15 p. MBC; MiD-B; RPB. 5856

Bailey, Phinehas, 1787-1861.
A pronouncing stenography, containing a complete system of short hand writing, governed by the analogy of sounds and adopted to every language. St. Albans, Pr. by J. Spooner, 1831. 18 p. ICJ; MB; NN. 5857

[Bailey, Samuel], 1791-1870.
Essays on the formation and publication of opinions, and on other subjects. From the last London ed. Philadelphia, R. W. Pomeroy, 1831. 240 p. CU; IEG; M; NGH; PHi; ScC. 5858

---- Essays on the pursuits of truth, on the progress of knowledge and the fundamental principle of all evidence and expectation. By the author of essays on the formation and publication of opinions. Philadelphia, R. W. Pomeroy, 1831. 233 p. CSmH; DLC; IEG; LNH; MH; NjP; ScC. 5859

Baker, Edmund James.
A map of the Towns of Dorchester and Milton, 1831... Boston [1831] MB. 5860

Balcom, D. A.
Confession of the Prince of darkness, concerning his devices in politics and religion...by D. A. Balcom. 3d ed. Cincinnati, Pr. for the publisher, 1831. 44 p. NNUT; OCHP. 5861

Baldivia; an original tragedy, founded on the history of the Spanish Wars with the aborigines of South America. In three Acts. Nashville, Pr. at the Herald Office, 1831. 253 p. DLC; DSG; MoS; TU; TxU. 5862

Baldwin, Ebenezer, d. 1837.
Annals of Yale College... from its foundation, to the year 1831. With an appendix containing statistical tables, and exhibiting the present condition, of the institution. By Ebenezer Baldwin. New York, New Haven, H. Howe, 1831. 324 p. N; OrU; PPL; PDULC. 5863

---- Catalogue of the phenogamous plants and ferns growing, without cultivation, within five miles of Yale College. See Tully, William, 1785-1859.

Balfour, Walter, 1776-1852.
Reply to Professor Stuart's exegetical essays on several words relating to future punishment. By Walter Balfour... Boston, Pr. for the author, 1831. 238 p. Ct; IEG; InU; MB; MiD; PPL. 5864

---- Tricks of Revivalists Exposed. Substance of two discourses, delivered in the First Universalist Church in Boston, on the morning and afternoon of Sunday, April 17th, 1831. By Walter Balfour. Boston, Pr. and pub. by G. W. Bazin, Trumpet Office, 1831. 24 p. CBPSR; MBUPH; MMeT-Hi; MNtCA; MWA; NCH. 5865

Ballantine, W[illiam]
The Infant School Reader. Being an improved edition of The Book of Words of One Sound: With 150 Spelling Lessons of Words of One Syllable the meanings of which are also well explained by words of one syllable. By W. Ballantine. Pittsburgh, John I. Kay and Co.; Philadelphia, Key and Milke, 1831. 146 p. DLC; ICBB. 5866

Ballou, Hosea, 1771-1852.
Fox sermon: a sermon delivered in the second Universalist Meeting-house in Boston, on the morning of the third sabbath in November, 1829. 5th ed. Exeter, 1831. 12 p. MH; MWA; MiD-B; Nh-Hi; NjR. 5867

---- Notes on the parables of the New Testament, scripturally illustrated and argumentatively defended. By Hosea Ballow. 4th ed. Rev. by the author. Boston, Marsh, Capen & Lyon, 1831. 296 p. DLC; KyLxT; MH. 5868

[Ballow, Henry], 1707-1782.
A treatise of equity. With the addition of marginal references and notes, by John Fonblanque ... 3d American ed.: with references to American chancery decisions and additional notes, by Antony Laussat... Philadelphia, J. Grigg, 1831. 2 v. in 1. CU; DLC; KyU-L; NcD; OClW. 5869

Baltimore. City Council. First Branch.
Journal of the proceedings of the First Branch of the City Council of Baltimore. January session, 1831. Baltimore, Pr. by Sands and Neilson, 1831. 342 p. DLC; ICJ; MdBB; MdBP; MdHi. 5870

---- ---- Second Branch.
Journal of the proceedings of the Second Branch of the City

Council of Baltimore. January session, 1831. Baltimore, Sands and Neilson, 1831. 192 p. MdBE; MdHi. 5871

No entry. 5872

---- Mayor.
Mayor's communication, January 3, 1831. Baltimore, Lucas and Deaver, 1831. 10 p. DLC; IU; MB; NN. 5873

---- ---- Message to City Council. (1800-1830. Bd. in 1 vol.) Baltimore, 1831. MdLR. 5874

---- Ordinances, etc.
The Ordinanaces of the Mayor and City Council of Baltimore, passed at the extra sessions in 1830, and at the January session, 1831. To which is annexed, Sundry acts of Assembly, passed Dec. session, 1830; a list of officers of the corporation, the summary of the register and the annual reports and returns of the officers of the Corporation. Baltimore, Pr. by Lucas & Deaver, 1831. 121 p. MdBB; MdHi; MH-L; NNLI. 5875

---- County. County Jail.
Report of the Visitors and Governors of the Jail of Baltimore County. [Baltimore, 1831] 11 p. MdHi; PP; PPULC. 5876

---- Province.
[Report of the first provincial council of Baltimore held October 1829 and reports of the diocesan and provincial councils...] Baltimore, J. D. Toy, 1831-1868. NNF. 5877

---- Archdiocese. Synod. 1831.
Synodus Diocesana Baltimorensis II. habita ab Illustrissimo ac Reverendissimo Jacob, archiepiscope Baltimorensi. Anne reparatae salutis 1831. Mense Novembri Baltimori, Ex typis J. D. Toy, 1831. 10 p. MdBS; MdW; MiDSH; PLatS. 5878

Baltimore and Havre-De-Grace Turnpike Co.
Act... Baltimore, 1831. PPL; PPULC. 5879

Baltimore and Ohio Railroad Co.
Argument, delivered at Anapolis, on behalf of the Baltimore and Ohio rail road company, on the final hearing, before the chancellor of Maryland, of the case of The Baltimore and Ohio Rail Road Company, against The Chesapeake and Ohio Canal Company. October, 1831. Baltimore, Pr. by William, Wooddy, 1831. 255 p. DLC; MdHi; MiU-T; NN. 5880

---- Communication from the Baltimore and Ohio Railroad Company, to the mayor and city council of Baltimore. Presented February 7th, 1831. Baltimore, Pr. by Lucas and Deaver, 1831. 8 p. CtY; DLC; MdHi; MH-BA; PH. 5881

---- Fifth annual report...Baltimore, 1831. ICU; MdBP; WU. 5882

---- Instructions to contractors, superintendents, etc. for laying the stone rail way, on the Baltimore and Ohio Railroad. Baltimore, 1831. PHi; PPULC. 5883

---- Laws and ordinances relating to the Baltimore and Ohio rail road company. Baltimore, 1831. DLC; MdHi; MH; NNE. 5884

---- Report from the President, P. E. Thomas, to the Governor and to the Executive of the State of Maryland. Baltimore, 1831.

8 p. CSt; DLC; MdHi; MH-BA. 5885

---- Report of the chief engineer of the Baltimore and Ohio Railroad Company to the president of said company. Annapolis, Jonas Green, 1831. 12 p. MdBJ; MdHi; MiU-T; NN. 5886

---- Report of the directors of the Baltimore and Ohio Railroad Company, to the Legislature of Maryland. Annapolis, Jonas Green, 1831. 43 p. MdBJ; MdHi; NiU-T; NN. 5887

---- To the Honorable the General Assembly of Maryland, The memorial of the Baltimore and Ohio Rail Road Company, counter to the statements contained in a memorial to the General Assembly of Maryland, at its present session, by the Chesapeake and Ohio Canal Company;--respectfully represents: [Baltimore, 1831?] 11 p. MiU-T; NN. 5888

Baltimore and Susquehanna railroad Company. Laws and ordinances relating to... See Maryland, laws, etc.

---- Report of the city director of the Baltimore and Susquehanna rail road, to the mayor. Baltimore, Pr. by Lucas & Deaver, 1831. 6 p. MdHi; NN; PHi; PPULC. 5889

Baltimore Directory, corrected up to June 1831. Baltimore, R. J. Matchett, 1831. 403 p. MBAt; MdBB; MdBP; NcWfC. 5890

Baltimore eastern dispensary.
An appeal to the patrons of the Baltimore eastern dispensary, by the board of directors. 1831. Baltimore, Pr. by Lucas and Deaver [1831] 26 p. DLC; MdHi. 5891

Baltimore. Library Company.
Third supplement to the catalogue of books, etc. belonging to the Library Company of Baltimore. 1831. Baltimore, Pr. by John D. Toy, 1831. 21 p. MdHi. 5892

Baltimore life insurance company.
Proposals and rates of the Baltimore life insurance company. Baltimore, Pr. by John D. Toy, 1831. 26 p. DLC; MH; NNC; PHi; PPULC. 5893

Balzac, Honore de, 1799-1850.
The quest of the absolute and other stories. By Honore de Balzac. With photogravures. Boston, E. B. Hall and Locke Co, 1831. 386 p. NJost. 5894

---- The works of Honore de Balzac. With introductions by George Saintsbury. University ed. New York, The University Society [1831?] 16 v. PPULC; PU. 5895

Bancroft, George, 1800--1891.
The bank of the United States, an article reprinted from the North American review, for April, 1831. Boston, Hale's steam-power-press, 1831. 44 p. DLC; InHi; MdHi; MnHi; NIC; PU. 5896

[----] Review of the Report of the Committee of Ways and Means; and of the Message of the President of the United States, relative to the United States Bank. From the American Quarterly Review--March, 1831. Philadelphia, Carey & Lea, 1831. 38 p. MH; NNC; PHi; PPAmP; PPULC. 5897

Bangor, Maine. First Congregational Church.
Confession of faith and covenant adopted by the First Congregational Church in Bangor Maine at its organization November 27, 1811. Bangor, Pr. by Burton and Carter, 1831. 18 p. CtY. 5898

---- ---- Manual. 1831. MBC. 5899

---- Forensic Club.

An argument delivered before the Bangor Forensic Club on the question, "Ought the law, requiring the opening of our postoffices, and the transportations of our mails, on the Christian Sabbath, to be repealed?" Thursday evening, January 6, 1831. Bangor, Pr. by Burton and Carter, 1831. 28 p. MeHi; NjR; MNtCA; MeBA. 5900

Bank of the United States, 1816-1836.

Letters from the secretary of the treasury transmitting the monthly statements of the Bank of the United States for the year 1830. January 22, 1831. Read and laid upon the table [Washington, 1831] NIC; NNC. 5901

---- Report of the proceedings of the triennial meeting of the stockholders of the Bank of the United States. Held according to the thirteenth article of the eleventh section of the charter, at Philadelphia, on the first day of September 1831. Philadelphia, Joseph Kite, 1831. 31 p. DLC; MdHi; MHi; P; RP. 5902

Banner of the Church. Boston, Stimpson and Clapp, September 3, 1831. DLC; MWA; PHi; PPULC. 5903

Banner of the Constitution. Philadelphia, Pr. by T. W. Ustick, 1831. 2 vols. NhD. 5904

Baptist confession of faith, and a summary of church discipline, to which is added, an appendix. Charleston, Pr. by W. Riley, for Daniel Sheppard, 1831. 303 p. GMM; KyLoS; LNH; NHC-S. 5905

Baptists. Alabama. Bethlehem Association.

Minutes of the Bethlehem Baptist Association convened at the Fellowship Church, Wilcox county...Mobile, Pr. at the office of the Mobile Commercial Register [1831] 8 p. NRAB. 5906

---- ---- Cahawba Association.

Minutes of the Fourteenth Anniversary of the Cahawba Baptist Association, held at the Five Mile Creek Church, Greene County, Alabama. From the 22d to the 25th October, 1831, inclusive. Selma, Ala., Pr. by Thomas J. Frow, 1831. 8 p. NHC-S. 5907

---- ---- Mulberry Association.

Minutes of the Fourth Session of the Mulberry Baptist Association, begun and held at the Baptist Church at Chesnut Creek, Autauga County, Alabama; from the tenth to the thirteenth of September-inclusive. 1831. 8 p. NHC-S. 5908

---- Arkansas. Spring River Association.

Minutes of the Spring River Baptist Association, held at the Richland meeting-house, in Richland, on the first, second and third days of October, 1831. [Little Rock, 1831] 6 p. NRAB. 5909

---- Board of Foreign Missions.

Report of the Baptist Board of Foreign Missions, at its annual meeting in Providence, April 27, 1831. Boston, Lincoln & Edmands [1831?] 32 p. IAlS. 5910

---- Connecticut. Stonington Union Association.

Minutes of the fourteenth anniversary of the Stonington Union Baptist Association; held in South Kingstown, R.I. June 22d and 23d, 1831. Wickford, R.I., Pr. by James J. Brenton, 1831. 8 p. PCA; RWe. 5911

---- Delaware.
Minutes of the Delaware Baptist Association, held at Rock Springs, on the 4th, 5th and 6th of June, 1831. 8 p. PCA. 5912

---- Georgia. Canoochie association.
Minutes of the Canoochie association, convened at Upper Black Creek meeting house, Bullock County, commenced on the 24th day of September, 1831. 8 p. NRAB. 5913

---- ---- Flint River association.
Minutes of the Flint River association, convened at Lebanon, Henry County, on the 15th, 16th, 17th and 18th days of October, 1831. 12 p. NRAB. 5914

---- Illinois. United Association.
Minutes of the Illinois United Baptist Association, begun and held at... Clinton County, Illinois, October 1st, 2nd, and 3rd, 1831. Edwardsville, Ill, Pr. by Sawyer and Angeuin, 1831. 5 p. IAlS; ISB. 5915

---- Illinois and Missouri. Friends to Humanity.
Minutes of three separate associations, held by the Baptized Churches of Christ, Friends to Humanity, in Missouri and Illinois, for the year 1831. [Rock Spring, 1831] 8 p. IHi; ISB; ISBHi. 5916

---- Indiana. Coffee Creek Association.
Minutes. Fifth annual meeting of the Coffee Creek Baptist Association, begun and held at Harbert's Creek meeting house, 3rd, 4th and 5th days of September, 1831. 3 p. InFrlC; NRCR-S. 5917

---- ---- Flat Rock Association.
Minutes of the Flat Rock Association of Baptists, begun and held at Sand Creek meeting house, Decatur county, Indiana, on the first, second and third days of October, 1831. 4 p. InFrlC. 5918

---- ---- Laughery Association.
Minutes of the 14th annual meeting of the Laughery Association of Baptists, held at Hartford, Dearborn co. Indiana. Commencing the 3d Wednesday in September, 1831. 4 p. NRCR-S. 5919

---- ---- Lost River Association.
Minutes of the 6th annual meeting of the Lost River Association held at Oxford meeting house, Scott County, Indiana, on the first Saturday, Lord's day, and Monday, in September 1831. [Salem, Ind., John Allen, 1831] 4 p. InFrlC; NRCR-S. 5920

---- ---- North Bend Association.
(Minutes of the 29th annual meeting of the North Bend Association of Baptists, held on the 3d Friday in August, 1831) Lawrenceburgh, Statesman Office, 1831. 4 p. ICU. 5921

---- ---- Union Association.
Minutes of the 7th annual meeting of the Union Association of United Baptists, held at Veal's Creek meeting house, Daviess county, Indiana, September 16, 17 and 18, 1831. 4 p. InFrlC; NRCR-S. 5922

---- ---- Whitewater Association.
Minutes of the proceedings of the 22nd annual meeting of the Whitewater Baptist Association. Begun and held at Little Flat Rock meeting house on Friday and Saturday, the 12th and 13th days of August, A.D. 1831. [Rushville, Indiana, William D.

M. Wickham, 1831] 4 p. NRCR-S. 5923

---- Kentucky. Bethel Association.

Minutes of the seventh Bethel Baptist Association, held at New Providence church in the town of Hopkinsville, on the 24th, 25th and 26th days of Sept. 1831. Saturday, an introductory sermon was delivered by Elder J. S. Wilson. Russellville, Ky., Pr. by Charles Rhea, 1831. 8 p. LNB. 5924

---- ---- Laurel River Association.

Minutes. 1831-. PCA. 5925

---- ---- Paint Union United Association.

Minutes. 1831. PCA. 5926

---- Maine. Convention.

Minutes of the Maine Convention, seventh anniversary, held in Bloomfield, October 12 and 13, 1831. Hallowell, Glazier, Masters and Co., 1831. 21 p. PCA. 5927

---- ---- Cumberland Association.

Minutes of the Cumberland Association. Portland, Advocate Office, 1831. 8 p. TxHuT. 5928

---- ---- ---- Minutes of the twentieth anniversary of the Cumberland Association, held at the Baptist meetinghouse in North Yarmouth on Wednesday and Thursday, August 31 and September 1, 1831. Portland, Pr. at the Advocate Office, 1831. 12 p. PCA. 5929

---- ---- Eastern Maine Association.

Minutes of the thirteenth anniversary of the Eastern Maine Association, held in the Baptist meeting house in Addison on Wednesday and Thursday September 7 and 8, 1831. Eastport, Pr. by Benjamin Folsom, 1831. PCA. 5930

---- ---- Oxford Association.

Minutes of the third anniversary of the Oxford Baptist Association, held at the Baptist meeting-house in Hebron on Wednesday, Thursday and Friday, October 5, 6, and 7, 1831. Norway, Pr. by William E. Goodnow, at the Oxford Observer Office, 1831. 8 p. PCA. 5931

---- ---- Penobscot Association.

Minutes of the Sixth anniversary of the Penobscot Association held at the Baptist meeting-house in Charlestown, September 14 and 15, 1831. Bangor, Pr. by Burton and Carter, 1831. 15 p. MeBa. 5932

---- ---- Waldon Association.

Minutes of the Waldon Association, holden at the meeting-house in Knox, August 31 and September 1, 1831, together with the circular and corresponding letters. Also the articles of faith and practice, and covenant. Augusta, Me., Washburn and Jewall, 1831. CSmH. 5933

---- ---- York association.

Minutes of the York Baptist Association holden at the Baptist meeting-house in South Berwick, Me., June 8 and 9, 1831. Together with the circular and corresponding letters. Portland, Pr. at the office of Zion's Advocate, 1831. 16 p. CSmH. 5934

---- ---- ---- A summary declaration of the faith and practise of the York Baptists Association. Adopted unanimously June 29, 1831, and adopted by the Baptist Church in Acton; September 1,

1829. Kennebunk, Pr. by James K. Remick, 1831. 12 p. MNtCA. 5935

---- Massachusetts. Boston Association.

Anniversary. Boston, 1831. MB. 5936

---- ---- ---- Minutes... meeting at Roxbury. Boston, Lincoln and Edmands, 1831. 24 p. IAiS; MiD-B. 5937

---- ---- Franklin County Association.

Minutes. 1831-. PCA. 5938

---- ---- Massachusetts Baptist Convention.

Minutes of the Massachusetts Baptist Convention, held in Framingham, October 26th & 27th, 1831. Seventh anniversary. Worcester, From N.W. Grout's Power Press, 1831. 27 p. M; MWA; NRAB. 5939

---- ---- Salem Association.

Minutes of the fourth anniversary of the Salem Baptist Association, held at the Baptist Meeting House Haverhill Village, Wednesday & Thursday, Sept. 28 & 29, 1831. Haverhill, Essex Gazette Office [1831] 22 p. MBevHi; PCA. 5940

---- ---- Worcester Association.

Minutes of the Worcester Baptist Association, held at Ward, Mass. August 17th & 18th, A.D. 1831. Twelfth anniversary. Worcester, Pr. by Moses W. Grant, 1831. 19 p. MWborHi. 5941

No entry. 5942

---- Mississippi. Mississippi Association.

Minutes of the Mississippi Baptist Ass'n., held at New Providence Church, Amite County, Miss., on the 21st, second & third days of Oct., 1831. Monticello [Miss.], Pr. at the office of the Monticello Gazette, 1831. 13 p. LNB. 5943

---- Missouri. Salem Association.

Minutes of the Salem Association, held at Union meeting-house, Boone Co., Mo. on the 3rd, 4th, and 5th of September, 1831. Columbia, Mo., Pr. by N. Patten, 1831. 7 p. MoHi. 5944

---- New Hampshire.

Proceedings of the Baptist Convention of the State of New Hampshire, at their annual meeting in Hopkinton, June 22 & 23, 1831. Concord, Pr. by Fisk and Chase, 1831. 15 p. PCA. 5945

---- ---- Meredith Association.

Minutes of the forty-second anniversary of the Meredith Baptist Association, held at the Centre meeting-house in Meredith, on Wednesday and Thursday, Sept. 14 & 15, 1831. Concord, Pr. by Fisk & Chase, 1831. 14 p. PCA. 5946

---- New Jersey.

Minutes of the second annual meeting of the New Jersey Baptist State Convention for missionary purposes; held at the meeting house of the New Brunswick Baptist Church. November 2, 1831. Trenton, N.J., Pr. by P. J. Gray, 1831. 8 p. PCA. 5947

---- [West] New Jersey Association.

Minutes of the New Jersey Baptist Association, held in the Meeting-House of the Baptist

Church at Haddonfield, September 17th, 19th and 20th, 1831. Bridgeton, Pr. by S. S. Sibleey, 1831. 16 p. MiD-B; PCA. 5948

---- New York. Black River Association.

Minutes of the Twenty-second Anniversary of the Black River Baptist Association, convened at Watertown, Jeff. Co., N.Y., June 8 and 9, 1831. Watertown, Pr. by Knowlton & Rice, 1831. 12 p. NHC-S; NRCR; PCA. 5949

---- ---- Bottskill Association.

The constitution and minutes of the first session of the Bottskill Baptist association, held at Hartford, Washington County, N.Y. September 13 and 14, 1831, together with their circular letter. Union Village, Pr. by W. Lansing & Co., 1831. NRAB; NRCR. 5950

---- ---- Cortland Association.

Minutes of the fourth anniversary of the Cortland Baptist association, convened at Tully, Onondaga county, on Thursday and Friday, September 15 & 16, 1831. Utica, from the press of Bennett & Bright, 1831. 16 p. NRCR. 5951

---- ---- Franklin Association.

Minutes of the Twentieth Anniversary of the Franklin Baptist Association, Convened at the Baptist Meeting House, in West Meredith, Delaware County, N.Y. June 15, & 16, 1831. Utica, Pr. by Bennett & Bright, 1831. 16 p. PCA. 5952

---- ---- Hartford Association.

Minutes of the Forty-Second Anniversary of the Hartford Baptist Association, held in the meeting house of the Baptist Church in Northeast, New York, Oct. 12, and 13, 1831. 15 p. NHC-S. 5953

---- ---- Holland Purchase Association.

Minutes of the Annual Meeting of the Holland Purchase Baptist Association. Held by appointment with the Baptist Church. Buffalo, Pr. by Steele & Faxon, 1831. 12 p. NHC. 5954

---- ---- Hudson River Association.

The Sixteenth Anniversary of the Hudson River Baptist Association. New York, George F. Bunce, 1831. 16 p. RPB. 5955

---- ---- Lake George Association.

Minutes of the Fifteenth Anniversary of the Lake George Baptist Association in Session at the Baptist Meeting house in Chester, Warren County, N.Y., September 7th & 8th, 1831. Glen's Falls, Pr. at the Messenger Office, 1831. 8 p. PCA. 5956

---- ---- Madison Association.

Minutes of the twenty-third anniversary of the Madison Baptist Association, convened at Cazenovia, Madison County, on Tuesday and Wednesday, September 13 and 14, 1831. Utica, From the press of Bennett & Bright, 1831. 16 p. NN; NRCR; PCA. 5957

---- ---- New-York Association.

Minutes of the Forty-First Anniversary of the New York Baptist Association, held in the Meeting-House of the First Baptist Church in the City of New York, May 31, June 1, 2, 1831. New York, Pr. at the Office of the Baptist Repository, 1831. 20 p. PCA. 5958

---- ---- Oneida Association.

Minutes of the eleventh anniversary of the Oneida Baptist association, held at Holland Patent, Trenton, on Wednesday and

Thursday, September 7, & 9, 1831. Utica, from the press of Bennett & Bright, 1831. 12 p. DLC; NN; NRCR; PPULC. 5959

---- ---- Otsego Association.

Minutes of the thirty-sixth anniversary of the Otsego Baptist Association, convened at Warren, Herkimer County, on Wednesday Aug. 31, and Thursday Sept. 1, 1831. Utica, From the press of Bennett & Bright, 1831. 16 p. NHC-S; NRCR; PCA; R. 5960

---- ---- Union Association.

Minutes of the Twenty-Second Anniversary of the Union Baptist Association, held with the Baptist Church in York-Town, New York, September 7 & 8, 1831. Danbury, Pr. by W. & M. Yale, at the office of the Recorder, 1831. 8 p. PCA. 5961

---- ---- Warwick Association.

Minutes of the Warwick Baptist Association, held in the Meeting-House of the First Baptist Church at Wantage, N.J. June 8 & 9, 1831--statement of belief. New York, Pr. by Watt & Ball, 1831. 12 p. PCA. 5962

---- ---- Washington Association.

Minutes of the fifth anniversary of the Washington Baptist Association, convened at the Baptist Meeting-House, West Granville, June 8, and 9, 1831. Brandon, Vermont Telegraph Office, 1831. 8 p. PCA. 5963

---- North Carolina. Tar River Baptist Association.

Minutes. 1831-. PCA. 5964

---- Ohio.

[Minutes of] Fifth Anniversary held in Lancaster. Commencing the Fourth Monday in May, 1831. 3 p. PCA. 5965

---- ---- Bethel Association.

Minutes. 1831-. OClWHi. 5966

---- ---- Columbus Association.

Minutes of the Columbus Baptist Association. Saturday, Sept. 3, 1831. ... 8 p. OClWHi. 5967

---- ---- Eagle Creek Association.

Minutes. 1831. OClWHi. 5968

---- ---- East Fork of the Little Miami Association.

Minutes of the East Fork of the Little Miami Baptist Association, Held at the Clough Creek Meeting House, Hamilton County, Ohio, on the 3rd, 4th, and 5th of September 1831. 6 p. OClWHi; PCA. 5969

---- ---- Geauga Association.

Minutes [1831?] OClWHi. 5970

---- ---- Grand River Association.

Minutes of the fifteenth session of the Grand River Baptist Association held by appointment with the church in Perry, Ohio September 14th and 15th, 1831; together with their circular and corresponding letter. Jefferson, Ohio, Pr. by L. B. Edwards, 1831. 10 p. NHC-S; OClWHi. 5971

---- ---- Huron Baptist Association.

Minutes of the tenth annual meeting of the Huron Baptist Association, at their session in the village of Norwalk, Huron County, Ohio, August 19, 20 & 21, 1831. Norwalk, Ohio, Pr. by S. Preston & Co., 1831. 8 p. OClWHi. 5972

---- ---- Little Miami Union Regular Association.

Minutes. 1831-. OClWHi. 5973

---- ---- Lorain Association.

Minutes [1831?] OClWHi. 5974

---- ---- Maumee River Association.
Minutes. 1831. OClWHi. 5975

---- ---- Meigscreek Association.
Minutes of the Ninth Anniversary of the Meigscreek Baptist Association, Held by Appointment, with the Brookfield Church, Morgan County, O. on the 12th, 13th, and 14th days of August, A.D. 1831. M'Connelsville [Ohio] Wilkins and Christy, 1831. 8 p. OClWHi. 5976

---- ---- Miami Association.
Minutes of the Miami Baptist Association, Held at Elkcreek Church, Butler Co., Ohio, on the 9th, 10th and 11th days of September, 1831. 8 p. OClWHi; PCA. 5977

---- ---- Miami Old School Association.
Minutes [1831?] OClWHi. 5978

---- ---- Mohican Association.
Minutes [1831?] OClWHi. 5979

---- ---- Portage Regular Association.
Minutes [1831?] OClWHi. 5980

---- ---- Rocky River Association.
Minutes [1831?] OClWHi. 5981

---- ---- Sandusky Association.
Minutes 1831. OClWHi. 5982

---- ---- Scioto Predestinarian Association.
Minutes. [1831?] OClWHi. 5983

---- ---- Trumbull Association.
Minutes. 1831. OClWHi. 5984

---- ---- Wills Creek Association.
Minutes. 1831. OClWHi. 5985

---- ---- Wooster Regular Association.
Minutes [1831?] OClWHi. 5986

---- ---- Zoar Regular Association.
Minutes [1831?] OClWHi. 5987

---- Pennsylvania.
Minutes of the convention of delegates of Baptist Associations in Pennsylvania, for the formation of a State convention for domestic missions, with the constitution, and list of officers, to which is prefixed the circular of the convention, together with an appendix, containing the tenth annual report of the Baptist Missionary Association of Pennsylvania. Philadelphia, Pr. by C. Sherman & Co., 1831. 24 p. PCA. 5988

---- ---- Centre Association.
First annual publication. Minutes of the Centre Baptist Association, held in the meeting house of the Williamsburg Church, Huntingdon County, Pennsylvania, August 19 & 20, 1831. Harrisburg, Pr. by G. S. Peters, 1831. 11 p. NRAB; PCA. 5989

---- ---- Philadelphia Association.
A confession of faith, put forth by the elders and brethren of many congregations of Christians, (baptized upon profession of their faith,) in London and the country. Adopted by the Baptist association, met at Philadelphia, September 25, 1742. With two additional articles, viz: Of public worship... Pittsburgh [Pa.] Pr. by D. & M. Maclean, for W. Williams, 1831. 108 p. CSmH; ICBB; LNB; MWA; PCA; PPeSchw. 5990

---- ---- ---- Minutes of the Philadelphia Baptist Association, held in Philadelphia, in the meeting house of the First Baptist Church, Spruce Street, from the 4th to the 7th, October, 1831, inclusive. Philadelphia, Pr. by T. W. Ustick, 1831. 16 p. PCA; ViRM. 5991

---- ---- Redstone Association.

Minutes of the Redstone Baptist Association held by appointment at Big Redstone, Fayette County, Pennsylvania. September 2, 3, and 4, 1831. Greensburgh, Pr. by Jacob S. Steck, 1831. 15 p. PCA. 5992

---- Rhode Island. Warren Association.

Sixty-fourth anniversary. Minutes of the Warren Baptist Association, held with the Second Baptist Church, in Providence, on Wednesday, and Thursday, September 14, and 15, 1831. Providence, H. H. Brown, 1831. 16 p. PCA; RHi; RPB; RPJCB. 5993

---- Vermont. Lamoille Association.

Minutes of the Fairfield Baptist Association, convened at Union Meeting-House in Berkshire, on September 21, 22 and 23, 1831... Brandon, Vermont Telegraph Office, 1831. 8 p. PCA. 5994

---- ---- Woodstock Association.

Minutes of the Woodstock Baptist Association, held at the Union Meeting-House, in Chester, on Wednesday and Thursday, Sept. 28 & 29, 1831. Windsor, Vt., Pr. at the Chronicle Press, 1831. 12 p. PCA. 5995

---- Virginia.

Minutes of the eighth annual meeting of the General Association of Virginia for missionary purposes, held at Lynchburg, Va., June 4-7, 1831.... Richmond, Pr. at the Office of the Religious Herald, 1831. 25 p. NRAB; PCA; ViRU. 5996

---- ---- Albemarle Association.

Minutes of the Baptist Association, of the Albemarle District, held at Eschol Church, Albemarle County, Virginia, on the 20th and 22d of August, 1831. Lexington, Virginia, Pr. by Elliot & Ware, 1831. 11 p. ViRU. 5997

---- ---- Columbia Baptist Association.

Minutes of the Twelfth Annual Meeting of the Columbia Baptist Association, Maintaining Held, by the appointment, at Mount Pleasant Meeting-house. August 25th, 26, 27 & 28, 1831. Washington City, Pr. by Stephen C. Ustick, 1831. 16 p. DLC; IU; ViRU. 5998

---- ---- Daver Baptist Association.

Minutes... 1831. Richmond, Va., 1831. CHH; DLC. 5999

---- ---- Goshen Association.

Minutes of the Goshen Baptist Association, Held at Liberty Meeting-house, Caroline County, Virginia, commencing on the 24th of September, 1831. Fredericksburg, Va., Pr. at The Herald Office, [1831] 16 p. ViRu. 6000

---- ---- Ketocton Association.

The 65th annual publication. Minutes of the Ketocton Baptist Association, held by appointment at Bethel, Frederick County, Va. August 18, 19 and 20, 1831. Winchester, Pr. by J. G. Brooks, [1831] 8 p. ViRU 6001

---- ---- Parkersburg Association.

Minutes of the Parkersburg, Union, Broad Run, Mt. Pisgah, Judson and Northwestern Virginia Regular Baptist Associations, 1831. 8 p. DLC; ViRU. 6002

Barbauld, Mrs. Anna Letitia (Aikin), 1743-1825.
Lessons for children. New-York, Pendleton and Hill, 1831. 180 p. MH; MPeHi; PPULC; PPPM. 6003

Barber, C. F.
A letter to the Lord Bishop of Lincoln, on the trial for libel Robinson v. Bontoft, and also on the bill of indictment Bontoft v. Robinson, for willful and corrupt perjury. With an address to the public. Boston, Pr. and pub. by C. F. Barber, 1831. 26 p. PPM. 6004

Barber, Edward Downing, 1806-1855.
An address, delivered before the Rutland County Antimasonic Convention, holden at Rutland on the first day of June 1831. By E. D. Barber. Pub. by request of the Convention. Castleton, Pr. by George Collingwood Smith, 1831. 14 p. MWA; PPFM; VtBrt; VtHi; VtU. 6005

Barber, John Warner, 1798-1885, comp.
History and antiquities of New Haven, (Conn.) from its earliest settlement to the present time. Collected and comp. from the most authentic sources... New Haven, J. W. Barber 1831-[32]. 120 p. CtY; DLC; OFH; MB; WHi. 6006

---- History of the New Testament; being an outline history of the principal events recorded in the New Testament. Illustrated by numerous copper-plate engravings. New Haven, Durrie & Peck, 1831. 124 p. CtY; MBC. 6007

---- Interesting events in the history of the United States: Being a selection of the most important and interesting events which have transpired since the discovery of this country to the present time. 3d improved ed. Carefully selected from the most approved authorities. By J. W. Barber. New-Haven [Connecticut] Pr. by Nathan Whiting for J. W. Barber, 1831. 307 p. CtW; CtY; MWA; RPB. 6008

Barber, Jonathan, 1784-1864.
A practical treatise on gesture, chiefly abstracted from Austin's Chironomia... Cambridge [Mass.] Hilliard and Brown, 1831. 116 p. CSmH; DLC; ICU; MnU; NN; TNP. 6009

Barbour, I[saac] Richmond.
A statistical table, showing the influence of intemperance on the churches. By I. Richmond Barbour. Boston, Perkins & Marvin, 1831. 24 p. CtY; MBC; MH-AH; MHi; MWA. 6010

Barclay, Robert, 1648-1690.
An apology for the true Christian divinity, as the same is held forth and preached by the people called in scorn Quakers... New York, Pr. by R. & G. S. Wood, repub. by Benjamin C. Stanton, 1831. GEU-T; KWiF. 6011

---- An epistle of love and friendly advice, to the ambassadors of the several princes of Europe, met at Nimeguen, to consult the peace of Christendom, so far as they are concerned... Which was delivered to them in Latin the 23d and 24th days of the month called February, 1677-8, and now published in English for the satisfaction of such as understand not the language. Philadelphia, Repub. by Benjamin C. Stanton, 1831. 252 p. KWiF. 6012

---- A true and faithful account of the most material passages of a dispute betwixt some students of divinity (so called) of the University of Aberdeen, and the people called Quakers. Robert Barclay and George Keith. Philadelphia, Pub. for preventing mis-reports, by Alex. Skein, John Skein, Alex. Harper, Thomas Mercer and John Cowe. Repub. by Benjamin C. Stanton, 1831. 598 p. MBevHi; PPF. 6013

---- Truth Triumphant, through the spiritual warfare, Christian labor and writing of that able and faithful servant of Jesus Christ, Robert Barclay. To which is prefixed an account of his life and writing... From the octavo end of 1718, collated with the folio ed. of 1692... Philadelphia, Repub. by B. L. Stanton, 1831. 3 v. ICU; MB; MWA; NcD; OHi; PHC. 6014

Barker, John W.
A map of Europe... Middletown, Conn., Hunt, 1831. MB. 6015

Barker, Luke, comp.
A collection of Psalms, hymns, and spiritual songs; selected from different authors; the whole being classed and arranged according to their respective subjects. By Luke Barker... New York, Pr. by G. F. Bunce, 1831. 303 p. DLC; NNUT; NjMD. 6016

Barnard, Daniel Dewey, 1797-1861.
An address delivered...before the Adelphic union society of Williams college; the evening preceding the annual commencement. Williamstown, 1831. 36 p. CtY; DLC; ICN; MB; MWA; PP; RPB. 6017

Barnes, Albert, 1798-1870.
Questions on the historical books of the New Testament. 2d ed. stero. New-York, J. Leavitt, etc., etc., 1831. 195 p. DLC; MH; NjR. 6018

---- The Way of Salvation; a sermon delivered at Morristown, New Jersey, February 8, 1829. By Albert Barnes. 3d ed. Newburyport, Mass., Pr. by Joseph H. Buckingham, for Charles Whipple, 1831. 20 p. CSmH; DLC; MB; NN; OClW. 6019

Barnes, Edwin.
Inconsistencies of Universalism exposed: A sermon, delivered in Boonville, Oneida County, March 18, 1831, by Rev. Edwin Barnes, pastor of the Congregational Church in that town. Utica, Press of William Williams, 1831. 28 p. CtY; MWA. 6020

Barnum, H. L.
Directions for cultivating valuable field products; stating the quantity of seed to be sown, and all the particulars to be observed in securing good crops of the most profitable kind. With recipes for their preservation. To which is appended a calandarial index, giving the course to be pursued by farmers in every month in the year. By H. L. Barnum. Cincinnati, 1831. 128 p. MWA. 6021

---- Family receipts, or practical guide for the husbandman and housewife. Cincinnati, Pr. by Lincoln & Co., for A. B. Roff, 1831. 391 p. INU; IU; KmK; OCHP; PPULC. 6022

---- Farmer's farrier, illustrating the peculiar nature & characteristic of the horse, & the diseases to which he is liable, with the symptoms & remedies familiarly explained... Cincinnati, 1831. 108 p. OCHP; OClWHi; OHi. 6023

---- The spy unmasked; or, Memoirs of Enoch Crosby, alias Harvey Birch, the hero of Mr. Cooper's tale of the neutral ground: being an authentic account of the secret services which he rendered his country during the revolutionary war. By H. L. Barnum. Embellished with a correct likeness of the hero ... 2d ed. Cincinnati, A. B. Roff, 1831. 216 p. ArU; DLC; KyHi; MdBJ; NjR; OCHP; TxH. 6024

Barr, John.
A Help to Professing Christians, in judging their spiritual state and growth in Grace... by the Rev. John Barr, author of the Scripture Students' Assistant, Plain Catechetical Instructions on the Lord's Supper and on Infant Baptism. From the Edinburgh ed. Boston, Perkins & Martin, 1831. 307 p. CtY; ICP; MB; MBC; MWA; NcCJ; OO. 6025

Barrett, Samuel, 1795-1866.
A discourse delivered before the Ancient and Honourable Artillery Company, June 6, 1831, being the 192d Anniversary By Samuel Barrett, Minister of the Church in Chambers Street, Boston. Cambridge, Pr. by E. W. Metcalf and Company, 1831. 19 p. DLC; MB; MHi; OMC. 6026

---- The Doctrine of Religious Experience Explained and Enforced. By Samuel Barrett. 2d ed., No. 29. Printed for the American Unitarian Association. Boston, Pr. by L. R. Butts, for Gray and Bowen, 1831. 24 p. ICMe; MB; MBC; MB-FA; MeB; MeBat; MNF. 6027

---- Sermons before Ancient & Ancient & Hov. Artillery Co. Boston. Jan. 6, 1831, Cambridge, 1831. OCHP. 6028

Barringer, Daniel Laurens.
To the freeman of Orange, Person and Wake. March, 1831. 3 p. NcU. 6029

Bartlett, Montgomery Robert.
A celestial planisphere or Map of the heavens. By M. R. Bartlett, Hartford, Engraved by V. Balch & S. Stiles, 1831. MH. 6030

Bartow, Robert.
A true exposition of the transactions which led to the failure of the late Franklin bank; together with a brief history of some of the detected acts, and malpractices of its late president, Samuel Leggett, in relation to that institution. By Robert Bartow. New York, Pr. by J. H. Turney, 1831. 29 p. DLC; MB; MHi; PPL; TxU. 6031

Bates, Elisha, 1780?-1861.
The doctrines of Friends: or, principles of the Christian religion, as held by the Society of Friends, commonly called Quakers. 3d ed. Mountpleasant, Pr. and pub. by the author, 1831. 320 p. CSmH; MB; MH; MNan; OClWHi; PHC; PHi. 6032

Bates, William, 1625-1699.
The Harmony of the Divine Attributes, in Accomplishment of Man's Redemption. By William Bates, D.D. With an Introductory Essay by A. Alexander, D.D. New York, Jonathan Leavitt; Boston, Crocker & Brewster, 1831. 348 p. GMM; ICP; MeB; NNUT; PPPrHi; ScU; WaPS. 6033

Baudelocque, Auguste César, 1795-1851.
Treatise on puerperal peritonitis, by A. C. Baudelocque...to which was awarded the prize by by Royal society of medicine of Bordeaux. Translated from the French by G. S. Bedford... New-

York, Pr. by Elliott & Palmer for Collins and Hannay [etc.] 1831. 480 p. CtY; DLC; MA; RPM; ViRA. 6034

Baxter, Richard, 1615-1691.

A call to the unconverted, to which are added, several valuable essays. By Richard Baxter, With an introductory essay by Thomas Chalmers, D.D., from the last London ed. ...New York, J. K. Porter, 1831. 220 p. ICU; RP. 6035

---- The dying thoughts of the late Richard Baxter, abridged by Benjamin Fawcet... New York, C. Wells, 1831. 187 p. MH-AH; MMeT-Hi; NNC; OO; PPM. 6036

---- The Saints' everlasting rest, by the Rev. Richard Baxter. Abridged by Benjamin Fawcett, A.M. New York, American Tract Society [183-?] 453 p. DLC; NIC; PPULC; ViU; WaPS. 6037

---- The Saint's everlasting rest: or, A treatise of the blessed state of the Saints, in their enjoyment of God in glory. Extracted from the works of Richard Baxter, By John Wesley... New York, Pub. by J. Emory and B. Waugh for the Method. Episcopal Church, 1831. 271 p. CoFS; DLC; NcD. 6038

---- Select Practical Writings of Richard Baxter, With a life of the author. By Leonard Bacon... New Haven, Durrie & Peck, 1831. 2 v. CU; IaCrM; MBC; NNUT; TWcW. 6039

[Bayard, Richard Henry] 1796-1868, comp.

Documents relating to the presidential election in the year 1801: containing a refutation of two passages in the writings of Thomas Jefferson, aspersing the character of the late James A. Bayard, of Delaware. Philadelphia, Pr. by Mifflin & Parry, 1831. 14 p. CtY; ICU; MB; MWA; NjR. 6040

Baylies, Francis, 1783-1852.

An address before the Members of the Taunton Lyceum. Delivered July 4, 1831. [Pub. at their request.] By Francis Baylies. Boston, J. H. Eastburn, 1831. 37 p. MBat; MBC; MiD-B; MWA; NjPT; PPL. 6041

[Beaconsfield, Benjamin Disraeli, 1st earl of] 1804-1881.

...The young duke...By the author of "Vivian Grey"... (Harper's stereotype ed.) New York, J. & J. Harper, 1831. 2 v. CtHT; DLC; LU; MWA; NjR; OkU; RJa; TxU. 6042

Beaman, Charles C.

Poem delivered before the Franklin Debating Society at their anniversary, January 17, 1831. Being the birthday of Franklin. By Charles C. Beaman, Boston, 1831. 12 p. CtY; DLC; MB; MH; MHi. 6043

Beard, E.

The Bee Sheperd; or, E. Beard's Practical Bee Manager. Boston, 1831. MHi. 6044

Beard, John Reilly, ed., 1800-1876.

Sermons, accompanied by suitable prayers; designed to be used in families. 1st Amer. ed. from the 2d London ed. Edited by the Rev. J. R. Beard. Boston, Leonard C. Bowles, 1831. 480 p. MH-AH; MNF; MW; NCaS; NhPet; OO. 6045

Beaumarchais, Pierre Augustin Caron de, 1732-1799.

Le barbier de Seville, un La precaution inutile, opera-comique en quartre actes, d'apres Beaumarchais et le drame italien, parales ajustees sur la musique de Rossini par Castil-Blaze, a comic opera in four acts: The words adapted to the music of Rossini, by Castil-Blaze. Tr. for the American publishers. Boston, 1831. 99 p. CtY. 6046

Beauties of Sentiment or an original collection of Moral Anecdotes for the young... Boston, John Punchard, 1831. 110 p. CSmH; MB; MH. 6047

The Beauties of the British poets, with a few introductory observations by the Rev. George Croly. New York, C. Wells, 1831. 393 p. CtY; MH; NN; PPA; PPULC. 6048

Beaver Meadow Railroad and Coal Company.

Acts of Assembly incorporating Beaver Meadow rail road and coal company, and address to the public by the directors. Philadelphia, 1831. 19 p. DBRE; PHi; PPAmP; PPULC. 6049

Bebb, William, 1802-1873.

An Address delivered before the Butler County Agricultural Society at the first annual meeting... Hamilton, O., Pr. by Woods & Campbell, for the Society, 1831. 12 p. NB; OOxM. 6050

Beck, Frederick.

The young accountant's guide; or, An easy introduction to the knowledge of Mercantile book-keeping... By Frederick Beck ... Boston, Stimpson & Clapp, 1831. 116 p. DLC; MB; MH; MH-BA; NBatHL. 6051

Beck, John Brodhead.

Report of trial on an indictment for libel. New York, 1831. 48 p. DLC; MB. 6052

Beck, Lewis C[aleb], 1798-1853.

A manual of chemistry, containing a condensed view of the present state of the science, with... references to more extensive treatises, original papers, &c. ... By Lewis C. Beck... Albany, Webster and Skinners, 1831. 458 p. CSt-L; DLC; NjR; OClWHi; TWeW; WaPS. 6053

Beckwith, George Cone, 1800-1870.

A dissuasive from controversy respecting the mode of baptism. By G. C. Beckwith. Pastor of a Church in Lowell, Massachusetts. 3d ed. Hartford, Pr. by G. F. Olmsted, for D. F. Robinson, 1831. 35 p. Ct; KyLoS; MiD-B. 6054

---- A sermon on the mode of baptism, by G. C. Beckwith. Castleton, Pr. by H. H. Houghton, 1831. 24 p. CtY; ICP; MH; OCHP. 6055

Beecher, Catherine Esther, 1800-1878.

The elements of mental and moral philosophy, founded upon experience, reason, and the bible. Hartford, P. B. Gleason & Co., 1831. 452 p. CBPSR; GDecCT; IaDuU; MH-AH; NNUT; OClW. 6056

Beechey, Frederick William, 1796-1856.

Narrative of a voyage to the Pacific and Beering's Strait, to co-operate with polar expeditions: performed in His Majesty's ship Blossom, under the command of Captain F. W. Beechey... in the years 1825, 26, 27, 28... Philadelphia, Carey & Lea, 1831. 493 p. CMiC. 6057

Beede, Samuel.

Questions designed to assist the pupil in acquiring a knowledge of English grammer, particularly adapted to Putnam's grammar.

Concord, [N. H.] Hoag & Atwood, 1831. 12 p. CU; MH. 6058

Beers' Carolina and Georgia Almanac for 1832. Charleston, S.C., S. Babcock & Co. [1831] DLC; MWA; NcU. 6059

Beers' Louisiana and Mississippi almanac for the year 1832.
Being Bissextile, or leap year, and until July 4, the fifty-sixth year of American Independence. Calculated for the meridian of Natchez... The astronomical part examined and corrected by Elijah Beaumont, 1831. 36 p. Ms-Ar. 6060

Behr, Charles de
A catalogue of French, Latin and Greek school books, published and for sale at the foreign and classical book store, Charles de Behr. New York, Philadelphia, Cincinnnati, C. D. Bradford & Co., 1831. [22] p. PPAmP; PPULC; TxSaO. 6061

Belfast. Maine. First Congregational Church.
Confession of Faith and Covenant, with ecclesiastical principles and rules of the First Congregational Church in Belfast. Belfast, John Derr, 1831. 22 p. MBC. 6062

[Belknap, Jeremy], 1744-1798.
The foresters, an American tale: being a sequal [!] to the history of John Bull, the clothier. In a series of letters to a friend. Exeter, B. H. Meder, 1831. 156 p. CFrT; DLC; ICU; MB; MeU; PPL-R; RPB. 6063

---- The history of New Hampshire. By Jeremy Belknap... From a copy of the original edition, having the author's last corrections. To which are added notes, containing various corrections and illustrations of the text, and additional facts and notices of persons and events therein mentioned by John Farmer... V. 1 Dover [N. H.] S. C. Stevens and Ela & Wadleigh, 1831. CoD; DLC; KHi; MB; RPJCB; ViU. 6064

Belknap, Philander W., comp.
A choice collection of hymns, and spiritual songs. For the use of all those who love our Lord and Savior Jesus Christ. Warsaw, N.Y., Pr. by A. W. Young, 1831. 96 p. RPB. 6065

Bell, Henry Glassford, 1803-1874.
Life of Mary Queen of Scots. By Henry Glassford Bell, Esq. New-York, J. & J. Harper, 1831. 2 v. DLC; NjPT; PHi; PU; ScC; TNP; ViL. 6066

Bell, John, 1796-1872.
On baths and mineral waters ... By John Bell... Philadelphia, H. H. Porter, 1831. 532 p. CtY; DLC; MaU; PPAmP; TxU; VL. 6067

Bell, Solomen.
Tales of travels. See Snelling, William Joseph, 1804-1848.

Bell, Thomas, 1792-1880.
The anatomy, physiology and diseases of the teeth. By Thomas Bell, F.R.S., F.L.S., F.G.S.,... Philadelphia, Carey & Lea, 1831. 351 p. KyU; MB; MH; NBMS; PPCP; ViNoM; WPA. 6068

Bell, William, 1791-1871.
Letters addressed to Rev. J. Clark, a presiding Elder of the Methodist Connexion, on the subject of a discourse delivered by him at the Methodist chapel, St. Albans, Vt. From Psalms ix. 27. Woodstock, [n.p.] 1831. 56 p. MMeT-Hi; MWA. 6069

Bellarmino, Robert, Francesco Romolo, Saint, 1542-1621.
Doctrina Cristiana. Philadelphia, 1831. MdW. 6070

Benedict, George Wyllys, 1796-1871.
An exposition of the system of instruction and discipline pursued in the university of Vermont. By the faculty. 2d ed. Burlington, Chauncey Goodrich, 1831. 32 p. DLC; MB; MH; NNUT; RPB. 6071

Benengeli, Cid Hamet, pseud.
The dedication; or, An essay on the true modern Caesar. By Cid Hamet Benengeli the second. Baltimore, Pr. and pub. by Sands and Neilson, 1831. 76 p. MdBLC; MdHi; PPL. 6072

Benezet, Anthony.
Plain path to Christian perfection, tr. from the French. Philadelphia, 1831. 99 p. KKcBT; OO; PSC-Hi; PHC. 6073

Bennett, James.
The history and prospects of the church. New York, Westly & Davis, 1831. 178 p. IaPeC. 6074

Bennett, James Arlington.
The American system of practical book-keeping... New York, Collins and Hannay, 1831. 104 p. MiU; OLak; PPULC. 6075

Bennett, Mrs. Mary E.
The Cottage Girl; or, An Account of Ann Edwards. Revised by the Committee of Publication of the American Sunday School Union. Philadelphia, I. Ashmead, 1831. 35 p. ICBB. 6076

Bennett & Walton's almanac for 1832. Philadelphia, Pa., Bennett & Walton [1831] MWA. 6077

Bennington, Vermont. Bennington Academy.
Catalogue for the summer and fall term ending November 29, 1831. 8 p. 6078

---- Second Congregational Church.
Articles of faith and covenant. Bennington [n.p.] 1831. 8 p. MBC. 6079

Bentley, Rensselaer.
The English reader. By R. Bentley. Poughkeepsie, P. Potter, 1831. NPV. 6080

Benton, Thomas Hart, 1782-1858.
Speech of Mr. Benton, of Missouri, on introducing a resolution against the renewal of the charter of the bank of the United States. Delivered in the Senate of the United States, February 2, 1831. Washington [D.C.], Pr. by Duff Green, 1831. 23 p. CSmH; DLC; GEU; MH; NcD; PPM; WHi. 6081

---- Speech of Mr. Benton of Missouri on the bill to abolish the duty on alum salt. Delivered in the Senate February 8, 1830. Washington, Pr. by Gales & Seaton, 1831. 46 p. DLC; ICRL; InFuoL; MH; NN; WHi. 6082

Berkley jail. [Philadelphia, Pr. by James Kay, 1831] 328 p. TxSani. 6083

Berkley, Massachusetts. Congregational Church.
"Better Edification a Good Plea." Proceedings of an Ecclesiastical Council, in the town of Berkley, October 19, 1831, and the documents connected therewith. Taunton [Mass.], James Thurber, 1831. 26 p. CSmH; MH; MH-AH; NN. 6084

Berkshire County Sunday School Teachers Union.
... Report of the Berkshire County Sunday School Teacher's

[!] Union, auxiliary to the American Sunday School Union. First- for the year. 1831-. Pittsfield, Pr. by Phineas Allen & son [1831?] Ct. 6085

Bernays, A.
German prose anthology. New York, Harper, 1831. 337 p. LN. 6086

[Berquin, Arnaud], 1749-(c 1791)
The Looking-Glass for the Mind; or, Intellectual Mirror. Chiefly trans. from L'Ami des Enfans. Philadelphia, 1831. 216 p. PHi. 6087

The Best Friend. Written for the American Sunday School Union and revised by the Committee of Publication. American Sunday School Union. Philadelphia, 1831. 24 p. DLC; ICBB; InLogCH; NjR. 6088

Bethune, George Washington, 1805-1862.
The cross of Christ, the only theme of the preacher of truth; an inaugural discourse: with an exhortation to prayer and exertion for the peace of Jerusalem. Delivered before the congregation of the Reformed Dutch Church, Utica, November 14th, 1830. By George W. Bethune. Utica, Pr. by Northway & Porter, 1831. 48 p. MH-AH; MiD-B; NAuT; NCH; NjR; NN; NUt; PPPrHi. 6089

---- Occasional sermons and addresses. Utica, 1831-45. 17 nos. in 1 v. NIC. 6090

Bevan, Joseph Gurney, 1753-1814.
An account of the life and writings of Robert Barclay. Philadelphia, Stanton, 1831. 3 v. NcGu; PPULC; PPWI. 6091

---- A short account of the life and writings of Robert Barclay. Philadelphia, Repub. by Benjamin C. Stanton, 1831. 66 p. InRchE; KyWAT; OHi. 6092

Bible. Abridged.
[History of the Bible, America, 183-?] 192 p. MB. 6093

---- Die Bibel, oder die ganze Heilige Schrift des Alten und Neuen Testaments...nach Dr. Martin Luthers uebersetzung. Philadelphia, 1831. PPL. 6094

---- The Christian Miniature Library. Vol. I. The Daily Scripture Expositor. New York, H. C. Sleight, Clinton Hall; Boston, Pierce and Parker, 1831. MBev-F; RNHi; ViRut. 6095

---- The daily Scripture expositor: containing a text of scripture for every day in the year; with explanatory notes and brief reflections. New-York, H. C. Sleight, Clinton Hall; Boston, Pierce & Parker, 1831. 280 p. CtY-D; NNQ. 6096

---- Daily texts, with verses of hymns; adapted for general use... New York, 1831. 128 p. IU. 6097

---- The English Version of the Polyglot Bible, containing the Old and New Testaments, with original selections of references to parallel and illustrative passages, and marginal readings... Baltimore, Armstrong and Plaskitt, 1831. 999 p. IEG; MdBAHi. 6098

---- The gospel of our Lord and Saviour Jesus Christ, according to Saint Matthew, tr. into the Mohawk language, by A. Hill, and corr. by J. A. Wilkes, jr. ... New York, The Young Men's Bible Society of New York, 1831. 197 p. CSmH; WHi. 6099

---- ---- Philadelphia, Key and

Meilke, 1831. 587, 189 p. Ct; MH; MNam; NN; OO. 6100

---- Ἡ καιτὴ διαδηκη. Novum Testamentum, cum versione latina Ariae Moutani, in quo turn selecti versiculi 1900, quibus omnes Novi Testamenti voces continentur, asteriscis notantur; tum omnes et singulae voces, sernel vel saepius occurrentes, peculiari nota distinguuntur. Auctore Johanne Leusden... New York, Collins & Hannay, 1831. 755 p. CBPSR; DLC; TxMinw. 6101

---- ---- Philadelphia, Towar et Hogan, 1831. 369 p. DLC; MWA; OU; PU; TU. 6102

---- A harmony of the gospels, on the plan proposed by Lant Carpenter. Boston, Gray & Bowen, 1831. 260 p. CBPac; CtHC; GDecCT; ICP; MH; RNR. 6103

---- A help to the Book of Genesis, on the lesson system of teaching. New York, J. Leavitt; Boston, Crocker & Brewster, 1831. 288 p. AmSSchU; GDccCT; IEG; MBC; MH. 6104

---- Holisso holitopa, chitokaka Chisus in anumpeshi Luk, Chani itatuklo kut holissochi tok Mak o, a kashapa kut Chahta im anumpa isht holisso hoke. [By Rev. Alfred Wright] Utica, Press of William Williams, 1831. 152 p. MBAt; MHi; NN; NHi; OMC. 6105

---- The Holy Bible containing the old and New Testament according to the authorized version; with explanatory notes, poetical observations and copious marginal references by Thomas Scott. Boston, Samuel T. Armstrong and Crocker and Brewster; New York, J. Leavitt; stereotyped by T. H. Carter & co., Boston type and stereotype foundry, 1831. 6 v. CtSoP; GAlN; IaFamP; TNP. 6106

---- ---- Boston, George Clark, 1831. CSmH; MTaHi; NcSalL. 6107

---- ---- Boston, Gray and Bowen, 1831. 2 vols. MdBCC; MeB; MHi; NN. 6108

---- ---- Boston, Hilliard, Gray, Little, 1831. 2 vols. MH-AH; NN. 6109

---- ---- Boston, Lincoln and Edmands, 1831. GDecCT; MHy; NbOM. 6110

---- ---- Boston, Wait and Dow, 1831. 2 v. IEN-M; MB. 6111

---- ---- Concord, 1831. 792 p. Nh-Hi. 6112

---- ---- New York, Pr. and pub. by T. Kinnersley, 1831. 1216 p. NbCrD; NNAB. 6113

---- ---- Stereotype edition. New York, Pr. by D. Fanshaw, for the American Bible Society, 1831. 852 p. CtY-D; PCDHi; PHC; WHi. 6114

---- ---- Diligently compared and revised by Harvey Wilbur, New York, White Gallaher and White, 1831. 4 vols. in 1. DLC. 6115

---- ---- Philadelphia, The Bible Association of Friends in America, 1831. CtY; DLC. 6116

---- ---- Pittsburgh, Pub. by H. Holdship, and sons, 1831. 1 vol. PPi. 6117

---- ---- Woodstock [Vermont], Rufus Colton, 1831. 486, 162 p. VtHi. 6118

---- The Holy Bible, containing the old and new testaments,

translated out of the original tongues, and with the former translations diligently compared and revised with Canne's marginal notes and references together with the Apocrapha. Boston, Langdon Coffin, 1831. 552 p. IEG; IaScW; MBD; MNoanNP; MWHi; NN. 6119

---- ---- Stereotyped, Cooperstown, H. and E. Phinney, 1831-1832. 768 p. NNAB. 6120

---- ---- New York, Daniel D. Smith, 1831. CtY; MBC. 6121

---- ---- Saratoga Springs [New York] G. M. Davison, 1831. 768 p. PHi. 6122

Bible English

The Holy Bible... with references and illustrations... summary... paraphrase... analysis... by John Brown. Embellished with a series of... engravings. New York, T. Kinnersley, 1831. NNAB. 6123

---- Mesah oowh menwohjemoowin owh St. Mathew. Kahkeway wonnably Kiya Tyentennagen Kahahnekahnootah moobeungig Keahnoonegoowod enewh York Auxiliary Bible Society. New York, Pr. by J. Baxter at the Colonial Advocate Office, 1831. 67 p. DLC. 6124

---- Das Neue Testament unsers Herrn und Heilandes Jesu Christi unbersezt [sic] von Dr. Martin Luther. Harrisburg (Pa.), 1831. 377 p. CSmH. 6125

---- ---- Philadelphia, G. W. Mentz, 1831. PPeSchw. 6126

---- The New Testament of our God and Savior Jesus Christ, translated out of the Latin vulgate; diligently compared with the original Greek; and first published by the English College of Rhemes [sic], anno, 1582. Newly revised and corrected according to the clementine edition of the scriptures; with annotation to clear up the principal difficulties of holy writ. As approved by the Right Reverend John DuBois, Catholic Bishop of New York... Bellows Falls, [Vt.] Pr. by Cook & Taylor, for J. I. Cutler & Co., 1831. 344 p. CSmH; RPB. 6127

---- ---- Boston, Stimpson and Clapp, 1831. 480 p. CSt; MNe; MoBolS. 6128

---- ---- Exeter, 1831. 259 p. Nh-Hi. 6129

---- ---- Hartford, Conn., Silas Condrus, 1831. 378 p. Ct; MWiw; WaPS. 6130

---- ---- Lancaster [Mass.], Carter, Andrews & Co., 1831. 335 p. MLanc; MWHi. 6131

---- ---- New York, Schayer, 1831. PPL; PPM. 6132

---- ---- Philadelphia, Pub. by Eugene Cummiskey, Stereotyped by J. Howe, 1831. 10 p. ICMBI. 6133

---- ---- Philadelphia, Pr. and pub. by William F. Geddes, 1831. 201 p. MMhHi; TSewU. 6134

---- ---- Utica, Pr. by William Williams for the proprietors, [1831] 344 p. ICLoy. 6135

---- The New Testament of our Lord and Saviour Jesus Christ. The text carefully printed from the most correct copies of the present authorized version including the marginal readings and parallel texts, with a commentary and critical notes designed as a help to a better understanding of the sacred writings, by Adam

Clarke... New York, S. Hoyt & co., Carlton & Lanahan, J. Emory and B. Waugh, etc., 1831. LNH; NGow; PALM; WaPS. 6136

---- Notes...on...Genesis. New York, 1831. 2 v. NbCrD. 6137

---- Le Nouveau Testament de notre seigneur Jesus Christ. Imprime sur L'edition de Paris, de L'Annee. 1805. Edition stereotype, revue et corrigee avec soin d'apres le texte grec. A New York, Imprime avec des planches solides par D. Fanshaw, aux frais de La societe Biblique Americaine, 1831. 207 p. AWA; MWA; MoSpD; NStC; OO. 6138

---- El Nuevo Testamento de nuestro Senor Jesu Christo, tr. de la Biblia Vulgata Latina en espanol por Felipe Scio de S. Miguel...conforme a la 2 ed. hecha en Madrid...1797 rev... New York, Soc. Amer. de la Biblia, 1831. 376 p. MB; MWA; PPLT. 6139

---- A new translation of the book of Psalms, with an introduction. By George R. Noyes. Boston, Gray and Bowen, 1831. 232 p. CtY; MBAt; MH-AH; MNe; MnM. 6140

---- Outline history of the principal events recorded in the New Testament. New Haven, Durrie, and Peck, 1831. 128 p. MH-AH. 6141

---- Pocket Reference Testament. The New Testament of our Lord and Saviour Jesus Christ: with original selections of references to parallel and illustrative passage; and marginal readings; together with other valuable additions; the whole designed to facilitate the acquisition of scripture knowledge in Bible Classes, Sunday Schools. Stereotyped by L. Johnson. Baltimore, Armstrong & Plaskett, 1831. 281 p. NBuG; NN. 6142

---- Psalms carefully suited to the Christian worship in the United States of America. Being an improvement of the old Psalms of David... New York, White, Gallaher & White, 1831. 300 p. DLC. 6143

---- The symbolical Bible for the amusement and instruction of children; being the hieroglyphical Bible, corrected and much enlarged. To which is added, The Life of Our Blessed Saviour, and Brief Sketches of the Apostles with questions on each. New York, M. B. Holmes, 1831. 72 p. MH; MH-AH. 6144

---- The whole book of Psalms, in metre; with Hymns... New York, Protestant Episcopal Church, 1831. 2 v. in 1. NNG. 6145

The Biblical repository devoted to Biblical and general literature, theological discussion, the history of theological opinions, etc. v 1-12, 1831-38; v 1-12 2d ser., 1839-44; v 1-6, 3d ser., 1845-50. Andover [Mass.] 1831-36; New York, 1837-50. Ct; MS; NbCrD; NUt. 6146

Bickersteth, Edward, 1786-1850. Bickersteth's Treatise on the Lord's supper: adapted to the services of the Protestant Episcopal Church in the United States, with an introduction and an essay, by G. T. Bedell... 3d ed. Philadelphia, Key & Mielke, 1831. 210 p. DLC; ICP; MB; ViRu. 6147

---- The chief concerns of man for time and eternity. Being a course of valedictory discourses preached at Wheler chapel in the autumn of 1830. By the Rev. E. Bickersteth, rector of Watton, Hertfordshire. Philadelphia, Clarke & Raser, 1831. 208 p. MB; PPM; PPULC; ViU. 6148

Biddle, Richard, 1796-1847.
A Memoir of Sebastian Cabot: with a review of the history of maritime discovery... Philadelphia [Pr. by James Kay and co.] for Carey and Lea, 1831. 327 p. CU; DLC; OCHP; PPA; WaU. 6149

Bigelow, Andrew, 1795-1877.
Travels in Malta and Sicily, with sketches of Gibralter in MDCCCXXVII. By Andrew Bigelow... Boston, Carter, Hendee & Babcock; New York, E. Bliss, 1831. 528 p. Ct; DLC; MSU; NjP; PPM. 6150

Bigelow, Jacob, 1787-1879.
Elements of Technology, taken chiefly from A Course of Lectures Delivered at Cambridge on the Application of the Sciences to the Useful Arts. Now published for the use of Seminaries and students. By Jacob Bigelow, M.D. Professor of Materia Medica, and late Rumford Professor in Harvard University; Member of the American Academy of Arts and Sciences; of the American Philosophical Society; of the Linnaean Societies of London and Paris, etc. 2d ed., with additions. Boston, Hilliard, Gray, Little and Wilkins, 1831. 521 p. DLC; IaHi; MH; NjR; PPWa. 6151

Bigland, John, 1750-1832.
A natural history of animals. Philadelphia, Grigg, 1831. 189 p. MB; PHi; PPULC. 6152

---- A natural history of birds, fishes, reptiles and insects. By John Bigland... Philadelphia, John Grigg, 1831. 179 p. CtY; NUt; NjR. 6153

Billerica [Mass.]
A statement of the expenses of the Town of Billerica, from May 3, 1830, to May 3, 1831. Lowell, Pr. by E. C. Purdy, 1831. Broadside. MBilHi. 6154

Billing, Archibald, 1791-1881.
First principles of medicine. Philadelphia, Pr. by O. S. Cooke, & Co., 1831. 246 p. PPiAM. 6155

Billy Gorham; the little infant scholar. New Haven, S. Babcock, Sidney's press, 1831. 17 p. CtY. 6156

Bingham, Caleb, 1757-1817.
The American preceptor improved; being a new selection of lessons for reading and speaking. Designed for the use of schools. By Caleb Bingham, A.M. ... 68th (8th improved) ed. Boston, J. H. A. Frost, 1831. 228 p. CtEhad. 6157

---- The Columbian orator: containing a variety of original and selected pieces; together with rules; calculated to improve youth and others in the ornamental and useful art of eloquence. Boston, J. H. A. Frost, 1831. 300 p. CtY; PPULC; ViU. 6158

Binney, Horace, 1780-1875.
Speech of Horace Binney, of Pennsylvania, on the contested election of Letcher and Moore. Washington, 1831. PPL-R; PPULC. 6159

Biography of Master Burke, the Irish Roscius; the wonder of the world: and the paragon of actors ... 7th ed. Philadelphia, Shakespeare press [1831?] 11 p. CtY; MB. 6160

The Birds, the thornbushes & the sheep... Providence, H. H.

Brown, 1831. 16 p. Mi. 6161

Birth-day present; from an affectionate friend. New Haven, S. Babcock, Sidney's press, 1831. 17 p. DLC; WHi. 6162

Bishop, Robert Hamilton.
An address delivered to the graduates of Miami university, September 28, 1831. By R. H. Bishop... Oxford [O.] Pr. at the Oxford press, 1831. 12 p. ICU; NNUT; PPPrHi. 6163

---- A manual of logic. By Robert H. Bishop, D.D., President of Miami University. Oxford, Societies' press, 1831. 172 p. OClWHi; WRHist. 6164

Blackstone Canal National Bank, Providence.
Charter...Granted Jan. 1831. Providence, R.I., Pr. by William Simons, Jun, 1831. 8 p. MH-BA; RPB. 6165

Blair, David, pseud. see Phillips, Sir Richard, 1767-1840.

Blair, Hugh, 1718-1800.
Dr. Blair's Lectures on Rhetoric. Abridged, with Questions. New York, Pr. by W. E. Dean, for Collins & Co., 1831. 268 p. Ct; KWiU; OC; OClWHi; Vi. 6166

---- ... Lectures on rhetoric and belles lettres...to which are added copious questions and an analysis of each lecture, by Abraham Mills... 3d ed. New York, Carvill, 1831. 557 p. ICU; Md; OT; PMA; TxShA. 6167

Blair, John, 1790-1863.
To the voters of the first Congressional district of Tennessee. [Washington, 1831] DLC. 6168

Blair, William, fl. 1820.
Sketch of the life and military services of Gen. John Adair, written principally in 1820 by Judge William Blair, and continued to the present time by a friend... Harrodsburg, Ky., Pr. at the American office, 1831. 20 p. KyHbHi; MH; WHi. 6169

Blake, J[ohn] L[auris], 1788-1857.
First book in astronomy, adapted to the use of common schools. Illustrated with steel plate engravings. By Rev. J. L. Blake, A. M. ... Boston, Lincoln and Edmands; Portland, S. Colman, [etc., etc.] ...1831. 115 p. CSt; MB; MH; NNC; NcD; NjR; OUrC; PU. 6170

---- Geography for children. With eight copper-plate maps and thirty wood cuts. By Rev. J. L. Blake, A. M. ... Boston, Richardson, Lord and Holbrook, 1831. 68 p. CSt; MB; MH; NNC; NhD; Nh-Hi; RHi. 6171

---- The historical reader, designed for the use of schools & families. On a new plan. By Rev. J. L. Blake...Stereotype ed. Concord, N.H., H. Hill & Co., 1831. 372 p. DLC; ICN; MH; Nh; OKU. 6172

---- Natural philosophy. Boston, 1831. CtHWatk. 6173

[Blanchard, Amos] of Cincinnati.
American military biography: containing the lives and characters of the officers of the revolution who were most distinguished in achieving our national independence. Also, the life of Gilbert Motier LaFayette... [Cincinnati] B. Crosby, 1831. 615 p. C-S; IU; MoK; WaSP. 6174

---- ---- Philadelphia, William Starely, 1831. 607 p. AAP; AU;

PPULC; PU; WaSP. 6175

Blanchard, Amos, 1801?-1869.
Book of martyrs, or, a history of the lives, sufferings, and triumphant deaths of the primitive Protestant martyrs, from the introduction of Christianity to the latest periods of pagan, popish, and infidel persecutions... Comp. from Fox's Book of Martyrs, and other authentic sources. Embellished with twenty four engravings. Cincinnati, Robinson, 1831. 516 p. ICBB; OCLWHi; MHi; PPLT; ViU. 6176

---- Original sin and the atonement. A trial sermon, preached before the Cincinnati presbytery, July 20, 1831... Cincinnati, Pr. by Robinson and Fairbank, 1831. 23 p. M; OClWHi; PPPrHi. 6177

Blanchard, J.
An address delivered before the Temperance Society in Weathersfield, Vermont. September 16, 1831. Windsor, Pr. at the Chronicle Press, 1831. 8 p. PPPrHi. 6178

Blaze, Francois Henri Joseph, called Castil-Blaze, 1784-1857.
La pie voleuse, opera, entrois actes., sur la musique de Rossini, par M. Castil Blaze. The magpie and the maid, an opera, in three acts. Music by Rossini. Translated literally, for the use of visitors to the French opera. By G. B. C. Baltimore, E. J. Coale, 1831. 126 p. DLC; ICU; MdBJ; MdHi; MH. 6179

The Blessed Family. Stereotyped by James Connor, New York. New York, Pr. at the Protestant Episcopal Press, 1831. 8, [1] p. MBD. 6180

Bloodgood, S. De Witt, 1799-1866.
Some account of the Hudson and Mohawk Railroad, communicated for the October number of Silliman's Journal 1831... Albany, Pub. by Tracy Doolittle, 1831. 22 p. NN. 6181

---- Some account of the Jacotot System of universal instruction; with a preliminary reference to the systems of Lancaster, Fellenburgh, and Pestalozzi, read before the Albany Institute... April, 1831. By a member of the Third Department. New York, Bliss, 1831. 33 p. CtY; MB; MH; NIC; NjR. 6182

Bloomfield, (Bishop).
Bishop Bloomfield's Manual of Family Prayers; with alterations. New York, Protestant Episcopal Tract Society, 1831. 36 p. MdBD. 6183

Blue-light beacon; or, The lost boy found in a tea-pot. A comedy in two acts. By the author of the "Pig's tail untwisted." Concord, 1831. 17 p. Nh-Hi; RPB. 6184

Blunt, John James, 1794-1855.
Undesigned coincidences in the writings both of the Old and New Testaments, and argument of their veracity. Paley, William Horae Paulinae... New York, Robert Carter, 1831. TxAuPT. 6185

Boaden, Caroline.
The first of April: a farce; printed from the acting copy, with remarks, biographical and critical, by D.-G. (With) stage business, etc. New York, Clayton, 1831. 36 p. DLC; MB; MBr; MH; PU; TxU. 6186

Bochsa, Robert Nicolas Charles, 1789-1856.
I pity and forgive: the last words of Gen. Simon Bolivar... Poetry by S. Woodworth. Music from Beethoven; arranged with an accompaniment for the pianoforte

by N. C. Bochsa... New York, Firth & Hall, c1831. 3 p. MNF. 6187

Boen, William.
Memorial of Mt. Holly Monthly Meeting. Philadelphia, 1831. PSC-Hi. 6188

Boeuf, Joseph F. A.
French reader: or, A step to translation by progressive exercises on a new plan: in which the English translation of the French is entirely excluded... containing also a treatise on pronunciation. By Jos. F. A. Boeuf... New-York, Sold by C. de Behr [etc.] 1831. iv, 125 p. MiD-B; OFH. 6189

Bogatzky, Carl Heinrich.
A Golden Treasury, for the children of God, whose treasure is in Heaven. Consisting of select texts of the Bible, with practical observations, in prose and verse, for every day of the year. C. H. V. Bogatzky. Together with a few Forms of Prayer, for private use. New York, M'Elrath & Bangs, 1831. 389 p. CtMW; GAGTh; NArge; PAtM; WJan. 6190

Bogle, Joseph M.
To the Freemen of Iredell County. Fellow-Citizens: On returning home from the arduous and responsible labours of a protracted session of our State Legislature, I, as one of your representatives, feel it no less my duty to impart such information as I possess.... A bill was before the Senate, to establish a Bank on the funds of the State; but after considerable discussion in that House, the bill was lost by the casting vote of the Speaker .... There was a bill passed by the House of Commons known by the name of Homestead bill, the provisions of which were that each individual owning lands in this state might, if he thought proper, have fifty acres of land laid off, including his dwelling, which should, for any debts contracted after the fourth day of July next, be and remain free from any execution.... Joseph M. Bogle. Raleigh, Jan. 8th, 1831. North Carolina, 1831? Broadsheet. NcD. 6191

Boieldieu, Francois Adrien, 1775-1834.
La Dame blanche; or, The white lady; a comic opera by M. Scribe. Music by Boieldieu. Translated literally... by W. P. W. Baltimore, E. J. Coale, 1831. 70 p. MB; MH; MiU-C; RPB. 6192

---- Le petit chaperon rouge. The little red riding hood; a fairy opera in three acts by Theaulon. Music by M. Boieldieu. Translated for the use of visitors to the French opera by W. F. F. Baltimore, E. J. Coale, 1831. 24 p(?). MH; NN; PU. 6193

Bolles, William, 1800-1883.
A spelling book: containing exercises in orthography, pronunciation and reading. Rev. and enl. By William Bolles. Stereotyped by A. Pell & brother, New-York. New-London, W. & J. Bolles, 1831. 179 p. CTHWatk; DLC; NNC. 6194

Bolmar, Antoine.
A book of the French verbs wherein the model verbs and several of the most difficult are conjugated affirmatively, negatively, interrogatively, and negatively, and interrogatively... To which is added a complete list of all the irregular verbs. By A. Bolmar. Philadelphia, Carey & Lea, 1831. 173 p. ArBaA; MH; OMC; PPL; RPB. 6195

---- A collection of colloquial phrases, on every topic necessary to maintain conversation: arranged under different heads... The whole so disposed as considerably to facilitate the acquisition of a correct pronunciation of the French. By A. Bolmar... Philadelphia, Carey & Lea, 1831. 208 p. DLC; KyDC; MB; Nh-Hi; PHi. 6196

---- A complete treatise on the genders of French nouns... Philadelphia, 1831. 15 p. DLC; KyHi. 6197

---- Key to the first eight books of the Adventures of Felemachus, son of Ulysses, by A. Bolmar. Philadelphia, Lea, 1831. 221 p. MnDu. 6198

Bonar, Horatius.
The Night of Weeping; or, Words for the Suffering Family of God. By Horatius Bonar. From the 3d London ed. New York, Robert Carter & Brothers, 1831. 180 p. 6199

Bonnycastle, John.
An introduction to algebra with notes and observations... To which is added an appendix, on the application of algebra to geometry. New York, Collins and Hannay [etc.] 1831. 316 p. MoU; NjR; PU; RPB; ViU. 6200

---- An introduction to mensuration and practical geometry. To which is added, A treatise on guaging: and also the most important problems in mechanics. By James Ryan... Philadelphia, Kimber & Sharpless, 1831. 251 p. NNC; OU; P; PPL-R. 6201

---- A key to the last New York Edition of Bonnycastles Algebra; and also adapted to the former American and latest London ed. of that work... By James Ryan. New York, Collins & Hannay, 1831. 261 p. NjP; NRivHi. 6202

A book for the children of Maine for the use of families and schools. Portland, S. Colman, 1831. 118 p. MB; MH; MeBa; NN; Nh. 6203

The book of accidents. Designed for young children. New Haven, S. Babcock, Sidney's press, 1831. 23 p. CtY. 6204

Booth, Abraham, 1734-1806.
The reign of grace from its rise to its consummation... A new ed. Washington, Ohio, Pr. by Hamilton Robb, 1831. 395 p. CSmH; ICP; NNUM; OClWHi; PPPrHi. 6205

Borgia, Experience, pseud.
The confessions of a Magdalen, or, Some passages in the life of Experience Borgia, in letters to Forgiveness Mandeville, esq. ... New York, Pr. for the publisher, 1831. 31 p. DLC; KMK; MB; MnU; ViU. 6206

Bossuet, Jacques Benigne.
An exposition of the doctrines of the Catholic Church, in matters of controversy. By the Right Rev. James B. Bossuit, D.D. Bishop of Meaux. Chambersburg, Pr. by Pritts & Oswald, for the publisher, 1831. 72 p. MdBLC; MdBS; PRosC. 6207

Bossut, M. L'Abbe.
The explanatory and pronouncing French word book see Phillips, Sir Richard, 1769-1840.

Boston, Thomas, 1676-1732.
Human nature in its fourfold state, of primitive integrity, entire depravation, begun recovery, and consumate happiness or misery, in the parents of mankind

in paradise, the unregenerate, the regenerate all mankind in the future state. In several practical discourses. 5th ed. Pittsburgh, Richard Hanna, 1831. 400 p. IaDmD. 6208

Boston. Board of Alderman.
[Report of the Committee on the jail and the house of correction...the Leverett Street jail] [Boston, 1831] 8 p. MB. 6209

---- City Council.
Joint committee to whom was referred the petition of Daniel Sargent and others...for an extension of Commercial Street to 7th Street...report. [Boston, 1831] 7 p. MB; OClWHi. 6210

---- [Report of the Joint Committee to divide the City into 12 equal wards. Boston, 1831] 8 p. MH; MHi; MMal. 6211

---- Common Council.
[Report of the committee of the Common Council to whom was committed the report of the Board of Aldermen and the resolutions annexed thereto relating to the lease of the Chambers of Quincy Hall. Boston, 1831.] DLC. 6212

---- ---- Report of committee on the memorial of the New England Society for the Promotion of Manufactures. Boston, 1831. MBAt. 6213

---- ---- Rules and orders of the Common Council of the city of Boston, Boston, John H. Eastburn, city printer, 1831. 54 p. DLC. 6214

---- Primary School Committee.
Semi-annual report of the examination of the Boston primary schools made by the standing committee in September, 1831. Boston, J. H. Eastburn, city printer, 1831. 10 p. DLC; MB. 6215

---- School Committee.
At a meeting of the...held on the tenth day of May, A.D. 1831, it was voted, that the regulations of this committee be altered and amended as follows...(regarding corporal punishment) [Boston, 1831] Broadside. MHi. 6216

---- ---- (Pamphlets on school questions, 1831). Boston, 1831. MBAt. 6217

---- ---- Report of a committee of the school committee on truant absences from schools. Boston, 1831. 15 p. MHi. 6218

---- ---- Report [of] the Committee appointed "to consider the expediency of adopting an uniform made of classification of the schools, of prescribing and assigning the studies to each class, and the term of time to be applied to them. [Boston, 1831] 15 p. DLC; MNV; MHi. 6219

---- Associated Engine and Hose Co. No. 7.
Constitution of the Associated Engine and Hose Company No. 7. Adopted April 1827. Boston, Pr. by Leprell & Hart, 1831. 24 p. MBB. 6220

---- Bowdoin Street Congregational Meeting House.
Plan and valuation of the Pews in the...Boston, 1831. The Pews will be offered for sale by auction... June 16, 1831. Broadside. MHi. 6221

---- Citizens.
Proceedings of the public meeting held in Boston to aid the American Sunday School Union in their efforts to establish Sunday Schools throughout the valley of

the Mississippi. Philadelphia, American Sunday School Union, 1831. 23 p. DLC. 6222

---- Independent electors.
For Mayor. At a meeting of independent electors, held on Wednesday evening, 21st, it was voted unanimously to support John C. Gray, esq. for Mayor. (Dated) Dec. 22, 1831. Broadside. MHi. 6223

---- King's Chapel.
A liturgy for the use of the church at King's Chapel in Boston; collected principally from the Book of common prayer 4th ed. ...by F. W. P. Greenwood. Boston, Carter and Hendee, 1831. DLC; MB; MH-AH; MdBP; MnH. 6224

---- Old South Church.
Manual of the Old South Church. Boston, 1831. 88 p. MWA. 6225

---- ---- Order of Exercises at the Old South Church, Commemorative of the Death of James Monroe, on Thursday, August 25, 1831. Boston, J. H. Eastburn, city printer, 1831. 8 p. MB; MBAt; MHi; MWA; Me; MiD-B. 6226

---- Salem Church.
The articles of faith and covenant of the Salem Church, Boston, with a list of the members. Boston, Pr. by T. R. Marvin, 1831. 16 p. M. 6227

Boston and Lowell Railroad Corporation.
Articles of agreement... [Boston, 183-?] 3 p. MB. 6228

Boston and Providence Railroad Corporation.
Annual report of the directors ... [to the Legislature] Boston, 183-. CSt; MB; MH; NN; PPULC. 6229

Boston and Taunton Railroad Co.
Charter of the Boston and Taunton Rail Road Company. Granted June, 1831. Boston, Pr. by Dutton and Wentworth, 1831. 12 p. MiU-T; NN. 6230

Boston and Worcester railroad corporation.
The act of incorporation and by-laws of the Boston and Worcester rail road corporation. Boston, From Hale's steam press, W. L. Lewis's printer, 1831. 18 p. CSmH; DBRE; ICJ; MB; NN. 6231

---- Two leaves giving agreement for the purchase of stock of the Boston and Worcester Rail Road Corporation. Financial statements attached. Signed by the committee. Boston, July 4, 1831. MH-BA; MWA; NN. 6232

Boston Asylum for indigent boys.
An account of the Boston Asylum for indigent boys... Boston, N. Hale's steam-power-press, 1831. 24 p. DLC; DNLM. 6233

---- Being a statement of the present depressed condition of the funds of that institution and an appeal to the benevolent of the community in its behalf. Boston, 1831. 12 p. DLC; MBAt; MHi; MWA; MiD-B. 6234

Boston Athenaeum Gallery.
Catalogue of the fifth exhibition of paintings in the Athenaeum gallery. Boston, Press of John H. Eastburn, 1831. 8 p. MB; MBAt; MWHi. 6235

---- Remarks upon the Athenaeum Gallery of paintings, for 1831. 35 p. DLC; MB. 6236

Boston Investigator. A. Kneeland, editor, etc. vol. 1-vi. Ap. 2, 1831- Mar. 10, 1837. Boston,

1831-37. fol. OMidt; Tuttle; BrMus. 6237

Boston morning post. see Boston post.

The Boston post. V 1- December 5th, 1831-. DLC; MBAT; PPPH; PPULC. 6238

Boston Sabbath School Union.
Celebration of American independence... July 4, 1831. Boston, 1831. "Earliest publication of words of "America." Broadside. MWA; NN. 6239

Boston Seaman's Friend Society.
Third Annual Report of the Board of Directors of, The Boston Seaman's Friend Society, Jan. 19, 1831. Boston, 1831. CtY; DLC; MB. 6240

Boston Society for the Diffusion of Useful Knowledge.
Circular. Boston, June, 1831. 1 p. MHi. 6241

Boston two hundred years ago; or, The romantic story of Miss Ann Carter, and the celebrated Indian chief, Thundersquall; with many humorous reminiscences and events of olden times. Boston, n.p., 1831. 156, 26 p. 1 illus. CLU-C; DLC; InU; MBat; ViU. 6242

Boston Young Men's Benevolent Society.
Constitution of the... Boston, 1831. 8 p. MHi. 6243

Boswell, James, 1740-1795.
The life of Samuel Johnson, LLD. including a journal of a tour to the Hebrides, by Jas. Boswell, esq. ...New York, Harper and brothers [1831] 2 vols. NSpriVi; OC; OrCa; WyLar. 6244

---- ---- With numerous additions and notes by J. W. Croker. New York, 1831. 2 vols. IaAS; MHolY; WyU. 6245

The Bouquet: flowers of polite literature...Hartford, Joseph Hurlbut, v 1- 1831- . 2 vols. CtHW; CtY; MHa; WHi. 6246

Bourdon, Louis Pierre Marie, 1779-1854.
Elements of Algebra. By Bourdon. Translated from the French ... Boston, Hilliard, Gray, Little and Wilkins, 1831. viii, 304 p. ICP; MeB; MH; NjP; PLFM. 6247

---- ---- New York, E. B. Clayton, 1831. 389 p. CtY; IEN; MH; NjP; ViU. 6248

Bourne, George.
Picture of slavery in the U.S. Boston, 1831. 227 p. PHC. 6249

Bourrienne, ([Louis Antoine Fauvelet] de)
Private memoirs of Napoleon Bonaparte, during the periods of the Directory, the Consulate, and the Empire. Philadelphia, Carey & Lea, 1831. 2 vols. MoS; PPM; ScC; ViR; WM. 6250

Bouton, Nathaniel, 1797-1878.
Instructions on prayer. Concord, N.H., Pub. by Oliver L. Sanborn, Press of Luther Roby, 1831. 167 p. ICBB; ICP; MeBat; NhD. 6251

---- (Six sermons, etc.) Concord, 1831-77. MB. 6252

---- Two sermons preached 21st November, 1830, in commemoration of the organizing of the First Church in Concord, and the settlement of the first minister, on the 18th November, 1730. By Nathaniel Bouton. Concord, Pr. by Asa M'Farland, 1831. 102 p. CtSoP; IaHA; PPPrHi; RPB;

WHi. 6253

The bow in the cloud... American Sunday School Union, Philadelphia, 1831. 24 p. MeBaHi; BrMus. 6254

Bowden, John, 1751-1817.
The apostolic origin of episcopacy asserted. In a series of letters, addressed to Rev. Dr. Miller, 1808. New York [Protestant Episcopal Press?] 1831. CtY; MCE. 6255

---- A full length portrait of Calvinism. By an old fashioned churchman. 4th ed. Newburyport, J. H. Buckingham, 1831. 32 p. KyLx; MH; MH-AH. 6256

---- Letters of Dr. Bowden; and essays, by Dr. Cooke and Bishop Onderdonk's works on episcopacy. New-York, The Protestant Episcopal press, 1831. 454 p. CtY; DNC; GDecCT; IU; MiU. 6257

---- Works on episcopacy, containing the first series of Dr. Bowdens, letters to Dr. Miller with a preface. By the Right Rev. Benjamin T. Onderdonk, D.D. New York, Protestant Episcopal Press, 1831. 2 vols. CtHT; GEU; InID; MBuDD; MdBD; TChU; ViAl. 6258

Bowdoin College.
Catalogue of the officers and students of Bowdoin College and medical school of Maine, April 1831. Brunswick, Me., Press of Joseph Griffin, 1831. 24 p. ICS; MeHi; Me. 6259

---- Catalogue senatus academici, et eorum qui mupera et officia gesserunt, quique adicusjus laurea donati suift in opllegio Bowdoinensi, Brunsvici, Republica Mainensi. Brunsvici, E. Typhis. Joseph Griffin, 1831. 23 p. MeB; MeBat; MeHi. 6260

---- Papers relating to the powers of the corporation of Bowdoin College. Brunswick, Me., J. Griffin, 1831. 16 p. CtY; MHi; MeHi. 6261

Bowen, Nathaniel, 1779-1839.
Christian consolations; or, The sorrows of Christian people, in their design and influences variously considered; in sermons adapted to different occasions and kinds of human affliction. By Nathaniel Bowen, D.D. Charleston, A.E. Miller, 1831. 96 p. MB; NcD; NcU; ScCoT; ScU. 6262

---- The moral efficacy of the Christian ministry, how best secured; a charge to the clergy of the Protestant Episcopal Church in the State of South Carolina, delivered in St. Michael's Church on the 10th February, 1821. By Nathaniel Bowen... Charleston, Pr. by A. E. Miller, 1831. 30 p. MBD; NNG; ScU. 6263

---- Pastoral advice affectionately tendered in relation to the practice of the frequent or occasional neglect by members of the Church, of its offices for those of other places of Christian worship. Charleston, A. E. Miller, 1831. 10 p. PPM; ScCC. 6264

Boyd, George, 1788-1850.
Sermon on death of Dan'l H. Miller. May 1831. Philadelphia, 1831. 18 p. PHi. 6265

Boyd, James R.
Memoir of the life, character, and writings of Philip Doddridge, D.D. With a selection from his correspondence. Compiled by Rev. James R. Boyd. New York, American Tract Company, 1831.

(4) (4-480) p. KyLoP. 6266

Boyer, Abel.
Boyer's French Dictionary; comprising all the additions and improvements of the latest Paris and London editions, with a very large number of useful words and phrases. ...Stereotyped by T. H. Carter & Co., Boston... Boston, Hilliard, Gray, Little and Wilkins, 1831. 250 p. IaCrM; OClW. 6267

Bozman, John Leeds.
History of Maryland, 1633-60. Baltimore, 1831. 2 vols. NBLIHI. 6268

[Brackenridge, Henry Marie], 1786-1871.
The History of the late war between the United States and Great Britain, containing a brief recapitulation of the events which led to the various brilliant land and naval victories, including the battle of New-Orleans. Wheeling, A. & E. Picket, 1831. 144 p. CSmH; DLC; PPL; WHi. 6269

Bradburn, Eliza Weaver.
The Story of Paradise Lost, for children. By Eliza Weaver Bradburn. New York, Pub. by J. Emory and B. Waugh, for the Sunday School Union of the Methodist Episcopal Church at the conference office, Pr. by J. Collord, 1831. 112 p. DLC; MH; MsAb; ViU. 6270

Braddeley, T.
A sure way to find out the true Religion: in a conversation between a father and his son, by the Rev. T. Braddeley. if any man preach any other gospel unto you than that you have received, let him be accursed. - Gal. 1-9. 1st Amer. ed. Boston, Pub. by William Smith, for the Editors of "the Jesuit," 1831. 126 p. MdBLC; MiDSH. 6271

Bradford, Alden, 1765-1843.
A discourse delivered before the Society of Propagating the Gospel among the Indians and others in North America, 1830. With report of Select Committee, Boston, 1831. 51 p. ICT. 6272

Bradstreet, Martha.
Statement of facts in relation to dismissal of Mrs. Bradstreet's suits from the district court of the U.S. Albany, 1831. 27 p. MB; MBAt; MBC; MH; NN. 6273

Braman, Isaac, 1770-1858.
A sermon in the Second parish meeting house in Rowley, March 27, 1831. Haverhill, Cummings, Hilliard & co., 1831. 16 p. CtY; DLC; MiD-B; NN; RPB. 6274

Braugham, Henry Peter.
Objects, advantages, and pleasures of science. Boston, Simpson and Clap, 1831. 320 p. WBEloC. 6275

Bray, Anna Eliza (Kempe) Stothard, 1790-1883.
The Talba; or, Moor of Portugal: a romance. By Mrs. Bray. New York, J. & J. Harper, 1831. 2 vols. DLC; GMWa; MdBP; PPULC. 6276

Breckinridge, Robert Jefferson, 1800-1871.
An address delivered before the Colonization society of Kentucky, at Frankfort, on the 6th day of January, 1831. by Robert J. Breckinridge... Frankfort, K., Pr. by A. G. Hodges, 1831. 24 p. CSmH; DLC; MB; PHi; PPPrHi. 6277

Brewster, David, 1781-1868.
The life of Sir Isaac Newton,

by David Brewster. New York, J. & J. Harper [1831] 323 p. CtY; MoS; PU; TxH; WHi. 6278

Brice, John, ed.
Selection of laws of the United States in force relative to Commercial subjects. Baltimore, 1831. 579 p. DLC; MH-L; Mi-L; NNC-L; PU. 6279

Bridge, Bewick, 1767-1833.
A treatise on the construction, properties, and analogies of the three conic sections. By the Rev. B. Bridge... From the 2d London ed., with additions and alterations by the American editor. New Haven, H. Howe, 1831. 132 p. CtY; LNT; MBBC; NhD; PHC. 6280

Bridges, Charles, 1794-1869.
The Christian ministry with an inquiry into the causes of its inefficiency by the Rev. Charles Bridges, B. A. ...1st Amer. from 2d London ed., corr. and enl. New York, Jonathan Leavitt; Boston, Crocker & Brewster, 1831. 2 vols. CBPac; KyLoP; MeB; NCH; OMC. 6281

A brief history of the Island of Hayti...revised by the publishing committee. Boston, Pr. by T. R. Marvin, for the Massachusetts Sabbath School Union, 1831. 68 p. CtMW; MH; MH-AH; NjR; ViHaI. 6282

A brief sketch of parties, the British and American, as connected with the American system; together with an account of the extraordinary doings of the Maine Legislature for 1831. Portland, 1831. 88 p. ICU; IaU; MBC; MeBat; MeHi. 6283

A brief treatise on the culture of silk. Boston, Russel, 1831. 14 p. MP; PPULC. 6284

Brief view of the system of internal improvement of Pennsylvania. 1st ed., Philadelphia, June 13, 1831. 40 p. PHi; PPULC. 6285

---- 2d ed., Philadelphia, July 9, 1831. 30 p. PHi; PPULC. 6286

Brigham, Charles, jr.
Book of questions and answers relating to the Town of Grafton, designed for the young children in schools of that Town. By Charles Brigham, Jr. Worcester, Pr. by M. Spooner and Co., 1831. 20 p. MWA; MWHi. 6287

Bristol County, Mass. Auxiliary. Bible Society. See. Auxiliary Bible Society of Bristol County.

British Charitable Society.
First annual rep., (for 1817), 1818-1828, 1828-31; also, Rules and regulations of the Society, and list of subscribers. Boston, 1831. MBAt. 6288

The British satirist. Comprising the best satires of the most celebrated poets, from Pope to Byron. Accompanied by original critical notices of the authors. New York, Charles P. Fessenden, 1831. 388 p. ArL CtHT; MB; TNP; ViL. 6289

Broad Grins, or Fun for the New Year, 1832. Boston, Mass., Arthur Ainsworth [1831] MWA. 6290

Broaddus, Andrew, 1770-1848, comp.
The Dover selection of spiritual songs; with an appendix of choice hymns, on various occasions: compiled by the recommendations of the Dover Association. By Andrew Broadhus. Richmond [Va.] Smith, 1831. 412 p. GDC; NNUT; NcD; NjPT. 6291

---- "The Extra Examined. A reply to Mr. A. Campbell M. Harbinger, Extra on remission of sins, etc. With an appendix, By Andrew Broaddus. Richmond, Pr. at the office of the Religious Herald, 1831. 56 p. CSmH; NeWfC; NRAB; OClWHi. 6292

---- ---- Pittsburgh, J. Green, 1831. 39 p. CtY; KyLoS; OClWHi. 6293

Brockway, Maria J.
[Manuscript books of poetry and prose, original and gathered from other sources. Newbury, Mass., 1831-36?] 2 vols. RPB. 6294

Brodhead, Jacob, 1782-1855.
A discourse on education, delivered in the Reformed Dutch Church in Broome stree[sic] on ... the 30th of January, 1831, for the benefit of the Sunday schools connected with said church. By Jacob Brodhead... New York, Pr. by William A. Mercein, 1831. 38 p. M; NNUT; PPPrHi. 6295

---- A sermon delivered in the Reformed Dutch Church in Broome Street, in the City of New York, on the ninth of December, 1830, being the day recommended by the acting Governor of the State, to be observed as a day of Thanksgiving. By Jacob Broadhead, D.D. Published by request of the Consistory of said church. New York, Pr. by William A. Mercein, 1831. 22 p. NjNBS; NjR; PLT; PPPrHi; PPULC. 6296

Bronson, [Hon. G. C.]
Report of the Select Committee, relative to the Conduct of Elam Lynds, late Keeper of Sing Sing Prison [n.p.] 1831. MB. 6297

Brooklyn. Fire Department.
Constitution and by-laws. Brooklyn, 1831. NBLIHI. 6298

Brooklyn Savings Bank.
Charter, by-laws and regulations. Brooklyn, 1831. 2 vols. NBLiHi. 6299

Brooks, Joseph.
A defence before the Congregational Church in Upton, Mass. ...against a charge of heresy for believing the doctrine of Universal Salvation [Upton? 1831?] CtY; BrMus. 6300

Brooks, Nathan Covington, 1809-1898.
The Amethyst, an annual of literature. Edited and published by N. C. Brooks. Baltimore, Pr. by William A. Francis, 1831. 290 p. CoU; DLC; MBAt; MBMu; MdBe; NjR; PPL. 6301

Brooks, William Hathorne.
The education of the five senses; lecture before the American Institute of Instruction, Aug. 1831. Boston, 1831. MBAt. 6302

Brougham and Vaux, Henry Peter Brougham, baron.
The working man's companion; the results of machinery, namely; cheap production & increased employment exhibited anon. Boston, Stimpson and Clapp, 1831. 230 p. MMe; MW; NhPet; NvHi; WU. 6303

---- ---- Amer. ed., Philadelphia, Carey, 1831. 216 p. Mi; PPULC; PHi. 6304

Broussais, Francois Joseph Victor, 1772-1838.
History of chronic phlegmasiae or inflammations founded on clinical experience and pathological anatomy...tr. from the French of the 4th ed. by Isaac Hays... and R. Eglesfeld Griffith. Philadelphia, Carey & Lea, 1831. 2 vols. IU; Nh; PU; ScC;

ViRA. 6305

---- On irritation and insanity; a work, wherein the relations of the physical with the moral conditions of man, are established on the basis of physiological medicine. By F. J. V. Broussais... tr. by Thomas Cooper...to which are added two tracts on materialism, and an outline of the association of ideas. By Thomas Cooper... Columbia, S.C., Pr. by S. J. M'Morris, 1831. 408 p. CU; MBM; NB; PU; ScU. 6306

Brown, Alling.
The musical cabinet; a collection of sacred music, comprising a great variety of psalm and hymn tunes, set pieces and anthems...together with a concise introduction to psalmody. Compiled and arranged by Alling Brown. 2d imp. ed. New Haven, Durrie & Peck, 1831. 230 p. ICN; MU; NRU; VtU. 6307

Brown, Bartholomew, 1772-1854.
Templi Carmina. Songs of the temple, or Bridgewater collection of sacred music. 21st ed. Boston, Richardson, Lord & Holbrook, 1831. 349 p. ICN; MH; MEab; NBuG; RPB; VtU. 6308

Brown, Goold, 1791-1857.
The child's first book... By Goold Brown. 26th ed. New York, Pr. by Mahlon Day, at the new juvenile book-store, 1831. 35 p. NNC. 6309

---- Lecture on grammar, delivered in Boston, before the American institute of instruction, August 1831. Boston, Hilliard, 1831. 46 p. MB; PPAmP; PPULC. 6310

Brown, James.
The American grammar. By James Brown. Prepared for the use of schools by the author... Philadelphia, Clark & Raser, 1831. 192 p. DLC; MB; NIC; PLFM. 6311

Brown, James Baldwin, 1785-1843.
Memoirs of Howard, comp. from his diary, his confidential letters, and other authentic documents. By James Baldwin Brown. Abridged by a gentleman of Boston, from the London quarto edition. Boston, Lincoln and Edmands, 1831. 352 p. CSmH; GDecCT; MB; RNR; WHi. 6312

Brown, John, 1722-1787.
A brief concordance to the Holy Scriptures of the Old and New Testaments: by which all or most, of the principal texts of scripture may be easily found out. Revised and corrected. [Philadelphia, 1831?] 92 p. NN; PPULC. 6313

---- A concordance to the Holy Scriptures of the Old and New Testaments. By the Rev. John Brown, of Haddington. New-York, Pr. by J. & J. Harper, 1831. 254 p. MH; MH-AH; ViRC. 6314

---- Two short catechisms, mutually connected... To which is added an address to the rising generation. Washington, Ohio, Hamilton Robb, 1831. 91 p. OClWHi; PPM. 6315

Brown, Nathaniel.
An address, delivered before the Wyne County Education Society, at its first meeting, held in Newark, Jan. 22, 1831. Palmyra, N.Y., The Western Spectator Office, 1831. 24 p. MBL; MH. 6316

[Brown, Rezeau], 1808-1833.
Memoirs of Augustus Herman Francke. Prepared for the American Sunday School Union,

and revised by the committee of publication. Philadelphia, American Sunday School Union, 1831. 180 p. GDecCT; KyLoS; NNNG; OSW. 6317

Brown, Samuel F.

An address delivered before the Livermore, Temperance Society, June 20, 1831. By Samuel Brown. Pub. by request. Portland, Pr. by A. Shirley, 1831. 25 p. MBAt; MWA. 6318

Brown, Thomas.

Lectures on the philosophy of the human mind. By the late Thomas Brown, M.D., professor of moral philosophy in the university of Edinburgh, in two volumes. Corrected from the last London ed. Stereotyped by T. H. Carter & Co., Boston, Hallowell, Pr. and pub. by Glazier, Masters & Co, 1831. 2 vols. IaCrC; IaPeC; MoSpD; NGlf; NcMfC. 6319

---- Philosophy of the human mind. New York, Glazier, Masters and Co., 1831. 514 p. IaPeC. 6320

Browne, D. J., ed.

The Naturalist, containing treatises on natural history, chemistry, domestic and rural economy, manufactures and arts ...Edited by D. J. Browne. Boston, Peirce & Parker, and Carter & Hendee, 1831. 2 vols. CU; ICJ; MH; MSaP; NIC-A. 6321

---- Trees of America. New York, 1831. MB. 6322

Browne, Sir Thomas, 1605-1682.

Miscellaneous works of Sir Thomas Browne. With some account of the author and his writings. Cambridge [Mass.], Hilliard & Brown, 1831. 304 p. CtY; ICMe; MB; NjP; ScU. 6323

Buck, Charles, 1771-1815.

Anecdotes; Religious, moral, and entertaining, by the Late Rev. Charles Buck...with a Preface, by Ashbel Green, D.D. Some time president of Princeton College. New York, J. C. Riker, 1831. 2 vols. in 1. CSt; KyLoP; MH-AH; NjPT; TBriK. 6324

---- ... A theological dictionary, containing definitions of all religious terms... By the late Rev. Charles Buck. Woodward's new ed. Pub. from the last London ed.; to which is added an appendix, containing an account of the Methodist Episcopal, and Presbyterian churches, in the United States, to the present period. Philadelphia, J. J. Woodward, 1831. 624 p. CtY; GDecCT; KyLo; MiU; WHi. 6325

Buck, Rueben.

An address delivered before the York County Temperance Society at Alfred, October 18, 1831. By Rueben Buck, M.D. Pub. at the request of the society. Kennebunk, Pr. by K. Remich, 1831. 15 p. MBC; MeHi; MnHi. 6326

Buckingham, J. H.

The Amaranth, a literary and religious offering, designed as a Christmas and New Year's present. Edited by J. H. Buckingham. Newburyport, Charles Whipple, 1831. 180 p. CtMW; CtY; HCL; MDux; MWA; MPiB; OO. 6327

Buckstone, John Baldwin, 1802-1879.

...Popping the question: a farce in one act. By J. B. Buckstone, esq. ...Printed from the acting copy (Cumberland's ed.) with remarks, biographical and critical, by D-G. To which are added, a description of the costume, cast of characters...and the whole of the stage business.

As performed at the Theatres Royal, London. New York, E. B. Clayton; Philadelphia, C. Neal, 1831. 26 p. DLC; MH; NN; PR. 6328

Budd, Richard Hayward.
A practical treatise on the diseases of the foot of the horse; containing, a correct description of their nature, causes, and methods of prevention: with suggestions of improved plans of treatment, founded on physiological principles. Also rules of shoeing, by which the ordinary evils attending this process may be in some measure prevented. ... New York, D. Murphy, 1831. [21]-195 p. NIC-V; NN. 6329

Buffon, Georges Louis Leclerc, comte de, 1707-1788.
A natural history of the globe of man, of beasts, birds, fishes, reptiles, insects and plants; from the writings of Buffon, Cuvier and other eminent naturalists; edited by John Wright. New ed. Boston, Gray and Bowen, 1831. 5 vols. GEU; ICJ; LNH; OCHP; ViU. 6330

---- ---- New York, Collins & Hannay, 1831. 5 vols. Nh; ODaU. 6331

---- ---- Philadelphia, Thomas Desilver, 1831. 5 vols. CoFoS; NN; PPAN; PPULC; PU. 6332

Bullions, Alexander.
A history of the trial of the Rev. Alexander Bullions, D.D. before the Associate Presbytery of Cambridge on a libel exhibited against him by that reverend body, in May, 1829; and before the associated Synod of North America at their meeting in Philadelphia, in May, 1830, whither the cause was carried by appeal... New York, William Stodart, 1831. DLC; MB; MH; MH-AH; MWA; NjR. 6333

Bunker, (Elihu S.)
A Reply to "The Proceedings and Minutes" of the "New York and Boston Steam-boat Company." (Motto.) New York, Pr. by George F. Nesbitt, 1831. 24 p. NN; RPB. 6334

Bunker Hill monument association.
Address on the concerns of the...to the citizens of Massachusetts and especially to the inhabitants of Boston and Charlestown. Boston, Buckingham, 1831. 8 p. MB; MHi. 6335

Bunnell, David C., b. 1793.
The travels and adventures of David C. Bunnell, during twenty-three years of a sea-faring life; containing an accurate account of the battle on Lake Erie, under the command of Com. Oliver H. Perry; together with ten years' service in the navy of the United States. Also service among the Greeks, imprisonment among the Turks, &c. &c. Written by himself... Palmyra, N.Y., J. H. Bortles, 1831. 199 p. CSmH; DLC; ICU; MWA; OCHP. 6336

Bunyan, John, 1628-1688.
Eines christen reise nach der seligen ewigkeit... In englischer sprache beschrieben durch Johann Bunyan... Harrisburg, Pa., Gedruckt und zu haben bey G. S. Peters, 1831. 2 vols. in 1. DLC; NN; PLFM. 6337

---- The Holy War made by King Shaddai upon Diabolus; to regain the metropolis of the world. or, The Losing and Taking Again of the Town of Mansoul. By John Bunyan. Author of "Pilgrim's Progress," &c. &c. ...Pittsburgh, John I. Kay & co.; Philadelphia, James Kay, Jun & co., 1831. 252 p. CtMW; ICP; KyDC; MdBD; OKU. 6338

---- The Pilgrim's progress from this world to that which is to come. Delivered under the similitude of a dream. In two parts. By Thos. Scott. Hartford, S. Andrus, 1831. 2 vols. in 1. InBC; MH; NPtW; PHC; PU. 6339

---- ---- New York, J. H. Turney, 1831. 341 p. MWA; InVi. 6340

---- The works of that eminent servant of Christ, John Bunyan, Minister of the Gospel, and formerly pastor of a congregation at Bedford. New Haven, Nathan Whiting, 1831. 3 vols. ArBaA; GMM; MeB; TxBrdD; Vi. 6341

Burder, George, 1752-1832.
Twelve sermons to the aged. New York, American Tract Society [183-?] 178 p. IaU. 6342

---- Village sermons; or, Fifty-two plain and short discourses on the principal doctrines of the gospel; intended for the use of schools, or companies assembled for religious instruction in country villages. Revised. New York, American Tract Society [183-?] 571 p. CtY; NIC. 6343

Burges, Tristam, 1770-1853.
Abstract of the debate in the house of representatives of the United States, on the general appropriation bill, for 1831, containing the whole of Mr. Burge's two speeches on the subject. New York [1831] 36 p. PHi; PPULC; RHi; WHi. 6344

---- An oration delivered before the Rhode Island federal Adelphia, Thursday, September 9, 1831. Providence, Weeden, 1831. 36 p. CtY; MBAt; MeWaC; MWA; RP. 6345

---- An oration, pronounced before the citizens of Providence on the Fourth of July, 1831... 2d ed. Providence, William Marshall & co. [1831] 32 p. CtY; DLC; MBAt; MH; MiD-B; MoKU; NjPT; RPB; WHi. 6346

---- Speech on the motion to strike from the general appropriation bill the salary appropriated for the minister to Russia, delivered in the house of representatives, February 3, 1831. Washington, Pr. by Gales & Seaton, 1831. 53 p. CtHT; ICN; MBAt; RHi; WHi. 6347

---- Speech of the Hon. Tristam Burges, of Rhode Island, at the public dinner given him by the citizens of New York, March 30, 1831. [New York, 1831] 31 p. CtY; DLC; MiU-C; PHi; ScU. 6348

Burgoyne, John.
Richard coeur-de-lion; an opera. New York, Richard Hobbs, 1831. 32 p. MB; MdB; MH. 6349

Burns, John, 1775-1850.
The principles of midwifery: including the diseases of women and children. By John Burns... From the 7th London ed., rev. and enl., with additions... New-York, C. S. Francis; Boston, Munroe & Francis, 1831. 754 p. CSt-L; CtY; DLC; NNN; PPCP. 6350

Burns, Robert.
The complete works of Robert Burns, with an account of his life, and criticism, on his writings, with observations on the character and condition of the Scottish peasantry, and a copious glossary. By James Currie, M.D. New York, Solomon King, 1831. 168, 163 p. 4 v. in 1. IaG; PWeHi. 6351

---- The works of Robert Burns; with an account of his life, and a criticism on his writings. To which are prefixed, some observations on the character & condition of the Scottish peasantry. By James Currie... New York, Solomon King, 1831. 168 p. MH; MeWC. 6352

---- The works of Robert Burns: with an account of his life, and criticism on his writings. To which are prefixed, some observations on the character and condition of the Scottish peasantry. By James Currie... A new ed., four volumes complete in one. With many additional poems and songs, and an enl. and corr. glossary. From the last London ed. of 1825. Philadelphia, J. Crissy and J. Griggs, 1831. 4 vols. in 1. NN; PP; PPULC; PPRF; PPWe; PWeHi. 6353

Burr, David H. (1803-75).
Maine; drawn and published by David H. Burr. New York, D. H. Durr, 1831. NIC. 6354

---- A new universal atlas;... New York, D. S. Stone, c 1831-1835. (4), p. 63 maps. ICJ; MH. 6355

Burrough, M.
Letter to D. Hosack [on Indian cholera]. [Philadelphia, 1831] 8 p. MWA; PPULC. 6356

---- [On spasmodic cholera... n.p., 1831] DNLM. 6357

Burt, Adam.
Journeyman, weaving; a poem, by Adam Burt.... New York, Press of the Old Countryman, 1831. NBuG; RPB. 6358

Bush, George, 1796-1859.
The life of Mohammed; founder of the religion of Islam, and of the Empire of the Saracens. (Stereotype ed.) New York, Pr. by J. & J. Harper, 1831. 261 p. CtHT; GHi; MW; OCl; WvW. 6359

---- Questions and notes critical and practical upon the book of Genesis; designed as a general help to Biblical instruction. By George Bush... New-York, J. P. Haven, 1831. 467 p. KyLoP; MB; OO; PPLT; ViRut. 6360

Butler, Benjamin Franklin, 1795-1858.
Opinion of the relative rights of the Mohawk and Hudson Rail Road Company, and the Albany and Schenectady Turnpike Company. Schenectady, Pr. by C. G. & A. Palmer, 1831. 15 p. DBRE; MH-BA; NN; NRom. 6361

Butler, Mann, 1784-1852.
An address on the value of the physical sciences, compared with other great branches of knowledge; delivered before the Louisville lyceum, October 1, 1831. By Mann Buttler, A.M. Louisville, Ky., Pr. by J. W. Palmer, 1831. 12 p. ChU; ICU; MWA; PHi. 6362

Butler, Samuel, bp. of Lichfield and Coventry, 1774-1840.
An Atlas of Antient Geography. By Samuel Butler, D.D. ...Stereotyped by J. Howe. Philadelphia, Carey & Lea, C. Blanchard, 1831. 91 p. AU; DLC; NjR; PU; ViRut. 6363

---- Geographia classica: or, The application of antient geography to the classics. By Samuel Butler... 2d American, from the 9th London ed., with questions on the maps, by John Frost. Philadelphia, Carey & Lea, 1831. 262 p. CtHT; ICP; NjP; PU; TU. 6364

Butler, Samuel, 1612-1680.
Hudbris [sic] (Hudibras) in three parts, written in the time of the late wars. By Samuel Butler, Esq. With a life of the author, annotations, and an index.

Hartford [Conn.] Andrus & Judd, 1831. 312 p. IaPeC. 6365

Butterworth, John.

A new concordance to the Holy Scriptures. Being the most comprehensive and concise of any before published... By the Rev. John Butterworth... A new ed., with considerable improvements. By Adam Clarke, LL.D...Stereotyped at the Boston, Stereotype foundry. Boston, Crocker & Brewster; New York, Jonathan Leavitt, 1831. [4], 516 p. ICU; IEG; MdW; TNMPH; ViFTBE. 6366

Buttmann, Philip Karl, 1764-1829.

Greek grammar for the use of schools, from the German of Philip Buttmann. 3d ed. of the translation. Boston, Hilliard, Gray, Little and Wilkins, 1831. 336 p. CtY; LNB; OO; ViU; WaPs. 6367

Buttrick, Tilly, b. 1783?

Buttrick's voyages, travels and discoveries 1812-1819; reprint of the original edition. Boston, 1831. 89 p. CO; MoSHi; OT; TNV; TxElp. 6368

---- Voyages, travels and discoveries of Tilly Buttrick, jr. Boston, Pr. for the author, 1831. 58 p. CtHWatk; DLC; MB; MH; MWA; OClWHi. 6369

Buzzell, John, comp.

Psalms, hymns, and spiritual songs, selected for the use of the United Churches of Christ, commonly called Freewill Baptist, and for saints of all denominations, by John Buzzell. 2d New-York ed. Rochester, Pr. by Hoyt, Porter & Co., 1831. 352 p. NBuG; NRU. 6370

Bynum, Jesse Atherton, 1797-1868.

Speech against the expediency and right of the general government to carry on works of internal improvement within the individual states. Delivered in House of Commons of State of North Carolina, Dec. 1830. Raleigh, Lawrence, 1831. NcD. 6371

Byron, George Gordon Noel Byron; 6th Baron, 1788-1824.

Childe Harold's Pilgrimage, a romaunt by (George Gordon Byron) Byron, 6th baron. (With notes). Campe's ed. Nurnberg and New-York, F. Campe and co. [1831] 33 p. MBAt; MH; NNUT; PU; PPULC. 6372

---- ... letters and journals of Lord Byron: with notices of his life. By Thomas Moore... New York, J. & J. Harper [1831] 2 vols. FTU; IEG; MdBP; NcU; WU. 6373

---- The Works of Lord Byron, including the suppressed poems. Also a sketch of his life. By J. W. Lake. Complete in one volume. Philadelphia, Henry Adams, 1831. 716 p. NICLA. 6374

C

C, G. B.

La muette; or the dumb girl of Portici, an opera in five acts. Baltimore, Coale, 1831. 46 p. PU. 6375

Cabell, Joseph Carrington, 1778-1856.

Speech on the anti-tariff resolutions passed at the session of the Legislature of Virginia, 1828-9. Accompanied by sundry notes and documents. By Joseph C. Cabell... Richmond, Pr. by T. W. White for an Association of gentlemen in Nelson County, Va. 1831. 58 p. CtY; MB; OCHP;

PHi; Vi. 6376

Caesar, C. Julius.
J. Julii Caesaris, quae extant, Interpretione et notis illustravit Johannes Grodvinus, Professor Regius in usum Delphine. Notes and interpretations translated and improved by Thomas Clark. 7th ed. Philadelphia, Thomas DeSilver, Jr., John Grigg, Uriah Hunt & M'Carty & Davis, 1831. 410 p. CtHT; GHi; IaHi; MnU; PP. 6377

Caldwell, Charles, 1772-1853.
An essay on the nature and sources of the Malaria or Noxious Miasma... By Chas. Caldwell, M.D. Philadelphia, Carey & Lea, 1831. 80 p. DLC; DSG; MeB; NNN; WHi. 6378

---- Essays on Malaria and Temperament. By Charles Caldwell, M.D. Professor of the Institutes of Medicine and Clinical practice in Transylvania University. Lexington, Ky., Pr. by N. L. Finnell & J. F. Herndon, 1831. ix, 300 p. ArBaA; CU; ICU; KyLxT; NBMS; OC; PU. 6379

Caldwell, Samuel B. T.
To the voters of Loudoun. Fellow-citizens, When I became a candidate for your sufferages ... Leesburg? Va., 1831. ViU. 6380

Caley, Cornelius Caley.
Power of Truth Exemplified. In three parts. Part 1. Seraphic Shepherd, trans. from the French and interspersed with notes. By Cornelius Caley, Jr. Part 2. Letters addressed to an Awakened Sinner. By Andrew Fuller. Part 3. (Extracts from) Advice to a Young Christian. By a village pastor. Boston, Jonathan Howe, 1831. 208 p. KyBC; MB. 6381

The Calhoun doctrine of State nullification discussed; originally published in the "Irishman and Southern Democrat." By a democratic republican. Charleston, S.C., 1831. 33 p. GU; MH; MH-L; MHi; ScCC. 6382

Calhoun, John Caldwell, 1782-1850.
Correspondence between Gen. Andrew Jackson and John C. Calhoun, President and Vice-President of the United States, on the subject of the course of the letter, in the deliberations of the cabinet of Mr. Monroe, on the occurrences in the Seminole War. Washington, Pr. by Duff Green, 1831. 52 p. CtHT; ICU; PHi; ScC; WHi. 6383

---- Mr. Calhoun's sentiments, upon the subject of state rights, and the tariff; together with copies of the Virginia resolutions of 1798; of the Kentucky resolutions of 1799; and of the decision of the Supreme court of Pennsylvania, pronounced in 1799, by Chief Justice M'Kean. [Documents referred to in the exposition of Mr. Calhoun] Boston, Pr. by Beals & Homer, 1831. 18 p. DLC; MBAt; TxH; WHi. 6384

---- ... Opinions of the Vice President of the United States, on the relations of the states and the general government... Charleston, The State rights and free trade association, 1831. 34 p. CtHWatk; CtY; DLC; NcD; PHi; WHi. 6385

The Calumet. New series of the Harbinger of Peace. Published under the direction of the American Peace Society. 1831-1836. Vol. I & II, New York, L. D. Dewey, 1831. 2 vols. MB; MeB; MH; NjP; OHi. 6386

Calvin, Jean, 1509-1564.
A selection of the most celebrated sermons of John Calvin, minister of the Gospel, and one of the principal leaders in the protestant Reformation. To which is prefixed a biographical history of his life. Philadelphia, T. Desilver, 1831. 200 p. CBPSR; IEG; NGH; OO; ScNC. 6387

Cambridge, Mass. Episcopal Theological School.
Constitution and statutes of the Massachusetts Episcopal Theological School. Boston, Stimpson and Clapp, 1831. 14 p. MBD; MH; MdBD; NNN. 6388

Cambridge University.
Cambridge classical examinations, second series; containing question papers on the Greek Testament, specimens of the examination for Tyrwhit's Hebrew scholarships and of the examinations for fellowships and scholarships at Trinity and St. John's colleges. Cambridge, Grant, 1831. 295 p. NB; ScSpW. 6389

Cameron, Lucy Lyttelton (Butt), 1781-1858.
My Bible, and my calling, by Mrs. Cameron. New York, General Protestant Episcopal Sunday School Union, Depository, Press Buildings, 1831. 26 p. DLC; NNC; WHi. 6390

Campbell, John Campbell.
The lives of the Lord Chancellor and Keeper of the great seal of England, from the earliest times till the reign of King George IV. By John Lord Campbell... 2d American ed., from 3d London ed. Philadelphia, Blanchard & Lea, 1831. NcD. 6391

Campbell, John M'Leod, 1800-1872.
The whole proceedings before the Presbytery of Dumbarton, and Synod of Glasgow & Ayr, in the case of the Rev. J. M. Campbell minister of Row, including the libel, answers to the libel, evidence and speeches. Greenock, Lusk, 1831. xxxvi, 371 p. CtY; MH; NNUT; NjPT; PPP. 6392

Campbell, Thomas.
The poetical works of Thomas Campbell, including Theodoric and many other pieces not contained in any former edition. Philadelphia, Pa., J. Crissy and J. Grigg, 1831. 38 p. CtMW; IaB; NjP; PU; TxBrdD. 6393

---- ---- Philadelphia, James Locken, 1831. 179 p. CoCsC; MdBLC; NjP; PPeSchw. 6394

Campbell, William W., 1806-1881.
Annals of Tryon county; or, The border warfare of New York, during the revolution... New York, J. & J. Harper, 1831. 191, 78 p. CtMW; IaHa; MiU; NGH. 6395

Canajoharie and Catskill railroad company.
Report on the surveys of a route for the proposed Canajohorie and Catskill rail-road, with an estimate of its cost, to the president and directors of the company. New York, Pr. by Sleight & Robinson, 1831. 23 p. CSt; DBRE; MBC; NN. 6396

Canning, Josiah W.
Sermon at Williamstown, Mass. Feb. 20, 1830, at the funeral of Elisha M. Chase. Williamstown, 1831. MWA; N. 6397

Cardell, William Samuel, 1780-1828.
...Story of Jack Halyard, the sailor boy; or, The virtuous

family...30th ed. with appropriate questions by M. T. Leavenworth. Philadelphia, Uriah Hunt, 1831. 234 p. NNC-T; PPULC; PWcHi. 6398

Carey, Mathew.
Address of the Committee of Superintendence to the public. [1831?] 4 p. MWA. 6399

---- Address to the wealthy of the land, ladies as well as gentlemen, on the character, conduct, situation, and prospects, of those whose sole dependence for subsistance, is in the labour of their hands... [Philadelphia] Pr. by W. F. Geddes, 1831. 28 p. DLC; MBAt; MdHi; PHi; PPuA. 6400

---- Annals of liberality, generosity, public spirit, etc. 3d ser., no. 4. Philadelphia, 1831. 4 p. MBAt; MWA. 6401

---- Brief view of the system of internal improvement of the state of Pennsylvania; containing a glance at its rise, progress, retardation--the difficulties it underwent, its present state, and its future prospects. By M. Carey, M. A. P. S. and the Antiquarian society. Pub. by order of the Society for the Promotion of Internal Improvement. Philadelphia, Pr. by Lydia R. Bailey, 1831. 36 p. CtY; DBRE; MiU; PPL; PU. 6402

---- Miscellaneous pamphlets. By M. Carey... Collected, April, 1831. [Philadelphia, 1831] [554] p. DLC; MiU; PPL; PPULC; ViU. 6403

---- The new olive branch: Addressed to the citizens of South Carolina... Philadelphia, Pr. by Clark & Raser, 1831. 59 p. MB; MH-BA; MdHi; PHi. 6404

---- ---- 2d ed. [Philadelphia, 1831] MHi; MWA. 6405

---- ---- 3d ed., Oct. 10, 1831. 27 p. MdHi. 6406

---- A plea for the poor, Nos. 1-3. Philadelphia, 1831 and 1832. 4, 4 p. MWA; MdHi; PPAmP. 6407

---- State rights... Philadelphia, 1831. PPL. 6408

---- Thoughts on penitentiaries and prison discipline... Philadelphia, Pr. by Clark & Raser, 1831. 76 p. DLC; IEG; MWA; NjR; PHi; PPAmP; PPL. 6409

---- Thoughts on the advantages of Infant Schools, and on the delay of their establishment at the public expense, in the city and liberties of Philadelphia. By M. Carey. Philadelphia, Pr. by Wm. F. Geddes, 1831. 8 p. DHEW; In; MWA; MiU-C; PPPrHi. 6410

---- To the citizens of the United States. Review of the address of the free-trade convention. Nos. I, II. [Philadelphia, 1831] 19 p. CtY; MdHi; MiU-C; PU; ScCC. 6411

---- To the public. (Address on infant schools.) 2d ed. Philadelphia, 1831. 12 p. CtY; MWA; PPAmP; PPL; PPPrHi. 6412

---- To whom it may concern. [n.p.] 1831? 8 p. ICU. 6413

Carisomo, Juan.
Carnestolendas; obra original por su objeto y producciones. Philadelphia, n.p., 1831. 272 p. NNH; PPULC; PPWI. 6414

Carlyle, Thomas, 1795-1881.
Carlyle's choice works, Sartor Resartus, the Life and opinions of Herr Teufelsdrockh, by Thomas Carlyle. Boston, Estes and

Lauriat [1831] 231 p. WMonr. 6415

---- Critical and miscellaneous essays collected and republished... Boston, Houghton, Mifflin & Co. [1831?] 4 v. in 2. NeU; OO; WBeloC. 6416

---- Heroes and hero-worship. New York, International Book Company, 1831. InGref. 6417

---- Sartor resartus, the life and opinions of Herr Teufelsdrocke. Boston, Estes and Lauriat, 1831. 231 p. IE; IaBl; InNdS; MNee; MS; Wa. 6418

---- ---- New York, Caldwell, 1831. 231 p. PW. 6419

---- ---- New York, C. Scribner's Sons, 1831. 250 p. IaDa; MdAS; NN; PHC; PP; PPULC. 6420

Carnahan, James, 1775-1859.
The character & blessedness of the good man. A discourse, delivered in the chapel of Nassau-hall on the Sabbath, January 9, 1831... Princeton, Pr. by Wm. D. Hart, 1831. 24 p. DLC; MH-AH; MnSM. 6421

The Carolina law journal... Edited by A. Blanding & D. J. McCord. v. 1; [July] 1830-Apr. 1831. Columbia, S.C., Pr. at the Times and gazette office, 1831. 669 p. DLC; IaU; PPiAL; RPL; WaU. 6422

Carpenter, George W., 1802-1860.
Essays on some of the most important articles of the materia medica...to which is added A catalogue of medicines, surgical instruments... By Geo. W. Carpenter. Philadelphia, G. W. Carpenter, 1831. 226 p. DLC; IEN-M; MnU; PU; RPM. 6423

---- On the mineralogy of Chester County, with an account of some of the minerals of Delaware, Maryland, &c. Philadelphia, 1831. PPL. 6424

Carpenter, Lant, 1780-1840.
The beneficial tendency of Unitarianism printed for the American Unitarian Association. Boston, Gray & Bowen [1831] 32 p. MH. 6425

---- The Scripture Doctrine of Redemption by Christ Jesus. By Lant Carpenter, LL.D. of England. No. 52. Pr. for the American Unitarian Association. Boston, Gray & Bowen, October, 1831. 12 p. MBAU; MCon; MH; MHi; MeB; NUt; OO. 6426

Carpenter, Thomas.
Scholars' spelling assistant. Charleston, S.C., S. Babcock & Co., 1831. MH. 6427

Carrier's address to the patrons of the Boston Press, January 1, 1831. [Boston, 1831] Broadside. MB; MH. 6428

Carson, Samuel Price, 1798-1832.
To the freemen of the twelfth congressional district of North Carolina, n.p. [1831?] ScU. 6429

Carter, James Gordon, 1795-1849.
An essay on teaching geography, being an extract from Mr. Carter's lecture, delivered before the American Institute of Instruction, August 23, 1830. Boston, Hilliard, Gray, and Co., 1831. 12 p. DLC; MWA. 6430

---- A geography of New Hampshire...for families and schools ...Portsmouth, N.H., N. March; Boston, Hilliard, Gray, Little, and Wilkins, 1831. 246 p. DLC;

MH; MLanc; MiD-B; Nh. 6431

---- A geography of Worcester county; for young children. Embracing 1. A short topographical and historical sketch of every town. 2. A general view of the county, and the employments of the people. 3. A glossary, explaining the geographical and other difficult terms. By J. C. Carter and W. H. Brooks. With a new map of the county.... Lancaster, Mass., Carter, Andrews, and co., 1831. 61 p. OCHi; OClWHi. 6432

---- On the development of the Intellectual Faculties... Boston, 1831. 94 p. MLanc. 6433

---- Southern portion of Lancaster, 1830. Pub. in 1831. MB. 6434

Cary, Mrs. Virginia.
Letters on female character; addressed to a young lady on the death of her mother. 3d ed. Hartford, Conn., 1831. 230 p. CtHWatK; MBAt; MWH; MiD; PPM. 6435

Casender, Don Pedro.
The Lost virgin of the South. A tale of truth. Connected with the history of the Indian war in the South, in the year 1812-13-14 and 15, and Gen. Jackson, now President of the United States... Tallahassee, M. Smith, 1831. 327 p. GMWa; NN. 6436

Castle, Thomas, ed.
A Manual of Surgery, founded upon the principles and practice lately taught by Sir Astley Cooper, Bart. F.R.S. and Joseph Henry Green, Esq. F.R.S. 4th ed., considerably enlarged, containing many additional notes from the writings of other distinguished surgeons. Edited by Thomas Castle. Boston, Republished by Munroe & Francis, and Joseph H. Francis; New-York, Charles S. Francis, 1831. x, 467 p. ViRA. 6437

Caswell, Alexis, 1799-1877.
Lectures on astronomy. [Boston, 1831] 52 p. MNtCA. 6438

Catalogue of Music. Thompson and Homans. Georgetown, Homans, 1831. 18 p. DLC. 6439

... A catechism on the tariff for the use of plain people of common sense... Pub. by the State rights and free trade association. Charleston, Pr. by E. J. Van Brunt, 1831. 22 p. A-Ar; ICU; MBAt; PHi; ScCC. 6440

Catherine and James; or The cross girl. New Haven, S. Babcock, Sidney's press, 1831. 23 p. CtY. 6441

Catholic Almanac, or Laity's Directory for 1832. Baltimore, Md., James Myres [1831] MWA. 6442

Catholic Church in the United States.
Concilium Baltimorenes, provinciale primum; Habitum Baltimori. Anne reparatae salutis 1829 Mense Octobori. Baltimore, Ex typis J. D. Toy, 1831. 28 p. DLC; MdBLC; MdW; Mo-FloSS. 6443

---- Benevolent Society of the City of New York.
Petition and remonstrance. To the honourable the board of assistant aldermen of the city of New-York, the petition and remonstrance of the Roman Catholic Benevolent Society of the said city. [New York, 1831] 23 p. MH. 6444

Causes of the progress of Liberal Christianity. Boston, Pr. by

Gray and Bowen, 1831. 16 p. MMeT. 6445

Cecil, John. see Hone, William.

Cecil, Richard, 1748-1810.
A Friendly visit to the House of Mourning. Hartford, Henry Benton, 1831. (3), 4-179 p. MHi. 6446

---- ---- New York, T. & J. Swords, 1831. 128 p. NNG. 6447

---- The life of John Newton, Rector of the United Parishes of St. Mary Woolnoth and St. Mary Woolchurch-Haw, Lombard St. London. Compiled for the American Sunday School Union and rev. by the Committee of Publication. Philadelphia, American Sunday School Union, 1831. 160 p. DLC; GDecCT; ICCB; PHi. 6448

Cennick, John, 1718-1755.
Village discourses on important subjects... Harrisburg, Pr. by J. S. Wiestling & Co., 1831. 444 p. PLT. 6449

Census of the several towns, plantations and other places in the state of Maine for the years 1820 and 1830. Portland, Todd and Holden, 1831. 16 p. 6450

Centerbrook, Conn., Centerbrook Congregational church.
Confession of faith & covenant of the Second church of Christ in Saybrook. n.p. 1831. 8 p. Ct. 6451

Challoner, Richard, Bp., 1691-1781.
The garden of the soul; a manual of fervent prayers, pious reflections and solid instructions... By Right Rev. Dr. England... With the approbation of the Right Rev. Dr. Hughes... New York, D. & J. Sadlier [1831?] GEU. 6452

Chambers, Ezekiel Forman, 1788-1867.
Addresses delivered at Chestertown, Kent County, Md. at the dinner given... in honor of Gen. Ezekiel F. Chambers, of the United States' Senate. [Baltimore, Sands and Neilson, 1831?] 16 p. MiU-C. 6453

---- Speech of the Hon. Ezekiel F. Chambers, at the public dinner in Cambridge, Md., given to him by citizens of Dorchester county, 10th of Aug., 1831. n. t.-p. [Baltimore, Pr. by Sands & Neilson, 1831] 16 p. MBAt; MiU-C; NIC; NN. 6454

Champlin, Henry L.
Notes of a voyage from Portsmouth, England, to New York, United States. In the packet ship President, Capt. Henry L. Champlin, in the autumn of 1831. [New York, 1831] 27 p. CtHC; DLC; MB; MWA; WHi. 6455

Channing, William Ellery, 1780-1842.
Elements of Morality and Religion, in the form of C[atechism] 7th ed. Boston, 1831. 6456

---- Remarks on the character of Napoleon Bonaparte, occasioned by the publication of Scott's life of Napoleon. Ascribed to Dr. Channing. From the Christian examiner. Vol. IV. No. V. New-York, G. F. Hopkins & Son, prs. and stationers, 1831. 51 p. CSmH; LNH; MWA; Nh; NjR; RHi. 6457

---- A sermon delivered at the ordination of the Rev. Jared Sparks, to the pastoral care of the First Independent church of Baltimore, May 5, 1819. By

William Ellery Channing, minister of the Church of Christ on Federal street, Boston. 7th ed. Boston, Cummings & Hilliard; [Cambridge, University press, Hilliard and Metcalf] 1831. 51 p. MNF. 6458

Chapin, Alphalus
Description of the picture of Christ healing the sick, painted by Alphalus Chapin. Boston, 1831. 16 p. MBC; MBMu. 6459

Chapin, Graham H.
An address, delivered before the Domestic horticultural society of the western part of the state of New York, at the annual meeting, held at Lyons, on the 21st day of Scripture, 1831. By Graham H. Chapin...Lyons [N.Y.], Pr. by E. J. Whitney, 1831. 20 p. CSmH; NRHi; NRU. 6460

Chapman, Ezekiel Jones.
Critical and explanatory notes, on many passages of Scripture, (of the New Testament chiefly), which to common readers are hard to be understood. Containing, also, an illustration of the genuine beauty and force of several other passages. By Ezekiel J. Chapman, A. M., minister of the gospel. 2d ed., with many additions and improvements. Utica, [N.Y.], Pr. by Hastings & Tracy, 1831. 308 p. CtSoP; ICP; NBuDD; OMC; TxAuPt. 6461

Chapman, George Thomas.
A funeral sermon, preached at Pittsfield, Sunday, February 6, 1831, and occasioned by the death of the Hon. John Chandler Williams, who departed this life, January 31, 1831. By G. T. Chapman, D.D. Boston, Stimpson and Clapp, 1831. 16 p. CSmH; MH; MHi; RHi; RPB. 6462

Chapman, Nathaniel.
Elements of therapeutics and materia medica; to which are prefixed two discourses on the history and improvement of the materia medica...By N. Chapman, M.D. ...6th ed., enl. and rev. Philadelphia, Carey & Lea, 1831. 2 vols. ICU; MBM; NBU-M; OCo; PPCP. 6463

Chapone, Hester (Mulso), 1727-1801.
Letters on the improvement of the mind, addressed to a lady. A father's legacy to his daughters, by Dr. Gregory. A mother's advice to her absent daughters, with an additional letter on the management and education of infant children. By Lady Pennington. New York, S. King, 1831. 279 p. IU; ViU. 6464

Charles, Thomas, 1755-1814.
Egluraad byr ar y deg gor chymyn. Utica, Pr. by Northway & Porter, 1831. 49 p. Trans.: Guide to the principles of Christian devotion. NUt. 6465

---- Hyfforddwr yn egwyddorion y grefydd gristionogol. Can y diweddar Barch. Thomas Charles of Bala. Hy argraffiad cyntaf yn America. Utica, Argraffedig gan Northway & Porter, 1831. NH; NUt. 6466

Charleston and Hamburg Rail Road Company.
...Report, exhibiting the present state of the work and probable progress of operations on the Charleston and Hamburg Rail Road, submitted to the direction October 18, 1831, by Alexander Black, Commissioner. Charleston, S.C. Pr. by William S. Blain, 1831. 14 p. DLC; NN; ScHi. 6467

---- ---- 2d ed. Charleston, Pr. by A. E. Miller, 1831. 14 p.

DBRE; DLC; NN. 6468

The Charlestown directory, for the year 1831. Charlestown, Waitt and Dow, 1831-1874. 113 p. MB; MBNEH; MHi; MWA. 6469

Charleston library society, Charleston, S.C.

A supplemental catalogue, alphabetically arranged, of all the books, maps & pamphlets which have been procured by the Charleston library society, since the publication of the first volume of their catalogue in 1826. Charleston, J. S. Burges, 1831. 46 p. DLC; NN; PPAmP; ScU. 6470

Charleston. State Rights and Free Trade Association of South Carolina.

A catechism on the tariff, for the use of plain people of common sense. Pub. by the State Rights and Free Trade Association. Charleston, E. J. Van Brunt, 1831. 22 p. MH. 6471

---- ---- The Constitution of the state rights and free trade Association of South Carolina, with the address prefixed, as adopted by the State Rights and free trade party of Charleston, at a public meeting at Charleston, on the evening of the 26th July, 1831. Charleston, Pr. by A. E. Miller, 1831. 8 p. NN; RPB. 6472

---- ---- The proceedings of the first meeting of the Charleston State Rights and Free Trade Association of South Carolina. Pub. by the Association. Charleston, Pr. by E. J. Van Brunt, 1831. 18 p. DLC; ScCC; ScU. 6473

---- ---- State Rights and free trade Association Convention. Charleston, 1831-1832. PHi. 6474

---- ---- ...Taxes! Taxes! Taxes! or tables showing the form and amount of the tribute money, levied by the government; on agriculture and commerce, to be transferred into the pockets of the manufactures and sugar planters. Charleston, Van Brunt, 1831. 24 p. A-Ar; DLC; ICU; WHi. 6475

---- State Right and Free Trade Party.

Proceedings of the celebration of the 4th July, 1831, at Charleston, S.C. by the State Rights and Free Trade Party: containing the speeches and toasts, delivered on the occasion, with a description of the procession; the pavilion, etc. Charleston, Pr. by Archibald E. Miller, 1831. 84 p. CU; DLC; NcD; OCHP; PPAmP; RPB. 6476

Chase, Irah, 1793-1864.

The duty of giving Christian instruction to children. A letter written by Irah Chase; addressed, in 1831, by the Boston Association, and now by the Tract Society to parents and others connected with Baptist Churches. [Philadelphia, Baptist General Tract Society, 1831?] 16 p. NRAB; PCA; ScGF. 6477

Chase, Philander, 1775-1852.

Bishop Chase's defence of himself, against the late conspiracy at Gambier, Ohio. n.p. [1831?] 60 p. CSmH; ICN; LNHT; MiD-B; PHi. 6478

---- Defense of Kenyon college: by the Right Rev. P. Chase, D.D. Columbus, O., Pr. by Olmstead & Bailhache, 1831. 72 p. CSmH; ICP; NNUT; OMC; PPL. 6479

Cheever, George Barrell, 1807-1890, comp.

The American commonplace book of poetry, with occacional notes. By George B. Cheever.

Boston, Carter, Hendee and Babcock; Baltimore, C. Carter, 1831. 405 p. GHi; LNH; MB; PP; RPB. 6480

---- The American commonplace book of prose, a collection of eloquent and interesting extracts from the writings of American authors. By G. B. Cheever. Boston, Carter and Hendee, 1831. 468 p. CtY; GHi; IU; MH; NcD. 6481

Cheney, John Milton.

An address delivered before the society of Middlesex Husbandmen and Manufacturers, at Concord, Mass. Oct. 5, 1831. By John M. Cheney. Concord, Herman Atwill, 1831. 22 p. MBC; MH; MWA; NN; PPL. 6482

Cherokee Nation.

Memorial of a delegation from the Cherokee Indians. Presented to Congress, January 18, 1831. ...[Washington? 1831] CtHWatk; ICN; MBAt; MH; PPL; RP. 6483

Cherry and Fair Star; a grand eastern spectacle in two acts. New-York, R. Hobbs, 1831. 38 p. MH; MWA. 6484

Chesapeake and Ohio Canal Company.

Chesapeake and Ohio Canal Company. December 19, 1831. Referred to the Committee on internal improvements. Dec. 20, 1831. Ordered to be printed. [Washington, Pr. by Duff Green, 1831] U.S. 22 Cong. 1 sess. House of Representatives. 222 p. Doc. No. 18. CtY; DLC; ICJ; MB; PPULC. 6485

---- The correspondence between the Chesapeake and Ohio Canal and the Baltimore and Ohio Railroad companies, and the proceedings of the former in relation to a compromise of the conflicting claims of these companies to the left bank of the river Potomac, Between the point of Rocks and Harper's Ferry or Williamsport. Washington, Pr. by Peter Force, 1831. 152 p. DLC; NN; NcD; OCHP; ViU. 6486

---- ... The memorial of the Chesapeake and Ohio Canal Company by the president and directors thereof, pursuant to a resolution of the stockholders, in general meeting, most respectfully represents. [Annapolis?] 1831. 222p. DLC; NN; ViU. 6487

---- Regulations for navigating the Chesapeake and Ohio Canal: rules for the collection of tolls, and division of the canal into Lock-keepers' Districts. Adopted July 16, 1831. Washington, Pr. by Way & Gideon, 1831. 16 p. MiD-B. 6488

---- Report from the president of the Chesapeake and Ohio canal company, to the Legislature of Maryland; Annapolis, Pr. by J. Green, 1831. 24 p. MdBE; MdBJ; MdHi. 6489

---- Report of the general committee of the stockholders... appointed June 6, 1830; to whom the 3d annual report of the president and directors was then referred. Presented to the stockholders, in general meeting, Dec. 3, 1831... Washington, Gales & Seaton, 1831. 12 p. CtY; MdHi; PPL; ScU; Vi. 6490

Chesterfield, Philip Dormer, 4th Earl of, 1694-1773.

The Beauties of Chesterfield, consisting of selections from his works. By Alfred Howard, Esq. 4th Amer. ed. Boston, Charles Ewer, 1831. 261 p. MTaHi; PPWa. 6491

---- Practical morality, or, A guide to men and manners, consisting of Lord Chesterfield's Advice to his son. To which is added, a supplement containing extracts from various books, together with The polite philosopher... Dr. Blair's Advice to youth... New York, J. A. Clussman, 1831. 5, 275 p. NUtHi; WHi. 6492

[Child, Lydia Maria (Francis)], 1802-1880.
The frugal housewife, dedicated to those who are not ashamed of economy...4th ed. corr. and arranged by the author to which are added hints to persons of moderate fortune. Boston, Carter, Hendee and Babcock, 1831. MH; MWA; MoK. 6493

---- ---- 5th ed. Boston, Carter, Hendee, and Babcock, 1831. MH; MU; MnH. 6494

---- The little girl's own book ... 2d ed. Boston, Carter, Hendee, and Babcock, 1831. viii, 263 p. CSmH; MH; MPiB; PHi; WaSp. 6495

---- The mother's book. By Mrs. Child... Boston, Carter, Hendee and Babcock, Boston Classic Press: I. R. Butts; Baltimore, C. Carter, 1831. 168 p. CSmH; DLC; NcU; PU; RPB. 6496

---- ---- 2d ed. Boston, Carter and Hendee, 1831. 169 p. CtY; ICNC; KyLxT; MNBedf; NN; NcWsS. 6497

[Children in the Wood]
The Affecting History of the Children in the Woods. (Second Series---No. 8) Concord, Hoag & Atwood, 1831. 8 l. PP; PP-Rosenbach; PPULC. 6498

Children's lyre: or Hymns and songs, religious, moral, and cheerful, set to easy music. For the use of primary and common schools. Boston, Richardson, Lord & Holbrook, etc., etc., 1831. 58 p. MH. 6499

The Child's Annual, or, conversations instructive and entertaining, for the use of Children. By a lady. Philadelphia, 1831. DLC. 6500

The child's assistant in acquiring useful and practical knowledge. 4th ed. Brookfield, Mass., E. & G. Merriam, 1831. 70 p. DLC; MH; NNC. 6501

Child's book, The, of Sunday reading... Worcester, Hervey & Co. [183-?] 24 p. MB. 6502

The child's books of nature. Number IV. Lancaster, Carter, Andrews & Company, 183-? 15 p. DLC; MH; NN; PPULC. 6503

The child's instructer; consisting of easy lessons for children, on subjects which are familiar to them, in language adapted to their capacities. By a teacher of little children in Philadelphia. ... 4th Canandaigua ed. [Canandaigua?] Bemis and Ward, 1831. 105 p. DLC; MH; MHi; MtBC; OCl. 6504

Child's Picture book of Indians... Boston, Carter, Hendee & Co., 1831. 205 p. MLanc. 6505

Chilton, Thomas.
The circular address of Thomas Chilton, of Kentucky, to his constituents. Washington City, Feb. 27, 1831. Washington, D.C., Pr. by Stephen C. Ustick, 1831. 20 p. MB; MHi; MWA; OClWHi. 6506

Chitty, Edward, 1804-1863.
An index to all reported cases, statutes and general orders, in,

or relating to the principles, pleadings, and practice of equity and bankruptcy in the several courts of England & Ireland... from the earliest period to 1831. 1st American ed. from the last London ed. Philadelphia, R. H. Small, 1831. 2 vols. C; Ky; NjP; PP; ViU. 6507

Chitty, Joseph.
Law of contracts. 2d American ed. Philadelphia, 1831. OCLaw. 6508

---- A Practical treatise on the law of contracts not under seal; and upon the usual defences to actions thereon by Joseph Chitty, Jun., with corrections and additional references, by a member of the Massachusetts bar. 2d American ed., with copious notes of recent English and American decisions by Francis J. Troubat. Philadelphia, John Grigg, 1831. 504 p. CtMW; MoSp; NhM; TxU-L; WU-L. 6509

The Choctaw Indians; or, the Indian imploring he may not be denied the Gospel of Jesus, in his wanderings after another home beyond the Mississippi. [Boston, American Board of Commissioners for Foreign Missions, 1831?] 8 p. CtY; WHi. 6510

Choctaw Treaty.
Choctaw treaty. Erie, Ala., Greene County Gazette, 1831. HBF. 6511

Christian Almanac for Connecticut 1832. Hartford, Conn., Pub. for Connecticut Branch American Tract Society [1831] MWA. 6512

The Christian Almanac for Maryland and Virginia...1832. Baltimore, Pub. for the American Tract Society [1831] 36 p. MWA; MdBE. 6513

The Christian Almanac, for New England for the year of our Lord and Savior, Jesus Christ, 1832, being Bissextile, or Leap Year and the fifty-sixth of the Independence of the United States. Calculated for the meridian of Boston. Lat. 42° 20' 58, 4"N. Long. 71° 4' 9" W.[sic] Boston, Pub. by Lincoln & Edmands, for the American Tract Society [1831] 36 p. ICMcHi; MWA; MeHi; NjR; WHi. 6514

Christian Almanack for New York, Connecticut and New Jersey for 1832. New York, N.Y., American Tract Society [1831] MWA; NjR. 6515

Christian almanac for Pennsylvania and Ohio, for the year of our Lord and Savior Jesus Christ, 1832; being bissextile, or leap year, and the fifty sixth of the independence of the United States; adapted to the meridian of Pittsburgh. Pittsburgh, American Tract Society [1831?] 36 p. OClW. 6516

The Christian almanac, for Pennsylvania, Delaware, and West New-Jersey, for the year of our Lord and Savior Jesus Christ, 1832: being bissextile, or leap year and the fifty-sixth of the independence of the United States. Calculated for the meridian of Philadelphia, lattitude 39° 56' 55", long. 75° 11' 30" ... Philadelphia, Pub. by the Pennsylvania Branch of the American Tract Society [1831] 36 p. MWA; NjP; PPFM. 6517

No entry. 6518

The Christian almanac for Tennessee, for the year of our Lord and Savior Jesus Christ, 1832, being bissextile, or leap year, and the fifty-sixth of the independence of the United States. Calculated for the meridian of Knoxville...Knoxville, American Tract Society [1831] 36 p. T. 6519

... The Christian almanac, for Virginia, for the year of our Lord and saviour Jesus Christ, 1832. Richmond, American Tract Society [1831] 2 vols. CSmH; NN; Vi; ViU. 6520

The Christian almanac, for the western district, for the year of our Lord and Savior Jesus Christ, 1832: being bissextile, or leap year, and the fifty-sixth of the independence of the United States. Calculated for the meridian of Utica. Lat. 43° 6', long. 75° 12°. Utica, American Tract Society [1831] 36 p. MWA; MiD-B. 6521

The Christian almanac, for the Western Reserve...Ohio, for the year of our Lord and Savior Jesus Christ, 1832: being bissextile, or leap year, and the fifty-sixth of the Independence of the United States. Calculated for the meridian of Cleveland. Lat. 41° 31', Long. 81° 46'. Hudson, The American Tract Society [1831] 36 p. MWA; WHi. 6522

Christian and Farmer's Almanac for 1832. By Zadock Thompson. Burlington, Vt., E. & T. Mills [1831] DLC; MWA; MiD; NIC. 6523

The Christian economy translated from the original Greek of an old manuscript found in the island of Patmos where St. John wrote his book of the revelation. Boston, J. Punchard, and J. Gay, 1831. 94 p. MB; MBC; MBevHi. 6524

The Christian messenger, Vol. 1-4. Oct. 1831 to Oct. 1836. New York, Pr. by J. M. Danforth, for P. Price 1831[-36] 4 vols. MBUPH. 6525

The Christians Manual-Designed for Families and Sunday Schools. Boston, Pr. by Leonard C. Bowles, 1831. 216 p. MMeT. 6526

The Churchman. Vols. 1-114. New York, Churchman Co., 1831 [-95]. CtHT; DLC; MBAt; PHi; PPL. 6527

The churchman's almanac for 1832. ...Calculated for the meridian of New York. By D. Young. New York, New York Protestant Episcopal Press, 1831. 36 p. CSmH; MWA; NNA; OrPD. 6528

Ciceronis, Marcus Tullius.

M. T. Ciceronis orationes quaedam selectae, notis illustratae. In usum academiae exoniensis. Editio Stereotypa. Tabulus analytices instructa. Bostoniae, Hilliard, Gray, Little, et Wilkins, 1831. 278 p. ICartC; MAnP; MB; MNan; TxU; TxU-T. 6529

---- ---- Stereotyped from the 2d ed. corrected and improved with a life of Cicero in English. Philadelphia, J. Towar and D. M. Hogan, 1831. 367 p. IEG; NNP; PMA; ViSwC. 6530

Cincinnati. Independent fire company, no. 1.

Constitution or articles for the government of the Independent fire company, no. 1. Rev. and amended, 4th June, 1831. I. The officers of this company [etc.] Cincinnati? 1831? OCHP. 6531

Cincinnati. University. Medical College.

Annual catalogue and circular of the Medical College of Ohio during its session of 1830 & 1831. Pub. by the class. Cincinnati, Pr. by W. J. Ferris, 1831. 12 p. CSmH; NNN; NNNAM; OCHP. 6532

Cincinnati Angling Club.
Proceedings of the Cincinnati Angling Club. (From the Cincinnati Chronicle, October 23, 1830.) Cincinnati, Pr. at the Chronicle office, 1831. 8 p. DLC; MH. 6533

The Cincinnati Directory, for the year 1831: containing the names of the inhabitants, their occupations, places of business, and dwelling-houses, and a complete list of the Streets and Alleys; with an appendix, containing the names of city, township, county and state officers, and the names of officers of the various Public, Literary, Scientific and Religious Institutions with a variety of interesting statistical notices. Cincinnati, Robinson & Fairbank, 1831. 213 p. DLC; OC; OClWHi; OMC. 6534

Cincinnati, Columbus and Wooster turnpike company.
Report of the engineer to the Cincinnati, Columbus and Wooster turnpike company. Cincinnati, Pr. by John H. Wood, 1831. 23 p. MBAt; OCHP; OCWO; OClWHi. 6535

The Cincinnati mirror, and western gazette of literature and science. v. 1- Oct. 1, 1831. OClWHi. 6536

Cincinnati savings institution.
An act to incorporate the Cincinnati savings institution. Passed March 7th 1831. [n.p., n.d. 1831] 3 p. OCHP. 6537

The Cinderella quadrilles, with new figures by M' Parker Arr. by P. A. Smith, New York, E. Riley, 1831. 7 p. DLC. 6538

Citizen's Almanack for 1832. Philadelphia, Pa., Griggs & Dickinson, for John Griggs [1831] MWA. 6539

The Citizen's and Farmer's Annual Magazine, or New Philadelphia Almanac for 1832. By Charles F. Egelmann. Philadelphia, Pa., John T. Hanzsche, [1831] MWA. 6540

Citizens' and Farmers' Almanac for 1832. Calculated by Charles F. Egelmann. Baltimore, J. T. Hanzsche [1831] 18 l. MWA. 6541

Citizens' and Farmers' Yearly Messenger for 1831. Calculated by Charles F. Egelmann. Baltimore, John T. Hanzsche [1831] 17 l. MWA. 6542

Clardy, William H.
To the Freeman of the County of Pitt. Fellow-citizens. It is probably already known to you that I am a candidate to represent you in the House of Commons in the next General Assembly of the State, for the county of Pitt. ... I am, fellow-citizens, with respect, Yours, etc. Wm. H. Clardy. Pitt County, N.C. May, 1831. Broadside. NcD. 6543

Clark, James, 1779-1839.
Circular Address to his constituents.- To the voters of the Third Congressional District of Kentucky, consisting of the Counties of Fayette, Woodford and Clar(k). [Remarks on the present state of the country. Dated Washington, Feb. 28, 1831. Washington, 1831] 42 p. DLC; KyLoF; MB; PP; ScU. 6544

Clark, Jonathan.
Like of General Washington... together with his farewell address, and a short account of the

American Revolutionary War... Albany, Packard, & Van Benthuysen, 1813. 143 p. MiU-C. 6545

Clark, Lucius Fayette.
The Child's Expositor and Sabbath School Teacher's assistant. 1st series. By. L. F. Clark, A.M., associate principal of Westfield Academy. 2d ed. Schenectady, Wilson & Wood, 1831. 203 p. ICP; MB; MH-AH. 6546

[Clark, Mary] 1792?-1841.
Conversations on the history of Massachusetts, from its settlement to the present period; for the use of schools and families. By a friend of youth. Boston, Munroe & Francis, 1831. 180 p. CtY; DLC; MH; MH-BA; MiD-B. 6547

Clarke, Adam, 1760?-1832.
Discourses on Various Subjects relating to Being and Attributes of God and his Works in Creation, Providence, and Grace. 3d ed. New York, McElrath & Bangs, 1830-1831. 3 v. CtW; GEU; MtHi; OO; ViU. 6548

---- The traveller's prayer. A discourse on the Third Collect for grace. From the 2d London ed. By Adam Clarke, LL.D. Albany, Pr. by M'Pherson and M'Kercher, 1831. 50 p. MeBat. 6549

Clarke, John (1755?-1798)
An Answer to the Question, Why are you a Christian? By John Clarke, D.D. Printed for the American Unitarian Association. Boston, Gray & Bowen, 1831. 34 p. ICMe; MCon; MH-AH; MHi; MW. 6550

Claverston; or, The infidel's visit. 1st American ed. New York, T. and Swords, 1831. 162 p. CtY; ICBB. 6551

Claxton, Timothy.
Explanation of a set pneumatic apparatus made by T. Claxton. Boston [1831?] 11 p. CtY. 6552

Clayton, David L., 1801-1854.
The Virginia harmony; a new and choice selection of psalm and hymn tunes, anthems and set pieces, in three and four parts, some of which have never before been published. Prepared for the use of singing societies, teachers of sacred music, and individual instruction. To which is prefixed and introduction explanatory of the system, and a series of progressive lessons. By David L. Clayton & James P. Carrell. Winchester, S. H. Davis, 1831. 167 p. IU; N; NcD; Vi; ViU. 6553

Clayton, John Middleton.
Speech of Mr. Clayton, of Delaware in the Senate of the United States Feb. 10, 1831, on the resolution of Mr. Grundy, to prohibit the select committee on the management of the Post Office Department, from investigating the principles upon which the removals have been made in that department. Washington, Pr. at the Office of the National Journal, 1831. 32 p. CSfCW; DLC; IU; NcD; PHi. 6554

Cleland, T., 1778-1858, comp.
Evangelical hymns, for private, family, social, and public worship. Selected from various authors. By Thomas Cleland, D.D. 4th ed. enl. Lexington, Ky., T.T. Skillman, 1831. 447 p. MdBD; NbOP; NNUT; OUrC. 6555

---- Hymns, selected and original, for public and private worship. Published by the General Synod of the Evangelical Lutheran Church. 4th ed. Pub. Gettysburgh, Pa. Stereotyped by L. Johnson, Philadelphia, 1831.

519, 16 p. ScCMu. 6556

Cleveland, Charles Dexter, 1802-1869.

Compendium of Grecian antiquities, by Charles Dexter. Cleveland, A. M. 2d ed. Boston, Hilliard, Gray, Little, and Wilkins, 1831. 251 p. CtY; LNT; PU; TNP; WaPS. 6557

---- First lessons in Latin: Upon a new plan; combining abstract rules, with a progressive series of practical exercises. 2d ed. By Charles Dexter Cleveland, A. M. Boston, Carter, Hende & Babcock; Baltimore, C. Cater, 1831. 214 p. CtMW; IEG; MB; RPB; TxBrdD. 6558

---- The national orator; consisting of selections, adapted for rhetorical recitation, from the parliamentary, forensic and pulpit eloquence of Great Britain and America: interspersed with extracts from the poets. 2d ed. carefully rev. and imp. by the addition of dialogues. By Charles Dexter Cleveland. New-York, White, Gallaher & White, 1831. 288 p. CtY; IC; IU; KyLoP; OMC. 6559

---- To my friends. (Concerning Dickinson College.) 1831. PPPrHi; PPULC. 6560

Cleveland, Dorcas Cleveland Hiller, 1773-1850.

A dialogue on providence, faith, and prayer. (Anon) 3d ed. Boston, 1831. MB-FA; MB-HP. 6561

---- A dialogue on some of the causes of Infidelity. By the Author of a dialogue on Providence, Faith, and Prayer, (Mrs. Cleveland). Boston, Gray & Bowen, 1831. 24 p. ICMe; MH; MMeT-Hi; MeBat; Me. 6562

Clifton, William.

The last link is broken, a favorite duett, composed, arranged and respectfully dedicated to Mrs Lydia McIntosh. Baltimore, George Willing, Jr. [1831?] 3 p. DLC; ViU. 6563

---- ---- New York, Bourne [1831?] 3 p. MB. 6564

---- ---- New York, J. L. Hewitt [1831?] DLC. 6565

Clowes, Timothy.

The root extractor, exhibiting new rules and processes... serving likewise as a key to all the cubic and higher equations in Bonnycastle's introduction to algebra. New York, Sleight, 1831. 70 p. CtY; NCH; NN; NSmb; PPM. 6566

Cobb, Jonathan Holmes, 1799-1882.

A manual containing information respecting the growth of the mulberry tree, with suitable directions, for the culture of silk. In three parts. By J. H. Cobb, A. M. Pub. by direction of His Excellency Gov. Lincoln, agreeably to a resolve of the commonwealth... Boston, Carter, Hendee & Babcock, 1831. 68 p. CtY; IU; MHi; OC; RPB. 6567

Cobb, Lyman, 1800-1864.

Cobb's juvenile reader, no. 1; containing interesting, moral, and instructive reading lessons, composed of easy words of one and two syllables. Designed for the use of small children, in families and schools. By Lyman Cobb... New York, Collins and Hannay, 1831. 72 p. CtHWatk; DLC; NN; NbCrD. 6568

---- ---- Baltimore, Joseph Jewett, 1831. 72 p. MdBE; ODaB; PPULC; PPeSchW; ViU. 6569

---- Cobb's Juvenile reader, No. 2, containing interesting moral and instructive reading lessons composed of words of one, two, and three syllables designed for the use of small children... Watertown, Knowlton & Rice, 1831. 144 p. N; NPDt. 6570

---- ---- Pittsburgh, Luke Loomis, 1831. 144 0. OClWHi. 6571

---- Cobb's juvenile reader, no. 3; containing interesting, historical, moral, and instructive reading lessons, composed of words of a greater number of syllables than the lessons in nos. I, and II... Designed for the use of larger children, in families and schools. By Lyman Cobb... Baltimore, J. Jewett, 1831. 212 p. DLC; MdBE; PLFM. 6572

---- ---- New York, Collins & Hannay, 1831. 212 p. DLC; PWCHi; RPB. 6573

---- ---- Pittsburgh, Loomis, 1831. OClWHi; PPi; WHi. 6574

---- ---- Indianapolis, Henkle and Chamberlain, 1831. 216 p. 6575

---- ---- Ithaca, Mack and Andrus, 1831. 216 p. NIDHi. 6576

---- ---- Philadelphia, Thomas L. Bonsal [1831] MH; PU. 6577

---- Cobb's spelling-book; being a just standard for pronouncing the English language, containing the rudiments of the English language, arranged in catechetical order; an organization of the alphabet; an easy scheme of spelling and pronunciation, intermixed with easy reading lessons: to which are added, some useful tables, with the names of cities, counties, towns, rivers, lakes, &c, in the United States; and a list of the proper names contained in the New Testament, and pronounced according to the best authorities. Designed to teach the orthography and orthoepy of J. Walker. Rev. ed. Ithaca, N.Y., Mack & Andrus, 1831. 168 p. MH; OClWHi. 6578

---- ---- New York, Caleb Bartlett, 1831. 158 p. NRivHi. 6579

---- ---- Rev. ed. St. Clairsville, Ohio, Heaton & Gressinger, [183-?] OCo. 6580

---- Critical review of the orthography of Dr. Webster's series of books for systematick [sic] instruction in the English language; including his former spelling-book, and the elementary spelling-book, compiled by Aaron Ely and Published under the name of Noah Webster, LL.D. By Lyman Cobb. New York, Collins and Hannay, 1831. 56 p. CSt; ICN; MiD; NjP; TxU. 6581

Cobbett, William, 1763-1835.
Advice to young men, and (incidentally) to young women. In the middle and higher ranks of life. In a series of letters, addressed to a youth, a bachelor, a lover, a husband, a citizen or a subject. By Wm. Cobbett. New York, John Doyle, 1831. 268 p. CtY; IU; KyU; MWA; PU. 6582

---- A full and accurate report of the trial of William Cobbett, Esq. (before Lord Tenterden and a special jury,) on Thursday, July 7, 1831, in the court of king's bench, London... New York, J. Doyle, 1831. 47 p. CSmH; CtY; NjR; RPB; ScU. 6583

---- A history of the Protestant Reformation in England and Ireland: Showing how that event has impoverished the main body of the people in those countries;... written by William Cobbett, M. P. in a series of letters, addressed to all sensible and just Englishmen. To which is now added three letters, by the same author, never before published in the United States. New York, D. & J. Sadlier & Co. [1831] 2 vols. MsMerStA; OWorP; PLatS; PPULC. 6584

Codman, John, 1782-1847.

Dr. Codman's speech in the Board of overseers of Harvard college, Feb. 3, 1831. [Cambridge? 1831] 15 p. CtY; DLC; ICMe; MB; MoU; PPPrHi. 6585

---- Ministerial courtesy. A sermon, delivered before the convention of Congregational ministers of Massachusetts, in Brattle street church, Boston, May 26, 1831. By John Codman, D.D. Pastor of the Second church in Dorchester. Boston, Peirce & Parker, 1831. 22 p. CtY; ICN; MBAt; MWA; NjPT. 6586

Coe, Truman.

Question on astronomy with answers designed to accompany a course of popular lectures on that science, New Haven, Tho. Z. Woodward, 1831. 36 p. RPB. 6587

Coffin, Charles, comp., 1779-1851.

History of the battle of Breed's Hill, by Major Generals William Heath, Henry Lee, James Wilkinson and Henry Dearburn. Comp. by Charles Coffin. Saco, Me., Pr. by W. J. Condon, 1831. 38 p. CtY; Me; MiU-C; NjN; RPB. 6588

[Cogswell, Joseph Green] 1786-1871.

Outline of the system of education at the Round Hill School, with a list of the present instructers and of the pupils from its commencement until... June, 1831. Boston, Hale, 1831. 24 p. CtY; ICHi; MB; NNG; NjP. 6589

Cogswell, William, 1787-1850.

Religious liberty. A sermon, preached on the day of the annual fast in Massachusetts, April 3, 1828... 2d ed. Boston, Peirce & Parker, 1831. 24 p. CtY; MWA; NcD; OO; RPP. 6590

---- The theological class book; containing system of divinity, in the form of question and answer ...designed for... theological classes, and the higher classes in Sabbath schools. By William Cogswell. Boston, Crocker & Brewster; New York, J. Leavitt [etc., etc.] 1831. 195 p. CtY; IAIS; MH; Nh-Hi; PPPRHi. 6591

Coke, Isaac P.

Coke's Juvenile Instructor, introductory to vocal music. By Isaac P. Coke. New York, Caleb Bartlett, 1831. 40 p. ICU. 6592

Coke, Thomas, bp., 1747-1814.

Account of the experiences of Hester Ann Rogers and her funeral sermon to which is added her Spiritual Letters. New York, 1831. 6593

Colburn, Warren, 1793-1833.

Arithmetic upon the inductive method of instruction: being a sequel to intellectual arithmetic. By Warren Colburn, A.M. Stereotyped at the Boston type and stereotype foundry. New York, R. Lockwood; Boston, Hilliard, Gray, Little, and Wilkins, 1831. 245 p. CSmH; DLC; ICBB; MH; NNC. 6594

---- First lessons. Intellectual arithmetic, upon the inductive method of instruction. By Warren Colburn. Boston, Hilliard, Gray, Little, and Wilkins, 1831. 172 p. KTW. 6595

---- ---- New York, Lockwood, 1831. 172 p. CtHwatk; NN; NPV; OCl; WHi. 6596

---- ...Intellectual arithmetic, upon the inductive method of instruction. By Warren Colburn, A. M. Stereotyped at the Boston type and stereotype foundry. New-York, R. Lockwood; Boston, Hilliard, Gray, Little, and Wilkins, 1831. 172 p. CtHWatk; ICBB; KTW; NN; WHi. 6597

---- An introduction to algebra upon the inductive method of instruction. By Warren Colburn ... Boston, Hilliard, Gray, Little, and Wilkins, 1831. 276 p. CtHT; InU; MBAt; OO; RPM. 6598

---- Key, containing answers to the examples in the sequel to intellectual arithmetic.... Boston, Hilliard, Gray & Co., 1831. 70 p. MH; MMhHi; NhD; PPM. 6599

---- ---- Stereotyped ed. Boston, Hilliard, 1831. 50 p. CtMW; MH. 6600

---- A lecture on the teaching of arithmetic, delivered in the representatives' Hall, Boston, August, 1830, before the American Institute of instruction. By Warren Colburn. Boston, Hilliard, Gray, Little and Wilkins, 1831. TxU-T. 6601

---- Second lessons in reading and grammar, for the use of schools: chiefly from the works of Miss Edgeworth. Selected and prepared by Warren Colburn... Boston, Hilliard, Gray, Little and Wilkins, 1831. 95 p. DLC; ICBB; MH. 6602

Colby, John, 1787-1817.
The Life, Experience and Travels of the Rev. John Colby. Written by himself. 3d ed. Portland, 1815. Newport, N.H., French and Brown, 1831-1832. 2 vols. CSmH; CtY; IU; RPAt. 6603

Colden, Cadwallader R.
An expose of the measures which caused a suspension of the races on the Union course, in October, 1830; and the proceedings since October, 1828, of the Association & Manager in their respective relations. By the late manager. New-York, 1831. 44 p. CtY; PHi. 6604

Cole, J.
A sermon preached at the closing of a Sunday School, October 31, 1830. By a Pastor. Boston, Leonard C. Bowles, 1831. 17 p. MH; MWA. 6605

Cole, John, 1792-1848.
A critique on the performance of Othello by F. W. Keene Alariage, the African Roscius. Scarborough, Cole, 1831. 4 p. MB. 6606

Coleridge, Henry Nelson, 1798-1843.
Introductions to the Study of the Greek Classic Poets. Designed principally for the use of young persons at school and college. By Henry Nelson Coleridge, Esq., M.A.... Part I. Containing- I. General introduction. II. Homer. Philadelphia, Carey & Lea, 1831. CoU; IaGG; MH; PPA; ViU. 6607

Coleridge, Samuel Taylor, 1772-1834.
The friend: a series of essays to aid in the formation of fixed principles in politics, morals, and religion. 1st Amer. from 2d London ed. Burlington [Vt.], C. Goodrich, 1831. 510 p. GEU; MB; RNR; ScU; WaU. 6608

---- The poetical works of

Coleridge, Shelley, and Keats, complete in one volume... Philadelphia, J. Grigg, 1831. 607 p. DLC; KyU; MB; NjP; TNP. 6609

Coles, Elisha.
A practical discourse of God's sovereignty. With other material points derived thence: namely, of the righteousness of God. Of election. Of redemption. Of effectual calling. Of perserverance. By Elisha Coles. With a recommendatory preface, by the Rev. William Romaine... Also by Dr. Owen and T. Goodwin... Pittsburgh, D. & M. MacLean, 1831. 298 p. IaFairP; KEmC; OSW; PPi; ScDue. 6610

A collection of hymns for the use of Unitarian Christians in public worship. Bristol [Conn.] 1831. unpaged. MH; MH-AH; NNUT. 6611

A collection of texts of Scripture, in which the different tenets of the Church of Rome are fully stated and fairly answered, from Scripture, and comment on Scripture. Baltimore, Lucas & Deaver, 1831. 168 p. NNUT; PLT; PPLT. 6612

Collections, topographical, historical and biographical, relating principally to New Hampshire; edited by J. Farmer & J. B. Moore... Concord, Hill and Moore, 1822. Vol. I. Repr. by H. E. & J. W. Moore, 1831. 296 (10) p. MIC; NIC; NjR; PHi; Vi. 6613

College for Colored Youth, New Haven. See Committee for superintending the applications for funds for the College for Colored Youth, New Haven.

Colles, Abraham, 1773-1843.
Treatise on Surgical Anatomy; by Abraham Colles, one of the professors of Anatomy and Surgery in the Royal College of Surgeons in Ireland, etc. etc. etc. 2d American ed. With notes by J. P. Hopkinson. Philadelphia, Carey & Lea, 1831. 186 p. CU; DLC; IU-M; MnU; OrUM; PU; TCh. 6614

Collins, Isaac, fl. 1830.
Copies of letters from Isaac Collins to Samuel Parsons, Flushing, Long Island, N.Y. 1831-36: chiefly relating to Haverford school. Philadelphia, 1831-36. 10 p. PHC. 6615

Colonization Society of Virginia.
Proceedings of the Colonization Society of Virginia. [Richmond? 1831?] 11 p. NN; TxU. 6616

Colton's Vermont miniature register and gentleman's pocket almanac for the year of our Lord, 1832. Astronomical calculations by Marshall Conant. No. 11. Woodstock, Rufus Colton [1831] 128 p. NHi; NN. 6617

Columbian almanac for 1832. Calculations by William Collom. Philadelphia, Pa., Joseph M'-Dowell [1831] MWA. 6618

The Columbus Almanac, for the year of our Lord 1832. Being besextile [sic], or leap year, and after the fourth of July, the fifty seventh year of American Independence. Calculated for the meridian of Columbus, In latitude 39° 56' north, and longitude 6° west from Washington City. By William Lusk. Columbus, Jenkins & Glover, 1831 [24] p. illus. 19.5 cm. MWA. 6619

Comer, Thomas, 1790-1862.
Auld Joe Nicholson's Nannie, a ballad... (T. accomp. for pianoforte). Boston, Bradlee

[1831] 3 p. MB. 6620

Comly, John.
Spelling and reading book... Philadelphia, 1831. CtHWatk. 6621

[Committee for Superintending the Application for Funds for the College for Colored Youth, New Haven]
College for colored youth, An account of the New-Haven city meeting and resolutions, with recommendations of the college, and strictures upon the doings of New-Haven. New York, Pub. by the Committee, 1831. 24 p. CtY; MiD-B; NcD; RPB; ScCC. 6622

Committee to investigate the evils of lotteries.
Report of a committee appointed to investigate the evils of lotteries in the commonwealth of Pennsylania and to suggest a remedy for the same. Philadelphia, D. B. Shrieves, 1831. 16 p. CU; MH; MdBJ; PHC; TxHuT. 6623

Common almanack for...1832 ... Watertown, N.Y., Knowlton & Rice, 1831. 1 v. DLC; NRU. 6624

Commonplace Book of Anecdotes. (Consisting of a choice collection of original and selected pieces.) Boston, n.p., 1831. 320 p. MiBatW. 6625

The Common-place book of romantic tales. Consisting of original and select pieces by the most eminent authors. New York, Charles Wells, 1831. 286 p. ICU; MBAt; MWA; MeB; PP. 6626

The Communicant's companion; containing prayers and meditations for use at the administration of the holy communion, with directions to the communicant, and the communion office... New York, Protestant Episcopal Press, 1831. 89 p. GDecCT; MBC; NNG; RNHi. 6627

A compendium of English grammar selected from Wells, Kirkham, Murray, Perry, &c. Union Village [Ohio] [Richard McNemarat] 1831. 12 p. OClWHi. 6628

Complete course of education according to Mr. J. J. Jacobott's natural method of Universal Instruction and intellectual emancipation. no. 2. writing-vernacular tongue-Grammar. Philadelphia, V. Guillou, 1831. 87 p. PHi; PPDrop; PPL. 6629

The complete New-England almanac, for the year of our Lord, 1832. by Marshall Conant. No. IV. Woodstock, Pr. by R. & A. Colton for Nahum Haskell [1831] 44 [4] p. DLC; MB; MWA; NjR. 6630

Comstock, John Lee, 1789-1858.
Elements of chemistry; in which the recent discoveries in the science are included, and its doctrines familiarly explained. Illustrated by numerous engravings, and designed for the use of schools and academies. 2d ed. Hartford, D. F. Robinson & co., 1831. 356 p. CtY; ICJ; MB; OClM; TNP. 6631

---- A system of national philosophy; in which the principles of Mechanics, Hydrostatics, Hydraulics, Pneumatics, Acoustics, optics, astronomy, Electricity, and Magnetism, and familiary explained, and illustrated by more than two hundred engravings, to which are added questions for the examination of the pupils, designed for the use of schools and academies. 2d ed. by J. L. Comstock, M.D. Hartford, D. F. Robinson & Co., 1831. 295 p. CtMW; ICT; MB;

NNC; OrC; PU; TxU; WWaHi. 6632

Comyn, Samuel

The law of contracts and promises upon various subjects and with particular persons, as settled in the action of assumpsit. In three parts. By Samuel Comyn... 3d American, from the last London ed.; with notes, and references to American authorities, by Thomas Huntington... New York, Collins and Hannay, 1831. 654 p. CU-L; CoU; ICP; NcD; WaU. 6633

Conant, Marshall.

Great solar eclipse of February 12, 1831; a rare magnificent phenomenon. Woodstock, L. A. Miller, 1831. Broadside. VtHi. 6634

Concilium Baltimorense, provinciale primum: Habitum Baltimori. Anno reparatae salutis 1829. Mense Octorbi. Baltimore, Ex typis J. D. Toy, 1831. 28 p. MdBLC; MdW; MoFloSS. 6635

A concise treatise upon the powers and duties of the principal state, county, and town officers. For the use of schools. By a gentleman of the bar. Utica, W. Williams, 1831. 144 p. GDecCT; IaHi; MH; NUt; OClW. 6636

Conclin, George.

...Conclin's new river guide, or A gazetteer of all the towns on the western waters: containing sketches of the cities, towns, and countries bordering on the Ohio and Mississippi rivers, and their principal tributaries... Comp. from the latest and best authority. With forty-four maps. Cincinnati, J. A. & U. P. James, 1831. 128 p. DLC; OClWHi. 6637

Concord, New Hampshire. First Congregational Church.

Pastors, deacons and members of the First Congregational Church, Concord. Concord, 1831. 211 p. MWA. 6638

Concordia parish, Louisiana.

Proceedings of the police jury of the Parish of Concordia... 1831. Natchez [Miss.] Pr. at the office of "The Natchez" [etc.] 1831-44. 4 v. CSmH; NN. 6639

[Conder, Josiah] 1789-1855.

The Modern Traveller. A popular description... Arabia. Boston, Lilly & Wait, 1831. 340 p. ICBB; NR; RNR; RP. 6640

---- ---- Russia. Boston, Lilly & Wait; Philadelphia, Thomas Wardle, 1831. 315 p. CSt; LU; NR; RP; ViAlTh. 6641

Condition and character of females in pagan and Mohammadan countries. 2d ed. Boston, Perkins, 1831. 12 p. MHi; OO. 6642

Confessio.

Der Bekenntnisz des Glaubens etlicher Fursten und Stadte, uberantwortet Kayserlicher Majestat zu Augspurg Anno MDXXX. Neu-Market, Virginia, gedruckt in Salomon Henkels Drunkerei, 1831. C; Cf; ViHarHi; ViU; ViW. 6643

Confessions and execution of the pirates Gibbs & Wansley on Ellis' Island, in the Harbour of New York, on the 22d April, 1831... New York, Christian Brown, 1831. NN; OClWHi; RHi. 6644

Congregational Churches in Connecticut.

Confession of faith owned to by the elders and messengers of the churches... New London, Pr. 1710; Bridgeport, Repr. by Lockwood & Backus, 1810. Hartford, Kappel, 1831. 79 p. CSmH; CtHT; CtY; MeHi. 6645

---- Saybrook Synod.
A confession of faith, owned and consented to by the elders and messengers of the churches in the colony of Connecticut in New-England, assembled by delegation at Saybrook, Sept. 9th, 1708. New London, Pr. 1710; Bridgeport, Repr. by Lockwood & Backus, 1810; Hartford, Conn., Pr. by G. W. Kappel, 1831. 79 p. CSmH; CtY; MH. 6646

Congregational Churches in Massachusetts.
Minutes of the General Association of Massachusetts, at their meeting in Groton, June, 1831, with the Narrative of the State of Religion, and the Pastoral Address. Boston, Pr. by Crocker & Brewster, 1831. 19 p. DLC; ICN; IEGG. OCC. 6647

---- Ecclesiastical council, Berkley.
"Better edification" a good plea. Proceedings of an Ecclesiastical council, in the town of Berkley, October 19, 1831. And the documents connected therewith. Taunton [Mass.] Pr. by James Thurber, 1831. 26 p. CSmH; NN. 6648

---- in U.S. Worcester Association.
A Catechism, in three parts, first part containing the elements of religion and morality; designed for children. Part second consisting of questions and answers, chiefly historical on the old testament. Part third consisting of similar questions and answers on the new testament; designed for children and young persons. Compiled and recommended by the Ministers of the Worcester association in Massachusetts. 5th ed. Boston, Hilliard, Gray, Little, and Wilkins, 1831. 54 p. MB; MBarn; MH-AH. 6649

Congregational Churches in Maine.
Minutes of the General Conference of Maine at their annual meeting at Fryeburg, June 21, 1831. Portland, Pr. by A. Shirley, 1831. 27 p. M; MeBat; MeLewB. 6650

Congregational Churches in New Hampshire.
Minutes of the General Association of New Hampshire, at their meeting in Concord, September, 1831. Published by order of the Association. Concord, Pr. at the Observer Press, 1831. 20 p. ICN. 6651

Congregational Churches in Vermont.
Extracts from the minutes of the General Convention of Congregational and Presbyterian ministers in Vermont, at their session at Windsor, September, 1831. Windsor, Pr. at the Chronicle Press, 1831. 16 p. MiD-B. 6652

Conkling, Alfred
Organization, jurisdiction and practice of the courts of the United States... Albany, 1831. 538 p. MH-L; RPB. 6653

---- A treatise on the organization, jurisdiction and practice of the courts of the United States, to which is added an appendix containing the rules of the Supreme court of the United States, of the courts of equity of the United States and also a few practical forms. By Alfred Conkling. Albany, W. & H. Gould; New York, Gould, Banks & co., 1831. 538 p. CU-Law; Ia; MH; NcD; RNR. 6654

Conkling, Thomas W.
Conkling's arithmetic, the young arithmetician's guide to a knowledge of numbers; being an easy practical system of arithmetic... By Thomas W. Conkling... adapted to the currency of the United States. New York, Ketcham & Aymar, 1831. 288 p. DAU; DLC; NN. 6655

Connecticut.
The public statute laws of the state of Connecticut, passed at the session of the General Assembly, in 1831. Published by authority of the General Assembly under the direction and superintendence of the Secretary of State. Hartford (Conn.), Pr. by Charles Babcock, 1831. 366 p. Ar-SC; DLC; IaU; MO; Wa-L. 6656

---- General Assembly. Building Committee.
Report of the case, relative to the State house, New Haven, between the Building Committee and Ithiel Town, architect, as decided by the arbitrators. [New Haven? 1831] CtY. 6657

---- ---- Committee on State prison.
Report of the directors and warden of the Connecticut State Prison; submitted to the legislature, May session, 1831. Pr. by order of the Legislature. Hartford, Pr. by Samuel Hanmer, jr., 1831. 19 p. Ct. 6658

---- Governor (John S. Peters)
Message of His Excellency John S. Peters, addressed to the Legislature of the state of Connecticut, May session, 1831. Hartford, Pr. by C. Babcock, [1831?] 12 p. CSmH; Ct; MdBJ. 6659

---- School fund commission.
Correspondence of the Connecticut school fund commission and the New Haven bank for 1831. 7 p. CtSoP. 6660

---- Secretary of State.
The Connecticut Annual register, and United States Calendar for 1832. Being the fifty-sixth of American Independence. Containing Almanack, executive, judicial, Civil and Military officers of the State of Connecticut. No. 42. [New London, Conn.] Samuel Green [1831?] 154 p. Mi; PHi. 6661

Connecticut Retreat for the Insane. see Hartford, Institute for the Living.

Connecticut State Medical Society.
Catalogue of the officers and members of the...and the Proceedings of the fellows, May, 1831. Hartford, P. Canfield, 1831. DNLM. 6662

---- Report of a committee of the Connecticut Medical Society respecting an asylum for the insane, with the constitution of the society for their relief. Accepted by the Medical Convention October 3, 1821, and by them ordered to be published. Hartford, Bowles & Francis, 1831. 16 p. MH. 6663

No entry. 6664

Conolly, John, 1794-1866.
...Cottage evenings. 1st Amer. ed. Philadelphia, Carey, Hart, 1831. 215 p. CtHT; MH. 6665

Conrad, Timothy Abbot, 1803-1877.
American marine conchology; or, Descriptions and colored

figures of the shells of the Atlantic coast of N. A., by Timothy A. Conrad. Philadelphia, Pr. for the author, 1831. 72 p. A-GS; DSI; MnU; PBa; TNV. 6666

Constitution of the temperance societies attached to the Methodist Episcopal church, of Baltimore city station, auxiliary to the Baltimore temperance society; with a list of the members. Baltimore, Pr. by J. D. Toy, 1831. DLC. 6667

Constitutional State Rights and Union Party.

Constitutional State Rights & Union Party of St. Johns Colleton. Manifesto and resolurions. Charleston, J. S. Burges, 1831. 24 p. CtY; MBAt; MH; MHi. 6668

Convention for the Improvement of the Free People of Color.

Minutes and proceedings of the first annual Convention of the People of Colour held in Philadelphia, June 6-11, 1831. Philadelphia, 1831. 16 p. KHi; MH; MeB; MiD-B; PHi; PPL. 6669

Convention of Congregational Ministers of Massachusetts.

Rules of the Massachusetts convention of Congregational ministers. Adopted May, 1830. Boston, Pr. by T. R. Marvin, 1831. 8 p. CtSoP; DLC; MBC; MWA; PPrHi. 6670

Convention of delegates appointed by persons interested in the growth and manufactures of wool, New York, May, 1831.

To the farmers, mechanics, and manufacturers of the United States. [Address by the committee appointed at the Convention, to take into concideration the expediency of forming a national association [New York, 1831] [2] p. Signed: Henry Shaw, Pater H. Schenck, Samuel D. Hubbard, Committee. New York, Aug. 15, 1831. CtY; ICU; MH-BA; PHi. 6671

Convention of delegates met to consult on missions, Cincinnati, 1831.

Minutes... Lexington, Ky., 1831. CtY; DLC; PPPrHi; OClWHi. 6672

---- A report of the minority in the Convention on domestic missions. Cincinnati, 1831. DLC; NjPT; OClWHi; OOxM; PPPrHi. 6673

Convention of delegates Representing Various Counties of the Western Division of the State of Virginia see Lewisburg Convention, Lewisburg, Va., 1831.

Convention of Mechanics, manufacturers and agriculturalists, New York, 1831.

Proceedings of a convention of delegates, appointed by persons interested in the growth and manufacture of wool, held at Clinton Hall, New York, New York, J. M. Danforth, 1831. 20 p. MH-BA. 6674

Convention of teachers and friends of education, Utica, N.Y.

Address of the state convention of teachers and friends of education, held at Utica, January 12th, 13th & 14th, 1831. With an abstract of the proceedings of said convention. Utica, Pr. by Northway and Porter, 1831. 16 p. MB; MH; MHi; TNP. 6675

Conversation on the subject of infant damnation between a professed Calvinist and a Universalist. Woodstock, Pr. by W. W. Prescott, Press of the Universalist Watchman, 1831. 12 p. MMeT; MMeT-Hi. 6676

Conversations on the attributes

of God. By the author of 'The badge', &c. Boston, L. C. Bowles, 1831. DLC; MH. 6677

Cook, Parsons.
The time-serving minister. A sermon preached at the installation of Rev. Joseph H. Patrick, as colleague pastor of the church in Greenwich. Nov. 17, 1830. By Parsons Cook... Together with the address, delivered by Rev. Sumner G. Clapp, pastor of the church in Enfield, on giving the right hand of fellowship. Greenwich [Mass.] Mervin Hale, 1831. 16 p. CtSoP; MBC; MDeeP; RPB. 6678

Cook, W.
Solutions of the Cambridge problems, proposed by the moderators to the candidates for honors at the examination for the degree of B.A. January, 1831, to which are added, essays on various points of pure and mixed mathematics. Cambridge, n.p., 1831. 134 p. IU; MB. 6679

The cook not mad, or rational cooking; being a collection of original and selected receipts ----to which, are added, directions for preparing comforts for the sick room;----Watertown, Knowlton & Rice, 1831. 120 p. DLC; ICRL; KMK; NNT-C; WBeaHi. 6680

Cooke, Parsons, 1800-1864.
A remonstrance against an established religion in Massachusetts. Boston, Peirce & Parker, 1831. 24 p. CtY; ICN; MH-AH; NN; PHi. 6681

Cooke, Phinehas, 1781-1853.
Historical recollections. A discourse delivered at Lebanon, N.H., on Thanksgiving Day, Nov. 15, 1830, embracing the leading events in the civil and ecclesiastical history of said town to the close of Rev. Isaiah Potter's Ministry. Concord, (N.H.) A. M'Farland, 1831. 17 p. CtSoP; ICN; MB; NjPT; PPAmP. 6682

Cooper, Astley Paston, bart, 1768-1841.
The lectures of Sir Astley Cooper, Bart., F.R.S. Surgeon to the King, &c., on the principles and practice of surgery. With additional notes and cases by Frederick Tyrrell, Esq. 3d Amer. from the last London ed. Boston, Lilly & Wait, 1831. 3 vols. CU; ICJ; MeB; NNN; WaU. 6683

Cooper, James Fenimore, 1789-1851.
The bravo, a tale by the author of The Spy, "The Red Rover," "The Water Witch," &c. Guistizia in palazzo, e pane in piazza, in two volumes. Philadelphia, Carey & Lea, 1831. 2 vols. CoU; DLC; NN; PPL; TxU. 6684

---- Home as found. Philadelphia, 1831. MB. 6685

---- The last of the Mohicans; a narrative of 1757. By the author of "the pioneers." 4th ed. Philadelphia, H. C. Carey & I. Lea, 1831. 2 vols. NcC; PPPCity. 6686

---- Lionel Lincoln; or, The Leaguer of Boston... (anon.). 5th ed. Philadelphia, Carey & Lea, 1831. 2 vols. DLC; NcD. 6687

---- The pilot: a tale of the sea. By the author of "The pioneers," &c.... 5th ed. Philadelphia, Carey & Lea, 1831. 2 vols. CtHWatk; ICP; IU; NcC; TNP. 6688

---- The Pioneers, or the

Sources of the Susquehanna; a descriptive tale. 6th ed. Philadelphia, Carey & Lea, 1831. 2 vols. CtHWatk; NcC. 6689

[----] The Prairie; a tale. By the author of the "Pioneers and the last of the Mohicans."... Philadelphia, Carey & Lea, 1831. 2 vols. MHaHi; NWattJHi; NcD. 6690

Cooper, J. G.
A plain and practical English grammar: in which the principles of our language are simplified, and more fully explained than in any work of the kind... By the Rev. J. G. Cooper, A.M. ...Philadelphia, Judah Dobson (agent), 1831. 210 p. MH; NNC; PWW. 6691

Cooper, Thomas, 1759-1839.
Address to the graduates of the South Carolina College at the public commencement, 1830. By Thomas Cooper. Pub. at the request of the senior class. May, 1831. Columbia, Pr. by S. J. Morris [1831] 12 p. CSmH; DLC; IU; RP; ScU. 6692

---- The case of Thomas Cooper ...President of the South Carolina College; submitted to the Legislature and the people of South Carolina, Dec. 1831. Columbia, Times & Gazette Office, [1831] vii, 44, 17, 5 p. CtY; DLC; MHi; NIC; ScC. 6693

---- Lectures on the elements of political economy...2d ed. Columbia, S.C., Pr. by M'Morris & Wilson, 1831. 1 p. l., vi, (7)-366 p. CSmH; CtY; ICU; NRU. 6694

[----] To any member of Congress. By a layman... [Columbia, S.C.] Pr. for the pub. by S. J. M'Morris, 1831. 16 p. MdBJ; PU; ScU. 6695

---- Two tracts, on materialism and on Outline of the Association of ideas (in Broussais, F.J.V. on intuition and insanity...Trans. Thomas Cooper. Columbia, S.C., 1831. ScU. 6696

Corinthian Hall Gallery, Boston.
Catalogue of the collection of oil paintings at the Corinthian Hall Gallery, Boston. Boston, 1841. 16 p. MB; MWA. 6697

[Corp, Harriet]
Antidote to the miseries of human life in the history of the widow Placid and her daughter Rachel. 5th Amer. ed. Philadelphia, W. S. Young, 1831. 126 p. ICBB; MB; OCU. 6698

Coster, Jacques, 1795-1868.
The practice of medicine, according to the principles of the physiological doctrine. By J. Coster... Trans. from the French. Philadelphia, Carey & Lea, 1831. viii, 5-319 p. CtY; ICJ; MeB; RPM; ViU. 6699

Cottage dialogues, on the mode of baptism; by Adelphos, author of cottage dialogues. Part I and II, and other tracts. Part III. (New York, 1831). 24 p. NjPT. 6700

Cottage Scenes; Revised by the Committee of publication of the American Sunday School Union. Philadelphia, 1831. BrMus. 6701

Cottin, Sophie Ristaud.
Elizabeth; or, The exiles of Siberia; A tale, founded upon facts. From the French of Madame Cottin. New-York, C. Wells, 1831. [8], 184 p. KyDC; MChiA; MWA; RPAt. 6702

Cottom's Virginia and North Carolina. Almanack. for the year of our Lord 1832. ...Richmond, P. Cottom, 1831. 36 p. ViU. ViW. 6703

Coues, Samuel Elliott.
Outlines of a system of mechanical philosophy: Being a research into the laws of force. By Samuel Elliott Coues... Boston, Charles C. Little and James Brown, 1831. MoCgSV. 6704

A course of Calesthenics for young ladies, in schools and families. With some remarks on Physical Education, with sixty-two engraved illustrations. Hartford, H. & F. J. Huntington, Carter and Hendie; Boston, J. Leavitt; New York, T. T. Ash, Philadelphia, 1831. 87 p. Ct; CtHWatk; MH; MPiB; PU. 6705

Courtney, John.
Selection of hymns from various authors. Richmond, Pr. by T. W. White, for R. D. Sanzay, [1831] 384 p. ICBB; MWHi. 6706

Coval, James.
Questions on the historical books of the New Testament, designed for bible classes and sabbath schools. New York, J. Emory & B. Waugh, 1831. 148 p. MdBD; NNMHi; NSyU. 6707

Cowley, Mrs. Hannah (Parkhouse) 1743-1809.
...A bold stroke for a husband; a comedy, in five acts... As performed at the Theatre royal, Covent Garden and Park theatre, New-York...with remarks by Mrs. Inchbald. New York, E. B. Clayton, 1831. iv, (5)-72 p. CtY; DLC; IU; PU; TxU. 6708

Cowper, William, 1731-1800
Fragments in prose, gathered from the correspondence of William Cowper... Boston, James Loring [c 1831] 96 p. DLC; MB; MnMau; ViU. 6709

---- Johnny Gilpin's diverting journey to Ware. Embellished with thirteen neatly coloured engravings. New York, S. Solomon King, 1831. 31 p. NRMA. 6710

---- Poems, with a sketch of his life. New York, J. H. Turney, 1831. 3 vols. RPB. 6711

---- Poems by William Cowper, esq., of the Inner Temple, with a sketch of his life... New York, S. King, 1831. 3 vols. LNDil; MWH; NcD; RPB; TxU. 6712

---- The task, and other poems, by William Cowper, esq., of the Inner Temple. Baltimore, Geo. M'Dowell and son, 1831. 179 p. CtMW; MdHi; NGH; OCMtSM. 6713

---- ---- New York, Pr. by J. H. Turney, 1831. 228 p. CSmH; KyOW; MH; MWA; NFred; NNF; NcU; OClW. 6714

---- The Works of Cowper and Thomas, including many letters and poems never before published in this country. With a new and interesting memoir of the life of Thomas. Complete in 1 vol. Philadelphia, J. Grigg, 1831. 539 p. CtY; DLC; KyU; PWcT; NjP. 6715

Cox, Francis Augustus, 1783-1853.
Female scripture biography: including an essay on what Christianity has done for women. By Francis Augustus Cox, A.M. Boston, Lincoln & Edmands, 1831. 2 vols. GMM; NjR; OMC; RPAt; TxDaM. 6716

Cox, [Ross], 1793-1853.
Adventures on the Columbia River, including the Narrative of a Residence of Six Years on the Western Side of the Rocky Mountains, among various Tribes of Indians hitherto Unknown; together with a Journey across the

American Continent... London, Henry Colburn and Richard Bentley; New York, J. & J. Harper, & Brother, 1831. DLC; ICU; PPL; OU; WHi. 6717

Cox, Samuel Hanson.
Quakerism not Christianity, or reasons for renouncing the doctrine of Friends. Boston, 1831-1833. InCW. 6718

---- Salvation achieved only in the present life, requiring a resolute effort, and forfeited inexcusably by the neglecters of the gospel: a sermon, from Luke XIII. 24. By Samuel Hanson Cox. New York, Jonathan Leavitt, 1831. 40 p. CU; MBAt; NjPT; OO; PPPrHi. 6719

Coxe, Daniel W.
Report in general convention of the Friends of domestic industry... on the coasting trade and internal commerce of the U.S. and the inquiry how far the protection of American manufactures had tended to improve them. New York, 1831. 20 p. DLC; MH. 6720

Coxe, John Redman.
The American dispensatory, containing the natural, chemical, pharmaceutical and medical history of the different substances employed in medicine; together with the operations of pharmacy: illustrated and explained, according to the principles of modern chemistry... 9th ed. By John Redman Coxe... Philadelphia, H. C. Carey & I. Lea, 1831. 832 p. CSmH; MH; NN; PP; Wu. 6721

Crabb, George, 1778-1851.
...English synonyms, with copious illustrations and explanations, drawn from the best writers. A new ed. enl. By George Crabb ... New York, J. J. Harper, 1831. 535 p. AMob; CtY; DLC; LNP; PHi; ViAl. 6722

---- A family encyclopaedia; or, An explanation of words and things connected with all the arts and sciences... enl. and improved, to which is added questions adapted to the text, by the author of popular lessons. New York, C. S. Dunning, 1831. 412 p. GAuY; IU; LNH; PHi; WaPS. 6723

---- A history of English law; or an attempt to trace the rise, progress, and successive changes, of the common law; from the earliest period to the present time. By George Crabb... 1st Amer. ed.: with definitions and translations of law terms and phrases, additional references, dates of successive changes, explanation of abbreviations, &c. Burlington, C. Goodrich, 1831. 595 p. CU; IEG; NBu; TxU; WaU. 6724

[Craik, George Lillie] 1798-1866.
...Paris, and its historical scenes (anon.) Boston, Lilly & Hait and Carter & Hendee, 1831-1832. 2 v. (Vol. 2 has title: Paris, and its historical scenes: the revolution of 1830.) CtHT; MB; NN; PU; RP. 6725

[----] The Pursuit of Knowledge under Difficulties...1831. Boston, Lilly and Wait and Carter and Hendee, 1831. 403 p. CtHT; KyDC; MeB; NRU; OClW. 6726

Cramer's magazine almanack, on a new and improved plan for the year of our Lord 1832, being a bissextile, or leap year, and after the fourth of July, the 57th year of American independence. Calculated by Sanford Hill... Pittsburgh, Cramer and Spear [1831] 72 p. OClWHi. 6727

Cramer's Pittsburgh almanack, for the year of our Lord 1832: being bissextile or leap-year, and after the fourth of July, the 57th year of American independence. Calculated by Sanford C. Hill. Pittsburgh, Cramer & Spear [1831] 36 p. OFH. 6728

Cramp, John Mockett, 1796-1881.
A text-book of popery; comprising a brief history of the council of Trent, a translation of its doctrinal decrees and copious extracts from the catechism published by its authority; with notes and illustrations. By J. M. Cramp. New-York, Daniel Appleton, 1831. 451 p. DLC; GDecCT; NjP; PU; ViRU. 6729

Cressy, Benjamin Cothen, 1798-1834.
A discourse on ministerial qualifications delivered at Hanover, Indiana, June 29, 1831, by Rev. Benjamin Cressy; together with an address by Rev. John Mathews, on occasion of the inauguration of the latter as Professor of Didactic and Polemic Theology in the Indiana Theological Seminary. Madison [Ind.] Pr. by Arion & Lodge, 1831. 30 p. CtY; In; MBC; MH-AH; MiD. 6730

Crist, Jacob Bishop.
The fog of Universalism dissipated by the light of nature. 2d ed. Reading, Pr. by R. Johnston, 1831. 20 p. DLC; NN; PHi. 6731

Crockett, David, 1786-1836.
David Crockett's circular. To the citizens and voters of the Ninth Congressional District in the State of Tennessee. [Washington, 1831] 16 p. DLC; MWA; ScU. 6732

Croker, J. W. see Boswell, James.

Croly, George, 1780-1860.
The Beauties of the British poets. With a few introductory observations. By the Rev. George Croly. New York, C. Wells, 1831. 391 p. CtY; KyBC; NjP; RPB; TNP. 6733

---- Croly's select British poets. C. Wells, New York, 1831. 393 p. WPdcV. 6734

---- Life and times of his late Majesty, George the Fourth; with anecdotes of distinguished persons of the last fifty years. By Rev. George Croly, A. M. Harper's stereotype ed. New York, Pr. by J. & J. Harper, 1831. 411 p. IaHi; MHi; MWA; NjP; ScNC; TNP; ViU. 6735

Cromwell.
The ocean spectre. [New York? 1831] MB. 6736

Crosby, Enoch.
Whig against Tory see under title.

Cross, Jeremy L., 1783-1861.
Triumphant deaths; or brief notices of the happy death of six Sabbath school scholars. New Haven, Jeremy Cross, 1831. 103 p. DLC; MB; MWO. 6737

---- Vacations at home. New Haven, S. Babcock, 1831. 2 v. MPB; NjR. 6738

Crothers, Samuel, 1783-1856.
An address to the churches on the subject of slavery. Georgetown, O., Pr. by D. Ammen & co., 1831. 24 p. OClWHi; PPPrHi; WHi. 6739

Crowe, Eyre Evans, 1799-1868.
The history of France. By Eyre Evans Crowe. Philadelphia, Carey & Lea, 1831. 3 vols. ArCH; DLC; ICMe; RPB; ViU. 6740

Cumberland Almanac, for the year of our Lord 1832...Calculating the motions of the sun and the moon... Nashville, Tenn., Pr. by Hunt Tardiff & Co. at the Whig & Banner Office [1831] 36 p. MWA. 6741

Cumberland Association.
Proceedings. Declaration of Independence, May 20, 1775. Raleigh, North Carolina, 1831. 29 p. MB. 6742

Cumberland Presbyterian Church.
Constitution... Confession of faith, catechism, etc., ratified and adopted by the Synod of Cumberland, held at Suggs Creek, Tenn., April 5, 1814. Russellville, 1831. 141 p. NN. 6743

---- A new selection of devotional hymns, compiled from various authors, for the use of the Friends of Zion. Adopted and recommended by the general assembly of the Cumberland Presbyterian church. Fayetteville, T[enn.], E. & J. B. Hill, 1831. 504 p. T. 6744

Cummings, Jacob Abbott, 1773-1820.
The pronouncing spelling book, adapted to Walker's critical pronouncing dictionary. Rev. and improved from the 4th ed. Worcester, Dorr & Howland, 1831. 157 p. MConA; MH. 6745

Cummins, Rev.
A sermon on confession and forgiveness of sins; preached in the Roman Catholic Church, of Utica. By the Rev. Dr. Cummins, pastor of said church. [Quotation. Bibl. Utica p. 177] Utica, Pr. by E. A. Maynard, 1831. 30 p. M; MWH; NAuT; NUt; WHi. 6746

Cunningham, Allan, 1785-1842.
Gowdie Gibbie: cf. Pickens Club Book. New York, J. & J. Harper, 1831. 41 p. MB; OCX; OCl. 6747

---- ... The lives of the most eminent British painters and sculptors. By Allan Cunningham ... New York, J. & J. Harper, 1831. 3 vols. CtHT; DLC; MiU; OCl; WaS. 6748

Cunningham, Francis.
Abstract of Vater's tables of ecclesiastical history. Boston, 1831. 37 p. MBAt; MWA. 6749

---- Tables of Ecclesiastical History from the origin of Christianity to the present time. Translated from Vaters "Synchronistischen Tafeln." By Francis Cunningham. Boston, Gray & Bowen, 1831. 1-37 p. CtHC; ICP; MH; MH-AH; MeBat; MiOC; NbOM; NBP; NhPet; NjPT; PPPrHi. 6750

Cunningham, John Williams.
Morning thoughts, in prose and verse, on single verses in the successive chapters, in the Gospel of St. Matthew. By J. W. Cunningham, M.A. ...2d Amer., from 3rd London ed. Philadelphia, A. Finley, 1831. 99 p. NNUT. 6751

Curtis, George Ticknor, 1812-1894.
History of the origin, formation, and adoption of the Constitution of the U.S. with notices of its principal framers. By George Ticknor Curtis. New York, Harper and bros., 1831-63. 2 vols. MoSHi. 6752

Curwine, Jonathan, 1640-1718.
A letter on the affairs of New England, 1663-or 1664. [In collection of Maine Historical Society] Pr. by Day, Fraser & Co., 1831. DLC; OCI. 6753

Cushman, Ralph.
An appeal to the Christian public, against the allegations contained in a pamphlet written by J. L. Wilson, entitled "Four Propositions Sustained against the Claims of the American Home Missionary Society." By Ralph Cushman... Cincinnati, Robinson & Fairbank, 1831. 20 p. NAuT; NjR; OClWHi; PPPrHi; WHi. 6754

Cutbush, Edward, 1772-1843.
An address delivered before the Domestic Horiticultural Society, of the western part of the state of New York; at the semi-annual meeting, held at Canadaigue, on the 30th day of June, 1831. By Edward Cutbush... Geneva (N.Y.), Pr. by J. Bogert, 1831. 33 p. DLC; MH; NGH; NIC; NBuG. 6755

Cutler, Benjamin Clarke, 1798-1863.
Letter to the parish of Christ Church, Quincy, on his resigning the charge of said parish. Boston, Freeman Hunt, 1831. 8 p. MBD; RPB. 6756

Cuvier, Georges, Baron, 1769-1832.
The animal kingdom arranged in conformity with its organization; the crustacea, arachnides and insecta, by P. A. Latreille. Tr. from the French with notes. ...by H. M'Murtrie. New York, G. & C. & H. Carvill, 1831. 20 pl., 4 v. CoU; KyU; MiU; PPL; WaU. 6757

---- A discourse on the revolutions of the surface of the globe, and the changes thereby produced in the animal kingdom... Tr. from the French with illustrations and a glossary. Philadelphia, Carey & Lea, 1831. iv, 252 p. CU; GAuY; NhO; PU; RPAt. 6758

D

Daboll, Nathan, 1750-1818.
Daboll's schoolmaster's assistant, improved and enlarged. Being a plain practical system of arithmetick. Adapted to the United States. By Nathan Daboll. With the addition of the Farmers' and mechanicks' best method of book-keeping, designed as a companion to Daboll's arithmetick. By Samuel Green. Ithaca, N.Y., Mark & Andrus, 1831. 228 p. CtHT-W; MH; MWA; MSyHi; NRioHi; OClWHi. 6759

---- Daboll's schoolmaster's assistant, improved and enlarged being a plain practical system of arithmetic... with the addition of the farmers and mechanics best method of bookkeeping, designed as a companion to Daboll's arithmetic, by Samuel Green. New York, W. C. Barradaile, 1831. 240 p. NHem. 6760

---- ---- Utica, Hastings and Tracy, 1831. 240 p. IU; N; NUt; MHi; ODW. 6761

Daggett, Herman, 1766-1832.
The American Reader, consisting of familiar, instructive, and entertaining stories. Selected for the use of schools. by Herman Daggett, A.M. "Tis our design. Instruction with amusement to combine." Poughkeepsie, N.Y., Paraclete Potter, 1831. 238 p. NP; NPot. 6762

Daily food for Christians, being a promise, and another scriptural portion for every day in the year: together with a verse of a hymn. 1st Amer. ed. Boston, Perkins & Marvin, 1831. 192 p.

MB; MWA; MWal; NPlaK. 6763

---- ---- Brookfield, E. Merriam & Co., prs., 1831. 192 p. NNUT. 6764

Dallas, George Mifflin, 1792-1864.
Address delivered in the church at Princeton, the evening before the annual commencement of the college of New Jersey, Sept. 27, 1831. By George M. Dallas. Pub. at the request of the American whig and cliosophic societies. Princeton, D'Hart and Connolly, 1831. 26 p. CSmH; KyLoS; NjP; PHi; WM. 6765

Dalzel, Andreas, 1742-1806.
ΑΝΑΛΕΚΤΑ 'ΕΛΛΗΝΙΚΑ ΜΕΙΖΟΝΑ, sive collectanea graeca majora, ad usum academicae juventutis, by Andreas Dalzel... Boston, Hilliard, Gray, Little and Wilkins, 1831. 2 vols. CtMW; IaGG; ICU; MB; NjMD. 6766

ΑΝΑΛΕΚΤΑ 'ΕΛΛΗΝΙΚΑ ΜΕΙΖΟΝΑ, sive, Collectanea graeca majora, ad usum academicae juventutis accomodata; cum notis philologicis, quas partim collegit, partim scripsit Andreas Dalzel... Ed. 4. americana, ex auctoribus correcta prioribus emendatior cum notis aliquot interjectis. Bostoniae, Hilliard, Gray & Co., 1831. CtMW; IaGG; MB. 6767

---- Collectanea graeca majora, ad usum academicae juventutis accomodata cum notis philologicis, quas partim collegit, partim scripsit, Andreas Dalzel, A.M. ...Tomus 11. complectens excerpta ex variis poetis. edito quarta Americana, ex auctoribus correcta. Bostoniae, Hilliard, Gray, Little, Et Wilkins, 1831. 344, 296 p. ICU; InCW; MnDu; MoFloss. 6768

Damphoux, Edward, 1788-1860.
Christian's Companion to Prayer, the Sacraments, and the Holy Sacrifice of the mass, Baltimore, James Myers, 1831. MdW. 6769

[Dane, Nathan] 1752-1835.
[Letter of Nathan Dane concerning the Ordinance of 1787. Indianapolis? Indiana historical society, 1831] 7 p. DLC; PHi. 6770

Daniel's Wiscom [Poem]
In wade, Mrs. D. B. L. Mrs. Wade's letter. New York, James Van Valkenburg, 1831. 16 p. RPB. 6771

Danville and Pottsville railroad Company.
An Act to incorporate the Danville and Pottsville railroad company. Pottsville, Pr. by B. Bannan, 1831. 12 p. CtY; NN. 6772

---- Central railroad. Reports of the engineers of the Danville and Pottsville rail road company. With the report of a committee of the board thereon. October 15, 1831. Philadelphia, Clark & Raser, 1831. 27 p. DBRE; ICJ; ICU; MB; PBL. 6773

---- Plan and profile... Philadelphia, Kennedy & Lucas, 1831. 1 p. PHi; PPAmP. 6774

Darby, William, 1775-1854.
The United States reader, No. 3 or Juvenile instructor, No. 1. 2d ed. rev. Baltimore Plaskitt and Co., 1831. 216 p. CLCM; DLC; FStar; MiU. 6775

Dard, Mme. Charlotte (Picard)
Perils and Captivity; comprising the sufferings of the Picard family after the shipwreck of the Medusa, 1816. Boston, Hill, 1831. 332 p. NcWfC; OMC. 6776

Dartmouth College.
A catalogue of the officers and students of Dartmouth College. Oct. 1831-2. Concord, Pr. by Fisk & Chase, 1831. 23 p. KHi; MeHi; OC; PAMPH. 6777

---- Catalogus Senatus Academici Collegei Dartmuthensi in Republica New-Hantoniensi... Leuphane, Typis Thomae Mann, 1831. 68 p. NhD. 6778

---- Social Friends Library.
Catalogue of the books belonging to the Social Friends' Library at Dartmouth College, October, 1831. Hanover, N.H., T. Mann, 1831. 64 p. CSmH; CtY; NN. 6779

D'Arusmont, Mme. Frances (Wright), 1795-1852.
A few days in Athens; being the translation of a Greek manuscript discovered in Herculaneum. Part. I... Repub. from the original London ed. New York, Wright & Owen, 1831. 114 p. DLC; InNhW; MB; NN; WHi. 6780

Davenport, Bishop.
History of the United States, containing all the events necessary to be committed to memory; with the declaration of independence, constitution of the United States, and a valuable table of chronology, for the use of schools. By B. Davenport... Philadelphia, U. Hunt, 1831. 144 p. CtY; ICBB; MH; RPB; TxU-T. 6781

Davenport, Matthew.
Brief historical sketch of the town of Boylston; in the county of Worcester; from its first settlement to the present time... Lancaster, Pr. by Carter, Andrews, and company, 1831. 28 p. ICN; MBC; NBLiHi; OCHP; WHi. 6782

Davidson, William B.
A report of the debates in the Presbytery of Philadelphia, at special meeting held in Philadelphia, on the 30th of Nov., and continued on the 1st and 2d of Dec., 1830. Phil[adelphia], 1831. 80 p. DLC; MH; NN; PPAmP; PPL. 6783

Davies, J.
Short sketch of the scripturians creed, arranged in contrast; with a number of important passages referred to. 1st American ed. Boston, Matthew M. Teprell, 1831. 24 p. NjN. 6784

Davis, Daniel, 1762-1835.
Precedents of indictments. By Daniel Davis. Boston, Carter, Hendee & Babcock, 1831. 319 p. Ct; FTU; LNT-L; NcD; PPB. 6785

Davis, George.
Petition. New Orleans, 1831. MB. 6786

Davis, Gustavus F., 1797-1836.
An address, by Gustavus F. Davis, A. M. Hartford, Hudson & Skinner, 1831. 30 p. C. 6787

---- The Bible doctrine of temperance. A sermon, delivered in the Baptist meeting house, Hartford, on Wednesday evening, May 25, 1831. By Gustavus F. Davis, pastor of the Baptist Church. (quotation.) Pub. by request. Hartford, Pr. by Philemon Canfield, 1831. 20 p. CBB; ICN; MBC; MWA; NjPT. 6788

---- Christ the Prince of Peace. An Address delivered before the Hartford County Peace Society, at their Semi-Annual Meeting in the Baptist Meeting House in Hartford, on the evening of October 30, 1831. By Gustavus F. Davis, A.M. Pastor of the Baptist Church. Hartford, Hudson & Skinner, prs., 1831. 20 p. CBB; CtY; MBC; NHC-S; NjPT. 6789

---- ... familiar dialogue between Peter and Benjamin, on the subject of baptism. By Suhploda. (Gustavus F. Davis.) New Haven, Pr. by J. L. Cross, 1831. CtY; NjPT. 6790

---- A familiar dialogue between Peter and Benjamin, on the subject of close communion. Hartford, J. W. Dimock, 1831. 8 p. MBC; NjPT. 6791

---- A familiar dialogue between Peter and Benjamin on the subject of close communion. By Gustavus F. Davis. 3d ed. Hartford [1831] NjPT. 6792

---- ---- 4th ed. Hartford [1831] NjPT. 6793

---- ---- 5th ed. Utica, Bennett & Bright, 1831. 11 p. DLC. 6794

Davis, John, 1787-1854.
The Post-Captain: or, The Wooden walls well mann'd: comprising a view of naval society and manners. Also a selection of favorite sea songs. 5th Amer. from 10th London ed. Boston, 1831. 180 p. CSmH. 6795

---- Report of the Hon. John Davis, agent for the prosecution of the claim of Massachusetts upon the United States for militia services during the last war; to his excellency Levi Lincoln, governor..., and transmitted by him to the legislature..., May 30, 1831. Boston [Dutton & Wentworth, prs. to the state] 1831. 76 p. InHi; MB; MnU; NNC; ScU; WHi. 6796

Davis, Peter B., defendant.
Trial of Peter B. Davis, for the murder of Baltus Roll. Held before a special term of the Court of oyer and terminer and general jail delivery for Essex county, June 28, 1831. Chief-justice Ewing presiding. Newark, [N.J.], Pr. and pub. at the office of the New-Jersey Eagle, 1831. 28 p. CSmH; NjR. 6797

Davis, William A. (comp.)
Acts of Congress in relation to the District of Columbia, from July 16th, 1790 to March 4th, 1831, inclusive; and of the Legislatures of Virginia and Maryland, passed especially in regard to that District, or to persons or property within the same. With preliminary notes of the Proceedings of the Congress, under the Convention, as well as under the Present Constitution, in regard to the Permanent Seat of Government of the United States.... Washington, Pr. by W. A. Davis, 1831. 8 vol. DLC; ICLaw; MH-L; RPL; ViU. 6798

Day, Jeremiah, 1773-1867.
The Christian preacher's commission. A sermon delivered before the General association of Connecticut at Saybrook, June 22, 1831. By Jeremiah Day, D.D., president of Yale college. New Haven, Hezekiah Howe, 1831. 20 p. CtY; IaGG; MWA; OO; PPPrHi. 6799

No entry. 6800

---- An introduction to Algebra; being the first part of a course of mathematics, adapted to the method of instruction in the American colleges. 6th ed. New Haven (Conn.), Hezekiah Howe, 1831. 332 p. IaDaP; MH; MNU; MoK; NRHi; NRivHi. 6801

---- The mathematical principles of navigation and surveying, with the mensuration of heights and

and distances, being the fourth part of a course of mathematics, adapted to the method of instruction in the American colleges, by Jeremiah Day... 3d ed. New Haven, Hezekiah Howe, 1831. 119 p. CtY; IaU; MH; MPB; MWiW; NIC; NNE; OClW. 6802

---- A practical application of the principles of geometry to the mensuration of superficies and solids: being the third part of a course of mathematics adapted to the method of instruction in the American colleges. By Jeremiah Day... 3d ed., with additions and alterations. New Haven, H. Howe, 1831. 96 p. DLC; ICBB; MPB; MWiW; OCl. 6803

---- The principles of plane trigonometry, mensuration, navigation and surveying, adapted to the method instruction in the American colleges. 3d ed. New Haven, Hezekiah Howe, 1831. 3 parts. CtW; IEN; MoU; NRU; OCl. 6804

---- A treatise of plane trigonometry. To which is prefixed a summary view of the nature and use of Logarithms; Being the second part of a course of mathematics adapted to the method of instruction in the American Colleges. By Jeremiah Day...3d ed. with additions and alterations. New Haven, Hezekiah Howe, 1831. 155 p. CtY; ILM; MH; MdBJ; OUrC. 6805

Day, Thomas, Esq.

Fragment of an original letter on the Slavery of the Negroes, written in the year, 1776. By Thomas Day, Esq., ...Boston, Garrison & Knapp, 1831. 12 p. ICN; MB; MiD-B; OClWHi; ViHal. 6806

[Dean, Christopher C.]

Letters on the Chickasaw and Osage Missions. Boston, 1821. ...Revised by the Publishing Committee, Boston, T. R. Marvin, for the Massachusetts Sabbath School Union, 1831. 161 p. WHi. 6807

---- The naval chaplain, exhibiting a view of American efforts to benefit seamen, by the author of Conversations on the Sandwish Island and Bombay missions, etc. Boston, Pr. by T. R. Marvin for the Massachusetts Sabbath School Union, 1831. 136 p. CtY. 6808

Dean, Paul, 1789-1860.

A discourse delivered at the annual election, January 4, 1831. Before His Excellency Levi Lincoln, governor, His Honor Thomas L. Winthrop, lieutenant-governor, the Honorable Council, and the Legislature of Massachusetts. By Paul Dean. Boston, Dutton and Wentworth, prs. to the state, 1831. 38 p. CSmH; ICN; MBAt; OO; WHi. 6809

Deane, Samuel, 1784-1834.

History of Scituate, Massachusetts, from its first settlement to 1831. By Samuel Deane. Boston, J. Loring, 1831. (iv), 406 p. CtY; KHi; MHi; NcD; PHi. 6810

Dearborn, Henry Alexander Scammel, 1783-1851.

Account (An) of the proceedings, in relation to the experimental garden and the cemetery of Mount Auburn. Boston, 1831. 60-84 p. NYPL. 6811

Decalogne, John Mary.

The life of John Mary Decalogne, student in the University of Paris. Trans. from the French. Chambersburg, Pa., Pr. by Fritts & Oswald, for the pub. 1831. 101 p. LU; MdBS; MidSH; MoW; PRosC. 6812

Decatur, Mrs. Susan (Wheeler)
...Case of Susan Decatur, et al. To accompany bill H.R. No. 98... [Washington, 1831?] 28 p. DLC; OO; RPB. 6813

Defence of country banks; being a reply to a pamphlet entitled An examination of the banking system of Massachusetts, in reference to the renewal of the bank charters. Boston, Stimpson, and Clapp, 1831. DLC; ICN; MBAt; MHi; WHi. 6814

[Defoe, Daniel] 1661?-1731.
The life and most surprising adventures of Robinson Crusoe, of New York, mariner. Embellished with elegant engravings. New York, John Lomax, 1831. CtY; MB; NCH. 6815

---- ---- Philadelphia, 1831. 159 p. MWA. 6816

De Ford, Samuel T.
An Address, delivered before the Brutus Fire Society, in Newburyport, at their annual meeting, Jan. 6, 1831. By Samuel T. De Ford...Newburyport, Pr. by E. W. Allen & Co., 1831. 14 p. CtSoP; MNe; ND; RPB. 6817

Dehon, Theodore, bp.
Sermons on confirmation; and an address delivered after administering that holy and apostolic rite. By the late Right Rev. Theodore Dehon...2d ed. New-York, T. & J. Swords, 1831. 71 p. CBCDS; NNG; NjPT; OrPD; ScCMu. 6818

De Lancey, William Heathcote, 1797-1865.
A Charge addressed to the Graduates in Medicine of the University of Pennsylvania at the Public Commencement held in the College Hall, on Thursday, March 24th, 1831. By William H. De Lancey, D.D. Provost of the University of Pennsylvania. Pub. at the request of the Graduates. Philadelphia, Pr. by Joseph R. A. Skerrett, 1831. CSmH; MWA; NBuDD; PPPrHi; PU. 6819

Delaware.
Laws of the state of Delaware, passed at a session of the General Assembly, commenced and held at Dover, on Tuesday the fourth day of January, in the year of our Lord, one thousand eight hundred & thirty-one, and of the independence of the United States, the fifty-fifth. By authority. Dover, Pr. by H. W. Peterson, 1831. 95 p. ArSC; DLC; InSC; MiL; Nj; R; T. 6820

---- Constitution.
The amended constitution of the state of Delaware adopted in the convention of the people of of the said state, at Dover, Dec. 2, 1831. Wilmington [1831?] 24 p. MH-L; N; PHi; PU-L. 6821

---- Constitutional Convention, 1831.
Debates of the Delaware convention, for revising the constitution of the state, or adapting a new one; held at Dover, November, 1831. (Reported for the Delaware gazette and American watchman,) by William M. Gouge. Wilmington, Del., S. Harker, 1831. 264 (3) p. CtY; MH-L; MnU; PHi; PPL; PPM; TxU. 6822

---- ---- Journal of the convention of the people, of the state of Delaware, etc... which assembled at Dover in the year 1831, and of the independence of the United States the fifty-sixth. Wilmington, Del., Pr. by R. & J. B. Porter [1831?] 129 p. MH-L; N; OCLaw. 6823

---- General Assembly. House

of Representatives.
Journal of the House of Representatives of the State of Delaware, at a session commenced and held at Dover, on Tuesday the fourth day of January, 1831, and in the fifty-fifth year of the independence of the United States. Wilmington, Del., W. A. Mendenhall, 1831. 234 p. IaHi. 6824

Delaware and Raritan Canal Company.
First annual report of the board of directors to stockholders... May 10, 1831. Princeton, N.J., Pr. by D'Hart & Connolly, 1831. 29 p. DBRE; ICU; MiU-T; NN; NjP; NjR; OClWHi; PPL; WHi. 6825

Democratic Republican Party. District of Columbia.
Rebublican [sic] Meeting of the Citizens of Washington City friendly to the re-election of Andrew Jackson to the Presidency. [Washington, 1831] 24 p. NbU; WHi. 6826

---- Michigan Convention.
Democratic republican convention. On Monday, the 18th inst. the delegates chosen agreeably to the invitation contained in the Democratic Republican address of the 24th ultimo, met at the mansion house in the City of Detroit... J. B. Breboort, chairman. James Q. Adams, secretary. Detroit, April 18, 1831. [Detroit, 1831] Broadside. MiU. 6827

---- New York General Committee., of Young men.
Address and Resolutions, of the General Committee of Democratic Republican Young Men, of the City of New-York. Pub. by order of the committee. October 18, 1831. New York, Pr. by Snowden, 1831. 12 p. NbU. 6828

---- ---- General committee of young men. Rules of the General committee of Democratic Republican young men of the city and county of New York, friendly to regular nominations. Passed January 28, 1831. New York. 1831. 8 p. CtY; NbU. 6829

---- New York (state).
Republican Legislative Meeting. At a meeting of the Democratic Republican members of the Senate and Assembly of the State of New-York, held in the Assembly Chamber, on Monday Evening, February 21st, 1831, pursuant to notice. 8 p. MBC; NbU. 6830

The demon ship, or The pirates of the Mediterranean. Albany, J. G. Shaw, 1831. 126 p. IU; NN; NSmb. 6831

De Morgan Augustus, 1806-1871.
[Contributions to] Companion to the Almanac, 1831-1857. 1 v. various pagings. DN-Ob. 6832

---- On the general equation of curves of the second degree. Cambridge, n.p., 1831. 8 p. IU. 6833

Demosthenes. Philippicae (English)
The orations of Demosthene pronounced to excite the Athenians against Philipi king of Hacedon, and on occasions of public deliberation, trans. by Thomas Leland, complete in one volume. New York, Harper, 1831-32. 2 vols. NN; PP; PPL; PPWe; PU. 6834

Description of Landis painting of Christ preaching and healing diseases...from a portion of the 6th chap. of Luke. Harrisburg, Pr. by G. S. Peters, 1831. 21 p. P. 6835

Desilver's annual almanac. The United State's almanac, comprising calculations for the latitude & meridians of the Northern, Southern, and Western States; with a variety of public information and interesting Masonic matter, together with a correct list of the civil and military of the United States... Philadelphia, William Sharples, 1831. 53 p. MWA; MWborHi; MdHi. 6836

Desmond, Daniel J.
The annual address of the Philodemic society of Georgetown college, delivered at the annual commencement...July 28, 1831. Philadelphia, Kay, 1831. 16 p. NN; PHi; PPAmP; PPM. 6837

Detroit, Michigan. Charters, ordinances, etc.
By-laws and ordinances of the city of Detroit, to which is prefixed the revised charter of said city, approved, April 4, 1827. Detroit, Pr. by George L. Whitney, 1831. 88 p. MiD-B; Mi-Hi. 6838

De Vinne, Daniel.
The Christian church; a sermon. By Daniel De Vinne. Boston, 1831. 18 p. NjPT. 6839

Devotional sonnets on some of the most striking texts in the Gospels of St. Matthew and St. Mark. By a member of the church of England... 1st Amer. ed. New York, Protestant Episcopal Church, 1831. 172 p. IC; NN; NNG; NNS; NNUT; NjMD. 6840

The Devout Christian's Vade mecum, being a summary of select and necessary devotions. New-York, J. H. Turney, 1831. Plates. MH. 6841

Dew-drops... New York, American Tract Society [1831?] 128 p. CtY; DLC; MH; MiD-B; NN. 6842

Dew Drops. "My speech shall distill us dew." Deut. 222. New York, Henry Sleight; Boston, Pierce and Parker, 1831. CtY; WSheHi. 6843

Dewees, William Potts, 1768-1841.
A treatise on the diseases of females. By William P. Dewees. M.D. 3d ed., rev. and corr. Philadelphia, Carey & Lea, 1831. 590 p. CtY; ICU; KU; MdBM; RPM. 6844

Dewey, Orville.
The Unitarian's Answer. By Rev. Orville Dewey. 6th ed. Pr. for the American Association. Boston, Gray and Bowen, 1831. ICME; MBC; MMeT-Hi; MeBat; OClWHi. 6845

DeWitt, Thomas.
The Gospel harvest and the Christian's duty. A sermon preached in Boston, Oct. 6, 1830, at the twenty-first annual meeting of the American Board of Commissioners for foreign missions. Boston, Pr. by Crocker & Brewster, 1831. 24 p. MB; MiD-B; NCH; PPPrHi; RPB. 6846

Dialogue between a Merchant and Planter. Charleston, 1831-32. PHi. 6847

Dibdin, Thomas.
The ruffian boy; a melo-drama, in two acts. New-York, E. B. Clayton, etc., etc., 1831. 35 p. MH; MWA. 6848

Dick, Thomas, 1774-1857.
The Christian philosopher; or, The connection of science and philosophy with religion. Illustrated with engravings. By Thom. Dick, author of a variety of literary and scientific communications in Nicholson's Philosophical Journal, the annals of

philosophy, &c., &c. New-York, Solomon King, 1831. 350 p. ANA; IaDuU; MB; NboP; OO. 6849

---- The philosophy of a future state... New York, Harper & Bros., 1831. 276 p. RPAt; RPB. 6850

---- ---- New York, Schoyer, 1831. 276 p. CU; MdW; MiU; PWW; ViU. 6851

---- ---- New-York, Solomon King, 1831. 276 p. KSalW; MA; NWM; ODaB; TChU. 6852

---- ---- Philadelphia, L. Johnson, 1831. 304 p. CtMW; MB; NNN; ScCMU; VtBru. 6853

---- The Philosophy of Religion; or An Illustration of the Moral Laws of the Universe. by Thomas Dick. New York, R. Schoyer, 1831. 391 p. CtY; KyDC; MNt; NRoM; ViL. 6854

---- ---- New York, S. King, 1831. GEU-T. 6855

Dickerman, Nathan W., d. 1830.
Memoir of Nathan W. Dickerman, who died at Boston [Mass.] January 2, 1830, in the eighth year of his age. Boston [Mass.] Peirce & Parker, 1831. MBAt; MWA. 6856

---- ---- 2d ed. Boston [Mass.] Peirce & Parker, 1831. 140 p. MBAt; MWA. 6857

---- ---- 3d ed. Boston, Peirce & Parker, 1831. 140 p. MBAt; MWA. 6858

Dickinson, Baxter.
Prize letters to students. New York, H. C Sleight, 1831. 85 p. CtY; GDecCT; InCW; NjR; OMC. 6859

Dickinson, Jonathan, 1688-1747.
Familiar letters on a variety of seasonable and important subjects in religion... (By Jonathan Dickinson). With an introductory essay by the Rev. David Young, of Perth. Pittsburgh, MacLeon, 1831. 300 p. CtY; GDecCT; ICBB; KyLoP; PPi. 6860

Dickinson, Samuel Fowler, 1775-1838.
An address delivered at Northampton, before the Hampshire, Hampden and Franklin, agricultural society, October 27, 1831. By Samuel F. Dickinson. Pub. by request of the society. Amherst [Mass.] Pr. by J. S. & C. Adams, 1831. 40 p. CSmH; ICU; MBAt; NjPT; RPB. 6861

Dickinson College, Carlisle, Pa.
Charter with Supplements. Carlisle, Pa., 1831. PCarlD. 6862

A dictionary of select & popular quotations, which are in daily use: Taken from the Latin, French, Greek, Spanish & Italian languages... 6th Amer. ed., corr. with additions. Philadelphia, J. Grigg, 1831. 312 p. KyDC; LNH; NbOM; OMC; RP. 6863

Dillaway, Charles Knapp, 1804-1889.
Roman antiquities and ancient mythology for classical schools. By Charles K. Dillaway... Boston, Lincoln & Edmands; New York, Collins & Hannay; etc., etc. 1831. 161 p. CtHT; GDecCT; LNH; MH; RPB. 6864

Dimmick, Luther Fraseur.
The duty of progress in the Christian calling: a new year's sermon, delivered in the North church, Newburyport, January 2, 1831. By L. F. Dimmick. Newburyport, Mass., Charles Whipple, 1831. 22 p. CBPSR; ICN;

MBC; NjPT; TxH. 6865

---- A Memorial of the Year Eighteen Hundred Thirty-One: A Sermon, delivered in Newburyport, Dec. 31, 1831, on occasion of a Public Thanksgiving of several of the Churches... By L. F. Dimmick, Newburyport, Ephraim W. Allen & Co. [1831?] 20 p. CBPSR; MB; MHi. 6866

No entry. 6867

Dimond, William, fl. 1800-1830.
The bride of Abydos; a tragick play, in three acts; as performed at the Theatre Royal, Drury-Lane (Robinson's 2d ed.) Baltimore, J. Robinson, 1831. 58 p. CtY; DLC; MH; NCH; NIC. 6868

Directions to persons just commencing a religious life. Andover, Mark Newman, 1831. 23 p. CSmH; MB. 6869

---- 5th ed. New-Haven, A. H. Maltby, 1831. CtY. 6870

Disbrow, Levi.
Disbrow's expose of water boring. [New York, Pr. by Marsh & Harrison, 1831?] 8 p. CSmH. 6871

---- Practice versus theory. On the methods of supplying New York City with water. [New York, Marsh & Harrison, 1831] 8 p. DNLM; DSG. 6872

The disobedient boy; an interesting story. New Haven, S. Babcock, Sidney's press, 1831. 23 p. CtY; NN. 6873

[Dix, Dorothea Lynde, 1802-1887]

Conversations on common things, or guide to knowledge, with questions. For the use of schools and families. By a teacher. 3d ed., rev., corr. and stereotyped. Boston, Munroe & Francis, 1831. 288 p. IU; IaFay; MH; NNQ; OO. 6874

Doane, George Washington, 1799-1859.
The Church of the Living God, the Pillar and Ground of the Truth: A Sermon, preached, by appointment, before the Prayer Book and Homily Society of Portland, Maine; on Monday, June 6, 1831, by George Washington Doane, A. M. Rector of Trinity Church, Boston. Boston, Stimpson & Clapp, 1831. 32 p. CtSoP; DLC; InID; MWA; NjR; RPB. 6875

---- The missionary argument: sermon before the Board of directors of the Domestic and foreign missionary society. 2d ed. Philadelphia, n.p. [1831] MCET; MdBD; NGH; PPL. 6876

---- The Missionary Spirit: Introductory to the Course of Monthly Lectures established by The Bishop and the Clergy of Boston and the Vicinity,...delivered in Christ Church, Boston... Nov. 27, 1831. By George W. Doane... Boston, Stimpson & Clapp, 1831. 34 p. CtHT; InID; MWA; NjR; PPPrHi. 6877

---- The Sunday School Teacher: A Sermon, preached, by appointment, before the Board of Managers of the General Protestant Episcopal Sunday School Union, in St. Paul's Chapel, New York ... June 26, 1831. by George W. Doane... Boston, Stimpson & Clapp, 1831. 32 p. CtHT; InID; MBAU; MdBD; NBuDD. 6878

Documents relating to the Dominguez grant of land in Texas. New York, G. Robertson, 1831. 19 p. CtY; CU-B; Cu; NN; PPAmP. 6879

Doddridge, Philip.
A dissertation on Sir Isaac Newton's scheme for reducing the several histories contained in the evangelists to their proper order. New York, 1831. NN. NYPL. 6880

---- The family expositor or, A paraphrase and version of the New Testament: with critical notes, and a practical improvement to each section. By Philip Doddridge, D.D., with memoirs of the author, by Job Orton, and extracts from Dr. Kippis, with a portrait engraved for an original picture in Wymondley House, Herts, by permission of the trustees of the late William Coward, Esq. New York, Jonathan Leavitt; Boston, Crocker & Brewster, 1831. 971 p. CtY; MdBD; NRom; ViU. 6881

---- The rise and progress of religion in the soul; illustrated in a course of serious and practical addresses suited to persons of every character and circumstances; with a devout meditation, or prayer, subjoined to each chapter; with an address to the master of a family... Andover, Flagg, 1831. 324 p. CL; ICP; MH-AH; OKU; PU. 6882

---- ---- Baltimore, 1831. BrMus. 6883

---- ---- Boston, Kimball & Johnson, 1831. 263 p. DLC; MB; MeLewB; OO. 6884

---- ---- New York, J. H. Turney, 1831. 252 p. ILM. 6885

---- ---- Last London ed. New York, Porter, 1831. 326 p. IU; LNB; MCET; NR. 6886

Dodsley, Robert, 1703-1764 (Supposed author.)
The economy of human life; with a biographical sketch of the author. Concord, Hoag & Atwood, 1831. 96 p. IaU; MWA; NhD. 6887

Donaldson, Peter.
Life of Sir William Wallace. The Governor General of Scotland, and the hero of the Scottish Chiefs, Containing his parentage, adventures, heroic achievements, imprisonments and death; drawn from authentic materials of Scottish history. By Peter Donaldson, Chirurgeon of the Store-Mount-Lock. Schenectady, N.Y., Wilson & Wood, 1831. IaIndianS; Nh-Hi. 6888

Done, Joshua, Jr.
The tuner's companion: being a treatise on the construction of piano-fortes, with rules for regulating and tuning them; prefaced with a notice of their origin & advice in the selection of them... 1st Amer., from 2d London ed. New York, Firth & Hall, 1831. 24 p. PPL; VtU; WHi. 6889

Donner, George.
The elegant horse, young (woodcut of horse with groom) Arabian Leopard, will stand the ensuing... George Donner, March 26, 1831. Springfield, Pr. by S. C. Meredith [1831] Broadside. IHi. 6890

Doodey, Joseph.
A Speech delivered in the House of Representatives, of the State of New-Hampshire, on the Discussion of the Bill respecting Ministerial Taxation. Dec. 1817. By Joseph Doodey, Esq. of New Durham, Pr. for the Publisher,

1831. 7 p. 6891

Dorr, Benjamin, 1796-1869.
The privileges and duties of an American Citizen. A sermon, preached in Trinity Church, Utica, on Thursday, December 8, 1831; The day of the annual Thanksgiving in the State of New York. By Benjamin Dorr, A.M. Rector of said church. Pub. by request. Utica, Pr. by E. A. Maynord, 1831. 22 p. InID; MBAt; NUtHi; NjR; RPB. 6892

Dorsey, John Larkin.
Address of John L. Dorsey to the Voters of the First Congressional District of Maryland. n.p., 1831. 72 p. MWA; PPAmP; PPGi. 6893

Dorsey, John Syng.
Elements of Surgery: for the use of students; with Plates, by John Syng Dorsey, M.D. Philadelphia, Edward Parker, Kimber & Conrad, 1831. 2 vols. NBatHi. 6894

Dort, Synod of, 1618-1619.
The articles of the Synod of Dort, and its rejection of errors: with the history of events which made way for that synod, as published by the authority of the States-General: and the documents confirming its decisions. Trans. from the Latin, with notes, remarks, and references. By Thomas Scott, rector of Aston Sandford, Bucks. Utica, William Williams; New York, Collins & Hannay, J. & N. White and H. C. Sleight; Philadelphia, Tower, J. & D. M. Hogan and John Griggs; Baltimore, F. Lucas, Jr.; Boston, Crocker & Brewster, and Richards, Lord & Holbrook; Andover, Flagg & Gould; Albany, B. D. Packard & Co., Little & Cummings and Oliver Steele; Hartford, D. E. Robins & Co.; New Haven, A. H. Maltby; Rochester, Hoyt, Porter & Co.; Auburn, H. Ivinson & Co., 1831. 304 p. DLC; InU; OMC; PPP; TxU. 6895

Douglas, James.
Errors regarding religion; and thoughts on prayer at the present. By James Douglas. New York, Jonathan Leavitt; Boston, Crocker & Brewster, 1831. 322 p. CU; DLC; ICP; MWA; PPM. 6896

---- The truths of religion. By James Douglas. Boston, Perkins & Marvin; New York, Jonathan Leavitt, 1831. 247 p. CtY; GMM; ICP; PW; RPB. 6897

Douglass, C.
An address...before the mechanics and other working men's association of New London, Conn. ...New London, n.p., 1831. 20 p. NjR. 6898

Dover, N.H. Niagara engine company, no. 2.
Constitution of the Dover fire engine company, no. 2. Organized Jan. 16, 1828. Dover [N.H.] Pr. by Ela and Wadleigh for Enquirer press, 1831. 9 p. CSmH; Nh. 6899

Dow, Daniel, 1772-1849.
A discourse, delivered in Chepachet, R.I., December 5, 1830, before the Gloucester temperance association...by Daniel Dow... Providence [R.I.] Pr. by H. H. Brown, 1831. 24 p. CSmH; MH; RPB. 6900

Dow, Lorenzo.
Chain of reason; consisting of 5 links, 2 hooks, 1 swivel: flattery--atheism--deism--universalism--predestination-perverseness --because--despair! By Lorenzo Dow... Erie, Pa., Rufus Clough, 1831. 118 p. CSmH; N. 6901

Drake, Benjamin, Esq., 1794-1841.
An address, delivered on the sixth anniversary of the Erodelphian Society of Miami University; September 27, 1831. By Benjamin Drake, Esq. Pub. by the Society. Cincinnati, Pr. at the office of the Cincinnati Chronicle, 1831. 15 p. DLC; ICP; MH; OClWHi; PPPrHi. 6902

Drake, Daniel, 1785-1852.
An oration on the causes, evils and preventives of intemperance, delivered and published by request, in the town of Columbus, Ohio, February 12th, 1831. Columbus, Olmsted & Bailhache, 1831. 21 p. CSmH; DLC; KyDC; MBAt; ScCC. 6903

---- An Oration on the Intemperance of Cities: including Remarks on Gambling, Idleness...Delivered in Philadelphia, January 24th, 1831. By Daniel Drake... Philadelphia, Griggs & Dickinson, prs., 1831. 30 p. DSG; MWA. 6904

Drayton, William, 1776-1846.
An oration delivered in the First Presbyterian church, Charleston, on Monday, July 4, 1831. By the Hon. William Drayton. To which is annexed, an account of the celebration of the 55th anniversary of American independence, by the Union and state rights party. Charleston, S.C., W. S. Blain and J. S. Burges, 1831. 104 p. A-Ar; DLC; ICU; ScC; WHi. 6905

Drew, Samuel, 1765-1833.
An original essay on the immateriality and immortality of the human soul...(founded solely on physical and rational principle) by Samuel Drew, A. M. Philadelphia, Leary & Getz, 1831. 288 p. MPiB; MnSM; OSW; PPL; PPLT. 6906

---- Remarks on the first part of a book, entitled "The age of reason," addressed to Thomas Paine, its author. By S. Drew ... 2d ed., rev. and considerably enl. New-York, S. King, 1831. 119 p. DLC; Mi; MOSHi; NjMD; PPL. 6907

Drew, William Allen, 1798-1879.
Original sermons on various subjects by living Universalist ministers. Vol. I. Pub. in monthly numbers during the year 1831 under the title of the Christian Preacher. By William A. Drew, writer. Augusta, Pr. by Sheldon & Dickman, for Gardiner, 1831. 206 p. MMeTHi. 6908

Dring, Thomas, 1758-1825.
Recollections of the Jersey prison-ship: taken, and prepared for publication, from the original manuscript of the late Captain Thomas Dring...one of the prisoners. By Albert G. Greene... New York, Davis, 1831. 167 p. DN; MH; NCH; NjP; OFH. 6909

Dryden, John, 1631-1700.
Poetical works; ed... by W. D. Christie. L. Macmillan, 1831. 662 p. OClW. 6910

Drysdale, Isabel.
Evening recreations. A series of dialogues on the history & geography of the Bible. Philadelphia, American Sunday School Union, 1831. 4 vols. ICBB; InCW. TxH. 6911

Ducachet, Henry William, 1796-1865.
A brief examen of a note appended to a letter on the Office of Sponsers in Baptism, by Henry W. Ducachet...By a Catholic [pseud.]. Norfolk, T. G. Broughton, 1831. 29 p. MdBS; NcH. 6912

---- The office of sponsors in baptism explained and vindicated in a letter to the congregation of Christ Church, Norfolk, Va.... Norfolk, Pr. by Shields and Ashburn, 1831. 14 p. DLC; MdBD; NjPT; RPB; Vi. 6913

Dukes, Joseph, 1811-1861.
The history of Joseph and his Brethren, in the Choctaw language. Revised by John Pitchlyn. Utica, 1831. 48 p. MBAt; MHi; NN. 6914

[Duncan, Mrs. Mary (Grey) Lundie]
Memoirs of the life and character of the Rev. Matthias Bruen, late pastor of the Presbyterian church in Bleecker-street, New-York. New-York, J. P. Haven and C. G. and H. Carvil; Boston, Pierce and Parker [etc, etc.] 1831. 358 p. CtY; DLC; MWA; NNUT; RNR. 6915

Dunlap, William, 1766-1839.
Address to the students of the National Academy of Design, at the delivery of the premiums, Monday the 18th of April 1831, by Wm. Dunlap... New York, Pr. by Clayton & Van Norden, 1831. 20 p. CtY; DLC; PHi; ScCC; ViU. 6916

Dunn, R. I.
A military pocket manual for militia officers, condensed, and agreeable to the system laid down for the United States army: with a short treatise on the cavalry and infantry swords. Also, by-laws for volunteer companies, &c. ... Cincinnati, J. Medary, 1831. 104 p. OClWHi; ViU. 6917

[Dunning, William M.] comp.
Domestic happiness portrayed; or, A repository for those who are, and those who are not married. By the most classic authors, ancient and modern... Including two prize essays, together with several articles written expressly for this work. New York, C. Spalding, 1831. 428 p. CtMW; IaKeos; MNe; NBuCC; RPB. 6918

Du Ponceau, Peter Stephen, 1760-1844.
Address delivered before the Law Academy of Philadelphia, on the opening of the session 1831-2, by Peter S. Du Ponceau, LL.D. provost of the Academy. Philadelphia, Law Academy, 1831. 20 p. DLC; MH; NN; PPAmP; PPL; P. 6919

---- An historical review of... the silk culture in Europe and America. See under title.

Durgin, Clement.
An oration, delivered before the Franklin debating society, at their anniversary, January 17, 1831, being the birthday of Franklin... Boston, J. H. Eastburn, 1831. 23 p. CtY; DLC; MHi; NN; PPL. 6920

[Dwight, Theodore] 1796-1866.
The northern traveller, and northern tour; with the routes to the Springs, Niagara and Quebec and the coal mines of Pennsylvania...new ed. Embellished with numerous engr. New York, Pr. by J. & J. Harper, 1831. 444 p. CSt; NcU; OClWHi; PHi; RPAt. 6921

Dwight, Timothy, 1752-1817.
Duration of Future Punishment Considered. Reading, S. C. Loveland [1831] 12 p. MMeT. 6922

---- Sermons of Timothy Dwight, D.D., late president of Yale college. New Haven, Hezekiah How and Durrie and Peck, 1831. 552 p. GAU; GAuP; TxAuPT. 6923

E

Eames, Theodore.
An address delivered at the opening of Eames and Putnam's English and classical hall, Brooklyn, Long Island, March 24th, 1831. By Theodore Eames... New York, Pr. by Sleight & Robinson, 1831. 32 p. CSmH; CtY; MH; MiD-B; NN. 6924

Eastman, Francis Smith, 1803-1846 or 7.
History of the State of New York from the first discovery of the country to the present time with a geographical account of the country, and a view of its original inhabitants, by F. S. Eastman. A new ed. New York, A. R. White, 1831. 455 p. CtY; IU; KyDC; MnU; Nh; WM. 6925

Eaton, John Henry, 1790-1856.
Candid appeal to the American public; in reply to Messrs. Ingham, Branch and Berrien, on the dissolution of the cabinet. Albany, 1831. CtY; NNC. 6926

---- ---- Washington, Pr. at the Globe Office, 1831. 55 p. DLC; IaU; MBAt; RPB; WHi. 6927

---- Leben des generals-majors Andreas Jackson, enthaltend eine geschichte des kriegs im Suden, vom anfange des feldzugs gegen die Creeks, bis zur beendigung der feindseligkeiton von Neu-Orleans. Zuzatze: anthaltend eine kurze geschichte des krieges gegen die Seminolen und uebergabe und regierung von Florida. Von Johann Heinrich Eaton... Uebers, von G. F. J. Jager... Reading [Pa.] Gedruckt bey J. Ritter und comp., 1831. 419 p. DLC; FU; MiU; NcD; PHi. 6928

---- Memoirs of Andrew Jackson, late major general and commander in chief of the southern division of the army of the United States... By Jerome Van Crowninshield Smith. Philadelphia, 1831. 334 p. NjP. 6929

Eberle, John, 1787-1838.
A treatise on the practice of medicine. By John Eberle, M.D., professor of Materia Medica and Botany in the Ohio Medical College, 2d ed., rev. and enl. Philadelphia, John Grigg, 1831. 2 vols. CU; ICJ; NjP; RPM. 6930

[Eddy, Zechdriah] 1780-1860.
Review of the Berkley Case. (By Zechariah Eddy.) Plymouth (Mass.), 1831. 28 p. MB; NN. 6931

The Edinburgh encyclopaedia, conducted by David Brewster... with the assistance of gentelemen eminent in science and literature. The 1st Amer. ed., cor. and imp. by the addition of numerous articles relative to the institutions of the American continent, its geography, biography, civil and national history, and to various discoveries in science and the arts... Philadelphia, Parker, 1831-1832. CtMW. 6932

[Edmands, Benjamin Franklin]
Boston school atlas. Boston, Lincoln & Edmands, 1831. CtY; MH. 6933

Edsall, John, b. 1788.
Incidents in the life of John Edsall... Catskill (N.Y.), Pub. for the author, 1831. 156 p. CtY; MiU; NcD; TxU; ViU. 6934

Edson, Theodore.
A sermon, preached in St. Anne's Church, Lowell, July 10th, 1831, the Sunday morning after the interment of Paul Moody, Esq. By Theodore Edson... Lowell, Mass, Thomas Billings,

1831. 7 p. MBNEH; MiD-B. 6935

Edson, William J.
The musical monitor; A collection of Church musick of the most approved character....to which are prefixed, the elements of musical science enlarged and carefully corrected. Ithaca, N.Y., Makc and Andrus; Pittsburgh, Pa., Loomis & Co., 1831. 262 p. IaKeos; NiDHi. 6936

Edward and Julia; or, Visits to the village... New Haven, S. Babcock, Sidney's press, 1831. 22 p. CtY. 6937

Edwards, Charles, 1797-1868.
The Juryman's Guide throughout the state of New York, and containing general matter for the Lawyer and Law Officer. By Charles Edwards (3 lines quot.) New York, D. Halstead, 1831. CU; In-SC; NIC-L; ViU. 6938

Edwards, Cyrus, 1793-1877.
An address delivered at the state house, in Vandalia, on the subject of forming a state colonization society, auxiliary to the American colonization society... Jacksonville, 1831. 22 p. CtY; IHi; NN; PHi. 6939

Edwards, Jonathan, 1703-1758.
A Narrative of the late Work of Work [sic] At the Near Northampton in New-England. Extracted from M. Ledward's Letter to Dr. Colman. By John Wesley, M.A. Late Fellow of Lincoln College, Oxon. ...Another ed., rev. from the ed. of 1738. Boston, 1831. MB. 6940

---- ... narrative of the surprising work of God in the conversion of many hundred souls in Northampton and the neighboring towns and villages...By Jonathan Edwards. Boston, James Loring, Sabbath school book-store, 1831. 140 p. ICBB; MBC; MeHi; NjPT; PPM. 6941

Eine Sammlung von geistreichen Sterk und Begrabniss-Liedern, fur Christen von allen Benennungen. Chambersburg, Pa., Heinrich Ruby, 1831. 162 p. PP; PPG; PSt; RPB. 6942

Eldridge, Lemuel B., 1777-1864.
The Torrent; or An account of a deluge occasioned by an unparalleled rise of the New-Haven River... Middlebury, E. D. Barber, 1831. 61 p. Ct; CtY; MHi; VtHi; WHi. 6943

Ellen, a tale by the author of Helen and Maria, etc. Boston, Carter, Hendee & Babcock, 1831. 64 p. DLC; ICBB; MiD-B. 6944

Ellen and Mary, or, The advantages of humility, 1st Amer. from the 2d London ed. Boston, Gray and Bowen, General agents for the Boston Sunday School Society. Sold also by Wait, Green & co., 1831. 36 p. DLC; MH. 6945

Ellis, Benjamin.
The medical formulary; being a collection of prescriptions... by Benjamin Ellis, M.D. ...3d ed. Philadelphia, Carey & Lea, 1831. 231 p. CtY; ICJ; MeB; OCGHM; ScNC. 6946

Ellis, William R.
A brief narrative of the religious experience of Dr. William R. Ellis, together with poems, composed on different subjects, by the same author... Rochester, S. H. Salisbury, 1831. 16 p. NRHi; RPB. 6947

Ely, Ezra Stiles, 1786-1861.
A Discourse...at the opening of the General Assembly of the Presbyterian Church in the U.S.

of America, May 21, 1829. Philadelphia, 1831. 16 p. CtY; MB; MBC; NjP; PPPrHi. 6948

Embury, Emma Catherine (Manley)
An address on female education, read at the anniversary of the Brooklyn Collegiate Institute for Young Ladies, by Fanning C. Tuker, president of the Board of Trustees. Written for the occasion by Emma C. Embury. New York, Pr. by Sleight & Robinson, 1831. 19 p. MB; NBLiHi; PPiW. 6949

Emerson, Benjamin Dudley.
The academical speaker: a selection of extracts in prose and verse, from ancient and modern authors. Adapted for exercises in elocution. New ed., rev. and enl. Boston, Richardson, Lord and Holbrook, 1831. 344 p. CtHWatk; MH; MHi; NCH; NN. 6950

---- The national spelling book and pronouncing tutor ... By B. D. Emerson, principal of the Adams grammar school, Boston. Boston, Richardson, Lord & Holbrook, 1831. 168 p. CSt; ICBB; MB; MH; NNC. 6951

Emerson, George Barrell.
A lecture on the education of females. Delivered before the American Institute of Instruction, Aug. 1831. Boston, Hilliard, Gray, Little and Wilkins, 1831. 27 p. MH; MHi; MWA. 6952

Emerson [Gouverneur], 1796-1874.
Medical Statistics, consisting of Estimates relating to the Population of Philadelphia, with its changes as influenced by the Deaths and Births, during ten years, viz. from 1821 to 1830, inclusive... Philadelphia, Jos. R. A. Skerrett, 1831. 32 p. CSt-L; ICJ; MBC; NNNAM; PP. 6953

Emerson, Joseph, 1779-1833.
The evangelical primer containing a minor doctrinal catechism and a minor historical catechism; to which is added the Westminster assembly's shorter catechism. With an appendix. Boston, Crocker & Brewster, etc., etc. 1831. 72 p. MBC; MH; MNowdHi; MWA; NNUT. 6954

---- Questions, adapted to Whelpley's Compend of history. 10th ed. Boston, Richardson & Holbrook, 1831. 69 p. MB. 6955

---- Questions and supplement to Goodrich's History of the United States. ...3d ed. stereotyped. Boston, Richardson, Lord and Holbrook, 1831. 204 p. MH; MeHi; Nh-Hi; OHi; RPB. 6956

---- Questions and supplement to Watts, on the improvement of the mind. By Joseph Emerson, jr. Boston, Loring, 1831. 68 p. CtSoP; MB; MWA; NjP; PPPrHi. 6957

Emma and her nurse; or The broken promise. New Haven, S. Babcock, Sidney's press, 1831. 23 p. CtY. 6958

Emmons, Richard, M.D., b. 1788.
Defence of Baltimore, and death of General Ross... [Poetry] 3d ed. Washington, William Emmons, 1831. 48 p. DLC; MdBP; TU; ViU; WHi. 6959

Emmons, William, b. 1792.
Authentic biography of Col. Richard M. Johnson, of Kentucky. Boston, Pub. for the proprietor, 1831. OC. 6960

The End and essence of Sabbath school teaching, and family religious instruction; in which the present defects in communicating religious knowledge to the young are investigated, and the lesson system of teaching the scriptures is fully developed. New York, Leavitt, 1831. 215 p. IEG; OO; WHi. 6961

Endless amusement, containing nearly four hundred interesting experiments in various branches of science,...to which are added, recreations with cards. Illustrated by engravings. ...New-York, W. C. Borradaile, 1831. 246 p. CtY; NNC. 6962

Erskine, Ralph, 1685-1752.
Gospel sonnets; or, Spiritual songs. In six parts...concerning creation and redemption,- law and gospel, - justification and sanctification, - faith and sense, - heaven and earth. By Rev. Ralph Erskine...to which is prefixed, an account of the author's life and writings... 1st Pittsburgh ed. Pittsburgh, L. Loomis & Co., 1831. 312 p. IEG; PPi; ViU. 6963

Erskine, Thomas.
Remarks on the internal evidence for the truth of revealed religion. By Thomas Erskine, Esq. Advocate. ...Philadelphia, E. Littell, 1831. 128 p. NcGu; ScCoB. 6964

The Essayist: a young man's magazine. By Geo. W. Light... Vol. 1. New series. Boston, Lyceum press, Geo. W. Light & co., 1831-33. IU; NjR. 6965

Essays on school keeping: comprising observations on the qualifications of teachers, on school government, and on the most approved methods of instruction in the various branches of a useful education. By an experienced teacher. Philadelphia, John Grigg, 1831. 200 p. ICBB; KyHi; NjR; PU; RPB. 6966

Essays on truth, knowledge, evidence, etc. Philadelphia, 1831. MWA; NWM. 6967

Essex Agricultural Society.
Reports of committees, and premiums awarded in 1830; and a list of premiums offered in 1831; with address of James H. Duncan, Esq. and remarks and hints to farmers, &c. Pamphlet No. X, 1830. Pub. by order of the society, March, 1831. Salem, Pr. by W. & S. B. Ives, Observer Office, 1831. 88 p. DLC; MHi; MNe; MToP. 6968

Essex County, Massachusetts. Bar Association.
Rules as adopted September, 1831. Salem, 1831. 17 p. DLC; MH-L. 6969

Estrange, Roger L.
Seneca's Morals. By way of abstract. To which is added, a discourse, under the title of an after-thought. By Sir Roger L'Estrange, Knt. 6th Amer. ed. Philadelphia, Henry Adams, J. Howe, 1831. 359 p. MNoanHi. 6970

Evangelical Association of North America.
Glaubenslehre und Kirchenzucht-Ordnung der Evangelischen Gemeinschaft, nebst dem Zweck ihrer Vereinigung mit Gott und untereinander. Dritte und verbesserte auflage. Neu-Berlin (Pa.), Gedruckt bey George Miller, fur obengesate Evangelische Gemein schaft, 1831. 135 p. MH-AH; OCl; PSt; ViHorEM. 6971

Evangelical Lutheran Church in the United States. General Synod.
Verhandlungen der Sechsten General-Synoda der Evangelisch Lutherischen Kirche in den Versigten Staaten. Versammelt su

Frisdbrichstadt Md. October 31, in die felgenden Tage 1831. Gettysburg, Pa., H. H. Neinstedt, Drucker, 1831. 40 p. PPLT. 6972

---- Synod of North Carolina.
Extract from the minutes of the Evangelical Lutheran Synod of North Carolina and adjacent states convened at Organ Church, Rowan County, N.C. on the First Sunday of May 1, 1831. Salem, Pr. by John C. Blun, 1831. 16 p. NcWsM. 6973

---- Synod of Virginia.
Minutes.... Saturday, October 15, 1831. 26 p. PPLT; ScCoT. 6974

---- Synod of West Pennsylvania.
Minutes of the session of the Evangelical Lutheran Synod, held October 2, 1830. Gettysburg, Pa., Pr. by the Press of the Theological Seminary, 1831. 18 p. PPLT. 6975

No entry. 6976

Evans [James], 1801-1846.
The Speller and Interpreter, in Indian and English, for the Use of Mission Schools, and such as may desire to obtain a knowledge of the Ojibway Tongue. ...New-York, D. Fanshaw, 1831. 195 p. MHi. 6977

Evans, John, 1767-1827.
Shakespeare's seven ages; or, The progress of human life; illus. by a series of ext. in prose and poetry, intr. by brief memoir of Shakespeare and his writings. By John Evans, LL.D. Embellished with 8 copper plate engravings. New York, C. P. Fessenden, 1831. 281 p. GDecCT; IaU; MdBP; NBuG. 6978

[Eveleth, Ephraim], 1801-1829.
History of the Sandwich Islands, with an account of the American mission established there in 1820. With a supplement embracing the history of the wonderful displays of God's power in these islands in 1837-1839. Rev. by the Committee of publication of the American Sunday-school Union: Philadelphia, American Sunday-school Union, [1831] 231 p. DLC; ICP; KGrb; OClWHi; PHC. 6979

[Everett, Alexander Hill] 1792-1847.
British opinions on the protecting system, being a reply to strictures on that system, which have appeared in several recent British publications... Repr. with a few alterations from an article in the North American review, for January, 1830. Boston, N. Hale [etc.] 1831. 85 p. CU. 6980

Everett, Edward, 1794-1865.
Address delivered before the American institute of the city of New York, at their fourth annual fair, October 14, 1831. ...New York, Van Norden and Mason, 1831. 50 p. CtY; ICU; NjR; PU; WHi. 6981

---- Address introductory to the Franklin lectures. Boston, 1831. PPL. 6982

---- A lecture on the Working Men's party... delivered October 6, (1830)...before the Charlestown Lyceum, etc. 2d ed. Boston, Gray and Bowen, 1831. NN. 6983

---- Speech in the house of representatives, on the 14th and 21st of February, 1831, on the execution of the laws and treaties in favor of the Indian tribes. [Washington, 1831] 28 p. CtY; ICN; OClWHi; PHi; WHi. 6984

Everett, L. S.
An exposure of the principles of the Free Inquirers'. By L. S. Everett. Boston, Benjamin B. Mussey, 1831. 44 p. CtHWatk; ICMe; MB; MMeT; WHi. 6985

Everett, Oliver.
An address delivered at Fitchburg on the Fifty-Fifth Anniversary of the Declaration of Independence of the United States of America. By Oliver Everett. Fitchburg, Mass., J. E. Whitcomb, 1831. 21 p. MFiHi; MHi; MWA; NCH. 6986

Everett, S.
Sermons, by the late Rev. Abiel Abbott, D.D. (With a memoir of his life, by S. Everett.) Boston, Wait, Green & Co., 1831. 297 p. MHa. 6987

The evidence of Christianity. By Alexander, Watson, Jenyns, Leslie, and Paley... Philadelphia, James Kay, Jun. & Co.; Pittsburgh, J. I. Kay & Co. [c 1831] 2 v. in 1. DLC; ICU; LNB; MH; NcD; OClW; PPAmP. 6988

Exercises for family and secret prayer...to which are annexed Hints on the common practical mistakes in family religion. 2d ed. enl. Boston, Munroe and Francis, 1831. 144 p. ICRL; WHi. 6989

F

Facts, important to be known by the manufacturers, mechanics, and all other classes of the community. Selected from a pamphlet, entitled "Remarks upon the Auction System as practised in New York." New York, Nov. 1831. 39 p. ICU; MB; MdBP; PHi; WHi. 6990

Fairchild, J[oy] H[amlet].
Objections to the Deity of Christ considered. A sermon, by J. H. Fairchild, Pastor of the Evangelical Congregational Church in South Boston. Pub. by request. Boston, Peirce and Parker, 1831. 36 p. CBPac; CtY; IEG; MBC; NjR. 6991

Faraday, Michael, 1791-1867.
Chemical manipulation, being instructions to students in chemistry, on the methods of performing experiments of demonstration or research, with accuracy and success. By Michael Faraday... 1st Amer. from the last London ed., edited by J. K. Mitchell... Philadelphia, Carey & Lea, 1831. 689 p. CtHT; IU; MnU; PPCP; ViU. 6992

[Farley, Frederick Augustus].
An explanation of the words: By nature children of wrath', found in Ephesians II. 3. Pr. for the American Unitarian Association. Boston, Gray & Bowen, 1831. 12 p. ICMe; IaHi; MH; MeB; OO; PPL. 6993

Farmer, John, 1789-1838.
The Constitution of New-Hampshire; approved by the people, and established by convention, September 5, 1792. To which are annexed questions, designed for the use of academies and district schools, in the State of New Hampshire. By John Farmer. Concord, 1831. 68 p. MHi; Nh-Hi. 6994

Farmer, John, 1798-1859.
Collections, topographical, etc. relating to New Hampshire. Concord, 1831. MH. 6995

---- The emigrant's guide; or, Pocket gazetteer of the surveyed part of Michigan. By John Farmer... 2d ed. Albany, Pr. by B. D. Packard & Co., 1831. 32 p. MiHi; MiPi; MiU-C; NjP. 6996

---- Map of the territories of Michigan and Wisconsin... Albany, N.Y., R. Clark & Co., 1831. ICN. 6997

Farmer, Miles, plaintiff.
Report of a trial: Miles Farmer, versus Dr. David Humphreys Storer, commenced in the Court of common pleas, April term, 1830, from which it was appealed to the Supreme judicial court, and by consent of parties, referred to referees, Dolph and George Washington Adams... Reported by the plaintiff. Boston, Pr. for the reporter, 1831. 44 p. CtY; DLC; MH-L; MHi; MoU. 6998

....The [old] farmers' almanack, calculated on a new important plan, for the year 1832... by Robert B. Thomas... Boston, Richardson, Lord & Holbrook [1831] (58) p. MPeHi; MWint; MeHi; NbU; NjR; RNR. 6999

The farmer's almanack, for the year of our Lord, 1832...By Zadock Thompson, A.M. No. 1. Burlington, E. & T. Mills [1831] 24 p. MWA. 7000

Farmer's Almanac. Hagerstown, Md., John Gruber, 1831. 28 p. IaHA. 7001

Farmer's Almanac for 1832. By James W. Palmer. Louisville, Ky., J. W. Palmer; J. A. Frazer and M. Kennedy, Lexington [1831] MWA; PPiU. 7002

---- By David Young. Philom ... New-York, Christian Brown, [1831] MWA; WHi. 7003

---- Calculations by John Ward. Philadelphia, Pa., M'Carty & Davis [1831] MWA. 7004

The (old) Farmers' Almanac, calculated on a new and improved plan for the year...1831. No. 60 calculated for the meridian of Portland and particularly intended for the state of Maine...By Robert B. Thomas. Portland, G. Hyde & Co., 1831. 36 p. MMhHi; MWA; MeHi. 7005

Farmers Almanac, for the middle states. Alphabetical chronology. [By Thomas Spafford] Utica, Hasting's and Tracy; New York, David Felt [1831] 37 p. CtY; MWA; N; NSyHi; PHi. 7006

Farmer's and Mechanic's Almanack for 1832. Calculations by Charles Frederick Egelmann. Baltimore, Md., Plaskett & Co. [1831] 18 l. MWA. 7007

Farmer's & Mechanic's Almanac for 1832. Calculations by Joshua Sharp. [Charles F. Egelmann] Philadelphia, Pa., George W. Mentz & Son [1831] CU; DLC; MWA; OMANS; P. 7008

The farmer's and mechanic's manual; or the present currency of the United States, concisely explained, by rules entirely original, and applied to practical purposes, in a manner not before published. Together with mensuration, and an appendix, containing rules that are seldom used, but sometimes necessary. By I. K. Torbert. Harrisburg, [Pa.] Pr. by F. Wyeth, 1831. 142 p. DLC. 7009

...The Farmer's, Mechanic's, and Gentleman's Almanack, for the year of our Lord, 1832, by Nathan Wild...Amherst, Mass., Pr. and sold by J. S. & C.

Adams; Chesterfield, N.H., sold by the author, and by many of the country traders [1831] 46 p. MH; MWA; WHi. 7010

The Farmer's receipt book; and Pocket farrier, being a choice selection of the most approved and valuable receipts, designed for the benefit of farmers, and heads of families generally. Concord, N.H., Fisk & Chase, 1831. 214 p. Nh-Hi; NjR. 7011

Farmer's reporter and United States agriculturist, ed. by H. L. Barnum. Cincinnati, 1831. O; OMC. 7012

Farr, Jonathan.
Gospel Temperance. A Sermon. Delivered in Gardner, Mass., the Sunday Morning after there had been a "protected meeting" in that town. By Jonathan Farr. Boston, Christian Register Office, 1831. 15 p. MBAU; MHi; MWA; Nh. 7013

---- ... On revivals. By Jonathan Farr. Pr. for the American Unitarian association. Boston, Gray and Bowen, 1831. 16 p. CBPSR; MBAt; MHi; MeLewB; RPE. 7014

---- ---- 2d ed. Boston, Gray & Bowen, 1831. 16 p. MBC; MH; MH-AH; OClWHi. 7015

---- A Pastoral letter to the Members of the First Congregational Society in Gardner, Mass. By Jonathan Farr, their Minister. Boston, Christian Register Office, 1831. 18 p. MH; MH-AH; MHi; MWA; NNUT. 7016

---- Plain letters on important subjects by Jonathan Farr. Boston, Leonard C. Bowles, 1831. 230 p. CtY; ICMe; MB; MH-AH; MWA. 7017

---- Religious Curiosity: or, The Great Concern. A Sermon, delivered in Gardner, Mass.; By Jonathan Farr. Boston, Christian Register Office, 1831. 14 p. MBAU; MHi; MWA; Nh. 7018

[Farrar, Mrs. Eliza Ware (Rotch)].
The story of the life of Lafayette, as told by a father to his children. Boston, Hilliard, Gray, Little, and Wilkins, 1831. 284 p. MAbD; MB; MH; Nh-Hi; O. 7019

Fay (Theodore Sedgwick), 1807-1898.
Views in New York and its environs from...drawings...by Dakin, architect: with historical, topographical and critical illustrations... New York, Peabody & Co., 1831. 41 p. DLC; MB; MBevHi; NjR; ScC. 7020

Fayette County, Illinois. Citizens.
Proceedings of a meeting... relative to the national road: held December 10, 1831. [Vandalia? 1831] 8 p. MWA. 7021

The Federalist.
The Federalist on the new Constitution, written in the year 1788, by Mr. Hamilton, Mr. Madison, and Mr. Jay: with an appendix containing the letters of Pacificus and Helvidius, on the proclamation of neutrality of 1793; also the original articles of confederation and the constitution of the United States, with the amendments made thereto. New ed., The numbers written by Mr. Madison corr. by himself. Hallowell, Glazier, Masters, & Co., 1831. 542 p. CtY; GEU; ICU; MdW; PU. 7022

Fellenberg institution at Bolton Farm near Bristol, Penna.
Circular. 1831. 2 p. PPAmP. 7023

Fellowship Society, Charleston, S.C.
(Certificate of membership of J. B. Robertson, Sept. 8, 1831.) Charleston [1831] MBAt. 7024

Felton, Cornelius Conway, 1807-1862.
Address Nov. 4, 1829 on anniversary of Concord Lyceum, Cambridge 1829, Lecture on Classical Learning Aug. 20, 1830 before American Institute of Instruction. Boston, 1831. OCHP. 7025

---- Lecture on Classical Learning delivered before the Convention of Teachers, etc. assembled to form the American Institute of Instruction. Aug. 20, 1830. B[oston] 1831. 34 p. MH; MHi. 7026

Female hospitable Society, Philadelphia.
Articles of association, act of incorporation & reports of the transactions of the... society... since its commencement. in 1808. Philadelphia, Bailey, 1831. 58 p. PPAmP; PPGi; PPL-R; PPL; ScU. 7027

Fenelon [Francois de Salignac de la Mothe] 1651-1715.
Selections from the writings of Fenelon. With a memoir of his life. By a lady. 3d ed., rev. and enl. Boston, Hilliard, Gray, Little, and Wilkins, 1831. 304 p. KyLoS; MBAt; MWA; OO; RPB. 7028

---- A treatise on the education of daughters. Tr. from the French of Fenelon, archbishop of Cambray. Boston, Perkins & Marvin, 1831. 182 p. ArCH; InCW; MH; OMC; TxSaO. 7029

Fennell, Samuel.
Elementary treatise on algebra designed to facilitate the acquirement of the first principles of science. Cambridge, Mass., Deighton, 1831. OO. 7030

Ferguson, John.
Letters addressed to the Rev. Moses Thatcher: together with the result of an ecclesiastical council, convened at North Wrentham, Dec. 14, 1830. By John Ferguson, pastor of the church in East Attleborough, Mass. Boston, Peirce & Parker, 1831. 32 p. CBPSR; IaCrM; MB; MH-AH; NNUT. 7031

Ferguson, Walter.
My early days. 3d ed. Boston, 1831. 151 p. MWA. 7032

[Ferrier, Susan]
Destiny; or the chief's daughter. By the author of "Marriage" and "The Inheritance." Philadelphia, Carey & Lea, 1831. 2 vols. MWalp; HCL; PPL; ScCMu; TNP. 7033

Fessenden, Thomas Green, 1771-1837.
Address delivered before the Charleston Temperance Society, January 31, 1831. By Thomas C. Fessenden...Charlestown, Pr. by William W. Wheildon, 1831. DLC; IaGG; MB; PPL; WHi. 7034

---- ... The new American gardner, containing practical directions on the culture of fruits and vegetables; including landscape and ornamental gardening, grapevine, silk, strawberries, &c. &c. By Thomas G. Fessenden. 5th ed. Boston, Carter, Hendee & Babcock, 1831. 306 p. MB; MWA; Mi; OCLloyd; OClW. 7035

Field, Barnum, 1796-1851.
The American School Geography, embracing a general view of mathematical, physical and civil geography adapted to the capacities of children. Boston, Pr. by Griffin & Co., for Wm. Hyde and Richardson, Lord &

Holbrook, 1831. 152 p. MB; MNBedf. 7036

Fielding, Henry, 1707-1754.
The history of Joseph Andrews, and his friend Mr. Abraham Adams. Written in imitation of the manner of Cervantes, author of Don Quixote... Philadelphia, 1831. CtY. 7037

---- The history of Tom Jones. Illus. by George Cruikshank. Philadelphia, Jacobs, 1831. 2 vols. TxBea. 7038

Fielding, Thomas, pseud. See Wade, John.

Fifty reasons, why the Roman Catholic Apostolic Religion ought to be preferred to all the sects, at this day in Christendom:... To which are added, three valuable papers, also Roman Catholic principles, in reference to God and the King. Boston, Wm. Smith, 1831. 108 p. MiDSH. 7039

Fine letters to Governor Hamilton. Charleston, 1831. MH. 7040

Finley, Anthony.
A new general atlas, comprising a complete set of maps, representing the grand divisions of the globe, together with the several empires, kingdoms and states in the world... Philadelphia, A. Finley, 1831. 3 p., 1, 60 maps. DLC; ICU; MdBP; NNC; PU. 7041

Finley, E. L.
An address delivered by request of the managers of the Humane Impartial Society, at their annual meeting, held on the 24th January 1831, in the First Presbyterian Church. Baltimore, Lucas and Deaver, 1831. 12 p. MBAt; MH; MdBE; PPL. 7042

---- An address delivered by request of the Managers of the Sunday School Union, for the State of Maryland, at their Annual Meeting, held on the 30th day of November 1830 in the First Presbyterian Church. Baltimore, Lucas and Deaver, 1831. 11 p. KyDC; MBAt; MWA; OCHP; PPL. 7043

---- Address delivered by request of the managers of the young men's preachers' aid Society, at their annual meeting, held on the 12th April, 1831... Baltimore, Pr. by Lucas & Deaver, ...1831. 11 p. MCET; MdHi; PPM. 7044

Finn, Henry J., 1785?-1840, ed.
American comic annual, Ed. by Henry J. Finn, and illustrated by D. C. Johnston. Boston, Richardson, Lord & Holbrook, 1831. 220 p. CtY; MBAt; MWA; PHi; RPB. 7045

---- Sayings and singings. Boston, 1831. 220 p. PU. 7046

---- Sayings & singings; a fragment of a farce. Boston, Richardson, 1831. 59 p. PU. 7047

Fire-side stories, or Recollections of my school-fellows. 2d Amer. ed. New York, William Burgess, 1831. 224 p. MH; NGH; NN; PU. 7048

Fisher, William Logan.
Pauperism and crime. By W. L. Fisher... Philadelphia, Pub. by the author, 1831. 119 p. ICJ; MMeT-Hi; MNBedf; PHi; WU. 7049

Fisk, Benjamin Franklin, d. 1832.
A grammar of the Greek language... 2d ed. Boston, Hilliard, Gray, Little, Wilkins, 1831. 263 p. ArCH; CtMW; NRU;

PPL-R; ScCC. 7050

---- Greek Exercises; containing the substance of the Greek Syntax, illustrated by passages from the best Greek authors, to be written out from the words given in their simplest form, by Benjamin Franklin Fisk. Adapted to the author's Greek Grammer. Boston, Hilliard, Gray, Little, and Wilkins, 1831. 171 p. CSt; NcU; ScCC; TxU-T; ViU. 7051

---- A Key to the exercises adapted to Fisk's Greek grammar. Boston, Hilliard, Gray, Little, and Wilkins, 1831. 82 p. CtY; ICU; MH; NcU; WBeloC. 7052

Fisk, Ezra, 1785-1833.
The inability of sinners considered. Being the first of a series of lectures now delivering ... in the sixth Presbyterian Church. Goshen, N.Y., 1831. 38 p. NcU. 7053

---- ---- Philadelphia, Russell and Martien, 1831. 10-38 p. NN; PPPrHi. 7054

Fisk, Wilbur, 1792-1839.
Discourse on Predestination and Election, preached on an Special Occasion at Greenwich, Mass., Springfield, Pr. by A. G. Tannatt, 1831. CBPSR; MBNMHi; MnHi; OClWHi; PPPrHi. 7055

---- ---- 2d ed. Brookfield, Pr. by E. & G. Merriam, 1831. 32 p. CtSoP; MBC; MiD-B; NNUT. 7056

---- ---- 3d ed. Springfield, Pr. by Merriam, Little & Co., 1831. (3), 4-32 p. CSt; CtSoP; ICU; MWA; MWo; MeLewB; MiD-B; NjR. 7057

Fiske, Oliver.
An address delivered before the Worcester agricultural society, October 20, 1831: being their thirteenth anniversary cattle show and exhibition of manufactures. By Oliver Fiske, M.D. Worcester [Mass.] From M. W. Gront's power press, 1831. 16 p. MB; MPB; MWA; MdBJ; NN. 7058

Fitzball, Edward, 1792-1873.
The innkeeper of Abbeville, or The ostler and the robber; a drama, in two acts. By Edward Fitz-Ball, (pseud.) New-York, R. Hobbs, 1831. 33 p. DLC; MB; MH; NBuG; PU. 7059

Flavel, John, 1630?-1691.
The fountain of life; or, A display of Christ in his essential and mediatorial glory. By Rev. John Flavel... New York, The American Tract Society [183-?] DLC; FMU; KMK; OCl; ViU. 7060

---- The touchstone of sincerity, or Trial of true and false religion. New York, American Tract Society [1831?] CtY; DLC; MH; PPPrHi; ViU. 7061

Fleetwood, John.
The life of Our Lord and Saviour Jesus Christ; containing a full, accurate, and Universal History from His taking upon himself our nature to his Crucifixion, Resurrection and Ascension: Together with the Lives, transactions, and sufferings of his Holy Evangelists, Apostles, Disciples, and other primitive Martyrs. to which is added The History of the Jews. By John Fleetwood, D.D. New Haven, Nathan Whiting, 1831. 608 p. ANA; CtSoP; IEG; NIC; OClW. 7062

Fletcher, James, 1811-1832.
...The history of Poland; from the earliest period to the present time. By James Fletcher... with

a narrative of the recent events obtained from a Polish patriot nobleman. New York, J. & J. Harper, 1831. 339 p. CtHT; LNL; RPB; TxU; WHi. 7063

Flint, (James), 1779-1855.
Card of invitation to the Ladies' Fair. By Rev. Dr. Flint. Salem, Dec. 1831. Broadside. MH. 7064

Flint, Timothy, 1780-1840.
History and geography of the Mississippi Valley. 2d ed. Cincinnati, E. H. Flint and L. R. Lincoln, c1831. 2 vol. in 1. InVi; KyBgW; MiD. 7065

Florian, Jean Pierre Claris de, 1755-1794.
William Tell; or, Switzerland delivered. By the chevalier de Florian; a posthumus work. To which is prefixed, the life of the author, by Jauffret. Trans. from the French by William B. Hewetson. Concord, N.H., L. Roby, 1831. 143 p. CtMW; IEN; MLanc. 7066

Florida.
Acts of the legislative council of the territory of Florida passed at their ninth session commencing January third, and ending February thirteenth, 1831. With also, the resolutions of a public or general character, adopted by the Legislative council at said session. Pub. by authority. Tallahassee, Gibson & Smith, Territorial printers, 1831. 123 p. DLC; ICLaw; MdBB; Nj; OCLaw; RPL. 7067

---- Opinion of the Superior Court of East Florida (concerning a Spanish grant, Nov. 1830). (Report 6th Pet. 691) Charleston, 1831. 68 p. FJ; MBS; MH; MdBJ. 7068

The flowers of anecdote, wit, humor, gayety and genius. With etchings. Boston, Frederic S. Hill, 1831. (2), 285 p. MBBC; MH; MWA; MWH; NcU. 7069

Follen, Charles Theodore Christian, 1796-1840.
Deutsches lesebuch fur anfanger: 2. aufl. (By C. T. C. Follen.) Boston, Hilliard, Gray, Little, and Wilkins, 1831. 256 p. CtY; DLC; ICU; MB; NjP. 7070

---- German reader for beginners. Boston, Hilliard, Gray, Little, and Wilkins, 1831. 256 p. CtY; KWiU; MH; PMA; ViU. 7071

---- Inaugural discourse, delivered before the university in Cambridge, Massachusetts, September 3, 1831... Cambridge, 1831. 27 p. CtY; MB. 7072

---- A Practical Grammar of the German Language, by Dr. Charles Follen. 2d ed. Boston, Hilliard, Gray, Little & Wilkins, 1831. 278 p. CtMW; ICP; MB; PPAmP; ViRut. 7073

Follen, Mrs. Eliza Lee (Cabot), 1787-1860.
Hymns, songs, and fables for children. Boston, Carter, Hendee and Babcock, 1831. DLC; MBAt. 7074

Foot, George, 1800?-1867.
A sermon on the connection between divine and human agency in the salvation of the soul: By George Foot, pastor... in Fairfield, N.Y. Utica, Press of William Williams, 1831. 17 p. MAnP; MnU; NNUT; PPPrHi. 7075

Ford, John, 1586-ca 1640.
Dramatic works; with an introduction, and notes critical and explanatory. New York, J. & J. Harper, 1831. 2 vols. CtY;

KyHi; MdBP; PPL; ViU. 7076

A form of Prayer at the laying of the corner-stone of a church or chapel. New York, Protestant Episcopal Press, 1831. 8 p. MdBD; PPL. 7077

Foster, Elijah, d. 1835.
An Address delivered before the Salisbury and Amesbury Society for the Suppression of Intemperance, February 6, 1831. By Elijah Foster, A. M. Pub. by request. Exeter, N.H., Pr. by J. C. Gerrish. Temperance Press, 1831. 21 p. CSmH; CoCsC; MBC; NN. 7078

Foster, Mrs. Hannah [Webster].
The Coquette; or, The history of Eliza Wharton. A novel, founded on fact. By a Lady of Massachusetts (anon.). 12th ed. New York, J. P. Clushan, 1831. 254 p. CtHWatk; MWA; NN. 7079

Foster, Jeremiah J.
An authentic report of the testimony in a cause at issue in the Court of Chancery of the State of New Jersey, between Thomas L. Shotwell, complainant and Joseph Hendrickson and Stacy Decow, defendants. Taken pursuant to the rules of the court, by Jeremiah J. Foster, master and examiner in chancery. Philadelphia, Pr. by J. Harding, 1831. 2 vols. DLC; NjP; OClWHi; PPF; WaU. 7080

Foster, Thomas Flournoy, 1790-1848.
Speech of Thoms F. Foster, of Georgia, on the powers of the federal judiciary. Delivered in the House of Representatives in the United States, February, 1831. Washington, Pr. by Duff Green, 1831. 8 p. DLC; OcLWHi; TxU. 7081

Foulke's almanac for the year 1832... astronomical calculations for the latitude and meridian of Philadelphia; by Joseph Foulke. Philadelphia, n.p., Pr. by John Richards, [1831] [50] p. MWA; NjR. 7082

Fowle, William Bentley, 1795-1865.
The French accidence. 2d ed. Boston, Hilliard, Gray, Little and Wilkins, 1831. 107 p. MB; MH; MWHi. 7083

---- Modern practical geography. 3d ed. with supplement. Boston, Lincoln & Edmands [1831] 162 p. MB; MH. 7084

---- Table of regular verbs, first prepared for Fowle's French accidence (and gender of all French nouns ending in unaccented E). [Boston, 1831?] MH. 7085

Fowler, William Chauncey, 1793-1881.
A lecture on the influence of academies and high schools on common schools. Delivered in Boston, before the American institute of instruction, August, 1831... Boston, Hilliard, Gray, Little and Wilkins, 1831. 22 p. CtHWatk; CtY; MnU. 7086

Fox, George, 1624-1691.
A collection of many select and Christian epistles, letters and testimonies, written on sundry occasions, by that ancient, eminent, faithful Friend, and minister of Christ Jesus, George Fox. Philadelphia, Marcus T. C. Gould; New York, Isaac T. Hopper, 1831. 2 vols. KWiF; MH; NBF; OHi; PPF. 7087

---- Gospel truth demonstrated, in a collection of doctrinal books, given forth by that faithful minister of Jesus Christ, George Fox: containing principles essential to Christianity and salvation, held among the people called Quakers... Philadelphia, Marcus T. C. Gould; New York, Isaac T. Hopper, 1831. 3 vols. MdToH; OHi; PPF; RNHS. 7088

---- The great mystery of the great whore unfolded; and Antichrist's kingdom revealed unto destruction. Philadelphia, also New York, 1831. 616 p. CtY; KyDC; MH; PU; ViU. 7089

---- A journal; or, Historical account of the life, travels, sufferings, Christian experiences, and labour of love in the work of the ministry, of that ancient, eminent and faithful Servant of Jesus Christ, George Fox; corr. by the first ed. Philadelphia, Marcus T. C. Gould; New York, Isaac T. Hopper, 1831. 2 vols. KWiF; NjR; OHi; PSC-Hi; RNHS. 7090

---- Saul's errand to Damascus, with his packet of letters from the high priests against the disciples of the Lord. Or, a faithful transcript of a petition contrived by some persons in Lancashire, who call themselves ministers of the gospel, breathing out threatenings and slaughter against a peaceable and godly people there, by them nicknamed Quakers. Together with the defense of the persons thereby traduced, against the slanderous and false suggestions of that petition and other untruths charged upon them. Pub. to no other end but to draw out the bowels of tender compassion from all that love the poor despised servants of Jesus Christ, who have been the scorn of carnal men in all ages. (4 lines quotations) London, Pr. 1654. Philadelphia, Marcus T. C. Gould; New York, Isaac T. Hopper, J. Harding, pr., 1831. KWiF. 7091

---- The works of George Fox. Philadelphia, M. T. C. Gould; New York, I. T. Hopper, 1831. 8 vols. DLC; ICU; NNUT; PHC; TxU. 7092

Foxe, John, 1516-1587.

Allgemeine Geschichte Des Christlichen Marterthums, bestehend in einer vollständigen und Glaub wurdigen nachricht von dem Leben, Leiden und Glorreichen Tode der Martyrer, sowohl aus der ersten "Christlichen Kirche in allen theilen der welt von der geburt unsers erlosers, biszuden spatesten zeiten der religiosen verfolgungen. Ursprunglich zusammengetragen von Dem Ehrwurdigen John Fox... Philadelphia, By Schafer und Koradi, [c1831] 934 p. InValU; MoSC; MoWgT; PPLT. 7093

---- Book of Martyrs; or, A History of the lives, sufferings, and triumphant deaths, of the primitive as well as Protestant martyrs: from the commencement of Christianity to the latest periods of Pagan and Popish persecution... Originally composed by the Rev. John Fox, and now by important alterations and additions, by Rev. Charles A. Goodrich. Embellished with numerous engravings. Cincinnati, A. B. Roff, 1831. 23, 594 p. CSt; ICBB; MsJMC; OkEnS; TxH. 7094

---- ---- Hartford, D. F. Robinson & co., 1831. 597 p. InCW; PFal; UPB. 7095

---- ---- New York, William W. Reed and Co., 1831. 597 p. NcP; PU; ViU. 7096

---- ---- Pittsburgh, John I. Kay and Co., Philadelphia, Key and Meilke, 1831. 403 p. NGH; PWW. 7097

Framingham, Mass., First Baptist Church.
The articles of faith, also the Covenant of the First Baptist Church of Church. Boston, Lincoln & Edmands, 1831. 16 p. MH. 7098

Francis, Convers, 1795-1863.
Life of John Eliot, the Apostle to the Indians... Boston, Hilliard, Gray and Co., 1831. 357 p. MB. 7099

---- On Experimental Religion. By Convers Francis. 2d ed. Pr. for the American Unitarian Association. Boston, Gray and Bowen, 1831. 20 p. CBPac; ICMe; MB-FA; MMeT-Hi; MeBat. 7100

---- A Sermon, preached at the Ordination of the Rev. Oliver Stearns, to the pastoral care of the Second Congregational Society in Northampton. Nov. 9, 1831. By Convers Francis. Northampton, Pr. by T. W. Shepard, 1831. 36 p. CtSoP; DLC; ICMe; OCHP; RPB. 7101

Francis, John W[akefield], 1789-1861.
An address delivered on the anniversary of the Philolexian Society of Columbia College, May 15, 1831. New York, G. & C. & H. Carville, 1831. 43 p. CtY; MB; NNC; PU; ScU. 7102

Franciscia, Julia.
Letter to Gen. Andrew Jackson, president of the United States. Philadelphia, J. Scarlet, 1831. 24 p. M; MB; PPAmP. 7103

Francois, C. P.
Researches on the chemical and medical properties of the root of Kahinca, trans. by John Baxter. New York, F. N. G. Carnes, 1831. 52 p. NNNAM; PPAN. 7104

Franklin, Benjamin, 1706-1790.
Life of Dr. Benjamin Franklin, written by himself, to which is added, his "Advice to a young tradesman," "Way to wealth," and other essays. Lewistown, Pa., C. Bell & sons, 1831. 240 p. CtY. 7105

---- ---- New York, S. King, 1831. 290 p. ICU; TNP. 7106

The Franklin Almanac for the year 1832...calculated by John Armstrong, teacher of Mathematics. Pittsburgh, Johnston & Stockton [1831] 80 p. MWA; WHi. 7107

Franklin Institute. Philadelphia.
Address of the committee on premiums and exhibitions of the Franklin Institute of the state of Penn, for the promotion of the mechanic arts. With a list of the premiums, offered to competitors at the exhibition to be held in Oct. Philadelphia, Pr. by I. Harding, 1831. 12 p. CSmH; DLC; MB; MdHi; MiD-B. 7108

Franklin society, Cincinnati.
Constitution and by-laws of the Franklin society of Cincinnati. Adopted February 19, 1829. Cincinnati, Pr. by W. J. Ferris & co., 1831. 8 p. OCHP. 7109

Frazer, James Baillie.
The Persian adventure; being a sequel of "The Kuzzilbash"; Philadelphia, Carey & Lea, 1831. 2 vols. CtY; GMWa; MBAt; PU; RPAt. 7110

Free Communion Baptist Black River Yearly Meeting.
Minutes...1831...Martinsburgh; Pr. by J. Wheeler,

1831. NN. 7111

Free trade convention, 1831.

Address of the Free trade convention, to the people of the United States. Held in Philadelphia, October, 1831. [Washington, City Pr. by J. Heart, 1831?] 8 p. DLC; GSDe; NcD; ScU. 7112

---- The journal of the Free trade convention, held in Philadelphia from September 30 to October 7, 1831; and their address to the people of the United States: to which is added a sketch of the debates in the convention. Philadelphia, Pr. by T. W. Ustick, 1831. 75 p. DLC; IU; MHi; TxU; Vi. 7113

---- Memorial of a committee appointed by the Free Trade convention, held in Philadelphia in September and October, 1831, upon the subject of the present tariff of duties. 22d Cong., 1st session, House of Reps. [Doc. no. 82] 53 p. DLC; In; PHi. 7114

---- A number of gentlemen from different states, then in the city of Philadelphia, having assembled at the house of Condy Raque... Monday the 6th of June, 1831, for the purpose of conversing upon matters connected with the advancement of the principles of free trade, there were present the following individuals... Henry D. Sedgewick... Theodore Sedgewick, of Stockbridge, Mass. ... it was resolved to have a convention in Philadelphia Sept. 30. Philadelphia, 1831. MHi. 7115

---- Review of the address of the Free-Trade Convention. Nos. III-IV. Philadelphia, 1831. 8 vols. MBAt; MHi; PPL. 7116

Freeman, Ann, 1797-1826.

A memoir of the life and ministry of Ann Freeman, a faithful servant of Jesus Christ, written by herself; and an account of her death by her husband, Henry Freeman; pub. by Nancy Towle. Exeter, N.H., L. F. Shepard, 1831. 216 p. MBNEH; MWA; NhD. 7117

Freeman, Charles, 1794-1853.

An account of Limerick, (In collection of the Maine Historical Society.) Portland, Day Frazer & co., 1831. 253 p. CSt; MiV; OCln; OFH; OO. 7118

Freeman, Enoch W.

A selection of hymns: including a few originals, designed to aid the friends of Zion in their private and social worship. By Enoch W. Freeman. Concord, N.H., Pr. by Luther Roby, 1831. 236 p. MPeHi; MPlyP; MWHi; NhD. 7119

---- ---- Exeter (N.H.); Peter T. Russell, 1831. 286 p. MLow; MNtCA; RPB. 7120

The Freeman's Almanack, for the year of our Lord, 1832: being bissextile or Leap Year, and (after July 4,) the 57th of American Independence, calculated for the meridian and parallel of Cincinnati, Lat. 39° 7' North; Long. 7° 25' West from Washington; but will serve with little variation for all the Western States. By Samuel Burr, Philom. Cincinnati, N. & G. Guilford, [1831] 30 p. CSmH; MWA; MiD-B. 7121

Freemasons. Alabama. Grand Lodge.

Proceedings of the Grand Lodge of the state of Alabama, at its annual communication in December, 1830. Tucaloosa [sic] Pr. by E. Walker, 1831. 28 p. DSC; MBFM. 7122

---- Indiana. Grand Lodge.

Proceedings of the Grand Lodge of...Masons of the State of Indiana, at its annual communication, held at Indianapolis, on Monday, the 4th day of October, A. L. 5830. Most worshipful Philip Mason, Grand Master. Right worshipful A. W. Morris, Grand Sec'y. Indianapolis, Pr. by A. F. Morrison, 1831. 31 p. IaCrM; MBFM; NNFM. 7123

---- ---- ---- Proceedings of the Grand Lodge of...Masons, of the State of Indiana, at its annual communication, held at Vincennes, on Monday, the 10th of October, A. L. 5831. Most worshipful William Sheets, Grand Master, Right Worshipful A. W. Morris, Grand Secretary. Indianapolis, Pr. by Douglass & Maguire, 1831. 26 p. MBFM; NNFM; OCM. 7124

---- Kentucky. Grand Chapter.
Proceedings of the Grand Chapter and of the Grand Council of the state of Kentucky, at a Grand annual convocation, begun and held at Mason's hall in the town of Lexington. Frankfort, Pr. by Albert G. Hodges, 1831. 15 p. NNFM. 7125

---- ---- Grand Lodge.
Proceedings of the Grand Lodge of Kentucky, at a grand annual communication in the town of Lexington, commencing on the 29th of August, 5831. Lexington, Pr. by N. L. Finnell & J. F. Herndon, 1831. 40 p. KyLx; NNFM. 7126

---- Louisiana. Grand Lodge.
Extracts from the proceedings of the Grand Lodge of free and accepted masons of the state of Louisiana, held in the city of New-Orleans. New Orleans, Pr. by B. Buisson, 1831. 9 p. NNFM; OCM. 7127

---- Maine. Grand Lodge.
Proceedings of the Grand Lodge of the Most Ancient and Honorable Fraternity of Free and Accepted Masons of the State of Maine. Portland, A. Shirley, 1831. 16 p. MNFM. 7128

---- Maryland. Grand Lodge.
Proceedings of the G. R. A. Chapter of the State of Maryland, at a Communication Held at the Masonic Hall, in the City of Baltimore, May 18th, A. T. 2831. Baltimore, Pr. by Lucas and Deaver, 1831. 18 p. MdBP; MdToH. 7129

---- Massachusetts. Grand Royal Arch Chapter.
Minutes of Grand Royal Arch Chapter, Massachusetts. Boston, 1831. 12 p. MWA. 7130

---- Mississippi. Grand Lodge.
Extracts from the proceedings of the state of Mississippi, at a grand annual communication, held at their hall in the city of Natchez, on the 21st February, A. L. 5831, A.D. 1831. Natchez, Andrew Marschalk, 1831. 29 p. MBFM; MsFM; MsMFM; NNFM. 7131

---- Missouri. Grand Lodge.
Proceedings of the Grand Lodge of the state of Missouri, at their several communications, begun and held in the city of St. Louis, on the fifth day of April, and 17th day of October (1831). St. Louis, Pr. at the St. Louis Book and Job Office, 1831. 16 p. DSC; IaCrM; MBFM; NNFM; PPFM. 7132

---- New Hampshire. Grand Chapter.
A journal of the proceedings of the Grand Royal Arch Chapter of the state of New Hampshire, at their annual communication, holden in Concord, June 9, A. L.

5831, Red river press, 1831. 10 p. LNMas; NNFM. 7133

---- New York. Grand Chapter.
Extracts from the proceedings of the Grand Chapter (Royal Arch Masons) of the State of New York, at its annual meeting February, 1831. Albany [N.Y.] E. B. Child, 1831. 7 p. IaCrM. 7134

---- ---- Grand Lodge.
Extracts from the proceedings of the Grand Lodge of the ancient and honorable fraternity of free and accepted Masons of the state of New York, at the annual communication, held at the Grand Lodge room, in the city of New York, on the 1st, 2d and 3d of June, A.L. 5831. New York, Pr. by William A. Mercein, 1831. 22 p. NNFM. 7135

---- ---- ---- Proceedings of Grand Lodge of Masonic Lodge, in New York State; Meeting held in 1831. New York, William A. Mercein, 1831. 8 p. IaCrM. 7136

---- North Carolina. Grand Lodge.
Proceedings of the Grand Lodge of ancient York Masons of North Carolina... Raleigh, Pr. by Lawrence & Lamey, 1831. 8 p. OCM. 7137

---- Ohio Grand Lodge.
Proceedings of the Grand Lodge of...Masons in...Ohio; at the Annual Grand Communication, A.L. 5831. Most Worshipful John Satterthwaite, Grand Master. Columbus, Pr. by Bros. Olmsted and Bailhache, 1831. 14 p. IaCrM; MBFM; NNFM. 7138

---- ---- Royal and Select Masters. Grand Council.
Proceedings of the Grand Council of Royal and Select Masters of the state of Ohio at its [1st] annual assembly... 1831- Chillicothe, Ohio. N; NIC; OClWHi; PHi. 7139

---- Pennsylvania. Philadelphia. Royal Arch Masons.
By-laws of Jerusalem. H.R. Arch Chapter. No. 3, Philadelphia, Pr. by T. S. Manning, 1831. 20 p. PPFM. 7140

---- Rhode Island. Grand Lodge.
Address of the Grand Lodge of the State of Rhode Island and Providence Plantations, to the people of said state. Providence, R.I., Pr. by R. Cranston, 1831. 16 p. CtY; DLC; MB; MWA; N. 7141

---- ---- ---- ---- Pawtucket [R.I.] Pr. by S. M. Fowler, 1831. 14 p. CSmH; MWA; NN; RPB. 7142

---- ---- ---- Memorial to the General Assembly, to be holden in East Greenwich... January, A.D. 1831. [From the Antimasonic Convention, at Providence, Dec. 29, 1830. Providence, 1831] 1 l. MB. 7143

---- ---- ---- Proceedings of the most worshipful Grand Lodge of the state of Rhode-Island and Providence plantations, at the annual meeting holden at the lodge room, East-Greenwich, R.I. Friday, June 24th, 1831. Providence, R.I., Pr. by Simons, jr., 1831. 8 p. NNFM. 7144

---- Tennessee. Grand Lodge.
Proceedings of the Grand Lodge of the state of Tennessee, at a grand annual communication held at the Masonic Hall, in the town of Nashville, on Monday, October 3d, A.D. 5831, A.L. 1831. Nashville, Pr. at the Herald office, 1831. 24 p. T; TxU. 7145

---- Vermont. Grand Lodge.
Journal of the Most Worshipful

Grand Lodge of Vermont, at the Communication, holden at Montpelier, Oct. 12, A. L. 5830. Montpelier, Pr. by G. W. Hill, 1831. 18 p. DSC; IaCrM; MBFM; NNFM; VtBFM. 7146

---- Virginia. Grand Council.
Proceedings of the Grand Council of Virginia... Richmond, in the years 1828, 1829 and 1830. Richmond, Pr. by John Warrock, 1831. 14 p. NNFM. 7147

---- ---- Grand Lodge.
Proceedings of a Grand annual communication of the Grand Lodge of Virginia, begun and held in the Mason's hall, in the city of Richmond, ... December 12th, A.D. 1831. Richmond, Pr. by John Warrick...1831. 35 p. NNFM. 7148

---- ---- ---- Proceedings of a Grand Lodge of Virginia, begun and held in the Mason's hall, in the city of Richmond, ...December 13th, A.D. 1830. Richmond, Pr. by John Warrock, 1831. 44 p. NNFM; OCM. 7149

---- West Virginia. Grand Encampment.
Proceedings of the Grand Encampment of the State of Virginia, held in the town of Petersburg. December 15th, 1831... Winchester, Pr. by Samuel H. Davis, 1831. 9 p. WvW. 7150

The Freewill Baptist Register and Saint's Annual Visiter for 1832.
By a member of the elder's conference. Linerick, Maine, Pr. by William Burr, for Elder Samuel Burbank, 1831. 54 p. MWA; MeLewB. 7151

French, D'Arcy A.
Parsing made easy an English grammar unfolding the principles of the English language with consistency and regularity; and exhibiting a theory of the moods and tenses more conformable than any other, to the definitions... By D'Arcy A. French. Baltimore, Pr. by Benjamin Edes, 1831. 168 p. DGU; MdBS; MoFloSS; NNC; PU-Penn. 7152

Frey, Joseph Samuel, C. F. d. 1850.
A new edition of a Hebrew Grammar, considerably altered and much enlarged. By Joseph Samuel C. F. Frey... New York, S. Hoyt & Co., 1831. 127 p. CtY; MH; MeB; PPLT. 7153

Friar and the boy. Jack the piper, or, The pleasant pastime of a fryar and boy. 2d ed. New-York, Pr. by D. G. Dunn, 1831. 26 p. MH. 7154

Frick, William, 1790-1855.
An address preparatory to opening the department of the arts and sciences in the University of Maryland. Delivered on behalf of the trustees, by Wm. Frick. Pub. at the request of the board. Baltimore, Pr. by John D. Toy, 1831. 37 p. DLC; MdHi; NIC; PHi; RPJCB. 7155

The Friend, or, Advocate of Truth. Religious publication. For the year, 1831. Philadelphia, Pr. by J. Harding, for Marcus T. C. Gould, 1831. 188 p. MBC; NN; PSC-Hi. 7156

A friendly letter to the Rev. Adam Wilson on the Mode of Baptism. By the author of the Examination. Norway, Maine, Wm. E Goodnow, 1831. 36 p. NHC-S. 7157

The Friends; a true tale of woe and joy, from the east Boston, Lindoln and Edmands, 1831. 178 p. CtY; RPB; ViU. 7158

Friend's Almanac. Philadelphia, Pa., M. T. C. Gould, 1831. MWA. 7159

Friends family library. Philadelphia, 1831. 5 vols. OO; PHC; PPFr; PSC-Hi. 7160

Friends' girls school, York. ...List of teachers and scholars. 1831-1881. 55 p. PHC 7161

[Friends of American industry] Report of manufactures of glass [and cabinet ware] New York, 1831. Reports submitted by Clarkson Crolins, 121-128 p. ScCC. 7162

Friends of domestic industry. Address of the Friends of domestic industry, assembled in convention, at New York, Oct. 26, 1831, to the people of the United States. Pub. by order of the convention. Baltimore [Pr. by Sands & Neilson] 1831. 44 p. CtHT; LNT; MBC; OCl; ScU. 7163

---- General convention of the Friends of domestic industry, assembled New York Oct. 26, 1831. Reports of committees. 31 p. CtY; InHi; PPL-R; ScU. 7164

---- Journal of the proceedings of the Friends of domestic industry, in general convertion met at the city of New York, Oct. 26, 1831. Pb. by order of the convention. Baltimore, H. Niles, 1831. 16 p. DLC; ICU; MWA; NcD; PBL. 7165

---- List of officers and members composing the New York convention held in the sessions room in that city, October 26th, 1831. 15 p. DLC; NcD; OClWHi. 7166

---- Report in the general convention of... 1831. See Coxe, Andiel W.

---- Committee on iron and steel. Report, Oct. 1831 [Baltimore, 1831?] 31 p. DLC; IU; OclW. 7167

---- Committee on the Coasting trade and internal commerce of the United States. Report, 1831. 20 p. PPPrHi. 7168

---- Committee on manufacture of glass, porcelain and other manufactures of clay. Report, 1831. 7 p. OClW. 7169

---- Twenty questions made by The Committee appointed by the Convention held in the City of New York, on the 26th of October last, "to report on the production and manufacture of Cotton." November, 1831. Broadside. MHi. 7170

Friends of free trade. Preamble and resolutions adopted at a meeting held at the Exchange coffee house, on Thursday evening, August 16, for the purpose of choosing delegates to the Anti-tariff convention. Boston, Beals and Homer, 1831. 12 p. MH-BA. 7171

Friends of Liberal Principles and equal rights. Proceedings of the Friends of Liberal Principles and Equal Rights, in Rochester... January, 1831. Rochester, S. H. Salisbury, 1831. 16 p. MdBJ; NRHi; NRU. 7172

Friends' miscellany; being a collection of essays and fragments, biographical, religious, epistolary, narrative, and historical; designed for the promotion of piety and virtue...Ed. by John & Isaac Comly, Byberry [Pa.] Philadelphia, Pr. by J. Richard for the editors, 1831-1839. 2 vols. MH; OCHP; PHC; PHi;

PPL. 7173

---- Alexandria [Va.] Monthly Meeting.
An address from Alexandria monthly meeting of Friends to each of its members [Alexandria? 1831] Broadside. DLC. 7174

---- Cambridge Preparative Meeting.
... Women Friends, 1831-1842. 1 vol. PSC-Hi. 7175

---- Cumberland and Northumberland Quarterly Meeting.
...the following report from the adjourned General Meeting for Wigton school has been brought in and read, and is satisfactory... 1831. 3 p. PHC. 7176

---- Indiana Yearly Meeting.
Minutes of the Indiana yearly meeting of Friends held at Richmond, Ind. 1831. 27 p. ICU; InHi. 7177

---- London Yearly Meeting.
The epistle from the yearly meeting, held in London, by adjournments, from the 18th of the fifth month, to the 27th of the same, inclusive. Baltimore, Pr. by Sands & Neilson, 1831. 7 p. DLC; MdToH. 7178

---- Mount Holly Monthly Meeting.
Memorial of Mt. Holly Monthly Meeting... Philadelphia, Wm. Boen, 1831. PSC-Hi. 7179

---- New York Yearly Meeting.
An address, to the youth of the Society of Friends. New York, Pr. by Mahlon Day, 1831. 8 p. PHC. 7180

---- ---- Epistle from the yearly meeting of friends, held in New York by adjournments from the 23d of 5th mo. to the 27th of the same, inclusive, 1831. n.p. [1831] 4 p. PHC; NNFL. 7181

---- New York Yearly Meeting of Women Friends.
Minute of Advice; from the New-York Yearly Meeting of Women Friends, 1831. New-York, Pr. by Mahlon Day, 1831. Double sheet. NNFL. 7182

---- North Carolina Yearly Meeting.
From the meeting for sufferings instituted by the yearly meeting of Friends of North Carolina for the purpose of acting in behalf of the general and special interests of the Society... [Greensborough, Pr. by Wm. Swaim, 1831] (2) p. NcU. 7183

---- Ohio Yearly Meeting.
The following pages contain all that could be procured (in time for publication) in relation to the petition of that part of the Society of Friends called Orthodox, to the legislature of this state, for an act to incorporate the Ohio yearly meeting ...1831, 32 p. OClWHi; PHC. 7184

---- Philadelphia Yearly Meeting.
The authenticity of the scriptures, and fundamental doctrines of Quaker Christianity. According to the Berean, and The investigation of Benjamin's Webb's case before a committee from the Quarterly meeting of Concord. Wilmington, Del., Pr. by W. M. Naudain, 1831. 94 p. PHC. 7185

No entry. 7186

---- ---- An epistle from the

Yearly Meeting held in Philadelhia, and a Report on Education. 1831. 8 p. DLC; MH; NjR; PHC; PPL-R. 7187

---- ---- Rules of discipline of the yearly meeting of Friends held in Philadelphia. Philadelphia, J. Richards, 1831. 102 p. DLC; ICN; NjR; PHi; TxU. 7188

---- ---- Statistics of the operations of the executive board of Friends' association of Philadelphia, & its vicinity for the relief of colored freedom. Philadelphia, [1831] 33 p. PPAmP. 7189

---- Scipio Quarterly Meeting.
An address to the youth of the Society of Friends. New York, Pr. by M. Day, 1831. 8 p. InRchE; MH; PHi; PSC-Hi. 7190

Friend's United States Almanac for 1832. Philadelphia, Pa., Marcus T. C. Gould [1831] MWA. 7191

Friendship's Offering. A literary album and Christmas and New Year's present, for 1831. London, Smith, Elder & Co.; Philadelphia, Thomas Wardle, 1831. 408 p. ScCliTO. 7192

Frieze, Jacob.
Address, delivered before the Grand Lodge of Rhode-Island, at the Anniversary Festival of St. John the Baptist, at East-Greenwich, R.I. Friday, June 24, 1831. By Jacob Frieze, G. Chaplain. Providence, R.I., Pr. by B. Cranston, 1831. 22 p. DLC; MWA; PPFM. 7193

Frost, John, 1800-1859.
Elements of English grammar: with progressive exercises in parsing, by John Frost... 2d ed. Boston, Richardson, Lord and Holbrook, 1831. 108 p. ICU; MB; MH; MNS; TxU-T. 7194

---- History of ancient and modern Greece. Boston, Lincoln & Edmands, 1831. 359 p. CtY; KyLx; MLy; MdW; PP; PPL. 7195

Frothingham, Nathaniel Langdon.
Signs in the sun; delivered on the day after the eclipse of Feb. 12. Boston, 1831. MBAt. 7196

Fuel Saving Society of the city and liberties of Philadelphia.
Constitution of the Fuel Savings Society of the City and Liberties of Philadelphia (Instituted May, 1821). ...Philadelphia, 1831. 8 p. 7197

Fuller, J. G.
Conversations between two laymen on strict and mixed communion; in which the principal arguments in favor of the latter practice, are stated, as nearly as possible, in the words of its most powerful advocate, The Rev. Robert Hall. By J. G. Fuller. With Dr. Griffin's Letter on Communion, and the Review of it by Professor Ripley, of Newton. Boston, Lincoln & Edmands, 1831. 321 p. GDecCT; KyLoP; LNB; PCA; ViRU. 7198

Fuller, S. W.
Letter to Rev. Edwin Barnes, of Boonville, Oneida county, in review of a sermon published by him entitled Inconsistencies of Universalism Exposed. By S. W. Fuller. Utica, Pr. by A. B. and R. K. Grosh, 1831. 24 p. MMeT-Hi. 7199

Fuller, Thomas, 1608-1861.
The holy and profane states. By Thomas Fuller. With some account of the author and his writings. Cambridge, Hilliard and Brown, 1831. 293 p. CtB; KTW; MB; MCR; NNG; OFH; TNP. 7200

Fuller, Timothy, 1778-1835.
An oration, delivered at Faneuil hall, Boston, July 11, 1831, at the request of the Suffolk anti-masonic committee, by Timothy Fuller. Boston, Pr. at the office of the Boston press for the Publishing committee, 1831. 11 p. CtY; MB; NjR; PHi; WHi. 7201

[Furman, Garrit]
The falls of the Genesee. A farce. In three acts... New York, Pr. by D. Mitchell, 1831. 37 p. ICU. 7202

Furness, William Henry, 1802-1896.
An address delivered in the First Congregational Unitarian Church in Philadelphia, Sept. 4, 1831, by the pastor of the Society. Philadelphia, 1831. 11 p. CtY; MH-AH. 7203

G

G. R. A. Chapter. Proceedings.
Proceedings of the GRA Chapter, of the State of Maryland, at a Communication held at the Masonic Hall, in the City of Baltimore, May 18th. Baltimore, Lucas & Deaver, 1831. 18 p. MdToN; NNFM. 7204

Gallatin, Albert, 1761-1849.
Considerations of the currency and banking system of the United States. By Albert Gallatin. Philadelphia, Carey & Lea, 1831. 106 p. CLU; DeWI; ICU; MBC; TNP. 7205

---- Extracts from Albert Gallatin's articles on the bank of the United States. Louisville, Ky., Prentise and Buxton, 1831. KyBgW. 7205

Gallaudet, Edward.
The progress of intemperance designed and engraved by E. Gallaudet. Boston, Gallaudet, 1831. DLC; MB; PPPrHi. 7206

Gallaudet, Thomas Hopkins, 1787-1851.
The Child's Book on the soul ... By Rev. T. H. Galludet... with questions, adapted to the use of Sunday Schools and of infant schools. Hartford, Cooke & Co., 1831. 2 vols. AU; DLC; IU; MWA; PP. 7207

Gallup, Joseph Adams, 1769-1849.
Outlines of an arrangement of medical nosology; founded on the physicology of the diseased system. Woodstock, Pr. by David Watson, 1831. 87 p. VtNN. 7208

Galt, John, 1779-1839.
The book of life. (In Picken, Andrew, editor, The club-book. Vol. 2. 241-253. New York, 1831.) MB. 7209

---- Haddad-Ben-Ahab; or the traveller. A tale of Stumboul. (In Picken, Andrew, editor, The book-club. Vol. 1. pp 69-75. New York, 1831) MB. 7210

---- ... The life of Lord Byron. [Harper's stereotyped ed.] New York, J. & J. Harper, 1831. 334 p. LNH; MHi; NNC; OM; WvW. 7211

---- The Lives of the Players. Boston, Frederic S. Hill [1831] 2 vols. IC; MWA; NcD; PHC; TNP. 7212

---- The painter... A Sicilian tale. (In Picken, Andrew, editor. The club-book. Vol. 2. 183-191. New York, 1831.) MB; OCX. 7213

---- The Progress of genius, or, Authentic memoirs of the early life of Benjamin West, esq., president of the Royal Academy, London, compiled from materials furnished by himself, by John Galt. Abridged for the use of young persons, by a lady. Boston, Leonard C. Bowles, 1831. 89 p. MH; MoSW; NjR; PSC-Hi. 7214

---- The unguarded hour. (In Picken, Andrew, editor. The book-club. Vol. 2. pp. 205-212. New York, 1831.) MB; OCl. 7215

Galveston Bay and Texas land company.
Address to the reader of the documents relating to the Galveston Bay and Texas land company, which are contained in the appendix. New York, Pr. by G. F. Hopkins & son, 1831. 69 p. CaBViPA; DLC; MWA; PHi; TxU. 7216

Gannett, Ezra Stiles, 1801-1871.
An address delivered before the Boston Sunday school society, on the celebration of the fiftieth anniversary of the Sunday School institution, at the Federal Street church, September 14, 1831. Boston, Gray and Bowen, General Agency for the Boston Sunday School Society, 1831. 42 p. CBPac; DLC; M; MB; MBAt; MiD-B; OO; RPB. 7217

---- A comparison of the good and the evil of revivals. 2d ed. by Ezra S. Gannett. Pr. for the American Unitarian Association. Boston, Gray and Bowen, Aug. 1831. 28 p. ICMe; MBC; MH-AH; MW; PPAmP. 7218

---- Necessity and sufficiency of religion. (A sermon.) [Boston, 1831] MH-AH. 7219

---- A sermon written for the children of his Society, and preached May 8, 1831. By Ezra S. Gannett, Junior minister of the Federal Street Society. Pub. by request. Boston, Leonard C. Bowles, 1831. 18 p. ICMe; ICN; MB; MBC; MH. 7220

No entry. 7221

Gardiner, John Sylvester John.
The American Gardener, containing ample directions for working a kitchen garden every month in the year, and copius instructions for the cultivation of flower gardens, vineyards, nurseries, hop yards, green houses, and hot houses. By John Gardiner, and by David Hepburn... A new ed. much enl. 4th ed. Washington City, Wm. Cooper, Jr., 1831. 294 p. CoFcS; DLC; NcWfC; NNBG; ViW. 7222

---- Catalogue of near two thousand volumes, being the entire library of the late Rev. J. S. J. Gardiner, D.D... to be sold at public auction... April 13, 1831. Boston, Pr. by Samuel Condon, 1831. MB; MBNEH; MHi; MWA; NIC. 7223

Garland, James, 1791-1885.
Remarks of Mr. Garland, on the resolutions on the subject of the judiciary, delivered in the House of delegates, Feb. 1, 1831. [n.p., 1831] CtY. 7224

The Garland; a collection of favorite waltzes, selected from the works of the most eminent composers. Philadelphia, J. Edgar [183-?] NcD. 7225

The garland for 1831. Designed as a Christmas and New Year's present... New York, C. H. Peabody, 1831. 2 vols. MnU; NNC; NjP; NjR. 7226

Garrison, Wm. Lloyd, 1805-1879.

An address, delivered before the Free People of Color... 1831. By William Lloyd Garrison. Boston, Pr. by Stephen Foster, 1831. 24 p. CtHWatk; MeB; NjR; PHi; RP. 7227

---- ---- 2d ed. Boston, Pr. by S. Foster, 1831. 24 p. CtY; DLC; MNA; OClWHi; TNF. 7228

---- ---- 3d ed. Boston, Pr. by S. Foster, 1831. 24 p. MBAt; MHi; MdBJ; OO; PPPrHi. 7229

---- Three addresses on the abolition cause... Boston & New York, 1831-1833. NN; PPPrHi. 7230

Gayarré, Charles.

Essai Historique sur La Louisiane. par Charles Gayarré. Second volume. Newelle-Orléans, Imprimé par Benjamin Levy, Au coin des rues de Chartres et Bienville, 1831. 231 p. AU; BWK; NN. 7231

Gems of sacred poetry. 1st Amer. ed. New York, H. C. Sleight, 1831. 256 p. DLC; IU; NN; NjR; PPL-R. 7232

Genealogy and family register of George Robinson, late of Attleborough, Mass., with some account of his ancestors. Hallowell, Glazier, Masters & Co., 1831. 36 p. DLC; MBNEH. 7233

General Protestant Episcopal Sunday School Union and Church Book Society.

Catalogue of Sunday School Books and Requisites published by the General Protestant Episcopal Sunday School (Union?) and for sale at the depositories of that institution. New-York: General Protestant Episcopal Sunday School Union, 1831. 12 p. MiD-B. 7234

General Society of Mechanics and Tradesmen of the City of New York.

Reports for 1830 of the School and library committees. New York, Pr. by Wm. A. Mercein, 1831. 24 p. NjR. 7235

---- [Supplement to the charter and by-laws] ...New York, Pr. by Wm. A. Mercein, 1831. 8 p. NjR. 7236

The Geneseee Farmer and gardner's journal. A weekly paper devoted to agriculture, horticulture & rural economy. N. Goodsell, Editor, Volume 1-9. Rochester, Luther Tucker & Co., 1831-1839. 416 p. IU; MBH; NRHi; NcD; PU. 7237

Geoffrey Crayon, pseud. See Irving, Washington, 1783-1859.

A geographical present: being descriptions of the several countries of Africa. Compiled from the best authorities. With representations of the various inhabitants in their respective costumes. New-York, Wm. Burgess, juvenile emporium, 1831. 130 p. CLCM; DLC; MB; MH; PHi. 7238

George, Noah J. T.

The gentlemen and ladies' pocket dictionary; to which is prefixed tables showing the day of the month for one hundred years. By Noah J. T. George, Esq. Author of the Vermont geographical and statistical gazetteer; gentlemen's pocket companion, &c., &c. Condord, Pr. by Luther Roby, 1831. 128 p. MH; NH-Hi; NRMA; NhD. 7239

---- The Gentleman's Pocket Companion: or, a series of valuable tables and useful forms of writing, compiled from most approved authors. By Dr. Noah J. T. George, author of the Vermont

Geographical and Statistical Gazeteer, etc. Concord, Pr. by Hill and Barton, 1831. 128 p. MH; MH-L; NH-Hi; WvU. 7240

Georgetown, D.C.

Ordinances of the Corporation of Georgetown, with a table of contents. Pr. by order of the Corporation Georgetown, D.C., Rind's Press, 1831. 37 p. DWP. 7241

Georgia.

Act of the General Assembly of the State of Georgia, passed in Milledgeville at an Annual Session in October, November and December, 1830. Pub. by authority. Milledgeville, Pr. by Camak and Ragland, 1831. 312 p. 7242

---- A compilation of the laws of the State of Georgia, passed by the General Assembly, since the year 1819 to the year 1829, inclusive, comprising all the laws passed within those periods, arranged under titles, with marginal notes, and notes of reference to the laws which are amended or repealed. To which are added such concurred and approved resolutions as are either of general, local, or private nature. Concluded with a full and ample index to the laws, and a separate one to the resolutions. By William C. Dawson... Milledgeville, Grantland and Orme, 1831. 488, 150 p. CSmH; DLC; GU-De; NcD; WaU-L. 7243

---- A digest of the laws of the State of Georgia: Containing all statutes, and the substance of all resolutions of a general and public nature, and now in force, which have been passed in said state from the year 1820 to the year 1829 inclusive: With occasional explanatory notes and connecting references, and a list of the statutes repealed or obsolete. To which is added an appendix, containing the Constitution of the state of Georgia, as amended; also references to such local acts as relate to towns, counties, internal navigation, county academies, etc. And a collection of the most approved forms used in carrying the above laws into effect. With a copious index to the whole. By Arthur Foster. Philadelphia, Towar,, J. & D. M. Hogan; Pittsburgh, Pr. by C. Sherman & co., for Hogan & co. 1831. 516 p. GA; GEU; InSC; MH; MdBB; Mi-L; NIC; Nv; RPL. 7244

---- Resolutions of the Legislature of Georgia on the subject of the Florida Boundry. January 10, 1831. [Washington, 1831] 4 p. 7245

Geschichte des Theologischen Seminars der Deutschen Reformiten Kirche. Nebst Beantwortung einer Schmahschrift von J. C. Ebaugh. Hannover, Pa., 1831. 64 p. PHi. 7246

Getty, John A.

Elements of rhetoric; exhibiting a methodical arrangement of all the important ideas of the ancient and modern rhetorical writers... By John A. Getty... Philadelphia, E. Littell, 1831. 117 p. MH; MdBLC; NjR; PPL. 7247

Geyer, Henry Sheffie.

Speech...on the expediency of a national bank of the validity of the currency, the American system. St. Louis, St. Louis Times Office, 1831. 47 p. PP; PU. 7248

Gibbon, Edward.

The History of the decline and fall of the roman empire. By Edward Gibbon, Esq. 5th Amer. from the last London ed. Complete in four volumes. New York, Pr. by J. & J. Harper, 1831. 446 p. MMarm. 7249

Gibbs, Charles, 1794?-1831.
Confessions to Judge Hopson et a. by Chas. Gibbs & Thos. J. Wansley. New York, n.p., 1831. 22 p. PHi. 7250

---- Horrible confessions of the pirate and murderer, Charles Gibbs, alias James Jeffreys, who acknowledges to taking the lives of no less than four hundred human beings, and who was condemned to be hanged, in the City of New York, April 23d, 1831, for the murder of the mate of the Brig Vineyard, and robbery of specie on board said vessel, being an authentic narrative compiled from his own confessions. See also Gibbs. 12 mo. [Newport] Pr. for the purchasers, April 1831. 28 p. 7251

---- Mutiny and murder. See under title.

---- Trial and sentence of Gibbs and Wansly, pirates; the inhuman murder of Capt. Thornby and his mate, Wm. Roberts, on board the brig Vineyard on her passage from New Orleans to Philadelphia. Philadelphia, Pr. by W. Johnson, 1831. 8 p. NjR. 7252

Gibson, Edmund, 1669-1748.
[Three Pastoral Letters to the people of the diocese of London...by Edmund Gibson, D.D. Bishop of London.] Standard Works adapted to the use of the Protestant Episcopal Church in the United States, volume v. Gibson's three pastoral letters. Hornis' letters on infidelity, and to Adam Smith, with prefaces, biographical memoirs, and notes, by W. R. Whittingham, A.M. New York, The New York Protestant Episcopal Press, 1831. 346 p. CtMW; IEG; NN; WNaE. 7253

Gibson, William.
The institutes and practice of surgery: being the outlines of a course of lectures. 3d ed. Philadelphia, Carey & Lea, 1831. 2 vols. GHi; GU-M; NBMS. 7254

Gieseler, Johann Karl Ludwig, 1792-1854.
A text-book of church history. By Dr. John C. L. Gieseler. Trans. and ed. by Henry B. Smith, professor in the Union Theological Seminary, New York. Vol. IV.-A.D. 1517-1648. The Reformation and Its Results to the Peace of Wesphalia. New York, & Brothers, 1831-1868. 4 vols. ViRut. 7255

Gilbert, Amos.
Strictures on "An Exposition of modern Scepticism by Wm. Gibbons." Wilmington, 1831. 30 p. PHi. 7256

[Gilbert, Ann (Taylor), 1782-1866]
Hymns for infant minds. Worcester, n.p., 1831. 108 p. MWA. 7257

Gilbert, Washington.
Sermon delivered before the 1st Cong. Society in Harvard, Oct. 23, 1831. Lancaster, Carter, Andrews & Co., 1831. 15 p. CtHC; MB; MBAt; MDovC; MiD-B; MWA. 7258

Gill, John, 1697-1771.
Infant baptism, a part and pillar of popery, being a vindication...with a preface and an appendix by C. C. P. Crosby. New York, Van Valkenburgh, 1831. MB; NHCS; PPPrHi. 7259

Gilleland, J. C.
The Ohio and Mississippi pilot, consisting of a set of charts of those rivers...to which is added a geography of the states and territories west and south of

the Allegheny mountains... Pittsburgh, H. Holdship and Son, 1831. [34] p. OClWHi. 7260

Gillies, John, 1747-1836.
The history of Ancient Greece, its colonies and conquests, from the earliest accounts till the division of the Macedonian Empire in the east: including the history of literature, philosophy, and the fine arts. By John Gillies, LL.D. F.A.S. Philadelphia, Thomas Wardle, 1831. 492 p. KyLo; MBC; OUrC; ScCC; TWaW. 7261

Gilman, Samuel, 1791-1858.
Address delivered at the anniversary meeting of the South-Carolina Society for the promotion of temperance, May 18th, 1831. By Samuel Gilman, Pastor of the Second Independent Church, Charleston. Pub. by request of the society. Charleston, Pr. by A. E. Miller, 1831. 28 p. CtY; ICMe; MH; ScHi; WHi. 7262

---- Unitarian Christianity free from Objectionable Extremes. By Samuel Gilman. 2d ed., no. 30. Pr. for The American Unitarian Association. Boston, Gray and Bowen, 1831. 24 p. CBPSR; ICMe; MB; MH; MeB. 7263

Gimcrack, Jeremy.
The circle of anecdote and wit; see [Gregson, John Stanley, d. 1837]

Girard almanac for 1832. Calculations by William Collom. Philadelphia, Pa., W. Johnson [1831] 7264

Gleig, George Robert, 1796-1888.
...The history of the Bible. By the Rev. G. R. Gleig...New-York, J. & J. Harper, 1831-32. 2 vols. CtY; GHi; MH; VtU; WaW. 7265

Globe Bank, Providence, R.I.
Charter granted Jan. 1831. In box with Providence-Banks. Providence, 1831. 8 p. CSmH; NN; RHi. 7266

Goddard, Henry, 1785-1871.
Ambition, an historical and argumentative poem in the abstract (as distinct from useful and laudable emulation) its origin, nature, effects and place of final abode. An essay verse. Portland, 1831. 25 p. MB; MBC; MH; MWA. 7267

Goddard, Thomas H.
A general history of the most prominent banks in Europe... Also A. Hamilton's report to Congress on currency, presented while secretary; and McDuffie's report on currency presented to the last Congress. By Thomas H. Goddard. New York, H. C. Sleight [etc.] 1831. 254 p. DLC; InHi; NjP; PHi; ScU. 7268

No entry. 7269

Godin, Des Odonais, Jean, 1712-1792.
Account of the adventures of Madame Godin des Odonais, in passing down the river of the Amazons, in the year 1770. (In Dard. Madame-Perils and captivity.) Boston, 1831. Nh-Hi. 7270

Godman, John Davidson, 1794-1830.
American natural history... By John D. Godman, M.D... 2d ed. Philadelphia, Key & Mielkie, 1831. 3 vols. DLC; KPea; MdW; NN; PP. 7271

Godwin, William, 1756-1836.
...Adventures of Caleb Williams. By William Godwin, Esq. New-York, J. & J. Harper, 1831. 2 vols. FTU; MWA; NjPT; RPB; TNP. 7272

Goffe, Joseph.
Report on Christian fellowship with freemasonry. Made to the convention assembled at Boston, May 19, 1831. By Rev. Josiah Goffee... Boston, Office of the Boston press, 1831. 8 p. ICU. 7273

Goldsmith, J., pseud. see Phillips, Sir Richard, 1767-1840.

Goldsmith, Morris.
Directory and Strangers' guide, for the City of Charleston and its vicinity, [from the 5th census of the United States] By Morris Goldsmith. Charleston, Pr. at the office of the Irishman, 1831. 191 p. DLC. 7274

Goldsmith, Oliver, 1728-1774.
An abridgement of the History of England from the Invasion of Julius Caesar, to the Death of George the Second. Continued to the present time, by several literary gentlemen. Stereotyped by Hammond Wallis & Co., New York. Imp. ed. continued to the close of the year 1828. Greenfield, Mass., A. Phelps, 1831. 348 p. ICMCC; NIDHi; REd. 7275

---- ---- Philadelphia, 1831. 346 p. MWA; MoS. 7276

---- The deserted village, traveller, and miscellaneous poems ... Middlebury, Vt., Pr. by A. Colton, for H. Richardson, 1831. 108 p. VtMidSM; VtMiS. 7277

---- Doctor Goldsmiths celebrated elegy on that glory of Her sex, Mrs. Mary Blaize. Baltimore, Joseph N. Lewis, 1831. 12 l. PP; RosenthC. 7278

---- Goldsmith's Roman history. Abridged by himself, for the use of schools. 1st ed., divided into sections, for a class-book... Hartford, S. Andrus, 1831. 316 p. TxU-T. 7279

---- History of animals; a sel. from (his) animated nature; with anecdotes of animals; with... Steubenville, J. & B. Turnbull, 1831. 204 p. MoS. 7280

---- Le ministre de Wakefield. Traduction nouvelle, precedee d'un essai sur la vie et les ecrits d'Olivier Goldsmith, par M. Hennequin... D'après l'edition de Paris. Boston, Gray et Bowen, 1831. 211 p. IaGG; MH; OHi; RPB; WaU. 7281

---- The vicar of Wakefield; a tale. By Oliver Goldsmith, M.B. With the life of the author, by Dr. Johnson. Knoxville, Pr. at the Knoxville republican office, 1831. 208 p. MoS; T; TKL-Mc. 7282

Gollet, John.
Elephant of Siam, and the fire fiend, a magnificent eastern drama in three acts including the words of the gallopading duet. Philadelphia, Turner, c1831. 67 p. ICU; PU. 7283

Gomez Pedraza, Manuel, 1789-1851.
Manifiesto, que Manuel Gomez Pedraza, ciudadano de la républica de Méjico, dedica á sus compatriotas; ó sea Una resena de su vida pública. Nueva-Orleans, B. Levy, 1831. 129 p., 1 l. CSmH; DLC. 7284

Good, John Mason, 1764-1827.
...The book of nature. By John Mason Good... From the

last London ed. To which is now prefixed, a sketch of the author's life... New York, J. & J. Harper, 1831. 467 p. OClW; ViU. 7285

---- Memoir of Caroline Campbell ... New York, J. Emory and B. Waugh, for the Methodist Episcopal Church, 1831. 7286

Goodard, T. H.
A general history of the most prominent banks in Europe, particularly England & France, the bank of North America, the bank of the U.S. Added a statistical & comparative view of the moneyed institutions of New York & twenty four other cities of the U.S. New York, [H.C. Sleight, Clinton Hall, G. C. H. Carnill] 1831. MH-BA; NIC. 7287

Goodhue, Josiah Fletcher, 1791-1863.
The Church of Christ one. A sermon delivered at Williston, Vermont, Sabbath, July 10, 1831. ... Malone [N.Y.] Pr. by John G. Clayton, 1831. [33] p. CSmH; NN. 7288

---- ---- Burlington [Vt.] Pr. by Foote & Stacy, 1831. 33 p. CSmH; MWA; Vt; VtMidSM; VtU. 7289

Goodrich, Charles Augustus, 1790-1862.
The childs history of the United States. Designed as a first book of history for schools. Illustrated by numerous anecdotes. Boston, Carter, Hendee and Babcock, 1831. 144 p. DLC. 7290

---- ... A history of the United States of America, on a plan adapted to the capacity of youth ... By Rev. Charles A. Goodrich. Bellows Falls, Vt., J. I. Cutler & Co., 1831. 296, 20 p. CtHWatk; MDeeP; NBLiHi; OClWHi; VtMidbC. 7291

---- ---- Boston, Carter, Hendee & Co., 1831. PPeSchW. 7292

---- ---- 35th ed. Boston, Richardson, Lord & Holbrook [1831] MB; MH. 7293

---- ---- Hartford [Conn.] D. F. Robinson & Co., 1831. 432 p. IU; MoU; NoGU; PHC. 7294

---- ---- And to which is added a geographical view of the United States. New-York, D. M. Jewett, 1831. 432, 119 p. OcLWHi; WMC. 7295

---- Lives of the signers of the Declaration of Independence. Philadelphia, Thos. Desilver, jr.; Hartford, H. & F. J. Huntington, 1831. 460 p. DGU; InU; MNF; MWA; MdW; PPLT. 7296

---- New family encyclopedia; or, Compendium of useful knowledge comprehending a plain and practical view of those subjects most interesting to persons, in the ordinary professions in life. 2d imp. ed. Philadelphia, 1831. 228 p. CtY; ICU; NGlo; ViU. 7297

Goodrich, Chauncey Allen, 1790-1860.
Elements of Greek grammar. By Chauncey A. Goodrich. Used in Yale college. Heretofore pub. as the Grammar of Caspar Frederic Hachenberg. 5th ed. enl. and imp. Hartford, O. D. Cooke & co., 1831. 260 p. IEG; MBC; Nh; RPB; ViRU. 7298

---- Lessons in Greek parsing; or, outlines of the Greek grammar, divided into short portions, and illustrated by appropriate exercises in parsing. By Chauncey A. Goodrich. [New Haven? 1831] 138 p. NN; TxU-T. 7299

[Goodrich, Samuel Griswold],

1793-1860.
The child's book of American geography: designed as an easy and entertaining work for the use of beginners. Boston, Waitt & Dow, etc., 1831. 64 p. DLC; IaHA; MB; MH; MHa. 7300

---- Child's Botany. 4th ed. Boston, Carter, Hendee, & Babcock, 1831. 103 p. InNd; MH; MLanc; OO. 7301

---- An Economical Atlas. For the use of families and young persons, containing thirty-four maps, as follows: (List of maps covering both hemispheres)-To which are added various tables of populations and extent; the height of mountains, and length of rivers; canals, roads, railroads, etc.; together with views, exhibiting the style of buildings, dress, etc. in various countries. Boston, Gray & Bowen; Philadelphia, Key & Meike; Baltimore, Charles Carter, etc. [1831] CtY; MH; Nh. 7302

---- The First Book of History: For Children and Youth. By the author of Peter Parley's Tales with sixty engravings and sixteen maps. Boston, Richardson, Lord and Holbrook, 1831. 180 p. MB; MH; NNC; NTi. 7303

---- ---- New York, Collins and Hannay, 1831. 180 p. CSmH; DLC; MiU; RPB. 7304

---- Outlines of chronology, ancient and modern; being an introduction to the study of history. On the plan of Rev. David Blair. For the use of schools. Accompanied by a chart. Boston, Richardson & Lord, 1831. 232 p. CtY; MB; MH; OClW; OMC; PLFM; RPG. 7305

---- Peter Parley's method of telling about geography to children. Boston, Carter, Hendee & Babcock, 1831. MH. 7306

---- ---- Hartford, H. & F. J. Huntington, 1831. CtY; MB; MH. 7307

---- Peter Parley's tales about the islands in the Pacific Ocean ... Boston, Gray & Bowen, 1831. 144 p. DLC; IU; MBBC; OClWHi. 7308

---- Peter Parley's tales about the sun, moon, and stars. Boston, Gray & Bowen, etc., 1831. 116 p. ICU; IEN; MH. 7309

---- Peter Parley's Tales of the Sea. With many engravings. Boston, Gray & Bowen and Carter, Hendee & Babcock, 1831. [2], 142 p. DLC; ViRVal. 7310

---- A present for Peter Parley to all his Little Friends. Philadelphia. R. W. Pomeroy, 1831. 168 p. NN; NNC; PHi; PU. 7311

---- The Tales of Peter Parley about Africa. 2d ed. Boston, 1831. PHi. 7312

---- The tales of Peter Parley about America. With engravings. 7th ed. Boston, Carter, Hendee and Babcock, 1831. [9]-160 p. CtY. 7313

---- The Tales of Peter Parley about Europe. With engravings. 6th ed. Boston, Carter, Hendee & Babcock, 1831. 148 p. PPF; WaS. 7314

Goodwin, Ezra S.
An address delivered at the third anniversary of the Barnstable Peace Society, Dec. 25, 1830. By Ezra S. Goodwin... Barnstable, Press of Barnstable Journal, 1831. 23 p. MH; MeB. 7315

Gordon, Thomas Francis, 1787-1860.
The history of America. By

Thomas F. Gordon. Volumes 1st and 2d, containing the history of the Spanish discoveries prior to 1520... Philadelphia, Carey & Lea, 1831. 2 vols. CtY; LNH; MH; PU; ViU. 7316

[Gore, Catherine Grace Frances (Moody) "Mrs. Charles Gore," 1799-1861.

The Tuileries. A tale by the author of "Hungarian Tales," "Romances of real life,"... New York, J. & J. Harper, 1831. 2 v. CtHT; KOt; MMilt; PPL; RJa. 7317

Gorman, Jane.

The acts of the Associate Reformed Church in its different courts for four years in the case of...West Union, O., Pr. by... 1831. 24 p. PPPrHi. 7318

Goshen Library (Goshen, N.Y.)

Bye-laws of the Goshen Library Association, together with a catalogue of books. October 22, 1831. 20 p. NGos. 7319

The Gospel anchor... V.1-July 2, 1831- Troy, N.Y. [Pr. by J. M. Austin, etc.] 1831-2. DLC; IaU; MH-AH. 7320

The Gospel harmony; chronologically arranged in separate lessons & particularly designed for the use of Sabbath schools & Bible classes, by a committee of teachers from those institutions. Utica, William Williams, 1831. 86 p. AmSSchU; PPAmS. 7321

Gould, Jacob, 1793-1840.

Trial for libel. Circuit court; Judge Vanderpoel presiding; Jacob Gould vs Thurlow Weed [Albany, n.p., 1831] 24 p. MB; MHi; NjR. 7322

[Gould, Marcus Tullius Cicero] 1793-1860.

[The art of short-hand writing. Philadelphia, 1831] 15-60 p. NN. 7323

Goupil, Jean Martin Auguste, 1800-1837.

An exposition of the principles of the new medical doctrine, with an analysis of the theses sustained on its different parts. Trans. from the French of J. M. A. Goupil, by Josiah C. Nott. To which is appended a short essay on leeches, by the translator. Columbia, Pr. at the Times and gazette office, 1831. 371 p. GU-M; KyLoJM; LNT-M; MoU; NcD. 7324

Gracchus, pseud.

...The Question, by Gracchus ...Columbia, S.C., Pr. at the Times and Gazette office, 1831. 24 p. PPL; ScU. 7325

Graeter, Francis.

German and English phrases and dialogues, for the use of students in the German language. By Francis Graeter. Boston, Hilliard, Gray, Little & Wilkins, 1831. 216 p. ICU; MBAt; OO; PMA; VtU. 7326

Graglia, C.

Italian pocket dictionary: in two parts: 1. Italian and English: II. English and Italian. Preceded by an Italian grammar. 1st Amer. from the 14th London ed. with corr. and additions. Boston, Hilliard, Gray, Little, and Wilkins, 1831. 484 p. CtMW; GAU; MH; MeB; MeBat; NBLiHi. 7327

Graham, Isabella (Marshall), 1742-1814.

The power of faith; exemplified in the life and writings of the late Mrs. Isabella Graham of New York. 8th ed. New York, Jonathan Leavitt; Boston, Crocker & Brewster, 1831. 303 p. MAbD; MH-AH; NRU; OCiR; WBeloc. 7328

Graham, Sylvester.

Thy Kingdom Come; A discourse, on the Importance of Infant and Sunday Schools, delivered at the Crown St. Church, Philadelphia, December 13th, 1829, by Sylvester Graham. Philadelphia, Pr. by Wm. F. Geddes, 1831. 28 p. CtHWatk; ICN; MH-AH; PHi; VtMidbC. 7329

Graham, Thomas John, 1795?-1876.
A treatise on indigestive, with observations on some painful complaints originating in indigestion, as tic douloureux, nervous disorder, etc. 1st Amer., from the last London ed., rev. and enl. with notes... Philadelphia, Key & Mielke, 1831. 206 p. CtY; GDecCT; ICU; MB; PPCC. 7330

Grandfather's story of Samuel Bennett. Worcester, Dorr & Howland, 1831. 16 p. MHi. 7331

Grattan, Thomas Calley, 1792-1864.
The heiress of Bruges: a tale of the sixteen hundred. By Thos. Calley Grattan. New York, Pr. by J. & J. Harper, 1831. 216 p. CtY; FTU; MWA; NcU; RLa. 7332

---- The history of the Netherlands. Philadelphia, Carey & Lea, 1831. 300 p. DLC; DeU; PPHa; PU; ViU. 7333

---- Jacqueline of Holland: a historical tale. New York, Harper, 1831. 2 vols. CtY; MBC; NjP; PU; VtU. 7334

Gray, Francis Calley, 1790-1856.
Letter to Governor Lincoln, in relation to Harvard University. By F. C. Gray. Boston, Pr. by W. L. Lewis, from Hale's Steam-Power-Press, 1831. 48 p. CBPSR; CBPac; CtHWatk; CtY; IC; ICN; M; MB; MBC; MFiHi; MH; MNBedf; MNF; MeB; MeHi; NjR; NNS; OO; PPAmP; PPL; PPPrHi; PU; WHi. 7335

---- ---- 2d ed., with an appendix. Boston, Carter, Hendee & Babcock, 1831. 60 p. CBPac; MHi; MnHi; NNC; ScCC. 7336

---- ---- 3d ed. Boston, By Carter, Hendee and Babcock. Pr. by W. L. Lewis on Hale's Steam Press, 1831. 63 p. LNH; MeB; NNUT; OClWHi; ScC. 7337

Gray, William Waller.
Names of the members of the legislature of Virginia. Now in session at Richmond, and their respective places of abode; together with the members of the convention, the civil list, and the census of 1820 & 1830, a calendar, &c. &c. Pub. by William Waller Gray, Feb. 1831. 1831. 24 p. MdBJ. 7338

Gray hairs made happy. An interesting story for children. Providence, Pr. by H. H. Brown, 1831. 16 p. DLC; RHi. 7339

Graydon, William, 1759-1840.
Graydon's forms of conveyancing & of practice in various courts and public offices...imp. arr. & cor. by Peter Thomson & John P. Owend. Philadelphia, Walker, 1831. 2 vols. IClaw; OrU-L; PP; PU-L; PV. 7340

Great Britain.
Condensed reports of cases decided in the High court of chancery in England [1807-1839]... Philadelphia, J. Grigg, 1831-1842. 13 vols. DLC; NcD; NjP; NcU; ViU-L. 7341

---- Reports of cases argued and determined in the English courts of Common Law. With tables of the cases and principal matters. Edited by Thomas

Sergeant and Hon. Thos. M'Kean Pettitt, Esqs. of the Philadelphia Bar. Vol. XVIII. containing cases in the Common Pleas and Exchequer Chamber from Trinity term 1828 to 1829, Geo. IV. Philadelphia, P. H. Nicklin and T. Johnson, Law Booksellers, 1831. NSsSC. 7342

---- Reports of cases argued and determined in the English ecclesiastical courts [1724-18]: with tables of the cases and principal matters... Philadelphia, P. H. Nicklin and T. Johnson, 1831-[1845?] DLC; GU-L; MiDB; NcD; PP; PPB; PU-L; WaU-L. 7343

---- Reports of cases argued and determined in the High court of Chancery, during the time of Lord Chancellor Brougham. By James Russel & J. W. Myline... 1831. New York, Albany, Bank & Bros., [1831] 18 vols. DLC. 7344

---- Reports of cases argued and determined in the time of Lord Chancellor Hardwicke, from the year 1746-7 to 1755. By Francis Vesey, Senior Esq. ... By Robert Belt, Esq. of the Inner Temple, Barrister at Law. 1st Amer. from the last London ed. Philadelphia, Robt. H. Small, 1831. 2 vols. DLC; MH-L; NN; NjP; ViU. 7345

---- Reports of cases principally on practice and pleading, determined in the Court of King's bench [1770-1822] By Joseph Chitty... [Philadelphia, P. H. Nicklin and T. Johnson, 1831] 2 vols. ViU-L. 7346

---- A supplement to the reports in chancery of Francis Vesey, senior...during the time of Lord Chancellor Hardwicke; comprising corrects of statement and extracts of the decrees and orders from the Registrar's books, references to cases cited, subsequent determinations on the several points, some manuscript cases, new marginal notes and a copious index; by Robert Bett... 1st Amer. from the last London ed. Philadelphia, R. H. Small, 1831. 529 p. InU; MH; MsU; NcD; ViU; WfW-L. 7347

[Greatrake, Lawrence]
Ministers portrait of Uricl B. Chambers by a regular baptist. Mountsterling, Ky., 1831. 42 p. NHCS. 7348

Green, Ashbel, 1762-1848.
An appeal to the Presbyterian Church... By the Rev. A. Green, D.D., also review and vindication, by the Rev. N. S. Beman. With notes and appendix. New York, Daniel Appleton, 1831. 71 p. CtY; DLC; MeBat; NjPT; PHi. 7349

---- Lectures on the Shorter Catechism of the Presbyterian Church in the United States of America. Addressed to youth. By Ashbel Green, D.D. Philadelphia, Presbyterian Board of Publication and Sabbath-school work, 1831. 2 vols. NbOP. 7350

Green, Benjamin, 1796-
The true believer's vademecum, or Shakerism exposed: together with an account of the life of the author, from his birth to the period of his joining and leaving that society of people called Shakers... Concord, Pr. for the author, 1831. 68 p. MB; MPiB; MWiW; Nh; OClWHi. 7351

Green, Richard W.
Inductive exercises in English grammar, designed to give young pupils a knowledge of the first principles of language: accompanied by progressive parsing lessons. The whole intended to

to inculcate habits of thinking reasoning, and expressing thought. By Richard W. Green. 3d ed, enl. and imp. Philadelphia, Pa., Uriah Hunt, 1831. 180 p. CtHWatk; CtY; OOxM. 7352

Green, Samuel.
The practical accountant, or farmers and mechanics best method of bookkeeping; for the easy instruction of youth, designed as a companion to Daboll's arithmetic by Samuel Green. New York, W. C. Barradaile, 1831. NHem. 7353

Green, William Mercer, 1798-1887.
The influence of Christianity upon the welfare of nations. An oration, delivered at Chapel Hill, on Wednesday, June 22, 1831, the day preceding Commencement at the University of North Carolina, according to the annual appointment of the two literary societies belonging to the University. by the Rev. William Mercer Green. Hillsborough, Pr. by Dennis Heartt, 1831. 32 p. CtHWatk; NcD; NcHiC; NcU; WHi. 7354

Greenbank's periodical library, containing in the cheapest possible form, a republication of new and standard works. Philadelphia, T. K. Greenbank [1831] 2 vols. MLy. 7355

Greenfield, Mass. Boarding School for Young Men.
Report of the teachers...G., 1831. 13 p. CtY; OCHP. 7356

Greenleaf, Jeremiah.
Grammar simplified; or, An ocular analysis of the English language. By J. Greenleaf. 20th ed., corr., enl. and imp. by the author. New-York, Stereotyped by James Conner; Hartford, D. F. Robinson & co., 1831. 50 p. CtMMHi; MBAt; NSyHi. 7357

Greenwood, Frances William Pitt, Comp., 1797-1843.
A collection of Psalms and Hymns for Christian worship. 2d ed. Boston, Carter, Hendee and Babcock, 1831. [424] p. MB; MBAU; MH-AH. 7358

---- ---- 3d ed. Boston, 1831. 560 p. MH-AH; MHi; MWA; NR. 7359

---- A liturgy for the use of the church at King's Chapel in Boston; collected principally from the Book of Common Prayer. 4th ed.; with family prayers and services, and...hymns for domestic and private use, by F. W. P. Greenwood. Boston, Carter & Hendee, 1831. 381 p. CtY; LNB; MH; OCHP; PPL. 7360

Gregory, George, 1790-1853.
Elements of the Theory and Practice of Physic; by George Gregory, M.D. with notes and additions adapted to the practice of the United States, by Nathaniel Potter, M.D. Professor of the Practice of Physic in the University of Maryland, and S. Colhoun, M.D... Philadelphia, Towar, J. & D. M. Hogan; Pittsburgh, Hogan & Co., 1831. 2 vols. CtY; MBM; NIC-V; PMA; TxSaO. 7361

[Gregson, John Stanley] d. 1837.
The circle of anecdote and wit; a choice collection of pieces of humour; including many never before printed. Collected by Jeremy Gimcrack (pseud.). Boston, F. S. Hill, 1831. 108 p. CtY; MB; MH; MWA. 7362

Gretry [Andre Ernest Modiste], 1741-1813.
William Tell: a lyric drama

in two acts by Pelissier, Music by Gretry. Trans. literally by W. P. W. Baltimore, J. Coate, 1831. 47 p. MH. 7363

Griffin, Ebenezer, b. 1789.
An address, delivered at Rochester, before the Monroe County Temperance Society, at their annual meeting, January 4, 1831. By Ebenezer Griffin, Esq. Pub. by request of the Society. Rochester, Pr. by E. Peck & Co., 1831. 16 p. NRHi. 7364

Griffin, Edmund Dorr, 1804-1830.
Remains of the Rev. Edmund D. Griffin compiled by Francis Griffin; with a biographical memoir of the deceased by the Rev. John McVickar... New York, G. & C. & H. Carvill; T. & J. Swords; E. Bliss; and O. Halstead, 1831. 2 vols. CtMW; MH; NjP; RPAt; WaS. 7365

---- A series of Lectures, delivered in Park Street Church, Boston, on Sabbath Evening, by Edward D. Griffin, D.D., Pastor of Park Street Church. Boston, Nathaniel Willis, 1831. 327 p. ICP. 7366

Griffin, Richard, ed.
Specimens of the novelists and romancers, with critical and biographical notices of the authors. By Richard Griffin. New York, J. Langdon, 1831. 2 vols. CtMW; MB; MH; OCY; RPAt. 7367

[Griffith, Mrs. Mary] d. 1877.
Our neighborhood, or, Letters on horticulture and natural phenomena: interspersed with opinions on domestic and moral economy. New York, E. Bliss, 1831. 332 p. CtY; IU; MH; NGH; NjR. 7368

Grigg, John, 1792-1864.
Grigg's southern and western songster; being a choice collection of the most fashionable songs, many of which are original. New ed., greatly enl. Philadelphia, J. Grigg, 1831. 324 p. CtHWatK; DLC; PAtM; ScMar; T. 7369

Grigg's City and County almanack, for the year of our Lord 1830-1831... Philadelphia, John Grigg [etc.] [1831] 2 vols. CtY; MWA. 7370

Grigsby, Hugh Blair, 1806-1881.
Oration, pronounced, at the request of the committee of arrangements, appointed by the Norfolk Volunteers, in the new Episcopal Church, in the borough of Norfolk, on the 4th of July, 1831... Norfolk, Va., Pr. by Shields and Ashburn, for C. Hall [1831] 43 p. CSmH; MH; NcD; TxU; ViU. 7371

Grimke, Thomas Smith, 1786-1834.
Address at the celebration of the Sunday school jubilee... By Thomas Smith Grimke. Charleston, Observer office press, 1831. 20 p. MA. 7372

---- Address of Thomas S. Grimke, at a meeting in Charleston, South Carolina...March 29, 1831, to consider the resolution of the American Sunday School Union, respecting Sunday Schools in the valley of the Mississippi. Philadelphia, American Sunday School Union, 1831. CtHC; ICU; KHi; NcU; TxU. 7373

---- Oration on the advantages, to be derived from the introduction of the Bible, and of sacred literature, as essential parts of an education in a literary point of view merely from the primary school to the university delivered before the Connecticut Alpha of the B K Society, Sept. 7, 1830. (With notes). New Haven, 1831. 162 p. MH. 7374

---- Reflections on the character and objects of all science and literature, and on the relative excellence and value of religious and secular education and of sacred and classical literature: in two addresses and with an oration with additions and improvements. With an appendix...by Thomas Smith Grimke... New Haven, H. Howe, 1831. 201 p. GU; KyBC; MWA; PU; ScCC. 7375

---- Sunday School Jubilee Address at the celebration of the Sunday School Jubilee or the 50th year from the institution of Sunday Schools, by Robert Raikes: delivered at Charleston, S.C., in the hall of the Sunday school depository, on Wednesday evening, 14th of September 1831. Charleston, Observer office press, 1831. 20 p. MA; MH; NN; OCHP; ScU. 7376

Grimshaw, William, 1782-1852.

The Merchants' Law Book; being a treatise on the law of Account Render, Attachment, Bailment, Bills of Exchange and Promissory Notes, Carriers, Insurance against Fire, Letters of Credit, Partnership, Principal and Agent, Stoppage in Transit, &c. Illustrated by many thousand judicial decisions, and designed expressly for the use of Merchants in the United States. By William Grimshaw. Philadelphia, Uriah Hunt, 1831. 346 p. IaK; KyLoF; MoS; NNLI; PU-L. 7377

---- Questions adapted to Grimshaw's History of England... Rev. and imp. Philadelphia, John Grigg, 1831. 72 p. ViU. 7378

Griscom, John, 1774-1852.

Address delivered before the Newark mechanics' assocation, on their third anniversary, January 25, 1831... Newark, Pr. by William Tuttle, 1831. 39 p. CtY; ICRL; MBAt; NjR; WHi. 7379

Groton, Massachusetts Union Church.

The confession of faith, covenant and principles of discipline and practice of the Union Church in Groton, Mass(achusetts). Lancaster, Pr. by Carter, Andrews and Co., 1831. 20 p. MBAt; MH; MHi; MiD-B. 7380

Grover, William, 1752-1825.

Selections from the letters and other papers of William Grover; preceded by a biographical notice of his life. Philadelphia, T. Kite, 1831. 99 p. CtY; ICN; MH; OHi; PSC-Hi. 7381

Groves, Rev. John.

A Greek and English dictionary, comprising all the words in the writings of the most popular Greek authors; with the difficult inflections in them and in the Septuagint and new Testament... By the Rev. John Groves with corr. and additional matter, by the American editor... Boston, Hilliard, Gray and company, 1831. 616 p. A-GS; CtSoP; IaGG; PMA; ViU. 7382

Grund, Francis Joseph, 1809-1863.

An elementary treatise on Geometry, simplified for beginners not versed in algebra. Part II, containing solid geometry... By Francis J. Grund. Boston, Carter & Babcock; Baltimore, Charles Carter, 1831. 195 p. ICBB; MDeeP; MH; MeU; NNC; OO. 7383

Grundy, Felix, 1771-1846.

Speech of Mr. Grundy, of Tennessee, relative to the Post Office Department. [Washington, 1831?] 8 p. N; NcD; OClWHi. 7384

The guardian, with notes, and a general index complete in one volume. Philadelphia, J. J. Woodward, 1831. 244 p. AMob; ICMe; PHi; TNP. VtBrt. 7385

Guilford, Nathan, 1786-1854.
The Western Spelling Book; being an improvement of the American Spelling Book, by Noah Webster. Cincinnati, N. & G. Guilford, 1831. 144 p. CtY; DLC; NN; OHi. 7386

Gundrum, G.
The American Interpreter, laid down in a plain and simple manner, for the English to learn the German and German the English language, without any more assistance. New-Berlin, Pa., Composed and pub. by G. Gundrum, 1831. 96 p. CSmH; MdBSHb. 7387

---- Der Amerikanische dolmetscher, niedergelegt auf eine deutliche und wohlerständliche art, für die Englishen Deutsch und die Deutschen Englisch au lernen ohne einige andere beihülfe... New-Berlin [Pa.], Gedruck für den verfasser durch D. Hachenberg, 1831. 96 p. NjR; PHi. 7388

Gunn [John C.]
Gunn's Domestic Medicine or Poor Man's Friend. Showing the diseases of men, women and children, and expressly intended for the benefit of families. Containing a description of the medicinal roots, and herbs and how they are to be used in the cure of disease. Arranged of a new and simple plan. 2d ed. Knoxville, F. S. Heiskell, 1831. 500 p. KyU. 7389

Guy, Joseph.
Guy's elements of astronomy, and an abridgement of Keith's New Treatise on the use of globes. 1s American ed., with additions and imp. Philadelphia, Key & Mielke, 1831. 136, 173 p. MH; NPV; PPL; PPL-R; TNP. 7390

---- The Pocket cyclopaedia, or Epitome of universal knowledge; designed for senior scholars in schools, and for young persons in general, containing multifarious and useful information on numerous subjects necessary to be known by all persons, yet not to be found in books of general use in schools. Brookfield, Mass., E. & G. Merriam, 1831. 467 p. CtMW; DLC; ICMe; MWA; NbOM. 7391

H

Haberman, John.
The Christian's Companion: Containing morning & evening prayers, for every day in the week; together with other devotions. By Dr. John Haberman. To which is added, Dr. Neuman's prayer of prayers; and a collection of morning and evening hymns. Trans. from the German. Harrisburg, Pa., G. S. Peters, 1831. 144 p. InPerM. 7392

Hackley, Richard S., comp.
Legal opinions on the title of Richard S. Hackley, to lands in east Florida. New-York, Pr. by Elliott and Palmer, 1831. 88 p. DLC; FJ; NNN; PPL. 7393

Händel, Georg Fredrich, 1685-1759.
Comfort ye my people from Handel's Messiah. Arranged for the piano... by P. K. Moran. New York, Firth and Hall, 1831. 7 p. MB. 7394

---- O lovely peace. Duett [S. A.] from Judas Maccabeus. Arranged for the pianoforte or organ by P. K. Morgan. New York, Firth & Hall [1831] 5 p. MB. 7395

Hale,
Thoughts on the Right Employment of Time, Selected from the Writings of the Eminent and Pious Chief Justice Hale. No. 16. New-York, Pr. by Mahlon Day, 1831. 12 p. MWA. 7396

[Hale, James W.]
An historical account of the Siamese twin brothers, from actual observations... New-York, Pr. by Elliott and Palmer, 1831. 16 p. CtHC; CtY; MH; NN. 7397

---- ---- 2d ed. New York, Pr. by Elliot and Palmer, 1831. 16 p. MBNEH. 7398

---- ---- 3d ed. New-York, Pr. by Elliott and Palmer, 1831. 16 p. MHi; MWA; NcU; TxHuT. 7399

Hale, Salma, 1787-1866.
History of the United States, from their first settlement as colonies, to the close of the war with Great Britain in 1815... Added questions, adapted to the use of schools. [Anon.] Keene, N.H., Prentiss, 1831. 298, 24 p. MB. 7400

---- A new grammar of the English language... New-York, Collins & Hannay, 1831. 78 p. MB. MH; NNC. 7401

Hale, Mrs. Sarah Josepha (Buell), 1788-1879.
Sketches of American character...4th ed. Boston, Freeman Hunt, 1831. 287 p. CtY; KWiU; MH; Nh; RPB. 7402

[Hale, Mrs. Sarah Preston (Everett)]
Boston reading lessons for primary schools. Boston, Richardson, Lord & Holbrook, 1831. 142 p. MH; OMC. 7403

Hall, Captain Basil, 1788-1844.
Fragments to voyages and travels. Including anecdotes of a naval life; chiefly for the use of young persons. By Captain Basil Hall, R.N., F.R.S. Philadelphia, Carey & Lea, 1831. 2 vols. CU; CtY; MH; PU; RJa; ScSoh. 7404

Hall, James.
Discourse in first Presbyterian Church, Trenton, N.J. Feb. 23, 1831 on death of Susannah L. Armstrong. by J. Hall. Philadelphia, 1831. 20 p. PHi. 7405

---- The soldiers bride; and other tales. By James Hall... Philadelphia, Key and Biddle, 1831. 272 p. RPB. 7406

Hall, John.
The life of Rev. Henry Martyn...By John Hall... Philadelphia, American Sunday School Union [c 1831] 246 p. ICT; MA; MoWgT; NSyU; PPal; ScCliP. 7407

Hall, O. A.
Treatise on astronomy. New York, 1831. MB. 7408

Hall, Samuel Read, 1795-1877.
The child's assistant to a knowledge of the geography and history of Vermont. 3d ed. Montpelier, Vt., J. S. Walton, 1831. 75 p. MH; Nh; VtMidSM; VtStjA. 7409

---- The child's book of geography. By S. R. Hall... Springfield [Mass.] Merriam, Little & co.; New York, Collins and Hannay; [etc., etc.] 1831. 96 p. DLC; ICHi; MH; MPiB. 7410

---- Lectures on school-keeping. By Samuel R. Hall. 3d ed. To which is added a lecture on the construction of school-houses, with a plan. Boston, Richardson, Lord & Holbrook, 1831. 148 p. CtY; MB; Nh; OO; WHi. 7411

Hall, Silas
A sermon and charge at the ordination of Wm. W. Hall in North Marshfield, Mass., Feb. 9, 1831. Plymouth, Allen Danforth, 1831. 24 p. MNtCA; MWA; RPB. 7412

---- A sermon,...at the ordination of Rev. Timothy C. Tingley ...in Foxborough, Mass., July 14, 1831. Dedham, Mann & Tolman, 1831. 16 p. MH; RPB. 7413

Hall, Thomas H., 1733-1853.
Circular to the freemen of the 3d Congressional district of North Carolina. [Tarboro, Free Press, 1831] 8 p. CU; NcD; NcU. 7414

Hall, Willard, 1780-1875.
Defence of the American Sunday School Union against the charges of its opponents, in an address delivered at the First Anniversary of the New Castle County Sabbath School Union, March 26, 1828. Philadelphia, Pa., Sunday School Union, Pr. by John Clarke, 1831. 16 p. MNtCA. 7415

Hall, William
Statement of some of the Principal Facts which took place in the Revolutionary War, in and about the County of Barnstable on Cape Cod... [Boston, 1831] 4 p. MB; MH; PHi. 7416

---- ---- New York [1831] 4 p. PP; ScU. 7417

Halsted, Oliver.
A full and accurate account of the new method of curing dyspepsia, discovered and practised by O. Halsted. With some observations on diseases of the digestive organs. 2d ed., with plates and explanatory notes. New York, O. Halsted, 1831. 155 p. CSt; GU-M; NjP; PPBP; ViRA. 7418

Hambden, pseud.
First reflections on reading the President's message to Congress, of December 7, 1830. By "Hampden"... Washington, Pr. by Gales & Seaton, 1831. 15 p. MB; MWA; PPL; ScU. 7419

Hamet, Benengeli, the second, cid, pseud.
The dedication; or An essay on the true modern Caesar. By Cid Hamet Benengeli the second. Mutato nomine, de te fabula narratur. Baltimore, Sands & Neilson, 1831. 76 p. DLC; MdBLC; MdHi; PPL. 7420

Hamilton, Alexander, 1757-1804.
The Federalist, on the new constitution, written in the year, 1788, by Alexander Hamilton, James Madison and John Jay, with an appendix, containing the original Articles of Confederation; the letter of General Washington as president of the convention, to the president of congress; the Constitution of the United States and the amendments to the Constitution. A new ed., with a table of contents, and index. The numbers written by Mr. Madison corrected by himself. Washington, Thompson & Homans, 1831. 420 p. DLC; InNd; LNDiA; ViU; WHi. 7421

Hamilton, James, 1786-1857.
The introductory address of Governor Hamilton, at the first meeting of the Charleston State Rights and Free Trade Association of South Carolina, held at Lege's Long-Room on August 1, 1831. [Latin quot.] Charleston, Pr. by E. J. Van Brunt, for the association, 1831. 15 p. ICU; MHi; NcD; ScHi; TxU. 7422

---- National and State rights. See McDuffie, George, 1790-1851.

---- Speech of Governor Hamilton, before the State rights and free trade association of Charleston, on the 12th September, 1831. Columbia, Times, 1831. 24 p. NcD; RPB. 7423

Hamilton, John.
A sermon on the subject and mode of baptism...Harrisburg, Pr. by Jacob Baab, 1831. 15 p. OSW. 7424

Hamilton, Thomas, 1789-1842.
Annals of The Peninsular Campaigns... Philadelphia, Carey & Lea, 1831. 3 vols. CtY; IU; MiU; NN; RPA. 7425

---- The youth and manhood of Cyril Thornton...a new ed. in 2 volumns. New York, J. & J. Harper, 1831. 2 vols. CtHT; ICU; LNB; MB; NjR; TxU. 7426

Hamilton, William T.
Infant baptism a scriptural ordinance and baptism by sprinkling lawful. Newark, Wm. Tuttle, 1831. 116 p. DLC; GDecCT; IEG; NjR; PPLT. 7427

Hamlin, Lorenzo F.
English grammar in lectures. Schenectady, N.Y., S. Wilson, etc., etc., 1831. 108 p. MH; NSchHi; WU. 7428

Hammond, Thomas, 1791-1880.
Journal of Thomas Hammond at the church family, Harvard, Mass., 1831-1879 (of the arrivals and departures of visitors, ministry, etc.) 206 p. Manuscript. 206 p. OClWHi. 7429

Hampden, pseud.
The genuine book of nullification: being a true--not an apocryphal--history, chapter and averse, of the several examples of the recognition and enforcement of that sovereign state remedy, by the different states of this confederacy, from 1798 down to the present day. (As originally pub. in the Charleston mercury.) To which are added the opinions of distinguished statesmen, on state rights doctrines. By Hampden... Pub. at the request of the State rights association. Charleston, Pr. by E. J. Van Brunt, 1831. 155 p. ICU; MB; NjP; RPB; ScU; WHi. 7430

Hampden Almanac, and Housewife's Companion for 1832. By Isaac Bickerstaff, Jun. Springfield, Mass., Pr. at the Office of the Hampden Whig [1831] MHi; MWA; NIC. 7431

Hampshire Education Society.
Report of the directors of the Hampshire Education Society, auxiliary to the American Education Society, October 12, 1831. Northampton, Pr. by T. W. Shepard, 1831. 12 p. AAS. 7432

Hampshire Sabbath School Union.
An Address of the Board of directors of The Hampshire Sabbath School Union, to the friends of Sabbath schools within the county. Northampton, Pr. by T. W. Shepard, 1831. 12 p. MWA. 7433

Hamton, James.
Narrative of the life & religious exercises of James Hamton, late of Bucks county, Pennsylvania. Together with diaries, soliloquies, essays & letters, written by himself. Philadelphia, W. Sharpless, 1831. 111 p. IaOskW; PHi; PPM; PSC-Hi. 7434

Hanaford, William G.
Lectures on chemistry, with familiar directions for performing experiments with a small apparatus. To which are added questions for the examination of scholars...By W. G. Hanaford,

M.D. Boston, Richardson, Lord and Holbrook, 1831. DLC; IEG; MWA; NNC; NbU. 7435

Handel and Haydn Society, Boston.
The Boston Handel and Haydn Society collection of church music; being a selection of the most approved psalm and hymn tunes, anthems, sentences, chants, etc. together with many beautiful extracts from the works of Haydn, Mozart, Beethoven, and other eminent composers... edited by Lowell Mason. 10th ed. with additions and imp. Boston, Richardson, Lord & Holbrook, 1831. 357 p. ICP; MeB; RPB; TxU. 7436

Handel harmony; a selection of sacred music from the best authors, adapted for public or private devotion. Boston, Perkins and Marvin, 1831. 301 p. CtY; NNUT; NhD. 7437

Handy, Jairus.
A Selection of Hymns, for Conference Meetings, designed for the use of Baptist Churches. By Jairus Handy. Buffalo, Steele & Faxon, 1831. 300 p. 7438

Hanning, John.
Dignity of the human character... Bedford, Gettsy [1831] PPPrHi. 7439

Hanson, Charles W.
Opinion of the law of warranty, by Judge Hanson of Baltimore. Baltimore, Lucas and Deaver, 1831. 32 p. DLC; Md; MdHi; N; PPL. 7440

Happy days. Part first. By the author of "Helen and Maria," and "The Happy Family." 2d ed. Boston, Gray and Bowen, 1831. 50 p. MHa. 7441

Hardy, Robert Spence, 1803-1868.
Travels in the Holy Land. New York, 1831. InCW. 7442

Harlan, Richard.
Description of the fossil bones of the megalonyx discovered in "white cave," Kentucky. [Philadelphia] 1831. 20 p. Ma-H; MH-Z; PPAmP. 7443

Harlem library, New York.
A catalogue of books... New York, J. Post, 1831. NN. 7444

Harlow, Samuel.
The botanist & physician; containing a description of the principal active medicinal plants found in the middle and northern states of America... Kingston, N.Y., Pr. by Wm. Culley, 1831. 151 p. CSmH; MWelC; NBMS; NNNBG. 7445

An harmony of the confessions of faith of the principal Christian churches in Europe and America, on the fundamental overtures of the gospel... Utica, Wm. Williams, 1831. 304 p. CtHC; MA; MeBat; NjP; OO. 7446

Harper [William], 1790-1847.
An address to a public meeting, of the citizens of Union District. Columbia, Times & Gazette Office, 1831. 48 p. PPAmP; ScC. 7447

Harpham, S.
An outline of the history and chronology of the world, from the creation to the present time. Cincinnati, O., S. Harpham, c1831. OClWHi. 7448

Harris, Moses Titcomb.
A sermon delivered at Alna, Me., March 6, 1831, by Moses Harris. Portland, A. Shirley, 1831 18 p. MH-AN; MeBat; P;

PHi; RPB. 7449

Harris, Thomas, of Baltimore.

Modern entries, or Approved precedents, of declarations, pleadings, entries, and writs, to which are prefixed forms of affidavits, references, awards and certificates, and select precedents in conveyancing, comprising all that is valuable in compilation of the late Thomas Harris, esquire, newly arranged, with additions and improvements, by Hugh Davey Evans... Baltimore, Lucas and Deaver, 1831-32. 2 vols. GU-L; ICLaw; LNT-L; MdHi; Tx-SC. 7450

Harris, Thomas, 1784-1861.

An oration delivered before the Philadelphia medical society, February 19, 1831. By Thos. Harris... Philadelphia, Pr. by J. Kay, jun. & co., for the society, 1831. 28 p. DSG; IEN-N; MH-M; PPM; PU. 7451

Harrison, John Pollard, 1796-1849.

Lectures on the responsibilities of the medical profession by John P. Harrison, M.D. Louisville, Ky., Pr. by W. W. Worsley, 1831. 11 p. CSmH; DNLM; DSG; MBCo. 7452

Harrison, William Henry.

An Address, delivered before the Hamilton County Agricultural Society, at their Annual exhibition, held on the 15th and 16th of June, 1831. by Gen. William H. Harrison. Cincinnati, Hamilton County Agricultural Society, 1831. 26 p. InHi; OClWHi; OHiML; PHi. 7453

Harrod, John J., comp.

The academical reader, comprising selections from the most admired authors, designed to promote the love of virtue, piety, and patriotism... Comp. by John J. Harrod... Baltimore, J. J. Harrod, 1831. 324 p. MH; MdBE; MiD-B; PPM. 7454

---- Compilation of hymns, adapted to public and social divine worship. 3d ed. Baltimore, J. J. Harrod, 1831. WaSp. 7455

---- The new and most complete collection of camp, social, and prayer meeting hymns and spiritual songs, now in use. Compiled by John J. Harrod. 2d ed. Baltimore, J. J. Harrod, 1831. 318 p. NNUT. 7456

---- A review of the constitution and discipline of the Methodist Protestant church, by a layman. Baltimore, John J. Harrod, 1831. 36 p. MdBP; MdHi; PPL; TxDaM. 7457

Hart, Cyrus Wadsworth.

Colloquy on the immortality of the soul, with an essay on prudence. To which is added, a love touch. By C. W. Hart. Steubenville, Pr. by James Wilson, 1831. 60 p. CSmH; KMC; NN. 7458

[Hart, Julia Catherine (Beckwith),] 1796-1867.

Tonnewonte, or The adopted son of America. A tale, containing scenes from real life. By an American... Exeter, B. H. Meder, 1831. 312 p. CtY; DLC; KyU; MiU; NNC. 7459

Hartford, Conn., Institute of living.

Seventh report of the Medical visitors of the Connecticut Retreat for the insane. Presented to the Society May 1831. With a tabular view commencing 1st April 1830, and ending 1st April 1831. Hartford, Pr. by Hudson and Skinner, 1831. 5 p. Ct; NNAM; PPPrHi; TxU. 7460

---- Second Church of Christ.

A brief summary of Christian doctrine & a form of covenant adopted by the South church in Hartford & publicly read on the admission of members, to which is added a historical sketch of the church & a catalogue of the members. Hartford, 1831. 28 p. Ct; CtSoP; MBC. 7461

Hartford County [Conn.] Temperance Society.
Annual report of the executive committee. (No.) 1. Hartford, 1831. NN. 7462

Harvard University.
Catalogue. Cambridge, Hilliard & Brown, 1831. 36 p. MS. 7463

---- Catalogue of students attending medical lectures. 1831. Harvard University. IEN-D. 7464

---- A catalogue of the maps and charts in the library of Harvard University in Cambridge, Mass. ...Cambridge, Pr. by E. W. Metcalf & co., printers to the university, 1831. 224 p. InCW; Nh; PPAmP; ScU. 7465

---- Statutes... relative to the degree of doctor in medicine. 1831. 8 p. MB; PU. 7466

---- Subjects of the Bowdoin prize dissertations from 1831. [Cambridge] 1831. RPB. 7467

---- Treasurer's Report, etc. (A collection of the annual reports and statements of the treasurer, from 1831 to 1842, inclusive.) 12 parts (Cambridge, 1831-42.) MB; MBAt; MdBJ. 7468

---- Divinity School.
Order of exercises at the exhibition, 1831. MBAt. 7469

Hastings, Thomas, 1784-1872.
The juvenile instructor for the use of teachers in infant, Sabbath and primary schools. Utica, Wm. Williams, 1831. NNUT. 7470

---- Musica sacra, or Utica and Springfield collections united: consisting of psalm and hymn tunes, anthems, and chants, arranged for two, three, or four voices, with a figured bass for the organ or piano forte. By Thomas Hastings and Solomon Warriner. 9th rev. ed.--with additions and imp. Utica, W. Williams, 1831. 300 p. CtMW; DLC; MS; NBuG; NUT. 7471

---- Selections from Musica sacra. [9th ed.] Pub. expressly for the Seneca county church music association, Utica, 1831. CtY. 7472

Haverhill Academy. Haverhill, Mass.
Catalogue 1831. MH. 7473

Hawes, Joel, 1789-1867.
Lectures to young men on the formation of character etc., originally addressed to the young men of Hartford and New Haven and pub. at their united request. By Joel Hawes. Hartford, Cooke & Co., 1831. 172 p. ICRL; MH; RPB; VtU; WHi. 7474

Hawes, Josiah Taylor.
Address before the Falmouth Temperance Society. Portland, 1831. 22 p. MBC. 7475

Hawes [Noyes Payson]
The United States spelling book and English Orthoepist; being an easy introduction to the English language and exhibiting the orthography and pronunciation of Walker, Hallowell, Glazier, Masters and Co., Union, Day, Bachelder and Co., 1831. BrMus. 7476

[Hawks, Francis Lister] 1798-1886.

American Historical Tales for Youth. New York, 1831. 204, 177, 174 p. (Sabin 1099) 7477

---- The history of New England, illustrated by tales, sketches, anecdotes, and adventures... By Lambert Lilly, schoolmaster (pseud.) Boston, W. Hyde, 1831. 184 p. CtY; DLC; ICCB; MWA; RPB. 7478

---- A narrative of events connected with the rise and progress of the Protestant Episcopal Church in Virginia. New York, 1831. NN. 7479

---- The story of the American revolution, illustrated by tales, sketches and anecdotes... By Lambert Lilly, schoolmaster (pseud.) Philadelphia, Key & Meilke, 1831. 204 p. DLC; MdBS; OClWHi; PPi. 7480

Hay, George, 1729-1811.
Devout Christian instructed in the faith of Christ, from the written word. By the Rt. Rev. George Hay. 1s Amer. ed. Philadelphia, Eugene Cumminskey, 1831. 2 vol. in 1. 412 p. MB; MWA; NNerC; OCMtSM; PU. 7481

Hayne, Isaac William, 1809- .
An oration, delivered in the Presbyterian Church in Columbia, on the Fourth of July, 1831. By Isaac William Hayne... Pub. by request of the citizens. Columbia, S.C., Pr. at the Times and Gazette office, 1831. 15 p. PPAmP; ScU. 7482

Hayne, Robert Y[oung], 1791-1839.
An oration, delivered in the Independent or Congregational church, Charleston... Charleston, A. E. Miller, 1831. 47 p. CtY; DLC; ICU; LNH; ScC; ViU. 7483

Haynes [Charles Eaton], 1784-1841.
Speech Mr. Haynes of Georgia, delivered in the House of representatives, January 21, 1831, in reply to Mr. Everett, of Massachusetts, on the Indian question. Washington[!] Pr. by D. Green, 1831. 13 p. DLC; NN. 7484

---- Speech of Mr. Haynes... (in the House of Representatives, Jan. 11, 1831) on his motion to reduce the duty on brown sugar. Washington, Gales & Seaton, 1831. 19 p. DLC; NN. 7485

Hays, Isaac, 1796-1879, ed.
Select medico-chirurgical transactions; a collection of the most valuable memoirs read to the medico-chirurgical societies of London and Edinburgh. Edited by Isaac Hays... Philadelphia. E. L. Carey and A. Hart, 1831. 420 p. CtY; IU-M; MdBJ-W; MiU; MoSU-M. 7486

Hayward, James, 1786-1866.
Report on the proposed railroad between Boston and Ogdenburgh. by James Hayward. Boston, Carter Hendee & Babcock, 1831. 46 p. CSt; DLC; MB; NjP; VtU. 7487

Hazen, Edward.
Das deutsche Sinnbildliche A.B.C. Büchlein, oder erstes buch für kinder besonders eingerichtet um den unterricht der jugend leicht und angenehm zu machen. Von E. Hazen... Vermehrt mit einem zweiter buche, enthaltend: weitere buchstabir- und lese-uebungen. Philadelphia, Denny und Walker, 1831. 72 p. DLC; MiU-C; P. 7488

---- ---- Philadelphia, W. W. Walter, 1831. 36 p. PHi. 7489

---- The Speller and Definer; or, Class Book, No. 2. Designed to answer the purposes of a spelling book, and to supersede the necessity of the use of a dictionary as a class book. By E. Hazen. Stereotyped by J. Howe, Philadelphia. New York, McElrath & Bangs; Hartford, Conn., D. F. Robinson & Co., and Denny & Walker and David Clark, Philadelphia; Baltimore, Armstrong & Plas-Kitt, and Cashing & Sons, 1831. 215 p. CSt; MA; MH; OHi; OKentC. 7490

Heath, William. See Pry, Paul (pseud.)

Heber, Amelia (Shipley)
Biography of Reginald Heber, Lord Bishop of Calcutta. Abridged for the use of young persons. Boston, Leonard C. Bowles, 1831. 352 p. IAIS; IEG; MBAt; MHi; N. 7491

Hedge, Levi, 1766-1844.
Elements of Logick; or a summary of the General Principles and different modes of reasoning. By Levi Hedge, LL.D. Professor of Natural Religion, Moral Philosophy, and Civil polity in Harvard University. Stereotype ed. Boston, Hilliard, Gray, Little & Wilkins, 1831. 178 p. DLC; LNP; NcD; OBerB; VtU. 7492

Heidelberg, catechism. English.
Heidelberg catechism; or, Method of instruction in the Christian religion, as the same is taught in the Reformed Churches ...tr. from the German. Philadelphia, G. W. Mentz & Sons, 1831. 71 p. HSMontgCo; PPLT; PPPrHi. 7493

Heiner, Henry.
Gesundheits-Schatzkammer; oder kurze, deutliche und richtige Anweisung zur Erhaltung der Gesundheit und Abwendung mancher Kravkheiten... Für Deutsche ganz deutlich und fasslich eingerich tet, und denselben zum nütlichen Gebrauch wohlmeinend anempfohlen und gekidmet. Lancaster [Pa.] Bör. 1831. 118 p. CtY-M; DNLM; MH; NNNAM; PHi. 7494

A help to the acts of the apostles. See American Sunday School Union.

Hemans, Mrs. Felicia Dorothea (Browne).
The poetical works of Hemans, Heber and Pollok. Stereotyped. Philadelphia, J. Crissy, etc., 1831. MH; RPB. 7495

---- ---- Philadelphia, J. Grigg, 1831. 43, 79, 348 p. DeWi; IU; KyDC; RPB; ViU. 7496

---- Songs of the affections, with other poems. By Felicia Hemans ... Philadelphia, Carey & Lea, 1831. 267 p. GDecCT; ICBB; LNL; NNUT; RPAt. 7497

Hemingway, Joseph.
History of the city of Chester, from its foundation to the present time; with an account of its antiquities, curiosities, local customs, peculiar immunities; and a concise political history... by ... Chester, Pr. by J. Fletcher, 1831. 2 vols. CtY; DLC; ICN; MB; OCl. 7498

Henderson, Ebenezer, 1784-1858.
Iceland; or, The journal of a residence in that island, during the years 1814 and 1815...by Ebenezer Henderson... Abridged from the 2d Edinburgh ed. Boston, Perkins & Marvin, 1831. 252 p. CtMW; GDecCT; KyLx; PHC. 7499

Henry, Joseph, 1797-1878.

On the application of the principle of the galvanic multiplier to electro-magnetic apparatus and also to the development of great magnetic power in soft iron with a small galvanic element. [New Haven? 1831] 12 p. MB; NN. 7500

Henry, Matthew, 1662-1714.
The communicant's companion or "Instructions and Helps for the Right receiving of the Lord's Supper," by Matthew Henry. 10th ed. Boston, 1831. 280 p. GDecCT; NN; RNHi. 7501

---- An Exposition of the Old and New Testament: Wherein each chapter is summed up in its content...by Matthew Henry. Ed. by The Rev. George Burder and the Rev. Joseph Hughes, A. M. with the life of the author by the Rev. Samuel Palmer. New York, John P. Haven; Boston, Peirce & Parker; Philadelphia, Towar, J. & D. M. Hogan; Pittsburgh, Hogan & co., 1831. 1181 p. ABBS; CtY; MBerl; TxAuTC; WvED. 7502

---- A Method for Prayer. Philadelphia, Towar, J. & D. M. Hogan, 1831. 233 p. NcCJ; PPM. 7503

---- A sermon, entitled, "disputes reviewed." By Matthews Henry. Philadelphia, 1831. NjPT; PPPrHi; PLT; PU. 7504

Henry, William, 1774-1836.
The elements of experimental chemistry. By William Henry. 11th ed. Philadelphia, Robert Desilver, 1831. 2 vols. Ia; LVP; MH; PPi; ViU. 7505

Henshaw, David, 1791-1852.
Remarks upon the Bank of the United States, being on examination of the Report of the committee of Ways and Means, Made to Congress, April, 1830. By David Henshaw, Esq. Boston, Pr. by True and Greene, 1831. 47 p. ICU; MBAt; NNC; PHi; WU. 7506

Henshaw, John Prentiss Kewley, 1792-1852.
The apostolic ministry: views of Calvin and the early Presbyterians, Wesley, Clarke and others, upon the apostolical succession... New York, Protestant Episcopal Tract Society [183-?] 26 p. WHi. 7507

---- The communicant's guide; or, An introduction to the sacrament of the Lord's Supper. By J. P. K. Henshaw, D.D. rector of St. Peter's church, Baltimore. Baltimore, J. N. Toy and W. R. Lucas, 1831. 227 p. MBAt; MBD; MDBD; MdBP; MdBe; MH-AH; MDBS; PPL-R; ViAl; VtU. 7508

Hentz, Nicholas Marcellus, 1797-1856, comp.
A classical French reader; selected from the best writers of that language, in prose and poetry; preceded by an introduction, designed to facilitate the study of the rudiments of the French. And attended with notes, explanatory of idioms, etc. throughout the work... Compiled for the use of the Round Hill school, by N. M. Hentz... In two parts. Boston, Richardson, Lord, and Holbrook, 1831. 270 p. KyLo; MB; MnHi; NjR; TxU-T. 7509

The Herald of truth; devoted to liberal Christianity, science, literature, and miscellaneous intelligence. Vol. 1, no. 1-52, Jan. 17-Dec. 24, 1831. Philadelphia, M. T. C. Gould, 1831. 414 p. CHtWatk; MdBJ; MnU. 7510

Herbert, Thomas.
The republican hymn book containing a new and original set of hymns and spiritual songs, suited to be sung at society meetings,

family worship, public and social prayer meetings, etc. Cincinnati journal office, pub. for the author, 1831. RPB. 7511

Hermann, pseud.
Letters which have appeared in the Banner of the Constitution, addressed to the editor, under the signature of Hermann. Philadelphia, Pr. by T. W. Ustick, 1831. 47 p. CU; DLC; PPAmP; ScU; ViU. 7512

Herrick's Almanac. See The National Calendar.

Herschel, John Frederick William, 1792-1871.
Discourse on the study of natural philosophy. By John Frederick William Herschel. Philadelphia, 1831. MA; PPWa; PWa. 7513

---- The general nature and advantages of the study of the physical sciences. (Boston Society for the Diffusion of Useful Knowledge, the American Library, etc. 1831). Boston, Stimpson & Clapp, 1831. V 1 p. [267]-320. CtY-M; MH. 7514

---- A preliminary discourse on the study of Natural Philosophy. By John Frederick William Herschel, Esq., A. M. Philadelphia, Carey & Lea, 1831. 279 p. CU; DLC; MeLewB; NNC; OOxM; PV. 7515

Hersey, John.
The importance of small things; or, A plain course of self-examination. To which is added, Signs of the times. By John Hersey... Georgetown, D.C., Rind's press, 1831. 227 p. CSmH; ViRU; ViU. 7516

Hervey, James.
Meditations and contemplations, by the Reverend James Hervey ... Together with the life of the author... New-York, John H. Turney, 1831. 2 vols. PSC-Hi; TBriK. 7517

Hervey, William, 1799-1832.
The Spirit of Missions. A sermon preached in Williamstown, Dec. 13, 1829. By Wm. Hervey, A. M. ... Williamstown, Pr. by Ridley Bannister, 1831. 24 p. CtY; MWiW; MnHi; NIC; RPB. 7518

Hicks, Edward, 1780-1849.
Sermon delivered by Edward Hicks, at Friends' Meeting, Rose Street, on First Morning, 11th mo. 21st, 1830. Taken in shorthand by Edward Hopper. 2d ed. New York, Isaac T. Hopper, 1831. 24 p. MH-AH; PSC-Hi. 7519

Hicks, Elias, 1748-1830.
The answers, by Elias Hicks to the six queries addressed to him, with his declarations upon the same points, on other occasions, contrasted with each other, and with the doctrines of the Society of Friends. New-York, Pr. by Mahlon Day, 1831. 32 p. MH; MWA; MiD-B; PSC-Hi; VtU. 7520

---- Two sermons and a prayer, delivered at Friends' Meeting Houses in New York, 1st mo. 31st. 1830... New York, Isaac T. Hopper, 1831. 32 p. DLC; MiD-B; NjR; OHi; RPB. 7521

[Hildreth, Hosea] 1782-1835.
An abridged history of the United States of America. For the use of schools. Intended as a sequel of Hildreth's View of the United States [anon.] Boston, Carter, Hendee & Babcock, 1831. 248 p. DLC; KyLa; MH; MnHi; NNC. 7522

---- A book for Massachusetts children, in familiar letters from a father, for the use of families and schools. 2d ed. Boston, Hilliard, Gray, Little and Wilkins,

1831. 142 p. DLC; MB; MHi; NNC; TxU-T. 7523

---- A view of the U.S., for the use of schools and families. 2d ed. Boston, Carter, Hendee & Babcock; Baltimore, C. Carter, 1831. 162 p. DLC; MB; MH; MNBedF; NhD. 7524

Hill, A.
Ne raorihwadogenhti ne shongwayaner Yesis Keristus, jinihorihoten ne Royatadogenhti Matthew. ... Gospel of our Lord and Saviour Jesus Christ according to St. Matthew, tr. into the Mohawk language, by A. Hill, and corr. by J. A. Wilkes, jr., Grand River, U. C. New York, 1831. CTHWatk. 7525

Hill, Alonzo.
Practical Error, and the Test of True Holiness. A sermon, delivered at the ordination of Rev. Josiah Moore, as Pastor of the First Church and Society in Athol, December 8, 1830. By Alonzo Hill, Junior, Minister of the Second Congregational Society in Worcester. Pub. by request. Worcester, Spooner and Church, 1831. 39 p. ICMe; MHi; MiU; OClWHi. 7526

[Hill, George] 1796-1871.
The ruins of Athens, with other poems... Washington, Thompson and Homans, 1831. 111 p. CtY; IU; MnU; NbU; RPB. 7527

Hill, Ira, 1783 ca. 1838.
Antiquities of America explained. By Ira Hill. Hagerstown, Pr. by W. D. Bell, 1831. 131 p. DLC; IaHA; MdBE; NNP; PBL; PHi. 7528

Hill and Barton vs. Upham, Timothy.
Report of the trial. Concord, 1831. Nh. 7529

Hilliard, Francis.
An address, delivered before the Lowell Temperance Society, Jan. 2, 1831. By Francis Hilliard. Pub. by request. Lowell, Pr. by T. Billings, 1831. 21 p. MHi; MWA; MeHi; NN; RPB. 7530

Hilliard, Gray & Co.
A list of works in press, and books. Boston, Hilliard, Gray & Co., January 1831. MHi. 7531

Hind, John, 1796-1866.
The principles of the differential calculus: with its application to curves and curve surfaces designed for the use of students in the University by John Hind... 3d ed. Cambridge, 1831. 525 p. DAU. 7532

Hinds, John see Badcock, John, pseud.

Hinton, John Howard, 1791-1873.
The means of a religious revival. By John Howard Hinton, M. A. ...With an introductory essay. Boston [Lincoln & Edmands, 1831] 103 p. DLC; ICU; OMC; PCA; ViRU. 7533

---- ---- 2d ed. Boston, Lincoln & Edmands, 1831. 90 p. GDecCT; GEU; IAlS; ICBB; ICP; MBC; MH-AH; MMeT; MoU; NbCrD; NjPT; OO. 7534

Hints for conversing with children of Infant Schools, upon the texts of Scripture hung round their room. by the author of Bible stories," &c. Boston, Munroe & F., 1831. 68 p. MB. 7535

Hints on scriptural instruction, designed to promote the voluntary study ...with questions on the scriptural proofs...and an historical appendix. Philadelphia, Thomas Kite, 1831. 101 p. CtHWatK; InRChF; MNBedf; NcD; PHC;

PLOcHi. 7536

Hints to a fashionable lady. By a physician. New York, Charles S. Frances; Boston, Munroe & Frances, 1831. 242 p. CRedwS; DLC; MdBP; OMC; PU. 7537

Hirsch, Meyer, 1765-1851.
A collection of arithmetical and algebraic problems and formulae; by Meier Hirsch: tr. from the original German, and adapted to the use of the American student. By Francis J. Grund... Boston, Carter, Hendee & Babcock, 1831. 340 p. DLC; ICU; MoS; PU; TNP; WU-WA. 7538

An historical eulogium on Don Hippolito Ruiz Lopez... Trans. from the Spanish. (Trans. by H. Hatcher). Salisbury, 1831. 55 p. CtY. 7539

An historical review of the rise, progress, present state & prospects, of the silk culture, manufacture, and trade, in Europe & America. Being an article extracted from the American quarterly review for December, 1831. Philadelphia, Pr. by L. R. Bailey, 1831. 34 p. DLC; MB; PPL. 7540

History of Constantious and Pulchera; or, Virtue rewarded. To which is added, Love and generosity. A tale founded on facts. Exeter, W. C. & S. Hardy, Sawyer and Meder, prs., 1831. 118 p. CtY; NNC; Nh-Hi; ViU. 7541

History of Massachusetts. Earliest Period and Present. Boston, Munroe & Francis, 1831. 180 p. NICLA. 7542

The history of Northampton and its vicinity; brought down to the present time. 2d ed. rev. Northampton, J. Birdsall, 1831. 152 p. DLC. 7543

History of the American Baptist African and Haytian Missions. For the use of Sabbath schools. By the author of Philip Everhard, or history of the Baptist Indian Missions. Rev. by the publishing committee. Boston, Pr. for T. R. Marvin, for the Massachusetts Sabbath School Union, 1831. 70 p. DLC; ICP; NRAB; PCA. 7544

History of the Bible. Bridgeport, Pr. by J. B. & L. Baldwin, 1831. 192 p. CtY; KyBgW; MB; NBuG; OClWHi. 7545

History of the Bible. New London, W. & J. Bolles, 1831. 192 p. CtNWchA; FCor; NN; NNC; NNP. 7546

The history of the English Bible with reflections. New York, American Tract Society [1831?] 36 p. DLC; NNC. 7547

A history of the most distinguished martyrs, in various ages and countries of the world; embracing accounts of their sufferings and death, with other interesting particulars. Compiled from the most authentic documents... Philadelphia, A. Salisbury, 1831. 528 p. MoCgSV; OClWHi; RPB. 7548

The History of the Pilgrims, or, A Grandfather's Story of the First Settlers of New England. 5th ed. Boston, Pub. by the Massachusetts Sabbath School Society, c1831. 142 p. CU; DLC; MH-AH; OCHP; ViU. 7549

A history of the revolutions in Europe since the downfall of Napoleon; comprising those of France, Belgium and Poland... By a counsellor at law. Hartford, S. Hanmer, Jun., 1831.

408 p. CtY; GColu; LNH; MWA; NGH. 7550

Hitchcock, Edward, 1793-1864.
Dyspepsy forestalled and resisted; or, Lectures on diet, regimen, and employment; delivered to the students of Amherst college, Spring term, 1830. By Edward Hitchcock... 2d ed. corr. and enl. by the addition of an address delivered before the Mechanical association in Andover theological institution, Sept. 21, 1830, and an appendix of notes. Amherst, J. S. & C. Adams; New York, J. Leavitt; [etc., etc.] 1831. 452 p. CtHC; DSG; MB; NjMD; PPCP; ViU. 7551

---- The geology and scenery of Massachusetts. (n.p.), c 1831. CTHWatk. 7552

---- The physical culture adapted to the times. An address delivered before the mechanical association, in Andover theological seminary. By Edward Hitchcock. Amherst, [Mass.] J. S. and C. Adams, 1831. DSG; MBC; NN; Nh; PPPrHi. 7553

Hitchcock, Ira Irvine, 1793-1868.
Key of Hitchcock's New Method of Teaching book-keeping. Baltimore, Hitchcock, 1831. 56 p. MB. 7554

---- Ledger of Hitchcock's New Method of teaching book-keeping. Pub. by the author, 1831. 40 p. CtY; MH; MH-BA. 7555

---- A new method of teaching book-keeping... accompanied by a key, by the assistance of which instructers are enabled to teach this art with facility and success to youth of proper age and capacity; and adult persons to acquire a knowledge of it without the help of a teacher; the whole comprised in fifteen lessons, and the rules and instructions exemplified in two sets of books kept by double entry. To which are added (in the key) specimens, showing the forms of the most important auxiliary books, connected, as such, with the preceding sets. 6th ed. By I. Irvine Hitchcock... Baltimore, Pub. by the author, 1831. 42 p. CtY; MH. 7556

Hmds, John. See Badcock, John, fl. 1816-1830.

Hobart, John Henry, 1775-1830.
The candidate for confirmation instructed, in a sermon explaining the office of confirmation; with suitable prayers. By John Henry Hobart. 3d ed. New York, Protestant Episcopal Tract Society, 1831. 56 p. DLC; NBLiHi; NcU. 7557

---- A Companion for the Altar; or Week's Preparation for the Holy Communion: consisting of a short explanation of The Lord's Supper, and meditations and prayers proper to be used before and during the receiving of the Holy communion; according to the form prescribed by the Protestant Episcopal Church in the United States of America. By John Henry-Hobart, D.D. Bishop of the Protestant Episcopal Church in the State of New-York. Stereotyped by A. Chandler. New-York, T. & J. Swords, 1831. OCX; ViRut. 7558

---- A companion for the book of common prayer, containing an explanation of the service. By John Henry Hobart, D.D. 4th ed., with additions. New York, Protestant Episcopal Tract Society, 1831. 83 p. MdBD. 7559

---- A Companion for the Festivals and Fasts of the Protestant Episcopal Church in the United

States of America principally selected and altered from Nelson's Companion for the festivals and fasts of the Church of England. with Forms of Devotion. By John Henry Hobart, D.D. Bishop of the Protestant Episcopal Church in the State of New York. 4th ed. Stereotyped by A. Chandler. New York, T. & J. Swords, 1831. 331 p. MeLewB; NTEW; OLiS; WKenHi. 7560

[Hobart, Nathaniel]
Life of Emanuel Swedenborg, with some account of his writings, together with a brief notice of the rise and progress of the New church. Boston, Allen & Goddard, 1831. 188 p. CtY; ICMe; OUrC; RPB; VtNofN. 7561

Der Hoch-Deutsche Americanische Calender, auf das jahr 1832... zum achtundvierzigstenmal herausgegeben. Germantaun, gedruckt und zu haben bey M. Billmeyer [1831] [34] p. MWA; P; WHi. 7562

Hodges, Richard Manning, 1794-1878.
An address, delivered before the Bridgewater society for the promotion of temperance. Jan. 4th, 1831. By R. M. Hodges... Boston, Carter, Hendee and Babcock, 1831. 15 p. MBAT; MWA; MWHi; NCH; NNUT; VtU. 7563

---- A sermon delivered before the Congregational Society in West-Bridgewater, 27th February, 1831, the Lord's Day after the interment of their minister, the Rev. John Reed, D.D. By R. M. Hodges, minister of the First Congregational Society in Bridgewater. Cambridge, E. W. Metcalf and Co., 1831. 32 p. CtY; DLC; ICMe; MBC; RPB. 7564

Hodgson, William Brown.
...Grammatical sketch and specimens of the Berber language: preceded by four letters on Berber etymologies, addressed to the president of the society... Read October 2d, 1829. Philadelphia, American Philosophical Society, 1831. 48 p. GHi; GSDe; MH. 7565

Hofland, Barbara Wreaks 1770-1844.
The affectionate Brothers. A tale. By Mrs. Hofland. Boston, Monroe and Francis, 1831. 119 p. MB. 7566

---- The Baradoes girl: a tale for young people. By the author of the Clergyman's widow and family, Marchant's widow and family, Affectionate brothers, Panoramo of Europe, The sisters, Daughter-in law, &c. &c. ...New-York, W. Burgess, Juvenile emporium, 1831. 155 p. CtY. 7567

---- The blind farmer and his children. By Mrs. Hofland... New York, W. B. Gilley 1831. DLC; LU; MH. 7568

Hogg, James.
The Laidlaws and the Scotts. ...New York, J. & J. Harper, 1831. 2 vols. OCX. 7569

Holbach, Paul Henrich.
Good sense: or natural ideas opposed to supernatural;...By Baron Holbach. 3d ed., repub. from the English ed. New York, Wright and Owen, 1831. 140 p. IU; MH; MHi; MMilf; NCale. 7570

Holbrook, Josiah, 1788-1854.
Easy lessons in geometry intended for infant and primary schools, but useful in academies, lyceums and families. 5th ed. Boston, Carter, Hendee & Babcock, 1831. 36 p. ArU; ICBB; MDeeP; OMC; WHi. 7571

[Holden, Oliver]
Incidents in the life of Oliver Holden... Manuscript. Charlestown, 1831. [2] p. MB. 7572

Holland, William M.
An address before the Hartford County Peace Society at its anniversary in May, 1831. By William M. Holland, Esq. Hartford, Hartford County Peace Society, 1831. 26 p. CtHC; MeB; NNF; OCHP; PPi. 7573

Holley, Myron, 1779-1841.
A discourse, upon education, delivered before the Wayne County education society, by their request, at Lyons, on the 2nd day of April, 1831. Lyons, New York, Pr. at the office of the country man, 1831. 24 p. CtY; N; NAuT; NCH. 7574

---- An oration delivered at Weedsport, the 4th of July, 1831; it being the fifty-fifth anniversary of the independence of the United States. By Myron Holley. Auburn, [N.Y.] Pr. by T. M. Skinner, 1831. 16 p. MBC; N; NBuG. 7575

Holloway, John.
The persecutions of the nonconformists, contrasted with the liberties of present dissenters. Bedford, White, 1831. PPPrHi. 7576

Holmes, John, 1773-1843.
An address, delivered at Waterville, before the Associated Alumni of Waterville College on the 28th July 1831. By John Holmes. Portland [Me.] Pr. by A. Shirley, 1831. 22 p. CSmH; MBC; MeWC. 7577

---- Post Office Inquiry. Speech on Mr. Grundy's resolution, delivered in the Senate U.S. Febr. 1831. Washington, 1831. 27 p. CtY; DLC; MBAt; OClWHi; WHi. 7578

The Home Missionary, and American Pastor's Journal, edited by Rev. Absalom Peters, Vol. 3, for the year ending April, 1831. New York, Executive Committee, 1831. 248 p. MA. 7579

Home Missionary Society. Eastern District of New-Haven County.
First annual report... New-Haven, Pr. by Baldwin and Treatway, 1831. 12 p. CtY. 7580

---- Hampden, Mass.
Address of the directors of the Hampden Home Missionary Society, to the churches. Constitution, and annual meeting. Springfield, 1831. 12 p. MBC. 7581

---- ---- Annual report. 1st. 1831. Springfield, Mass., G. & C. Merriam, 1831. MSHi. 7582

Honeywood, St. John, 1763-1798.
Poems, by St. John Honeywood, A.M., with some pieces in prose. New York, Pr. by T. & J. Swords, 1831. 159 p. CSt. 7583

[Hook, Theodore Edward]
Maxwell. By the author of "Sayings and doings." New York, J. & J. Harper, 1831. 2 vols. LU; MB; MBAt; MBL; PFal. 7584

Hooper, Robert.
Lexicon-medicum; or, Medical dictionary...4th Amer. from last London ed. with additions by Samuel Akerly. New York, Collins, 1831. 2 vols. in 1. LNOP; MH-M; OO; OWorP; PPCD. 7585

Hoover, Frederick.
Looking-glass for Orthodox Friends, where in they may not only see themselves, but also the path they are pursuing. Richmond, Ind., Pr. by T. J. Lorsh, 1831. PSC-Hi. 7586

[Hope, Thomas, 1770?-1831]
...Anastasius; or, Memoirs of a Greek, written at the close of the eighteenth century. New York, J. & J. Harper, 1831. 2 vols. DLC; LU; NjR; RPAt; TxU. 7587

Hopkins, Rev. John Henry, 1792-1866.
Religion the only safeguard of national prosperity. A sermon. By John H. Hopkins. Boston, Samuel H. Parker, 1831. 24 p. CtHC; ICMe; MH-AH; NNG; RPB. 7588

Hopkins Academy. Hadley, Massachusetts.
Catalogue of the officers and pupils of Hopkins Academy, Hadley, Mass. During the term ending November 22, 1831. Northampton, Pr. by T. W. Shepard, 1831. 4 p. AAS; FL. 7589

Hopkinson, Joseph, 1770-1842.
Annual oration delivered before the Zelosophic Society of the University of Pennsylvania, in the college hall, July 29th, 1831. By Hon. Joseph Hopkinson, LL.D. Philadelphia, Pr. by J. R. A. Skerrett, 1831. 20 p. DLC; NjPT; PPL; PPPrHi; ScU. 7590

Hopper, Isaac Tatem, 1771-1852.
Defence of Isaac T. Hopper, against the aspersions of Marcus T. C. Gould. [New York, 1831] 12 p. LfCG; MBC; NN. 7591

---- Facts from M. C. L. Gould. Philadelphia, 1831. PSC-Hi. 7592

Hoppus, John, 1789-1875.
An account of Lord Bacon's Novum Organon Scientiarum, or New method of studying the sciences, the first or introductory part. From the British library of useful knowledge. Boston, 1831. DLC; MH. 7593

Horatius Flaccus, Quintus.
Accedunt Clavis metrica et Notae Anglicae Cura. B[oston] B. A. Gould, 1831. MH. 7594

---- Quinti Horatii Placci opera. Accedunt Clavis Metrica et notae Anglicae... Cura B. A. Gould. Boston, Hilliard, Gray, Little, et Wilkins, 1831. AU; DLU; MBBC; MH; MnHi; NN; RPB. 7595

Horne, George, bp. of Norwich, 1730-1792.
The doctrine of the Trinity stated and defended; a sermon; added, comments from Mant & D'Olylys Bible, ed. by J. H. Hobart, New York, 1831. NN; Nh. 7596

---- Letters on infidelity [and a letter to Adam Smith...on... David Hume...] In: Gibson (F.) Three pastoral letters... New York, 1831. NN. 7597

Horne, Thomas Hartwell.
An introduction to the critical study and knowledge of the Holy Scriptures; 4th Amer. ed., illustrated with numerous maps and facsims, of Biblical manuscripts. Philadelphia, E. Littell, 1831. 4 vols. DLC; KyDC; OBerB; PPLT; ViRU. 7598

Horner, William Edmonds.
Introductory to a course of anatomy in the University of Pennsylvania, delivered November 7th, 1831... Philadelphia, J. G. Auner, 1831. 28 p. CtY; DLC; MnHi; OClWHi; PHi. 7599

Hoskins, James W.
An address, delivered before the Camden Equal Rights Society, May 16, 1831. Bangor, Pr. by Burton & Carter, 1831. 16 p. MeHi. 7600

Hoskins, Nathan, 1795-1869.
A history of the State of

Vermont, from its discovery and settlement of the close of the year 1830. Vergennes, J. Shedd, 1831. 316 p. CtY; DLC; ICU; MH; VtU. 7601

How, Samuel Blanchard, 1790-1868.
An address delivered to the graduates of Dickinson College, on Wednesday, September 28, 1831. By Samuel B. How, D.D. Principal of Dickinson College. Pub. at the request of the Board of Trustees. Carlisle, Pa., 1831. 21 p. MiD-B; NjR; OCHP; PHi; PPPrHi. 7602

Howard, Alfred, (ed.)
The beauties of Sheridan see Sheridan, Richard Brinsley Butler, 1756-1816.

Howard, William.
Communication from Messrs. Howard and M'Neill, in reply to a request from the committee on internal improvements, in accordance with the order of the House of Delegates, to ascertain the cost and advantage of a Rail-road, from Baltimore to Washington, to be made by the State. Annapolis, Pr. by Jonas Green, January 1831. 12 p. MdHi; NIC. 7603

Howe, Hezekiah, 1775-1838.
Architecture. Part I. Ancient architecture... New Haven, H. Howe, 1831. 74 pp. CtY; ICU; NNC; PU; ViU. 7604

Howell, R. B. C.
The deaconship; a sermon preached at the ordination of deacons in Smithfield, Va. By R. B. C. Howell. Richmond (n.p., n. pr.) 1831. 16 p. NjPT; PPL. 7605

Howitt, William.
The Book of the seasons; or, The Calendar of nature. By William Howitt. ...Philadelphia, Carey & Lea, 1831. (3), (25)-312, (36) p. GDecCT; LN; MB; RPAt. 7606

Howland, Mrs.
The infant school manual, or Teacher's assistant. Containing a view of the system of infant schools... By Mrs. Howland... Boston, Richardson, Lord & Holbrook, 1831. 274 p. DLC; ICHi; MH; NCH; RPB. 7607

Howland, Henry J.
Lessons for infant Sabbath schools: with a plan for conducting an infant class... By Henry J. Howland. Worcester, Pub. by Dorr & Howland, 1831. 106 p. MWHi. 7608

Howland, John.
Letter from John Howland, Esq. Relative to the Rhode-Island regiment, commanded by Col. Christopher Lippitt, in the years 1776 and 1777. Providence, Pr. by H. W. Brown, 1831. 11 p. MB; RHi; RNHi; RPB. 7609

Hoyt, A.
A. Hoyt's acquittal from the anonymous charges of Rev. J. Emory and B. Waugh, Agents of the Methodist Book Concern, his defense before the New-York Quarterly Conference. New-York, S. Hoyt & Co., 1831. 35 p. 7610

Hubbard, Jeremiah.
An account of Wells. By Jeremiah Hubbard and Jonathan Greenleaf. (In collection of the Maine Historical Society) Portland, Pr. by Day, Fraser and Co., 1831. v 1, p. (256)-268. DLC; F; MeHa; MiU; OCl; OFH. 7611

Huchins' [sic] improved almanac for the year of our Lord 1832, being bissextile, or leap year and until the fourth of July, the fifty-sixth of American independence, containing... By David Young... New York, Pr. by John C. Totten [1831] (34) p. MWA; NjMo; NRnHi. 7612

Hudson and Delaware Rail-Road Company.
Prospectus of the route from Newburgh to Carpenter's Point, together with the act of incorporation passed April 19, 1830. Newburgh, Pr. by Parrmenter and Spalding, 1831. 16 p. DLC; NN; NNC; ViU. 7613

Hudson river and the Hudson river railroad. with a complete map... Boston, 1831. PPL. 7614

Huger, Daniel Elliott, 1779-1854.
Speech of the Honorable Daniel E. Huger, in the House of Representatives of South Carolina, December 1830, on the Resolutions reported by the Committee on Federal Relations. Charleston, Pr. by W. Riley, 1831. 41 p. MH; MWA; NN; PPL; ScU. 7615

Hughs, Thomas.
The American popular reader; or, Lessons for junior classes. By Thomas Hughs... Philadelphia, Key & Mielke, 1831. 214 p. DLC. 7616

---- The new American speaker; being a selection of speeches, dialogues, and poetry... By Thomas Hughs... Philadelphia, Key & Mielke, 1831. 252 p. DLC. 7617

Hugo, Victor Marie.
...Notre-Dame de Paris, by Victor Hugo... Boston, Aldine Book Pub. Co., [1831] 2 vols. in 1. GA; IR; MB; RWoH; TxD-T. 7618

[Humbert, Stephen] 1768?-1849, comp.
Union harmony: or, British America's sacred vocal musick from approved English and American authors. To which is prefixed a concise introduction...3d ed. abridged. St. John (New Brunswick) Stephen Humbert... Boston, Pr. by James Loring, 1831. 164 p. CtY; MBNEC. 7619

Hume, David, 1711-1776.
Hume and Smollett's celebrated history of England, from its first settlement to the year 1760. Accurately and impartially abridged. And a continuation from that period to the coronation of George IV. July 19, 1821. Embracing a period of nearly two thousand years. By Rev. John Robinson... Illustrated by twenty-four pages of engravings together with an appendix, containing the succession of sovereigns--eminent and remarkable persons who have flourished in Britain--battles in English history, by sea and land, from 1588 to 1806--improvements and inventions--discoveries and settlements of British colonies. Hartford, D. F. Robinson & co., 1831. 494 p. GDecCT; MBBC; NPV; PP; RJa; VtMidSM. 7620

Humphrey, Heman, 1779-1861.
An address delivered at the opening of the convention of teachers, & of the friends of education, in the city-hall, in Hartford, November, 10th, 1830... Hartford, Cooke & co., 1831. 19 p. CtHC; CtY; MBC; MH; MeHi. 7621

---- Indian Rights and our duties. An address delivered at Amherst, Hartford, etc. December 1829. By Heman Humphrey, D.D. President of Amherst College. Stereotyped for the Association for diffusing information on the subject of Indian Rights, Albany, 1831. 24 p. DLC; MHi; NjR; PPL; PPWI. 7622

---- The way to bless and save

our country, a sermon, preached in Philadelphia, May 23, 1831 by Heman Humphrey, D.D. Philadelphia, American Sunday School Union, 1831. 24 p. DLC; MeB; Nh; OClWHi; TxDaM. 7623

Hunt, Halloway Whitfield, 1769-1859.
An ecclesiastical and historical catechism, for children and youth. By Halloway W. Hunt, A.M. Minister of the Gospel. 2d ed. Bethelehem, N.J., Geo. Sherman, 1831. 24 p. PPPrHi. 7624

Hunt, William Gibbes.
An address, delivered at Nashville, Tenn. April 6, 1831, at the request of the literary societies of the University of Nashville. By William Gibbes Hunt. Nashville, Hunt, Tardiff & Co., 1831. 20 p. KyLxT; MBAt; MWA; PHi; TxDaM. 7625

Huntington, J. F.
Annual (Connecticut) State Register...No. 5. 1831. By J. F. and H. Huntington. Hartford, [1831] 144 p. MHi. 7626

Huntington, Mrs. Susan [Mansfield]
Memoirs of Mrs. Susan Huntington, of Boston, Mass. Designed for the young. By an early friend. New Haven, A. H. Maltby, 1831. 131 p. CtHC; MH; PPF; PPT; OClWHi. 7627

Huntoon, Benjamin, 1792-1864.
A sermon preached May 18, 1831, at the ordination of Mr. William Farmer, at Belgrade, Me. by Benjamin Huntoon, of Bangor. Augusta, Pr. by Eaton & Severance, 1831. 23 p. CtSoP; MH; PPB; PPL; RPB. 7628

Hunt's Philadelphia almanack for 1832. By Joseph Cramer. Philadelphia, Pa., Uriah Hunt [1831] MWA. 7629

Hutching's revived almanack, for the year 1832... by David Young, philom. New York, Wm. Beastell, etc., etc. [1831] (16) p. MWA; NGos; NjR. 7630

Hutton, Charles, 1737-1823.
A course of mathematics; for the use of academies as well as private tuition in two volumes, by Charles Hutton, LL.D., F.R.S., late Professor of Mathematics in the Royal Military Academy. 5th Amer. from 9th London ed., with many corr. and imp., by Olinthus Gregory, LL.D., corresponding associate of the academy of Dyon, Honorary Member of the Literary and Philosophical Society of New York, of the New York Historical Society, of the Literary and Philosophical and Antiquarian Societies of Newcastle upon Tyne, of the Cambridge Philosophical Society, of the Institution of Civil Engineers, &c., &c., Secretary to the Astronomical Society of London, and Professor of Mathematics in the Royal Military Academy, with the additions of Robert Adrain, LL.D., F.A.P.S., A.A.S., &c. and Professor of Mathematics and Natural Philosophy. The whole cor. and imp. New York, Pr. by W. E. Dean, for E. & J. Swords; T. A. Ronalds; Collins and Co., Collins and Hannay; G. and C. and H. Carvill; White, Gallaher, and White; O. A. Roorbach; and M'Elrath and Bangs, 1831. 2 vols. CtY; LNT; MiU; PP; ScSP. 7631

Hutton, William.
Hutton's book of nature laid open. Adapted to the use of families and schools. By Rev. J. L. Blake... Boston, Waitt & Dow, 1831. 267 p. DLC; Nh-Hi;

NhPet; NjR; RPA. 7632

The Hyacinth... New York, J. C. Riker, 1831. 240 p. DLC; ICU; MWA; NNC; VtMicSM. 7633

Hyde, William A.
Christian imitation: sermon on the death of Mrs. Nancy Lay. Hartford [1831] 21 p. MBC. 7634

Hymers, John, 1803-1887.
A treatise on the integral calculus. Pt. I. Containing the integration of explicit functions of one variable; together with the theory of definite integrals and of elliptic functions. By J. Hymers... Cambridge, Pr. by J. Smith, for J. & J. J. Deighton, etc., etc., 1831. 282 p. OCU; OO; ViU. 7635

Hymns for Infant Sabbath Schools; selected from various compilations. Pittsburgh, Loomis, 1831. AmSSchU; PPi. 7636

Hymns for little children. Wendell, Metcalf, 1831. Tt. MA. 7637

Hymns for schools and families selected from various authors. n.p. Hallowell, 1831. 90 p. MH. 7638

I

Illinois.
Journal of the House of Representatives of the 7th General Assembly of the State of Illinois at their 1st session, held at Vandalia, Dec. 6, 1830. Vandalia, Ill., Robert Blackwell, 1831. 560 p. DLC; ICN; ICj; IHi; IU; NN. 7639

---- Journal of the Senate of the 7th General Assembly of the State of Illinois, at their 1st session, held at Vandalia, Dec. 6, 1830. Vandalia, Ill., Robert Blackwell, 1831. 472 p. IHi; ILM; IU; NN. 7640

---- The Laws of Illinois, passed at seventh General Assembly, at their Session held at Vandalia, commencing on the first Monday in December, 1830. Published in pursuance of law. Vandalia, Robert Blackwell, Public printer, 1831. 217 p. IHi; L; Mo; Nj; T. 7641

---- Reports of cases at common law and in chancery... Bloomington, Ill. [etc.] 1831. Ct; IHi; MWA. 7642

Illinois College. Jacksonville, Illinois.
An appeal in behalf of the Illinois College, recently founded at Jacksonville, Illinois. New York, Pr. by D. Fanshaw, 1831. 16 p. CtY; ICJ; MB; MH; MHi; NNUT; PPPrHi; WHi. 7643

---- Constitution of the Christian Union of Illinois College. 183? IJI. 7644

---- Order of exercises at the annual exhibition of Illinois College, August 17, 1831... [Jacksonville, 1831] IJI. 7645

Illinois Farmers' almanac for the year of our Lord, 1832. No. 1- By Benaiah Robinson... [1831] IH; IHi. 7646

Illinois monthly magazine, conducted by James Hall. v. 1- Vandalia, Pr. by Blackwell, 1831. ICHi; IGK; MH; NN; PU. 7647

Illinois State Lyceum.
Minutes of the meeting for the purpose of organizing...held at Vandalia, Dec. 8th, 1831.

[Vandalia, 1831] Broadside. IHi. 7648

Illinois Sunday School Union.
Proceedings of the First Annual Meeting of the... Vandalia, Robt. Blackwell, 1831. 16 p. IQHi; MiD-B; WHi. 7649

An imaginary conversation, between President Jackson and the ghost of Jefferson. Columbia, S.C., Pr. at the Telescope office, 1831. 22 p. ArAr; NoD; PPAmP; ScC; WHi. 7650

The imprisoned missionaries. [Washington? 1831] 8 p. Relating to the imprisonment of S. A. Worcester and others in the penitentiary for residing within the limits of the Cherokee Reservation without a license. MB; PPL. 7651

Incidents in the life of President Dwight, illustrative of his moral and religious character: designed for young persons. New Haven, Conn., A. H. Maltby, 1831. 156 p. CtSoP; IaB; MH; OSW; PPL-R; BrMus. 7652

Independent Messenger. Adin Ballou, ed. Vol. 1. Jan. 1, 1831. Mendon, Mass. 1831. MCon; MMet-Hi. 7653

Index to the printed minutes of the General Synod of the Reformed Dutch Church in North America, from June 1794 to June 1826 inclusive. Prepared by the Rev. Thomas M. Strong, stated clerk...[sic] New York, Pr. for the General Synod, 1831. 115 p. IaPeC; MiD-B; NcMHi; NNUT; NjR. 7654

Index to the subjects contained in the old and new testaments. [Philadelphia, 1831] 33 p. NN. 7655

Indiana.
An act to organize and regulate the militia of the state of Indiana. Passed at the 15th session of the General Assembly. Pub. by authority. Indianapolis, Douglass and Maguire, 1831. 74 p. DLC; InHi; In-SC; InU. 7656

---- Journal of the House of Representatives of the State of Indiana; being the 16th session of the General Assembly, begun and held at Indianapolis, in said state, on Monday the fifth day of December, A.D. 1831. Indianapolis, N. Bolton, state pr., 1831. 451 p. In; InU. 7657

---- Journal of the Senate of the State of Indiana; during the 16th session of the General Assembly, commenced at Indianapolis, on Monday the 15th of December, 1831. Indianapolis, A. F. Morrison, pr. to the Senate, 1831. 410 p. In; InU; N. 7658

---- The revised laws of Indiana, in which are comprised all such acts of a general nature as are in force in said state; adopted and enacted by the General Assembly at their 15th session. To which are prefixed the Declaration of Independence, the constitution of the state of Indiana, and sundry other documents, connected with the political history of the territory and state of Indiana. Arranged and pub. by authority of the General Assembly. Indianapolis, Douglass and Maguire, 1831. 596 p. In; InHi; InU; N. 7659

---- Special acts passed at the 15th session of the General Assembly of the State of Indiana, begun and held at Indianapolis, on Monday the 6th day of December, A.D. 1830. Indianapolis, Douglass and Maguire, 1831. 206 p. In; InHi; In-SC; InU; N. 7660

Indiana Historical Society.
Indiana Historical Society. On the 11th of December, 1830, a number of citizens of Indiana... formed themselves into an association under the name of the Indiana Historical Society, and adopted a constitution, from which the following articles are extracted:...[Indianapolis? 1831] Broadside. In; InHi. 7661

---- Published by order of the Indiana Historical Society. (A letter from the Indiana Historical Society to the Hon. Nathan Dane relative to that part of the Orinance of 1787 which excludes slavery from the Territory and Mr. Dane's reply.) [Indianapolis, 1831] 7 p. DLC; InHi; InU. 7662

Indiana Journal (Indianapolis).
Prospectus of the Indiana Journal on an imperial sheet, pub. twice a week during the session of the General Assembly... Indianapolis, Oct. 29, 1831. Broadside. In. 7663

Indiana University.
Indiana College. (A catalogue of the officers and students.) 7 p. InSU. 7664

The infant school and nursery hymn book; being a collection of hymns, original and selected; with an analysis of each, designed to assist mothers and teachers in developing the infant mind: to which are added, moral songs, and pieces for recitation. The whole adapted to the capacity of children under seven years. 3d ed., rev. and cor... New York, A. W. Corey [etc.], 1831. 126 p. AmSSchU; CLU; MB; MWA; NNUT. 7665

Infant School Society. Boston.
The Constitution and by-laws of the Infant School Society of the city of Boston, with the annual report... Boston, Pr. by T. R. Marvin, 1831. MB; MWA. 7666

---- New York.
A Colloquy on grammar between a little boy or girl and the children in the gallery; written for the fourth anniversary of the Society, May, 1831. New York, Pr. by J. Seymour, 1831. 8 p. MH. 7667

Infant stories; with beautiful pictures. New Haven, S. Babcock, Sidney's press, 1831. 17 p. CtY. 7668

The infernal secret! Or, The invulnerable Spaniard, who was for many years termed the terror of Madrid! Containing an account of the wonders of his withered arm ... Boston, H. Jenkins, 1831. 23 p. MB; MH; RPB; TxU. 7669

Infidelity unmasked.
Infidelity unmasked edited and published by Dyer Burgess V. 1; June 5, 1831-April 22, 1831 [1831-1832] 384 p. DLC; ICU; OClWHi; WHi. 7670

Ingersoll, Charles Jared.
Julian; a tragedy, in five acts. Philadelphia, 1831. 87 p. CSmH; MH; NCU; PU; RP; RPB. 7671

Ingersoll, Charles M.
Conversations on English grammar, explaining the principles and rules of the language... By Charles M. Ingersoll...9th ed. Boston, William Hyde, 1831. 251 p. MH; MdAS; ViU. 7672

Ingersoll, George Goldthwait.
A sermon, preached before the First Congregational Society, on Thanksgiving Day. By Geo. G. Ingersoll. Pub. by request. Burlington, Chauncey Goodrich, 1831. 24 p. CtHT; CtY; DLC; MiD-B; VtU. 7673

Ingles, John.
A sermon... 1831. 14 p. DLC. 7674

Inquiry into the nature and design of music; being a series of numbers, first pub. in the American traveller, signed: A friend to Stoughton collection of church music. Pub. by request. Boston and Concord, N.H., Marsh, Capen, and Lyon, 1831. 45 p. CtY; DLC; MB; PPAmP; RPB. 7675

Insect transformations. See Rennie, James, 1787-1867.

An interesting account of the persecution and martyrdom of several persons eminent for piety, under the reign of popery, as late as the fifteenth and sixteenth centuries. (1 line, biblical quotations) Rochester, N.Y., Pr. by Marshall & Dean, 1831. 56 p. 7676

Investigator (pseud.)
Corruption further exposed and falsehood refuted by Investigator [pseud.] [Providence, 1831?] 2 p. RPB. 7677

Ipswich Female Seminary.
Catalogue of the officers and members of Ipswich female seminary, for the year ending October 1831. Salem, Pr. by Warwick Palfray, Jun., 1831. 12 p. MMhHi. 7678

Irish eloquence...1831. See Speeches of Philips, Curran and Grattan.

The Irish Shield.
A historical and literary weekly paper, v. 1-4; 1829-31? Philadelphia [etc.] 1 Reel. 35 mm. (American periodical series: 1800-1850. APS 933). Title varies 1829-1830. The Irish Shield and monthly Milesian; 1831, Irish Shield and literary panorama. Vol. 3-4 called new series. Editor George Pepper. MoU; NcD; PHi; PSt. 7679

Irvine, James.
Particular, eternal, sovereign election to eternal life through means of grace; a discourse by Rev. James Irvine. New York, 1831. 22 p. NjPT. 7680

Irving, Christopher, d 1856.
A catechism of classical biography, containing an account of the lives of the most celebrated characters among the ancient Greeks and Romans, approved for the use of schools in the United States. 2d American ed., imp. and enl. New York, Collins & Hannay, 1831. 88 p. MB; MdHi; MiGr; NcWsS. 7681

---- A catechism of Grecian History from the earliest times to the period when Greece became a Roman Province...adapted to the use of schools in the U.S. 4th Amer. ed. New York, Collins & Hannay, 1831. 71 p. NcWsS. 7682

---- A catechism of Roman antiquities; ...an account of religion, civil, government, (etc.)... with description of the public buildings of the city of Rome... adapted to use of schools in the United States. 4th Amer. ed. New York, Collins and Hannay, 1831. 106 p. AH; MH; NcWsS; NPla. 7683

---- A catechism of Roman history, containing a concise account of the most striking events from the foundation of the city, to the fall of the Western Empire. With engraved illustrations. By C. Irving, LL.D. 4th Amer. ed. New York, Collins & Hannay, 1831. 83 p. IaB; MH. 7684

Irving, Washington, 1783-1859.
Bracebridge Hall; or, The Humourists. A medley by Geoffrey Crayon, Gent. (pseud.)... 4th ed. Philadelphia, Carey, Lea & Blanchard, 1831. 2 vols. MBat; MPlyA; MeBa. 7685

---- A chronicle of the conquest of Granada. By Fray Antonio Agapida (pseud.)... Philadelphia, Carey & Lea, 1831. 2 vols. InStmAS; MPlyA; MWA; MeBa; TxU. 7686

---- A history of New York, from the beginning of the world to the end of the Dutch dynasty. Containing among many surprising and curious matters, the unutterable ponderings of Walter the doubter, the disasterous projects of William the testy, and the chivalric achievements of Peter the headstrong, the three Dutch governors of New Amsterdam... By Dietrich Knickerbocker (pseud.) Philadelphia, Carey and Lea, 1831. 8 v. in 1. MH; MiU; NN; PPL; PU. 7687

---- The life and voyages of Christopher Columbus... A new ed., rev. and cor. by the author. New York, G. & C. & H. Carvill, 1831. 2 vols. CtY; DLC; GHi; ICHi; MBAt; MiD; NNF; PPAN; PU; OClWHi; TxU; WaU 7688

---- The sketch book of Geoffrey Crayon, gent. 7th Amer. ed. Philadelphia, Carey & Lea, 1831. 2 vols. 236 p. MH; NN; ViAl. 7689

---- Voyages and discoveries of the companions of Columbus. Philadelphia, Carey & Lea, 1831. 350 p. H Geno; MWA; NIC; NcWfC. 7690

---- Works of Washington Irving. New York, Hurst and co. [1831] 6 vols. FWpR. 7691

Ismar, F. A.
Emanuel Fellenberg's institution, at Hofwyl, in Switzerland; two lectures, delivered in Georgetown, D.C. Georgetown, D.C., Pr. at the Columbian Gazette Office, 1831. 52 p. DLC; MH. 7692

Iucho, Wilhelm.
Institute Rondo (for pf.). New York, Firth Hall & Co., 1831. fol. (In "Mus. Miscel.," 24) 5 p. CtY; KU. 7693

---- .... Lexington Rondo. Composed & dedicated Miss Adaline Van Doren by Wilhelm Iucho. 5th ed. New York, Firth & Hall, c1831. [2] p. CtY; ICN; ViU. 7694

---- My heart with love o'erflowing. Hope, air with variations. [S. or T. Accomp. for pianoforte.] New York, Hewitt [183-?] 4 p. MB. 7695

Ives, Elam, 1802-1864, comp.
American Psalmody: A collection of sacred music, comprising a great variety of Psalm and Hymn tunes, set-pieces, anthems, and chants, arranged with a figured bass for the organ or piano forte. To which is prefixed, a new system of teaching musical elocution, or the art of singing, upon the inductive plan of education adopted in other branches of science. Designed for the use of schools and private pupils. By E. Ives, Jr., and D. Dutton, Jr. 2d ed., greatly enl., with alterations and imp. Hartford, H. & F. J. Huntington; Boston, Crocker & Brewster; New York, J. Leavitt; Philadelphia, Towar, J. & D. M. Hogan, 1831. 368 p. MBC; NutHi. 7696

---- A manual of instruction in the art of singing, prepared for the American Sunday School

Union, rev. by the Committee of Publication. Philadelphia, American Sunday School Union, 1831. 40 p. AmSSchU; CtHWatk; CtMW; CtY; MeHi. 7697

Ives, Levi Silliman, 1797-1867, ed. New manual of private devotions. See Title.

---- A sermon preached in St. Luke's Church, New York, September 25, 1831, on taking leave of his congregation: by the Right Reverend Levi Siliman Ives, D.D. New York, Protestant Episcopal Press, 1831. 15 p. CtHT; DLC; MH; PPM; RPB. 7698

---- A sermon preached in Trinity Church, Southwark. By Rev. Levi Silliman Ives. New York, Protestant Episcopal Press, 1831. 19 p. NGH. 7699

J

J. C. M.
Savonarola, an attempted tragedy, in five acts. By J. C. M. ...Harrisburg, H. Welsh, 1831. 77 p. ICU. 7700

Jackson, Andrew.
A letter on the causes of the dissolution of his cabinet. 1831. PPL. 7701

Jackson, Daniel, b. 1790.
Alonzo and Melissa: or, The unfeeling father. An American tale... By Daniel Jackson, jr. Castleton, Vt., G. C. Smith, 1831. 254 p. DLC; MB; NSchU; Vt. 7702

---- ---- Concord, Luther Roby, 1831. 253 p. DLC; MB; MHi; OrPr; Vt. 7703

---- ---- Exeter, Mass., A. R. Brown, 1831. 256 p. CyMW; ICSX; MB; MHa; MWA; RPB. 7704

---- ---- Sandbornton [N.H. ?] D. V. Moulton, 1831? 253 p. CtY. 7705

Jackson, James, 1777-1867.
Memoir of James Jackson, jr. M.D. written by his father... Boston, Hilliard, Gray & Co. ? 1831. MWA. 7706

Jackson, Samuel
Observations on delirium tremens. Philadelphia, 1831. 24 p. PHi. 7707

Jackson, Thomas.
Memoirs of the life and writings of the Rev. Richard Watson, late secretary to the Wesleyan Missionary Society. By Thomas Jackson... New-York, Waugh and Mason, 1831. 488 p. OkOkU. 7708

Jacobs, Frederic, 1764-1847.
The Greek Reader, by Frederic Jacobs... 4th New York from the 9th German ed. with improvements, additions, notes and corrections by David Patterson, A. M. New-York, Collins & Hannay; Collins and Co.; White, Gallaher and White; G. and C. Carvill; and O. A. Roorbach, 1831. 258, 78 p. ArEs; CU; IU; MH; NjP. 7709

---- ... Jacob's Latin reader. With a vocabulary and English notes, for the use of schools, academies, &c. Boston, Hilliard, Gray, Little, and Wilkins, 1831. 2 vols. CSansS; IAlS; MH; PHi; TxU-T. 7710

James, D.
Fragments on the divinity and humanity of Christ; on the atonement and salvation through faith in Christ Jesus... Philadelphia, [Pr. by Griggs & Dickson] 1831. 40 p. OO; PPPrHi. 7711

James, George Payne Rainsford, 1799-1860.
The History of Chivalry. By G. P. R. James, Esq... New York, Pr. by J. & J. Harper, 1831. 342 p. CtY; MBC; NjR; TNP; ViU. 7712

---- Philip Augustus; or, The brothers in arms. By the author of 'Richelieu', 'Darnley', 'Do l'Orme', &c. (George Payne Rainsford James). New York, J. & J. Harper, 1831. 2 vols. MB; MBL; MH; RLa; RPB. 7713

James, John Argell, 1785-1859.
The Christian Father's present to his children. By J. A. James. Vol. 1. 6th Amer. ed. Boston, Leonard W. Kimball; New York, John P. Haven, 1831. 2 vols. in 1. ICBB; MB; MH; MWA; NNUT. 7714

---- Christian fellowship, or The church member's guide. By J. A. James, A. M. Birmingham, England. Edited by J. O. Choules, A. M. Pastor of the Second Baptist Church in Newport, R.I. Stereotype ed. Boston, Lincoln & Edmands, 1831. 240 p. CtHC; IEG; MBC; NcD; PPM. 7715

---- The family monitor, or a help to domestic happiness. By John Angell James, author of "The Christian Father's Present Christian Charity Explained" &c. From the 3d London ed., corr. and enl. Boston, Crocker & Brewster; New York, Jonathan Leavitt, 1831. 205 p. GU; KyLxT; MLow; MdBD; OMC. 7716

---- ---- Pittsburgh, D. & M. Maclean, 1831. 205 p. MsV; NcD; OO; OSW; PPi. 7717

James and Joseph; or The contrast between Industry and Indolence. Providence, 1831. 15 p. RHi. 7718

Jameson, Mrs. Anna Brownell (Murphy), 1794-1860.
Memoirs of celebrated female sovereigns, by Mrs. Jameson. Philadelphia, 1831. 2 vols. PPL-R. 7719

Jameson, Robert, 1774-1854.
...Narrative of discovery and adventure in Africa, from the earliest ages to the present time: ...by Professor Jameson, James Wilson, and Hugh Murray... [Harper's stereotype ed.] New York, J. & J. Harper, 1831. 359 p. CU; KyBC; NjR; PU; ScNC. 7720

Jamieson, Alexander.
A grammar of rhetoric and polite literature comprehending the principles of language and style, the elements of taste and criticism with rules. 5th ed. stereotyped. New Haven, A. H. Maltby, 1831. 36 p. CtHT; DLC; MH; MdBLC; OO; ViRU. 7721

---- ---- 7th ed. stereotyped. New Haven, A. H. Maltby, 1831. 306 p. CtY; MB; OClW. 7722

---- The rhetorical examiner, comprehending questions and exercises on the grammar of rhetoric and polite literature; for the use of schools and private students. By Alexander Jamieson, LL.D., ...New Haven, A. H. Maltby, 1831. 56 p. CtY; MB; NN; OClW. 7723

Jans, Anneke.
Copy of the will of Anneke Jans, and the proceedings of a general meeting of her heirs and descendants, together with the report and pledge of the executive committee and sundry resolutions... New York, Marsh &

Harrison, pr., 1831. 23 p. NjR. 7724

Jaquith, James, b. 1781.
The history of James Jaquith; being his travels through the United States and Upper and Lower Canada containing great geographical information. Written by himself. 4th ed. Pub. for the author, 1831. 34 p. MH. 7725

Jarrett, Thomas, 1805-1882.
An essay on algebraic development containing the principal expansions in common algebra in the differential and integral calculus...the general term...a new and comprehensive notation... Cambridge, J. J. Deighton, 1831. 192 p. CU; DAU; MH; NGH; PPAN. 7726

Jarrom, Joseph, 1774-1842.
The regard which is due from Christian societies to their deceased pastors. A sermon (on Heb. XIII. 7.) preached...on the occasion of the death of the Rev. William Taylor, etc. Boston, 1831. NAC-S. 7727

Jay, William, 1769-1853.
The Christian contemplated; in a course of lectures, delivered in Argyle Chapel, Bath...3d Amer. ed. New York, Solomon King, 1831. 264 p. CtHC; MB; MH; NbCrD; OO. 7728

---- Evening exercises, for every day in the year. By Rev. William Jay. From the ed. of his works revised by himself... New York, American Tract Society [1831] 771 p. DLC; ICP; LPL; MdBJ; NNUT. 7729

---- Exercises for the closet, for every day in the year. By William Jay. 2d Amer. ed. New York, John P. Haven, 1831. 2 vols. in 1. CBPSR; ICP; MnSM; NBuDD; PPiW. 7730

---- ---- 2d Boston ed. Boston, Crocker & Brewster; New York, Jonathan Leavitt, 1831. 333, 396 p. GAGTh; ILM; MBC; MDeeP; PMA; WHi. 7731

---- Prayers for use of families. Hartford, Silus Andrus, 1831. 266 p. NSyU. 7732

---- ---- Lewistown, Pa., Charles Bell & Sons, 1831. 300 p. NRCR; PAtM. 7733

---- ---- Philadelphia, Key, Meilke, 1831. 249 p. GDecCT; MBC; OMC. 7734

---- Short discourses to be read in families... Philadelphia, Towar, J. & D. M. Hogan, 1831. 2 vols. GDecCT; MdBD; OMC; ScCMa. 7735

Jebb, John, Bp. of Limerick, Alfred & Aghadoe, 1775-1833, ed.
...Piety without asceticism; or, the Protestant Kempis: a manual of Christian faith and practice, selected from the writings Scougal, Charles How, and Cudworth; with corrections and occasional notes by John Jebb...New-York, Protestant Episcopal press, 1831. 361 p. CtHT; MB; MPiB; NNG; PU. 7736

Jefferson college, Louisiana.
Status, plan d'education et reglemens, adoptés pous Jefferson [n.p., 183-?] 19 p. NN. 7737

Jefferson College. Pennsylvania.
Catalogue of the books in the library of the Phile Literary Society of Jefferson College, January 1, 1831. [Pittsburgh] D. & M. Maclean, pr., 1831. 8 p. PHi. 7738

---- Catalogue of the officers and students of Jefferson College,

Canonsburg, August, 1831. Pittsburgh, Pr. by D. & M. Maclean [1831] 12 p. PWW. 7739

Jefferson Insurance Company (New York City)
Charter and amendments thereto... rules of order and by-laws. ...New York, Pr. by Jared W. Bell, 1831. 24 p. MB; MH-BA. 7740

Jenkins, Charles, 1786-1831.
Address delivered before the Portland Association for the Promotion of Temperance, March 30, 1831. By Charles Jenkins. Portland, A. Shirley, 1831. 22 p. MBC; MeHi; NN; NjPT. 7741

Jenks, Benjamin.
Prayers and offices of devotion for families and for particular persons upon most occasions. New York, 1831. 336 p. InCW; MWA. 7742

Jennings, Isaac.
Jennings' family present... Natchez, Pr. by Andrew Marschalk, 1831. v, [6]-24 p. NN. 7743

Jennings, Samuel Kennedy, 1771-1834.
An exposition of the late controversy in the Methodist Episcopal church, of the true objections of the parties concerned therein, and of the proceedings by which reformers were expelled, in Baltimore, Cincinnati and other places... By a layman. Baltimore, John J. Harrod, 1831. GEU-T; IEG; MB; NcU; OSW; ScNC. 7744

Jerram, Charles, 1770-1853.
Conversations on infant baptism and some popular objections against the church of the United Kingdom. Philadelphia, Latimer, 1831. PPPrHi. 7745

Jewel, John, bp. of Salisbury, 1522-1571.
The Apology for the Church of England; and a treatise of the Holy Scriptures; by Bishop Jewell, with a preface, biographical memoir, and notes. By W. W. Whittingham. New-York, New York Protestant Episcopal Press, 1831. IaFair; MdBD; NN; NNUT; RPB. 7746

Jewsbury, Maria Jane, 1800-1833.
The three histories. The history of an enthusiast. The history of a nonchalant. The history of a realist. By Maria Jane Jewsbury. Boston, Perkins & Marvin, 1831. 268 p. DLC; KHi; MnU; RPB; VtU. 7747

Johnson, Alexander Bryan, 1786-1867.
A method of acquiring a full knowledge of the English language, propounded at their invitation, by A. B. Johnson, Utica, August 10, 1831, before the New-York state lyceum. Utica (N.Y.), Pr. by Northway & Porter, 1831. 16 p. CtY; MB; MBAt; NUt; PPmP. 7748

Johnson, Cave, 1793-1866.
[Circular to his constituents] Washington, 1831. 8 p. DLC. 7749

---- [Letter on the general condition of the country] Washington, 1831. 8 p. DLC. 7750

---- [Letter on the situation of the affairs of our Country] Washington, 1831. 8 p. DLC. 7751

Johnson, Edwin Ferry, 1803-1872.
Review of the project for a great western railway. Addressed to the author of the project, in May, 1829; and first published in the New York statesman, in Feb. 1830. By E. F. Johnson, engineer. [New York] Pr. by W. D.

Starr, 1831. 16 p. CSmH; Ct; MH-BA; NN. 7752

Johnson, James, 1777-1845.
Change of air, or The philosophy of travelling; being autumnal excursions through France, Switzerland, Italy, Germany, and Belgium; with observations and reflections on the moral, physical, and medicinal influence of travelling-exercise, change of scene, foreign skies, and voluntary expatriation. To which is prefixed, Wear and tear of modern Babylon. By James Johnson ... New York, S. Wood and sons, 1831. 326 p. CSt; LU; MeB; PHC; WHi. 7753

---- An essay on indigestion; or morbid sensibility of the stomach and bowels, as the proximate cause or characteristic condition of dyspepsy, nervous irritability, mental despondency, hypo-chondriasis...To which are added, observations on the diseases & regimen of invalids on their return from hot and unhealthy climates. By James Johnson, M.D. ...3d Philadelphia, from the 6th London ed., much enl. Philadelphia, Nathan Kite, 1831. 194 p. ANA; GU-M; IEN-M; PPCP; TNV. 7754

Johnson, John, 1706-1791.
The advantages and disadvantages of a marriage state: as entered into with religious or irreligious persons. Presented under the similitude of a dream. Salem, Ind., Pr. by John Allen, at the office of the Western annotator, 1831. 13 p. In; InSaHi. 7755

Johnson, Oliver, 1809-1889.
A dissertation on the subject of future punishment. Delivered at Framingham, and other places. By Oliver Johnson, Editor of the Christian Soldier. Boston, Peirce & Parker, 1831. 32 p. DLC; MB; MWA; NcD; PPPrHi. 7756

Johnson, Samuel, 1709-1784.
Rasselas, prince of Abyssinia. A tale, by Dr. Johnson. Stereotyped by T. H. Carter & co., Boston. Boston, T. Bedlington, 1831. 124 p. CtY; IaCrM; MH; MoS; PSC. 7757

Johnson, Walter Rogers, 1794-1852.
Description of an apparatus called the Rotascope for exhibiting several phenomenal and illustrating certain laws of rotary motion by Walter R. Johnson. 1831. PAN. 7758

---- A lecture on the importance of linear drawing, and on the methods of teaching the art in Common schools and other seminaries. Delivered in the Representatives' hall, Boston, August 23, 1830, before the American institute of instruction. By Walter R. Johnson. Boston, Hilliard, Gray Little and Wilkins, 1831. 19 p. CtY; PPAmP. 7759

---- Remarks on the nature and importance of enlarged education, in view of the present state of society in Europe and America. By Walter R. Johnson... [Philadelphia? 1831] 8 p. CtHWatk; DLC; MH; PPAN. 7760

Johnston, Josiah Stoddard, 1784-1833.
Letter of Mr. Josiah S. Johnston, of Louisiana to a gentleman in New York, in reply to an article on the expediency of reducing the duty on sugar... [Washington, 20th February, 1831] 8 p. DGU; MdHi; NcD; ScU; ScCC. 7761

---- Letter of Mr. Johnston, of Louisiana, to the secretary of the Treasury, in reply to his circular of the 1st July, 1830, relative to the culture of the sugar cane. Washington, Pr. by Gales & Seaton, 1831. 21 p. DLC; MB; MWA; PPL; PPWI; OCHP. 7762

---- Speech of Mr. J. S. Johnston... at a public dinner given to him and... E. D. White, in... New Orleans, 8 June, 1831. [New Orleans? 1831] MB; PPL. 7763

Johnstone, Christian Isobel, 1781-1852.
Lives and voyages of Drake, Cavendish, and Damaier; including an introductory view of the earlier discoveries in the South Sea, and the history of the bucaniers--with portraits on steel. New York, Harper & Bros., [1831] 332 p. MBAt; NBuCC; NNCoCi; RKi. 7764

[Jones, Epaphras]
On the ten tribes of Israel, and the aborigines of America, &c., &c. By a Bible professor ... Providence, Ind., May 2d, 1831. New-Albany, Ind., Pr. by Collins & Green, 1831. 32 p. DLC; IU; In; InNea; InU. 7765

Jones, James Athearn, 1791-1854.
Haverhill; or, Memoirs of an officer in the army of Wolfe. By James A. Jones... New-York, J. & J. Harper, 1831. 2 vols. CtY; DLC; IU; RPB; TNP. 7766

Jones, John.
Land of liberty...Composed by Mr. Jones, and sung by him with great applause at the Park Theatre. New York. New York, c1831. MB. 7767

Jones, (Mrs.) Thomas.
An account of the loss of the Wesleyan missionaries, Messrs. Hillier, Truscott, Oke, and Jones, with Mrs. White and Mrs. Truscott, and their children and servant in the Maria Mail Boat, off the island of Antiqua in the West Indies, February 28, 1828, by Mrs. Jones, the only survivor on that mournful occasion, second American ed. New York, Pr. by J. Collard, for J. Emory and B. Waugh, for the Methodist Episcopal Church, 1831. 24 p. ICP; MoS; TxDaM. 7768

Jones, Thomas P., 1774-1848.
New conversations on chemistry, adapted to the present state of that science; wherein its elements are clearly and familiarly explained. With one hundred and eighteen engravings...appropriate questions; a list of experiments, and a glossary. On the foundations of Mrs. Marcet's "Conversations on chemistry." By Thomas P. Jones... Philadelphia, J. Griff, 1831. 332 p. ICU; KyDC; MH; PPL; RPB. 7769

Jones, William.
The History of the Christian Church, from the birth of Christ to the eighteenth century, including the very interesting account of the Waldenses and Albigenses. By William Jones. 3d Amer. from the 4th London ed. Louisville, Ephraim A. Smith, 1831. 2 vols. in 1. 577 p. ArEs; KyLxT; KyRE; PCA; ViRU. 7770

Josephus, Flavius.
The genuine works of Flavius Josephus, the Jewish historian ...and the life of Josephus, written by himself; translated from the original Greek, according to Havercamp's accurate edition. Together with explanatory notes and observations... A complete index. By the late William Whiston, M.A...Revised and illustrated with notes, by Samuel Burder, A.M. ...Philadelphia, Kimber & Sharpless, 1831. 2 vols. CLSU;

FTaSC; PPiW; PNt. 7771

---- Works...to which are added three dissertations concerning, Jesus Christ, John the Baptist, James the Just, God's command to Abraham...trans. by Wm. Whiston... Baltimore, Md., Armstrong, 1831. PPLT. 7772

---- The Works...Translated from the Greek, according to Havercamps...edition. Together with...notes and observations... By...W. Whiston... Philadelphia, J. Grigg, 1831. 2 vols. CtY; OCH; OClWHi. 7773

Joslin, Benjamin Franklin, 1796-1861.
Electro-magnetic apparatus, by Benjamin F. Joslin, M.D. [Philadelphia, 1831] 7 p. NNNAM. 7774

---- Observations on vision, by Benjamin F. Joslin, M.D. ... Extracted from the American journal of the medical sciences, for May, 1831. Philadelphia, Pr. by Joseph R. A. Skerrett., 1831. 8 p. CtY; DSG; MBM; NNUT; NNN. 7775

Journal of the Free Trade Convention, held in Philadelphia, from Sept. 30-Oct. 7, 1831; and their Address to the People of the United States: to which is added a sketch of the Debates in the Convention. Philadelphia, 1831. 7776

Journal of the proceedings of a convention of literary and scientific gentlemen, held in the Common council chamber of the city of New York, October, 1830. New York, J. Leavitt and G. & C. & H. Carvill, 1831. 286 p. ABBS; CtY; DLC; NhD; Wa. 7777

Joutel, Henri, 1640?-1735.
Diario hostorico del ultimo viaje que hizo M. de la Sale para descubrir el desembocadero y curso del Missicipi. Contine la historia tragica de su muerte y muchas cosas curiosas del nuevo mundo. Escriot en idioma frances por M. T. Joutel... Tr. al español par J. M. Tarnel... Nueva York, J. Desnous, 1831. 156 p. CLCo; IGK; MiD-B; NN; Tx. 7778

Judson, A[doniram], 1788-1850.
A cry from Burmah. Mr. Judson's letter to Mr. Grow. 1831? 12 p. MB; PCC; PPC; PPCP. 7779

---- Letter from the author. American Missionary in Burmah, To female members of Christian Churches in the United States. 2d Boston ed. Boston, Pr. by J. Howe, 1831. 12 p. MNtCA. 7780

---- Letter on ornamental and costly attire to the female members of Christian churches in the United States of America. Providence, H. H. Brown, 1831. 8 p. MBC; NHC-S; PPC; PPCP. 7781

---- Rev. Mr. Judson's letter, to the female members of Christian churches in the United States of America. 2d ed. Providence, Pr. by H. H. Brown, 1831. 12 p. MWborHi. 7782

Judson, Andrew T.
Letter of Andrew T. Judson, state's attorney of Windham county to the Norwich republican regarding criticisms made upon his prosecution of Dr. Siah Fuller of Plainfield, for perjury in case of State vs. Oliver Watkins for murder. Canterbury, Conn., Apr. 22, 1831. 10 p. Ct. 7783

Julia Changed or A True Secret of a Happy Christmas. Philadelphia, American Sunday School Union, 1831. 71 p. NPlaK. 7784

Jung-Stilling, Johann Heinrich, 1740-1817.

The life of John Henry Stilling ...trans. by E. L. Hazelius... Gettysburg, Pr. at the press of the Theol. seminary, H. C. Neinstedt, 1831. 416 p. CoD; DLC; MdBP; PHi; ScNC. 7785

Juvenalis, Decimus Junius, 40-125?

Decimi Junii Juvenalis et Auli Persii Flacci Satiiae expurgatae, notis illustratae, curavit. F. P. Leverett. Boston, Bazin & Ellsworth [1831] 252 p. InU; MA; NjR; RWoH. 7786

---- ---- Bostoniae, Hilliard, 1831. 253 p. MA; NJR; NcG; OrPU. 7787

---- Juvenal. Translated. By Charles Badham... New ed. With an appendix containing imitations of the third and tenth satires. By Dr. Samuel Johnson. To which are added the Satires of Persius. New York, Harper [1831?] 227, 58 p. C; NbOC; OC; PLFM. 7788

---- Juvenalis et Anti Persü Flacci satirae expurgatae, notis illustratae, curvit F. P. Leverett. Boston, Bayin & Ellsworth, c1831. 252 p. RPB. 7789

---- Satires; trans. by Charles Badham. By D. J. Juvenalio. New York, 1831. UU. 7790

---- Ten expurgatae of Junius Juvenal and Persies Flaccus. Boston, Wilkin, 1831. 252 p. IaFairP; MiD; PP. 7791

The Juvenile forget me not. A Christmas and New Year's gift, or birthday present. For the year 1831. Edited by Mrs. S. C. Hall. Philadelphia, T. Wardle [1831] 224 p. TxU. 7792

The juvenile magazine, and youth's monthly visiter... New York, Turney, 183- V. OClWHi. 7793

The Juvenile miscellany...V. 1-4, Sept. 1826-July-1828; new ser. V. 1-6, Sept. 1828-Aug. 1831; 3d ser. V. 1-6 Sept. ? 1831-Aug. 1834. Boston, J. Putnam [etc.] 1826-34. MBL; MPlyA; MWat; MdBLC. 7794

Juvenile stories; for the instruction of children. 2d series - No. 9. Concord, Hoag & Atwood, 1831. 16 p. MHa; NN; OCl. 7795

K

Kain, John H.

An oration, pronounced before the medical society of the state of Tennessee, May 3d 1831. On medical emulation, by John H. Kain, A. M. member of the society. Nashville, Pub. by the Society, 1831. 13-29 p. CtY; MHi; NBMS; T. 7796

The kaleidoscope or, The spirit of the periodicals... Philadelphia, 1831-1832. 216, 252 p. MB; PHi. 7797

Kames, Henry Home, lord, 1696-1782.

An abridgment of Elements of criticism. By the Honorable Henry Home of Kames. Ed. by John Frost... Philadelphia, Towar, J. & D. M. Hogan; Pittsburgh, Hogan & co., 1831. 300 p. DLC; GEU; MH; OO; PPC. 7798

Kane, John Kintzing, 1795-1858.

A discourse pronounced before the Law academy of Philadelphia, on the 26th of October, 1831. By John K. Kane. Philadelphia, Law Academy, Pr. by Mifflin & Parry, 1831. 32 p. MH-L; MWA; OCLaw; PPM; PHi. 7799

Kater, Henry, 1777-1835.
Treatise on mechanics. By Henry Kater and Dionysus Lardner. Boston, 1831. 2-287 p. CtY; MB; MH; MNe; RP. 7800

---- ---- From the London ed. Cambridge, Hilliard & Brown, 1831. 388 p. CtHT; InNd; MB; MH; NNA; PFal. 7801

---- ---- Philadelphia, Carey & Lea, 1831. 287 p. ArCH; MoSU; NCH; NNF; OCx; OCY; OO. 7802

---- Useful knowledge. By Kater, Capt. Henry & Lardner, Rev. Dionysius. Boston, Stimpson & Clapp, 1831. 287 p. MWHi. 7803

Keach, Benjamin, 1640-1704.
The travels of True Godliness. By Rev. Benjamin Keach ... Rev. and imp., with occasional notes, and a memoir of his life; by Howard Malcom, A.M. 2d ed. Boston, Lincoln & Edmands, 1831. 212 p. CtY; DLC; MB; MH-AH; ScU. 7804

Keeler, John.
The South Sea islanders, with a short sketch of Captain Morrell's voyage to the north and south Pacific ocean, in the schooner Antarctic...to which is added a brief sketch of the sufferings of Leonard Shaw, while in captivity. New York, Pr. by Snowden, 1831. 34 p. MB; MBAt; MdBP; PPAmP; PPM. 7805

Keightley, Thomas, 1789-1872.
Outlines of history, from the earliest period to the present time. 1st Amer. ed. with additions. Philadelphia, Carey & Lea, 1831. 379 p. CtHT; IU; PU; RPB; WHi. 7806

---- ---- 2d Amer. ed. with additions and a set of questions for examination of students, by John Frost, A.M. Philadelphia, Carey & Lea; Boston, Hendee and Babcock, 1831. 466 p. DLC; MH-AH; MiDSH; NNC; OClWHi; PHi; ViRU. 7807

Kelley, Hall Jackson, 1790-1874.
A general circular to all persons of good character, who wish to emigrate to the Oregon territory, embracing some account of the character and advantages of the country; the right and the means and operations by which it is to be settled;--and all necessary directions for becoming an emigrant. [By] Hall J. Kelley, general agent, by order of the American society for encouraging the settlement of the Oregon territory. Instituted in Boston, A.D. 1829. Charlestown, Pr. by W. W. Wheildon; Boston, R. P. & C. Williams, 1831. 25 p. CtY; MnHi; OrP; WHi; WaU. 7808

---- A geographical sketch of that part of North America, called Oregon: containing an account of the Indian title...Indians; --number and situation of their tribes;--together with an essay on the advantages resulting from a settlement of the territory. To which is attached a new map of the country. 2d ed., enl. with an appendix embracing an account of the expedition, and directions for becoming an emigrant. [by] Hall J. Kelley... Boston, J. Howe [1831?] 104 p. DLC; MnHi; MoS; NN; WaSP. 7809

---- The Oregon Country... Charlestown, Mass.? 1831. 1 l. WaU. 7810

Kelly, John, 1763-1858.
A sermon, delivered at the funeral of Doctor William Cogswell, of Atkinson, (N.H.) January 3, 1831. Boston, Crocker & Brewster [1831] 16 p. CtY; MB;

MWA; MWc; RPB. 7811

Kelsey, Asahel E.
Select scriptures, or plain Bible facts theological questions, remarks, &c... Elyria, O., Park & Burrell, 1831. 22 p. OClWHi. 7812

Kemper, Frederick Augustus.
Consolations of the afflicted, written by Frederick Augustus Kemper, A.M. A native of Ohio. Cincinnati, Pr. by Wm. J. Ferris & co., 1831. 258 p. CSmH; ICP; OC; OClWHi; TxHR. 7813

Kempis, Thomas A.
The imitation of Christ, in three books. Rendered into English from the original Latin by John Payne, with an introductory essay by Thomas Chalmers, of Glasgow. By Thomas à Kempis. Boston, Lincoln & Edmands, 1831. 228 p. GAlN; MWA; WAsN. 7814

Kendall, James.
A sermon, delivered at the ordination of Rev. James Augustus Kendall, as pastor of the First Congregational Church and Society in Medfield, Mass. Nov. 10, 1830. By James Kendall, Pastor of the First Church in Plymouth. Pub. by request of the Society. Boston, Leonard C. Bowles, 1831. 24 p. ICMe; MH; MH-AH; MWA; RPB. 7815

Kendall, John, 1726-1815, ed.
Letters on Religious Subjects, written by Diver Friends deceased. First published in London by John Kendall. Philadelphia, Thomas Kite, 1831. 2 vols. in 1. CtHT; ICN; NjR; PHC; ScC. 7816

Kennebunkport, Me. Baptist Church.
Summary declaration of the faith and practise of the Baptist Church in Kennebunk-Port, Maine. Adopted by the church in 1831. Kennebunk, 1831. 8 p. CtY. 7817

Kennedy, A. W.
Map of Buck's County, Pennsylvania. Philadelphia, Tanner, 1831. PHi; PPL-R; PU. 7818

[Kennedy, Grace] 1782-1825.
Father Clement. Boston, Peirce, 1831. 246 p. PWW. 7819

Kennedy, John Pendleton, 1795-1870.
Address delivered on behalf of the faculty of arts and sciences, on the occasion of the opening of the collegiate department in the university of Maryland, on the 3d of January, 1831. By John P. Kennedy, Professor of History. Baltimore, Pr. by John D. Toy, 1831. 26 p. DLC; MdBA; NIC; PHi; WHi. 7820

Kennedy, Nathaniel.
The gospel Mason, or the beauty of unity; a sermon preached before the worshipful master, wardens, and brethren of Lodge no. 50, of Free and Accepted Masons, at West-Chester, on the anniversary of St. John the Evangelist... Philadelphia, Pr. for the author, 1831. 24 p. IaCrM; PHi; PPL. 7821

Kenney, James, 1780-1849.
Hernani; or, The pledge of honour; a play in five acts, from Victor Hugo, by James Kenney. New York, S. French, ltd. [1831?] 53 p. OCl. 7822

Kenrick, Francis Patrick.
Pastoral address of the Rt. Rev. Dr. Kenrick, to the clergy of the diocess of Philadelphia, on occasion of the promu[l]gation of the decrees of the Provincial council. Philadelphia, Eugene Cummiskey, 1831. 8 p. DLC; MdBLC; MdHi; NNF; PHi. 7823

---- Pastoral addresses (1) to the clergy July 30; (2) to the Laity, Aug. 1, 1831. Philadelphia, 1831. 8 p. PHi. 7824

---- Pastoral address to the congregation of St. Mary's April 22, 1831. Philadelphia, 1831. 8 p. PHi. 7825

Kenrick, John, 1788-1877.
A key to the complete course of exercises in Latin syntax; adapted to Zumpt's grammar, chiefly by the Rev. John Kendrick, M. A. New-York, G. & C. H. Carvill, 1831. 110 p. DLC; MH; NCU; NGH. 7826

[Kenrick, William] 1725?-1779.
The whole duty of woman... Written at the desire of a noble lord. By a lady. Georgetown, D.C., Rind, 1831. 80 p. DLC. 7827

Kent, James, 1763-1847.
An address delivered at New Haven before the Phi Beta Kappa Society, September 13, 1831. By James Kent. New Haven, Pr. by Hezekiah Howe, 1831. 48 p. CtHT-W; ICU; NN; PPPrHi; RPB. 7828

---- Opinions of Chancellor Kent and A. Van Vechten upon the case between the Albany and Schenectady Turnpike Company, and the Hudson and Mohawk Railraod Company. [New York? 1831.] Broadside. NN. 7829

---- Speeches of Chancellor Kent and the Hon. Daniel Webster at a public dinner given to the latter at the City Hall in New York, March 24, 1831. Boston, N. Hale's Steam Power Press, 1831. 24 p. CtY; NN. 7830

Kentucky.
Acts passed at the first session of the thirty-ninth General Assembly for the commonwealth of Kentucky, begun and held in the town of Frankfort, on Monday, the sixth day of December, 1830, and of the commonwealth the twenty-ninth. Thomas Metcalfe, governor. Pub. by authority. Frankfort, Jacob H. Holeman, 1831. 231 p. A-SC; IaU-L; KyLxT; MdBB; Nb; OrSC. 7831

---- Decisions, Court of Appeals, Kentucky 1817-1821. Frankfort, 1831. Md. 7832

---- Journal of the Senate. 1831 ... Frankfort, Jacob H. Holeman, 1831. 288 p. Ky; KyBgW; KyRmcl; KyU; MHi. 7833

---- Militia laws, comprising the Acts of Congress... and the Acts of Kentucky... Louisville [Ky.] 1831. 72 p. OCHP. 7834

---- Reports of cases at law and in equity, argued and decided in the Court of appeals, of the commonwealth of Kentucky, [1829-1832] By J. J. Marshall... Frankfort, Pr. by J. H. Holeman, [etc.] 1831-34. 7 vols. CSjoSCL; IaDaGL; MBNU-L; NCH; OCLaw; Sc-SC. 7835

---- Reports of selected civil and criminal cases decided in the Court of appeals of Kentucky... Louisville, Ky., J. P. Morton & Co., 1831. DLC. 7836

---- Rules of the House of Representatives of the commonwealth of Kentucky November session, 1831. Frankfort [Ky.] J. H. Holeman, public pr., 1831. ICU. 7837

Kentucky colonization society.
The...annual report of the Kentucky colonization society, with an address...1831-. Frankfort, Ky. [1831] DLC; KyDC; OC; TxU. 7838

Kenyon College, Gambier, Ohio.
By-Laws of Kenyon College and Grammar School. Acland Press, Gambier, Ohio, Pr. by George W. Myers, 1831. 16 p. MH; MHi. 7839

---- Catalogue of the officers and students of Kenyon College and Grammar School, 1831-1832. Gambier, Ohio, Pr. by George W. Myers, 1831. 12 p. MHi; OGaK. 7840

Kett, Henry.
The Flowers of Wit; or, A choice collection of bon mots, puns, epitaphs, bulls, etc., etc. Both ancient and modern, with biographical and critical remarks, by Henry Kett. New York, Pr. by S. & D. A. Forbes, 1831. 2 vols. in 1. 115 p. NBuG; NbU; PP. 7841

Key, Francis Scott, 1779-1843.
Oration delivered by Francis S. Key, esq., in rotundo of the Capitol of the United States, on the 4th of July, 1831. [Washington, 1831] 16 p. DLC; KyDC; MdHi; PPL. 7842

Key to the Analytical table of Mechanical Movements. Boston, S. N. Dickinson, 1831. 18 p. DLC. 7843

A key to the second initiatory catechism with an introduction explanatory of the lesson system of teaching and with directions for using the key. New York, Pr. by J. Leavitt, 1831. 216 p. CtHWatk; NCanHi; UPB. 7844

Kilbourn, John, 1787-1831.
The Ohio Gazetteer; or, Topographical dictionary describing the several counties, towns, villages, canals, roads, rivers, lakes, springs, mines, &c., in the state of Ohio. By John Kilbourn, carefully rev. and cor. Columbus [O.] J. Kilbourn [c 1829] 1831. 335 p. DLC; IU; MHa; OO; WM. 7845

Kimball Union Academy, Meriden Village, N.H.
A Catalogue...for the year ending May 11, 1831. [Windsor, Vt., Pr. by Simeon Ide, 1831] 12 p. MH. 7846

King, Thomas F.
A sermon delivered in the Universalist Church... "He that believeth and is baptized, shall be saved; but he that believeth not shall be damned." A sermon, delivered...in Portsmouth, N.H., in April, 1831. By Thomas F. King... Portsmouth, N.H., Nathaniel March, 1831. 8 p. NcA-S. 7847

Kinkead, George Blackburn.
An oration delivered in behalf of Transylvania Whig Society, on the 22d February, 1831. [Lexington, Pr. by Herndon & Savary, 1831] 8 p. KyLexP. 7848

Kinne, William.
Short system of practical arithmetic, compiled from the best authorities; to which is annexed a short plan of book-keeping. The whole designed for the use of schools...8th ed., with questions. Rev., corr. and greatly enl. by Daniel Robinson. Hallowell, Glazier, Masters and Co., 1831. 240 p. NNC. 7849

Kirby, Edmund.
Address delivered before the Jefferson County Agricultural Society, at the annual cattle show and fair, at Watertown, on the 27th Sept. 1831...Watertown, Pr. by Woodward & Calhoun, 1831. 24 p. N; NN; NbU; P. 7850

Kirkham, Samuel.

English grammar in familiar lectures...compendium embracing a new systematick [sic] order of parsing... etc. 24 ed. Rochester [N.Y.] Marshall, 1831. 228 p. OClWHi; OO. 7851

---- ---- 25th ed., enl. and imp. Louisville, Ky., Smith and Morton, 1831. 228 p. NBuHi. 7852

---- ---- 25th ed., enl. and imp. New York, M'Elrath & Bangs, 1831. 28 p. MoKCM; OBog. 7853

---- ---- 26th ed., enl. and imp. Cincinnati, Morgan and Sanxay; Stereotyped by Wm. Hagar & Co., New York, 1831. 228 p. CSt; IaBo. 7854

---- ---- 30th ed., enl. and imp. Baltimore, Plaskitt & Co., etc., 1831. MH. 7855

Kitchiner, William, 1775?-1827.
The art of invigorating and prolonging life...& peptic precepts...By the author of "The cook's oracle." From the 6th London ed., rev. and imp. by T. S. Barrett. New York, Harper, 1831. 281 p. PPA. 7856

---- ...The cook's oracle; and housekeeper's manual...by William Kitchiner, M.D... From the last London ed. New York, J. & J. Harper, 1831. 432 p. MB; MeHi. 7857

---- Directions for invigorating and prolonging life; or, The invalid's oracle. Containing peptic precepts...to prevent and relieve indigestion, and to regulate and strengthen the action of the stomach and bowels. From 6th London ed., rev. by T. S. Barrett. New York, J. & J. Harper, 1831. 252 p. CtHT; MB; OO; TNP; ViU. 7858

Knapp, Georg Christian, 1753-1825.
Lectures on Christian theology, by George Christian Knapp. Tr. by Leonard Woods, jun. ...New-York, G. & C. & H. Carvill, 1831-33. 2 vols. CtY; DLC; IAlS; KyLo; ViRut. 7859

Knapp, John Francis.
An authentic account of the last hours of John Francis Knapp ...with comments on the evidence produced at his trial for the murder of Capt. Joseph White. Milford, Ballou & Story, 1831. 15 p. MBAt; MBC. 7860

[Knapp, John Leonard] 1767-1845.
The journal of a naturalist... Philadelphia, Carey & Lea, 1831. 286 p. CU; CtY; ICBB; GDecCT; KyLx; MiU; PP; RPB; TNP. 7861

Knapp, Samuel Lorenzo, 1783-1838.
A memoir of the life of Daniel Webster. By Samuel L. Knapp. Boston, Stimpson and Clapp, 1831. 1 p. l., 234 p. ICMe; MH; MPlyP; NhD; Nh; VtB; WHi. 7862

Kneeland, Abner, 1774-1844.
A review of the evidences of Christianity; in a series of lectures, delivered in Broadway hall, New-York, August, 1829. To which is prefixed, an extract from Wyttenbach's Opuscula, on the ancient notices of the Jewish nation previous to the time of Alexander the Great. By Abner Kneeland...3d ed. Boston, Office of the Investigator, 1831. 204 p. DLC; MB; WHi. 7863

Knickerbocker, Diedrich, pseud.
See Irving, Washington, 1783-1859.

Knickerbocker's Almanac for 1832. By David Young. New York, Christian Brown [1831] MWA. 7864

Kniffin, W. G.
Historical catechism...history of the United States...3rd ed. Warsaw, Ind., 1831. CtHWatk. 7865

[Knight, Charles] 1791-1873.
...The results of machinery, namely, cheap production and increased employment, exhibited: being an address to the workingmen of the United Kingdom. American ed. Philadelphia, Carey & Hart, 1831. 216 p. CtHT; DLC; OClW; PU. 7866

---- The Working-men's companion: containing the results of machinery, Cottage evenings, and the rights of industry. Addressed to working-men. New York, Leavitt and Allen [1831?] 3 vols in 1. MH-BA. 7867

Knight, Edward.
The false one. A ballad... [with accompaniment for pianoforte]. The poetry by Thos. H. Bayley [sic] Esq. Composed... by Edw. Knight. New York, Firth & Hall, 1831. 3 p. MB. 7868

Knight, Henry C[ogswell], 1788-1835.
Lectures and sermons. Boston, Lilly & Wait, (late Wells & Lilly), 1831. 2 vols. CtHC; LNT; NBuDD; OO; PPL-R. 7869

Knight, Thomas, 1759-1838.
The turnpike gate; a musical farce, in two acts. New York, E. B. Clayton, 1831. 39 p. MH. 7870

Knight, W. C.
The juvenile harmony, or, a choice collection of psalm tunes, hymns and anthems...5th ed. rev. & cor. Cincinnati, Morgan & Sanxay, 1831. 143 p. OCHP; OClWHi. 7871

Knowles, James D(avis), 1798-1838.
Life of Mrs. Ann H. Judson, late Missionary to Burmah; with an account of the American Baptist Mission to that empire. Philadelphia, American Sunday School Union [c 1831] 266 p. ArSsJ; FDef; Ia; IaGG; MHa; NBP; PPM; ScCoT. 7872

---- Memoir of Mrs. Ann Judson, late missionary to Burmah, including a history of the American Baptist mission in the Burman Empire. By James Knowles. 4th ed. Boston, Lincoln & Edmands, 1831. 406 p. C; IU; MB; OO; PCA. 7873

Knoxville Female Academy. Knoxville, Tennessee.
Catalogue of the trustees, instructors and students of the Knoxville Female Academy. Summer session, 1831. Knoxville, T., Pr. by F. S. Heiskell, 1831. 11 p. TKL-Mc; TU. 7874

Kuhff, Henry.
Elements of the calculus of finale differences with the application of its principles to the summation and interpolation of series... Cambridge, Hilliard & Co., 1831. 77 p. CtY; RPB. 7875

Kurtz, Benjamin, 1795-1865.
A door opened of the Lord; being an introductory sermon delivered in Chambersburg, Pa., on Sunday, Aug. 14, 1831, upon taking charge of the Evangelic Lutheran Congregation of said place. Chambersburg, Pa., Pr. by Pritts & Oswald [1831?] 10 p. CSmH; PHi. 7876

---- The "ministerial appeal," a valedictory sermon delivered in the Evangelical Lutheran Church in Hagerstown, Md., on Sunday the 4th of September, 1831. [Hagerstown, Md.] Pr. at the "Free Press" office [1831]

14 p. NcU; PPLT. 7877

Kurzefasstes Weiber-Büchlein; enthalt Aristoteli und A. Magni Hebammen-Kunst mit endarzu gehörigen Recepten. Canton (O.), Gedruckt fur J. Sala, 1831. 64 p. NN. 7878

L

Labarraque, Antoine Germain, 1777-1850.

Instructions and Observations concerning the use of the chlorides and soda and lime. By A. G. Labarraque, pharmaceutist of Paris... Tr. by Jacob Porter. 2d ed. New-Haven, Pr. by Baldwin & Treadway, 1831. 32 p. Ct; MB; PPL-R; ScU; WU. 7879

Lacroix, Silvestre François, 1765-1843.

Elements of algebra, by S. F. Lacroix. Tr. from the French for the use of the students at the University at Cambridge, New England. By John Farrar... 3d ed. Boston, Hilliard, Gray, Little & Wilkins, 1831. 298 p. DLC; ICP; MdBD; NjP; PPi; ViU. 7880

Lacy, Michael Rophino, 1795-1867.

Songs, duets, concerted pieces, and choruses, in the new comic opera, in three acts, called Cinderella, or the Fairy queen and the glass slipper. The music composed by Rossini, containing choice selections from his operas of Cenerentola... The scenery by Mr. Evers. The whole arranged and adapted to the English stage by M. Rophino Lacy. Performed for the first time at the Park Theatre. New York, Monday, Jan. 24, 1831. New York, J. C. Spear, 1831. 16 p. TxU. 7881

[Ladd, William] 1778-1841.

A brief illustration of the principles of war and peace, showing the ruinous policy of the former, and the superior efficacy of the latter, for national protection and defence; clearly manifested by their practical operations and opposite effects upon nations, kingdoms and people. By Philanthropos [pseud.] ... Albany, Pr. by Packard and Van Benthuysen, 1831. 112 p. CtY; IU; NBuG; RPB; WHi. 7882

Ladies Greek Association. New Haven.

First annual report. New Haven, Nathan Whiting, 1831. 64 p. Ct; MH; MHi; PPPrHi; WHi. 7883

LaGarrigue, John Francis.

Geometry of Motion: Trisection of Angles and Arches. Trisection-Compass; or, The Compass of Proportions, Improved. In other words: Construction of a mathematical instrument, whereby any angle and arch may be divided into three equal parts. By John Francis LaGarrigue, formerly an Advocate in Cahors, (France); now, and three years since, a resident in the United States of America. New York, 1831. 68 p. MCM; MWA; ScC. 7884

[LaHarpe, Barnard de]

Journal historique de L'etablissement des Francaisa la Louisiane. Nouvelle, Orleans, A. L. Boimare [etc., etc.] 1831. 412 p. CSmH; ICN; IGK; LNL; MB; TxU; ViU. 7885

Laird, Robert M.

A discourse on Christian baptism. Princess-Anne, Me., 1831. 23 p. MBAt; NHC-S. 7886

---- A discourse on the witnessing of the Holy Spirit, in regard to the divine adoption of true believers. By Robert M. Laird.

Princess-Ann, Md., 1831. MBAt; NjPT. 7887

---- The Shorter catechism of the Presbyterian Church briefly explained, in the way of question and answer. By Robert M. Laird. Princess-Anne, Md., Pr. by J. S. Zieber, 1831. 149 p. CSmH; MdHi; PPPrHi. 7888

Lallemand, Charles Francois Antoine Baron.
Catalogue des livres provenant de sa bibliotheque... New York, Desnoues, 1831. 38 p. PPAmP. 7889

Lamarck, Jean Baptiste Pierre Antoine de Monet, chev de, 1744-1829.
Genera of shells; partly copied from the London quarterly; of science, literature and the arts... Philadelphia, 1831. PPAmP. 7890

Lamb, Jonathan.
The child's primer or first book for primary schools. Burlington, C. Goodrich, 1831. 72 p. MH. 7891

---- A present for a little niece. Burlington, C. Goodrich, 1831. 16 p. MB. 7892

Lancasterian school.
Circular. New Haven, 1831. MB. 7893

[Lancelot, Claude] 1615-1695.
The Greek Primitives, of the Messieurs DePort-Royal, to which are added rules for derivation, or the formation of words; selected principally from Buttman's Greek Grammar. Boston, Perkins and Marvin, 1831. 183 p. CoU; IJI; MH; RPB; WU. 7894

Landreth, David.
Periodical catalogue of green house and hardy herbaceous plants and shrubs, etc. to which is added a treatise on the cultivation of vegetables... Philadelphia, W. Stavely, 1831. 109 p. PPM. 7895

Langdon, J.
A new map of the City of New York. New York, 1831. MB. 7896

Larcom, Lucy, comp.
Hillside and seaside in poetry; a companion to "Roadside poems," ed. by Lucy Larcom. Boston, J. R. Osgood and company, 1831. 303 p. MLy. 7897

Lardner, Rev. Dionysius, 1793-1859.
History of the Netherlands. Philadelphia, Carey & Lea, 1831. 300 p. CtY; MH; OCX; PU; WvW. 7898

Larrabee, Rev. William C.
Inaugural address of Rev. William C. Larrabee, A.M. delivered November 10th, 1831, on being inducted into office as Principal of the Oneida Conference Seminary, Cazenovia, N.Y., Pr. by J. F. Fairchild & Son, 1831. 27 p. KyLx; PPL. 7899

Last hours of several eminently useful and pious individuals, of the Baptist denomination, in the United States. Philadelphia, 1831. 36 p. NjPT. 7900

Lathrop, John, Jr., 1772-1820.
An address before the associated instructors of youth in Boston... Aug. 19, 1831. 20 p. MB. 7901

Lathrop, Leonard E.
Sermons on the nature & influence of evangelical faith. By ...pastor of the Congregational church & society, Salisbury, Conn. Hartford, Hudson & Skinner, 1831. 103 p. CtHC; Ct;

IEG; InCW; NSyU. 7902

Lathrop, Samuel K.
Anniversary address I. C. C. Oct. 19, 1831 by the Rev. Samuel K. Lathrop. Philadelphia, Carey & Lea, 1831. 3 vols. MBVAFCC. 7903

Latreille, P. A.
Crustacea, Arachnides aux insecta. New York, G. & C. & H. Carvill, 1831. 4 vols. in 2. INovmN; PPAN. 7904

Law, William, 1686-1761.
An address to the clergy and a short account of the author. Exeter, N.H., 1831. 192 p. MB. 7905

---- A humble, earnest, and affectionate address to the clergy, by William Law... To which is prefixed a short account of the author. Exeter, N.H., Pr. by B. H. Meder, 1831. 188 p. IaMp; MB; MHi; Nh; TxGR. 7906

---- The nature and design of Christianity... Philadelphia, 1831. RPJCB. 7907

---- ---- Providence, Pr. by H. H. Brown, 1831. 12 p. RPJCB. 7908

Lawrence & Lemay's North Carolina Almanack for the year of our Lord, 1832...Carefully calculated for the latitude and meridian of Raleigh. By William Collom. Raleigh, Pr. by Lawrence & Lemay...[1831] 40 p. NcD; NcU. 7909

Lawson, John, d. 1712.
History of North Carolina. By John Lawson...presented by James Maddison in the year 1831. Charlotte? Observer printing house? 1831. 171 p. RP. 7910

[Lea, Pryor]
Circular of Mr. Lea, to his constituents of the Second Congressional District of Tennessee. Washington City, March 3, 1831. 8 p. DLC. 7911

Leavitt, Humphrey Howe, 1796-1873.
Speech of Mr. Leavitt, of Ohio on the amendment offered by Mr. Vance to the general appropriation bill [proposing to reduce the compensation of the president of the United States, vice-president, heads of department, auditors, clerks, postmasters, etc.] [Washington, 183-] DLC. 7912

Leavitt, Joshua, 1794-1873.
The Christian lyre, by Joshua Leavitt. New York, Jonathan Leavitt; Boston, Crocker & Brewster, 1831. 2 vols. Ct; DLC; MB; NjP; NNMHi. 7913

---- Easy lessons in reading; for the use of the younger classes in common schools. By Joshua Leavitt; 3d ed. Watertown, Knowlton & Rice, 1831. 156 p. NjHi. 7914

---- Supplement to the Christian lyre; containing more than one hundred psalm tunes, such as are most used in churches of all denominations. By Joshua Leavitt. New York, Jonathan Leavitt; Boston, Crocker & Brewster, 1831. 106 p. CtY; MPiB; NN; PCA; RPB. 7915

No entry. 7916

Leavitt's farmers almanac.
Leavitt's Improved Farmer's and Scholar's Almanack, for 1832. Dudley Leavitt. Concord, N.H., Horatio Hill & Co. [1831] MWA; MiD-B. 7917

Leben August Herman Frankes, Professor der Theologie in Halle. Stifter und Director des Hallischen Waisen Hauses. Gettysburg, Pa., Pr. by H. C. Neinstedt, 1831. 72 p. CSmH. 7918

Le Clerc, Paul, 1657-1740.
Man's only affair: or, Reflections on the four last things to be remembered. Tr. from the French, to which are added, morning and evening prayers; prayer of Mass, accompanied with a short explanation of its ceremonies; and Vespers. 2d Amer. ed. Boston, William Smith, for the editors of "The Jesuit," 1831. 208 p. MdBLC; MiDSH. 7919

Lecture on the resurrection of the body; compiled from the writings of Paul, Dick, Hall and others, by a layman. Albany, Joel Munsell, 1831. 24 p. MBC. 7920

Lee, George Alexander, 1802-1851.
Oh 'twas sweet to hear her singing. As sung by Miss Shirrif; poetry by Miss Fitzroy; composed by Alexander Lee. Baltimore, G. Willig, Jr. [183-?] 3 p. ViU. 7921

[Lee, Gideon] 1778-1841.
To the honorable the legislature of the state of New York. [New York, 1831?] 3 p. MH-BA. 7922

Lee, Mrs. Rebecca.
Address at Marlborough, Ct. to the Female Benevolent Association... and the members of the Female Bible Class. Hartford, 1831. 12 p. MBC. 7923

Lee, Thomas Jones, d. 1835.
A spelling-book, containing the rudiments of the English language, with appropriate reading lessons. Imp. ed. Hallowell, Me., Glazier, Masters and Co., 1831. 207 p. DLC. 7924

Leeds, Joseph.
Address delivered before Dorchester Temperance Society, at Public Meeting, Dec. 4, 1830. 1st Anniversary of the Society. Boston, T. R. Marvin, 1831. 36 p. DLC; ICN; MB; MHi; MWA. 7925

[Lees, Thomas J.]
The musing of Carol (pseud.). Containing an essay on Liberty; The desperado, a tale of the ocean, and other original poems. By Thomas J. Lees... Wheeling, Pr. by A. & E. Picket, for the author, 1831. 178 p. MB; NcD; OCOV; ViU. 7926

Leeth, John, 1755-1832.
A short biography of John Leeth, giving a brief account of his travels and sufferings among the Indians for eighteen years, together with his religious exercises, from his own relation, by Ewel Jeffries. Lancaster, O., Pr. at the Gazette Office, 1831. OFH; PPL; WHi. 7927

LeFevre, C. F.
...A discourse... By Rev. C. F. LeFevre. Troy, N.Y., Kemble & Hill, 1831. 16 p. MMeT-Hi. 7928

Legendre, Adrian Marie.
Elements of geometry, by A. M. Legendre...Tr. from the French for the use of the students of the University at Cambridge, New England, by John Farrar...New ed., enl. Boston,

Hilliard, Gray, Little & Wilkins, 1831. 235 p. CV; IaHi; MBAt; RNR; TxU-T. 7929

[Leggett, Samuel]
The explanation and vindication of Samuel Leggett, late president of The Franklin Bank of the City of New-York. New-York, Pr. by E. Conrad, 1831. 87 p. CSmH; CtY; MH; NNC; PHi. 7930

LeGuire, Amos.
A juvenile poem, entitled, The Heliad, or Christ, the light of world, in numbers, at different intervals. Cooperstown, H. & E. Phinney, 1831. RPB. 7931

Lehigh Coal and Navigation Company.
Report(s) of the board of managers... Philadelphia, Pr. by Wm. F. Geddes, 1831-33. MH-BA. 7932

Leib, James Ronaldson.
Lecture on Scientific Education. Delivered Saturday, December 18, 1830, before the members of the Franklin Institute. By James R. Leib, A.M. Philadelphia, Pr. by Clark & Raser, 1831. 16 p. MBAt; MWA; PPAmP; PHi; PPL. 7933

[Leigh, Benjamin Watkins]
Essays on the American system, its principle and object, originally published in the Boston com. gazette, in October, 1831. Under the signature of Algernon Sydney, and repub. in the Banner of the constitution. Philadelphia, Pr. by T. W. Ustick, 1831. 28 p. ICU; MB; MH-BA; NNE. 7934

Leighton, Robert, abp. of Glasgow, 1611-1684.
The Select Works of Archbishop Leighton. Prepared for the practical use of Private Christians. With an introductory view of the Life, Character, and Writings of the Author. By George B. Cheever. Boston, Peirce & Parker, 1831. 2 vols. 7935

Lempriere, John, 1765?-1824.
Bibliotheca classica: or, A classical dictionary; containing a copious account of the principal proper names mentioned in ancient authors...By J. Lempriere, D.D. 3d New York ed., enl., remodelled, and extensively imp. by Charles Anthon... New York, G. & C. and H. Carvill, 1831. 2 vols. NNV; NSuf; PWW; ScSP. 7936

Leo-Wolf, Joseph.
Observations on the prevention and cure of hydrophobia. According to the latest and popular publications in Germany. Read before the New York Medical and Philosophical Society. New York, Carvill, 1831. 31 p. CtHWatk; MH-M; MoKJM; NNN; PPL-R. 7937

Leonard, Benjamin G.
An oration, delivered at Chillicothe on the fourth day of July, 1831. Chillicothe, O., 1831. 19 p. OCHP; OClWHi; PPAmP. 7938

Leonard, Levi W.
The literary and scientific class book, embracing the leading facts and principles of science. Illustrated by engravings ...Selected from the Rev. John Platts' literary and scientific class book. ...By Levi W. Leonard. Boston, Keene, N. H. J. & J. W. Prentiss, 1831. 318 p. NNC; TxU-T. 7939

Le Sage, Alain Rene, 1668-1747.
The adventures of Gil Blas of Santillane. Tr. from the French of Monsieur Le Sage. By Dr. Smollet... Hartford, Andrews, 1831. Paged separately. 3 vols. in 1. CtHWatk; LNT; MH; PPL-R; WHi. 7940

---- The devil upon two sticks translated from the Diable Borteux of M. LeSage... New York, J. A. Clusman, 1831. 337 p. CtHT-W; NICLA; RPE. 7941

Leseur, Francis.
The universal triune: a new and universal system of Christian philosophy, embracing every department of science; theology, metaphysics, and physiology, on a short and concise plan. Discovered by Francis Leseur. Hartford, Pr. [by Folsom & Hurlburt] for the author, 1831. 31 p. CtY; MBAt; MWA; MWo; NNG. 7942

Leslie, Eliza, 1787-1858.
American girls' book; or, occupation for play hours. By Miss Leslie... Boston, Munroe & Francis; New York, C. S. Francis, 1831. 303 p. CS; DLC; MH; PHi; ScCliTO. 7943

---- ---- 16th ed. New York, James Miller, c1831. 383, 309 p. ScCliTO. 7944

---- Cards of Boston, comprizing a variety of facts and descriptions relative to that city in the past and present times; so arranged as to form an instructive and Amusing Game for Young People [Boston] 1831. MHi. 7945

Leslie, John, 1766-1832.
...Narrative of discovery and adventure in the Polar seas and regions:...and an account of whale-fishery, by Professor Leslie, Professor Jameson, and Hugh Murray. [Harper's stereotype ed.] New York, J. & J. Harper, 1831. 373 p. CSmH; LNL; ScNC; TxDaM; ViU. 7946

Let not the faith nor the laws of the commonwealth [Pennsylvania] be violated. [relative to the Union canal company's claims to a double lottery grant]. 1831. 30 p. WHi. 7947

A letter on the Principles of the Missionary Enterprise. 3d ed. Boston, Gray and Bowen, for the American Unitarian Association, 1831. 39 p. MB-HP; MeBat. 7948

The Letter Writer: containing a great variety of letters on the following subjects: relationship-busines-love, courtship and marriage-friendship-and miscellaneous letters: selected from judicious and eminent writers. Boston, C. Gaylord, 1831. 6-144 p. CtY; ICN; NN. 7949

The letters of "Republicus," with explanations and remarks, by Mr. Buchan. Rochester, Pr. by Marshall & Dean, 1831. 26 p. MdBLC. 7950

Letters of [Richard] Rush, [John Quincy] Adams, and [Wm.] Wirt. on Free masons. Boston, Leonard W. Kimball, and John Marsh, & Co., 1831. 47 p. MBAt; MBNEH; MdHi; WHi. 7951

Letters on religious subjects between a dissenting minister in Birmingham and a Roman Catholic. Boston, Mooney, 1831. 106 p. MBrigStJ; MDB; MdBLC; MiDSH. 7952

Letters to a mother. Boston, 1831. 67 p. MB; MWA. 7953

Letters to James Fener [sic] esq. in 1811 and 1831. [Providence? 1831?] 16 p. DLC; MH; NN; NNC; RPB. 7954

Leverett, Frederick Percival, 1803-1836.
...The new Latin tutor; or, Exercises in etymology, syntax and prosody: comp. chiefly from the best English works. By

Frederic P. Leverett... Boston, Hilliard, Gray, Little and Wilkins, 1831. 350 p. CtY; ICP; KyLxT; MB; NjR; TxU-T. 7955

Levizac, Jean Pons Victor Leroutz de.
A theoretical and practical grammar of the French tongue; in which the present usage is displayed, agreeably to the decisions of the French academy; rev. and corr. by Stephen Pasquier. 7th Amer. ed., with the Voltarian orthography, according to the dictionary of the French academy. New York, Dean, 1831. 444 p. KyLo; NCH. 7956

Lewis, Alonzo, 1794-1861.
Poems. By Alonzo Lewis. Boston, J. H. Eastburn, 1831. 208 p. DLC; MBAt; MH; RPB. 7957

Lewis, Enoch, 1776-1856.
The Practical analyst; or, A treatise on algebra, containing the most useful parts of that science, illustrated by a copious collection of examples designed for the use of schools. 2d ed. Philadelphia, Kimber and Sharpless, 1831. CtY; MBBC; MH; PHC; PHI; PU. 7958

---- Some observations on the militia system addrssed to the serious consideration of the citizens of Pennsylvania. Philadelphia, Pr. by A. Waldie, 1831. 35 p. MWA; NjR; PHi; PU; ScCC. 7959

[Lewis, Evan]
An address to Christians of all denominations, on the inconsistency of admitting slave holders to communion and church membership... Philadelphia, Pr. by S. C. Atkinson, 1831. 19 p. DLC; ICN; MB; PHi; RPB. 7960

Lewis, Freeman.
The beauties of harmony; containing the rudiments of music on an improved plan. A musical dictionary, or glossary of musical terms, with their explanations, and an extensive collection of sacred music, short tunes, fuges and anthems. Pittsburgh, Pa., Johnston and Stockton, 1831. 208 p. ICN; ODaB; PPiHi. 7961

Lewis, John.
A brief account of the school, for the liberal education of boys, proposed to be established at Covington, Kentucky, opposite Cincinnati, Ohio. By John Lewis. Teacher at Llangallen, in Spottsylvania County, Virginia. Covington, Ky., Pr. by R. C. Langdon & W. A. Cameron, 1831. 8 p. KyU; MHi; OCHP. 7962

Lewis, Seth.
Remarks on the Hon. Edward Livingston's introductory report to his system of penal law, prepared for the State of Louisiana ... New-Orleans, Pr. by A. T. Penniman & Co., 1831. 142 p. M; MH; NN; PPL. 7963

Lewisburg convention, Lewisburg, Va.
Journal and proceedings of the Lewisburg convention, convened on the 31st of October 1831, to deliberate on the subject of internal improvement in Virginia. Kanawha C.H., Va., Pr. by Campbell & Walker, 1831. 36 p. MH; NcD; OClWHi; Vi. 7964

Lexington, Mass. Social Library.
Catalogue of books in the Lexington Social Library. Boston, Monroe & Francis, 1831. 4 p. MLex. 7965

Lhomond, Charles Francois, 1727-1794.
Elements of French grammar, by M. Lhomond...trans. from

the French, with additional notes, for the use of schools. By H. W. Longfellow... 2d ed. Boston, Gray and Bowen, 1831. 102 p. MB; MH; NNC; NNUT; NNT. 7966

---- French exercises; selected chiefly from Wanostrocht and adapted to the elements of French grammar. By an instructer(!) 2d ed. Boston, Gray and Bowen, 1831. 95 p. CtHWatk; MB; MH. 7967

Libellus precum et piarum exercitationum in usum pie vivere, et feliciter mori desiderantium Permissu superiourum. Georgiopoli, D.C. typis Samuelis. S. Rind, 1831. 191 p. DWP; MdW. 7968

The liberal preacher; a monthly publication of sermons by living ministers, conducted by an association of clergymen. Vol. 1, new series. Boston, Leonard C. Bowles, 1831. 201 p. IEG; MB; MWal. 7969

The Liberator. William Lloyd Garrison and Isaac Knapp, publishers. [Boston, Pr. by Stephen Foster] 1831-1865. DLC; MB; NjP; PHi; TxU. 7970

Library Company of Baltimore.
Third supplement to the catalogue of books, &c. belonging to the Library company of Baltimore. 1831. Baltimore, Pr. by John D. Toy, 1831. 21 p. MdHi. 7971

Library of Foreign Literature and Science.
Report. [Philadelphia, 1831] 8 p. PHi; PPL. 7972

Library of practical medicine. Published by order of the Massachusetts medical society. Boston, 1831-1843. 7 vols. MA. 7973

Lieber, Francis, 1800-1872.
France: A series of articles reprinted from the Encyclopedia Americana contents, part of the article France. Department. Codes, les cinq. Election. Charles X. Louis Philip I. Philadelphia, Carey & Lea, 1831. [79] p. DLC; KHi; MBAt; PPAmP; WHi. 7974

The life and death of Lady Jane Grey. Prepared for the American Sunday School Union, and rev. by the Committee of Publication. Philadelphia, American Sunday-School Union, 1831. 35 p. DLC; MnU. 7975

The life of the Rev. John Fletcher. Abridged from authentic sources. By a friend of Sabbath schools. New York, J. Emory and B. Waugh, for the Sunday School Union of the Methodist Episcopal Church, 1831. 91 p. CtHC; CtMW; GEU; GEU-T; ICBB. 7976

Lincoln, Almira H.
Familiar lectures on botany, including practical and elementary botany...and a vocabulary of botanical terms...By Mrs. Almira H. Lincoln. 2d ed. Hartford, H. & F. J. Huntington, 1831. 426 p. IaTO; InVi; NNC; NNNBG. 7977

Lincoln, E.
The Sabbath School Class Book comprising copious exercises on the sacred scriptures. Boston, Lincoln & Edmands, 1831. 104 p. ICBB; MBC; MCanHi. 7978

Lindley, John, 1799-1865.
An introduction to the natural system of botany...By John Lindley...1st Amer. ed. New York, G. & C. & H. Carvill, 1831. 393 p. IaAS; MB; NjR; PPi; WU. 7979

Lindsley, Philip, 1786-1855.

Baccalaureate address, pronounced on the sixth anniversary commencement of the University of Nashville, October 5, 1831. By Philip Lindsley. Nashville, Pr. at the Herald office, 1831. 36 p. DLC; MWA; NjPT; PHi; TNP. 7980

Lingard, John, 1771-1851.
History of England, from the first invasion by the Romans. By John Lingard, D.D. 1st Amer. from the last London ed. Baltimore, Fielding Lucas, Jr., 1831. MiDU; PPL-R; ScNC. 7981

Little, William.
The easy instructor, or, A new method of teaching sacred harmony. rev. enl. ed. Albany, Websters, 1831. 127 p. PPPrHi. 7982

Little and Cummings, booksellers.
Catalogue of Popular Periodicals; annuals and engravings; law, school, medical, botanical, chemical, theological and miscellaneous books. Albany, Little and Cummings, 1831. NT. 7983

Little Frank's Almanack for 1832. Concord, N.H., J. W. Moore & Co [1831] MWA. 7984

The little gentleman. nos. 1-6; Jan. 1, 1831-April 29, 1831. New Haven, Conn., Hezekiah Howe, 1831. 174 p. Ct; OHi. 7985

The little idle girl, and the Sunday scholar. New Haven, S. Babcock, Sidney's press, 1831. 23 p. CtY. 7986

Little Jane, or playing with fire. New York, J. A. Clussman, c1831. 4 l. PP. 7987

Little Mary; a story for children from four to five years old. Pt. I. By a mother. Boston, Cottons and Barnard, 1831. 36 p. DLC; MH. 7988

Little warbler. Vol. V. Naval songs. Providence, Hutchens & Shepard, 1831. 110 p. MSaP; RPB. 7989

Littlefield, Myra.
Christian perfection. A letter from Miss Myra Littlefield, of Sloughton to the church in North Bridgewater, under the pastoral care of Rev. Daniel Huntington. ... Boston, Pr. by David H. Ela, 1831. 12 p. MB; MBC; MBNEH. 7990

The lives and characters of the officers of the revolution who were most distinguished in achieving our national independence. Also, the life of Gilbert Motier La Fayette. Published for subscribers. Philadelphia, Pr. by Wm. Stavely, 1831. 607 p. LNB. 7991

Livingston, Edward.
An address delivered on the 1st of August, 1831, before the Philolexian and Peithologian Societies, of Columbia College. By Edward P. Livingston.. New-York, G. & C. & H. Carvill, 1831. 28 p. MBC; NNC; PU; ScU; WHi. 7992

---- Lessee of E. Livingston et al., plaintiffs in error, vs. John Moore, et al...defendants. n.p., 1831. MH. 7993

---- Remarks on the expediency of abolishing the punishment of death. By Edward Livingston. Philadelphia, Pr. by Jesper Harding, 1831. 42 p. DLC; MBAt; NdU; PPL; ScC. 7994

---- Speech in the Senate of the United States, Feb. 1831; on the Turkish mission, in answer to Mr. Tazewell of Virginia. Washington, Gales & Seaton, 1831.

47 p. DLC; NN; NNC; PPAmP; WHi. 7995

Livingston, John H., 1746-1825.
Analysis of a System of theology, compiled from lectures by the late John H. Livingston, D.D. New York, J. F. Sihel, 1831. Nos, 1, 2, 3. MBC; NN. 7996

Livingston, R. L.
Memorial to H. of R. Dec. 1831. New York, 1831. 49 p. CtY; MB. 7997

Livius, Titus
Titi Livii Patavini historiarum liber primus et selecta quaedam capita. Curavit notulisque instruxit Carolus Folsom, A. M. ... Editio stereotypa. Cantabrigiae, Sumptibus Hilliard et Brown, 1831. 287 p. DLC; IaFayU; KOtU; MiD-B; ViRU. 7998

Lobstein, Johann Georg Christian Friedrich Martin, 1777-1835.
A treatise on the structure, functions and diseases of the human sympathetic nerve... By John Fred. Lobstein...Tr. from the Latin with notes, by Joseph Pancoast, M.D. Philadelphia, J. C. Auner, 1831. 157 p. CSt-L; DSG; ICJ; NjP; ViRA. 7999

Locke, John, 1632-1704.
An essay for the understanding of St. Paul's Epistles. By John Locke. No. 45. Pr. for The American Unitarian Association. Boston, Gray & Bowen, March, 1831. 24 p. CtHC; DLC; ICMe; Meb; MMeT; MNF. 8000

---- Treatise on the conduct of understanding. By John Locke. Boston, C. D Strong, 1831. 138 p. KySoPL; MFiHi; OMC. 8001

---- ---- Boston, Timothy Bedlington, 1831. 132, 218 p. IEG; MB; MH; PHi; RNR. 8002

Lockhart, John Gibson, 1794-1854.
The history of Napoleon Bonaparte. By J. G. Lockhart, Esq. New York, J. J. Harper, 1831. 2 vols. ArCH; CtHT; MoS; NBuG; TxD-T. 8003

---- Life of Robert Burns. By J. C. Lockhart...With an essay on his writings, prepared for this edition. New York, W. Stodart [etc.] 1831. 320 p. CtHC; GAuP; ICN; OClW; TNP. 8004

The London Carcanet. Containing select passages from the most distinguished writers. From the 2d London ed. New York, C. H. Peabody, 1831. 244 p. DLC; MLex; NN; OT; PPL. 8005

Londonderry, Charles William Vane, 3d marquis of, 1778-1854.
Narrative of the war in Germany and France, in 1813 and 1814. By Lieut. General Charles William Vane... Philadelphia, Carey & Lea, 1831. 300 p. CU; LNH; NcU; PU; ScDue. 8006

Long, Stephen Harriman, 1784-1864.
Report to the canal commissions in reply to strictures passed by Mr. Robinson. Philadelphia, 1831. 12 p. MBAt; MWA; NIC; PHi; PPL. 8007

Longstreet, Augustus Baldwin.
An oration delivered before the Demosthenian and Phi Kappa Societies of the University of Georgia, at the Commencement of August, 1831... Augusta, Pr. by W. Lawson, 1831. 23 p. GEU; NcD. 8008

Longworth's American Almanac, New-York register, and city directory, for the fifty-sixth year of American independence... New-York, Thomas Longworth,

1831. 722 p. NNMuCN; NNS; NjR. 8009

Loomis' calendar, or the New York and Vermont almanack, [sic]: for the year of our Lord 1831. Being the third after bissextile or leap year; and ('till July 4th) the fifty-fifth of American independence. By a successor of the late Andrew Beers. Containing a variety of useful and interesting matter. Albany, G. J. Loomis, 1831. [24] p. MWA; NT. 8010

Lord, Eleazar, 1788-1871.

Memoir of the Rev. Joseph Stibbs Christmas. New York, Haven, and J. Leavitt, 1831. 213 p. CSmH; DLC; ICP; MB; NjP; PHi; RPB. 8011

Lord, Nathan.

A sermon preached at the annual election, at Concord, 2 June, 1831, before the executive and legislative authorities of the state of New-Hampshire. By Nathan Lord, D.D. ...Concord, Pr. by Hill and Barton, for the state, 1831. 34 p. MH-AH; MiD-B; Nh-Hi; NjR; RPB. 8012

Louisa's tenderness to the little birds in winter. Concord, Hoag & Atwood, 1831. 16 p. MHaHi. 6013

Louisiana.

Acts passed at the extra session of the tenth legislature of the State of Louisiana, begun and held in the City of New-Orleans, on Monday the fourteenth day of November, A.D one thousand eight hundred and thirty-one. Pub. by authority. New-Orleans, John Gibson, 1831. 204 p. LNBA; MdBB; Mo; Nv; Wa-L. 6014

---- Acts passed at the first session of the tenth legislature of the State of Louisiana, begun at Donaldsonville, on Monday the third day of January, one thousand eight hundred and thirty-one, and of the independence of the United States of America the fifty-fourth, and adjourned to and held in the City of New Orleans on the eighth of January. Pub. by authority. New Orleans, John Gibson, 1831. 143 p. IaU-L; In-SC; LNBA; MdBB; Mi-L; NN; Nb; Nj; NNLI; PU; T. 8015

---- Reports of cases argued and determined in the Supreme court of the State of Louisiana. By Branch W. Miller & Thomas Curry... Vol. I-[XIX]. New Orleans, Pr. by Atherton T. Penniman & co., 1831-[1842] 19 vols. CoSC; KyU-L; LNBA; MdBB; OCLaw. 8016

Louisville [Ky.] Temperance Society.

Annual Report of the Louisville Temperance Society, [1831] 20 p. MHi. 8017

Love and generosity, a tale founded on facts. Exeter, W. C. & S. Hardy...1831. With history of Constantius & Pulchere. 97, 113 p. MHi; Nh-Hi. 8018

Lovell, S.

A plain statement of the reasons which led to a dissolution of the connection of the author with the Methodist Episcopal Church. Portsmouth, 1831. MH. 8019

Lowe, Abraham T.

Second Class Book, principally consisting of historical geographical and biographical lessons, adapted to the capacities of youth, and designed for their improvement. By A. T. Lowe, M.D. ... Stereotyped at the Boston Type and Stereotype Foundry, Late T. H. C. Carter & Co. Worcester, Dorr & Howland, 1831. 122 p. CoGrS; MH; OClW. 8020

Lowe, R. T.
Primitae faunae et florae Maderae et Portus Sanet... Cambridge, 1831. 70 p. MH-Z. 8021

Lowell, Charles, 1782-1861.
Gospel Preaching. A sermon, preached at the ordination of Mr. Thomas B. Fox, as pastor of the First Church and Religious Society in Newburyport, on Wednesday, August 3, 1831. By Charles Lowell, Minister of the West Church in Boston, with the right hand of fellowship [By F. H. Hedge], Charge [by John Pierce], address to the Society (by Convert Francis), and an appendix. Cambridge, Hilliard and Brown, 1831. 44 p. CBPac; ICU; MH; NjR; OClWHi; PHi; RPB. 8022

---- Men accountable only to God for their religious opinions; a sermon preached at the ordination of William Barry, jr. to the pastoral care of the South Congregational Church in Lowell, Nov. 17, 1830. Boston, N. S. Simpkins & Co., 1831. 16 p. CBPac; ICMe; MH; OClWHi; PPL; RPB. 8023

---- The world passeth away. A sermon, preached in the West Church in Boston, Jan 2, 1831, being a quarter of a century from the settlement of the present minister. By Charles Lowell... Boston, Boston Press, 1831. 20 p. ICMe; MH-AH; OClWHi; PHi; RPB; WHi. 8024

Lowell, Massachusetts. First Baptist Church.
A summary declaration of the faith and practice of the church. [Lowell] Pr. at the Lowell Evangelist Office, 1831. 8 p. MH; PCA. 8025

---- First Congregational Church. Articles of faith. Lowell, Mass. [1831] 8 p. NN. 8026

Lowell journal and tri-weekly advertiser. Lowell, Mass., July 1, 1831-. DLC; MLow; MWA. 8027

Lowry, L. A.
An earnest search for truth in a series of letters to Cumberland Presbyterians... Cincinnati, Thorpe, 1831. 160 p. PPPrHi. 8028

The lumiere; containing a variety of topographical views in Europe and America. New York, H. R. Piercy & co., 1831. 74 p. MB; MiU; OHi. 8029

Luther, Martin D.
Der kleine catechismus des sel. D. Martin Luther. Harrisburg, 1831. 125 p. MWA. 8030

---- Luthers Bibel-erklavungen über die wichtigsten spruche aus dem Alten und Neuen Testament, gesammelt und nrsg. zum gesegneten gebrauch heilsbegienger seelen, von Heinrich Gind. York, Pa., Gedruckt bey D. May und B. Flory, 1831. 372 p. DLC; PHi; PPG; PPLT. 8031

---- Luther's smaller catechism. York, Pa., 1831. 66 p. MWA. 8032

---- A selection of the most celebrated sermons of Martin Luther ... Never before published in the United States. To which is prefixed a biographical history of his life. Philadelphia, C. Desilver, 1831. 204 p. CtHC; IJ; NB; PWW; WM. 8033

Lutheran. Connecticut. General Association.
(Proceedings of the General Association of Connecticut, June 1831.) Hartford, Pr. by P. B. Gleason & Co., 1831. 24 p. MoWgT; NcMHi. 8034

Lutheran Observer, Baltimore, Morris, 1831. MB; PP; PPL; PPLT; PPPrHi; ScNC. 8035

Lynd, Samuel W.
Discourse before Cincinnati, Sunday School Union, Sept, 1831. 16 p. RPB. 8036

---- Narrative of Catharine Helfenstein, who died at Carlisle, Pennsylvania, June 14, 1830, aged thirteen years. Written by Rev. S. W. Lynd. New York, American Tract Society, 1831? RPB. 8037

Lytton, Edward George Earle Lytton Bulwer-Lytton, 1st baron, 1803-1873.
Devereux. A tale. By Edward Lytton Bulwer. New York, J. & J. Harper, 1831. 2 vols. CtHT; MEab; MeU. 8038

---- The Disowned. By Edward Lytton Bulwer. New York, Pr. by J. & J. Harper, 1831. 2 vols. MeU; NPla. 8039

---- Paul Clifford. By the author of "Pelham"; "The Disowned"... A new and enl. ed. New York, Harper, 1831. 2 vols. KyU; NcD. 8040

---- Pelham; or, the adventures of a gentleman. By the author of "England and the English, Fanaticism." New York, J. & J. Harper, 1831. 2 vols. PFal. 8041

---- Sculpture; a poem: by Edward Lytton Bulwer... New York, Peabody & co., 1831. 14 p. DLC; MB; NIC; NjR; PPL. 8042

---- The Sea-captain. New York, 1831. NhD; NjP. 8043

---- ...The Siamese twins. A satirical tale of the times. With other poems. By the author of "Pelham" [etc.]... New York, Pr. by J. & J. Harper, 1831. 308 p. CSmH; DLC; KyU; MdBP; NjP; ViU; WHi. 8044

---- A strange story and Eugene Aram. By Edward Bulwer Lytton. New York, Edward Bulwer Lytton, 1831. 356 p. KyHop; MoCgSV; WyU. 8045

M

McAdam, John L.
Remarks on the present system of road making; with observations, deduced from practice and experience with a view to the introduction of improvement in the method of making, repairing, and preserving roads. By John L. McAdam, Esq. Baltimore, 1831. PPL-R. 8046

McAfee, Robert Breckinridge, 1784-1849.
Speech of Gen. Robert B. McAfee, in the legislature of Kentucky showing his views of the policy the State should pursue, in making internal improvements. January 14th, 1831. Harrodsburg, Pr. at The American Office, 1831. 15 p. KyLoF; NN. 8047

Macaulay, Thomas Bagington Macaulay, 1st baron.
Miscellaneous works of Lord Macaulay. Edited by his sister Lady Trevelyan. New York, Harper & Bros., 1831. 5 vols. ArBaA; CSlu. 8048

McCalla, William Latta, 1788-1859.
A discussion of Christian baptism, as to its effects upon civil and religious society. In opposition to the views of Mr. Alexander Campbell, as expressed in a seven days debate with the author at Washington, Kentucky, October, 1823, and in his

spurious publication of that debate and of a previous one, of two days with the Rev. John Walker, of Ohio. And in opposition to the views of the celebrated Mr. Robinson, and other Baptist authors. By W. L. M'Calla... Philadelphia, G. M'Laughlin, 1831. 397 p. CU; KyDC; MBC; NNUT; OAU. 8049

---- A discussion of Unitarianism; or, A condensed defence of the divinity of Christ, against the heresy of Christianism as advocated by... William Lane, in the debate at Milford, Hunterdon county, New Jersey, December, 1830. By W. L. M'Calla... Philadelphia, Pr. by Russell & Martien, 1831. 32 p. CtHC; NjR; OCHP; PPPrHi; VtU. 8050

---- A fair hearing? Philadelphia, 1831. PPPrHi. 8051

---- A Faithful report of the theological debate held at Milford, New-Jersey, December, 1830... prepared for the press, by Isaac C. Goff... New-York, Pr. at the office of D. Mitchell, 1831. 88 p. KyDC; NN. 8052

McCarrell, Joseph, 1795-1864.
Speech delivered before the General Assembly of the Presbyterian church of 1831, in support of a claim of the Associate Reformed Synod of New York, to the property transferred to the General Assembly by the General Synod of the Associate Reformed church in 1822. ...Newburgh, Pr. by Charles U. Cushman, 1831. 24 p. MH-AH; NN; PLT; PPPrHi; WHi. 8053

McComas, David.
Substance of the remarks of Mr. M'Comas, of Wythe, in the Senate of Virginia, on the judiciary bill, and the substitute proposed thereto by the Committee of fifteen. Delivered on the 28th day of March, 1831. [Richmond, 1831] 8 p. Vi. 8054

MacCoy, Isaac, 1784-1846.
Address to Philanthropists in the United States, generally, and to Christians, in particular, on the condition and prospects of the American Indians. [Washington? 1831?] DLC; MWA; NN; PPL. 8055

McCrie, Thomas, 1772-1835.
Life of John Knox; containing illustrations of the history of the reformation in Scotland: with biographical notices of the principal reformers, and sketches of the progress of literature in Scotland during the sixteenth century; and an appendix, consisting of original papers. By Thomas M'Crie ...1st complete Amer. ed. Philadelphia, Presbyterian board of publication [1831] 579 p. CU; ICP; LPL; MoSM; Vi. 8056

McDuffie, George, 1790-1851.
Defence of a liberal construction of the powers of Congress, as regards internal improvement, etc. with a complete refutation of the ultra doctrines respecting consolidation and state sovereignty. Written by George M'Duffie, esq. in the year 1821. Over the signature of "One of the people." To which are prefixed an encomiastic advertisement of the work by Major (now Governor) Hamilton, and a preface by the editor ... Philadelphia, Pr. by L. R. Bailey, 1831. 22 p. DLC; LNH; MBAt; NB; OClWHi; ScU. 8057

---- National and state rights, considered by the Hon. George M'Duffie, under the signature of "One of the people," in reply to the "Trio," with the advertisement prefixed to it, generally attributed to Major James Hamilton, jr. when published in 1821. Columbia [S.C.] Free press and Hive office, 1831. 40 p. DLC; ICU; RP; ScU; ViU. 8058

---- Speech of the Hon. George McDuffie, at a public dinner given to him by the citizens of Charleston, (S.C.), May 19, 1831... in support of the Rights and Interests of the Southern States. Charleston, Pr. by A.E. Miller, 1831. 29 p. ICU; MBAt; MHi; ScC; ScCC. 8059

MacEwen, A. R.
The Erskines. New York, Charles Scribner & sons, 1831. 160 p. NjN. 8060

McEwen, William.
Grace and Truth; or the Glory and Fulness of the Redeemer, displayed in an attempt to explain, illustrate, and enforce the most remarkable types, figures, and allezonies of the Old Testament. By the Rev. Wm. M'Ewan, late minister of the gospel in Dundee. Cincinnati, Pr. at the Chronicle Office, 1831. 300 p. GAGTh; OC. 8061

McFarlan, John.
The signs of the times, behind the substance of a discourse ... Paris, Ky., Joel R. Ryle, 1831. 7 p. ICU. 8062

McGready, James, 1758-1817.
The posthumous works of the Reverend and pious James M'-Gready...edited by the Reverend James Smith... Louisville, Ky., W. W. Worsley, 1831-1833. 2 vols. ArCT; GEU; KyBgW; PW; TNP. 8063

[McHenry, James] 1785-1845.
Meredith; or, The mystery of the Meschianza. A tale of the American revolution. By the author of "The betrothed of Wyoming"... Philadelphia, Sold by the principal booksellers; and in New York, Boston, Baltimore, and Washington, 1831. 260 p. CSmH; DLC; LNH; MWA; WaU. 8064

McIlvaine, Charles Pettie.
Pastor's address to a candidate for confirmation in St. Ann's Church, Brooklyn. Brooklyn, 1831. 8 p. NBLiHi; NN. 8065

McIntyre, Archibold.
Memorial to the Senate and House of Representatives. Pennsylvania, 1831. 7 p. TxHuT. 8066

McKee, Joseph.
An apology for the Protestant Methodists, in which thirty of their principle [sic] objections to the government and discipline of the Methodist Episcopal church are laid down, being thirty reasons why they have rejected the Episcopal government, and formed one more agreeable to the Holy Scriptures... Wilmington, Del., Pr. by Samuel Harker...[1831?] 28 p. PPL. 8067

Mackenzie, Colin, 1753?-1820.
...Mackenzie's five thousand receipts, in all the useful and domestic arts: constituting a complete practical library relative to agriculture, bees, bleaching... A new American, from the latest London ed. with numerous and important additions generally; and the medical part carefully rev. and adapted to the climate of the United States. And also a new and copius index. By an American physician. Philadelphia, J. Kay, jr.; Pittsburgh, J. I. Kay and Co., 1831. 456 p. CLSU; KyU; MtHi; PPi; RPB. 8068

---- Secrets of all trades and arts, being an abridgement of the latest London edition of

Mackenzie's five thousand receipts ... Hamilton, O., Taylor Webster, 1831. 312 p. OClWHi; OSW. 8069

[McKim, John]
To the Honorable Levi Woodbury, Secretary of the Navy. Charlestown, 1831. 56 p. MB; PPL. 8070

Mackintosh, James, 1765-1832.
The history of England. By the Right Hon. James Mackintosh, M. P. Sir Walter Scott, Bart. and Thomas Moore, Esq. England. Philadelphia, Carey & Lea, 1831. 3 vols. InU; MB; NGH; NjR; RNR. 8071

McLean, John, 1785-1861.
An address prepared at the request of the Union and Jefferson societies of Augusta college. by John McLean. Cincinnati, Pr. by John Whetstone, jr. & co., 1831. 28 p. KyRE; MBAt; OC; PPAmP. 8072

---- ---- 2d ed. Philadelphia, Pr. by S. C. Atkinson, 1831. 16 p. A-Ar; OClWHi. 8073

---- An eulogy on the character and public services of James Monroe, late president of the United States: delivered in Cincinnati, August 27, 1831, in compliance with an invitation from the citizens. By the Hon. John M'Lean. Pub. by order of the City council, from a copy submitted by the committee of arrangements. [Cincinnati] Pr. by Looker and Reynolds, 1831. 32 p. CSmH; DLC; MiD-B; OClWHi; WHi. 8074

McLeod, Rev. Alexander, 1774-1833.
The Ecclesiastical catechism, being a series of questions relative to the Christian Church, stated and answered with the scripture proofs. New York, G. F. Bunce, 1831. 144 p. ICP; ICT; MBC; NBuG; PPins. 8075

McLeod, John.
An address to the mayor, aldermen and common council of the city of Washington, respecting the management and condition of the western free school. [Washington, 1831] 23 p. DLC. 8076

Maclure, William, 1763-1840.
Opinions on various subjects, dedicated to the industrious producers. By William Maclure. Vol. I. New Harmony, Indiana, Pr. at the School Press, 1831-1838. 3 vols. in 2. Ct; DLC; IEG; IU; IaBo; In; MS; OC; BrMus. 8077

McMahon, John Van Lear, 1800-1871.
An historical view of the govt. of Maryland from colonization to present day. Baltimore, F. Lucas Jr., Cushing & Son, and Wm. & Joseph Neal, 1831. 539 p. IaGG; MdBP; OClWHi; RPB; TxU. 8078

McMurray, William.
A sermon occasioned by the death of Mr. Aaron A. Hand, preached in the Reformed Dutch Church. (New York) Jan. 16, 1831. New York, Fanshaw, 1831. NN; PPPrHi. 8079

McNemar, Richard, 1770-1839.
A review of the most important events relating to the rise and progress of the United society of believers in the West; with sundry other documents connected with the history of the society. Collected from various journals, by E. Wright (pseud.) Union Village, O., 1831. 34 p. CSmH; DLC; NN; OClWHi. 8080

McVickar, John.

Memoir of Edmund D. Griffin. New York, 1831. 2 vols. MBL. 8081

Maddox, John Medex, 1789-1861.
The king and deserter: a drama, in two acts. New York, Samuel French [1831] 22 p. OCl. 8082

Madison, James, bp., 1749-1812.
A discourse on the death of General Washington, late president of the United States: delivered on the 22d of February 1800, in the church in Williamsburgh. By James Madison...3d ed., with additions. Philadelphia, Pr. by J. Kay, jun. and co., 1831. 40 p. CtMW; MBAt; NjR; PPAmP; RPB; Vi. 8083

---- Papers of James Madison. Edited by Henry D. Gilpin. New York, 1831. 3 vols. OCLaw. 8084

Madison Insurance Company.
Charter of... Madison, Ind., 1831? 8 p. In; MH-BA. 8085

Maine.
An act additional to an act regulating elections, 1831. Portland, Todd and Holden, 1831. 8 p. MeHi. 8086

---- An act additional to an act to promote the sale of public lands. Portland, Todd and Holden, 1831. 8 p. MeHi. 8087

---- An act additional to the several acts regulating judicial process and proceedings. Portland, Todd and Holden, 1831. 2 p. MeHi. 8088

---- An act for the abolition of imprisonment of honest debtors for debt. Portland, Todd and Holden, 1831. 21 p. MeHi. 8089

---- An act for the encouragement of agriculture. Portland, Todd and Holden, 1831. 3 p. MeHi. 8090

---- An act to encourage literature and the useful acts and sciences. Portland, Todd and Holden, 1831. 8 p. MeHi. 8091

---- Adjutant General's report. Adjutant General's Office, Portland, January 8, 1831. Portland, Thomas Todd, 1831. 12 p. MeHi. 8092

---- The constitution of the state of Maine and that of the United States; with marginal references; containing the census of several towns and plantations in Maine in 1830. Pr. by order of the legislature. Portland, Todd and Holden, 1831. 93, [1] p. CSmH; ICJ; MH-L; NN; OCLaw. 8093

---- Extracts from records in the county of York (1636-1690) (In collection of the Maine Historical Society.) Portland, Day & Fraser & Co., 1831. v. 1, p. [269]-286. WeBa. 8094

---- The form of a bill to incorporate the city of Portland, as reported by a committee October 12, 1829, with the amendments adopted by the town, December 7, 1829. State of Maine, act to incorporate the city of Portland. Portland, Todd and Holden, 1831. 8 p. MH. 8095

---- Governor's message and documents on the subject of the doings of the arbiter, with the report of the committee of the legislature, in relation to the north-east boundry. Pr. by order of the Legislature. Portland, Todd and Holden, 1831. 52 p. CSt; DLC; MB; NHi; WHi. 8096

---- A petition from the inhabitants of Maine to Oliver Cromwell, 1656. (In collection of the Maine Historical Society.)

Portland, Day, Frazier and Co., 1831. v. 1, p. 296-299. DLC. 8097

---- Private and special acts of the state of Maine, passed by the eleventh Legislature, at its session commencing January 5, 1831. Pub. agreeable to the resolve of June 28, 1820. Portland, Todd and Holden, 1831. [3], 128, [10] p. CSf-Law; IaU-L; Mi-L; MeP; TxU-Law; Wa-L. 8098

---- Public acts of the state of Maine, passed by the eleventh Legislature at its session, held in January, 1831. Pub. agreeable to the resolve of June 28, 1830. Portland, Todd and Holden, 1831. 1270-1355, [10] p. A-SC; MdBB; MeU; Nj; TxU-Law. 8099

---- Report of the Bank Commissioners. Portland, Pr. by Todd and Holden, 1831. 8 p. MeHi. 8100

---- Report of the Committee appointed to inquire into the expediency of making an appropriation to improve the notch of the White Hills, February 23, 1831. Portland, Todd and Holden, 1831. 16 p. MeHi. 8101

---- [Report of] the Joint Standing Committee on Claims, to which was referred the petition of Edward Russel, 1831. Portland, Todd and Holden, 1831. 15 p. MH. 8102

---- Report of the Land Agent to the Hon. the Governor and the Executive Council of the State of Maine. January 6, 1831. Portland, Todd and Holden, 1831. 12 p. MeHi. 8103

---- Report of the Military Committee. (n.p.) 1831. 110 p. NbU. 8104

---- Reports of decisions in the Circuit Courts Martial of questions arising on trials had in said courts. Compiled from original papers in the office of the Adjutant General, in conformity to a resolve of the Legislature of Maine passed March 31, 1831. To which is added an appendix of Practical Forms of Proceedings in Circuit Courts Martial. By Francis O. J. Smith, Counsellor-at-law. Portland, Pr. by Todd and Holden, 1831. 113 p. CoCs; IU-Law; MB; OrSC; PPB; WaU. 8105

---- Resolve making provision for managing and settling the wild lands in this state, February 23, 1831. Portland, Todd and Holden, 1831. 2 p. MeHi. 8106

---- Resolves of the eleventh Legislature of the State of Maine, passed by the session commenced on the fifth day of January and ended on the second day of April, 1831. Published agreeably to the resolve of June 28, 1820. Portland, Todd and Holden, 1831. [6], 147-325, [14] p. IaU-Law; InSc; MeBa; Nj; T. 8107

---- Rules and orders to be observed in the House of Representatives of the State of Maine during the continuance of the eleventh Legislature, 1831. Portland, Todd and Holden, 1831. 204 p. MeHi. 8108

---- Supplement to the laws of Maine, 1821-1831. Portland, Todd, 1831. 413 p. ORSc. 8109

The Maine Farmers' Almanac for the year of our Lord 1832. Calculated for the meridian of Portland particularly intended for the State of Maine. Portland, Shirley Hyde and Co., 1831. 48 p. MWA. 8110

Maine Historical Society.

Act of incorporation, by-laws and lists of members. Portland, Day, Fraser and Co., 1831. [i], viii p. CSt; DLC. 8111

---- Collections of the Maine Historical Society [1st. ser.] V. 1-10; 2d ser., v. 1-10; 3d ser., V.1- . Portland, The Society, 183- . DLC; MnM; NN; OO; PHi; WHi. 8112

Maine Register and United States Calendar for the year of our Lord (1832). Portland, G. Hyde and Co.; Hallowell, Glazier, Masters and Co. [1831] 112 p. MHi. 8113

Maine State-Lyceum.
Constitution. Portland, March 23, 1831. 2 p. MHi. 8114

Mair, D. M.
The bridal of Borthwick... New York, J. & J. Harper, 1831. 2 vols. OCX. 8115

Mair, Hugh, 1797-1854.
A sermon on the love of Christ. Johnstown, New York, 1831. 24 p. CtY; MH-AH. 8116

Malcom, Howard.
Dictionary of important names, objects and terms, found in the Holy Scriptures. Intended principally for youth. By Howard Malcom, A.M. 4th ed. Boston, Lincoln & Edmands, 1831. 276 p. DLC; MH-AH; NhCon; OO; PCA; RJa. 8117

Malin, William Gunn.
Some account of the Pennsylvania hospital, its origin, objects and present state. By W. G. Malin... Philadelphia, Pr. by Thomas Kite, 1831. 46 p. DLC; MH; MnU; PHi; PU. 8118

[Malkin, Arthur Thomas]
Historical parallels. By Lilly & Wait and others. Boston, Lilly & Wait, 1831. 408 p. ArFs; ICBB; KyDC; MoSW; RAu. 8119

Maltby, A. H., ed.
Incident in the life of President Dwight illustrative of his moral and religious character. Designed for young persons. New Haven, Baldwin and Treadway, 1831. 156 p. CtSoP; DLC; IC; MH; PPL. 8120

Maltby, Erastus, 1796-1883.
A sermon, preached at the installation of Reverend William M. Cornell, as pastor of the First Congregational Church and Society in Woodstock, Connecticut, June 15, 1831. Taunton, Edmund Anthony, 1831. 26 p. CtSoP; MBC; NN; PPPrHi; RPB. 8121

Malthus, Thomas Robert, 1766-1834.
Additions to An essay on the principles of population...1st Amer. ed. Georgetown, D.C., Charles Cruikshan, Rind's press, 1831. 230 p. DLC; InBrD; MD; MWA; PU. 8122

Manchester, William C. B., 1794.
Songs of Zion, or Conference hymns, selected and original; to which is added, a brief sketch of the author's life and experience. Providence, H. H. Brown, 1831. 224 p. RPB. 8123

Manhattan gas light company. New York.
An act to incorporate the Manhattan Gas Light Company. New York, 1831. DLC. 8124

Manley, James R., 1781-1851.
An address...by James R. Manley before the Association of the alumni of Columbia college at their anniversary. New York, G. & C. & H. Carvill, 1831.

31 p. MB; MH; NNC; NjR. 8125

Mann, Cyrus.
An Epitome of the Evidences of Christianity; designed for families, Sabbath Schools, and Bible Classes. By Cyrus Mann, Pastor of the Congregational Church in Westminster, Mass. (Quotations) 2d ed. Boston, Pr. by T. R. Marvin, for the Massachusetts Sabbath School Union, 1831. 148 p. DLC; ICP; MBC; RNHi. 8126

Manning, Robert.
The shortest way to end disputes about religion. In two parts. by the Rev. Robert Manning, author of England's Conversion and Reformation Compared.... 1st Amer., rev. and corr. from the best London ed. Boston, Wm. Smith, 1831. 292 p. ArLSJ; CtHT; MBAt; MWH; MdBS; MoW; NbOC. 8127

Manual of the practical naturalist; or Directions for collecting, preparing, and preserving subjects of natural history... Boston, Lilly and Wait, and Carter, Hendee & Babcock, 1831. 214 p. CSmH; DLC; LNH; MB; ViRA. 8128

Manvill, Mrs. P. D.
Lucinda or The Mountain Mourner. 7th ed. Erie, Pa., Rufus Clough, 1831. 119 p. MBevHi. 8129

Marblehead Charitable Society.
By-Laws of the Marblehead Charitable Society. Instituted Feb. 12, 1831. 8 p. MMhHi. 8130

Marcet, Jane Haldimand, 1769-1858.
Bertha's visit to her uncle in England. Illustrated and imp. from the London ed. Boston, Lilly and Wait; Carter, Hendee & Babcock; G. & C. & H. Carvill; E. Bliss. New York, Carey & Hart. Philadelphia, W. & J. Neal. Baltimore, Little & Cummings. Albany, M. Carroll, New Orleans, and S. Colman, Portland, 1831. 2 vols. 335 p. DLC; LU; MB. 8131

---- Conversations on chemistry; in which the elements of that science are familiarly explained, and illustrated by experiments and 38 engravings on wood. 13th Amer. from the last London ed. with old and corr. to which are now added, explanations of the text... by J. L. Comstock, M.D. Together with a new and extensive series of questions by Rev. J. L. Blake, A.M. Hartford, O. D. Cooke & Co., etc., 1831. 356 p. CtHT; NBuG; OMC; RPB; ViL. 8132

---- Conversations on natural philosophy, in which the elements of that science are familiarly explained, and adapted to the comprehension of young pupils...Improved...also by illustrative notes, and a dictionary of philosophical terms. By Rev. J. L. Blake... Boston, Lincoln and Edmands, 1831. 252 p. CtHT; GDecCT; MH; NNC; TxD-T. 8133

Margaret and Delia: or temper corrected. Boston, 1831. MB. 8134

Marks, David, 1805-1856.
The life of David Marks, to the 26th year of his age. Including the particulars of his conversion, call to the ministry, and labours in itinerant preaching for nearly eleven years. Written by himself. Limerick, Pr. at the office of the Morning Star, 1831. 396 p. ICN; ICU; MH; MeHi; RPB. 8135

Marsh, C[hristopher] C[olumbus].
Science of double-entry bookkeeping...2d ed., rev. Baltimore, G. M'Dowell & Son, etc., 1831.

DLC; MH; MdHi; OSW; PPWl. 8136

Marsh, John, 1788-1864.
An epitome of general ecclesiastical history, from the earliest period to the present time. With an appendix, giving a condensed history of the Jews... 3d ed. New York, W. E. Dean, 1831. 449 p. CBPac; MMedHi; NB; NcCJ; WaPS. 8137

---- An exhibition of the Religious Sentiments of the Presbyterian, Baptist and Methodist denominations as set forth in their respective creeds, by the sanction of the highest judicatories of those orders without disguise, Being designed to settle questions relating to the real sentiments of those churches. Compiled by John Marsh. Buffalo, Pr. for the compiler, by Horace Steele, [1831] 88 p. MiGr. 8138

Marshall, Elihu F.
A spelling book of the English Language, or the American tutor's assistant. Intended particularly for the use of "Common Schools." The pronunciation being adapted to the much approved principles of J. Walker. By Elihu F. Marshall. Concord, N.H., March, Capen & Lyon, 1831. 156 p. 8139

Marshall, John, 1755-1835.
The life of George Washington, Commander-in-Chief of the American Forces... Philadelphia, J. Crissy, 1831-36. 2 vols. InNd; InNdS; NR; PCD-Hi; PPiHi; TxD-W. 8140

Marshall, William L.
The annual address delivered before the Maryland Institute for the Promotion of the Mechanic Arts by W. L. Marshall on Monday 31st October, 1831. Baltimore, Pr. by Joseph Robinson, 1831. 27 p. MdHi. 8141

Martin, J. L., d. 1848.
Native bards; a satirical effusion: with other occasional pieces. By J. L. Martin. Philadelphia, E. L. Carey & A. Hart, 1831. 114 p. CtMW; MH; OC; PHi; TxU. 8142

Martin, Morgan Lewis.
Caution, In pursuance of an order of the Circuit court of the County of Brown... a certain farm in the township of Green Bay... and of late owned and occupied by George Johnson was sold... Morgan L. Martin. Att'y for the mortgagee. Nov. 11, 1831. [Detroit, 1831] WHi. 8143

Martin, Robert, and Whitney, George Clinton.
The scholar's exercise and review, containing the principal rules of English grammar and arithmetic and key to many difficult questions in the latter. The whole designed for use of schools and private instructions. Brunswick, Noyes and Fairfield, 1831. 168 p. MH; MeU; NNC. 8144

Martineau, Harriet.
The times of the Saviour. By Harriet Martineau. Repr. after revision, from the English ed. Boston, Leonard C. Bowles, 1831. 132 p. CtHC; MB; MWA; NN; PU. 8145

Martyn, Francis, 1782-1838.
Homilies on the book of Tobias, or a familiar explication of the practical duties of domestic life. By the Rev. Francis Martyn. Baltimore, Fielding Lucas, Jr. [1831] 264 p. IEG; MWH; MoSU; OCX; PPM; TxH. 8146

Martyrs of Lyons and Vienne in France. Philadelphia, American Sunday School Union, Entered

1831 by American Sunday School Union [1831] 24 p. NNC; BrMus. 8147

The marvelous doings of Prince Alcohol. An allegory. By one of alcohol's enemies. Philadelphia, Pr. by Martien & Boden, 1831. 79 p. MBC; NbOP; NcU. 8148

Maryland.

(Document No. 1) Accompanying the general report of the Committee on Internal Improvement. Abstract of the accounts of the Washington and Baltimore Turnpike Road Company. Annapolis, Pr. by Jonas Green, 1831. 2 p. MdHi. 8149

---- (Document No. 2) Accompanying the general report of the Committee on Internal Improvement. Letter from William Lorman, President of the Baltimore Turnpike Road Company. Annapolis, Pr. by Jonas Green, 1831. 3 p. MdHi. 8150

---- (Document No. 3) Accompanying the general report of the Committee on Internal Improvement. Extract of a letter from J. Stull, Treasurer of the Washington Turnpike Company. Annapolis, Pr. by Jonas Green, 1831. 3 p. MdHi. 8151

---- (Document No. 4) Accompanying the general report of the Committee on Internal Improvement. A letter from the president of the Chesapeake and Delaware Canal Company, to the chairman of the Committee on Internal Improvement. Annapolis, Pr. by Jonas Green, 1831. 5 p. MdHi. 8152

---- (Document No. 5) Accompanying the general report of the Committee on Internal Improvement. Eleventh general report of the president and directors of the Chesapeake and Delaware Canal Company. Annapolis, Pr. by Jonas Green, 1831. 12 p. MdHi. 8153

---- A compilation of the insolvent laws of Maryland, together with the decisions of the Court of Appeals of Maryland, and of the Supreme Court of the United States, on the subject of insolvency. With a copious index. By a member of the Baltimore Bar. 1831. Baltimore, J. J. Harrod, 1831. 325 p. MH; MdBE; MdHi; MH-L; MdBP; OCLaw. 8154

---- General Report of the Committee on Internal Improvement. Annapolis, Pr. by Jonas Green, 1831. 12 p. MdHi. 8155

---- Journal of the proceedings of the House of Delegates of the State of Maryland at a session of the General Assembly of Maryland, begun and held in the State House of the City of Annapolis on the last Monday of December 27th A.D., 1830. By authority. Pr. by J. Green, 1831. 418 p. MdBB; MdHi. 8156

---- Journal of the proceedings of the Senate of the State of Maryland, at a session of the General Assembly, begun and held at the Capitol in the City of Annapolis, in the County of Anne Arundel on the last Monday of December, the 27th day of the month 1830 to February 25th 1831 and in the 55th year of the Independence of the United States of America. Pub. by authority. Annapolis, Pr. by J. Green, 1831. 153 p. MdBB; MdBP; MdHi. 8157

---- Laws and ordinances relating to the Baltimore and Susquehanna rail road company. Baltimore, Pr. by J. Lucas & E. K. Deaver, 1831. 24 p. DLC; MdBJ; NNE; PHi; PPlrankT. 8158

---- Laws made and passed by the General Assembly of the State of Maryland, at a session of the said Assembly, which was begun and held in the State House at the City of Annapolis, in the County of Anne Arundel on the last Monday of December 1831 pursuant to the constitution and form of government of the said state, and concluded on Thursday the 24th day of February 1831... Pub. by authority. Annapolis, Pr. by J. Green, 1831. 326 p. IaU-L; MdBP; Mi-L; Mo; Nj; Nv; T. 8159

---- Message from the executive to the Legislature of Maryland, at the December session 1831. Annapolis, Pr. by Jeremiah Hughes, 1831. 10 p. NN. 8160

---- Select Committee on the Establishment of a Bank. Report of Mr. Teackle, Chairman of the Select Committee, upon the Memorials of sundry citizens of different counties praying the establishment of a financial institution under the style of the Bank of the State of Maryland. Annapolis, Pr. by Jonas Green [1831] 48 p. CSmH; DLC; MH-BA; MdBE; MdHi. 8161

---- Report of the Committee of Claims to the House of Delegates. January 5th 1831. Annapolis, Pr. by Jonas Green, 1831. 8 p. MdHi. 8162

---- Report of the Committee on internal improvement, delivered by Archibald Lee, esq., Chairman. December session, 1830-31. Annapolis, Pr. by J. Green, 1831. 6 p. DLC. 8163

---- Report of the Joint Committee relative to the obstructions in the river Susquehanna delivered by J. S. Heath, Chairman. December session, 1830-1831. Annapolis, Pr. by Jonas Green, 1831. 6 p. MdHi. 8164

---- Reports of cases argued and determined in the Court of Appeals of Maryland. By Richard W. Gill, and John Johnson. Containing cases in 1829-1830. Baltimore, Pub. by Fielding Lucas, Jr., Lucas and Deaver, 1831. 2 vols. CU; InSC; ICU; MdU-L; PLL; Vi-L. 8165

---- Penitentiary, Baltimore.
Report of the directors of the Maryland penitentiary, made to the executive, and communicated by his excellency Governor Howard, to the legislature, at December session, 1831. Baltimore, Pr. by James Lucas and E. K. Deaver, 1831. 2 vols. MdHi; PHi; PPL; PP; PJ. 8166

---- Treasurer of the Eastern Shore.
Report of William K. Lambdin, treasurer of the Eastern Shore. Delivered by Charles Stewart, esq. Chairman of the Committee on Claims. December session, 1830-31. 5 p. MdHi. 8167

---- Treasurer of the Western Shore.
The annual report of the treasurer of the Western Shore for December session 1830 to the general assembly of Maryland, in pursuance of an act of the Legislature, passed at the December session 1824 entitled an act relating to the treasurers of the Western and Eastern Shores. Annapolis, Pr. by Jonas Green, 1831. 38 p. MdHi. 8168

---- ---- Annual report of the treasurer of the Western Shore, for the December session 1831 to the General Assembly of Maryland. Annapolis, Pr. by J. Green, 1831. 37 p. PHi. 8169

---- ---- Report from the Treasurer of the Eastern Shore, containing a list of balances outstanding on the books of his office. January 15, 1831. Annapolis, Pr. by J. Green, 1831. 10 p. MdHi. 8170

---- ---- Report of the Treasurer for the Western Shore, concerning the Washington monument in obedience to an order of the House of Delegates 22nd January, 1831. Annapolis, Pr. by J. Green, 1831. 15 p. MBAt; MdHi. 8171

---- ---- Report of the Treasurer for the Western Shore, in obedience to an order of the House of Delegates of the 20th January 1831. Annapolis, Pr. by J. Green, 1831. 6 p. MdHi. 8172

---- University.

Report of the trustees of the University of Maryland to the General Assembly of Maryland. December session, 1830-31. Annapolis, Pr. by J. Green, 1831. 7 p. MdHi; PHi. 8173

Maryland State Colonization Society.

Address of the Society, to the people of Maryland; with the constitution of the Society, and an appendix. Baltimore, Lucas & Deaver, 1831. 24 p. MH; MdHi; PPPrHi. 8174

Mason, John, 1646?-1694.

Gems of piety, from the Select remains...recommended by Dr. Watts. Boston, Lincoln & Edmands, 1831. 192 p. CtHC. 8175

Mason, Lowell, 1792-1872, comp.

Church Psalmody; a new Collection of Psalms and Hymns, adapted to public worship. Selected from Dr. Watts, and other Authors. Boston, Perkins & Marvin, 1831. 576 p. CtMW; ICT; MH; NNUT; WStC. 8176

---- Juvenile Lyre; or hymns and songs, religious, moral and cheerful, set to appropriate music. For the use of primary and common schools. Boston, Richardson, Lord & Holbrook; Hartford, H. & F. J. Huntington, 1831. 72 p. CtHWatk; DLC; MB; NIC; PPL. 8177

Mason, Stevens Thomson.

To the public. An address to the President of the United States, remonstrating against my appointment as Secretary of the Territory... [Detroit, 1831] WHi. 8178

Mason, William, 1719-1791.

Crumbs from the Master's table; or, Select sentences, doctrinal, practical and experimental. By W. Mason. New York, D. Appleton, 1831. 192 p. CSmH; MB; NN; ViU. 8179

Masonic apology...by a friend to truth. Philadelphia, 1831. PPL. 8180

Massachusetts. Commissioners on Isolvency and Imprisonment for Debt.

Report, May 31. Boston, 1831. MBAt. 8181

---- Committee on Railways & Canals, Reports.

Report of a committee on the Boston and Lowell rail road. Boston, 1831. 14 p. MB; MHi; NNE. 8182

---- General Court.

Rept. ...Freemasonry... Grand Lodge of Massachusetts. [Boston, 1831] MB. 8183

---- ---- Report of a Special committee of the Senate relating to the state printers. Reported and accepted in Senate, June 20, 1831. [Boston, State printers,

1831] 7 p. M. 8184

---- ---- Report on punishment by death. June 9, 1831. [Boston, 1831] 17 p. M. 8185

---- ---- House of Representatives.

...Report of the select committee of the House of Representatives, on so much of the governor's speech, at the June session, 1830, as relates to legalizing the study of anatomy... Boston, Dutton & Wentworth, Prs. to the state, 1831. 118 p. DLC; IU-M; MBAt; NNN; PPAmP. 8186

---- ---- ---- [Report of] the special committee, to whom was referred so much of the Governor's message as related to the subject of the Lunatic Hospital at Worcester. Boston, 1831 (House Report 19) 4 p. MH. 8187

---- ---- ---- Report on the Suspension of Specie Payments. [1831] (House Report 21) 24 p. MHi. 8188

---- ---- Library.

Catalogue of the library of the General Court. Boston, Dutton and Wentworth, Prs. to the state, 1831. 43 p. IaHi; LNH; M; NN. 8189

---- ---- Senate. Report on the late resolutions of the State of Georgia. 1831. 24 p. MBC; PPL. 8190

---- ---- ---- Rules and Orders. Boston, Dutton and Wentworth, State prs., 1831. 36 p. MWHi. 8191

---- Governor.

Commonwealth of Massachusetts. By His Excellency Levi Lincoln, Governor of the Commonwealth of Massachusetts, A Proclamation, for a day of public fasting, humiliation and prayer... I appoint Thursday 7th of April ...as a day of fasting and prayer ...Given at ...Council Chamber ... Boston, 1st March... 1831. Levi Lincoln, Edward D. Bangs, Sec. Broadside. MAtt; MBB; MHi. 8192

---- ---- Message of His Excellency, Levi Lincoln, communicated to the two branches of the Legislature, Jan. 5, 1831. Boston, State pr., 1831. 36 p. MHi; PU; WHi. 8193

---- ---- Message of the Governor reporting on Commissioners on insolvency and imprisonment for debt with a bill for relief of insolvent debts. Boston, Dutton & Wentworth, Prs. to the State, 1831. 103 p. DLC; Ia; M. 8194

---- Laws, Statutes, etc.

Acts regulating banks and banking. Passed in 1829 and 1831. Boston, Pr. by Beals and Homer, 1831. 32 p. MB. 8195

---- ---- ... (Grant to Seward Porter of a portion of the flats in Boston Harbor to construct a breakwater) [Boston? 1831?] 3 p. MB; MH-BA. 8196

---- ---- Laws of the Commonwealth of Massachusetts, passed by the General Court at their session, which begun on the 24th day of January and ended 23d day of June, 1831. 556 p. MdBB. 8197

---- ---- Resolves of the General Court of the Commonwealth of Massachusetts, passed at the several sessions of the General Court, commencing May, 1828, and ending June, 1831. Published agreeably to a resolve of the 16th Jan. 1812. Boston, Dutton and Wentworth, prs. to the state, 1831. 657 p. MKiTH; Mi-L; Mo; NNLI. 8198

---- Treasury Department.
Statement of the sums allowed from the treasury for the support of state paupers. 1831. 18 p. (Senate doc. no 13) MBC; PU. 8199

Massachusetts Almanac, or the Merchants & Farmers Calendar for 1831. Boston, Allen & Co. [1831] MHa; MWA; PHi. 8200

Massachusetts Colonization Society.
...American Colonization Society, and the Colony at Liberia. Published by the Massachusetts Colonization Society. Boston, Pr. by Peirce & Parker, 1831. 16 p. DLC; ICN; MnHi; NjR; PPPrHi. 8201

---- A statement of facts respecting the American Colonization Society, and the colony at Liberia. By the Massachusetts Colonization Society. 2d ed. Princeton, N.J., Pr. by W. D'Hart, 1831. 14 p. IU; MH; NcMHi; P. 8202

Massachusetts Convention of Congregational Ministers.
Rules of the Massachusetts Convention of Congregational Ministers. Boston, 1831. MBC. 8203

The Massachusetts family almanac. Boston [1831] DLC; MB. 8204

Massachusetts Medical Society.
Library of practical medicine, pub. by order of the Massachusetts Medical Society for the use of its fellows. V. 1- Boston, Stimpson and Clapp, 1831. DLC; DSG; MB; Nh; PU. 8205

---- Southern district Medical Society.
The medical police and regulations... Boston, T. R. Marvin, 1831. 16 p. DLC. 8206

The Massachusetts Register and United States Calendar, for the year 1832. Also City Officers in Boston, and other useful information. Boston, James Loring [1831] 252 p. C; MBB; MBevHi; MNe; MToP; MWHi; MeBa; MeHi. 8207

Massachusetts Temperance Society.
A letter to the mechanics of Boston, respecting the formation of a city temperance society, from a committee of the Massachusetts society for the Suppression of Intemperance. Boston, 1831. 26 p. DLC; MB; MH; MH-AH; MHi; WHi. 8208

---- Report of a committee of the Massachusetts Society for the Suppression of Intemperance, adopted at a meeting of the Society, June 3, 1831. Boston, Boston Power Press, 1831. 12 p. DLC; MBC; MWA; NIC; WHi. 8209

Masset, Madame E.
...Deliciosa or Leonore polka. Merz. ... Baltimore, G. Willig Jr.; Cincinnati, W. C. Peters & sons; New Orleans, H. D. Hewitt [183-?] 5 p. ViU. 8210

Massinger, Philip, 1583-1640.
The Plays of Philip Massinger. Adapted for family reading, and the use of young persons, by the omission of objectionable passages. New York, J. & J. Harper, 1831. 3 v. DLC; IU; NjPT; ScNC; TNP. 8211

Mathers, William.
The rise progress and downfall of aristocracy. Taken from ancient and modern history, sacred and profane. By William Mathers. Wheeling, W. Va., Pub. by the author, 1831. 205 p. ICNi; OClWHi; PWW; Vi; WvW. 8212

Matthews, John.
Address on occasion of his

inauguration as professor of didactics and polemic theology in the Indiana Theological Seminary, 1831. Madison, Arion & Lodge, Republican office, 1831. 17 p. In; MBC. 8213

Maturin, Charles Robert, 1780-1824.
Melmoth, the wanderer; a melo dramatic romance in three acts (Founded on the popular novel of that name.) Baltimore, J. Robinson, 1831. 41 p. DLC; MH; PU. 8214

Maxson, W. B.
Investigator, being a review of President Hunphrey's fourth question, in his essay on the Sabbath. Homer, 1831. 24 p. NHCS. 8215

May, Samuel Joseph, 1787-1871.
Letters to Rev. Joel Hawes ... in review of his tribute to the memory of the pilgrims. By Samuel J. May. Hartford, Philemon Canfield, 1831. 72 p. CSmH; MH; NjPT; PHi; RPB. 8216

---- On Prejudice. 2d ed. 1st series. No. 41. American Unitarian Association. Boston, Gray & Bowen, 1831. 16 p. MB-HP; MHi; MeB. 8217

Mayer, Alfred M.
Light: a series of simple, entertaining, and inexpensive experiments in the phenomena of light, for the use of students of every age by A. M. Mayer and Charles Barnard. New York, Appleton, 1831. 112 p. PPFrankI. 8218

Mayes, Daniel, 1792-1861.
An Address delivered before the trustees and faculty of Transylvania University, at the opening of the session of the Law Department...17th Nov. 1831. Lexington [Ky.], Pr. by N. L. Finnell & J. F. Herndon, 1831. 17 p. DLC; NN. 8219

Mayhew, Horace, 1816-1872.
The Toothache imagined, by Horace Mayhew. Boston, Bradford [1831] Illus. MH-D. 8220

Maynard, William Hale, 1787 or 8-1832.
Speech of William H. Maynard on the bill for the construction of the Chenango canal. Delivered in the Senate of New York, February 23 and 24, 1831. Utica, Press of W. Williams, 1831. 32 p. CSt; DLC; NN; NUt; NUtHi. 8221

Mayo, Elizabeth, 1793-1865.
Lessons on things, intended to improve children, on the system of Pestalozzi. Philadelphia, Carey & Lea; Boston, Carter, Hendee & Babcock, 1831. 324 p. DLC; MBAt; RPB; ScSp. 8222

Mead, Asa, 1792-1831.
Memoir of John Mooney Mead, who died at East Hartford, April 8, 1831, aged 4 years, 11 months, and 4 days... Boston, Peirce & Parker, 1831. 92 p. CtSoP; DLC; MAJ; MH-AH; MH. 8223

Meade, Richard Worsam.
Catalogue of Italian, Spanish, Flemish & Dutch paintings, collected in Europe & brought to this country by him, now exhibiting in the gallery of the National Academy of Design, Clinton hall... New York, Clayton and Van Norden, 1831. PPAmP; PPM. 8224

Meade, William, bishop, 1789-1862.
Sermon on confirmation...December 12, 1830. Georgetown, D.C., Pr. by James C. Dunn, 1831. 58 p. CSmH; DLC; Ky; PHi; Vi. 8225

Mease, James, 1771-1846.

On the causes cure and means of preventing the sick headache. 3d ed. Philadelphia, Porter, 1831. 52 p. PPAmP; PPL-R; PaHosp. 8226

---- Pictures of Philadelphia, giving an account of its origin, increase and improvements in arts, sciences, manufactures, commerce and revenue... By James Mease, and continued by Thomas Porter. Philadelphia, Pub. by Robert Desilver, 1831. 2 vols. in 1. DLC; MBAt; NNC; PHi; PPFM. 8227

Medical Society of the County of New York.

By-laws of the Medical Society of the county of New-York. Revised and adopted July, 1831. New-York, Pr. by J. Seymour, 1831. 18 p. NNN. 8228

---- Report of the Committee of the Medical Society of the City and County of New York, appointed to investigate the subject of a secret medical association. New York, 1831. 12 p. CSt-L; MBM; MHi; NNN; OC. 8229

Medical Society of the County of Rensselaer, New York.

By-laws, medical ethics and list of members. 1831. PPCP. 8230

Medical Society of the State of New York.

Transactions of the Medical Society of the State of New York, for the year 1831, with the annual address by Jonathan Eights, M.D. ... Albany, Pr. by Websters and Skinners, 1831. 52 p. NNN; NjR. 8231

Medway Classical Institution.

Catalogue... 1831. Dedham, Mass., Politician & Advocate Press, 1831. 8 p. MHi. 8232

Megede, Wilhelm, ed.

Sammlung vorzueglicher poesien, gesaenge und lieder von deutschen dichtern gesammelt und herausgegeben. Reading, Roths, 1831. 492 p. DLC; MnU; NN; PU; ScC. 8233

Meikle, James, 1730-1799.

Solitude sweetened; or Miscellaneous meditations on various religious subjects, written in different parts of the world. Exeter, 1831. 2 vols. in 1. MBC; Nh-Hi. 8234

---- ---- New-York, John E. Turney, 1831. 369 p. MTr. 8235

[Melish, John] 1771-1822.

The traveller's manual; and description of the United States: comprising geographical, historical, and statistical details of the union, and of each state; being a compendium of information, and a useful accompaniment to a map of this country. New York, A. T. Goodrich, 1831. 497 p. MH-BA. 8236

Memes, John Smythe.

History of sculpture, painting, and architecture... Boston, Allen & Goddard, 1831. 299 p. CtMW; KyLo; MB; OCL; RPB. 8237

Memorial of Bishop Hobart See Schroeder, John Frederick, ed.

Menard, P.

Melanges philosophiques et Litteraires Par P. Menard. Dedies A La Loge. La Grandeur. Charleston, Pr. at the office of The Irishman, 1831. 31 p. NNFM. 8238

Mental friend and rational companions, consisting of maxims and reflections which relates to the conduct of life. Newark, Benjamin Olds, 1831. 119 p.

NjN. 8239

Merriam, George, 1803-1880.
The child's guide: comprising familiars lessons, designed to aid in correct reading, spelling defining, thinking and acting. By George Merriam. Brookfield, Eon G. Merriam, 1831. 178 p. MH-AH; NCanHi. 8240

Merrimack Mutual Fire Insurance Company.
By-laws. Andover, 1831. 8 p. Nh-Hi. 8241

Merritt, Timothy, 1775-1845, comp.
The Christian's manual, a treatise on Christian perfection; with directions for obtaining that State. Compiled principally from the works of the Rev. John Wesley. By the Rev. T. Merritt... New-York, Pub. by J. Emory and B. Waugh for the Methodist Episcopal Church, 1831. 144 p. CtMW; NjP. 8242

---- Review of a pamphlet entitled, Letters on Methodism: purporting to have been written by one or more clergymen, in answer to the inquiries of a female. Brookfield, Mass., Lewis Merriam; New York, J. Emory and B. Waugh, 1831. 35 p. ICN; MB; MBC; NjPT; TxU. 8243

[Merry, Barney]
Address of the Grand Lodge of the State of Rhode Island and Providence Plantations, to the people of said State. Providence, R.I., Pr. by B. Cranston, 1831. 16 p. DLC; PPFM; RHi. 8244

Methodist Episcopal Church.
A collection of hymns for the use of the Methodist Episcopal Church principally from the collection of John Wesley. New York, J. Emory & B. Waugh, 1831. 543 p. MNBMHi; PAnL. 8245

---- A collection of interesting tracts explaining several important points of Scripture doctrine. Pub. by order of General conference. New York, J. Emory and B. Waugh, for the Methodist Episcopal Church, at the conference office, J. Collord, pr., 1831. 388 p. CtMW; NbOP. 8246

---- The doctrines and discipline of the Methodist Episcopal Church. Stereotyped by J. Conner. New-York, Pr. by Hoyt, for the use of the Methodist Episcopal Church in the United States, 1831. 60 p. NNMHi; NNMP; NPla; TNMPH. 8247

---- Minutes of the annual conferences of the Methodist Episcopal Church, for the year 1831. New-York, J. Emory and B. Waugh, for the Methodist Episcopal Church, at the conference office, J. Collord, pr., 1831. 48 p. CoDI; GAuP; NNMHi; TxGeoS. 8248

The Methodist harmonist, containing a great variety of tunes collected from the best authors, adapted to all the various metres in the Methodist hymn-book, and designed for the use of the Methodist Episcopal Church in the United States. To which is added a choice selection of anthems and pieces, for particular occasions. New-York, J. Emory and B. Waugh, for the Methodist Episcopal Church; and to be had of the Methodist preachers in the cities and country. J. Collord, pr., 1831. 247 p. CtHWatk; CtY-D; MAnHi; MiD; WBeloHi; WHi; WPri. 8249

Methodist Protestant Church.
Constitution & discipline of the Methodist Protestant Church. Baltimore, 1831. 159 p. Ct;

DLC; KyLxT; MdBP; NcD; ViRut. 8250

Miami University, Oxford, Ohio.
Catalogue of the officers and students of Miami University, Oxford, Ohio, July 1831. Pr. by W. W. Bishop [1831] DLC; OOxM. 8251

---- Extracts from the catalogue of Miami University. Oxford [1831] Broadside. PPPrHi. 8252

---- Miami University Erodelphian Society address 1831-1856. Anniversary addresses delivered before the Erodelphian and Union Literary Societies. [1831] 154 p. Ohi. 8253

Michener, Ezra.
Essay designed briefly to illustrate the foundation and constitution of religious society. Philadelphia, Atkinson, 1831. 43 p. PHi; PPAmP; PSC-Hi. 8254

Michigan.
Acts passed at the second session of the fourth legislative council of the Territory of Michigan, begun and held at the council chamber, in the city of Detroit, on Tuesday, the fourth day of January, in the year of our Lord one thousand eight hundred and thirty-one. Detroit, Pr. by Sheldon M'Knight, 1831. 85 p. C-L; DLC; NHi; OCLaw; RPL; WaU-L. 8255

---- Address to the electors of the Territory of Michigan. 1831. 7 p. MiD-B. 8256

---- Journal of the legislative council of Michigan, being the second session of the fourth council. Begun and held at the city of Detroit, January 4th, 1831. Detroit, Pr. by George L. Whitney, 1831. 192 p. DLC; ICU; MiU; NHi; WHi. 8257

---- Message to the legislative council of Michigan, from Governor Cass, at the commencement of the second session, of the fourth council, with the accompanying documents. January 5, 1831. Pr. by order of the council. Detroit, Pr. by George L. Whitney, 1831. 20 p. MiD-B. 8258

---- Public meeting. At a numerous meeting of the citizens of Detroit, without distinction of party, convened at the city council house on the evening of the 28th of January, for the purpose of freely discussing certain measures of the executive of the Territory... [Detroit, 1831] MiD-B. 8259

Mickel, Johann Friedrich, 1781-1833.
Manual of general, descriptive, and pathological anatomy, by J. F. Mickel... Tr. from German into French, with additions and notes, by A. J. L. Jeurdan... and G. Breschet. Tr. from the French with notes, by A. Sidney Doane... New York, H. C. Sleight [etc.] 1831-2. 3 vols. ArU-M; CSt-L; MeB; NjR. 8260

Middlebrook's almanac by Elija Middlebrook. New Haven, S. Babcock, 1831. DLC; MWA. 8261

Middlebury Female Seminary. Middlebury, Vermont.
Catalogue of the officers and members of the Middlebury Female Seminary, 1831. Middlebury, Pr. at the office of the Free Press, 1831. 8 p. MH. 8262

Mildmay, Sir N. P. St. John.
Life of Tucker. Cambridge, 1831. 4 vols. MBL. 8263

Milledoler, Philip, 1775-1852.
Address delivered to the graduates of Rutgers college at commencement, held in the Reformed Dutch Church, New Brunswick, N.J., July 20, 1831, by Philip Milledoler... New York, Pr. by William A. Mercer for Rutgers Press, 1831. 24 p. CSansS; DLC; MH-AH; NjR; PPL. 8264

Miller, E.
The life of Joseph, a Scripture narrative. New York, M. Day, 1831. 23 p. N. 8265

Miller, G. B.
A discourse delivered at Schaghticoke, on the first Sunday in Sept., 1831, before the Evangelical Lutheran ministerium of the state of New York, on the fundamental principle of the Reformation. By G. B. Miller. New York, Ludwig & Tolefree, 1831. 16 p. CBPSR; NBuG; NjR; OClWHi; PHi. 8266

Miller, H.
A new selection of psalms, hymns and spiritual songs, from the best authors... 9th ed. Cincinnati, Pr. by Morgan and Sanxay, 1831. [25] p. OCHP. 8267

Miller, Samuel.
Duty, benefits, and the proper method of religious fasting. By Samuel Miller... New York, 1831. 145-160 p. NjP. 8268

Miller, Samuel, 1769-1850.
An essay on the warrant, nature and duties of the office of the Ruling Elder in the Presbyterian Church. By Samuel Miller, D.D. ...New York, Jonathan Leavitt; Boston, Crocker & Brewster, 1831. 322 p. ArCH; CBPSR; KyLoS; NjP; WaPS. 8269

Miller's Planters' & Merchants' Almanac for 1832. Columbia, S.C. B. D. & T. H. Plant [1831] MWA. 8270

Milman, H. H.
The history of the Jews...By Rev. H. H. Milman. New York, J. & J. Harper, 1831. 3 vols. FU; GMM; NGH; Nj; ScC; ViA. 8271

Milton, John, 1608-1674.
Paradise Lost. A poem in twelve books by John Milton. Stereotyped by T. H. Carter and Co. Boston, Langdon Coffin, 1831. 294 p. CtHT; MH; PHi; ScC; WHi. 8272

---- Paradise regained and other poems. New York, S. King, 1831. 215 p. MdW; NPV; NWefa; WBeloC. 8273

---- Poetical works...together with the life of the author. New York, C. Wells [183-?] DLC. 8274

---- ---- Philadelphia, Gregg, 1831. 858 p. LNP; PPA. 8275

---- ---- A new ed. with notes. Philadelphia, Porter and Coates, [1831?] 2 vols. in 1. InFtw; MH; OKEnS; PLor. 8276

Miniature Almanack, for the year of our Lord 1832... Boston, Richardson, Lord & Holbrook [1831] [28] p. MWA; Whi. 8277

The mirror of the graces. Containing general instructions for combining elegance, simplicity, and economy with fashion in dress... Boston, F. S. Hill, 1831. 192 p. NCH; OrP; PPL; PU. 8278

Mischief its own punishment; exemplified in the history of William and Harry. Providence, 1831. 15 p. RHi. 8279

The missions of the Moravians

among the North American Indians inhabiting the middle states of the Union. Written for the American Sunday School Union, and rev. by the committee of publication. Philadelphia, American Sunday School Union, 1831. 162 p. DLC; ICN; NcWsM; WHi. 8280

Mississippi.
Auditors Office, Jackson, November 26, 1831. In obedience to a resolution of the State requiring the Auditor of Public Accounts, and State Treasurer to lay before them their respective reports as Auditor and Treasurer on this day... T. B. Hadley, Auditor of Public Accounts, [Jackson, Peter Isler, 1831] MsJS. 8281

---- Bank, State Mississippi, Natchez, 22d Nov. 1831. Gerard C. Brandon, Governor of State Mississippi. Sir, - I have the honor to enclose a Report, shewing the affairs of the Bank of the State of Mississippi for the past year, and am your most obedient servant, Gabriel Tichenor, Cashier. Statement exhibiting the condition of the Bank of the State of Mississippi, and its Offices, on the first day of November, 1831. Pr. by the State prs. at Natchez, 1831. Broadside. MsJS. 8282

---- Constitution and form of government of the State of Mississippi. Port-Gibson, Pr. by Benj. F. Stockton, 1831. 36 p. Ms-Ar; MsJS; NN. 8283

---- General orders. Head Quarters, Jackson, Miss. Jan. 22d, 1831. The following uniform is hereby prescribed for the officers of the militia State... [Jackson, 1831] 2 p. Ms-Ar. 8284

---- Governor's message. Fellow-Citizens of the Senate and of the House of Representatives. [Jackson, 1831] Broadside. Ms-Ar. 8285

---- Journal of the Convention of the western part of the Mississippi Territory. Begun and held in the town of Washington, on the seventh day of July, 1817. Port Gibson, Repr. by B. F. Stockton, 1831. 108 p. Ms; Ms-Ar; NN; OCLaw. 8286

---- Journal of the House of Representatives, of the State of Mississippi, at their fifteenth session, held in the town of Jackson. [Nov. 21-Dec. 20, 1831] Pub. by authority. Jackson, Pr. by Peter Isler, 1831. 273 p. CSmH; Ms; WHi. 8287

---- Journal of the Senate of the State of Mississippi, at their fifteenth session, held in the town of Jackson. Pub. by authority. Jackson, Peter Isler, 1831. 219 p. Ms; Ms-Ar; WHi. 8288

---- Laws of the state of Mississippi, passed at the fifteenth session of the General Assembly ... Pub. by authority. Jackson, Pr. by Peter Isler, 1831. 172 p. IaU-L; Ms; NN. 8289

Missouri.
House Journal, of the first session, of the sixth General Assembly of the State of Missouri, begun and held at the City of Jefferson, on the third Monday, being the fifteenth day of November, in the year of our Lord, one thousand eight hundred and thirty. Fayette, Pr. at the office of the Western Monitor, 1831. 285 p. Mo; MoHi. 8290

---- Laws of the state of Missouri, passed at the first session of the sixth General Assembly, begun and held at the city of

Jefferson, on Monday, the fifteenth day of November, in the year of our Lord, one thousand eight hundred and thirty. [Jefferson, 1831] 136 p. DLC; MH-L; Mo; MoHi. 8291

---- Senate Journal of the first session, of the sixth General Assembly, of the state of Missouri, begun and held at the city of Jefferson, on the third Monday being the fifteenth day of November, in the year of our Lord one thousand eight hundred and thirty. Fayette, Pr. at the office of the Western Monitor, 1831. 43 p. Mo; MoHi. 8292

Mitchell, Elisha.
Arguments for temperance; a sermon addressed to the students of the University of North Carolina, March 13th, 1831 and pub. by their request. Raleigh [N.C.] Gales, 1831. 29 p. NcU; PHi; PPPrHi. 8293

Mitchell, J. Murray.
Once Hindu: Now Christian. The early life of Baba Padmanji. An autobiography. Edited by J. Murray Mitchell. New York, 1831. 135 p. ViRut. 8294

Mitchell, Samuel Augustus, 1792-1868.
Map of Kentucky, and Tennessee, compiled from the latest authorities. Philadelphia, Pa., Mitchell, 1831. KyLx. 8295

---- Map of Maine, New Hampshire and Vermont. Philadelphia, 1831. 1 p. Nh-Hi; PHi. 8296

---- Map of Massachusetts, Connecticut & Rhode Island: map, constructed from latest authorities, with statistical table. Philadelphia, 1831. IP. 8297

---- Map of New York State. Philadelphia, 1831. 1 p. PHi. 8298

---- Map of Pennsylvania, New Jersey & Delaware. Philadelphia, Samuel Augustus. Mitchell, 1831. P. 8299

---- Map of South America. Philadelphia, 1831. 1 p. PHi. 8300

---- A new American atlas designed principally to illustrate the geography of the United States of North America...the whole compiled from the latest and most authentic information. Philadelphia, S. Augustus Mitchell, 1831. 15 maps. MHi; MiU-C. 8301

Mitchell, Thomas Rothmaler, 1783-1837.
Speech of Mr. Mitchell, of South Carolina, on the resolution of Mr. Mercer, to appoint a standing committee of seven members, to be styled a committee on roads and canals, delivered in the House of Representatives, December 15, 1831. City of Washington, Pr. by the Globe office, by F. P. Blair, 1831. 12 p. A-Ar; DLC; MBaT; ScU. 8302

Mitford, Mary Russell.
Narrative poems on female character...by Mary Russell Mitford... Vol. 1. New York, Eastburn, Kirk & Co., 1831. 206 p. NGos. 8303

Moat, Thomas.
The Practical proofs of the soundness of the hygeian system of physiology... Brooklyn, H. Shepheard Moat, 1831. 30 p. ICJ; KyDC; NN. 8304

The Modern Traveller. A popular description, geographical, historical and topographical, of the various countries of the globe. Arabia. Boston, Lilly & Wait, 1831. 340 p. ICBB; NGH;

RNR; ViAl. 8305

Moister, W[illiam] 1808-1891.
Africa: past and present. New York, American Tract Society, 1831. ViRVU. 8306

Monfort, David.
A sermon on justification, from Romans 111, 24. With an appendix. By David Monfort, minister of the gospel at Franklin, Johnson county, Indiana, pub. by request. Indianapolis, Douglass & Maguire, 1831. 35 p. In; InHi. 8307

Monita Secreta Societatis Jesu.
Secret instructions of the Jesuits. Printed verbatim from the London copy of 1725, to which is prefixed an historical essay; with an appendix of notes, by the editor of the Protestant... Princeton, N.J., J. & T. Simpson, 1831. 232 p. (Text in Latin and English.) ICN; KyDC; MdBL; MdBP; PPL. 8308

Monroe County, Michigan (territory). Citizens.
Voice of the French citizens of the county of Monroe. At a large and respectable meeting of the inhabitants of Frenchtown... [Monroe, 1831] MiD-B. 8309

Montgomery, George Washington, 1804-1841.
El serrano de las alpujarras: y El cuadro misterioso. Brunswick, Imprenta de Griffin. Se halla de venta en la liberia de Colman; Portland, 1831. 80 p. MB; MH. 8310

Monthly American Journal of Geology and Natural Science. Conducted by G. W. Featherstonhaugh, Philadelphia, July 1831-June 1832. CtY; MH-G; PPAN; TV; WHi. 8311

Montolieu, Isabelle (polier) de baronne de, 1751-1832.
Caroline of Lichtfield: a novel. By Thomas Holcroft. I dole d'un coeur juste & passion du Sage, Amitie, que ton nom soutienne cet ouvrage; Regne dans mes ecrits, ainsi que dans mon coeur, Tu m'appris a comoitre, a sentir, le bankeur. Voltaire. New York, Pr. by S. & D. Forbes, 1831. 2 vols. MB; NRMA; NjR. 8312

Montresor, John.
Journey of a tour from the St. Lawrence to the Kennebec, supposed to have been made by Colonel Montresor, chief of the engineer department, about the year 1769. Me. Historical Society Collection. Portland, Pr. by Day, Frazer & Co., 1831. DLC. 8313

Moor, James, 1712-1779.
Elements of the Greek language, exhibited, for the most part, in New Rules, made easy to the memory by their brevity: Being a translation of Dr. Moor's celebrated Greek Grammar. With large additions and improvements from the latest editions, by Professors Dunbar and Neilson, and from the late works of Mattilae, Buttman, Thiersch, and others. By the Rev. Peter Bullions, Professor of Language in The Albany Academy. New-York, Collins and Hannay; Albany, Webster and Skinner, and Little & Cummings, 1831. 408 p. CtY; InCW; NjPT; OWoC; TNP; ViRU. 8314

Moore, Henry.
The life of Mrs. Mary Fletcher, consort and relict of the Rev. John Fletcher. Compiled from her journal, and other authentic documents. By Henry Moore... Stereotyped by H. Simmons &

co. Baltimore, Mordecai Stuart, 1831. 420 p. ABBS; GEU-T; MdAS; MdHi; ViPet. 8315

Moore, James Wilson.
The Bible a revelation of God. A discourse by the Rev. James Moore, minister of the Presbyterian Church in Little Rock, A.T. Little Rock, Pr. by Wm. E. Woodruff, 1831. 28 p. ArBaA. 8316

Moore, Samuel W.
A memoir of the life and character of John Watts, M.D. late president of the College of Physicians and Surgeons. With an address to the gentlemen who were graduated doctors of medicine at the annual commencement of the College of Physicians and Surgeons, held April 5th, 1831. New York, 1831. 28 p. MBAt; MdBD; NNN; PPcP; RNR. 8317

Moore, Thomas, 1779-1852.
The complete works of Thomas Moore. With a biographical sketch by Nathan Haskall Dole. By Thomas Moore. New York, Thomas V. Crowell Co., 1831. 800 p. LAlS. 8318

---- The Epicurean, a tale. By Thomas Moore, dedicated to Lord John Russell. Boston, N. H. Whitaker, 1831. 192 p. KAL; MdBL; NNUT; OMtv; RJa. 8319

---- The life and death of Lord Edward Fitzgerald, by Thomas Moore, in two vols. New York, J. & J. Harper, Peabody & Co., and Carey & Lee, 1831. 2 vols. CtMW; LU; PPA; ScU; VtU. 8320

---- The poetical works of Thomas Moore, including his melodies, ballads, etc. Philadelphia, J. Crissy and J. Grigg, 1831. 419 p. KyOw; LNB; NjN; PHi; TxHR. 8321

More, Hannah, 1745-1833.
The young lady abroad; or, Affectionate advice on the social and moral habits of females. By Hannah More... Boston, James Loring [1831?] 216 p. NjR. 8322

Morgan, Nathaniel H[arris].
A lecture on party spirit; together with a valedictory address, delivered to the members of "Goshen lyceum" in Lebanon, Connecticut, April 1st, 1831. Hartford, 1831. 16 p. ICBB; NNC. 8323

Morgan, Rev. Richard.
Consolation in the death of infants; a sermon preached in St. Martin's Church, Marcus Hook, Feb. 13th, 1831. Wilmington, Del., 1831. 16 p. NIC. 8324

Morison, John, 1791-1859.
Counsels on matrimony; or, Friendly suggestions to husbands and wives and a remembrance for life... Newark, Worts & Co., 1831. 126 p. CtMW; NjN. 8325

---- Counsels to young men on modern infidelity and the evidences of Christianity. New York, American Tract Society [183-?] MH. 8326

Morrell, Benjamin.
A narrative of four voyages to the South Sea, North and South Pacific Ocean, Chinese Sea, Ethiopie and Southern Atlantic Ocean, Indian and Antarctic Ocean. From the year 1822 to 1831... By Capt. Benjamin Morrell. New York, J. & J. Harper, 1832. 492 p. NIC. 8327

Morris, John Gottlieb, 1803-1895.
Catechumen's and Communicant's Companion, designed for the use of young persons of the Lutheran Church, preparatory to

confirmation and the Lord's Supper; by a Pastor. Baltimore, Wright, 1831. MoS; PPhT. 8328

Morse, Pitt.
Sermons in vindication of Universalism, by Pitt Morse, pastor of the First Universalist Church and Society in Watertown, N.Y. ... In reply to "Lectures on Universalism: by Joel Parker, pastor of the 3d Presbyterian Church, Rochester," Watertown, Pr. by Woodward & Calhoun, 1831. 135 p. CSmH; MMeT-Hi; NBuG; NRHi; ScNC. 8329

Morse, William.
On "Revivals of religion." A sermon, delivered in New Bedford, April 17, 1831. New Bedford, Benjamin T. Congdon, 1831. 20 p. MMeT-Hi; NHi; NNUT. 8330

[Morton, Henry]
[Original poems, songs and letters by Henry Morton of Spottsylvania, Va. and Richmond, Va. Richmond, Va., 1831] Manuscript notebook. RPB. 8331

Morton, Samuel George, 1799-1851.
Introductory lecture to a course of demonstrative anatomy; delivered December 11th, 1830. By Samuel George Morton, M.D. ... Philadelphia, Pr. by Mifflin and Parry, 1831. 16 p. NBMS; NNN; PHi; PPAN; PU. 8332

Moses, Myer.
Oration, delivered at Tammany-Hall, on the twelfth of May, 1831, being the forty-second anniversary of the Tammany Society, or, Columbian Order, by Myer Moses, a member of said Society, New York, Pr. by P. Van Pelt, 1831. 31 p. LNH; MiD-B; NutHi; PPDrop. 8333

Moulton, Joseph White, 1789-1875.
The chancery practice of the state of New York, by Joseph W. Moulton, solicitor and counsellor. New York, O. Halstead [1831?] 489 p. In-SC; NSyCA. 8334

Mount Pleasant Classical Institution, Amherst, Massachusetts.
Catalogue of the students of the Mount Pleasant Classical Institution, Amherst, Mass. From June 1, 1827 to January 1831. [Amherst] Pr. by J. S. and C. Adams [1831] 8 p. MA-H; MH; NN. 8335

Mount Vernon Female School. Boston.
Catalogue of the...January, 1831. Boston, 1831. 12 p. MHi. 8336

Moyamensing Township, Pa. Ordinances.
Digests of Acts of Assembly of Moyamensing, with ordinances and rules of order, 1831. Philadelphia, 1831-48. MH-L; PHi; PPB. 8337

Muhlenberg, William Augustus and Seabury, S.
Christian education: being an address delivered after a public examination of the students of the institute at Flushing, L.I.; The studies and discipline of the institute; and an essay on the study of the classics on Christian principles. New-York, Protestant Episcopal Press, 1831. 34 p. MdBD; NCH; PPL; RPB. 8338

Muller, Albert Arney.
Address delivered before the members of Rising Virtue Lodge, and various officers and members of the Grand Lodge of the State of Alabama, on the occasion of laying the corner stone of the Masonic Hall in Tuscaloosa, on Monday the 11th of April, A.D.

1831, and in the year of Masonry 5831. By Brother Albert A. Muller, Rector of Christ Church, Tuscalossa. Tuscaloosa, Pr. by Wiley, M'Guire & Henry, 1831. 13 p. AMFM; DSC; MB; MBFM. 8339

Muller, Johannes von, 1752-1809.
An universal history, in twenty-four books. Trans. from the German of John von Muller. Boston, Stimpson and Clapp, 1831-1832. 4 vols. CtHC; InCW; MB; OClWHi; TNP. 8340

Murray, John.
Records of the life of Rev. John Murray, late minister of the reconsiliation, and senior pastor of the Universalists, congregated in Boston. Written by himself. Rev. John Murray the... quot. 3d ed. with notes and remarks, by Rev. L. S. Everett. Boston, Marsh Capen and Lyon, and Waitt & Dow, 1831. 328 p. MBarn. 8341

Murray, Lindley, 1745-1826.
Abridgement of Murray's English Grammar. With an appendix, containing exercises in ortnography, phrasing, syntax, and punctuation. Designed for the younger class of learners. By Lindley Murray. Hallowell, U.C. J. Wilson, 1831. 105 p. NN. 8342

---- ---- 8th Hallowell ed., rev. and corr. Hallowell, Glazier, Masters & Co., 1831. 68 p. MeHi. 8343

[----] ... English grammar. "Remove not the ancient landmark." Edited by Silas Blaisdale. Boston, Marsh, Capen and Lyon, 1831. 88 p. DLC; NNC. 8344

---- English grammar. Adapted to the different classes of learners, with an appendix, containing rules and observations for assisting the more advanced students to write with perspicuity and accuracy... By Lindley Murray... Baltimore, Geo. M'Dowell & son, 1831. 300 p. AzU; OO; TJon; ViU. 8345

---- ---- Bridgeport, Conn., Baldwin, 1831. 232 p. NRivHi; OO; WU. 8346

---- ---- Philadelphia, Key and Mielke, 1831. 210 p. 8347

---- ---- From the 28th English ed. Stereotype ed. Utica, W. Williams, 1831. KHi; NE; NPotN; NUt. 8348

---- The English reader; or, pieces in prose and poetry selected from the best writers... By Lindley Murray. ...Boston, Lincoln & Edmands, 1831. 264 p. MLaw. 8349

---- ---- Concord, N.H., Marsh, Capen & Lyon, 1831. 304 p. CSt; MH; NCH. 8350

---- ---- New York, White, Gallaher & White, 1831. VtCas. 8351

---- ---- Philadelphia, L. Johnson, 1831. 263 p. MsClim; NjR; OCl. 8352

---- ---- Philadelphia, Neall, 1831. 252 p. P; PLFM; PU-Penn. 8353

---- ---- Philadelphia, S. Probasco, 1831. 252 p. IaHi. 8354

---- The English reader... To which a key representing the different sounds of the vowels referred to by the figures. By Rensselaer Bentley. By Lindley Murray. Poughkeepsie, P. Potter, 1831. 204, 60 p. MH; MdBS-P; NP. 8355

---- Introduction to the English

reader; or a selection of pieces in prose and poetry... By Lindley Murray... Philadelphia, Simon Probasco, 1831. 162 p. MiU; TxD-T. 8356

---- Murray's Grammar simplified with questions. Philadelphia, 1831. MB. 8357

---- Murray's System of English Grammar, improved and adapted to the present mode of instruction in this branch of science. Larger arrangement. By Enoch Pond. Stereotyped by Lyman Thurston and Co., Boston. Worcester, Dorr and Howland, 1831. 228 p. CoGrS. 8358

---- Sequel to the English reader; or, Elegant selections in prose and poetry. Designed to improve the highest class of learners in reading; to establish a taste for just and accurate composition; and to promote the interests of piety and virtue. By Lindley Murray. New York, Collins, 1831. 299 p. MS; OHi; VtU. 8359

---- ---- Philadelphia, S. Probasco, 1831. 244 p. InI; KWiF; NNUT; OC; PHi. 8360

Musical Fund Society of Philadelphia.

Act of Incorporation and by-laws. Philadelphia, 1831. PHi. 8361

Mutiny and murder. Confession of Charles Gibbs, a native of Rhode Island. Who, with Thomas J. Wansley, was doomed to be hung in New-York on the 22d of April last, for the murder of the captain and mate of the brig Vineyard, on her passage from New-Orleans to Philadelphia, in November 1830. Providence, I. Smith, 1831. 36 p. DLC; MBNEH; MH; NIC; RPA. 8362

Mutual rights and Methodist Protestant; a weekly periodical containing various original select essays on religion, literature and church policy; with literary, biographical, and historical sketches, and also, religious and miscellaneous intelligense... Edited by Gamaliel Bailey...Vol. 1. Baltimore, John J. Harrad, 1831. Vol. 1. 414 p. DLC; F. 8363

Myers, James.

Narrative of two wonderful cures, wrought in the Monastery of the Visitation at Georgetown, in the District of Columbia in the month of January, 1831. Baltimore, Myers, 1831. 24 p. MH; MdBS; MdW; PHi; PPL. 8364

N

National Academy of Design.

The sixth exhibition of the National Academy of Design. New-York, Pr. by Clayton & Van Norden [1831] 15 p. MH; PPAmP. 8365

The national calendar, for 1831, by Peter Force. Published annually. Washington, Peter Force, 1831. 372 p. MdHi; MiD; NCH; RNR. 8366

[National Republican party. Kentucky]

Proceedings of the National Republican convention, held at Frankfort, Kentucky, on Thursday, Dec. 9, 1830. [Frankfort? 1831?] 19 p. DLC. 8367

---- National Convention, Baltimore, 1831.

An Address to the freemen of Vermont, by their delegation to the National Republican Convention, holden at Baltimore, Maryland, In December, 1831. Middlebury, Vt., Pr. by H. H.

Houghton, [1831?] 16 p. VtU. 8368

---- ---- ---- Journal of the National Republican convention, which assembled in the city of Baltimore, Dec. 12, 1831, for the nominations of candidates to fill the offices of president and vice president. Pub. by order of the convention. Washington, Pr. at the office of the National Journal, 1831. 32 p. DLC; MBC; ScU; TxU; WHi. 8369

---- ---- Washington. ... Proceedings of the National Republican party in the city of Washington, on the 3d day of May, 1831... Washington, F. P. Blair, 1831. 24 p. MHi; WHi. 8370

---- New York (State).
New-York National Republican state convention... Address to the electors of the state of New York... [Albany, Office of the Daily freeman's advocate, 1831] 4 p. DLC. 8371

---- Rhode Island.
Address of the National Republican Convention to the freemen of the state of Rhode-Island and Providence Plantations. [Political handbill in favor of Lemuel H. Arnold against Gove. James Fennar, Providence? 1831] RPA; RPB. 8372

---- ---- Examination of certain charges against Lemuel H. Arnold, esq., the National Republican candidate for governor, being a report of the committee, appointed April 12, 1831. Providence, 1831. 28 p. DLC; MH; RHi; RNHi; RP. 8373

---- Vermont.
An address to the Freemen of Vermont, by their Delegation to the National Republican Convention, holden at Baltimore, Maryland, in December 1831. Middlebury, Vt., Pr. by H. H. Houghton, [1831] 16 p. CSmH; VtMidbC; Vt; VtU. 8374

The Nautical almanac and astronomical ephemeris for the year 1833. Pub. by order of the Board of Admiralty. New York, Patten, 1831. 1 vol. CtMW. 8375

The naval chaplain, exhibiting a view of American efforts to benefit seamen. By the author of Conversations on the Sandwich Islands and Bombay missions, &c. &c.... Boston, Pr. by T. R. Marvin, for the Massachusetts Sabbath School Union, 1831. 136 p. OClWHi; OMC; PHi; TNP. 8376

Neal, John, 1793-1876.
An address delivered before the M. C. Mechanic Association. Thursday evening, January 13, 1831, by John Neal, Portland, Day and Fraizer, 1831. 17 p. MMeT; MnHi; NN. 8377

Needham [Mass.] Temperance Society.
Constitution and... Members of the Needham Temperance Society. Dedham, Mass., 1831. 7 p. MH. 8378

Neilson, William, 1760?-1821.
Exercises on the syntax of the Greek language. By the Rev. William Neilson, D.D. A new ed., cor. and enl. To which are subjoined, exercises in metaphrasis, paraphrasis, dialects, and prosody. Together with an historical sketch of the dialects; the doctrine of the middle voice, with explanatory examples; a statement of opinions respecting the Greek accents; and two appendices, illustrative of the leading principles of the Greek syntax. By Charles Anthon... New York, T. & J. Swords, Stanford & Co.,

1831. 211 p. NGH; NNC; OClU; OO; TWcW. 8379

Nelson, John, 1707-1774.
Extract from the "Journal of John Nelson": being an account of God's dealing with him, from his youth to the forty-second year of his age, written by himself. ...New York, Pr. by J. Collord, at the conference office, for J. Emory and B. Waugh, 1831. 227 p. CtMW; IRA; NNMHi. 8380

---- Life of John Nelson: embracing an account of God's dealing with him from his youth to the forty second year of his age. Written by himself. To which is added, an account of his death. Exeter [N.H.] Pr. by Sawyer & Meder, for James J. Wiggin, 1831. 272 p. MB; Nh; NhD; Nh-Hi. 8381

Nelson, Robert.
The practice of true devotion ...By Robert Nelson, esq. New York, T. & J. Swords, 1831. 252 p. ICCB; GDecCT; MdBD; NNG; PCC. 8382

Netherlands, Sovereigns.
The decision of the King of Netherlands considered in reference to the rights of the United States and of the State of Maine. Portland, T. Todd, 1831. 35 p. ArU; CtSoP; DLC; MB; OClWHi. 8383

Nettleton, Asahel, 1783-1844.
Village hymns for social worship. Selected and original. Designed as a supplement to be the psalms and hymns of Dr. Watts ...Stereotype ed. New York, E. Sands, 1831. 488 p. ICT; MdBD; PPPrHi; RNR; ViAl. 8384

Neue Americanische Landwirthschafts Calender, 1832. Von Carl Friedrich Egelmann. Reading, Pa., Johann Ritter [1831] MWA. 8385

Neuman, Henry.
Dictionary of the Spanish and English languages, where in the words are correctly explained and a great variety of terms relating to art, science, manufacture, etc., stereotype ed., carefully rev. and enl. Boston, Hilliard, Gray, Little & Wilkins, 1831. 2 vols. MCon; MiD; MoSW. 8386

---- A pocket dictionary of the Spanish and English languages. Comp. from the last imp. eds. of Neuman and Baretti. In 2 parts. Spanish-English and English-Spanish. Philadelphia, Carey, 1831. 714 p. CtHC; MH. 8387

Nevin, John Williamson.
The claims of the Bible urged upon the attention of students of theology. A lecture, delivered November 8, 1831, at the opening of the winter session of the Western theological seminary of the Presbyterian church... Pittsburgh, Pr. by D. & M. Maclean, 1831. 26 p. NjR; OClWHi; OMC; PPM; PPPrHi; PPiW. 8388

New Bedford, Mass.
Report of the Selectmen, for the expenses of the town of New Bedford, as paid by them for the year ending March 21, 1831. New Bedford, B. T. Congdon, 1831. 20 p. MHi; MNBedf. 8389

---- First Baptist Church.
Articles of faith and the covenant adopted by the First Baptist Church in New Bedford. New Bedford, B. Lindsey & Son, 1831. 14 p. ICN. 8390

New Bedford Port Society.
First annual report of the board of managers of the New Bedford Port Society for the moral improvement of seamen, presented

at the annual meeting, June 7, 1831. New Bedford, B. T. Congdon, 1831. 24 p. MB; MH; MNBedf. 8391

A new collection of genuine receipts, for the preparation and execution of curious arts, and interesting experiments... To which is added, a complete and much approved system of dyeing, in all its varieties. Stereotype ed. Concord, N.H., Fisk & Chase, 1831. 102, 6 p. DLC; MHi; NCaS. 8392

The New-England almanac, and Methodist register...1831. By Aaron Lummus. Boston, Putnam & Hunt [1831] [54] p. NhD. 8393

The New England almanack, and farmer's friend, for the year of our Lord Christ, 1832... Fitted to the meridian of New London ...The astronomical calculations performed by Nathan Daboll... New London, Samuel Green [1831] [34] p. CtNwchA; RWe; WHi. 8394

New England Anti-masonic almanac, 1832. Boston, Pr. by John Marsh and Co. [1831] 48 p. IaCrM; MBC; MWA; MeHi; PPFM. 8395

New England Anti-Slavery Society.

Proceedings, Boston, May 28 & 29, 1831. OCHP. 8396

New England Comic Almanac for 1830. Full of whims, scraps, and odd it is!! Woodstock, Vt., Nahum Haskell [1831] 48 p. VtHi. 8397

The New England Farmer's almanac, by Thomas G. Fessenden, 1832... Boston, Pr. by I. R. Butts, for Carter, Hendee & Babcock, 1831. 45 p. MBilHi; MDovC; MWA; MeHi; WHi. 8398

The New England farmer's almanack, with an ephemeris for the year of the Christian era, 1832. By Truman W. Abell, Winsor, Simeon Ide...[1831] 24 l. DLC; MBUPH; MWA. 8399

The New England farmer's diary and almanac...for 1832. ...By Truman Abell. Windsor, Vt., Pr. by Simeon Ide, 1831. MBUPH; MWA. 8400

The New-England magazine. v. 1-9; July 1831-Dec. 1835. Boston, J T. and E. Buckingham [etc., 1831-35] 9 v. CU; IaU; MiU; RNR; WHi. 8401

New New England Primer, or, An easy and pleasant guide to the art of reading. Adorned with cuts. To which is added The Catechism. Boston, John Punchard, and James Gay...1831. [64] p. CtSoP; MB; MHi; MWA; OCHP. 8402

New Hampshire.

Constitution of New Hampshire. Concord, 1831. MH. 8403

---- Journal of the Honorable Senate by the State of New Hampshire at their session holden at the Capitol in Concord. Commencing Wednesday June 1, 1831. Pub. by authority. Concord, Pr. by Luther Roby, for the state, 1831. 126 p. Mi; Nh; NhPet. 8404

---- Journal of the House of Representatives, of the state of New-Hampshire, at their session, holden at the capitol in Concord, commencing Wednesday, June 1, 1831. Pub. by authority. Concord, Pr. by Luther Roby, for the state, 1831. 266 p. Mi. 8405

---- Sessions Laws.

June 1831. Concord, Pr. by

Hill and Barton, 1831. 47 p. MH-L. 8406

The New-Hampshire Annual Register, and United States Calendar. By John Farmer... Concord, Horatio Hill & Co., 1831. 144 p. MHa; MWA; MiD-B; NhHi. 8407

New Hampshire Medical Society.
The charter by-laws, regulations and police of the New Hampshire Medical Society... Concord, Pr. by Fisk & Chase, 1831. 28 p. DLC; Nh; OC; OCGHM. 8408

New Hampshire Temperance Society.
Third Annual Report of the executive committee.. June 1, 1831. Concord, Pr. by Morrill & Chadwick, 1831. 24 p. DLC. 8409

New Haven. School Fund. Commissioners of.
Correspondence between the commissioners of the school fund and the New Haven bank, Hartford, Dec. 23, 1831. 7 p. MiD-B. 8410

---- Classical and commercial school.
Catalogue, 1831. 7 p. CtY. 8411

---- Franklin Institute.
Outline of the Franklin, institution of New Haven. [New Haven, Pr. by Baldwin and Treadway, 1831] 10 p. MiD-B. 8412

---- Third Congregational Church.
The Constitution, Confession of Faith, & Covenant, of the Third Congregational Church in New Haven. New Haven, 1831. MWA. 8413

---- Young men's institute.
Constitution of the Young Mechanics' institute [Instituted in 1826] [New Haven, 1831] 1 l. CtY. 8414

New Haven County Horticultural Society.
Notice. An exhibition of the "Horticultural Society of New Haven," will be made at Washington Hall, on Friday, the 9th instant... [New Haven] Sept. 6, 1831. Broadside. CtY. 8415

New Haven Ladies Greek Association.
First Annual Report of the New Haven Ladies Greek Association. New-Haven, Pr. by Nathan Whiting, 1831. 64 p. Ct; MBC; MH; PPPrHi; WHi. 8416

New Jersey.
Acts of the fifty-fifth General Assembly of the state of New Jersey. At a session begun at Trenton, on the twenty-sixth day of October, one thousand eight hundred and thirty: being the second sitting. Trenton, Pr. by Joseph Justice, 1831. 10 p. Ky; MiL; Nj; T. 8417

---- Journal of the proceedings of the Legislative council of the state of New Jersey, convened at Trenton, October, 1830...first sitting of the fifty-fifth session. Bridgeton, N.J., Pr. by Samuel S. Sibley, 1831. 162 p. Nj; NjR. 8418

---- Journal of the votes and proceedings of the convention of New Jersey, begun at Burlington the 10th day of June, 1776, and thence continued by adjournment at Trenton and New Brunswick, to the 21st of Aug. following... Trenton, N.J., Pr. by Joseph Justice, 1831. 100 p. InHi; MH-L; NHi; NjMp; PHi; PPL. 8419

---- Opinion of the Circuit Court of New Jersey, on rights of fishing in the Delaware. Delivered by Justice Baldwin. Philadelphia, 1831. PHi; PPL; PPL-R. 8420

---- Public acts, also Various acts of the General Assembly of the State of New Jersey... at the different sessions held in 1822-1830. Princeton, D. A. Borrenstein [1831] 6 v. KyU; Ky; NjP. 8421

New Jersey almanack for the year 1832... New Brunswick, Pr. by Griggs & Dickinson, Philadelphia, for Joseph C. Griggs [1831] [40] p. NjR. 8422

---- Newark, Benjamin Olds [1831] [34] p. NjMOW; NjR. 8423

New Jersey and New York Almanac for 1832. By David Young, Philom. New-York, C. Brown [1831] MWA. 8424

New Jerusalem Church.
A catechism for the children of the New Church. Boston, Allen & Goddard, 1831. 36 p. CBPac; MH. 8425

New Jerusalem Western Missionary Society.
Proceedings of the first annual meeting of the New Jerusalem Western Missionary Society, held in the temple, Cincinnati, October 2, 1831: together with the reports of the missionaries. Cincinnati, Pr. by John H. Wood, 1831. 16 p. OClWHi; WRHist. 8426

New manual of private devotions, in three parts, containing prayers for families and private persons... Corr. and enl. by The Right Reverend Levi Silliman Ives, D.D. ...3d New York ed. To which is added, A Friendly visit to the house of mourning, by The Rev. Richard Cecil, M.A.... New York, T. and J. Swords, 368 p. DLC; NcU. 8427

New Orleans.
A general digest of the ordinances and resolutions of the corporation of New-Orleans. Made by order of the City council by their Secretary, D. Augustin... [New Orleans] Pr. by J. Bayon, 1831. 415 p. IU; L; MH-L; NN; PU; WaU. 8428

New-Orleans Canal and Banking Company.
An Act to incorporate the subscribers...to the New Orleans Canal and Banking Company, and for other purposes. New-Orleans, Pr. by Benjamin Levy, 1831. 42 + 16 p. AU; DLC; NN; OCHP; PPAmP. 8429

New Orleans wholesale prices current. March 12, 1831-New Orleans, weekly, B. Levy, 1831-MH-BA. 8430

New York (City). Board of Assistant Alderman.
Documents. New York 1831-[1834] 13 v. in 10. DLC; MB; MH. 8431

---- ---- Report of the special committee in relation to the fifth ward election... (July 18, 1831). 16 p. NNC. 8432

---- Common council.
Names and places of abode of the members of the Common council, and of the officers who hold appointments under them. New York, Pr. by Peter Van Pelt, 1831. 24 p. NIC; NjR. 8433

---- ---- Report [on the propositions of W. J. Hubard to dispose of a copy of the Hondon statue of Washington to the city of New York] [1831] Vi. 8434

---- ---- Remarks of Mr. Dibblee, in common council, on discussing the following Resolution offered by Alderman Stevens, [on forming city corporation to supply water. New York (City),

1831?] 56 p. MBC; WHi. 8435

---- Comptroller's office.

Annual report of the comptroller, with the accounts of the corporation of the city of New-York, for the year ending the 31st day of December, 1830. Also, the account current of the commissioners of the sinking fund, for the same period. New-York, Pr. by Peter Van Pelt, 1831. 39 p. DNASD; MnU; ScU. 8436

---- Inspector. Annual reports.

Annual Report of Deaths in the city and county of New York for the year 1831. New York, Peter Van Pelt, 1831. 15 p. 8437

---- Superior Court.

Reports of cases argued and determined in the Superior court of the city of New York: [1828-1829] By Jona. Prescott Hall... New York, O. Halsted, 1831-33. 2 vols. IN-SC; MH-L; NhD; Nj; Ok. 8438

---- University.

Constitution and statutes for the present government of the university. New York, Pr. by W. A. Mercein, 1831. 21 p. MB; MH; NIC; NNUT. 8439

New York (County) Court of General Sessions.

Report of the trial on an inditement for libel. New York, 1831. NN. 8440

New York (State).

Memorial to the Legislature of Lyman A. Spalding, relative to the surplus waters at Lockport. Albany, 1831. 19 p. MBC. 8441

---- Attorney General's office.

Report of the Attorney-General, on the communication of the Hon. Smyh Thompson, one of the justices of the Supreme court of the United States, 1831. MdBJ. 8442

---- Bank commissioners.

Annual report. [New York, 1831-] ICLAW; ICU; PPAmP. 8443

---- Canal Commissioners.

Report of the Canal Commissioners, in obedience to the act entitled "An act directing the survey of a canal route from Rome to the High Falls of the Black River." 23 p. DLC; NbU. 8444

---- Commissioners for constructing the Sodus Canal.

Reports and estimates for uniting Lake Ontario with the Erie Canal at Sodus Bay, Oct., 1831. 22 p. NIC. 8445

---- Commissioners of the Canal fund.

... Annual report of the commissioners of the canal fund... Albany, by Croswell and Van Benthuysen, 1831. 24 p. DLC; MiD-B. 8446

---- Committee to investigate the affairs of the New York Hospital.

Report. Albany, 1831. NN. 8447

---- Court of Common Pleas, Dutchess Co.

Rules and orders of the court of common pleas of the County of Dutchess adopted February 8, 1831. Poughkeepsie, E. B. Killey and A. Low, 1831. 51 p. NP. 8448

---- Dept. of public instruction.

Report of the Superintendent of Common Schools of the State of New-York. Made to the Assembly, January 15, 1831. Albany, Pr. by Croswell and Van Benthuysen, 1831. 71 p. NbU. 8449

---- General Assembly.

... An act for the appointment of a measurer-general of grain in and for the city and county of

New York... [Albany, 1831] 2 p. NN. 8450

---- ---- Documents of the Senate of the state of New York, fifty-fourth session, 1831. From no. 1 to 78, inclusive. Albany, Pr. by E. Croswell, pr. to the state, 1831. 987 p. NNLI. 8451

---- Governor. E. T. Throop, 1829-1832.

Communication from the governor, relative to the boundary line between this state and the state of New Jersey, March 11, 1831. [Albany, N.Y., 1831] 31 p. DLC; NbU. 8452

---- Laws, Statutes, etc.

An act incorporating the University of the City of New York, passed April 18, 1831. New York, Pr. by W. A. Mercein, 1831. 8 p. GDecCT; NNUT; RPB. 8453

---- ---- An act to provide for sick and disabled seamen. The people of the state of New York represented in Senate and Assembly, do enact as follows... New York, [1831] 7 p. NjR. 8454

---- ---- Laws of the state of New-York, passed at the fifty-fourth session of the Legislature. ...Albany, Pr. by E. Croswell, for Wm. & A. Gould & Co.; and Gould Banks & Co., 1831. 487 p. Az; CoU; MdBB; MiD-B; NNLI. 8455

---- ---- Manual of the revised statutes of the state of New York... With appropriate directions, explanations and references, to cases adjudged in the Courts of said state, and in the Supreme Court of the United States; and designed for the use of professional men; officers, civil and military, and other citizens of said state. In five parts. Prepared and compiled by a Counsellor at Law. Glen's Falls, Pr. by Abial Smith, 1831. 412 p. DLC; MH-L; MWiW; MdBB; NNLI. 8456

---- ---- Revised Statute relating to Common Schools, being Title II. of Chapter XV. passed at the Extra Session of the Legislature of the State of New-York, December 3, 1827; together with Amendments, including those adopted at the Session of 1831... Albany, Pr. by Croswell and Van Benthuysen, 1831. 72 p. KyDC; MB; NbU. 8457

---- ---- Revised Statutes relating to the New York State Canals... Albany, Pr. by Croswell and Van Benthuysen, 1831. 34 p. NRom. 8458

---- ---- Synopsis of the laws of the state, relative to imprisonment for debt, and a statement of their effects, etc. Refutation of Mr. Stilwell. New York, 1831. 37 p. MBC. 8459

---- Legislature. Assembly. Committee on canals and internal improvements.

...Report of the Committee on canals and internal improvements, relative to the construction of the Black River canal. [Albany? 1831] 33 p. DLC. 8460

---- ---- ---- Select Committee

[Report of the Committee appointed by the Legislative Assembly of 1830, to investigate "the manner in which the Hospital in the City of New-York, and the Asylum connected therewith, have disbursed the funds which they have received from the State"; etc.] [Albany, 1831] 79 p. NbU. 8461

---- ---- Senate.

Journal of the Senate of the state of New-York, at their fifty-fourth session, begun and held at the capitol, in the city of Albany, the 4th day of January, 1831. Albany, Pr. by E. Croswell, pr. to the state, 1831. 418 p. NNLI. 8462

---- ---- ---- Committee on Canals.

....Report of the Committee on canals, to whom was referred "so much of the message of the governor as relates to canals, and internal improvements by means of canals." [Albany, 1831] 40 p. DLC. 8463

---- ---- ---- Committee on Finance.

...Report of the Committee on Finance, on the bill from the Assembly entitled "An act concerning the Interest of Money." ...[Albany, 1831] 7 p. NbU. 8464

---- ---- ---- Select Committee.

...Report of the Select Committee on sundry memorials of the manufacturers and others interested in making salt in the Count of Onondaga... [Albany, 1831] 21 p. NbU. 8465

---- Secretary of State.

...Census of the state of New York, for the years 1825 and 1830... [Albany, 1831?] 15 p. MH-BA; N. 8466

---- ---- Report of the Secretary of State, giving an Abstract of the Returns of the Superintendents of the Poor in the several counties. No. 66, Jan. 25, 1831. Albany, 1831-1832. 48 p. PHi. 8467

---- Superintendent of Common Schools.

Report of the superintendent of common schools of the state of New York. By A. C. Flagg. Albany, 1831. 71 p. NjPT. 8468

---- Supreme Court.

Bishop Perkins, ad'sm. David B. Ogden. Arguments for the defendant. New York, 1831. 32 p. CtY. 8469

---- ---- Digested Index to nine volumes of his reports, Supreme Court, and Court for trial for Impeachments and Corrections of Errors (1823-29). Albany, 1831. MBS; MD. 8470

---- ---- A general digested index to the nine volumes of Cowen's Reports of cases argued and determined in the Supreme court and in the court for the trial of impeachments and the correction of errors of the state of New-York. Albany, W. & A. Gould & Co.; New York, Gould Banks & Co., 1831. 559 p. DLC; ICLaw. 8471

---- ---- Rules and orders of the Supreme Court of the state of New York... with additional rules & notes of cases arising under the rules. Also precedents of bills of costs, and of pleadings, etc. in the action of ejectment, approved by the judges. Albany, Pr. by B. D. Packard & Co., 1831. 52 p. Ct; NIC-L; NNLT. 8472

---- University.

Annual report of the regents of the university of the state of New-York. ...Albany, Pr. by Creswell and Van Benthuysen, 1831. 97 p. NbU; NCanHi; NNLI. 8473

New-York Almanack for 1832. By David Young. New York, N.Y. Benjamin Olds [1831] MWA; NjR. 8474

New York. American Academy of the Fine Carts.

Catalogue of fine paintings.

New York, 1831. DLC. 8475

New York and Erie Railroad Company.
Preliminary surveys, memorials, reports, broadsides, and maps and miscellaneous pamphlets, relating to... New York, 1831. PPL. 8476

---- Report on a railroad route from the Hudson through New Jersey and Pennsylvania to Western New York. New York, 1831. PPL. 8477

New-York and New-Jersey Almanac for 1832. By David Young. New York, N.Y. John C. Totten, [1831] MWA. 8478

New York and Vermont Almanac see Loomis' Calendar.

New York Annual Register see Williams, Edwin.

New York Association for the gratuitous distribution of discussions of political economy--political essays. [New York, 1831] 24 p. MB. 8479

New York City Directory. New York, Thomas Longworth, 1831. 722 p. NE. 8480

New York Debating Society.
Address to the young men of ... New York... (with) the Constitution of the society. New York [1831] 11 p. NNC. 8481

New York Institution for the Instruction of the Deaf and Dumb.
By-laws of the Directors of the New-York Institution for the Instruction of the Deaf and Dumb; with the Act of Incorporation, and other Legislative Acts. New York, Pr. by B. Curtis Brown, 1831. 23 p. NbU. 8482

New York Life Insurance and Trust Company.
In Chancery. Before the Chancellor. The separate answer of Robert Smith...to bill of complain of Elisha Tibbitts--complainant. New-York, Pr. by J. Seymour, 1831. 134 p. NNLI. 8483

---- Report...made to the Chancellor of the State of New- York, March 20, 1831. Albany, Pr. by Croswell and Van Benthuyse, 1831. 31 p. MB; NN. 8484

New York Magdalen Asylum. Board of Directors.
Address of the Board of Directors, to the benevolent public, in behalf of the New-York Magdalen Asylum. New York, John T. West & Co., prs., 1831. 12 p. CtHWatK; MB; MBC; MeBat; MiD-B; NjR. 8485

New York Magdalen Society.
Anti-Magdalen report. Proceedings of a meeting of the citizens of New York...September 9, 1831, on the subject of the Magdalen report... New York, 1831. 8 p. MHi. 8486

---- First annual report of the executive committee of the New-York Magdalen society. Instituted January 1, 1830. New-York, Pr. by J. T. West & co., 1831. 32 p. DLC; MBC; MHi; NGeno. 8487

---- ---- From the 2d New-York ed, with corroborative notes and a plate. Philadelphia, 1831. 24 p. MH-AH; MdBD; MdBJ; MiD-B. 8488

New York Mechanics Institute.
First report of the board of directors, of the Mechanics' Institute, of the City of New York. October, 1831. New York, Pr. for the Institute, 1831. 15 p. PP; PPL; RP. 8489

New York Mechanics' Society.
Report of the Special Committee of the General society of Mechanics and tradesmen of the city of New York, to whom was referred the resolution for extending the usefulness of that institution. Also, the annual reports for 1830, of the School and library committees. New York, Pr. by Wm. A. Mercein, 1831. 24 p. 8490

New York medico-chirurgical bulletin. Edited by George Bushe. [New York,] Ludwig & Tolfree, 1831-32. 2 vols. DLC; MH-M; MdBM; PPCP. 8491

New York Protestant Episcopal City-mission society.
Account of the origin and formation of the New York Protestant Episcopal city mission society, with constitution and a list of the officers and managers. New York, Protestant Episcopal press, 1831. 15 p. MHi; MdBD; NjR; WHi. 8492

---- Constitution of the New-York Protestant Episcopal city-mission society with the by-laws of the managers. New York, Protestant Episcopal Press, 1831. 8 p. MdBD; NjR. 8493

New York Register and Anti-masonic review. January 1-March 15, 1831. New York, Henry Dana Ward, 1831. MH; NjR. 8494

New York Society for the Promotion of Temperance. See New York State temperance society.

New York State Colonization Society.
African Colonization. Proceedings of the New-York State Colonization Society, on its Second Anniversary; together with an Address to the Public, from the Managers thereof. Albany, Pr. by Webster and Skinners, 1831. 36 p. DLC; MBC; MH; NGH; NbU. 8495

New-York State Lyceum.
Proceedings of the first annual meeting...held at Utica, August 10th and 11th, 1831. Utica, Pr. by Northway & Porter, 1831. CSmH; MB; MH; NN; NUt. 8496

New York state temperance society.
Second annual report of the New-York state society for the promotion of temperance. Presented by the executive committee, January 18, 1831. Albany, Pr. by Packard & Van Benthuysen, for the society, 1831. 95 p. KyLx; MdHi; NbU; OC; ScU. 8497

The New-York Western pocket almanac for 1832; being bissextile or leap year's. Auburn, Pub. and sold wholesale and retail, by H. Ivison & Co., Oliphant's Press [1831] [24] p. NN. 8498

New York Young Men's Society.
Annual report, with the constitution, by-laws, and standing rules. New York, 1st [1831] MH. 8499

---- Constitution, & charter of the New-York young men's society. New York, Pr. by J. & J. Harper, 1831. 10 p. MBC; NNUT; WHi. 8500

Newburyport, Mass. School Committee.
Rules and regulations. 1831. MH. 8501

[Newcomb, Harvey 1803-1863]
Memoir of Phebe Bartlett of Northampton, Mass. Philadelphia, American Sunday School Union, 1831. 35 p. DLC; MH; MH-AH; MNF. 8502

Newell, Mrs. Harriet (Atwood), 1793-1812.

The life and writings of Mrs. Harriet Newell. Revised by the committee of publication. Philadelphia, American Sunday School Union, 1831. 267 p. ArLAB; ICP; KyLo; NjT; PHi. 8503

Newhall, Isaac.
Letters on Junius, addressed to John Pickering, esq., showing that the author of that celebrated work was Earl Temple. By Isaac Newhall... Boston, Hilliard, Gray, Little, and Wilkins, 1831. 276 p. DLC; IU; LNH; MiD; WHi. 8504

No entry. 8505

Newman, John.
The Tennessee Judiciary. Memorial and Remonstrance to the Honorable General Assembly of Tennessee, in session at Nashville, September 1831: by J. Newman. Nashville, Pr. at the Herald Office, 1831. 22 p. NcD; T. 8506

Newton, John.
Forty-one letters on religious subjects, originally published under the signature of Omicron and Virgil; and fourteen letters addressed to the Rev. Mr. B-, by Rev. John Newton, late rector of St. Mary's Weelneth, and St. Mary Weelehursh, London; with a preface by Rev. Elisha P. Swift, pastor of the Second Presbyterian Church, Pittsburgh. Pittsburgh, Lake Loomis & Co., 1831. 240 p. CSmH; ILM; MH; PPi; ViRUT. 8507

Newton Theological Institution.
Catalogue. December 1831. Boston, 1831. OCHP. 8508

The Newtonian Reflector, or New-England Almanac, for the year of our Lord 1832... Hartford, H. Burr, 1831. [24] p. CtHWatk; MWA; MWHi; MiD-B; NCH. 8509

Nichlin, P. E.
Conchyliology of North America. Philadelphia, 1831. PPAN. 8510

Nichols, Andrew.
The spirit of free-masonry; A poem. By Andrew Nichols. Boston, J. Punchard, 1831. 24 p. IaCrM; MB; MHi; PPFM; WHi. 8511

Nichols, Ichabod.
A catechism of natural theology... By I. Nichols... 2d ed., with additions and improvements. Boston, Wm. Hyde, 1831. 215 p. ICMe; ILM; MBAt; NNUT; RNR; BrMus. 8512

Nicholson, John.
The operative mechanic, and British machinist; being a practical display of the manufactories and mechanical arts of the United Kingdom. 2d American from the 3d London ed., with additions. Philadelphia, T. Desilver, 1831. 2 vols. NGH; PPL-R; RPB; TxHR; ViU. 8513

Nicholson, Peter.
The mechanic's companion, or the elements and practice of carpentry, joinery, brick laying... containing a full description of the tools belonging to each branch of business... also an introduction to practical geometry. By Peter Nicholson. Illustrated with forty copper plate engravings. New York, W. C. Borradaile, 1831. 333, 40 p. IaHi; OCOMI; RPA; RP. 8514

Nicklin, P. H. and T. Johnson,

Law-Booksellers.
Catalogue of law books for sale by P. H. Nicklin and T. Johnson, Law-booksellers. Philadelphia, Pr. by Miffin and Parry, 1831. 15 p. IaHi. 8515

Niles, Hezekiah.
Journal of the proceedings of the Friends of Domestic Industry in General Convention at the city of New York, Oct. 26, 1831. By Hezekiah Niles. Baltimore, Pub. by order of the Convention, 1831. MA. 8516

---- Politics for working men, an essay, on labor and substance; addressed to the free productive people of the United States. [Baltimore, 1831] 15 p. MB; MBAt; MdBP; MdHi. 8517

Noble, Birdsey G.
Lectures on the catechism of the Protestant Episcopal church. New York, 1831. 208 p. MA; NNG. 8518

Noble, Samuel.
The true object of Christian worship demonstrated and the doctrine of the Trinity elucidated, and cleared of the difficulties in which it is commonly involved. By Samuel Noble. 2d ed. Boston, Allen & Goddard, 1831. 31 p. MLow. MWA; NNG; OUrC; PPL-R. 8519

Norfolk County. Massachusetts Auxiliary Foreign Missionary Society.
Addresses. 1831. MB; MBC. 8520

The North American Calendar; or, The Columbian almanac for the year of our Lord 1832, being bissextile, or leap year, and 56th year of American independence, calculated for the meridian of the middle states...Wilmington, Del., R. Porter & Co., [1831] 36 p. DLC; DeHi; MWA; NjR. 8521

North American journal of geology and natural science; by G. W. Featherstonebaugh. v. 1-1831-. Philadelphia. PPCP. 8522

North Carolina.
Acts passed by the General Assembly of the State of North Carolina, at the session of 1830-31. Raleigh, Pr. by Lawrence & Lemay, prs. to the State, 1831. 142 p. Ia; IaU-L; In-SC; Ms; Mo; NNLI; NcU. 8523

---- Cases argued and determined in the Supreme Court of North Carolina, from Dec. term, 1828 to Dec. term, 1830. By Thomas P. Devereux, Reporter. Vol. II. Raleigh, Pr. by J. Gales & Son, 1831. 611 p. MH-L; MWCL; MdBB; Ms; NCH; Nb; NcU; NV; PPiAL; TxU; ViU; WML; Wy. 8524

---- The declaration of independence by the citizens of Mecklenburg county, on the twentieth day of May, 1775, with accompanying documents, and the Proceedings of the Cumberland association. Pub. by the governor, under the direction of the General Assembly of the state of North Carolina. Raleigh, Pr. by Lawrence and Lemay, 1831. 32 p. MdHi; NN; NcAS; NcD; NcU; P; Vi; WHi. 8525

---- Equity cases argued and determined in the supreme court of North Carolina, from June term, 1826, to December term, 1830. By Thomas P. Devereux, reporter, &c. Raleigh, J. Gales & son, 1831. 566 p. Ia; Md; Mi-L; MoU; Ms; ViU; Wy. 8526

---- The journal of the proceedings of the Provincial congress of North Carolina, held at Halifax, on the fourth day of April, 1776. Pub. by authority. Newbern, Pr. by James Davis, pr. to the honourable the House of assembly, 1826. Repr. in pursuance of a resolution of the General assembly of North Carolina, passed at the session of 1830-31. Raleigh, Pr. by Lawrence & Lemay, prs. to the state, 1831. 66 p. DLC; IU; NcU; OCLaw; TxU. 8527

---- Journal of the Senate and House of Commons of the General Assembly of the State of North Carolina at the session of 1830-31. Raleigh, Pr. by Lawrence & Lemay, prs. to the state, 1831. 284 p. NcWfC; Nc. 8528

---- Message of His Excellency, Montford Stokes, to the General Assembly of North Carolina. Raleigh, Pr. by Lawrence and Lemay, prs. to the State, 1831. 8 p. Nc. 8529

---- Report of the Adjutant General of North Carolina, 1831. Raleigh, Pr. by Lawrence and Lemay, prs. to the state, 1831. 24 p. (Leg. Doc. No. 4) Nc. 8530

---- Report of the Committee of Finance on procuring Specie Change. Raleigh, Pr. by Lawrence and Lemay, prs. to the state, 1831. 4 p. (Leg. Doc. No. 10) NcD; Nc. 8531

---- Report of the Committee of Finance on the State of the Public Treasury, 1831. 4 p. (Leg. Doc. No. 9) Nc. 8532

---- Report of the joint committee on the legality of the Legislature holding its sessions without the limits of Raleigh. Raleigh, Pr. by Lawrence & Lemay, prs. to the State, 1831. 4 p. (Leg. Doc. No. 3) Nc. 8533

---- Report of the Public Treasurer on the State of the Finances of North Carolina, transmitted, according to Act of Assembly, on the 24th November, 1831. Raleigh, Pr. by Lawrence and Lemay, 1831. 32 p. (Leg. Doc. No. 2) Nc. 8534

---- Report of the Select Committee raised to inquire into the amount dividends and Bonus divided by the Banks of North Carolina, etc. Raleigh, Pr. by Lawrence & Lemay, prs. to the state, 1831. 12 p. (Leg. Doc. No. 8) NcD; Nc. 8535

---- Report on a communication from the waters of Albemarle Sound to the ocean. Raleigh, Lawrence, 1831. 4 p. (Leg. Doc. No. 12). NcU. 8536

---- Report on Incorporating the Mecklenburg Gold Mining Company. Raleigh, Pr. by Lawrence & Lemay, prs. to the State, 1831. 4 p. (Leg. Doc. No. 6) NcD (RBR); Nc. 8537

---- Report on the progress and present condition of the affairs of the Roanoke navigation co. Raleigh, Lawrence, 1831. 8 p. NC; NcU. 8538

---- Report relative to the government of slaves and free persons of color. Raleigh, 1831. NcD. 8539

----Report relative to the Statue of Washington. Raleigh, Pr. by Lawrence & Lemay, prs. to the State, 1831. 4 p. (Leg. Doc. No. 7) 8540

---- Statements of the affairs of the banks, received at the Treasury department since the date of the annual report of the public treasurer. Raleigh, Lawrence, 1831. 2 p. (Leg. Doc. No. 18) NcU. 8541

---- Treasurer's Report of the funds belonging to the State. Raleigh, Pr. by Lawrence and Lemay, prs. to the State, 1831. 4 p. (Leg. Doc. No. 5) Nc. 8542

The Northern traveller.
Routes to the Springs, Niagara, and Quebec, and the Coal Mines of Pennsylvania; also, the tour of New-England. New ed. Embellished with numerous copperplate engravings. New York, Pr. by J. & J. Harper, 1831. 444 p. NRSB. 8543

Norton Detecting Society.
Detecting society. A correct list of the officers and members of the Norton detecting society. Formed for the purpose of detecting horse thieves. Pr. by Taunton E. Anthony [1831?] Broadside. NN. 8544

Norwich, Conn. Second School Society.
To the members of the Legislature, (remarks on) the importance of a good system of common school instruction. [Norwich] 1831. Broadside. MH. 8545

Norwich and Worcester Railroad Company.
Norwich and Worcester railroad. [183-?] 8 p. CSt; M. 8546

Notes of a voyage from Portsmouth, England, to New York, United States. In the packet ship President, Capt. Henry L. Champlin, in the autumn of 1831. [New York, 1831] 27 p. MA. 8547

Notice of the Academy of Natural Sciences of Philadelphia... 2d ed. Philadelphia, Pr. by Mifflin & Parry, 1831. 15 p. KyLxT; PPAN; PPL; PPL-R. 8548

Nott, Samuel, Jun.
Temperance and Religion: or the Best Means and Highest End of the Temperance Reformation, in two parts, by Samuel Nott, Jun. Boston, Peirce & Parker, 1831. 36 p. ArCM; MB; MH-AH; PPPrHi. 8549

Noyes, George Rapall.
The Gospel exhibited, a discourse delivered before the Second Congregational Society in Brookfield, Nov. 7, 1831, by George R. Noyes, minister of said society. Brookfield, Pr. by E. Merriam & Co., 1831. 35 p. MB; MBC; MH-AH; MNe; RPB. 8550

Noyes, Matthew.
Address delivered in Northford, at the admission of a large number of persons to that church in that place, July 3d, 1831. By the Rev. Matthew Noyes. Pub. by request. New Haven, Journal Office, prs., 1831. 12 p. CBPSP; Ct; MB; MBC; MHi. 8551

Nutting, William.
An address to the Orang County Lyceum at their first meeting, June 23, 1831. Chelsea, Pr. by B. Avery, for the Lyceum, 1831. 14 p. M; VtHi; VtU. 8552

O

Oakland College, Clairborne Co., Miss.
Oakland College, Clairborne Co., Miss. Constitution and laws. ...Carlisle, Pa., Herald off., 1831. 12 p. MiU. 8553

Oalton, Ann Elizabeth.
Clara and Albina or, The ill effects of prejudice. A juvenile tale by Ann Elizabeth Oalton.

New-York, Pub. by R. Schoyer, at his juvenile repository, 1831. 35 p. MH; NNC; PP; TSewU. 8554

Obedience, the test of friendship with Christ. An appeal from a country clergyman, to the young members of his parish, on the duty of coming to the Lord's supper... Auburn, Pr. by H. B. Ten Eyck, at the C. K. Society's press, 1831. 16 p. NNC. 8555

Odd-fellows, Independent order of, Maryland Grand Lodge.
An account of the grand celebration of the independent order of Odd-Fellows, for the dedication of the new hall in the city of Baltimore, which took place on the 26th day of April 1831, being the anniversary of Odd-Fellowship in the United States. Baltimore, Sands & Neilson, 1831. 52 p. DLC; MB; MdHi; PPL. 8556

---- Proceedings of the R. W. G. Lodge of Maryland at its Annual Grand Communication, held in the City of Baltimore May 1831. 19 p. MdToN; PP; 8557

---- Report, rules of order and circular. Baltimore, 1831. PPL. 8558

Ohio.
Acts of a general nature enacted, revised and ordered to be reprinted, at the first session of the 29th General Assembly of the state of Ohio. Pub. by authority. Columbus, Pr. by Olmsted & Bailhache, 1831. 618 p. CLSU; NIC-A; NIC-L. 8559

---- Cases decided in the courts of common pleas in the fifth circuit of the state of Ohio, commencing with May term, 1816. To which is added the opinion of Judge McLean in the case of Landerback vs. Moore. By Benjamin Tappan... Steubenville, James Wilson, 1831. 321 p. Ct; DLC; Ms; PPB. 8560

The Ohio pocket lawyer, form book, or self-conveyancer: containing all the necessary legal forms, used in the state of Ohio. By a member of the Ohio bar. Wheeling, Va., A. & E. Pickett, 1831. 140 p. CtY-L; DLC; IaU-L; OC; OClWHi. 8561

Old Colony Baptist Association.
Ninth anniversary. Minutes of the Old Colony Baptist Association, holden with the Baptist Church in Barnstable, Wednesday and Thursday, October 5 and 6, 1831. Plymouth, Allen Danforth [1831] 16 p. PCA. 8562

Old Stoughton Musical Society.
Stoughton Collection of Church Music. Selected and arranged by the Stoughton Musical Society. 2d ed. Boston, Concord, N.H., Marsh, Capen, and Lyons, 1831. 360 p. DLC; MH; MHi. 8563

Oliphant, David.
Why sinners cannot come to Christ. A sermon preached to the Third Congregation church and society in Beverly, May 1, 1831. Salem, Pr. by Warwick Palfray, 1831. 16 p. MB; MBC; MH-AH; NjR; RPB. 8564

Oliver, Benjamin Lynde, 1788-1843.
The law summary; a collection of legal tracts on subjects of general application in business. By Benjamin L. Oliver...Boston [etc.] Marsh, Capen & Lyon, 1831. 348 p. CSt; MB; MH-BA; MH-L; OMC; RPL. 8565

Oliver, Henry Kemble.
A lecture on the advantages and defects of the monitorial system...delivered...before the

American Institute of Instruction. By Henry K. Oliver, of Salem, Mass. Boston, Hilliard, Gray, Little and Wilkins, 1831. 26 p. MB; MBVAFCC; MH; NNS. 8566

Ollendorff, Heinrich Gottfried, d. 1865.
Ollendorff's mew method of learning to read, write, and speak: the Spanish language: with an Appendix, and Rules for the Spanish Pronunciation, the whole designed for young learners, and persons who are their own instructors. By M. Velazquez and T. Simmons. New York, D. Appleton & Co., 1831. 558 p. KyLoS. 8567

Olmsted, Denison, 1791-1859.
An introduction to natural philosophy: in two volumes. Vol. I. mechanics and hydrostatics. Compiled from various authorities. By Denison Olmsted, A. M. New Haven, Hezekiah Howe, 1831. IGK; KyLoS; MH; PU; RPB. 8568

Olney, Jesse, 1798-1872.
The national preceptor: or selections in prose and poetry; consisting of narrative, descriptive, argumentative, didactic... and humorous pieces...3d ed. Hartford, Goodwin & co., 1831. 336 p. Ct; CtHWatk; OMC; WHi. 8569

----The National preceptor: or, selections in prose and poetry; consisting of narrative, descriptive, argumentative, didactic, pathetic, & humorous pieces; together with dialogues, addresses, orations, speeches, &c. ...Designed for the use of schools and academies. 6th ed. By J. Olney. New York, Robinson, Pratt & Co. [1831] 336 p. MAshlHi; ONC. 8570

---- A new and improved School Atlas to accompany the practical system of Modern Geography by J. Olney. Hartford, D. F. Robinson & Co., 1831. 14 maps. MH; RNHi. 8571

---- A new and improved school atlas, to accompany the practical system of modern geography... New York, Pratt, Woodford & co., 1831. 294 p. MiD-B; PHi. 8572

---- A practical system of modern geography; or, A view of the present state of the world...Accompanied by a new and improved Atlas. By J. Olney. 7th ed. Hartford, D. F. Robinson & co., 1831. 283 p. CtHWatk; MH; MWfo; TxU-T; WJan. 8573

Onderdonk, Benjamin Tredwell, bp., 1791-1861.
The character of the Protestant Episcopal church, in its prominent distinctive features, considered in reference to its duties thence resulting, in a primary charge to the clergy of the diocese of New York...delivered in Trinity church in the city of New York, at the opening of the convention, on Thursday, Oct. 6, 1831. New York, Pr. at the Protestant Episcopal Press, 1831. 18 p. MdBD; NjR; PHi; RPB; WHi. 8574

---- Memorial of Bishop Hobart; a collection of sermons on the death of the Right Reverend John Henry Hobart... (By Onderdonk, Berrian, Schroeder)... New York, Pr. by Edward Swords, for T. & J. Swords, 1831. 250 p. NjR. 8575

---- A sermon, on the excellence the benefits and the obligations of the divine law. Preached at the consecration of the Mission Church of the Holy Evangelists in the city of New-York, on Saturday, Nov. 19, 1831. By Benjamin T. Onderdonk. D.D. New-

York, Pr. at the Protestant Episcopal Press, 1831. 19 p. InID; MNF; NjR; PPL; RPB. 8576

---- Sermon preached in the chapel of the General Theological Seminary of the Protestant Episcopal Church in the United States, on occasion of the inarticulation of the newly admitted students of that seminary, November 6, 1831... New York, Pr. at the Protestant Episcopal press, 1831. 16 p. MB; MBD; NCH; NNG; NNUT. 8577

---- A sermon, preached in Trinity Church, Southwark, Philadelphia, at the Consecration of the Right Reverend Levi Silliman Ives, D.D. Bishop of the Protestant Episcopal Church in the State of North Carolina, on Thursday, Sept. 22, 1831. By Benjamin T. Onderdonk, D.D. Bishop of the said Church in the State of New-York, and Professor of the Nature, Ministry, and Polity of the Church in the General Theological Seminary of the Protestant Episcopal Church in the United States. Pr. for the benefit of The Missionary Society of North Carolina. New York, Pr. at the Protestant Episcopal Press, 1831. 19 p. MH; MWA; MdBD; NGH; PHi. 8578

Onderdonk, Henry Ustick, 1789-1858.

Episcopacy tested by Scripture. By Henry U. Onderdonk, D.D.... New York, Pr. at the Protestant Episcopal press, for the Protestant Episcopal Tract society [1831] 46 p. CtHC; ICP; MdBD; NjR; WHi. 8579

---- The foundation and extent of duty: An address delivered at the commencement in the General Theological Seminary of the Protestant Episcopal Church...on the 1st of July, 1831. By the Rt. Rev. Henry U. Onderdonk...New York, Pr. by the Protestant Episcopal press, 1831. 15 p. CSansS; InID; NNUT; PHi; WHi. 8580

Oneida Institute, Whitesboro, New York.

Proceedings of a meeting held at the Masonic Hall on the subject of manual labor in connexion with literary institutions, June 15, 1831. Together with some particulars respecting the Oneida Institute at Whitesboro, N.Y. New York, L. Booth, 1831. 19 p. MHi; NNUT; NjR; OClWHi. 8581

---- Third Report of the Trustees of the Oneida Institute of Science and Industry. Whitestown, January 1831. Utica, Press of William Williams, 1831. 30 p. MHi; NN; NUtHi; NjR; PPL. 8582

O'Neill, Rev. P.

A sermon on the mystery of the real presence, preached in the courthouse in the borough of Butler. By the Rev. P. O'Neill ...with an analysis of a sermon, said to be preached against transsubstantiation, in the Associate Reformed Church in the borough of Butler. By the Rev. Isaiah Niblock, A.M. Audiatur et Altera Parts... Pittsburg, (Pa.), Pr. by Johnston & Stockton, 1831. 80 p. IaDuTM; McMHi; MdW. 8583

Orme, William, 1787-1830.

The life and times of the Rev. Richard Baxter: with a critical examination of his writings. By Rev. Wm. Orme,...Boston, Crocker & Brewster; New York, Jonathan Leavitt, 1831. 2 vols. ArCH; NcU; OClW; PU; ViU. 8584

[Osborn, Laughton] 1809-1878.

Sixty years of the life of Jeremy Levis...in two vols. (anon.) New York, G. & C. H. H. Carvill,

1831. 2 vols. DLC; ICU; KyLxT; MBat; OC. 8585

Osbourn, James.
A glimpse of the building of mercy; or, An outline of the mystical building of Christ... Baltimore, Pr. by John D. Toy, 1831. 325 p. NcD. 8586

Otey, James H.
A discourse on the evils of intemperance; delivered on Thursday evening, 12th of October, 1830, before the Lynchburg, Temperance Society. Lynchburg, Va., Fletcher & Toler, 1831. 12 p. T. 8587

Otis, Harrison G[ray], 1765-1848.
Address to the board of aldermen, and members of the Common council, of Boston on the organization of the city government, Jan. 3, 1831. Boston, J. H. Eastburn, city pr., 1831. 12 p. CtHT; MHi; BrMus. 8588

Otis, William F[oster] 1801-1858.
An oration delivered before the "Young men of Boston," on the fourth of July, 1831...Boston, Carter, Hendee & Babcock, 1831. 36 p. Ct; OCHP; PPL; RPB; WHi. 8589

---- The reviewer reviewed. A defence of "An oration delivered before the young men of Boston, 4th July, 1831, by W. F. Otis." Boston, Carter, Hendee and Babcock, 1831. 29 p. M; MB; MBAt; MH; MHi. 8590

Our neighbourhood; or, Letters on horticulture and natural phenomena: interspersed with opinions on domestic and moral economy. New York, E. Bliss, 1831. DLC; PPL. 8591

Ovidius, Naso, Publius.
Excerpta Ex Scriptis Publii Ovidii Nasonis. Accedunt Notulae et Questiones in usum Scholae Bostoniensis. Editio Secunda. Bostoniae, Sumptibus Hilliard, Gray, Little, et Wilkins, 1831. 287 p. ArCH; CtHWatK; ICP; MH; OBerB; RNR. 8592

Owen, Robert Dale, 1801-1877.
Moral physiology; or, A brief and plain treatise on the population question. New York, 1831. 72 p. WHi. 8593

---- ---- 2d ed. New York, Wright & Owen, 1831. 74 p. MoSW; PU; ViU. 8594

---- ---- 3d ed. New York, Wright & Owen, 1831. 72 p. MH. 8595

---- ---- 5th ed. New York, Wright, 1831. 83 p. NB; NNN. 8596

---- ---- 6th ed. New York, Wright & Owen, 1831. 83 p. OO. 8597

P

P's and Q's... Hingham, Mass., C. & E. B. Gill, 1831. 200 p. CSmH; MB; RPB; WU. 8598

Paddock, Zachariah, 1798-1879.
A brief defence of the doctrines, government, and usages of the Methodist Episcopal Church against the New-York Baptist Register. By Zechariah Paddock, minister of the M.E. Church, Cazenovia. Utica, Northway & Porter, prs., 1831. 32 p. IU. 8599

Paddon, John.
I'll think of thee. Ballad (T.) Boston, Dickson, 1831. 3 p. MB. 8600

Page, Edward Postlehayt.
The reminiscence of nature, and clue to Bible astrology, by

Edw. P. Page, High Priest of Nature... Marietta, O., 1831. PPL; PPL-R. 8601

Paine, Thomas, 1737-1809.
The age of reason. By Thomas Paine. New York, Wright & Owen, 1831. 159 p. MH; MMilf; MnSH. 8602

---- The Theological Works of Thomas Paine. To which are added the Profession of Faith of a Savoyard Vicar, by J. J. Rousseau; and other miscellaneous pieces... Boston, Pr. by the advocates of common sense, 1831. 384 p. InFtwL. 8603

---- ---- New York, W. Carver, 1831. 424 p. CBPSR; InID; NCaS; TxHR. 8604

Paley, William, 1743-1805.
Natural Theology: or, evidences of the existence and attributes of The Deity, collected from the appearances of nature. By William Paley, D. D. with illustrations and descriptive letter press, by James Paxton. Boston, Richardson, Lord & Holbrook, and Crocker & Browester; New York, Jonathan Leavitt, 1831. 336 p. NBuDD. 8605

---- ---- Stereotype ed. Boston, Lincoln & Edmands, 1831. 344 p. ICT; McU; NcD; OClWHi; PPi. 8606

---- Paley's moral philosophy, abridged and adopted to the constitution, laws and usages of the United States of America. New York, Collins and Hannay, 1831. 180 p. Ct; MT. 8607

Paley, William See also Questions adapted...

---- The principles of moral and political philosophy. By William Paley, D.D. With additions and improvements. New York, Collins and Hannay, 1831. 2 v. in 1. CtMW; ICT; KyHi; NNUT; OO; ViU. 8608

---- The Works of William Paley, D.D. Archdeacon of Carlisle. Containing his life, moral and political philosophy, evidences of Christianity--natural theology, tracts, Horae Paulinae, Clergyman's Companion and Sermons. Printed verbaitm from the original editions. Complete in 1 vol. Philadelphia, J. J. Woodward, 1831. 604 p. DLC; MBBC; MiU; NSsA. 8609

Palfrey, Cazneau.
On Change of Heart. By Cazneau Palfrey. No. 53. 1st series. American Unitarian Association. Boston, Gray & Bowen, 1831. 20 p. CtHC; ICMe; MCon; MH-AH; MeB. 8610

---- ---- 2d ed. Boston, James Munroe & Co., for the American Unitarian Association, 1831. 20 p. CBPac; ICMe; MB-FA; MH; NUt. 8611

Palfrey, John Gorham, 1796-1881.
An address delivered before the Society for promoting theological education, June 5, 1831... Boston, Gray & Bowen, 1831. 18 p. CBPac; CtHT; MHi; Nh; WHi. 8612

---- An oration pronounced before the citizens of Boston, on the anniversary of the Declaration of American Independence, July 4, 1831. By John G. Palfrey. Boston, Press of John H. Eastburn, city pr., 1831. 42 p. CtHWatk; CtSoP; MeB; OCHP; PHi; RPB. 8613

---- Sketch of a plan for a Sunday School. Boston, etc., 1831. 7 p. MH-AH. 8614

Palmer, John C. R.
Explanation; or, 1830: being a series of facts connected with the life of the author, from 1825 to the present day. By John C. R. Palmer. Boston, Pr. for the author, at the office of S. N. Dickinson, 1831. 191 p. DLC; MB; MNF; NhD. 8615

Palmer, Ray.
Memoirs and Select Remains of Charle Pond, late member of the sophomore class in Yale college. Compiled by a classmate. Revised by the publishing committee. 5th ed. Boston, Massachusetts Sabbath School Society, [1831] 140 p. MA; MBC; NSYU. 8616

Palmer's New England almanac for 1832 by J. N. Palmer. New Haven, Durrie and Peck, 1831. 22 p. MWA. 8617

The Pamological manual. See Prince William, 1766-1842.

Paris, John A.
Pharmacologia. 4th Amer. from 7th London ed. By John A. Paris, M.D...With notes and add. by John B. Beck, M.D... New York, Pr. by W. E. Dean, for Collins & Hannay and White, Gallaher & White, 1831. 550 p. MBP; OCU-M; TU-M; ViRMC. 8618

Paris and its Historical Scenes. Boston, Lilly & Wait, and Carter & Hendee; New York, Carey & Hart, and S. Colman, Portland, 1831. 385 p. ICarTC; MeB; NcSalL. 8619

Parker, Joel.
Sermon C. By Rev. Joel Parker, New York. The Conviction of Sinners at the Judgement. 162-176 p. MB; PPPrHi. 8620

[Parker, John]
The pilgrimage of Ormond, or Chile Harold in the New World ... Charleston, Pr. by W. Riley, 1831. RPB. 8621

Parker's miniature almanac for the year...1832. Boston, Amos B. Parker [1831] 28 p. MHi; MWA; NNT-C. 8622

Parkes, Mrs. Frances (Byerley)
Domestic duties; or, Instructions to young married ladies, on the management of their households, and the regulation of their conduct in the various relations and duties of married life. By Mrs. William Parkes. New York, J. & J. Harper, 1831. 408 p. MB; PFal. 8623

Parkhurst, John L.
Lecture on the means...to stimulate the student without the aid of emulation...By John L. Parkhurst. Boston, Hilliard, Gray, Little and Wilkins, 1831. 13 p. M. 8624

Parkinson, William, 1774-1848.
The Romish Antichrist. A sermon delivered in the meeting-house of the First Baptist church in the city of New-York, Lord's day, Nov. 28, 1830. By Wm. Parkinson, A.M...New-York, Pr. by G. F. Bunce, 1831. 28 p. NHC-S; NNC; NjR; OClWHi; PCC. 8625

---- A series of sermons on the xxxiii Chapter of Deuteronomy. By Wm. Parkinson, A.M. Pastor of the First Baptist Church, New York. Pub. at the request of said Church. New York, Pr. by G. F. Bunce, for J. M. Morgan, 1831. 2 vols. CU; ICU; MNtCA; MoInRC; PCA. 8626

Parsons, Usher, 1788-1868.
An address, delivered before the Providence Association for the promotion of Temperance, May 27, 1831. Providence, Pr.

by Weeden & Knowles, 1831. [3]-16 p. CtHT-W; MBAt; MnHi; RPaw; WHi. 8627

---- Directions for making anatomical preparations formed on the basis of Pole, Marjolin and Breschet...By Usher Parsons. 1st ed. Philadelphia, Carey & Lea, 1831. 316 p. CU; ICT; MB; PU; TxU. 8628

Pascal, Blaise.
Provincial letters, containing an exposure of the reasoning and morals of the Jesuits. By Blaise Pascal...Translated from the French. To which is added a view of the history of the Jesuits... Washington, James Turner, 1831. 296 p. DLC; KLaw; MdW; NbL; PPP. 8629

Pascalis Ouviere, Felix.
Eulogy on the life and character of the Hon. Samuel Latham Mitchill, M.D. Delivered at the request of the New-York city and county medical society...by Felix Pascalis, M.D....New-York, from the American argus press, 1831. 25 p. MH; MdBJ; NjR; PHi; RPB. 8630

The pastime of learning, with sketches of rural scenes... Boston, Cottons & Barnard, 1831. 260 p. MB; MH; NhPet; NjR; PMA. 8631

A Pastoral Address to the members of St. James Church. By the rector. Poughkeepsie, Jackson & Schram, 1831. 14 p. NGH. 8632

A pastoral letter, by a Unitarian minister. 2d ed. Boston, Gray & Bowen, 1831. 16 p. DLC; MBAU; MHi; OClWHi. 8633

Pattie, James Ohio, b. 1804?
The personal narrative of James O. Pattie, of Kentucky, during an expedition from St. Louis, through the vast regions between that place and the Pacific Ocean, and thence back through the City of Mexico to Vera Cruz...with a description of the country, and the various nations through which they passed. Edited by Timothy Flint. Cincinnati [John H. Wood] 1831. 300 p. KyHi; OCHOP; MoSU; PPiU; WHi. 8634

Paul (pseud.).
The question whether, a man may lawfully marry the sister of his deceased wife, examined, in a letter...Philadelphia, 1831. 96 p. PHi; PPPrHi. 8635

Paul Pry.
V 1-5; Dec. 3, 1831-Nov. 18, 1836. Washington, D.C., 1831-36. 5 vols. in 2. DLC. 8636

Paulding, Hiram, 1797-1878.
Journal of a cruise of the United States schooner Dolphin among the islands of the Pacific Ocean; and a visit to the Mulgrave Islands, in pursuit of the mutineers of the whaleship Globe ...By Lieut. Hiram Paulding... New-York, G. & C. & H. Carvill, 1831. 258 p. CU; ICU; MB; NUt; PPA; WHi. 8637

Paulding, James Kirke, 1778-1860.
The Dutchman's Fireside. A tale. By the author of "Letters from the South," "The Backwoodsman,"... New-York, J. & J. Harper, 1831. 2 vols. CtY; DLC; MnU; NcD; WU. 8638

Paulison (Christian Z.)
A development of facts and circumstances justifying a Union with the True Reformed Dutch Church...of Hackensack and English Neighbourhood. New York, J. T. West & Co., 1831.

48 p. N; PPL. 8639

Payson, Edward, 1783-1827.
Sermons by the late Rev. Edward Payson, D.D...Boston, Wm. Hyde, 1831. 400 p. CtHT; IEG; MBC; Nh; OMC. 8640

Peabody, Ephraim, 1807-1856.
The sins of the temperate, a prize essay, read before the Crawford county temperance society, January 1, 1831. By the Rev. Ephraim Peabody. Meadville, Pa., Pr. by T. Atkinson [1831] 24 p. ICMe; MiU-C; PPL; WHi. 8641

[Peabody, William Bourn Oliver] 1799-1847.
Address to the Calvinistic society in Springfield. Springfield, Mass., Pr. by S. Bowles, 1831. 15 p. Ct; MH-AH; MiD-B; NjPT; WHi. 8642

Peake, Richard Brinsley, 1792-1847.
The chancery suit! A comedy, in five acts. First performed at the Theatre Royal, Covent Garden, Tuesday, November 30, 1830. By R. B. Peake. Baltimore, J. Robinson, Circulating library and dramatic repository, 1831. 76 p. CSt; DLC; MH; MWA; MdBJ. 8643

Peale, Rembrandt, 1778-1860.
Catalogue of Peale's Italian Pictures, now exhibiting at Sully & Earle's Gallery, opposite the State House. Philadelphia, 1831. 18 p. MB; PHi. 8644

---- Notes on Italy, by Rembrandt Peale. Written during a tour in the years 1829 and 1830. Philadelphia, Carey & Lea, 1831. 328 p. GHi; ICP; LU; RPB; ScC. 8645

Peale, Titian R[amsey], 1800-1835.
Circular of the Philadelphia museum, containing directions for the preparation & preservation of objects of natural history. Philadelphia, Kay, 1831. 29 p. OCHP; PHi; PPAmP. 8646

Pearl, Cyril.
The Sabbath a divine institution. A reply to arguments on the negative of the question "Ought the law requiring the opening of our post offices & the transportation of our mails on the Christian Peirce, 1831. MeHi; PPPrHi. 8647

No entry. 8648

The Pearl, or Affections gift; a Christmas and New Years present. Philadelphia, Thomas T. Ash, [1831] 222 p. WU. 8649

Pearson, Eliphalet.
A letter to the candid; occasioned by the publications of Rev. Bernard Whitman... Boston, Peirce & Parker, 1831. 36 p. CBPac; ICMe; MB; MHi; VtU. 8650

Pease, Bartlet.
The Retrospect. A New-Year's discourse, preached to the Baptist congregation in Newburyport, Lord's-Day morning, Jan. 2, 1831. By Bartlet Pease, Pastor of the Baptist Church and society in Newbury and Newburyport. Pub. by request. Newburyport, Pr. by W. & J. Gilman, 1831. 16 p. MBC; MNe; NHC-S. 8651

Pease, David.
Good man in bad company, or Speculative Freemasonry a wicked and dangerous combination: a

sermon delivered at Belchertown, (Mass.), July 8, 1830. By David Pease, pastor of Baptist church in Conwayon, what influenced him to become a Mason and the cause of his renouncing and denouncing it. Brookfield, Pr. by E. & G. Merriam, 1831. 27 p. IaCrM; MA; MB; MBC; NNUT. 8652

Peck, John, 1735-1812.
A descant on the universal plan, corrected or universal salvation explained. Madison, Arion, 1831. PPPrHi; RPB. 8653

---- The spirit of methodism; a poem supposed to be sung at a love feast to the tune of Rochdale. With notes. New-York, Pub. for the trade, 1831. 91 p. CtY-D; MH. 8654

Peck, John Mason, 1789-1858.
A guide for emigrants, containing sketches of Illinois, Missouri, and the adjacent parts. By J. M. Peck... Boston, Lincoln & Edmands, 1831. 336 p. DeWi; IGK; OCHP; RPB; WHi. 8655

Pedraza, Manuel Gomez.
Manifesto, que Manuel Gomez Pedraza, Ciudadano de la Republica de Mejico, Dedeca A Sus Compatriotas; O sea Una Resena De Su Vida Publica. Nueva-Orleans: En la Imprenta de Benjamin Levy, Calle de Chartres, esquina a la de Bienville, 1831. 129 p. + errara p. BWK; NN. 8656

A Peep at the various nations of the World. A Concise description of the Inhabitants. Embellished with several Engravings. Concord, Hoag & Atwood, 1831. 14 l. PP. 8657

Peirson, Abel Lawrence.
Remarks on puerperal fever. By A. L. Peirson... Boston, Pr. by W. L. Lewis, from N. Hale's steampower press, 1831. 30 p. CtSoP; NjR. 8658

[Peisse, Louis] 1803-1880.
Sketches of the character and writing of eminent living surgeons & physicians of Paris, tr. from the French of J. L. H. P. by Elisha Bartlett... Boston, Carter, Hendee & Babcock, 1831. 131 p. CU; ICJ; MB; NcD; TNV. 8659

Peixotto, Daniel L.
Address delivered before the Medical society... city and county of New-York on the 25th day of July, 1831, by Daniel L. M. Peixotto, M.D....New York, Pr. by J. Seymour, 1831. 30 p. NNN; PU; WU-M. 8660

Pemberton, A. H.
Calumny refuted, or, A defence of the drama. Columbia, Times & gazette office, 1831. 19 p. ScCC. 8661

Pembroke Academy, Pembroke, New Hampshire.
Catalogue. Concord, 1831. MB. 8662

Pendergrass, Peter.
The Magdalen report: a farce, in three acts. By Peter Pendergrass, senior... New York, Pr. for the publisher, 1831. 25 p. ICU; MWA. 8663

Pendleton, Nathaniel Greene, 1793-1861.
Oration, delivered on the Fourth of July, 1831... Cincinnati, Pr. by Lodge and L'Hommedieu, 1831. 28 p. CSmH; MBAt; MH; OCHP. 8664

Pennell, Alice Hart.
A key to the questions in Adams' geography, together with an Account of the principal countries, kingdoms, states, cities and towns: with a description of the most remarkable mountains,

rivers, &c. &c., of the world. Baltimore, J. J. Harrod, etc., 1831. 63 p. MH; NNC; PHi; PP. 8665

Pennington, Isaac, 1616-1679.
Memoirs of the life of Isaac Penington, to which is added a review of his writings, by Joseph Gurney Bevan. Philadelphia, T. Kite, 1831. 208 p. CtY; DLC; MB; NcD; RP; TxHuT. 8666

Pennsylvania.
An abridgement of the laws of Pennsylvania, being a complete digest of all such acts of assembly, as concern the commonwealth at large...By Collinson Read...Philadelphia, Pr. for the author, 1831. 468, 28 p. WaU. 8667

---- An act to re-charter certain banks, passed the twenty-fifth day of March, 1824, and the By-Laws of the Miners' bank of Pottsville. Pottsville, Pr. by B. Bannan, 1831. DLC. 8668

---- Acts relating to Eastern State Penitentiary and to New Prisons of City and County of Philadelphia. Philadelphia, J. Allen, 1831. MH-L; MWA; OClW; PHi; ScC. 8669

---- Communication to the Pennsylvania Legislature, with a statement of certain banks. Harrisburg, Henry Welsh, 1831. 32 p. P; PPDrop; RPB. 8670

---- A Digest of the Laws of Pennsylvania, from the year one thousand seven hundred, to the seventh day of April, one thousand eight hundred and thirty. By John W. Purdon. Philadelphia, M'Carty & Davis, 1831. 976 p. Ct; Ia; IU; PAtM; WaU. 8671

---- Laws of the General Assembly of the State of Pennsylvania, passed at the session of 1829-30, in the fifty-fourth year of Independence. Pub. by authority. Harrisburg, Pr. by James Cameron, 1831. 412, 33 p. PLL. 8672

---- Laws of the General Assembly of the state of Pennsylvania, passed at the session 1830-31, in the fifty-fifth year of independence. Pub. by authority. Harrisburg, Pr. by Henry Welsh, 1831. 512 p. NN; P; Sc; W; Wa-L. 8673

---- Nisi prius, first period special jury, Monday, 14th February 1831. A list of special jurors. Philadelphia, Jan. 24, 1831. 1 p. PHi. 8674

---- Purdon's digest, 1830: laws of Pennsylvania by John Purdon. Philadelphia, M'Carty & Davis, 1831. 976 p. OrSC. 8675

---- Report of the Canal Commissioners of Pennsylvania, relative to the Pennsylvania Canals and Railroads. Read in Senate, December 15, 1831. With table of canal and railroad lettings. Harrisburg, Pr. by Henry Welsh, 1831. 38 p. C-S; OCHP; PReaHi. 8676

---- Report of the Committee of Ways and Means, relative to the finances of the commonwealth. January 19, 1831...Harrisburg, 1831. 23 p. MHi; PPCC. 8677

---- Report of the Committee on Internal Improvement and Inland Navigation...House of Representatives, January 11, 1831. Harrisburg, 1831. 16 p. MHi; PPL-R. 8678

---- Report to the Canal Commissioners in reply to strictures passed by Mr. Robinson on the views entertained by Lieut. Col. Long in relation to the manner of crossing the Allegheny Mountain by means of a rail-road, dated March 24th, 1831. Philadelphia,

1831. 12 p. NIC. 8679

---- Report of the Commissioners appointed to revise the civil code of Pennsylvania. (1st-8th) Harrisburg, Pr. by H. Welsh, (etc.), 1831-36. 8 vols. in 1. IAU-L; MH-L; NIC-A; NIC-L; PPAmP; WaU. 8680

---- Reports of cases, abridged, in the courts of Common Pleas. Quarter sessions, Oyer and terminer and Orphans Court of the First Judicial District of Pennsylvania, with notes and references. By John W. Ashmead. Philadelphia, Towar, J. and D. Hogan; Pittsburgh, J. and D. Hogan, 1831-1841. 2 vols. PP; PPiU-L; PU-L; ViU-L. 8681

---- Reports of cases adjudged in the Court of Common Please, quarter sessions, oyer and terminer and orphan's courts of the First Judicial District of Pennsylvania...By John W. Ashmead. Philadelphia, Towar, J. and D. M. Hogan; Pittsburgh, Hogan & Co., 1831 (-1841). 2 vols. Ct; DLC; KyU-L; MH-L; OrSC; PPB; RPL. 8682

---- Reports of the committee on education; read... January 27, 1831. Harrisburg, Welsh, 1831. 16 p. NjR; PPAmP; PPPrHi. 8683

---- Robert Morris' Property. Philadelphia, Pr. by King & Baird, 1831. 45 p. CSfLaw; WHi. 8684

---- Several acts of assembly providing for the education of children at public expense within the city & county of Philadelphia. Philadelphia, Stavely, 1831. 40 p. PHi; PPL-R; PU. 8685

---- State Penitentiary for the eastern district, Philadelphia.
Annual report of the inspectors... Philadelphia, 1831-1903. 70 vols. in 10, various paging. CU; ICJ; MH; NjP; PHC; RPB. 8686

Pennsylvania Academy of the Fine Arts, Philadelphia.
The act of incorporation and standing regulations of the Pennsylvania Academy of the Fine Arts. Philadelphia, Pr. by James Kay, Jun. & Co., 1831. 24 p. MdBJ; PHAmP; PHi; PHiPPWa; PPL; PU. 8687

Pennsylvania Almanac for 1832. Calculated by John Ward. Philadelphia, Pa. [1831] MWA; PHi. 8688

Pennsylvania & New Jersey Almanac for 1832. Calculated by Joseph Cramer. Philadelphia, Pa. Thomas L. Bonsal [1831] MWA. 8689

Pennsylvania Artillery. First Regiment.
Constitution of the 1st regiment of Volunteer Artillery of the 1st Brigade, 1st Div. of Pennsylvania militia. Philadelphia, 1831. 8 p. PHi. 8690

Pennsylvania Horticultural Society, Philadelphia.
Constitution and by-laws of the Pennsylvania Horticultural Society. Philadelphia, Pr. by T. A. Conrad, 1831. 20 p. MdHi; P; PHi; PPAmP. 8691

---- Report of the Committee appointed by the Horticultural Society of Pennsylvania, for visiting the nurseries and gardens in the vicinity of Philadelphia, July 13, 1830. Philadelphia, 1831. 16 p. DLC; MBHo; PHi; PPAmP; PPL; RPB. 8692

Pennsylvania Library of Foreign Literature and Science.
Report & constitution, 1831. Philadelphia, 1831. 8 p. PHi. 8693

Pennsylvania Society for discouraging the use of ardent spirits. See Pennsylvania State Temperance Society.

The Pennsylvania State register, for 1831. Published annually. Philadelphia, J. Conrad, 1831. DLC; PHi; PPA; PPL. 8694

[Pennsylvania State Temperance Society]
The anniversary report of the managers of the Pennsylvania society for discouraging the use of ardent spirits. Read on the 27th day of May 1831, and ordered to be published by the society. Philadelphia, Henry H. Porter, 1831. 80 p. IG; KyLx; PPAmP; PHC; PPCP; PPGi; PHi; PU. 8695

Pennsylvania University.
Catalogue of the trustees, officers, & students of the University of Pennsylvania. Philadelphia, Pr. by L. R. Bailey, 1831. 38 p. MHi; TNP. 8696

.... People of Providence (a plea for the "American system") [Providence, 1831] Broadside. RPB. 8697

People of Rhode Island, read, examine, and judge for yourselves. [Providence, 1831] Broadside. RPB. 8698

[Perkins, Ephraim]
A serious address to the Presbytery of Oneida, on the manner of conducting the late revivals... [Utica, 1831] 12 p. MHi. 8699

Perkins, Jonas.
Sermon, delivered before the Auxiliary education society of Norfolk county, at their annual meeting in Stoughton, June 8, 1831. Boston, Pr. by T. R. Marvin, 1831. 24 p. MBC; MH; NNUT; NhD; RPB. 8700

Perrin, Jean Baptiste, fl. 1786.
Fables amusantes, avec une table generale et particuliere des mots et de leur signification en anglais selon l'ordre des fables, pour en rendre la traduction plus facile a l'ecolier. Par M. Perrin. Edition revue et corrigee par un maitre de langue francaise. Stereotype de A. Chandler. Philadelphia, Key & Mielke, 1831. 180 p. ICP; MdW; MoSW. 8701

---- A selection of one hundred of Perrin's fables, accompanied by a key... also a figured pronunciation of the French... The whole preceded by a short treatise on the sounds of the French language... By A. Bolmar, professor of the French language ... Stereotyped by L. Johnson. Philadelphia, Carey & Lea, 1831. 185 p. IaHi; MB; MH. 8702

Perrin, John.
Elements of French and English conversation. Philadelphia, Key & Mielke, 1831. 216 p. MDeeP; NSyU. 8703

Peters, Absolom, 1793-1869.
A brief answer to an official reply of the Board of Missions of the general assembly to Six letters of the Rev. Absalom Peters, corresponding secretary of the American Home Missionary Society, entitled "A Plea for Union in the West," Pub. in the Cincinnati Journal, in the course of the months of December and January last. Also, Mr. Peters' Reply to the Rev. Dr. J. L. Wilson's four propositions sustained against the claims of the American Home Missionary Society. With an appendix. New-York, Pr. by Clayton & Van Norden, 1831. 48 p. ICN; MiD-B; NjR; PPPrHi; WHi. 8704

---- An official reply of the board of missions of the general assembly, to six letters of the Rev. Absolom Peters... Philadelphia, Pr. by Clark & Raser, 1831. 32 p. IU; MiD-B; PHi; OClWHi; PLT; WHi. 8705

Peters, Richard, 1780-1848.
The case of the Cherokee nation against the state of Georgia; argued and determined at the Supreme court of the United States, January term 1831. With an appendix containing the opinion of Chancellor Kent on the case; the treaties between the United States and the Cherokee Indians; the act of Congress of 1802, entitled 'An act to regulate intercourse with the Indian tribes, &c.'; and the laws of Georgia relative to the country occupied by the Cherokee Indians, within the boundary of that state. By Richard Peters... Philadelphia, J. Grigg, 1831. 286 p. IU; OFH; PU; RPB; WHi. 8706

Pettersdorff, Charles, 1800-1886.
A Practical and Elementary Abridgment of the Cases argued and determined in the courts of King's Bench, Common pleas, Exchequer, and at Nisi Prius and of the Rules of Court, from the Restoration in 1660, to Michaelmas term, 4 George IV. With Important Manuscript Cases, alphabetically, chronologically, and systematically arranged and translated; with copious notes and references to the Year Books, analogous adjudications, text writers, and statutes, specifying what decisions whave been affirmed. Recognized qualified, or overruled. Comprising, under the several titles, a practical treatise on the different braches of the Common Law. By Charles Petersdorff, Esq. of the inner temple. Vol. X. New York, W. R. H. Treadway and Gould & Banks, 1831. 508 p. AzPh; In-SC; LNB; MdBB; WU-L. 8707

[Pettis, F. H.]
To the people of the United States. [An appeal from conviction of perjury and a threat to draw his sword on any one who ever again mentions the case.] Washington, 1831. 7 p. MB; MWA; MdHi. 8708

[Peyre Ferry, François]
Conseils de l'esprit d'un vieillard septuagenaire à son âme et la métamorphose de l'âme en perroquet; poéme[!] moral et burlesque en 4 chants, avec des notes historiques. Par P**** F****. Philadelphia, imprimé par Clark & Raser, 1831. 61 p. MH; PPCP. 8709

The Phantasmagoria of New York; a poetical burlesque upon a certain libellous pamphlet, written by a committee of notorious fanatics, entitled The Magdalen Report. New York, Pr. for the publisher [1831] RPB. 8710

The pharmacopoeia of the United States of America. By authority of the National Medical Convention held at Washington, A.D. 1830. Philadelphia, John Grigg, 1831. 268 p. Ia; KyLxT; MiU; PU; WaPS. 8711

Phelps, [A. R.]
Circular letter to the public. [Worcester] 1831. 7 p. MWA. 8712

Phelps, Mrs. Almira (Hart) Lincoln, 1793-1884.
Familiar lectures on botany. Including practical and elementary botany, with generic and specific descriptions of the most common native and foriegn plants, and a vocabulary of botanical terms. For the use of higher schools and academies. By Mrs. Almira H. Lincoln... 2d ed.

Hartford, H. & F. J. Huntington, 1831. 428 p. CtHT; GEU; MH; PPM; ScC; WU. 8713

Phelps, Ansel, b. 1815.
Secondary lessons, or the improved reader. 5th ed. New Haven, Durrie & Peck, 1831. 186 p. NNU. 8714

Phelps, Dudley.
The making of a new heart a reasonable duty. A discourse ... First Parish Meeting House, Haverhill, Lord's day, Dec. 11, 1831. Haverhill, 1831? 40 p. MHaHi. 8715

Phenix mining company.
Proposals of the Phenix mining company; with a statement of the history and character of their mines, property, and leases, course of investigation and its results. New-York, Pr. by J. Seymour, 1831. 30 p. Ct; ScU. 8716

Philadelphia. Academy of Natural Sciences of Philadelphia.
Notice of the Academy of Natural Sciences of Philadelphia ... 2d ed. Philadelphia, Pr. by Mifflin & Parry, 1831. DLC; PPAN; PPL-R; PPULC. 8717

---- American Hose Company.
Constitution of the American Hose Company. Instituted September 2d, 1828. Philadelphia, Pr. by order of the Company. 1831. 24 p. PPM. 8718

---- (City) Councils.
Report of the Watering committee, to the select and common councils. Read February 10, 1831. Published by order of the councils. Philadelphia, Pr. by Lydia R. Bailey, 1831. 32 p. THi. 8719

---- ---- Report... respecting the proposed canal near the western abutment of the permanent bridge over the River Schuylkill. Philadelphia, Bailey, 1831. 15 p. MH; PPAmP. 8720

---- City Mission.
Address and Constitution. [Philadelphia, 1831] MHi. 8721

---- ---- Quarterly report. 1831- . Philadelphia, Geddes, 1831- . PHi; PPFrankI; PPPrHi. 8722

---- City Tract Society.
Annual report... 1831-. Philadelphia, Geddes, 1831-. PHi; PPPrHi. 8723

---- Collegiate Institution for Young Ladies.
Third annual catalogue of the scholars of the Collegiate Institution for Young Ladies. Philadelphia, W. F. Geddes, 1831. MH; PPPrHi. 8724

---- Friends' Library.
Catalogue of the books belonging to the library of the four monthly meeting of Friends of Philadelphia; with the rules for the government of the library, Philadelphia, Pr. by J. Rakestraw, 1831. 152 p. DLC; MH; P; PSC-Hi. 8725

---- Library and Reading Room Company of the Northern Liberties.
Constitution; rules and regulations. [Philadelphia? 1831?] MH. 8726

---- Mayor's Court.
A full and accurate report of the trial for riot before the Mayor's court of Philadelphia on the 13th of October, 1831... Philadelphia, Pr. by J. Harding, 1831. 104 p. DLC; MH-L; PPB; PPL. 8727

---- Public Instruction, Joint committee on.

Report on the state of education in Pennsylvania, accompanied with two bills for the establishment of a general system of public instruction... Philadelphia, Garden, 1831. 22 p. PU. 8728

---- St. Mary's Church.

Address of the trustees of St. Mary's Church, to the congregation. April 16, 1831. Philadelphia, [1831] 12 p. DLC; MdW; PHi; PPL. 8729

Philadelphia, Germantown, and Norristown Railroad Company.

Act... incorporating the Philadelphia, Germantown, and Norristown Railroad Company. Philadelphia, 1831. 24 p. PHi. 8730

Philadelphia Reading Railroad Company. See An Address to the friends of the railroad...

Philadelphia Saving Fund Society.

Act of Incorporation. Philadelphia, 1831. 16 p. PHi. 8731

Philadelphia Young Men's Society.

Constitution, 1831. 8 p. MBC. 8732

Philanthropes (pseud.).

Adventures of a French soldier, exemplifying the evil, crime, and sufferings of war. With reflections by Philanthropos, author of "The Sword," "Howard and Napoleon," &c. Boston, 1831. 108 p. MHi; Mh-Hi. 8733

Philip, Alexander Philip Wilson, 1770-1851?

A treatise on the nature and cure of those diseases, either acute or chronic, which precede change of structure; with a view to the preservation of health, and, particularly, the prevention of organic diseases. By A. P. W. Philip...With notes and appendices, by J. H. Miller...Baltimore, E. J. Coale; Washington City, Cole & co., 1831. 328 p. DLC; ICJ; KyLxT; TNV; ViU. 8734

Philip Everard; or, A history of the Baptist Indian Missions in North America...Revised by the Publishing Committee. Boston, Massachusetts Sabbath School Union, 1831. 108 p. A-Ar; IHi; InHi; MH-AH; NNUT. 8735

Philleo, Calvin, 1787-1874.

Calvin Philleo's light on Masonry and anti-Masonry, and a renunciation of both, with undissembled esteem for Masons and anti-Masons. Providence, H. H. Brown, 1831. 23 p. DLC; MB; MH; RHI; RPB. 8736

Phillips, Jonas B.

...The evil eye: a melo-drama, in two acts. Written by Jonas B. Phillips...Pr. from the acting copy...New York, E. B. Clayton; Philadelphia, C. Neal, 1831. 27 p. ICU; MH; PU; RPB. 8737

[Phillips, Sir Richard] 1767-1840

The explanatory and pronouncing French word-book;...To which is annexed the French phrase-book. By M. L'Abbe Bossut. (pseud.) 3d ed. Boston, Richardson, Lord & Holbrook, 1831. 96, 29 p. MH; NNC; RPB. 8738

---- A geographical view of the world, embracing the manners, customs, and pursuits, of every nation; founded on the best authorities. By Rev. J. Goldsmith (pseud.)...6th Amer. ed., rev. corr., and imp. by James G. Percival... Hartford, Robinson, 1831. 406 p. DeWi; GAuY; InCW; MoSM. 8739

---- Outlines of chronology, ancient and modern; being an

introduction to the study of history... Boston, Richardson, Lord & Holbrook, 1831. 232 p. RPE. 8740

---- Reading exercises for the use of schools. 6th ed. Philadelphia, Kimber & Sharpless, 1831. 204 p. MH; PHi. 8741

---- The Universal Preceptor: being a general grammar of arts, sciences, and useful knowledge. By the Rev. David Blair...From the 13th English ed., rev. and imp. Greenfield, Mass., Pr. by Phelps & Ingersoll, for A. Phelps, 1831. 294 p. KyBC; MLy. 8742

Phillips, Stephen Clarendon.
A lecture on the usefulness of lyceums...delivered in Boston, before the American Institute of Instruction, August, 1831. Boston, Hilliard, Gray, Little and Wilkins, 1831. 38 p. M; MHi; MWA; PCA; PHi. 8743

---- An oration, delivered at the request of the young men of Salem, July 4, 1831. Salem, Warwick Palfray, jun., 1831. 40 p. MHi; OClWHi; PHi; RPB; VtU. 8744

Phillips, Williard.
A digest of the Pickering's report from the second to the eighth volume, inclusive. By Williard Phillips and others. Boston, Richardson, Lord, and Holbrook, 1831. 434 p. CU; MBS; MH; NCH; PU-L. 8745

Phinney, Elias, 1780-1849.
Address delivered before the Middlesex society of husbandmen and manufacturers, at their annual festival, October 7, 1830. By Elias Phinney. Charlestown, Pr. by W. W. Wheildon, 1831. 28 p. MBHo; MH; MiD-B; NNC; NjR; WU-A. 8746

Phinney's calendar or, Western Almanac...1832...by Edwin E. Prentiss...Cooperstown, Pr. by H. & E. Phinney...1831. 36 p. NUtHi; WHi. 8747

[Picken, Andrew], 1788-1833, ed.
The club-book, being original tales, &c. by various authors. Edited by the author of "The Dominie's Legacy." New York, J. & J. Harper, 1831. 2 vols. FTU; ICN; MB; MH; NSyHi; TNP; VtU. 8748

---- The Deer-Stalkers of Glenskrach... New York, J. & J. Harper, 1831. 122 p. OCX. 8749

Pickering, David.
Lectures in defence of divine revelation, delivered at the Universalist Chapel in Providence, R.I. 2d ed. Providence, S. W. Wheeler, 1831. MB; MBC; MH; PPM; RP; RPB; ScNC. 8750

[Pickering, Henry] 1781-1838.
The buckwheat cake, a poem ... Boston, Carter, Hendee and Babcock, 1831. 14 p. DLC; MBAt; NN; RPB; TxU. 8751

Picket, Albert
Juvenile spelling book...New York, 1831. CtHWatk. 8752

---- The new juvenile expositor, or Rational reader, and key to the Juvenile spelling book: comprising the definitions of all the syllabic words in that work... being American school class book no. 4. By A. & J. W. Picket...Cincinnati, Picket & co., 1831. 384 p. OC; Vi. 8753

Pictorial narratives. J. A. Ackley, New-York, 1831. 256 p. KyHopB. 8754

Picture primer...By a friend to youth...New Haven, S. Babcock,

[1831] MH. 8755

Piepe, J. L. H.
Surgeons and physicians of Paris. Tr. by E. Bartlett. Boston, 1831. MB. 8756

Pierce, I.
A reference and distance map of the State of New York. New Haven, I. Pierce, 1831. 1 fold. col map. NIC. 8757

Pierpont, John, 1785-1866, comp.
The American First Class Book; or, Exercises in Reading and Recitation: selected principally from modern authors of Great Britain and America; and designed for the use of the highest class in publick and private schools. By John Pierpont, Minister of Hollis Street Church. Boston, Author of Airs of Palestine Etc. Boston, Hilliard, Gray, Little, and Wilkins; and Richardson, Lord & Holbrook, 1831. 480 p. CoD; IU; MB; OCl; PMA. 8758

---- Introduction to the National reader; a selection of easy lessons, designed to fill the same place... By John Pierpont, compiler of the American First class book, and the National reader. Boston, Richardson, Lord & Holbrook, 1831. 168 p. Ct; ICU; MiU-C; MLy; RPB. 8759

---- The national reader; a selection of exercises in reading and speaking, designed to fill the same place in the schools of the United States that is held in those of Great Britain, by the compilation of Murray, Scott, Enfield, Mylius, Thompson, Ewing, and others. Boston, Richardson, Lord, and Holbrook; and Hilliard, Gray, Little, and Wilkins, 1831. 276 p. MH; OMC; PWW; RPE; TxU-T. 8760

---- The young reader: to go with the spelling book. By John Pierpont... Boston, Richardson, Lord and Holbrook, 1831. 162 p. CSt; MB; MH; MPeHi; RPB. 8761

Pierson, Josiah.
Millenium, a poem in five books. By Rev. Josiah Pierson... Rochester, N.Y., Pr. by Tyler & Chipman, 1831. 81 p. CSfCW; NRHi; NjP; OO. 8762

Pike, Samuel, 1717?-1773.
Religious cases of conscience, answered in an evangelical manner, at the casuistical lecture in Little St. Helen's... Philadelphia, Towar, J. & D. M. Hogan; Pittsburgh, Hogan & co., 1831. 1 vol. 436 p. ArAO; CSmH; ICP; NcD; TBrik. 8763

Pike, Stephen, comp.
The teacher's assistant; or A system of practical arithmetic; wherein the several rules of that useful science are illustrated by a variety of examples...the whole designed to abridge the labour of teachers, and to facilitate the instruction of youth. A new ed., with corr. and add. by the author. Compiled by Stephen Pike. Philadelphia, M'Carty & Davis, 1831. 198 p. ICACS; MH; PHi; PU; TxU-T. 8764

The pilgrimage of Ormond, or Childe Harold in the New World ...Charleston, W. Riley, 1831. 94 p. DLC; MH; NIC-L; PPAmP; ScC. 8765

The Pillar of Divine Truth...the word of God... New York, Peter P. Good, 1831. 337 p. PRea. 8766

Pinkney, Charles.
The last serenade (song) arranged for the pianoforte and guitar, the words and music by Charles Pinkney. Baltimore,

John Cole, 1831. 2 p. ViU. 8767

The pious sister of Roseneath, a pathetic narrative. Boston, James Loring, 1831. CtY. 8768

[Pise, Charles Constantine] 1802-1866.

Father Rowland, a North American tale. 2d ed., enl. Baltimore, Fielding Lucas, Jr. [1831] 195 p. DLC; ICBB; MdHi; ODa. 8769

---- The Indian cottage: a Unitarian story...By the author of "Father Rowland"... Baltimore, Lucas [1831] 159 p. DLC; MdBE; MdHi; MiDSH. 8770

Pitkin, Timothy.

A political and civil history of the United States of America, from the year 1763 to the close of the administration of President Washington, in March, 1797: including a summary view of the political and civil state of the North American colonies, prior to that period. By Timothy Pitkin. New Haven, Hezekiah Howe and Durrie & Peck, 1831. 2 vols. GA; Nj; RPaw; ScU; TMeC. 8771

Pittsburgh songster; containing a choice collection of approved popular songs. Selected from the best authors. Pittsburgh, Cramer & Spear, 1831. 93 p. MB. 8772

A plain account of the ordinance of baptism: in which all the texts in the New-Testament relating to it, are proved; and the whole doctrine concerning it, drawn from them alone; in a course of letters to the Right Rev. Benjamin Hoadly, late Lord Bishop of Winchester; author of the Plain account of the Lord's Supper ...Canondaigua, Pr. by Morse & Harvey, for J. Bignall, 1831. 72 p. N. 8773

Plain facts for the people. From the Morning Courier & New-York Enquirer, June 23, 1831. 12 p. MdHi; NbU. 8774

The Planters Almanac, for the year of our Lord, 1832, being bissextile or leap-year, and the fifty-sixth--seventh of the Independence of the United States. Calculated for the latitude and longitude of Mobile, but will answer for the adjoining states. The Astronomical part of the "American Almanac." Mobile, Odiorne, and Smith, 1831. 36 p. MH. 8775

Platt, Jonas, 1769-1834.

Address delivered before the Temperance society of Plattsburgh, Sept. 14th, 1831. Plattsburgh, 1831. CtHWatk. 8776

Playfair, John, 1748-1819.

Elements of geometry containing the first six books of Euclid, with a supplement...By John Playfair, F. R. S. New York, Collins & Hannay; Collins and co., G. & C. and H. Carvill, 1831. 333p. LNT; MH; NRHi; OO; WM. 8777

The Plebeian, and Millbury Workingmen's Advocate. Millbury, Pr. by Josiah Snow... V. 1, January 5, 1831. MBedfHi; MWA. 8778

Plutarchus, ca. 50-120.

The beauties of Plutarch; consisting of selections from his works. By Alfred Howard, esq. Boston, Frederick S. Hill, 1831. 192 p. DLC; InHan; MBBC; MH; Msa. 8779

---- Plutarch's Lives, tr. from the original Greek: with notes, critical and historical, and a life of Plutarch. By Long Langhorne, D.D. and William Langhorne, A.M. a new ed.

carefully rev. and corr. Baltimore, Neal, 1831. 748 p. CtMW; IEG; LNL; TxU; WHi. 8780

The Pocket lawyer and family conveyancer; comprising a selection of forms necessary in all mercantile, and money transactions, including every direction essential to the magistrate and private individual... To which is added and abridged law dictionary, comp. by a gentleman of the bar... Lewistown, Pa., C. Bell & Sons, 1831. 132 p. NcD; PHi; PPB. 8781

The Pocket lawyer; or, Self-conveyancer; containing all the most useful forms, rendered so plain that every man can draw any instrument of writing without the assistance of an attorney. In a method entirely new. 4th ed. Pittsburgh, Robert Patterson, 1831. 107 p. PPi. 8782

Pocock, Isaac, 1782-1835.
Maggie; or, The maid. A melodrama in three acts. Translated and altered from the French by I. Pocock, Esq., Baltimore, J. Robinson, 1831. 48 p. DLC; LNH; LNHT; MB; NN. 8783

---- The Miller and his men; a melodrama in two acts, by J. Pocock, Esq. Philadelphia, C. and J. C. Neal, 1831. 34 p. MB; MH. 8784

Poe, Edgar A[llan].
Poems. 2d. ed. New York, E. Bliss, 1831. IGK; MH; NNC. 8785

The poetical works of Milton, Young, Gray, Beattie, and Collins. Complete in one volume. Stereotyped by J. Crissy and G. Goodman. Philadelphia, John Grigg, 1831. KyU; MB; MH; MeBaT; PHi. 8786

Poetry for children under ten years of age. New Haven, S. Babcock, Sidney's press, 1831. 22 p. [Binder's title: A present from sister] CtY. 8787

Polite present; or manual of good manners. Boston. Munroe & Francis, 1831. 72 p. MBC; NNC. 8788

Pollock, George, 1802-1840.
The beauties of Scottish & Irish melody. No. 1. for the piano forte or flute & violoncello. Boston, 1831. 22 p. MH. 8789

Pollok, Robert, 1798-1827.
The Course of Time. A poem...New-York, Charles Wells, 1831. 328 p. CtHT; IU; MH; PEaL; WHi. 8790

---- ---- 10th Amer. ed. New York, M'Elrath & Bangs, 1831. 240 p. CLU; CoNo; MnSM; MiToC; MiMarsHI; MW; NOx; OBerB; ViU; WBeloHi. 8791

---- ---- 12th Amer. ed. New York, M'Elrath & Bangs, 1831. 240 p. OO; PU. 8792

---- ---- 13th ed. New York, M'Elrath & Bangs, 1831. 240 p. NNG; OO. 8793

The Polyanthos, or Flowers of literature; being selections from the most approved authors, in prose and verse. 1831. New-York, C. Wells [1831] 192 p. MB; MH; PP; WrU. 8794

Pomeroy, Swan Lyman, 1799-1869.
The dead in Christ blessed. A discourse preached at the funeral of the Rev. John Smith, D.C., professor of Theology in the Seminary at Bangor, April 12, 1831. By S. L. Pomeroy, pastor of the First Congregational Church in Bangor. Augusta,

Pr. by Eaton and Severance, 1831. 15 p. MBAt; MHi; Nh-Hi; PHi; RPB. 8795

[Pond, Enoch], 1791-1882.
Review of Mr. Whitman's Letters to Prof. Stuart, on religious liberty. 2d ed., with an appendix not before published. Boston, Peirce & Parker, 1831. 84 p. CBPac; MA; MH-AH; NjR. 8796

Poor Richards' almanack for the year of our Lord 1832; being bissextile, or leap year, and of American Independence the 56th. Adapted to the meridian of Rochester, Monroe Co. Rochester, Marshall & Dean, [1831] [24] p. MWA; NRU; NUtHi. 8797

Poor Will's Pocket almanack for 1832. Philadelphia, Pa., Kimber & Sharpless [1831] MWA. 8798

Porcher, Frederick Adolphus.
An oration delivered before the inhabitants of Pineville, South Carolina on Monday, July 4, 1831. Charleston, S.C., J. S. Burges, 1831. 15 p. 8799

Porter, Ebenezer, 1772-1834.
Analysis of the principles of rhetorical delivery as applied in reading and speaking. By Ebenezer Porter... 4th ed. Andover, Flagg & Gould; Boston, Crocker & Brewster; Richardson, Lord & Holbrook; and Lincoln and Edmands. New-York, J. Leavitt, 1831. 404 p. DLC; KyLxT; MH; PPWa; TxU-T. 8800

---- The Christian Citizen: or the Duty of Praying for Rulers. Two sermons, preached in the chapel of the Theological Seminary, Andover, on the State Fast. April 7, 1831. By Ebenezer Porter, D.D. ...2d ed., with an appendix. Boston, Peirce & Parker, 1831. 44 p. CtHC; ICMe; MB; NjR; WHi. 8801

---- Duty of praying for rulers; sermons 104 and 105, preached on the day of annual state fast, 1831. New York, 1831. p. 193-208. CtSoP. 8802

---- The rhetorical reader consisting of instructions for regulating the voice. By Ebenezer Porter. Andover, Mass., Flagg & Gould; New York, Leavitt, 1831. 300 p. DLC; GDecCT; MiD; NcD; RPB. 8803

---- ...Two sermons preached in the chapel of the Theological Seminary, Andover, on the state fast. April 7, 1831. By Ebenezer Porter, D.D. 2d ed., with an appendix. Boston, Peirce & Parker, 1831. 44 p. GDecCT; MAnHi; MNe; MeHi; OCHP; PPL; RPB. 8804

Porter, George Richardson.
The nature and properties of the sugar cane; with practical directions for the improvement of its culture, and the manufacture of its products. By George R. Porter. Philadelphia, Carey & Lea, 1831. 354 p. DLC; InLPU; LU; NcD; ScC; TxU. 8805

[Porter, Henry H.]
The catechism of health; or, Plain and simple rules for the preservation of the health and vigour of the constitution from infancy to old age. Ladies ed. Philadelphia, Journal of health and Journal of Law, 1831. 195 p. ICBB; MWA; MdBM; OC; RPM. 8806

---- ---- 5th ed. Philadelphia, Journal of health and Journal of law, 1831. 202 p. DLC; NNT-C; OMC; OO. 8807

---- ---- 7th ed. Philadelphia, Journal of health, 1831. 202 p.

DLC; PBM. 8808

Porter, Miss Jane, 1776-1850.
The Scottish chiefs. By Miss Jane Porter, authoress of "Thaddeus of Warsaw," etc. etc. Complete ed. New York, New York Publishing Co., etc., 1831? 3 vols. FDU; IaLeo; LNL; NMerk; OkMuV. 8809

---- Sir Edward Seaward's narrative of his shipwreck, and consequent discovery of certain islands in the Caribbean Sea: with a detail of many extraordinary and highly interesting events in his life, from the year 1733 to to 1749, as written in his own diary. Ed. by Miss Jane Porter. New York, J. & J. Harper, 1831. 3 vols. DLC; IaCeC LNB; MB; TxU. 8810

---- Thaddeus of Warsaw. By Jane Porter. New and rev. ed. Philadelphia, Porter & Coates, 1831. 536 p. NRU; NRU-W; PNt; ViR; VtV. 8811

No entry. 8812

The Portland directory, containing names of the inhabitants, their occupations, places of business and dwelling houses. With lists of streets, lanes, and wharves. The town officers, public offices and banks. Portland, S. Coleman [1831] 86 p. DLC. 8813

[Potter, Elisha Reynolds], 1764-1835.
An address, to the freemen of Rhode-Island. By a landholder. Providence, Pr. at the Herald Office, 1831. 16 p. DLC; RHi-RP; RPB. 8814

[Potter, Paraclete]
Every man his own lawyer, or The clerk and magistrate's assistant. By a gentleman of the bar. Stereotyped by James Conner, New-York. Poughkeepsie, P. Potter & co., 1831. 126, 62 p. CSmH; MH; WMMD. 8815

Potter, Ray.
Lecture on the Covenant of Circumcision, showing the impossibility of supporting or inferring from it the doctrine of infant baptism. Delivered...March 25, 1831. Providence, Brown, 1831. PPPrHi; RPB; RPaw. 8516

Potts, S. G.
The pet lamb; by S. G. Potts. Auburn [N. Y.] H. Ivison & co., 1831. 17 p. CU. 8817

Potts, William S.
"Death desireable to the Christian." A sermon, St. Louis, November 20, 1831, occasioned by the death of Stephen Hempstead, Sen. St. Louis, 1831. 30 p. WHi. 8818

---- Importance of early education and family government, and obligations of parents to Sunday schools. An annual sermon, preached at St. Louis, July 17, 1831. For the Presbyterian Sunday School Society of St. Louis ... St. Louis, Pr. at the St. Louis Times office, 1831. 20 p. IU; WHi. 8819

Poughkeepsie News Telegraph Weekly.
Poughkeepsie: Poughkeepsie News Company. 1831 (-1876). 1 vol. for each year from 1831 to 1876. Tot. vols. 46. NP. 8820

Poulson, Charles A.
Monographs of the several genera of terrestrial & fluviatile shells of the U.S. ... Philadelphia, 1831. PPAN. 8821

Powell, Benjamin F.
Bible of reason: or, Scriptures of ancient moralists. Collected and rendered by B. F. Powell... New York, Wright & Owen, 1831. 2 vols. DLC; ICP; MMilf; OC; WHi. 8822

[Power, Tyrone] 1797-1841.
The King's secret. By the author of "The lost heir"... New-York, J. & J. Harper, 1831. 2 vols. DLC; MW; RjA; ViU; VtU. 8823

---- Married lovers: a petite comedy, in two acts; as performed at the Theatre Royal, Covent Garden, on February 2, 1831. By T. Power i.e. William Grattan Tyrone...Baltimore, J. Robinson, 1831. 42 p. DLC; ICU; MH. 8824

Praed, Winthrop Mackworth.
The poems of Winthrop Mackworth Praed. Rev. and enl. ed. With a memoir by the Rev. Derwent Coleridge... New York, Frederick Stokes & Co., 1831. 2 vols. WyU. 8825

Prayer, considered experimently and practically, in reference to the existing state of the churches and of the world. New York, Jonathan Leavitt, 1831. 122 p. ICCB; GDecCT; MBC. 8826

Prayers suitable for children & Sunday Schools. Philadelphia, American Sunday School Union (V.T.P.) 1831? 86 p. ICP; MB; NcMHi. 8827

Preamble and resolutions adopted a meeting held at the Exchange Coffee house. See Free trade convention, Philadelphia, 1831.

Preble, William Pitt, LL.D., 1783-1857.
The decision of the king of the Netherlands considered in reference to the rights of the United States and of the state of Maine. Portland, Thomas Todd, 1831. 35 p. Williamson 8290. 8828

Prentice, George Denison, 1802-1870.
Biography of Henry Clay. By George D. Prentice, Esq. Hartford, Samuel Hanmer, Jr. and John Jay Phelps, 1831. 304 p. CtHC; GAU; MnHi; OO; RP. 8829

---- ---- 2d ed. New York, J. J. Phelps, 1831. 312 p. CLU; ICU; KyU; ViL; WHi. 8830

The Presbyterian. 9 vols. in 4. Philadelphia, 1831-39. MBC; PCC; PP; PPWe. 8831

Presbyterian Church in the U.S.A.
Address of the board of directors of the Presbyterian Education Society to the Christian public. Pub. by order of the directors. October, 1831. New York, Pr. by Sleight & Robinson, 1831. 16 p. MHi; PHi; PPPrHi. 8832

---- The consitution and laws of the board of education of the general assembly of the Presbyterian church in the United States. Philadelphia, Russell & Martier, 1831. 16 p. ICU; KyDC. 8833

---- Minutes of the convention of delegates, met to consult on Missions, in the city of Cincinnati, A.D. 1831. Lexington, Ky., Skillman, 1831. 22 p. ICP; ICU; NjPT; PPPrHi. 8834

---- Minutes of the General Assembly of the Presbyterian church in the United States of America: with an appendix A.D. 1831. Philadelphia, Pr. by Wm. F. Geddes, for the stated clerk of the assembly, 1831. 153-306 p. InU; NNG; NcMHi; ViRut. 8835

---- Psalms and hymns adapted to public worship, and approved by the General assembly of the Presbyterian church in the United States of America. Philadelphia, Pub. for the General assembly, by S. Allen, 1831. DLC; LV; MBC; PPC; PPPrHi. 8836

---- Reply to six letters of Rev. A. Peters. Philadelphia, 1831. MB. 8837

---- A report of the minority in the Convention on domestic missions, held in Cincinnati, November, 1831. By a committee. Cincinnati, Pr. at the Cincinnati journal office, 1831. 48 p. CSmH; MBC; MH; MiD-B; TxDam. 8838

---- Presbytery of Baltimore. Circular. 1831. PPPrHi. 8839

---- Presbytery of Detroit. Articles of faith and covenant, adopted by the Presbytery of Detroit, September 1, 1831, and recommended for adoption to the churches under their care. Detroit, Pr. at the office of the Courier, 1831. 12 p. MiD-B. 8840

---- Presbytery of Geneva. Summary confession of faith, and form of covenant: adopted by the Presbytery of Geneva, and recommended to the churches under their care. Geneva [1831?] 4 p. NRU. 8841

---- Presbytery of Oneida. Confession of faith and covenant adopted by the Presbytery of Oneida, February, 1831, and recommended to the Churches under its care. Utica, Pr. by Hastings & Tracy, 1831. 8 p. MBAt; MBC. 8842

---- Presbytery of Philadelphia. Complaint from the minority of the Presbytery of Philadelphia presented to the general assembly, May 20, 1831. Philadelphia, Pr. by Wm. F. Geddes, 1831. 14 p. CtY; MH-AH; NNG; NjPT; PHi; PLT; PPL. 8843

---- ---- Debates in the Presbytery of Philadelphia on the case of the Rev. Albert Barnes, at a special case held in the city of Philadelphia... Philadelphia, Pr. by Geddes, 1831. 80 p. MBC; MiD-B; PHi; PPL. 8844

---- Presbytery of Watertown. The second report of the executive committee of the benevolent association of the Presbytery of Watertown, New York, & the Black River, New York Association, Feb. 9, 1831. Watertown, Knowlton, 1831. PPPrHi. 8845

---- Synod of Cincinnati. An Address to the churches, on the subject of slavery. Georgetown, Ohio, August 5, 1831. [Georgetown?] D. Ammen and co., prs. [1831] 24 p. DLC. 8846

---- Synod of Illinois. Extracts from the Minutes of the Synod of Illinois held at Hillsborough Sept. 15, 1831. No. I. Alton, [Ill.] E. Breath, 1831. 10 p. PPPrHi. 8847

---- Synod of South Carolina and Georgia. Presbyterian Church. Minutes of the Synod of South Carolina and Georgia, at their Sessions in Augusta, Dec. 1830. With an

Appendix. Charleston, Observer Office Press, 1831. 35 p. MB. 8848

The Presidency.
(Political essays, subscribed, An Old Man; directed against the re-election of General Jackson. By J. M. White? Repr. from the Baltimore Chronical.) [Baltimore, 1831] MB; MBAt; MdHi. 8849

Prest, J. A.
The monitorial primer, on new and improved principles, consisting of monosyllables, roots of words, etc. arranged according to the vowel sounds, in the order of grammar, natural history, etc. Being an introduction to the Juvenile lexicon, by J. A. Prest... [Part 1] Harrisburg [Pa.] F. Wyeth, 1831. CtHWatk; DLC. 8850

Preston, Charles Henry.
Descendants of Roger Preston of Ipswich and Salem Village. Salem, Mass., Essex institute, 1831. 355 p. OClWHi. 8851

Preston, Lyman, b. 1795.
Preston's complete time table: showing the number of days from any date in any given month to any date in any other month, embracing upwards of one hundred and thirty thousand combinations of dates. New York, Sheldon, 1831. 12 p. CoD; DLC; MH-L; NBuG. 8852

---- Preston's cubical estimates of boxes, bales, and casks: adapted to the use of merchants and carriers. By Lyman Preston... New York, Pr. by Sleight & Robinson, 1831. 3-13 p. DLC; GHi; MH; MiDT; NNC. 8853

---- Preston's pocket reckoner and Almanack. By Lyman Preston... New York, Pr. by Sleight & Robinson, 1831. 23 p. DLC; MiU. 8854

---- Preston's Tables of Interest computed at seven per cent., allowing three hundred and sixty-five days to be a year. The interest on dollars and cents being shown at one view together with calculations of rebate, or discount. By Lyman Preston. New ed., enl. New York, Sheldon & Co. [1831] 267 p. NBuG. 8855

---- Preston's treatise on book-keeping: or Arbitrary rules made plain: in two parts... The first part being designed for the use of mechanics of all classes; the second...showing the method of keeping accounts by double entry ...By Lyman Preston... New York, Pr. by Sleight and Robinson, [1831] 174 p. DLC; KyU; MoS; NRU; OSW. 8856

Priest, Josiah, 1788-1851, comp.
A view of the expected Christian millenium... Albany, Pub. for subscribers, Loomis' press, 1831. 408 p. NN. 8857

Priestman, William.
Catalogue...library to be sold ... Philadelphia, 1831. PPL. 8858

Prince, William, 1766-1842. See Prince, William Robert, 1795-1869. The Pamological manuel.

Prince, William, 1766-1842.
Annual catalogue of fruit and ornamental trees and plants, cultivated at the Linnaean botanic garden and nurseries...26th ed. New York [1831] 91 p. MH; NNC. 8859

Prince, William Robert, 1795-1869.
An oration, pronounced in the Methodist Episcopal Church, Hempstead, July 4, 1831. Being the 55th anniversary of American independence. By Wm. R. Prince, esq. Hempstead (L.I.), N.Y., Pr.

by W. Hutchinson, 1831. 15 p. DLC; MBAt; NBLiHi; NNQ; NSmb. 8860

---- The Pamological manual: or a treatise on fruits: containing descriptions of a great number of the most valuable varieties for the orchard and garden... By Wm. Robert Prince... Aided by Wm. Prince... 1st ed. New York, T. & J. Swords, G. & C. & H. Carvill, E. Bliss, Collins & Co., G. Thornburn & Sons, Judah Dobson; Philadelphia, I. B. Russell; Boston, Gideon B. Smith; Baltimore, James Winston; Richmond, Jos. Simons, Charleston, S.C. 2 pts. in 1. DLC; IaAS; KMK; MH; NN. 8861

Princeton Theological Seminary.
Catalogue of the officers and students of the Theological Seminary, Princeton, New Jersey, Jan. 1831. Princeton, Pr. by Wm. D'Hart, 1831. 8 p. CoU. 8862

Prindle's almanac for the year of our Lord 1832. Calculated for the meridian of New Haven by Charles Prindle, successor to Andrew Beers. New Haven, A. H. Maltby, 1831. 22 p. CtMW; MWA. 8863

Prison discipline society. (Boston)
Annual reports, 5th, 1831. Boston, 1831. CtHWatk. 8864

---- [Sixth annual report of the Board of Managers of the Prison Discipline Society. Boston, May 24, 1831. Boston, Perkins & Marvin. Stereotyped at the Boston Type & Stereotype Foundry, 1831] 100 p. CtHC; GDecCT; ICP; MeBat; MiD. 8865

The Progressive reader or Juvenile monitor. Concord, N.H., Hoag & Atwood, 1831. MH; VtHi. 8866

Protestant Episcopal Church in the U.S.A.
The Book of Common Prayer, and administration of the Sacraments...with the psalter or psalms of David. Boston, Massachusetts Episcopal Missionary Society, 1831. 405 p. MH; MMeT; MWA. 8867

---- Livre des prieres publiques, de L'administration des sacremens, et des autres rites et ceremonies de l'eglise, selon l'usage de l'eglise Protestante Episcopale dans les e'tats Unis d'Amerique: avec le psautier ou les psaumes de David: nouvelle edition revue et corrigee...par Rev. A. Verren. New York, T. et J. Swords, 1831. 464 p. CtHT; LNT; MWA; PPP; ScC. 8868

---- ---- New York, Protestant Episcopal Press, 1831. 394, 56 p. NjR; OHi; PHi; PPi; VtU. 8869

---- ---- Philadelphia, Latimer, 1831. 50, 371 p. GDecCT; NNP; OClW. 8870

---- ---- Standard ed. Philadelphia, J. Johanson, 1831. 421 p. IaDmDC; MdBD. 8871

---- General theological seminary. Proceedings of the board of trustees, June 28, 1831. New-York, Protestant Episcopal Press, 1831. 24 p. MdBD. 8872

---- Alabama Diocese.
Journal of a convention of the Protestant Episcopal Church, in the state of Alabama, held in Christ Church, Tuscaloosa, on Monday, January 3, 1831. To which is added, a Discourse delivered before that body by the Rev. Albert A. Muller, rector of Christ Church, Tuscaloosa.

Pub. by the Convention. Tuscaloosa, Pr. by Wiley, M'Guire & Henry, 1831. 28 p. ABCA; NN; NcD. 8873

---- Church Scholarship Society.
Appeal to the members of the Protestant Episcopal Church, in behalf of the Church Scholarship Society. By order of the Board of Directors... Hartford, H. & F. J. Huntington, 1831. 20 p. CtHT; MBD; MHi; PPL. 8874

---- Committee on the Psalms in metre.
Report of the Committee on the Psalms in metre appointed by the General convention of 1829. New York, Protestant Episcopal press, 1831. 42 p. CtHT; ICU. 8875

---- Delaware Diocese.
Journal of the Proceedings of the 41st Annual Convention of the Protestant Episcopal Church in the diocess of Delaware. June, 1831. Dover, Pr. by A. M. Schee [1831] 14 p. MBD. 8876

---- Domestic and foreign missionary society.
Periodical paper of the Domestic and foreign missionary society, of the Protestant Episcopal Church in the United States of America. New series-Vol. I. March, 1831-[September, 1832] [Philadelphia] Pr. by Wm. Stavely. TSewU. 8877

---- ---- Proceedings of the Board of Directors of the Domestic and Foreign Missionary Society of the Protestant Episcopal Church. Philadelphia, Pr. by Wm. Stavely, 1831. 44 p. CtHT; InID; MBD; MHi; MnHi. 8878

---- Eastern diocese.
Journal of the proceedings of the annual convention of the Protestant Episcopal Church, in the Eastern Diocese, held in Trinity Church, Boston, September 29 and 30, 1830, and in St. Peter's Church, Salem, Sept. 28 and 29, 1831. Boston, Stimpson and Clapp [1831] 33 p. MBD; MHi; WHi. 8879

---- General Convention.
Revision of the Canons of the Protestant Episcopal Church in the United States, by the Committee of the General Convention ...1831. [New York, 1831] 23 p. MH. 8880

---- Hymnal.
Hymns of the Protestant Episcopal church... Hartford, S. Andrus, 1831. 91 p. NNG. 8881

---- Kentucky Diocese.
Journal of the proceedings of the third convention... in Christ Church, Louisville...June 1831. Louisville, Pr. by Norwood & Palmer, 1831. 34 p. MBD; MHi; NN. 8882

---- Maryland Diocese.
Journal of a convention of the Protestant Episcopal Church of Maryland, held in Chestertown, Kent County, June 1st, 2d and 3d, 1831. Baltimore, Joseph Robinson, 1831. 56 p. MBD; MdBD; NBuDD. 8883

---- Massachusetts Diocese.
Journal of the proceedings of the annual convention of the Protestant Episcopal Church in the Commonwealth of Massachusetts, held in Saint Paul's Church, Boston, June 15 & 16, 1831. Cambridge, Pr. by E. W. Metcalf and Co., 1831. 60 p. InID; MiD-B; WHi. 8884

---- New Hampshire Diocese.
Journal of the proceedings of the thirty-first convention...

Great Falls, in Somersworth... July 25, 1831. Concord, Pr. by M'Farland and Ela-Statesman office, 1831. 16 p. MiD-B. 8885

---- New York Diocese.
Journal of the proceedings of the forty-sixth convention of the Protestant Episcopal Church in the state of New York: held in Trinity Church, in the city of New York on Thursday, October 6th, Friday, October 7th, and Saturday, October 8th. A.D. 1831. To which is prefixed a list of the clergy of the diocese. New York, Protestant Episcopal Press, 1831. 87 p. InID; MBD; NBuDD; NGH. 8886

---- New-York Protestant Episcopal Sunday School Society.
Annual report. New York, 1831- 1 nos. WHi. 8887

---- Ohio Diocese.
Journal of the Proceedings of the Fourteenth Annual Convention of the Protestant Episcopal Church in the Diocese of Ohio, 1831. Gambier, O., Pr. by Geo. W. Myers, at Acland Press, 1831. 39 p. MBD; NN; OCHP. 8888

---- Pennsylvania Diocese.
Journal of the proceedings of the forty-seventh convention of the Protestant Episcopal Church in the state of Pennsylvania, held in St. James' Church, in the city of Philadelphia, on Tuesday, May 17, and Wednesday, May 18, 1831. Philadelphia, Pr. by Jesper Harding, by order of the convention, 1831. 55 p. InID. 8889

---- South Carolina Diocese.
Journal of the proceedings of the 43 annual convention, of the Protestant Episcopal Church, in the diocese of South Carolina; held in St. Michael's Church, Charleston, on the 9. and 10. of February, 1831. Charleston, A. E. Miller, 1831. 42 p. MBD; NBuDD; NN; ScCC. 8890

---- Tennessee Diocese.
Journal of the proceedings of the third Convention of the Clergy and Laity of the Protestant Episcopal Church in the State of Tennessee, held in the Masonic Hall at Columbia, on Thursday, June 30,--Friday, July 1--and Saturday, July 2, 1831. Nashville, Pr. by Hunt Tardiff & Co., by order of the convention, 1831. 14 p. NBuDD; NH; NN. 8891

---- Vermont Diocese.
Journal of the proceedings of the Convention of the Protestant Episcopal Church in the State of Vermont, 1831. Woodstock, Pr. by David Watson, 1831. 15 p. MB; MHi. 8892

Protestant Episcopal Sunday & Adult School Society.
Annual report of the Protestant Episcopal Sunday and Adult School Society of Philadelphia. For 1831. Read May 24th, 1831. Philadelphia, Pr. by Wm. Stavely, 1831. 23 p. MdBD; WHi. 8893

Protestant Episcopal Tract Society.
The dairyman's daughter; an authentic and interesting narrative, in five parts. Communicated by a clergyman of the church of England. 3d ed. Stereotyped by James Conner. New York, Pr. at the Protestant Episcopal Press, for the Society [1831] 34 p. WHi. 8894

Protestant Female Tract Society.
Series of Tracts, No. 79. Morning visits to the rector's study; or, Conversations between a clergyman and a parishioner with his friend, on the subject of Baptism, published by the Protestant Episcopal Female Tract

Society of Baltimore. Baltimore, Pr. by John D. Toy, 1831. 36 p. ICP; MdBD; MdHi. 8895

Providence. Board of Assessors.
A list of persons assessed in the Town-Tax of thirty-five thousand dollars, voted by the Freemen of Providence, June, 1831, with the amount of valuation and tax of each. Providence, Hutchens & Shepard, 1831. 38 p. RHi; RNHi. 8896

---- Charters.
City Charter, proposed for the adoption of the Freemen of Providence, at a town meeting, to be holden October 22, 1831. Pr. for the use of the Freemen, by order of the town. Providence, R.I. Pr. by Cranston & Hammond, 1831. 16 p. DLC; RHi; RPB; RP. 8897

---- Committee on riots, 1831.
History of the Providence riots, from September 21 to September 24, 1831. Providence, H. H. Brown, 1831. 20 p. Ct; MWA; RH; RP; RPB. 8898

---- M. Robinson's Circulating Library.
Catalogue of additions, for 1830 & 1831. Providence, Cranston & Hammond, prs., 1831. 16 p. RPB. 8899

---- Second Baptist Church.
Confession of faith of the Church of Christ in Providence, unanimously received and appointed to be read by the church, and asserted to by each person offering themselves for membership. Providence, H. H. Brown, 1831. 8 p. RHi. 8900

Providence Atheneum.
Charter, Constitution and By-Laws of the Providence Atheneum. Providence, Cranston & Hammond, 1831. 14 p. MnU. 8901

Providence dispensary.
Rules and Regulations of the Providence Dispensary, instituted March, 1829... With a list of the original contributors, and also the managers and officers, for 1831. Providence, Pr. by H. H. Brown, 1831. 12 p. MH; RHi; RP; RPB. 8902

No entry. 8903

Provident Institution for Savings, Boston.
The plan and by-laws of the Provident institution for savings in the town of Boston, with the regulations of the trustees and rules of the board of investment. Boston, Pr. by Hugh H. Tuttle, 1831. 18 p. WHi. 8904

Pry, Paul (pseud.), 1795-1840.
Letters from England description of various scenes and occurrences during a short visit to that country, by Paul Pry. Boston, Munroe & Francis, 1831. 112 p. RNHi. 8905

The Psalmist, or Chorister's Companion, consisting of psalm tunes, adapted principally for the use of public worship; with a few hymn tunes and longer pieces, suited to other religious occasions. Boston, Richardson, Lord and Holbrook, 1831. 152 p. ICN; ICP; MEab; MH; MHi. 8906

Punctuation Personified; or, pointing made easy. By Mr. Stops. Steubenville, J. & B. Turnbull, 1831. 10 l. PP. 8907

Purify, John.

A selection of hymns and spiritual songs, in two parts--Part I, containing the songs. Part II, containing the hymns--Designed for the use of the congregation. By John Purify... Raleigh, J. Gales & Sons, 1831. 225, 68 p. NcD. 8908

Putnam, John March.
English grammar, with an improved syntax. Part I. Comprehending at one view what is necessary to be committed to memory. Part II. Containing a recapitulation, with various illustrations and critical remarks. Designed for the use of schools. By J. M. Putnam. Concord, N.H., Hoag & Atwood, 1831. 162 p. MB; MH; Nh-Hi. 8909

Putnam, John Milton, 1794-1871.
The Pilgrim fathers and American independence. An address to the Sabbath School children in Dunbarton, delivered July 4, 1831. By John M. Putnam, pastor of the Congregational Church in that place...Concord, Pr. by M'Farland & Ela, 1831. 16 p. DLC; MBC; MiD-B; Nh; Nh-Hi. 8910

Putnam, Samuel.
The Analytical reader; containing lessons in simultaneous reading and defining; with spelling from the same... 9th ed. Dover, N.H., S. C. Stevens, 1831. 228 p. CtMW; MH; Nh-Hi. 8911

---- Sequel to the Analytical Reader; in which the original design is extended so as to embrace the explanation of phrases and figurative language. By Samuel Putnam. 2d ed., Dover E. French; Boston, Perkins & Marvin, 1831. 300 p. CtMW; MDeeP; MeHi; MsG; NRU-W; NSyU. 8912

Q

Questions, adapted to Paley's Moral and Political Philosophy. By a citizen of Massachusetts... New-York, Collins and Hannay, 1831. 41 p. MoInRC. 8913

R

No entry. 8914

Rafferty, Patrick.
A short history of the Protestant reformation; chiefly selected from Protestant authors...Pittsburgh, Johnston & Stockton, 1831. 236 p. MdBS; NcMHi; NPStA; OCMtSM; OCX; PPPrHi; PV. 8915

Raffles, Thomas.
Memoirs of the Life and Ministry of... T. Spencer Liverpool, with a poem, occasioned by his death, and an appendix, containing a selection from his papers 2d ed., etc. Philadelphia, American Sunday School Union, 1831. IAlS; Nh-Hi. 8916

Rafinesque (Prof. Constantine Samuel)
Continuation of a Monograph of the Bivalve Shells of the River Ohio, and other Rivers of the Western States...With a supplement on the Fossil Bivalve Shells...[Philadelphia, William Sharpless, pr., 1831] MB; MH-Z. 8917

----Enumeration and account of some remarkable objects of the cabinet of Prof. Rafinesque... being animals, shells, plants, and fossils...Philadelphia, Wm. Sharpless [1831?] 8 p. MB;

MH-Z; MWA. 8918

Railroad journal, pub. by D. K. Minor, v. 1-. New York, 1831. PHi; PPL. 8919

Rainsford, J. A.
An oration, pronounced at Abington on the fifty-fifth anniversary of American Independence, July 4, 1831, by J. A. Rainsford, published by request. Boston, Light & Harris, Lyceum press, 1831. 24 p. MWeyHi. 8920

Ramsay, Edward Bannerman.
Reminiscences of Scottish life and character. By E. B. Ramsay. From the 7th Edinburgh ed. Boston, Ticknor & Fields, 1831. 297 p. MWiW. 8921

Rancher, Abraham.
Circular of Mr. Rancher, to his constituents of the tenth Congressional District of North Carolina. Washington, 1831. NcU. 8922

Randall, Phineas.
A treatise on Christian Baptism and open communion. Entered according to act of Congress, in the year 1831, by Phineas Randall, in the Clerk's Office of the District Court of Vermont. [n.p., n.d.] 12 p. DLC. 8923

Randolph, Mrs. Mary.
The Virginia housewife: or, Methodical cook. By Mary Randolph... Stereotype ed., with amendments & additions. Baltimore, Plaskitt & Cugle [1831?] 180 p. MB; MdHi; NPV; Vi; ViU. 8924

---- ---- Washington, Thompson. & Homans, stereotyped by Lucas & Neal, 1831. 180 p. MB; NGlf. 8925

Randolph, Thompson.
The Practical Teacher; being an easy and rational introduction to Arithmetic. Designed for beginners of every age, adapted to every mode of instruction and particularly the monitorial. By Thompson Randolph. 3d ed., rev. and corr. Philadelphia, Uriah Hunt, 1831. 192 p. ICP; NcWsHi. 8926

Ratcliffe, Mrs.
The Romance of the Forest, interspersed with some pieces of Poetry. New York, Pr. by Wm. Broadwell & Co., 1831. 2 vols. MBilHi; WRichM. 8927

Ratier, F. S.
A practical formulary of the Parision hospitals; exhibiting the prescription employed by the physicians and surgeons of those establishments. With remarks illustrative of their doses, mode of administration, and appropriate application...Trans. from the 3d ed. of the French, with notes and illustrations, by R. D. M'Lellan. New York, Pr. by Clayton & Van Norden, for F. & N. G. Carnes, 1831. 262 p. MB; MdBJ; NBMS; NNN; ViNoM. 8928

Rawson, Susanna (Haswell)
Rebecca...3d American ed. Boston, Pr. for the booksellers, 1831. 288 p. ICU. 8929

Ray, Joseph.
Inaugural dissertation on some of the abuses of blood letting, by Joseph Ray, M.D. Cincinnati, 1831. 33 p. OC. 8930

Rayner, Menzies, 1770-1850.
St. Paul, a Universalist; a sermon delivered in the Universalist Church in Portland, November 6, 1831. By Menzies Rayner, pastor of said Church. Pub. by Menzies Rayner, Jr. Portland, Day, Frazer & Co., 1831. 16 p. MBC; MMeT-Hi. 8931

Reading, Pa. Ordinances.

Ordinances of the Corporation of the Borough of Reading. Together with the Act of Incorporation. Reading, Pr. by Robert Johnson, 1831. 42 p. PReaHi. 8932

The ready reckoner; or, Traders' companion, showing at one view the wholesale or retail value of any commodity, from one quarter of a cent up to twelve dollars. in dollars & cents. With a variety of useful tables. Harrisburg, Pa., G. S. Peters, 1831. 120 p. MnHi. 8933

Reasons for embracing the Catholic Religion or the motives which lately influenced a Protestant gentleman to unite himself with the Catholic church. Hartford, Conn., U.S. Catholic press, 1831. 62 p. MD-B; MiDSH; MoSU. 8934

The Recluse: a semi-monthly literary journal. Edited by Geo. W. Warren. Vol. 1, No. 1, [July 1st, 1831] New Bedford, 1831. 16 p. 8935

The red book and Mary Anne. By the author of "Little Henry and his bearer." New York, Pendleton & Hill, 1831. 69 p. MdBD. 8936

The Red Rover, a tale. By the author of the Pilot, &c. &c. "Ye speak like honest man: pray God Ye prove so!" 2d ed. Philadelphia, Carey, Leo & Carey, 1831. 2 vols. KyU; NcC. 8937

Redfield, William C.
Remarks on prevailing storms. New York, 1831. 36 p. MB; N. 8938

Reed, John, 1786-1850.
Pennsylvania Blackstone; being a modification of the Commentaries of Sir William Blackstone with numerous alterations and additions... Laws of Pennsylvania, in three volumes by John Reed. Carlisle, Pr. by Geo. Fleming, 1831. 3 vols. IaU-L; MH-L; NjP; PHi; PU. 8939

A reference and distance map of the state of New York. New Haven, Conn. [I. Pierce, 1831] 1 fold. col. map. NIC. 8940

Reformed Church in America.
The Acts and Proceedings of the General Synod of the Reformed Dutch Church... From June 1827, to June 1831, inclusive. With a copious index. New York, Vanderpool & Cole, 1831. 397 p. IaPeC; MiD-B. 8941

---- Additional hymns, adopted by the General Synod of the Reformed Dutch Church in North America at their session June, 1831, and authorized to be used in the churches under their care. New York, Mercien, 1831. 190 p. DLC; RPB; TxU. 8942

---- Proceedings of the German Reformed Synod of Pennsylvania Adjacent States, held at Beanestown, Lancaster county, September 4th, 5th, & 6th, 1831. Reading, Pr. by John Ritter & Co., 1831. 16 p. PLT. 8943

---- Verhandlungen der Deutsch Reformirten Synode von Pennsylvanien und den angränzenden Staaten. Gehalten zu Riemstaun, Lancaster County, den 4ten, 5ten und 6ten September, 1831. Reading, Gedruckt bey Yohann Ritter und Comp., 1831. 16 p. PLERCHi. 8944

---- General Synod.
The acts and proceedings of the General Synod of the Reformed Dutch Church in North America, at Albany, June, 1831. New York, Pr. for General

Synod, 1831. 90 p. IaPeC. 8945

---- ---- Acts and proceedings of the General Synod of the Reformed Dutch Church in North America, convened in extra session at New York on Wednesday, November, 9, 1831. New York [1831] 14 p. IaPeC. 8946

---- ---- Synodal Verhandlungen der Hochdeutschen Reformirten Kirche in den Vereinigten Staaten von Nord Amerika. Gehalten in Harrisburg, Pa. den 2sten September, 1831, und folgenden tagen. Harrisburg, Pa., Gedruckt bey Heinrich Boute, 1831. 29 p. PLERCHi. 8947

Refutation of two passages in writings of Thomas Jefferson aspersing character of Jas. A. Bayard. Philadelphia, 1831. 14 p. PHi. 8948

Reid, Robert, 1781-1844.
Doctor Watts' Preface to the Psalms of David, imitated in the language of the New-Testament... West-Union, Ohio, Repr. by J. T. Crapsey, 1831. 48 p. CSmH; NN. 8949

Reid, Robert W.
William Rollinson Engraver, a monograph prepared by Robert W. Reid, & Charles Rollinson. New York, 1831. 62 p. PHi. 8950

Reinhard, Franz Volkmar, 1753-1812.
Plan of the founder of Christianity, by F. V. Volkmar. Tr. from the 5th German ed., by Oliver A. Taylor... New York, Carvill, 1831. 359 p. CU; DLC; GDecCT; MBC; NjR; OO; RPA; TNT; VtU. 8951

The Religious Monitor, and Evangelical Repository. Albany, N.Y., B. D. Packard & Co., 1831. IaK; NAl; NcMHi; NcWfC. 8952

Remarks on the auction system ... New-York, Elliott & Parker, 1831. 20 p. NN. 8953

Remarks on the militia system... New York, American Peace Society, 1831. 8 p. NHi; OC. 8954

[Rennie, James], 1787-1867.
The architecture of birds. illus. Boston, Lilly & Wait, and Carter and Hendee; New York, G. & C. & H. Carvill, and E. Bliss [etc., etc.] 1831. 390 p. MB; MB-FA; MiDU; NCH; NRU; Nj. 8955

---- ... Insect transformation. Boston, Lilly & Wait (late Wells & Lilly), 1831. 415 p. GU; InNea; MB; MeBat; MiDU; NRU; Nj; RP; ViU; WHi; WU. 8956

---- The Menageries. Quadrupeds, described and drawn from living subjects. Boston, Lilly & Wait, 1831. 419 p. CtHT; KyDC; MH; NbOM; PHarU; ScNC. 8957

---- ... The natural history of insects... New York, J. & J. Harper, 1831-35. 2 vols. ArCH; CtHT; GU; LNP; MdHi; NjP; PU; TNP. 8958

Rensselaer County, N.Y. Medical Society.
By-laws, medical ethics & list of members. 1831. PPCP. 8959

Renwick, James, 1790-1863.
Syllabus of lectures on chemistry. By James Renwick, LL.D., in Columbia College. New York, G. F. Hopkins & Son, prs. & stationers, 1831. 55 p. DLC; NNC. 8960

Reply to "An examination of the banking system of Massachusetts." Boston, Cottons and Barnard, 1831. 24 p. MH-BA. 8961

A reply to the address of John L. Hunter, Senator of St. Bartholomew's Parish, By a constituent... October, 1831. 15 p. ScU. 8962

Report of a committee on the Boston and Lowell railroad. Boston, 1831. 14 p. DLC. 8963

Report of the Committee, appointed, at the "Free Trade Meeting" holden at Portland, August 24, 1831. To preface an address on the subject of the Tariff Laws and Free Trade. Portland, Eastern Argus Extra, 1831. 8 p. MeLewB. 8964

Result of an ecclesiastical council, convened in the Vestry of the Howard St. Church, Salem, on Wednesday, July 27, 1831. Boston, Pr. by Peirce & Parker, 1831. 16 p. CtSoP; MB; MBC; MBD; NjR. 8965

A review of "An oration delivered before the young men of Boston, on the Fourth of July, 1831." [Boston, 1831] 16 p. DLC; MH; WHi; WaPS. 8966

A review of the constitution and discipline of the Methodist Protestant church, by a layman. Baltimore, John J. Harrod, 1831. 36 p. MdHi; PPL; TxDaM. 8967

Review of the late negotiation and arrangement with the British government, respecting the West India trade; being the letters which appeared in the United States gazette, signed X. Y., in the summer of 1831, now first collected, with an appendix. Philadelphia, 1831. 47 p. MH-BA. 8968

Review of the speech of Harrison Gray Otis, mayor of the city of Boston...By a citizen of Boston. Boston, Pr. by Beals and Homer, 1831. 40 p. CtY; DLC; KyDC; MB; MdHi; PPAmP. 8969

Review of the speech of Mr. Benton, against the renewal of the charter of the Bank of the United States. Delivered in the Senate of the United States, February 2, 1831. Intended for the American Quarterly Review, but published originally in the National Gazette. Nashville, Hunt Tardiff and co., prs., 1831. 39 p. T. 8970

Rhinehart, William R.

The American or union harmonist; or a choice collection of psalm tunes, hymns and anthems, selected from the most approved authors, and well adapted to all Christian Churches, singing schools and private families. Chambersburg, Pa., Pr. by Henry Ruby, 1831. 146 p. TKL-Mc. 8971

Rhode Island.

At the General Assembly of the State of Rhode-Island and Providence Plantations, begun and holden (by adjournment) at East Greenwich, within and for said state, on the second Monday of January, in the Year of Our Lord one thousand eight hundred and thirty- one, and of Independence the Fifty-fifth. Present: His Excellency James Fenner, Governor. His Honor Charles Collins, Lieut.-Governor. Providence, Pr. by J. Jones, 1831. 51 p. DLC; RNCH. 8972

---- At the General Assembly of the State of Rhode Island and Providence Plantations, begun and holden (by adjournment) at Newport, within and for said State, on the Third Monday of June, in the Year of Our Lord One thousand eight hundred and thirty-one, and of Independence the Fifty-

Fifth. Present, His Excellency Lemuel H. Arnold, Governor. His Honor Charles Collins, Lieut. Governor. Providence, Wm. Marshall, pr. to State, 1831. 67 p. DLC; Nb; RNCH. 8973

---- At the General Assembly of the State of Rhode-Island and Providence Plantations, begun and holden at Newport, within and for said State, on the First Wednesday of May, in the Year of Our Lord one thousand eight hundred and thirty-one, and of Independence the Fifty-fifth. Present His Excellency James Fenner, Governor. His Honor Charles Collins, Lieut. Governor. Providence, Pr. by J. Jones, 1831. 36 p. DLC; RNCH. 8974

---- At the General Assembly of the State of Rhode Island and Providence Plantations, begun and holden at South Kingstown, within and for said State, on the last Monday of October, in the Year of Our Lord one thousand eight hundred and thirty-one, and of Independence the Fifty-sixth. Present His Excellency Lemuel H. Arnold, Governor. His Honor Charles Collins, Lieut. Governor. Providence, Wm. Marshall, pr., Oct. 1831. 90 p. DLC; Nb; RNR. 8975

---- Public laws of the state of Rhode Island and Providence Plantations, passed since the session of the General Assembly, January, 1831. [Providence? 1831?] 749-810 p. In-SC; MdBB; Ms. 8976

The Rhode-Island Almanack... 1832...By Isaac Bickerstaff, Esq., Philom. Providence [R.I.] H. H. Brown [1831] 23 p. CSmH; DLC; NN; TxU; WHi. 8977

Rhode-Island anti-masonic state convention, Providence, 1831.

Proceedings of the Rhode-Island Anti-Masonic State Convention. September 14, 1831. Providence, Pr. at The Daily Advertiser Office, 1831. 28 p. DLC; MB; PPFM; RP; WHi. 8978

Rhode Island Medical Society.

The act of incorporation; together with the medical police, by-laws and rules of the Rhode Island Medical Society... Providence, Pr. by Cranston & Hammond, 1831. 31 p. DLC; MH; MH-M; RPB. 8979

The Rhode-Island Register, and Counting House Companion...1832 ...Providence, H. H. Brown [1831] 48 p. WHi. 8980

Richardson, William Merchant.

The New-Hampshire justice of the peace. 2d ed. imp. Concord, Horatio Hill & co., 1831. 299 p. MH; MH-L; NcBe; OClWHi. 8981

Richey, Matthew.

Effective benevolence inculcated by our Lord's example; a sermon preached in Trinity Church, on Wednesday, March 23, 1831, in order to promote the objects of the Methodist Benevolent Society of Charleston, S.C. Charleston, S.C., J. S. Burges, 1831. 22 p. NcD. 8982

Richmond, Legh.

Little Jane, the young cottager. By the Rev. Legh Richmond, Rector of Turvey, Bedfordshire. Complete ed. Stereotyped by Jas. Conner, for the New York Protestant Episcopal Tract Society. New York, Pr. at the Protestant Episcopal Press, for the Society [1831] 43 p. WHi. 8983

Richmond, Virginia.

Ordinances of the corporation of the city of Richmond, and the acts of the Assembly relating thereto. Pub. by the authority of the Common council. Richmond, Pr. by John Warrock, 1831. 140 p. C; DLC; IU; MH-L; MiU; NN; NcD; NcU; PHi; Vi; ViRVal; ViU; ViW. 8984

---- Common Council. Finance Committee.

Estimate of the Resources and expenditures of the City of Richmond... Mar. 1st, 1831, to Feb. 29th, 1832, inclusive. [Richmond, 1831] CSmH; DLC. 8985

---- Union Theological Seminary in Virginia.

Plan of the Union Theological Seminary of the General Assembly under the care of the Synods of Virginia and North Carolina with a brief sketch of its history. Richmond, Pr. by J. Macfarlan, 1831. 16 p. CSmH; IEG; MWA; NN; PPPrHi; ViRUT. 8986

Riley, James, 1777-1840.

An authentic narrative of the loss of the American Brig "Commerce," wrecked on the western coast of Africa, in the month August, 1815...By James Riley. Preceded by a brief sketch of the author's life...Illustrated and embellished with ten copper-plate engravings; revised and his life continued, by the author, in January. 1828. Hartford, S. Andrus & Son, 1831. 271 p. MoSHi; TMeSC. 8987

Ripley, George, 1802-1880.

The Divinity of Jesus Christ. 3d ed. No. 33. Boston, Gray & Bowen, for The American Unitarian Association, 1831. 28 p. DLC; ICMe; MB-MP; MH; MeB; MeBat; Nh. 8988

Ripley, Thomas Baldwin, 1795-1876.

A selection of hymns, for conference and prayer meetings and other occasions. By Thomas B. Ripley, pastor of the Baptist Church in Bangor. Md. ed., with numerous additions and improvements. Bangor, Burton & Carter, 1831. 160 p. CBB; NNUT; RPB. 8989

Rishworth, Edward.

Letter from Edward Rishworth to Gen. Endicott, 1656. (In collection of the Main Historical Society.) Portland, Day, Frazer & Co., 1831. (1st ser.) v. 1. p. 299-300. DLC; MeBa. 8990

Ritchie, Leitch.

The romance of history. France. By Leitch Ritchie. New York, J. & J. Harper, 1831. 2 vols. CtHT; LNH; MB; PPA; RJa. 8991

Riverhead Temperance Society, Riverhead, L.I.

Annual report. New York, 1831. DLC. 8992

Rivinus, Edward Fiorens.

A catalogue of the medical library of the Philadelphia almshouse, prepared agreeably to a resolution of the Board of managers, by E. F. Rivinus, M.D. Philadelphia, 1831. 174 p. DSG; NNN; PPL; WHi. 8993

---- On the operation of physical causes upon the constitution, the health, and diseases of man. Philadelphia, Skerrett, 1831. 26 p. DLC; NN; PHi; ScC. 8994

Robbins, Archibald, 1792-1865.

A journal, comprising an account of the loss of the Brig Commerce, of Hartford, (Conn.) James Riley, master, upon the western coast of Africa, Aug. 28, 1815, also the slaver & sufferings of the author and the rest of the crew upon the desert of Zahara, in the years 1815-16-17; with accounts of the manners, customs, and habits of the wandering Arabs; also, a brief hist. and geog. view of the continent of Africa. By A. Robbins. 20th ed. Hartford, S. Andrus, 1831. 275 p. NN; NbO; OClWHi; OMC; TNP; WHi. 8995

[Robbins, Clement]
Vampires of New York. (No. 1) [New York?] Pub. for the proprietor, 1831. MH. 8996

Robbins, Eliza, 1763-1853.
Introduction to popular lessons, for the use of small children in schools... New York, M'Elrath and Bangs, 1831. 180 p. DLC; MH; PPM. 8997

---- Tales from American history; containing the principal facts in the life of Christopher Columbus. For the use of young persons, and schools. By the author of American popular lessons. New York, Wm. Burgess, 1831. (x), 238 p. DLC; MB; MH; NcDaD; Pu-Penn. 8998

Robbins, Royal, 1787-1861.
The world desplayed in its history and geography, embracing, A history of the world, from the creation to the present day; with general views of the politics, religion, military and naval affairs, arts, literature, manners, customs, and society of ancient as well as modern nations...to which is added, An outline of modern geography... New York, W. W. Reed & co., 1831. 2 vols. in 1. CLCM; Ct; NN; OO. 8999

Robert & William or the beauties of nature. ...New-York, Pr. and sold by Mahlon Day, at the new juvenile book-store, 1831. 23 p. MSherHi. 9000

Roberts, Daniel, b. 1811.
Address delivered before the Temperance Society of Wallingford and its vicinity, July 4, 1831. Rutland, Herald Office, 1831. 14 p. WHi. 9001

Roberts, Joseph Jr.
Observations made at Friends' Observatory in Philadelphia during the solar eclipse of Febr. 12, 1831. PPAN. 9002

Roberts, William, 1767-1849.
The portraiture of a Christian gentleman. By W. Roberts... New York, T. & J. Swords, 1831. 170 p. LU; MB; MdBD; PPL-R; VtU. 9003

Robertson, William, 1721-1793.
...An historical disquisition concerning the knowledge which the ancients had of India; and the progress of trade with that country, prior to the discovery of the passage to it by the Cape of Good Hope. With an appendix... New-York, Pr. by J. & J. Harper, 1831. 146 p. CtHC; KyLo; LNH; MoS; OClWHi; RPA. 9004

---- History of America. By W. Robertson. New York, Harpers, 1831. 520 p. WvSht. 9005

---- ... The history of Scotland during the reigns of Queen Mary and of King James VI till his accession to the crown of England. With a review of the Scottish history previous to the period; and an appendix, containing original letters. New York, Harper, 1831. 460, 146 p. CBPSR; MoS; RPA; ScDue; TNP. 9006

---- The history of the discovery and settlement of America, by William Robertson, D.D. ... Harper's stereotype ed. New-York, Pr. by J. & J. Harper, 1831. 570 p. DLC; GU; MH; OO; P; WvW. 9007

Robertson, William.
Sacred harmony or council of peace; A divine poem by Rev. William Robertson. 2d ed. New York, Pr. at the Greenwitch Printing Office, 1831. 36 p. DLC; MB; MCNC; RPB. 9008

Robinson, Charles.
An address delivered before the Hartford county agricultural society at their annual meeting, October 28, 1830. By Charles Robinson... Hartford, Pr. by Hudson & Skinner, 1831. 11 p. CtHT-W; CtSoP; NNUT. 9009

Robinson, Frederick.
Letter to the Hon. Rufus Choate containing a brief exposure of Law Craft and some of the encroachments upon the rights and liberties of the people. Boston, 1831. 21 p. MH-L. 9010

Robinson, James.
A compend of book-keeping by single entry; designed for the use of schools... By James Robinson ... Boston, Hilliard, Gray, Little and Wilkins, 1831. 28 p. DLC; MH. 9011

---- Elementary lessons in intellectual arithmetic, illustrated upon analytic and inductive principles: By James Robinson... Boston, Hilliard, Gray, Little and Wilkins, 1831. 84 p. ICBB; MB; MBAt; MH; MWfo. 9012

Robinson, John.
A description of, and critical remarks on the picture of Christ healing the sick in the temple; painted by Benjamin West... and presented by him to the Pennsylvania hospital. By John Robinson ... Philadelphia, 1831. 24 p. CtHC; MH. 9013

Robinson, Moncure, 1802-1891.
Reports on Routes for crossing the Allegheny Mountain, Read in the Senate of Pa. March 14, 1831. By M. Robinson and Stephen H. Lang. Harrisburg, 1831. 32 p. NIC; PHi. 9014

Robinson, Thomas.
The last days of Bishop Heber. By Thomas Robinson. New York, Y. & J. Swords, 1831. MNe; MdBD; NjR; OClW; PPiW; ViAl; WM. 9015

Rochester, New York. Fire Department. Company No. 4.
By-laws of Fire Company, No. 4. Adopted January 17, 1831. Rochester, Marshall and Dean, 1831. 8 p. NRHi. 9016

Rodriguez, Alonso.
The practice of Christian and religious perfection. Written in Spanish by V. F. Rodriguez of the Society of Jesus. Tr. from the French copy of M. l'abbe Regnier des Marais... Philadelphia, E. Cummiskey, 1831. 2 vols. MdW; MoSU; NjR; OCX; PV. 9017

Rogers [David L.], 1799-1877.
Description of a new instrument for exercising enlarged tonsils. New York, Clayton & Van Norden [1831] 3 p. DSG. 9018

Rogers, Mrs. Hester Ann, 1756-1794.
Account of the experience of Hester Ann Rogers, and her funeral sermon, by Rev. T. Coke, LL.D. to which is added her spiritual letters... New York, J. Emory & B. Waugh, 1831. 243 p. ICU; MB; NNG. 9019

Rogers, Robert, 1731-1795.
Reminiscences of the French war: containing Rogers' expeditions with the New-England rangers under his command, as published in London in 1765; with

notes and illustrations. To which is added an account of the life and military services of Maj. Gen. John Stark; with notices and anecdotes of other officers distinguished in the French and revolutionary wars. Concord, N.H., L. Roby, 1831. 275 p. IHi; MiD-B; MnM; OCl; P. 9020

Rogers, Samuel, 1763-1855.
The poetical works of Rogers, Campbell, J. Montgomery, Lamb, and Kirke White. Complete in 1 vol. Philadelphia, Carey & Lea, 1831. CoD; CoPu; MH; NBuCC; TMeL; ViAl; ViU. 9021

Roland, John.
The shepherd's song. Composed for the piano forte, and respectfully dedicated to Miss Rebecca Keim, by John Roland. Philadelphia, G. Willig [183-?] 3 p. ViU. 9022

Rollin, Charles, 1661-1741.
The ancient history of the Egyptians, Carthaginians, Assyrians, Babylonians, Medes and Persians. Grecians and Macedonians. By Charles Rollin...Tr. from the French. To which is prefixed, a life of the author, by the Rev. R. Lyman, A.M. From the 15th London ed., rev. and corr. Philadelphia, J. P. Ayres, 1831. 8 vols. TJoT; TxDa. 9023

Romaine, William, 1714-1795.
Treatises upon the life, walk and triumph of faith. By the Rev. W. Romaine. Hartford, Conn., Silas Andrus, 1831. 392 p. GDecCT; NWatt; NcMHi; OO; ScCoB; TxAuPT. 9024

Ross, Edward C.
Elements of algebra, translated from the French of Mr. Bourdon. for the use of the cadets of the U.S. Military Academy. By Lieut. Edward C. Ross ...New York, Pr. by Clayton & Van Norden, for E. B. Clayton, 1831. 389 p. IaDaM; NICLA; PReaA. 9025

Ross, Frederick A.
Faith, according to Common Sense, written for the Calvinistic Magazine, by Fred Ross. Part I. Rogersville, Tennessee, 1831. 21 p. T. 9026

Rossini, Gioacchino Antonio. 1792-1868.
Le barbier de Séville, on La précaution inutile, opéra-comique en quatre actes, d'aprés Beaumarchais et le drame italien, paroles ajustées sur la musique de Rossini par Castil-Blase. The barber of Sevill, or The useless precaution a comic opera in four acts; altered from Beaumarchais and the Italian drama. The words adapted to the music of Rossini. By Castil-Blaze. Tr. for the American publishers. Boston, 1831. 99 p. CtY; PPL. 9027

---- Cinderella, or the fairy queen & glass slipper. Comic opera in three acts...The music composed by Rossini, being selections from his operas of La Cenerentola, Maometto secondo, Armida, & Guillaume Tell. The whole arranged and adapted to the English stage by M. Rophino Lacy. With additions by Signor G. Pons. (Vocal score.) New York, Bourne [1831] Irreg. paged. Plates. MB; MH. 9028

---- Le comte Ory, opera, en deux actes, par M. Scrib and Delestre Poirsan. Sur la musique de Rossini. Translated literally for the use of visitors to the French opera... Baltimore, E. J. Coale, 1831. 61 p. NN; RPB. 9029

---- Midst doubts confusing. Quintett (S. J. Bar. B.B.) in the opera of Cinderella. (accomp. for pianoforte.) New York, Bourne [1831?] 6 p. MB. 9030

---- (Sir a secret.) The celebrated comic duet (Bar. B.) in the opera of Cinderella. (accomp. for pianoforte.) New York, Bourne [1831?] 17 p. MB. 9031

---- Songs, duetts, concerted pieces and choruses in the new comic opera, in three acts called Cinderella, or The Fairy Queen and the Glass Slipper. The music by Rossini. New York, J. C. Spear, 1831. 19 p. MB; MH; NNMvCN. 9032

---- Swift as the flash! (Solo, S., and choruses. T.T.B.) In the opera of Cinderella. Air from Rossini's opera, Guillaume Tell. Arranged & the variations composed, by G. Pons. (Accomp. for pianoforte.) New York, Bourne, 1831. 12 p. MB. 9033

Rousse, M. B.
Instinct, habits, and sagacity of animals, in a series of letters on natural history, translated from the French of M. B. Rousse, with additions and cuts. New York, Sleight, 1831. 285 p. CtMW; MH. 9034

Rowbotham, John, 1793-1846.
A practical grammar of the French language. By J. Rowbotham. 1st Amer. ed., with alterations and additions. By F. M. J. Surault... Cambridge, Hilliard and Brown, 1831. 324 p. DLC; MBC; NNC. 9035

Rowe, Elizabeth (Singer), 1674-1737.
Mrs. Rowe's Devout exercises of the heart. Revised at her request, by Rev. Isaac Watts... with notices of her life, compiled by Rev. William Jenks... Boston, William Hyde, 1831. 192 p. MB; NN. 9036

Rowland, Daniel.
Eight sermons on practical and experimental religion, preached by Daniel Rowland, minister of the Gospel, South Wales. First translated into English in the year of our Lord 1774, now revised and published with a hymn and short prayer, suitable to each subject. By Stephen Gerrish. New York, Pr. by G. F. Bunce, 1831. 39 p. ICU. 9037

Rowlett, John.
Rowlett's tables of discount; or, Interest showing at sight the interest on each and every dollar... By John Rowlett. Philadelphia, Adam Waldie, 1831. 208 p. In; KyLo; LNH; MB; MiU. 9038

Rowson, Mrs. Susanna (Haswell), 1762-1824.
Charlotte Temple, a tale of truth. By Mrs. Rowson, late of the New Theatre, Philadelphia; author of 'Victoria,' 'The Inquisitor,' 'Fille de Chambre,' &c. Cincinnati, Wm. Conclin, 1831. 155 p. IdHi; MWA; MWH. 9039

---- ---- New York, John Lomax, 1831. 138 p. MB-AT; MiD-B; NN. 9040

---- Rebecca; or, The Fille de Chambre. 3d Amer. ed. Boston, Pr. for the booksellers, 1831. 288 p. ICBB; IUC. 9041

Roxbury, Massachusetts. Second Church.
Order of exercises at the ordination of Mr. George Whitney, as pastor of the Second Church and Society in Roxbury, on Wednesday, June 15, 1831. Boston, Pr. by I. R. Butler [1831] Broadside. MB; MHi. 9042

---- Yoeman Association.
Regulations of the Roxbury Yoeman Association for the detection and prosecution of trespassers on fields, orchards and gardens, in the town of Roxbury, and vicinity. Boston, Pr. by Wm. Smith, 1831. 12 p. MBB. 9043

Royall, Mrs. Anne (Newport), 1769-1854.
Mrs. Royall's southern tour, or, Second series of the Black book. By Mrs. Anne Royall... Washington, 1831. 3 vols. CtHC; ICLoy; MdBJ; PHi; ScU. 9044

Rudd, John Churchill, 1779-1848.
A series of discourses addressed to young men, on the principles and duties by which their conduct should be regulated. By John C. Rudd, D.D., rector of St. Peter's Church, Auburn, N.Y. 2d ed. Auburn, Pr. by Henry B. Ten Eyck, at the Gospel Messenger Office, 1831. 132 p. MH; MoS; NNG. 9045

Ruddiman, [Thomas]
The rudiments of the Latin tongue... New York, Collins & Hannay, 1831. 168 p. NN. 9046

Ruggles [Thomas], 1704-1770.
The usefulness and expediency of soldiers as discovered by reason and experience, and countenanced and supported by the Gospel. A sermon preached to an Artillery Company at Guilford, May 25, 1736. On the day of their first choosing their officers and now made publick [sic] at their earnest desire and charge. By Thomas Ruggles. Hartford, Pr. by Geo. W. Kappel, 1831. 29 p. DLC; MB; NN. 9047

Rumford Institute, Waltham, Mass.
Catalogue of the books belonging to the Rumford institute. Cambridge, E. W. Metcalf & Co., 1831. 28 p. MB. 9048

Ruschenberger, William Samuel Waithman, 1807-1895.
Elements of Herpetology and of Ichthyology. By W. S. W. Ruschenberger. Philadelphia, Grigg & Elliot, 1831. ScNC. 9049

Rush, Benjamin, 1745-1813.
An account of the life and character of Christopher Ludwick... By Benjamin Rush, M.D. First published in the year 1801. Rev. and repub. by directions of the Philadelphia Society for the establishment and support of charity schools. To which is added, an account of the origin, progress, and present condition of that institution. Philadelphia, Pr. by Garden & Thompson for the Society, 1831. 61 p. Ct; MNU; MWA; PU; TNU. 9050

Rush, Richard, 1780-1859.
A letter of "Temple" on the present Whig party in England. York, Pa., 1831. PPL. 9051

---- Letter on Freemasonry, by Hon. Richard Rush, to committee of citizens of York co., Pennsylvania. Boston, Kimball and Johnson, 1831. 16 p. IaCrM; MB; MBAt; MH; NjP. 9052

---- ---- Boston, J. Marsh & Co., 1831. 20 p. DLC; MH; NjP; PHi; WHi. 9053

---- Letter of Hon. Richard Rush, in reply to anti-masonic committee of York county, Pa., on subject of Masonry to which is added notices of opinion of Judge Nelson, and decisions of jury, in case of Elisha Adams, and report of the special counsel relating to all Masonic trials at Lockport. Lyons, N.Y., Holley and Whitney, pr., 1831. 40 p.

IaCrM. 9054

---- Proceedings at a meeting of the Antimasonic young men of the city of Schenectady, held in said city on the 21st day of July, 1831... To which is added the Hon. Richard Rush's views of Masonry, contained in his letter addressed to the York committee... Schenectady, 1831. 16 p. WHi. 9055

---- Two letters of Hon. Richard Rush of Pennsylvania, on subject of Freemasonry; and New Berlin trial, embracing judicial evidence of Masonic obligations. Utica, William Williams, 1831. 32 p. CSmH; IC; ICJ; IaCrM; NCH; NN. 9056

The Rushbearing. A tale. Boston, Perkins & Marvin, 1831. 71 p. MHad; MPlyA. 9057

[Rushton, Edward]
Expostulatory letter to George Washington. Boston, Garrison & Knapp, prs., Office of the Liberator, 1831. 8 p. CSmH; MB; MBAt; MHi; MWA. 9058

Russell, Bertrand.
The scientific outlook. By Bertrand Russell. New York, W. W. Norton & Co., 1831. ICU. 9059

Russell, Michael, 1781-1848.
Palestine; or, the Holy Land, from the earliest period to the present time. By the Rev. Michael Russell, LL.D., author of "View of Ancient and Modern Egypt." ...With a map and nine engravings. New York, Harper & Bros. [Pref. 1831] 330 p. NBuCC; NjNbR; ScAb. 9060

---- View of ancient and modern Egypt; with an outline of its natural history, by the Rev. Michael Russell, LL.D. with a map and engravings. New York, J. & J. Harper, 1831. 348 p. IaOsa; MoSU; OClW; PP; ViL. 9061

Russell, Samuel.
Review of a pamphlet, entitled "Trial of the action in favor of the Rev. Samuel Russell of Boylston, against John Howe of Boylston, for defamation at the Supreme judicial court, holden at Worcester, April, A.D. 1831." By Samuel Russell. Boston, Peirce and Parker, 1831. 31 p. DLC; ICN; M; MBAt; MH; Nh-Hi. 9062

---- Trial of the Action in favor of the Rev. Samuel Russell of Boylston, against John Howe of Boylston, for defamation, at the Supreme Judicial Court, holden at Worcester, April, A.D. 1831. Worcester, 1831. 27 p. MBC; MH_ MH-AH; MNBedf; MWA; PHi. 9063

Russell, William, 1798-1873.
The infant school system of education (may be a lecture)... Boston, 1831. 124 p. MLanc. 9064

---- Lessons in enunciation; comprising a course of elementary exercises, and a statement of common errors in articulation, with the rules of correct usage in pronouncing. To which is added an appendix. Boston, Richardson, Lord, and Holbrook, 1831. 81 p. MB; MH. 9065

Russell, Sir William Oldnall.
A treatise on crimes & indictable misdemeanors...By Wm. Oldnall Russell... With additional notes of decisions in the American courts, by Daniel Davis... 2d Amer., from the 2d English ed., with additional references, by Theron Metcalf... Philadelphia, P. H. Nicklin & T. Johnson; Boston, Lilly & Wait, 1831. 2 vols. C-L; DLC; MBPL; NcD;

NjP; TxSao; ViU. 9066

Ruter, Martin, 1785-1838.
The juvenile arithmetick and scholars' guide, illustrated with familiar questions, and containing numerous examples in federal money. To which is added, a short system of bookkeeping: by Martin Ruter... Rev. and enl. by Nathan Guilford. Cincinnati, N. & G. Guilford, 1831. 179 p. OCA; OCHP; OHi; OCO; TxU-T. 9067

---- The martyrs, or a history of perseuction, from the commencement of Christianity to the present time: including an account of the trials, tortures, and triumphant deaths of many who have suffered martyrdom. Compiled from the works of Fox and others. By Martin Ruter, S. T.D. President of Augusta College. Cincinnati, E. Deming, 1831. 561 p. InCW; InRchE. 9068

Ryan, Edward George, 1810-1880.
The hero's repose; a monody on the late Commodore Decatur, written by E. G. Ryan, composed by Geo. Geib. New York, Geo. H. Geib, 1831. 3 p. WHi. 9069

Ryan, James.
A key to the last New-York edition of Bonnycastle's algebra. New-York, Collins & Hannay, 1831. CtMW; CtY; MH; MdB; MoSU. 9070

---- The mathematical diary containing new researches. New York, Ryan, 1831. DLC; NN. 9071

---- The new American grammar of the elements of astronomy, on an improved plan: in three books ... The whole systematically arranged and scientifically illustrated; with several cuts and engravings; and adapted to the instruction of youth in schools and academies. By James Ryan: author of "An elementary treatise on algebra, theoretical and practical." New York, Collins & Hannay, 1831. 375 p. CtMW; InCW; NNC. 9072

---- A treatise on the art of measuring: containing all that is useful. In Bonnycastle, Hutton, Howney, Ingram, and several other modern works on mensuration: to which are added trigonometry, with its application to heights and distances. surveying; gauging: and also the most important problems in mechanics. By James Ryan... New York, Collins & Hannay-White, Gallaher & White- and James Ryan, 1831. 344 p. NBuG; NjP; OClWHi; PPM; ViRVMI. 9073

---- See also Bonnycastle, John.

Ryder, Thomas P.
An address delivered at Dorchester before the Norfolk Juvenile Lyceum, on Tuesday, 10th of May. Dedham, L. Powers, 1831. 16 p. MB; MH. 9074

S

S. M.
Hark! Hark! The soft bugle. Composed and inscribed to his friend, J. H. Hewitt. Baltimore, Geo. Willig, Jr., c1831. 4 p. ViU. 9075

The Sailor Boy, or, The first and last...4th Amer. ed. Concord, Fisk and Chase, 1831. 16 p. CtY; ICN; NBatHi. 9076

St. Clair, Henry.
The criminal calendar, or An awful warning to the youth of America; being an account of the most notorious pirates,

highwaymen, and other malefactors who have figured in this hemisphere...By Henry St. Clair, Boston, Frederic S. Hill, 1831. 356 p. CtMW; NIC-L; NNLI. 9077

St. John's College. Annapolis.
Rules and regulations of St. John's College as established by the Board of Visitors and Governors. Annapolis, Pr. by J. Hughes, 1831. 11 p. MdAS; MdBP; MdHi. 9078

St. Mary's Seminary. Somerset, Ohio.
St. Mary's Seminary. Somerset, Ohio. The system of education terms for boarding and tuition are as follows: Terms for day scholars, necessary regulations for entrance into the seminary. Somerset, October 18, 1831. Broadside. WHi. 9079

Saint-Pierre, Jacques Henri Bernardin de, 1737-1814.
The history of the adventures, love and... Concord, H. E. & I. Moore, 1831. 72 p. 9080

Sairerille, comte de.
Catalogue of the celebrated Sairerille's collection, lately brought to New York from Paris ... New York, Pr. for the proprietor, 1831. 36 p. NN. 9081

Salem, Massachusetts.
Annual report of the receipts and expenditures to March 8, 1831. Salem, 1831. 2 p. MHi; MiD-B. 9082

---- Committee of inquiry on retrenchment: 1831.
Report (of the committee appointed March 7, 1831 to inquire into the expenses of the several boards of town officers... [Salem, Mass., 1831] 12 p. M; MB; MHi. 9083

---- East India Marine Society.
The East India Marine Society of Salem. [Salem, Oct., 1831] 178 p. DLC; ICN; MHi; MB; MH; MSaP; MWA. 9084

Salem mercury. Salem, 1831-33. Vol. 1-3. 3 vols. in 1. MB-FA. 9085

Sallustius Crispus, Caius, 86-34 B.C.
C. Crispi Sallustii de Catilinae conjuratione belloque Jugurthino historae asimadversionibus illus. Carolus Anthon... Ed. quarta, prioribus longe emendatior. xi, 374 p. Boston, Hilliard, Gray, Little and Wilkins; New York, G. & C. and H. Carvill, 1831. 386 p. ICN; MBrigst; MH; NCH; TxU-T. 9086

---- De Catilinae conjuratione belloque jugurthino historiae. Animadversionibus illustravit Carolus Anthon. Ed. 4A, prioribus longe emendatior. Boston, Hilliard, Gray, Little, and Wilkins, etc., etc. 1831. ICN; MH; NCH; OMC; PPLT; TxU-T. 9087

---- Sallust. Tr. by W. Rose. With improvements and notes. Harper's stereotype ed. New York, J. & J. Harper, 1831. 242 p. ArCH; CtMW; IJT; MoSU; ViL. 9088

Sammlung von Geistreichen Sterb und Begräbniss-Liedern für Christen von allen Benennungen. Chambersburg [Pa.], Heinr. Ruby, 1831. PPG. 9089

Samuel, J. M.
Letters to Reverend Hawes, in review of his Tribute to Pilgrims. Hartford, 1831. MH. 9090

[Sanderson, John] 1783-1844, ed.
Biography of the signers to the Declaration of independence. Rev., imp. and enl. ed. Philadelphia, Bennett & Walton and J.

P. Ayres, 1831. 5 vols. DLC; GEU; IP; LN; RPB; TxU. 9091

Sanford, Enoch.
Sketches of the pilgrims who founded the Church of Christ in New England. Boston, Perkins and Marvin, 1831. 71 p. DLC; MBAt; MBC. 9092

Sarah and her cousins, or, Goodness better than knowledge. By the author of The Sandfords, or, Home Scenes. Boston, Carter, Hendee and Babcock, 1831. 103 p. DLC; ICBB; MHi; OOC. 9093

Saratoga and Schenectady railroad co.
Act of incorporation...Saratoga Springs, Davison, 1831. 16 p. DLC. 9094

Sargent, John, 1780-1833.
A memoir of the Rev. Henry Martyn... From the 10th London ed., corr. & enl. With an introductory essay & an appendix, by the American ed. Boston, Perkins & Marvin; New York, J. Leavitt, 1831. 432 p. GHi; IEG; KyLo; PPPrHi; RHi; TxU; ViRut. 9095

Saunders, John Simcoe.
The law of pleading and evidence in civil actions, arranged alphabetically: with practical forms: and the pleading and evidence to support them. By John Simcoe Saunders... 2d Amer. ed., with considerable additions, by a member of the Philadelphia bar... Philadelphia, R. H. Small, 1831. 2 vols. DLC; IU; MiD-B; PU-L; TxU-L; WaU. 9096

[Savage, Sara]
Conversations on the attributes of God. By the author of "The badge." Boston, Bowles, 1831. 91 p. DLC; ICMe. 9097

Savonarola See J. C. M.

Sawyer, Matthias E.
Treatise on primitive or secondary disguised or misplaced fever, as a single disease with the varieties cause and treatment, as it appears in most of the particular forms of fever recognized by nosologists. New York, Peabody, 1831. 307 p. DLC; IC; MB; NbU-M; ViU. 9098

Say, Thomas, 1787-1834.
American conchology...New Harmony, Indiana, Pr. at the School Press, 1831. DLC; ICHi; MB; NbU; PHi. 9099

---- Descriptions of new species of curculionites of North America, with observations on some of the species already known. New-Harmony, Indiana, 1831. 30 p. In; InU; MH-Z; PHi; PPAN. 9100

---- Descriptions of new species of heteropterous hemiptera of North America. New-Harmony, Indiana, 1831. 31 p. InU; OClW; PPAmE. 9101

---- ---- (Additional text). New Harmony, 1831. 68 p. In; InHi; PPAN. 9102

---- Descriptions of new species of North American insects, found in Louisiana by Joseph Barabino. By Thomas Say... New-Harmony, Ind., Pr. at the School Press, 1831. 19 p. DA; DLC; MBN; MH-Z; PPAN. 9103

---- New terrestrial and fluviatile shells of North America. [New Harmony] 1831. [5] p. InU; PPAN. 9104

Schauffer, William Gottlieb, 1798-1883.
Fastidious hearers of the Gospel, admonished. A sermon preached at Park street meeting house, October 16, 1831. By

William G. Schauffer. Boston, Peirce & Parker, 1831. 20 p. CU; Ct; DLC; MBAt; MBC; MHi; MiU; NN; NjR; PPPrHi. 9105

---- The pious man happy in his sufferings. A sermon preached in the chapel of the Theological Seminary, Andover, Sept. 11, 1831. By William G. Schauffler ... Boston, Pr. by Peirce & Parker, 1831. 22 p. CU; MB; MBAt; MBC; NN; Nh; PPPrHi; RPB. 9106

Scholar's weekly gazette, Apr. 1831- , v. 1- . Philadelphia, 1831. DLC; PPL-R; PU. 9107

Schoolcraft, Henry Rowe.
Expedition into the Indian Country. [Washington, 1831?] 20 p. WHi. 9108

Schoyer, Jacob.
The lily, a holiday present, with steel embellishments. New York, E.Sands, 1831. 238 p. Ia-L-B; NjR. 9109

Schroeder, John Frederick, 1800-1857.
Memorial of Bishop Hobart, a collection of sermons on the death of the Right Reverend John Henry Hobart, D.D., by John F. Schroeder. New York, T. & J. Swords, 1831. 250 p. CtMW; DLC; ICU; MH; MiD; NNC; NjP; WHi. 9110

Schweinitz, Lewis David von, 1780-1834.
Synopsis Fungorum in America Boreali media degentium, Secundum observations, Communicated to the American Philosophical Society. Philadelphia, April 15, 1831. 141-316 p. DSl; MBHo; RPB. 9111

Scientific tracts, designed for instruction and entertainment, and adapted to schools, lyceums, and families. Conducted by Josiah Holbrook & others... Boston, Carter Hendee and Babcock, 1831-33. 3 vols. DLC; IaMu; LU; MB; MH; OPom; NR. 9112

Scott, Job, 1751-1793.
The works of that eminent minister of the Gospel, Job Scott, late of Providence, Rhode Island. Philadelphia, John Comly, 1831. 2 vols. DLB; NBF. 9113

Scott, O[range], 1800-1847, composer.
Camp meeting hymn book. Brookfield [Mass.], 1831. MB. 9114

---- The new and improved camp meeting hymn book: being a choice selection of Hymns from the most approved authors. Designed to aid in the public and private devotion of Christians by Orange Scott... 2d ed. Brookfield (Mass.), Pr. by E. & G. Merriam, for the composer, 1831. RPB. 9115

Scott, Robert.
The consequence proved; or, Strictures upon a pamphlet written by Doctor Hellenbrock, and lately introduced as a catechism for children... By Robert Scott. Kingston, N.Y., 1831. 12 p. NjR. 9116

Scott, Robert Wilmont.
An address delivered at the request of the Kentucky state temperance society, at Frankfort, on the 9th day of April, 1831... Frankfort, Ky., A. G. Hodges, 1831. 23 p. MoSHi; NjR. 9117

Scott, Thomas, 1747-1821.
An essay on repentance. By Thomas Scott. Boston, Peirce & Parker, 1831. 116 p. CtHC; GDecCT; MeBat; OO. 9118

Scott, Sir Walter, bart., 1771-1832.

...The abbot; being the sequel to The monastery. From the last revised ed., containing the author's final corrections, notes, etc. Parker's ed. Boston, Bazin & Ellsworth, 1831. 2 vols. in 1. CFrT; MB-FA; MCan; NNCoCi; NNF; NJam. 9119

---- ---- Boston, De Wolfe, Fiske & Co., [1831] 430 p. Ia; MHa; NLac; PNt. 9120

---- ... Anne of Geierstein; or, The maidens of the mist... From the last revised ed., containing the author's final corrections, notes, etc. Parker's ed. Boston, Bazin & Ellsworth [1831] 2 vols. in 1. CFrT; DLC; NNCoCi; NJam. 9121

---- ---- Boston, De Wolfe, Fiske, & Co., 1831. 463 p. Ia; OrP; PNT. 9122

---- Autobiography of Sir Walter Scott, bart. Philadelphia, Carey & Lea, 1831. 288 p. CU; DLC; ICMe; KyU; MH; TNP. 9123

---- ... Chronicles of the Canongate... From the last rev. ed., containing the author's final corrections, notes &c. Parker's ed. Boston, Bazin & Ellsworth [1831] 4 vols. in 2. CFrT; DLC; NNCoCi; NJam; ScFl. 9124

---- ---- Boston, De Wolfe, Fiske & Co., [1831] 410 p. KWiF; NcDurN; PNt. 9125

---- A discourse on the holy spirit. By Walter Scott... 2d ed., enl. and imp. Bethany, Va., Pr. by Alexander Campbell, 1831. 24 p. KyLxCB; OClWHi; ViRU. 9126

---- The Lady of the Lake. A poem... New York, S. King, 1831. 234 p. DLC; KyDC; NIC; TNV. 9127

---- ---- New York, J. Lomax, 1831. 232 p. DLC; MBev; MH; RPA; WvF. 9128

---- Kenilworth from the last revised ed., containing the authors final corrections, notes and etc. Parker's ed. Boston, Bazin & Ellsworth, 1831. 2 vols. DLC; NJam; ODa. 9129

---- ---- Boston, S. H. Parker, 1831. 2 vols. MB-FA; MH; RBr. 9130

---- ... Letters on demonology and witchcraft, addressed to J. G. Lockhart, Esq. by Sir Walter Scott, bart. (Harper's stereotype ed.) New York, J. & J. Harper, 1831. 338 p. MB; MNF; MoSpD; RNPL; WvW. 9131

Scott, William.

Lessons in elocution; or, A selection of pieces in prose & verse, for the improvement of youth in reading and speaking; to which are prefixed elements of gesture, also an Appendix containing lessons on a new plan. Concord, N.H., Marsh, 1831. 372 p. CtWatk; PU; ViU. 9132

Scougal, Henry, 1650-1678.

The life of God in the soul of man, by the Rev. H. Scougal. Boston, B. H. Greene and L. C. Bowles, 1831. GEU-T; IEG; MB; MH-AH. 9133

---- ---- New York, New York Protestant Episcopal Tract Society [1831] 48 p. KyLoF; MdBD; NBuDD; WHi. 9134

---- The works of the Rev. H. Scougal, A.M.S.T.P. containing the Life of God in the soul of man; with nine other discourses on important subjects, to which is added a sermon preached at the author's funeral, by George Gairden, D.D. ...Boston, Stereotyped from the last London ed., by Lyman Thurston and Co., Pierce and Williams, 1831. 272 p. GMi; MB; MH; MBC; NPV; RPB; VtU. 9135

---- The works of Rev. Henry Scougal...Together with his funeral sermon by the Rev. Dr. Gairden; and an account of his life and writings. Philadelphia, J. Kay, Jun. and bro.; Pittsburgh, J. I Kay & co. [183-?] 272 p. DLC. 9136

The Scrap book; or Traveller's pocket library... New York, J. A. Clussman, 1831. 216 p. NN. 9137

Scribe, Augustin Eugene, 1791-1861 La dame blanche. See Boseldiev, Francois Adrien.

The Scriptural interpreter. Ed. by Ezra S. Gannett. v. 1-7. July, 1831-1836. Boston, Leonard C. Bowles, 1831-1836. CBPac; MH; NhGrl; OClWHi; PSC. 9138

The Scripture directory to baptism, or, A faithful citation of the principal passages of the Old and New Testaments, which relate to the mode of administering this ordinance...By a layman... New-York, J. Leavitt; Boston, Crocker and Brewster, 1831. 45 p. MBC; NbOP; Nh; NjR; PCA. 9139

[Seabury, Samuel]

The study of the classics, on Christian principles. [Prospectus of a proposed edition of a few of the more popular classics, with the view of adapting them to a course of Christian education. Flushing, L.I., 1831] 12 p. MB; MH; NBLiHi. 9140

The Seasons. Wendell, Mass., Pr. by J. Metcalf, 1831. 8 p. NN. 9141

Seaton, Henry Wilmot.

Forms of decrees in equity, and of orders connected with them. With practical notes, by Henry Wilmot Seaton, of Lincoln's Inn, Barrister at law. New-York, O. Halsted, 1831. 321 p. CU; DLC; MoU; NcD; PP; TxU-L; ViU; WaU. 9142

Seaward, Sir Edward.

Narrative of his shipwreck, and consequent discovery of certain islands in the Caribbean Sea ...1733-1749; ed by Miss Jane Porter. New York, Harper, 1831. 3 vols. FTU; GMWa; In; MdAN; PNt. 9143

[Sedgwick, Catharine Maria]

The deformed boy. Springfield, 1831. 32 p. RPB. 9144

---- Sketch of Mary Dyre. Boston, 1831. PPL. 9145

Sedgwick, Henry Dwight, 1785-1831.

Mr. Clay's speech at Cincinnati. New York, The New York Evening Post, 1831. 32 p. MPiB. 9146

---- The Practicability of the Abolition of Slavery: a lecture, delivered at the Lyceum in Stockbridge, Mass. New York, Pr. by J. Seymour, 1831. 48 p. DLC; ICMe; KyDC; MB; MH; MHi; OClWHi; VtU. 9147

Seidenstuecker, Johann Henrich Philipp.

An elementary practical book for learning to speak the French language, expressly adapted to the capacity of children;...Tr. by Mrs. B. D. Addicks. New York, Charles Collins [1831]

130 p. MoS; NN; TxGUr. 9148

Selden, John, Table talk... See Sidney, Philip, 1554-1586. The defence of Posey.

A selection of wonderful and entertaining stories and romance. To which is added a few funny, droll, comical, serious, jovial, tragical, shimsical, sentimental, pathetical, curious and humorous songs. Concord, N.H., Fisk & Chase, 1831. 135 p. DLC; NIDHi; RPB. 9149

Selwyn, William, 1775-1855.
An abridgment of the law of nisi prius. By William Selwyn ... With notes and references to the decisions of the courts of this country. By Henry Wheaton ...4th Amer. from the 7th London ed., with additional notes and references, by Thomas I. Wharton... New Haven, E. F. Backus; Philadelphia, P. H. Nicklin & T. Johnson, 1831. 2 vols. DLC; MSU; NCHoc; OKHl; TMeB; ViL; WaU. 9150

Seneca, Lucius Annaeus, 4 B.C.-65 A.D.
Seneca's morals by way of abstract to which is added a discourse under the title of "An afterthought" by Sir Roger L'Estrange. By Lucius Annaeus Seneca. 6th Amer. ed. Philadelphia, Henry Adams, 1831. 359 p. CtHT; ICJ; KyLO; NP; RPA; TxU. 9151

Sergeant, John, 1779-1852.
Argument in the case of the Cherokee nation vs. the state of Georgia, before the Supreme court of the United States, March 5, 1831. DLC; IU; PPB. 9152

A sermon on Christ's sheep. Reading, Vermont, Pr. by David Watson, Woodstock, for Samuel C. Loveland [1831] 12 p. MMeT. 9153

A sermon preached at the closing of a Sunday school, October 31, 1830. By a pastor. Boston, L. C. Bowles, 1831. MH. 9154

Severance, Moses.
The American manual, or New English reader:...Waterloo, N.Y., M. Severance, 1831. 300 p. CSmH; DLC; NiDHi. 9155

Sewall, Edmund Q[uincy], 1796-1866.
On Human Depravity. By Edmund Q. Sewall. 5th ed., 1st ser., No. 3. Printed for The American Unitarian Association. Boston, Gray & Bowen, 1831. 42 p. ICMe; KMK; MeB; MeBat; PPLT. 9156

Seward, William Henry.
Oration delivered at anti-masonic celebration at Syracuse, July 4, 1831...Syracuse, Campbell and Newton, 1831. 16 p. CDU; IaCrM; MBC; MHi; N. 9157

---- Speeches of Wm. H. Seward on joint resolutions in honor of Louis Kossuth in Senate of United States. Washington [1831?] 12 p. OCHP; PHi. 9158

Seymour, J.
Lecture on Abolition of Slavery. New York, J. Seymour, 1831. 48 p. C. 9159

Seymour, James.
Report of an experimental survey of part of the proposed rail road from the Wyoming and Lackawanna coal vallies...By James Seymour...Montrose, Pa., C. L. Ward, 1831. 32 p. NN; PHi; PPAmP. 9160

Shakespeare, William, 1564-1616.
The dramatic works of William Shakespeare, accurately printed

from the text of the corrected copy left by the late George Steevens, esq. with a glossary, and notes, and a sketch of the life of Shakespeare...Hartford, Conn., S. Andrus, 1831. 2 vols. CtHT; GDecCT; IaBo; MDBJ; OClW. 9161

---- ---- New York, S. King, 1831. 2 vols. IaDuMte; MdBJ; MiDU; OClW; ViR. 9162

---- Much ado about nothing. New York, 1831. 72 p. CU. 9163

Shannon, Charles.
My wife; or, My place; a petite comedy, in two acts. By C. Shannon and T. J. Thackeray, Esqrs. First performed at the theatre Royal Haymarket... Baltimore, Jos. Robinson, 1831. 46 p. CU; LNH; MH; NN. 9164

Shaw, Edward.
Civil architecture: or, A complete theoretical and practical system of building. By Edward Shaw. Boston, Lincoln & Edmands, 1831. 175 p. MNBedf. 9165

Shaw, Lemuel, 1781-1861.
Address delivered before the bar of Berkshire on the occasion of his first taking his seat as Chief Justice of the Supreme Judicial Court, September term, 1830. By Lemuel Shaw. Boston, Stimpson & Clapp, 1831. 15 p. M; MB; Me; MeHi; OO; PPM. 9166

[Shaw, Oliver A.] 1779-1848.
Brief description of the nature and construction of the visible numerator. With directions for its use. By the patentee. New York, Pr. by Sleight & Robinson, 1831. 16 p. MB. 9167

---- The fountains of Marrah, a sacred song. Words by Mrs. Hemans. Providence, Pub. by the author, 1831. 3 p. MNF. 9168

Shea, John Augustus, 1802-1845.
Adolph and other poems: by J. A. Shea... New York, Pr. by W. E. Dean, 1831. 168 p. DLC; ICU; NBuG; RPB; TITB. 9169

Sheldon English and Classical School. Southampton, Massachusetts.
The annual catalogue, of the officers and students of the... November, 1831. Northampton, Pr. by T. W. Shepard, 1831. 12 p. FL. 9170

Shelley, Percy Bysshe, 1792-1822.
Poetical works. Philadelphia, 1831. 11, 275 p. 9171

---- Queen Mab: a philosophical poem, with notes. By Percy Bysshe Shelley... From the original London ed. New-York, Wright & Owen, 1831. 112 p. NIC; NN; OHi; PPL. 9172

[Shepard, William Biddle] 1799-1852.
To the electors of the First Congressional district of North Carolina. [Washington, 1831] 5 p. ScU. 9173

The Shepherdess. New-Britain.
Vol. I, no. 1-21 (July 18, 1831-June 5, 1832). Incomplete. MH. 9174

Sheppard, John Hannibal, 1789-1873.
An address delivered before Lincoln Lodge, Wiscasset, June 24, A. L. 5831. By John H. Sheppard. 2d ed. Boston, Pr. by Beals & Homer, 1831. 32 p. MB; MBC; MH; MHi; MWA; Me; MeHi. 9175

---- ---- 3d ed. Boston, Pr. by Beals and Homer, 1831. 32 p.

DLC; MH; Me. 9176

Sherburne, Andrew, 1765-1831.
Memoirs of Andrew Sherburne, a prisoner of the navy of the revolution. Written by himself... 2d ed., enl. and imp. Providence, H. H. Brown, 1831. 312 p. IU; MH; Mi; MnHi; NN; NjR; OMC; PHC; RPB. 9177

Sheridan, Richard Brinsley Butler, 1751-1816.
The beauties of Sheridan, consisting of selections from his poems, dramas, and speeches. By Alfred Howard, esq. Boston, Pr. by S. N. Dickinson, for Frederic S. Hill, 1831. 211 p. CSCA; KyDC; MDeeP; NGH; OClW. 9178

Sherman, Eleazer, b. 1795, comp.
Conference hymns, selected and original. Providence, H. H. Brown, 1831. 159 p. RHi; RPB. 9179

Sherwood, [Mary Martha] (Bott), 1775-1851.
The Lady of the Manor; being a series of conversations on the subject of Confirmation. Intended for the use of the middle and higher ranks of young females. By Mrs. Sherwood... Philadelphia, Towar, J. & D. M. Hogan; Pittsburg, Hogan & Co. Stereotyped by L. Johnson, 1831. 7 vols. KyHi; MB; MH; MW; PPL; ViAl. 9180

---- Little Robert and the owl. Wendell, Metcalf, 1831. MA. 9181

---- Questions for children, with answers from Scripture. By Mrs. Sherwood. New Haven, S. Babcock, Sidney's press, 1831. 22 p. CtY. 9182

---- ...Roxobel. By Mrs. Sherwood, author of "The lady of the manor," "Little Henry and his bearer," &c. &c. New-York, Pr. and pub. by J. & J. Harper, 1831. 3 vols. NCH; ODuU; ScCMu; TNP; ViAl. 9183

Shinn, Asa, M. G., 1771-1853.
An essay on the plan of salvation: in which the several kinds of evidence are examined, and applied to the interesting doctrine of redemption, in its relation to the government and moral attributes of the Deity. 2d ed. abridged and rev. By Asa Shinn, M.G... Cincinnati, (Ohio), John H. Wood, 1831. 326 p. IaDmD; IaMp; IEG; KyLxT; LNB; OClWHi; TNT; Wv. 9184

Shipherd, John Jay, 1802-1844.
The Sabbath School Guide: or, A selection of interesting and Profitable Scripture lessons, illustrated and applied, by questions and answers. Designed as a permanent system of Sabbath School instruction. (2d ed., rev. and cor.) Middlebury, Vermont Sunday School Union, 1831. MH. 9185

Short stories, for good children. New Haven, S. Babcock, 1831. 16 p. CtY. 9186

Shotwell, Thomas L., complainant.
An authentic report of the testimony in a cause at issue in the court of chancery of the state of New Jersey, between Thomas L. Shotwell, complainant and Joseph Hendrickson, and Stacy Decow, defendants. Taken pursuant to the rule of the court, by Jeremiah J. Foster, master and examiner in chancery... Philadelphia, Pr. by J. Harding, 1831. DLC; NjP; PHi. 9187

The sick man's friend... New York, Pr. by Mahlon Day, 1831. 12 p. PHC. 9188

Sidney, Algernon. Essays on the American System. See Leigh, Benjamin Watkins.

Sidney, Philip, 1554-1586.
The defence of poesy. By Sir Philip Sidney. Table talk. By John Selden. With some account of the authors... Cambridge, Hilliard & Brown, Booksellers to the University, 1831. 294 p. CtMW; ICMe; MB; NNS; NPV; PPF; PPins. 9189

Shimeall, Richard C.
Complete historical, chronological, geographical, & genealogical chart of the sacred scriptures, from Adam to Christ. By Richard C. Shimeall. Philadelphia, Tanner, 1831. Broadside. NjP. 9190

Silliman, Benjamin, 1799-1864.
Elements of chemistry. Arranged in the order of lectures given in Yale college. New Haven, H. Howe, 1831. 2 vols. CtHT; CtW; Ku; MBC; NNC; ViU. 9191

Simeon, Charles, 1759-1836.
The excellency of the liturgy; four discourses preached before the University of Cambridge, in November, 1811. Also, a university sermon containing the churchman's confession, or an appeal to the liturgy. 2d American ed. Columbus, Ohio, I. N. Whiting, 1831. 108 p. CSmH; ICMe; NSyU; OMC; PPL-R. 9192

[Simmons, Amelia]
American Cookery; or, the art of dressing viands, fish, poultry, and vegetables. And the best mode of making puff pastees, pies, etc. Also the best way of curing hams, corned beef, mutton and veal. Together with the rules of carving at dinner parties.... By an Orphan. 2d ed. imp. Woodstock, A. Colton, 1831. 110 p. VtMiS. 9193

Simpson, Stephen, 1789-1854.
The working man's manual: a new theory of political economy, on the principle of production the source of wealth... Philadelphia, T. L. Bonsal, 1831. 272 p. MH-BA. 9194

Sketches and views of scenery in various parts of the world, embellished with thirty-six engravings. New-York, Henry R. Piercy & Co., 1831. 74 p. NBu. 9195

Sketches of domestic life.
By an observer. Contents: The twin sisters, Aunt Ruth's jewels, The orphan, The broken stage-coach, The mother. Portland [Me.], Shirley, Hyde & Co., 1831. 339 p. DLC; MeHi. 9196

Skinner, C. R., ed.
A free pulpit in action. New York, 1831. MB. 9197

Skinner, Rev. George New translation of proverbs, 1831. See under Bible.

---- Sermon preached at Cambridge, Nov. 6, 1831. Cambridge, 1831. 20 p. MH. 9198

Skinner, Icabod Lord, d. 1852.
A Key to the Gospels: being a compendious exposition of the principal things contained in them, intended for Sunday-School teachers, Bible classes, and families ... By I. L. Skinner. Washington, Pr. by Wm. Greer, 1831. 276 p. ABBS; MDeeP; MiD; PPPrHi. 9199

Skinner, Rodger Sherman.
The New York State register, for the year of our lord 1831, with a complete United States calendar. By Rodger Sherman Skinner. New York, Rodger Sher-

man Kinner [1831?] 358 p. ICN; NBLiHi; NCanHi. 9200

Skinner, Thomas Harvey, 1791-1871.
Aids to preaching and hearing. New York, J. S. Taylor, 1831. KyLo. 9201

Slack, Elijah.
A discourse on agricultural chemistry delivered at a quarterly meeting of the Hamilton county Agricultural Society, held on the 4th of June 1831, by the Rev. Elijah Slack, M.D. [Cincinnati, Pr. by Wm. J. Ferris, for the Society [1831?] 14 p. IEN-M; OClWHi. 9202

Slocomb, William.
The American calculator; or a concise system of practical arithmetic; containing all the rules necessary for transacting the common business of life; together with questions for examination, under each of the rules. By Wm. Slocomb. Philadelphia, William Davis, 1831. 180 p. DLC; IHi; WHi. 9203

Slocum, Samuel, comp.
The cold water melodies. Providence, 1831. 9204

Smiley, Thomas Tucker.
Scripture geography; or, A companion to the Bible, being a geographical and historical account of the places mentioned in the Holy Scriptures. Philadelphia, Grigg, 1831. 344 p. CBPac; IAEv; ICP; PU. 9205

Smith, David Solon Chase Hall.
Suggestions with regard to the general treatment of fractures; with a ...new kind of splinting composed of felt. Boston, Carter, Hendee and Babcock, 1831. 11 p. MBM; MH-M; NIC; NNN; OC; RPB. 9206

Smith, Francis Ormond Jonathan, 1806-1876, comp.
Reports of decisions in the circuit courts martial, of questions arising on trials had in said courts compiled from original papers in the office of the adutant general in conformity to a resolve of the Legislature of Maine, passed March 31, 1831. To which is added an appendix of practical forms of proceedings in circuit courts martial...Portland, Pr. by Todd & Holden, 1831. 113 p. DLC; OCLaw. 9207

Smith, George Washington, 1800-1876.
Arguments in favour of the proposed canal around the western abutment of the Schuylkill permanent bridge, including some remarks on the report of a committee of the city councils to that body. Philadelphia, 1831. 24 p. NjP; PPAmP; PPL; PHi. 9208

Smith, Henry.
The church harmony...Approved psalms and hymn tunes... By Henry Smith. Chambersburg [Pa.] Pr. by Henry Ruby, 1831. 136 p. CtHT-W; CSmH; OClWHi; P; PPL-R. 9209

Smith, Horatio, 1779-1849.
Festivals, games and amusements...By Horatio Smith, Esq. With additions by Samuel Woodworth, Esq. New York, J. & J. Harper, 1831. 355 p. CtHT; IU; MH; NjR; OMC; RPB; ScC; TxU; ViU. 9210

Smith, James, 1737-1812.
An account of the remarkable occurrences in the life and travels of colonel James Smith... during his captivity with the Indians in the years 1755, 56, 57, 58, and 59, in which the customs, manners, traditions, theological sentiments, mode of

warfare, military tactics, discipline and encampments, treatment of prisoners, &c are better explained... Together with a description of soil, timber and waters.... Written by himself. Philadelphia, J. Grigg, 1831. 162 p. DLC; DeWi; ICHi; ICN; ICU; KHi; NcD; OClWHi. 9211

Smith, Jerome Van Crowninshield, 1800-1879.
An essay on the practicability of cultivating the honey bee, in maritime towns and cities, as a source of domestic economy and profit. By Jerome V. C. Smith, M.D. Boston, Perkins & Marvin; New York, J. Leavitt, 1831. 106 p. IEN-M; MAA; MBAt; MH; MWA; NGH; NIC; NICA; OMC; RPA. 9212

Smith, John.
An address, delivered before the associated mechanics and manufacturers of the state of New Hampshire, at the celebration of their anniversary, in Portsmouth, October 13, 1831. ...Portsmouth, R. Foster, 1831. 28 p. MH-BA. 9213

Smith, John Rubens.
A key to the art of drawing the human figure...comprised in twenty four lithographic plates... The whole designed and executed by John Rubens Smith...Philadelphia, S. M. Steward, 1831. (29) p. MdBG; PP; PPFrankI. 9214

Smith, Joseph L.
Opinions of Joseph L. Smith... upon claims... Charleston, 1831. MH. 9215

Smith, Joseph Mather, 1789-1868.
A discourse on the epidemic of cholera morbus of Europe and Asia; delivered as an introductory lecture, at the College of Physicians and Surgeons in the city of New-York, November 9, 1831. By Joseph Mather Smith, M.D Professor of the theory and practice of physic and clinical medicine. New-York, Pr. by J. Seymour, 1831. 36 p. DLC; MB; MBM; MH-M; MWA; NNN; PPL; PU. 9216

Smith, Nathan, 1762-1829.
Medical and Surgical Memoirs, by Nathan Smith, M.D... Edited and addenda, by Nathan R. Smith, M.D. ...Baltimore, Pr. by Wm. A. Francis, 1831. 374 p. CtSoP; DLC; ICJ; KyU; MdBJ; NNF; PU; TNV; VtU. 9217

Smith, Prudence.
Modern American Cookery: containing directions for making soups, roasting, boiling, baking, dressing vegetables, poultry, fish, made dishes, pies, gravies, pickles, puddings, pastry, sick cookery, etc. with a list of family medical receipts, and a valuable miscellany. By Miss Prudence Smith. New-York, J. & J. Harper, 1831. 220 p. NNT-C; TxHuT; ViU. 9218

[Smith, Richard Penn], 1799-1854.
The forsaken. A tale. By the author of "Caius Marius," "The deformed," etc., etc. ...Philadelphia, J. Grigg, 1831. 2 vols. MWA; MnU; NcWfc; PU; WaU. 9219

Smith, Roswell Chamberlain, 1797-1875.
English grammar on the productive system. Boston, Richardson, Lord & Holbrook, 1831. 204 p. MH; RPB. 9220

---- Intellectual and practical grammar, in a series of inductive questions, connected with exercises in composition. By Roswell C. Smith... Boston, Pr. by T. R. Marvin for Perkins and Marvin; New York, R. Lockwood,

1831. 123, 82 p. CtHWatk; ICP; MB; MH; MoU; RNHi; TxU-T; WU. 9221

---- Practical and mental arithmetic... By Roswell C. Smith. Boston, Richardson, Lord & Holbrook, 1831. 268 p. MB; MH; MeHi; MiU; MoS; NNC; O; OMC; RPB. 9222

---- Practical grammar. Boston, Perkins & Marvin; New York, Roe Lockwood, 1831. 123, 82 p. MWHi. 9223

---- Reply to the charges of Daniel Adams. [Providence, R.I., 1831] 12 p. MH; MHi; MWA. 9224

Smith, Samuel Francis, 1808-1895.

America. [1st printing] Program of the celebration of American independence, by the Boston Sabbath School Union, at Park St. Church, July 4, 1831. Boston, 1831. 1 p. PHi. 9225

Smith, Samuel G.

Report of an examination, made under a Resolution of the Legislature of Tennessee, into the situation of the Entry Takers Offices, and Bank Agencies in West Tennessee and the Western District. Nashville, Allen A. Hall, pr. to the House of Representatives, 1831. 21 p. T. 9226

Smith [Stephen Rensselaer], 1788-1850.

Sermons from Universalist preachers, printed monthly by G. W. Kappel, Hartford, Conn. [1831] 8 p. NNUT. 9227

Smith, T[homas] Southwood, 1788-1861.

Illustrations of the Divine government, by T. Southwood Smith, M.D. 1st Amer. from the last London ed. ...Boston, Benj. B. Mussey, 1831. 347 p. CSmH; MB; MBL; MW; MWA; MeBaT; PPWa. 9228

---- ---- Boston, Thomas Whittemore, 1831. 358 p. ICP; IEG; MH; NCaS. 9229

---- A treatise on fever... Boston, Stimpson and Clapp, 1831. 412 p. CSfCMS; CSt-L; ICJ; MB; MBM; RPM; TNV. 9230

---- ---- Philadelphia, Carey & Lea, 1831. 412 p. MBM; MdBM; MH; ViU. 9231

Smith, Rev. Thomas.

Walker's Critical Pronouncing Dictionary and Expositor of The English language, abridged... By Rev. Thomas Smith. Albany, G. J. Loomis, 1831. 411 p. OkGoP. 9232

[Snelling, William Joseph], 1804-1848.

A brief and impartial history of the life and actions of Andrew Jackson, president of the United States... By a Free man. Boston, Pr. by W. L. Lewis, for Stimpson and Clapp, 1831. 216 p. Ia; LNH; MH; OC; RPB. 9233

---- The polar regions of the western continent explored; embracing a geographical account of Iceland, Greenland, the islands of the frozen sea, and the northern parts of the American continent. Boston, W. W. Reed, 1831. 501 p. CtMW; ICJ; KyU; LNH; MB; MH. 9234

[----] Tales of travels in Central Africa, including Denham and Clapperton's expedition, Park's first and second journey, etc. By Solomon Bell (pseud.). Boston, Gray and Bowen, 1831. MH. 9235

[----] Tales of travels in the

north of Europe, including Brooks' travels in Lapland, Conway's travels in Norway, Sweden, and Denmark, and Granville's travels in Russia and Poland. By Solomon Bell, late keeper of the Traveller's Library, Province House court, Boston. With map and numerous engravings. Boston, Gray & Bowen; Philadelphia, Key and Mielke, 1831. 164 p. ICU; MH; MWA; NRHi; PU. 9236

[----] Truth; a New Year's gift for scribblers... Boston, Pr. by Stephen Foster, 1831. 52 p. DLC; ICU; IaU; MB; MBL. 9237

The snow drop; a story for good little girls. New-Haven, S. Babcock, Sidney's press, 1831. 23 p. CtY. 9238

Snyder, W. B.
The western lyre: a new selection of sacred music, from the best authors... By W. B. Snyder and W. L. Chappell... Cincinnati, J. H. Wood [c 1831] 184 p. OClWHi; TxD-W. 9239

Social and camp-meeting songs. 2d ed. Baltimore, 1831. MB. 9240

Social and camp-meeting songs for the pious. 26th ed., enl. Baltimore, Armstrong & Plaskitt, 1831. 215 p. MB; MoS. 9241

Société Francaise de Bienfaisance de Philadelphie.
Constitution, 1791 reprint, 1831-. Philadelphia, 1831-. PHi. 9242

Society for Propagating the Gospel.
Report of the Select Committee of the Society for Propagating the Gospel among the Indians and others in North America. Read and Accepted November 3, 1831. Boston, Pr. by Putnam & Damrell, 1831. 20 p. MPlyP; MeB; MiD-B; WHi. 9243

Society for the Reformation of Juvenile Delinquents.
Sixth annual report of the manners of the society for the reformation of juvenile delinquents, in the city and state of New-York. New-York, Pr. by Mahlon Day, 1831. 43 p. MiD-B; ScU. 9244

Society for the Relief of Orphan and Destitute Children. See Albany. Society for the Relief of Orphan and Destitute Children.

Society of the Sons of St. George, Philadelphia.
Charter and by-laws...together with the names of the present members. Philadelphia, Kay, 1831. 32 p. PPAmP. 9245

Socio, Clio Convivius, (pseud., comp.)
The post-chaise companion, and magazine of wit: original and selected. From the most favourite literary authors. 4th ed. ... Baltimore, 1831. 256 p. MdHi; NN; RPB. 9246

Somerset, C(harles) A.
"Yes!" an operatic interlude, in one act. New York, E. B. Clayton, etc., etc. 1831. MH. 9247

Sophocles, Evangelinus Apostolides, 1807-1883.
Romaic Grammar. Boston, 1831. MB. 9248

South Carolina.
Acts and resolutions of the General Assembly of the state of South Carolina, passed in December, 1830. Columbia, S. J. McMorris, 1831. 37, 62, 3 p. IaU-L; MdBB. 9249

---- General Assembly.
The debate in the South

Carolina Legislature, in December, 1830, on the reports of the committees of both houses in favor of convention, etc. Columbia, Pr. by S. J. M'Morris, 1831. 203 p. ScC; ScHi; ScSp; RPB. 9250

---- ---- House of Representatives.
Debates which arose in the House of Representatives of South Carolina, on the Constitution framed for the United States, by a convention of delegates assembled at Philadelphia...Charleston, Pr. by A. E. Miller, 1831. 95 p. A-Ar; DLC; MH; NNLI; NjP. 9251

---- ---- ---- Journal.
Columbia, S.C., 1831. ICU; IU. 9252

---- ---- Senate.
Journal. Charleston, S.C., 1831. IU. 9253

South Carolina Canal and Railroad Company.
Annual Report of the South Carolina Canal and Railroad co., by the director, submitted and adopted May 2, 1831. Charleston, Pr. at the office of the "Irishman and Democrat," 1831. 20 p. DLC; MB; NN; ScHi; WM. 9254

---- Report, exhibiting present state of work. See Charleston and Hamburg Rail Road Co.

South Carolina College.
Catalogue of the Trustees, Faculty and Students of the South Carolina College, January 1831. ...Times & Gazette Print., [1831] Broadside. MH. 9255

South Carolina Railroad Company See South Carolina Canal and Railroad Company.

Southern pioneer and gospel visiter. Ed. by an association of gentlemen. V.1- Oct. 1831- . Baltimore, Pr. by W. Woody, 1831-. PPPrHi. 9256

Southey, Robert, 1774-1843.
The life of Nelson. By Robert Southey, LL.D. Poet laureate... New York, Pr. by J. & J. Harper, 1831. 309 p. CtHT; GMM; IEG; MH; NjR; PU; ViU; WvW. 9257

The Souvenir of the Lakes. Detroit, George L. Whitney, 1831. 38 p. ICU; MB; MiD-B. 9258

Spalding, Horace.
Child's pocket companion... choice hymns for Sabbath schools. New York, 1831. CtHWatk. 9259

Sparks, Jared, 1789-1866.
The life and correspondence of Gouverneur Morris, with selections from his correspondence, and miscellaneous papers. Boston, Gray & Bowen, 1831. OM. 9260

Speeches of Phillips, Curran, and Grattan, the celebrated Irish orators. Selected by a member of the bar. Philadelphia, Kay & Mielke, 1831. 370 p. CtHT; KWiU; LNL; MH; MdBJ; NBu; PPL. 9261

Spencer, John Canfield, 1788-1855.
Report to the United States anti-masonic convention at Baltimore, September 1831. [Baltimore? 1831?] 15 p. MH-AH. 9262

The Spirit of the Annuals for MDCCCXXXI. Philadelphia, E. Littell, 1831. 467 p. CtMMHi; ICU; MiGr; PHi; PPeSchw. 9263

Spirit of the coming age. V. 1- No. 1- Philadelphia, 1831- PHi; PPPrHi. 9264

The Spiritual Mirror; or Looking-glass: exhibiting the human heart as being either the Temple of God or Habitation of Devils... By Peter Bauder. Newburyport, Charles Whipple, 1831. 80 p. MBC; Nh. 9265

Spofford, Luke A.
The Ten Commandments briefly explained and enforced, in the form of Questions and answers, with scripture proofs. For the use of families and schools of all Christian denominations. By Luke A. Spofford, Minister of the Gospel. Boston, Perkins & Marvin, 1831. 54 p. MB. 9266

Sprague, Charles, 1791-1875.
An oration: pronounced before the inhabitants of Boston, July the fourth, 1825, in commemoration of American Independence. By Charles Sprague. Boston, Pr. by order of the City Council, 1825. Repr. by John Eastburn, 1831. (6th ed.) 30 p. MB; MBAt; MHi; MPeaHi; MWA; MiD-B; ViU. 9267

Sprague, William Buell, 1795-1876.
Lectures to young people. By William B. Sprague, D.D. With an introductory address, by Samuel Miller, D.D. 2d ed. New York, John P. Haven, 1831. 310 p. CtHC; GDecCT; MB; PPLT; PPPrHi; PU; OMC. 9268

---- Letters on practical subjects, to a daughter. By Wm. B. Sprague... 2d ed. New York, John P. Haven, 1831. 214 p. MH-AH; MiU; OMC; PPPrHi; WM. 9269

---- The probability of perdition inferred from present impenitence. 177-192 p. ICP; MB; MPiB. 9270

Spring, Gardiner, 1785-1873.
Tribute to the memory of the late Jeremiah Evarts, secretary of the American Board of Commissioners for Foreign Missions; delivered and published at the request of the executive committee of the auxiliary Foreign Mission Society of New York and Brooklyn. New York, Pr. by Sleight & Robinson, 1831. 32 p. CtHC; IaGG; NjR; OC; PHi. 9271

The Sprite. From the Elves of Ginnistian. Amherst, J. S. & C. Adams, 1831. 3 vols. CSmH; MWA; NjR; RPB. 9272

Standefer, James.
Circular of James Standefer, to his constituents of the Third Congressional district of Tennessee, composed of the counties of Campbell, Anderson, Morgan, Roan, Monroe, McMinn, Rhea, Hamilton, Bledsoe and Marion. Washington, Pr. at the office of Jonathan Elliott, 1831. 7 p. DLC; TxH. 9273

Stanhope, Louisa Sidney.
The bandit's bride; or The maid of Saxony. A romance, in three volumes. By Louisa Sidney Stanhope... Hingham, C. & E. B. Gill, 1831. 3 vols. KyU; MsMerN. 9274

Stansbury, Arthur Joseph, 1781-1865.
Elementary catechism on the Constitution of the United States. For the use of schools. By Arthur J. Stansbury. Boston, Hilliard, Gray, Little, and Wilkins, 1831. 78 p. IU; MB; MH; MHi; OClW. 9275

Starck, Johann Friedrich, 1680-1756.
Johann Friedrich Starck's gewesenen Evangelischen Predigers und Consisterial-raths zu Frankfurt am Mayn tägliches handbuch

in guten und bosen Tagen, welchen beigefügt ist, ein tägliches Gebetbüchlein für Schwangere, Gebärende und Unfruchtbare. Philadelphia, Herausgegeben von Georg W. Mentz und Sohn Buchhandler, 1831. 538, 106 p. PAtM. 9276

Stark, John.
Life and military services of Maj. Gen. John Stark in Reminiscences of the French war. Concord, N.H., 1831. MDeeP. 9277

State Register, Civil, Judicial, Military and other officers in Connecticut: and United States Record. To which is prefixed An Almanack...No. 5. For the year of our Lord 1831. Being the fifty-fifth year of American Independence. Hartford, H. & F. J. Huntington, Pr. by P. B. Gleason and co. [1831] 144 p. Ct; OClWHi. 9278

The State-Rights and Free-Trade Almanac for 1832. Charleston [The State Rights and Free Trade Association, 1831?] MB; MHi; NcU. 9279

Staughton, James Martin, 1800-1833.
An address delivered on the anniversary of the Union Literary Society of Miami University. By James M. Staughton. Cincinnati, Pr. by W. J. Ferris & co., 1831. 23 p. CSmH; ICU; NjN; OCHP; PPPrHi. 9280

Stearns, Asabel, 1774-1839.
A summary of the law and practice of real actions; with an appendix of practical forms. 2d ed. with additions. Hallowell, Mass., Glazier, Masters & Co., 1831. 464 p. DLC; MSH; PPB; PU-L. 9281

Steel, John Honeywood, 1780-1838.
An analysis of the mineral waters of Saratoga and Ballston, with practical remarks on their medical properties; together with a history of the discovery and settlement of these celebrated watering places, and observations on the geology and mineralogy of the surrounding country. By John H. Steel, an entire new work. Saratoga Springs, G. M. Davison, 1831. 203 p. CtMW; MB; NBuG; NNN; PPCP. 9282

Steele, Richard.
The Father and Guardian. Philadelphia, J. J. Woodward, 1831. KyDC; NAl. 9283

Steele's Albany Almanack for 1832. By a Successor of Andrew Beers. Albany, N.Y., Oliver Steele [1831] MWA. 9284

Stephen, George Sir, 1794-1879.
The adventures of a gentleman in search of a horse. Philadelphia, Carey, Lea & Co., 1831. 288 p. PPM. 9285

Stephen, Henry John, 1787-1864.
A treatise on the principles of pleading in civil actions; comprising a summary view of the whole proceedings in a suit at law, from the last London ed., with corr. and imp. 2d Amer. ed. with large additions, by Francis J. Troubat. Philadelphia, Robt. H. Small, 1831. 511 p. MdBJ; MH-L; ViU. 9286

[Stephens, John Lloyd] 1805-1852.
Incidents of travel in Egypt, Arabia Petraea and the Holy Land. By an American, with a map and engravings. 8th ed. with additions. New York, Harper Bros., 1831. 2 vols. CtHWatk; NhLitt. 9287

Stephens, William.

A treatise on the nature and constitution of The Christian Church; wherein are set forth the form of its government, the extent of its powers, and the limits of our obedience. By Wm. Stephens, New York, The Protestant Episcopal Tract Society, 1831. 16 p. MdBD; NHC-S. 9288

Stephenson, Robert.
Observations on the comparative merits of locomotive and fixed engines, as applied to railways. Philadelphia, Carey & Lea, 1831. 71 p. MoSW. 9289

Sterret, James.
The Columbian standard; or, Critical pronouncing spelling book; a new guide to the English language, adapted to the juvenile understanding, wherein are exhibited in a clear, plain and comprehensive manner... By James Sterret, Esq. Philadelphia, Geo. W. Mentz & Con, 1831. 130 p. PReaHi. 9290

---- The young nobleman extricated from false friends; a tale, interspersed with admonition, and scenes of honorable love; others of gamesters' fraud; the latter terminating in misery, disgrace, and suicide; the former in happy marriage, etc... Lewisburg, Pa., Pr. by Daniel Gotshall, 1831. RPB. 9291

Stetson, Caleb, 1793-1870.
On Piety at Home. By Caleb Stetson. 1st series, No. 46. 2d ed. American Unitarian Assoc. Boston, Gray & Bowen, 1831. 16 p. MB-FA; MB-HP; MeB. 9292

Stevens, James.
Letter to Levi Lincoln, governor of the commonwealth of Massachusetts. Boston, 1831. 14 p. PU. 9293

[----] [Report of progress of the surveys on trigonometrical principles and astronomical observations of the territory of the commonwealth of Massachusetts for the purpose of making a correct map thereof. Boston, 1831] 14 p. DLC. 9294

Steward, Maria W.
Religion and the Pure Principles of Morality the sure foundation on which we must build. Productions from the pen of Mrs. Maria W. Steward. Boston, Oct. 1831. 12 p. MB. 9295

Stewart, Charles Samuel, 1795-1870.
Sketches of society in Great Britain and Ireland. Philadelphia, 1831. 2 vols. MdAN. 9296

---- A visit to the South seas, in the U.S. ship Vincennes, during the years 1829 and 1830; with scenes in Brazil, Peru, Manilla, the Cape of Good Hope, and St. Helena, by C. S. Stewart ... New York, J. P. Haven, 1831. 2 vols. DLC; MH; MnHi; NJ; OO. 9297

Stilwell, Silas Moore, 1800-1881.
An act to abolish imprisonment for debt, and to punish fraudulent debtors. Passed April 26, 1831. Also, a synopsis of the same, by S. M. Stilwell. New-York, Elliott & Palmer, 1831. 24 p. MWA. 9298

---- Report on imprisonment for debt. Albany, 1831. PPL. 9299

Stimpson's Boston directory... Boston, Stimpson & Clapp, 1831. 346 p. WHi. 9300

Stith, (Mrs.) Townsend.
Thoughts on female education. by Mrs. Townsend Stith... Philadelphia, Pr. by Clark & Raser, 1831. 31 p. MBAt; NjR; P;

PHi; Vi. 9301

Stoddard, Elijah W.
Funeral sermon, delivered... at the funeral of Mrs. Sarah Hotchkiss, wife of Carver Hotchkiss of Windsor...Binghamton, N.Y., Pr. at the Courier Office, 1831. 12 p. NN. 9302

The stolen fruit; an interesting story. New Haven, S. Babcock, Sidney's press, 1831. 17 p. CtY. 9303

Stone, John Seeley, 1795-1882.
Address delivered before the Young men's temperance society of New Haven, Conn. in Trinity Church, Dec. 20, 1830, by... associate rector of Trinity church in New Haven. New Haven, S. Babcock, 1831. 22 p. Ct; IEG; MB; MBC; MH; MdBC; MdBD; MiD-B; NNG. 9304

Stone, Thomas, Treadwell, 1801-1895.
An address on the introduction of historical studies into the course of common education delivered before Oxford County Lyceum, by Thomas T. Stone, preceptor of the Bridgton Academy, Paris [Me.], H. King, 1831. 16 p. MH. 9305

Stone, William Murray.
A primary charge, delivered to the clergy and laity of the Protestant Episcopal Church, assembled in the annual convention of said church, in Chestertown, Eastern shore of Maryland, June 1st, 1831, by William Murray Stone, D.D., Bishop of the Protestant Episcopal Church of Maryland. Baltimore, Pr. by Lucas & Deaven, 1831. 18 p. InID; MdBD; MdBE; MdHi; NGH. 9306

Stones, Samuel.
An essay on the nature and properties of the blood. Philadelphia, Pr. by W. F. Geddes, 1831. 15 p. PPM. 9307

Stories about Arnold, the traitor, André the spy, and Champe, the patriot: for the children of the United States... 2d ed. New Haven, A. H. Maltby, 1831. 72 p. MH; MiD-B; NWM; OMC. 9308

Stories about Dr. Franklin, designed for the instruction and amusement of children. A new and improved ed. New-York, Pendleton & Hill, Pr. by G. F. Bunce, 1831. 64 p. MBevHi; MfiHi; MFran. 9309

The Storm. A juvenile tale, with four coloured engravings. 1st Amer. ed. New York, J. A. Clussman, 1831. 34 p. MH; PP. 9310

Storrs, Charles Backus.
An address delivered at the Western Reserve College, Hudson, Ohio, Feb. 9, 1831. Pub. by request of the trustees. Boston, Pr. by Peirce & Parker, 1831. 19 p. ICHi; IEG; MBC; MH; OClWHi; RPB. 9311

Storrs, Richard Salter, 1787-1873.
The glory of the Lord; a discourse, delivered at the dedication of the North Meeting House in Braintree, December 29, 1830. By Richard S. Storrs, pastor of the First Church in Braintree. Boston, Pr. by Peirce & Parker, 1831. 32 p. MBC; MH-AH; Msbra; MiD-B; OClWHi; RPB. 9312

---- God's instrument for the conversion of men. A sermon delivered at the installation of the Rev. Josiah Powers, over the Evangelical church in Kingston, Mass. June 15, 1831. By Richard S. Storrs. Boston, Pr. by Peirce & Parker, 1831. 28 p. MA; MBC; MH; MKi; MiD-B; NcMHi; RPB; WHi. 9313

Story, Joseph, 1779-1845.
An address delivered on the dedication of the cemetery at Mount Auburn, September 24, 1831. By Joseph Story. To which is added an appendix, containing a historical notice and description of the place, with a list of the present subscribers. Boston, J. T. & E. Buckingham, 1831. 32 p. CU; ICU; M; MA; MB; MBC; MHi; NNUT; OCHP; PHi; RPB; WHi. 9314

The story of little Benjamin; or, confess your faults. Providence, Pr. by H. H. Brown, 1831. 16 p. MaM; RHi. 9315

Stow, Baron, 1801-1869.
An address, delivered before the Portsmouth Temperance Society, October 25, 1830...Dover, N.H., Pr. by John T. Gibbs, 1831. 16 p. MWA. 9316

The stranger's guide to all the public buildings, places of amusement, streets, alleys, roads, avenues, courts, wharves, principal hotels, steamboat landings, stage offices, &c. &c. of the city of Philadelphia and adjoining districts. Being a complete guide to everything interesting in the city and suburbs of Philadelphia. Philadelphia, Carey & Hart, 1831. 54 p. OU. 9317

Stratten, Thomas.
The Book of the Priesthood; an argument, in three parts by Thomas Stratten, Sunderland. 1st Amer. from the 1st London ed. New York, Jonathan Leavitt; Boston, Crocker & Brewater, 1831. 285 p. CU; ICP; MiD; NjP; PU. 9318

Streeter, Russell.
A sermon, delivered at the funeral of Miss Abigail Reed, of Westwood, Mass., aged twenty years...the victim of modern revivals. By Russell Streeter. Pub. by request. Worcester, Pr. by Spooner & Church, 1831. 20 p. MBUPH; MMeT-Hi. 9319

Stuart, Moses, 1780-1852.
A grammar of the Hebrew language. By Moses Stuart... 4th ed. corr. and enl. Andover, Flagg & Gould, Codman press, 1831. 248, 4 p. CtHC; GDecCT; IU; MH; NjR; PLT; ScDuE; ViRut; WBeloC. 9320

---- A letter to William E. Channing, D.D. on the subject of Religious liberty. 4th ed. Boston, Pr. by Perkins & Marvin, 1831. 43 p. ICMe; ICU; IaGG; M; MH-AH; MHi; MNe; RPB. 9321

---- Sermon at the ordination of the Rev. William G. Schauffler, as Missionary to the Jews. Preached at Park-Street Church, Boston, on the evening of November 14, 1831, by Moses Stuart. 2d ed. Andover, Pr. by Flagg & Could, 1831. 36 p. CtHC; GDecCT; ICN; MH-AH; NjP; RPB; ViRut. 9322

The Student's companion. v. 1, no. 1-4; Jan.-April 1831. By the Knights of the Round table [pseud.] New-Haven, Baldwin & Treadway, 1831. 200 p. Ed. by David Francis Bacon. Each number has a separate cover not included in the pagination. No more published. CtY. 9323

Sue, Eugene, 1804-1857.
Atar gull, a nautical tale. Translated from the French of Eugene Sue, by Wm. Henry Herbert, esq...New York, Garrett & Co. [1831] 94 p. ViU. 9324

---- The Wandering Jew. By Eugene Sue. Illustrated. New York & Boston, H. M. Caldwell Co., [1831] 3 vols. MoRH. 9325

[Sullivan, John Langdon] 1777-1865.
A report, descriptive of a route for a rail road from the Hudson through Paterson to the Delaware River, thence to the Susquehanna and the south western counties of New York...New York, Pr. by Clayton and Van Norden, 1831. 20 p. DLC; MBAt; NHi; PPAmP. 9326

Sullivan, William, 1774-1839.
The moral class book, or The law of morals; derived from the created universe, and from revealed religion. Intended for schools...By William Sullivan. Boston, Pr. by Wait & Dow, for Richardson, Lord & Holbrook, 1831. 282 p. MBL; MH; NCaS; NRU; OMC; RPB. 9327

---- The Political Class Book ... By William Sullivan, Counselor at Law. With an appendix. By Geo. B. Emerson. New ed. with amendments and additions. Boston, Richardson, Lord & Holbrook, 1831. 157 p. CU; IP; MB; Me; PU. 9328

Sumner, Bradford, 1782-1855.
An address delivered at the fifteenth anniversary of the Massachusetts Peace Society. January 19, 1831. By Bradford Sumner. Boston, Pr. by Samuel N. Dickenson, 1831. 30 p. MBAt; MBC; MH; MH-AH; MWA; MeB; MeHi; MnU; NN; OClWHi; PHi; RPB. 9329

Sumner, John Bird, 1780-1862.
A Practical Exposition of the Gospels of St. Matthew & St. Mark, in the form of lectures, intended to assist the practice of domestic institution and devotion by John Bird Sumner, D.D. Bishop of Chester. 1st Amer. ed. New York, Protestant Episcopal Press, 1831. 408 p. ICP; NBuDD; OrP; PSC; ViAl; ViRut. 9330

The Sun anti-masonic almanac. Philadelphia, J. Clarke, 1831. PPeSchw. 9331

The Sunday scholar who turned sailor boy. New Haven, Babcock, Sidney's press, 1831. 18 p. CtY; MB. 9332

Sunday School meeting, Washington, D.C., 1831.
Speeches of Messrs. Webster, Frelinghuysen and others at the Sunday School meeting in the city of Washington. February 16, 1831. Philadelphia, American Sunday School Union, 1831. CtHC; ICU; MBC; OClW; WHi. 9333

Sunday School Society, Boston.
The annual reports of the Boston Sunday School Society. For the year 1831. Boston, Gray & Bowen, 1831. 28 p. ICMe; MiD-B. 9334

---- Order of Performances at the celebration of the Jubilee of Sunday Schools, by the Boston Sunday School Society, in the Federal Street Church, Sept. 14, 1831. 1 p. MHi. 9335

Surault, Francois Marie Joseph.
An easy grammar of the French language, for young beginners. By F. M. J. Surault... Boston, Richardson, Lord & Holbrook, 1831. 287 p. MB; MH; NNC; Nh; OClW. 9336

Susan and Edward; or, A visit to Fulton Market. New York, Mahlon Day [c 1831] 8 l. PP. 9337

Swaim, William.
A collection of cases, illustrating the restorative and sanative properties of Swaim's panacea, in variety of diseases... Philadelphia, 1831. 120 p.

MnU; NNN. 9338

Swan, William.
Letters on missions, by William Swan, missionary to Siberia, with an introductory preface by the late William Orme... Boston, Perkins & Marvin; New York, J. Leavitt, 1831. 288 p. ICP; ICU; MA; MB; MeBat; NNMr; NjP; OClW; OMC; PPiW; PWW. 9339

Swedenborg, Emanuel, 1688-1772.
A brief exposition of the doctrine of the New Church...translated from the Latin of Emanuel Swedonborg. Boston, Allen & Goddard, 1831. 92 p. MCNC. 9340

---- The doctrine of life for the New Jerusalem, from the commandments of the decalogue translated from the Latin. From the 6th London ed. Boston, Allen & Goddard, 1831. MH. 9341

---- Life; with some account of his writings together with a brief notice of the rise and progress of The New Church. Boston, Allen, 1831. MWA. 9342

---- On the New Jerusalem and its Heavenly Doctrine, as revealed from Heaven, etc. 4th Amer. ed. Boston, Allen and Goddard, 1831. MH-AH; MLow. 9343

Swords' pocket almanack, churchman's calendar, and Ecclesiastical Register...1832...New York, Pr. by Edward J. Swords, for T. & J. Swords [1831] 100 p. MWA; WHi. 9344

T

The tablet... New-Haven, A. H. Maltby, 1831. 220 p. CtY; DLC; MB; RPB. 9345

Talbert, J. L.
The Western Youths' Geography, with eleven maps, designed for the use of schools and academies. "Do you aspire to eminence in the Republic, study its geography and resources." By J. L. Talbert. Cincinnati, Robinson and Fairbanks, 1831. 102 p. OMC. 9346

Tales of Egypt, comprising histories of Joseph, Moses, and Joshua. By the author of "The Family Temperance Meeting." Boston, James Loring, Sabbath School Book-Store, 1831. 10 p. ICBB. 9347

Tallmadge, James, 1778-1853.
Address of Gen. Tallmadge, delivered before the American Institute of the City of New-York, at Clinton Hall, August, 1831. New-York, Pr. by J. M. Danforth, for the American Institute, 1831. 8 p. MWA. 9348

Tappan, Henry Philip.
The progress of Christianity, the history of the world; a sermon delivered at Pittsfield, Mass. in the Congregational church, Jan. 2, 1831...by Henry Philip Tappan... Pittsfield, Allen [1831] 20 p. MHi; MPiB; NjP; RPB. 9349

Tappan, Lewis, 1766-1873.
Letter to Eleazer Lord, Esq., in defence of treasures for promoting the observance of the Christian Sabbath. New York, Sleight and Robinson [1831] 24 p. DLC; MB; MH; MWA; OO; PPPrHi. 9350

Tate, George.
A treatise on hysteria. By George Tate. Philadelphia, E. L. Carey & A. Hart, 1831. 134 p. ArU-M; LNOP; MdBJ; NbU-M; OClM; RPM. 9351

The Tatler and Guardian, chiefly

by Sir Richard Steel and Joseph Addison. And an account of the authors, by Thomas Babbington[!] Macaulay, complete in one volume. With notes and indexes. Philadelphia, Woodward, 1831. 444, 244 p. AMob; CSmH; ICMe; LNF; MH; TNP; ViU. 9352

Taylor, Benjamin Elder.
Memoirs of Ardelia A. Martin...who died July 26, 1830. Embracing sketches of her religious experience...by B. Taylor and J. Blackmarr. Fall River, Pr. by B. Earl, 1831. 24 p. RPB; Nh. 9353

Taylor, C. B.
A universal history of the United States of America, embracing the whole period from the earliest discoveries down to the present time; giving descriptions of the western country, its soil, settlements, increase of population, etc. New York, Ezra Strong, 1831. 494 p. MiDSH; NbOM; OClWHi; ViRVU; WHi. 9354

Taylor, Isaac.
Bunyan explained to a child being pictures and poems founded upon the pilgrim's progress. Hartford, D. F. Robinson & co., 1831. 96 p. MNF; NBi. 9355

---- Natural History of Enthusiasm. New York, Jonathan Leavitt; Boston, Crocker & Brewster, 1831. 300 p. GOgU; KyBC; MA; MaBat; PU; ViU. 9356

Taylor, James B.
A Memoir. New York, John S. Taylor, 1831. 400 p. IaPeC. 9357

Taylor, Jane, 1783-1824.
Bible thoughts for the young. Boston, 1831. MNan. 9358

---- The Contributions of Q. Q. By Jane Taylor. Boston, Perkins and Marvin, 1831. 268 p. NGH. 9359

---- Elizabeth Palmer; or, Display, a tale; from 12th London ed. Boston, Perkins, 1831. 180 p. PU. 9360

---- Essays in rhyme, on morals and manners. By the late Jane Taylor...From 4th London ed. Boston, Perkins & Marvin, 1831. 108 p. MeBaT; OO; PU. 9361

---- Little Ann, a true story: and other pleasing pieces for children. New York, M. Day, 1831. 23 p. CtY; NN. 9362

---- Scenes of early life... Boston, 1831. PPL; VtBarnd. 9363

---- The writings of Jane Taylor in five volumes... Boston, Perkins & Marvin; Philadelphia, French & Perkins, 1831-1832. IP; MB; MH; MHoly; OCL. 9364

Taylor, Jane E. J.
A memoir of Jane E. J. Taylor, who died in the fourteenth year of her age; revised by the committee of publication. Philadelphia, American Sunday School Union, 1831. 51 p. CtY; NTEN. 9365

Taylor, Jeremy, 1613-1667.
The comforts of piety, taught from four beads in religion: faith, hope, the Holy Spirit, and prayer... Boston, James Loring [1831] 96 p. CtHWatk; MBC; PHi; PU-Penn. 9366

---- Holy living and dying, with prayers, containing a complete duty of a Christian. By Jeremy Taylor. Amherst, J. S. and C. Adams, 1831. 431 p. CtHC; IJI; MA; MoSpD; OO; RPB. 9367

---- ---- Hartford, H. & F. J. Huntington, 1831. 431 p. Ct; MB; MLen; Nh; OHi; RPA. 9368

---- ---- Philadelphia, Thomas Wardle, 1831. 515 p. MdW; NSyU; PHi; TNP. 9369

Taylor, John, 1757-1832.
Records of my life. New York, 1831. 461 p. MWA. 9370

Taylor, John W., 1784-1854.
An address before the Republican Antimasonic County Convention... Ballston Spa, Oct. 1831. From proceedings. Saratoga County, N.Y., 1831. MB. 9371

Taylor, Thomas House.
An address, delivered before the Charleston Infant School Society, in St. Michael's Church, Charleston, on the evening of the 30th October, and in the Circular Church, on the evening of the 13th November, 1831. By Thomas House Taylor, Rector of St. John's Parish, Colleton. Pub. by request of the society. Charleston, Pr. by J. S. Burges, 1831. 15 p. MHi; MWA. 9372

Teachers and Friends of Education. New York.
Address of the state convention of Teachers and Friends of Education, held at Utica, January 12th, 13th & 14th, 1831. With an abstract of the proceedings of said convention. Utica, Pr. by Northway and Porter, 1831. 16 p. MB; MBAt; MH; MHi; MWA; N; NGH; NHi; TNP. 9373

The Teacher's Gift to his pupils. With numerous engravings. 2d ed. Boston, Gray & Bowen, Lincoln & Edmands, and N. S. Simpkins & Co., 1831. 144 p. DLC; MiK; NSchHi; RPB. 9374

Teaching. Essays on school keeping: comprising observations on the qualifications of teachers... and on the most approved methods of instructions... by an experienced teacher. Philadelphia, John Grigg, 1831. 200 p. MNF. 9375

Teall, Benjamin.
Universalism; or, The doctrine of the restoration of all men refuted in a short discourse. Newport, 1831. Nh. 9376

Tegg, Thomas, 1776-1845.
The Vocal Annual. 1831. MH. 9377

Temperance almanac, for the year of our Lord 1832: Being Leap-Year and the 56th-57th of American Independence. Calculated for the meridian of Rochester... Rochester, Pr. by Hoyt, Porter & Co. [1831] 36 p. NNHist; NUtHi. 9378

Temperance Calendar for 1832. Sandy-Hill, N.Y., Temperance Advocate Office [1831] MWA. 9379

Tennessee.
Journal of the Court of Impeachment, the State of Tennessee, vs. Joshua Haskell. [Nashville?] F. S. Heiskell and A. A. Hall, prs. to the state. "Knoxville Register" Office, 1831. 359-442 p. GEU; T; TKL-Mc; TMeC. 9380

---- Journal of the House of Representatives of the state of Tennessee, at the nineteenth General Assembly, held in Nashville. [Nashville?] F. S. Heikell & A. A. Hall, prs. to the state. "Knoxville Register" Office, F. S. Heiskell, pr., 1831. 414 p. T; TKL-Mc; TMeC. 9381

---- Journal of the Senate, of the state of Tennessee, at the nineteenth General Assembly, held at Nashville. [Nashville?] F.S. Heiskell & A. A. Hall, prs. to the state. "Knoxville register" office, F. S. Heiskell, pr., 1831. 442 p. This session began September 19, 1831 and adjourned

December 21, 1831. Pp. 259-442 contain the "Journal of the Court of Impeachment..." GEU; T; TKL-Mc; TMeC. 9382

---- Report of Mr. Brown, from the Select Committee against the Renewal of the Charter of the United States Bank. Nashville, Allen A. Hall, pr. to the House, 1831. 13 p. TKL-Mc. 9383

---- Report of the committee on internal improvement, in the House of Representatives, in relation to the Lynchburg and New-River Railroad, December 3, 1831. Pr. by order of the House. Nashville, A. A. Hall, pr., 1831. 17 p. MH-BA. 9384

---- Report of the standing committee on banks, in the House of Representatives, on the subject of closing the concerns of the bank of the state. Submitted December 10, 1831. Pr. by order of the House of Representatives. Nashville, Allen A. Hall, pr. to the House, 1831. 12 p. T. 9385

---- The statute laws of the state of Tennessee, of a public and general nature; revised and digested by John Haywood and Robert L. Cobbs. By order of the General assembly...Knoxville, T., F. S. Heiskell, 1831. 2 vols. GHi; IU; MoS; NcD; TCh; WaU. 9386

Tennessee State Medical Society.
Minutes of the proceedings of the Medical Society of Tennessee, at the second annual meeting, held in the City of Nashville, May 1831. Nashville, Pr. at the Herald Office, 1831. 29 p. MHi; PPAmP; T. 9387

Tenney, Caleb Jewett, 1780-1847.
Mysterious events to be explained; a sermon, at Glastenburg, December 8, 1830, funeral of Rev. Samuel Austin. Hartford, Pr. by Philoemon Canfield, 1831. 27 p. Ct; CtMW; MWA; MiD-B; NN; VtMidbC. 9388

Test, John, d. 1849.
Circular to his constituents. Washington, 1831. 16 p. DLC. 9389

A testimony on baptism, as practiced by the primitive Christians, from the time of the apostles; and on the Lord's Supper, according to the institution of Christ and his Apostles, and on the washing of feet, with regard to the right manner, in which the same ought to be performed, and also, on the leprosy and the sprinkle-water, and the signification thereof. Written by a lover of the Divine truth, and submitted to the reflection of all those who seek their eternal welfare. Baltimore, Pr. by Benjamin Edes, 1831. 71 p. PCA; RPB. 9390

Thacher, James, 1754-1844.
An essay on demonology, ghosts and apparitions and popular susperstitions. Also, an account of the witchcraft delusion at Salem, in 1692. By James Thacher. Boston, Carter & Hendee, 1831. 234 p. CSt; ICU; M; MB; PPA. 9391

Thacher, Peter Oxenbridge, 1776-1843.
An address, pronounced on the first Tuesday of March, 1831 before the members of the bar of the County of Suffolk, Massachusetts, by Peter Oxenbridge Thacher. Boston, Hilliard, Gray, Little & Wilkins, 1831. 40 p. CtHC; DLC; MB; MBC; MWA; MoS; NNC; PHi. 9392

Thackrah, Charles Turner, 1795-1833.

The effects of the principal arts, trades, and professions, and of civic states and habits of living, on health and longevity; with a particular reference to the trades and manufactures of Leeds: and suggestions for the removal of many of the agents, which produce disease, and shorten the duration of life. By C. Turner Thackrah. From the London ed., with imp. Philadelphia, H. H. Porter, 1831. 180 p. CtHT; ICJ; ICP; MB; MBM; OC; OO; PU. 9393

Thatcher, Benjamin Bussey, 1809-1840.
Polish war song. Written for the consecration of the Polish standards at Faneuil Hall, Boston, Sept. 12th 1831. By B. B. Thatcher Esq. Music composed by Ch. Zeuner. Boston, C. Bradlee, [1831] 2 p. ICPRCU. 9394

---- Tales of the Indians; being prominent passages of the history of the North American natives. Taken from authentic sources... Boston, Waitt & Dow, 1831. 253 p. ICN; InU; KyDC; MH; MiD; NBuG; WHi. 9395

Thayer, Nathaniel, 1769-1840.
An address delivered at the Berry street conference, May 25, 1831... Boston, Wait, Green, 1831. 15 p. CBPac; MH; MH-AH; MLanc. 9396

Theaulon, de Lambert, Marie Emmanuel Guillaume Marguerite, 1787-1841.
The little Red Riding Hood, a fairy opera in three acts, by Mr. Theaulon. Music by M. Boieldieu; tr. for the use of visitors to the French opera by W. F. F. Baltimore, 1831. 131 p. WHi. 9397

Theophrastus.
The characters of Theophrastus; illustrated by physionomical sketches. Boston, Frederick S. Hill, Jenkins & Greenough, Stereotypers, 1831. 64 p. CtSoP; IRoC; MH; MWA; MeBa; NGH; PHi; PP; PPL-R; RPA; Vi; WU. 9398

Third Congregational Church. New Haven.
The constitution, confession of faith, and covenant of the Third Congregational Church in New Haven. New Haven, 1831. 14 p. MWA. 9399

Thomas, Abel C.
Shipwreck of partialism. Review of..."The fog of Universalism dissipated by the light of truth" (a pamphlet by J. B. Crist). By Abel C. Thomas. Reading, Pa., Pr. by John Ritter & Co., 1831. 24 p. MMeT-Hi. 9400

Thomas, James.
The miscellaneous poems, together with some of the prose composition of James Thomas. Rutland [Vt.], Herald office print, 1831. RPB; VtHi. 9401

Thomason, Denny R.
Fashionable amusements...by Rev. D. R. Thomason, with a recommendatory preface, by Rev. G. Spring, D.D. New York, J. Leavitt; Boston, Crocker & Brewster, 1831. 205 p. CSmH; GDecCT; IaDuU; MiU; NjP; PMA; ScNC; TNP. 9402

Thompson, James William.
The Claims of Free-Masonry Stated, and Objections to it Considered. An address delivered before the Fraternity, at Leicester, Mass., on the anniversary of St. John The Baptist, June 24, A. L. 5831. By James W. Thompson, Pastor of the Church in South Natick. Cambridge, Pr. by E. W. Metcalf & Co., 1831. 32 p.

DLC; IaCrM; MB; MHi; MWA. 9403

---- Forms for the devotional exercises of Sabbath Schools. By a pastor. Boston, Wait, Green & Co., 1831. 33 p. MB; MHi; MiD-B. 9404

Thompson, John Samuel.
The Reformed Christian guide. ...By Rev. John Samuel Thompson...New York, Pr. by Daniel Mitchell, 1831. 72 p. ICU; MH; MMeT-Hi. 9405

Thompson and Homans.
Catalogue of Music. Thompson and Homans. Georgetown, Homans, 1831. 18 p. DLC. 9406

Thomson, James, 1700-1748.
Poetical works. Philadelphia? [Grigg, 1831] OSand. 9407

---- The seasons... To which is prefixed the life of the author, by P. Murdock...New York, Pr. by S. & D. A. Forbes, 1831. 192 p. OO. 9408

---- ---- Philadelphia, James Locken, 1831. 192 p. KMopc; Mchesh; MWA; MoSU; WvSh. 9409

Thomson, John.
Lectures on inflammation, exhibiting a view of the general doctrines, pathological and practical, of medical surgery. By J. Thomson, M.D. 2nd American from the last London ed. Philadelphia, Pr. by C. Sherman & Co., for Carey & Lea, 1831. CU; KyU; MNF; MoSW-M; NIC-M; PP; PU; TNV. 9410

---- A view of science and quackery...By John Thomson... Albany, N.Y., Pr. by S. Southwick, Jun., 1831. 48 p. NNN. 9411

Thomson, Mrs. Katherine (Byerley), 1797-1862.
Memoirs of the life of Sir Walter Raleigh, with some account of the period in which he lived. Philadelphia, Carey & Lea, 1831. 287 p. MB; NjP; PPL; OHi; VtB; WHi. 9412

Thomson, Peter.
Appendix to Graydon's Forms of Conveyancing and of Practice, in various courts and public offices. By Peter Thomson and John P. Owens. Philadelphia, 1831. 174 p. MH-L; PU-L. 9413

Thomson, Samuel.
New guide to health; or, Botanic family physician. Containing a complete system of practice on a plan entirely new. 3d ed. Boston, Howe, 1831. 156 p. PPCP; PPL-R; PHi. 9414

The Thomsonian and Botanic Medical adviser. Published Monthly under the superintendence of a Committee from the Thomsonian society of Baltimore, No. 1. Baltimore. Pr. by Richard J. Matchett, 1831. 24 p. ScU. 9415

Thoughts on Calvinism: a poem. Northampton, T. Taylor, Drapery, and J. Taylor, 1831. 15 p. PPM. 9416

Thoughts on the importance of Religion. 4th ed. New York, Mahlon Day, 1831. 12 p. MeB. 9417

Thucydides
Thucydides De bello peloponnesian libri octo. Hilpertolrusal et Novi Yorici, sumptibus et typis Instituti bibliographici, 1831. DLC; MH. 9418

[Thurston, John] 1774-1822.
Illustrations of Shakespeare, comprised in 230 vignette engravings by Thompson from designs by Thurston, adapted to all editions. New York, William

Jackson, 1831. 37 p. MH. 9419

[Ticknor, George] 1791-1871.
Remarks on the life and writings of Daniel Webster of Massachusetts. Philadelphia, Carey and Lea, 1831. 48 p. MH; MiU; OCLaw; RPB; WHi. 9420

Tillotson, John, 1630-1694.
A discourse against transubstantiation: by Archbishop Tillotson. Philadelphia, Pr. by W. F. Geddes, 1831. 38 p. CtHC; DLC; MWA. 9421

Tillson, John, Jr.
Hillsboro, March, 1831. Circular. Sir: It is with regret, that I inform you...the taxes... raised from $1.60 to $2.40 on each quarter section... Your obedient Servant, John Tillson, Jr.... [1831?] Broadside. MHi. 9422

Tilton, J.
Bill of mortality for Exeter, N.H , 1830. Exeter, 1831. Broadside. MBM. 9423

Timbs, John.
Knowledge for the people; or, The plain Why and Because. By John Timbs. Popular Chemistry-Mechanics-Arts and manufactures. Boston, Lilly & Wait, and Carter and Hendee; New-York, P. Hill; Philadelphia, Carey & Hart; New Orleans, M. Carroll; Portland, S. Colman, 1831. 72 p. MB; MBAt; MBL; MCM; MH; MShM; Nh; NjR. 9424

Tingry, P[ierre] F[rancois]
The painter's colourman's complete guide; being a practical and theoretical treatise on the preparation of colours, and their application to the different kinds of paintings in which is particularly described the whole art of house painting. 1st Amer., from the 3d London ed., corr. and imp. Philadelphia, E. L. Carey & A. Hart, 1831. MH; NbOM; NTiHi. 9425

Tinker, Reuben.
Ought I to become a missionary? An address to theological students by Rev. Reuben Tinker, missionary to the Sandwich Islands. Dedham, Mass., L. Powers, 1831. 15 p. CtHC; ICP; MB; MBC. 9426

The token; a Christmas and New Year's present: edited by S. G. Goodrich. Boston, Gray & Bowen, 1831. 320 p. ICN; MNS; MWHi; NT; PMA; RWe. 9427

Tooth, Miss.
Memoirs of Miss Sarah Jenkins, by Miss Tooth. New York, J. Emory, 1831. TxDaM. 9428

Toppan, Benjamin, 1788-1863.
The believers last enemy destroyed. A sermon delivered November 17, 1830 at the funeral of Rev. Fifield Holt, late pastor of the Congregational Church in Bloomsfield. By B. Toppan, pastor of a church in Augusta. Augusta, W. Hastings, 1831. 20 p. DLC; MBS; NBLiHi; OCHP; RPB. 9429

Torrey, John, 1796-1873.
Catalogue of North American genera of plants, arranged according to the orders of Lindley's introduction to the natural system of botany with the number of species belonging to each genus as far as they are at present determined. New York, Pr. by Sleight, 1831. 22 p. CtMW; MH; MoSB; NNN. 9430

Totten, John, comp.
Selection of hymns and spiritual songs, with the choruses affixed...as usually sung at campmeetings, etc. To which is added an Appendix, containing funeral hymns. Compiled by John Totten.

23d ed. New York, 1831. 192 p. InFoc; MHi. 9431

Towndrow, Thomas, b. 1810.
A complete guide to stenography, or an entirely new system of writing short hand. Formed upon rational principles, and combining simplicity, brevity and perspicuity, for the use of schools and private tuition. By T. Towndrow... Boston, Pr. by C. S. D. & B. F. Griffin, 1831. 28 p. MNan; MTemNHi; PP. 9432

Townsend, John.
Memoirs of the Rev. John Townsend, founder of the asylum for the deaf and dumb, and of the Congregational school...1st American ed. Boston, Crocker & Brewster; New York, J. Leavitt, 1831. 244 p. ICP; IJI; M; MA; MB; MBC; MH-AH; MNe; NNC; OMC; OO; PMA; PWW. 9433

Townsend, P[eter] S.
Result of observations made upon the black vomit, or yellow fever, at Havana & New York... read to the Board of health, New York, and pub. in the New York Medical Journal...1831. New York, Clayton, 1831. 65 p. NjR; PPCP; TxU. 9434

---- Speech...on the report presented by him, as chairman of the special committee, on the subject of the tax upon seamen. In Common Council, New York, April 4, 1831. [New York, Clayton & Van Norden, 1831] 8 p. MH-BA. 9435

Transylvania College, Lexington, Ky.
A catalogue of the officers and students of Transylvania University, Lexington, Ky. January 1831. Lexington, Pr. by Herndon & Savary, 1831. 16 p. KyU; MB. 9436

The Traveller's Pocket Directory and Stranger's Guide; exhibiting distances on the principal Canal and Stage routes in the State of New-York. Containing also descriptions of the rail roads now building and in contemplation in this state. With a list of broken banks--Rates of toll on the Canals for 1831--and a variety of other matter, highly valuable to the travelling community. Schenectady, Pr. by S. Wilson for the pub., 1831. 66 p. MB; MReu; NSchHi. 9437

Trelawny, Edward John, 1792-1881.
The adventures of a younger son. By Edward John Trelawny. New York, Humphrey, Milford, University Press, 1831. 544 p. PPL. 9438

Trenck, Friedrich, freiherr von der, 1726-1794.
The life of Baron Frederick Trenck, containing his adventures, his excessive sufferings during ten years imprisonment at the fortress of Magdeburgh, by command of the late king of Prussia. Philadelphia, Key, 1831. 264 p. OClW. 9439

Trial of Parkhusrt [sic] Whitney, Timothy Shaw, Noah Beach, William Miller, and Samuel M. Chubbuck; for a conspiracy; the abduction, false imprisonment, and assault and battery, of William Morgan: had at a special circuit court, held at Lockport, Niagara County, Feb. 1831... Pub. at the Balance office, Lockport [1831] 63 p. CSmH; NCH. 9440

The Trials of a school girl... Boston, Leonard C. Bowles, 1831. 134 p. MFiHi. 9441

Trimmer, Mrs. Mary.
A natural history of the most

remarkable quadrupeds, birds, fishes, serpents, reptiles, and insects. By Mrs. Mary Trimmer, abr. and imp. ...Boston, Hilliard, Gray, Little & Wilkins, 1831. 233 p. NjR. 9442

Triumphant deaths, or Brief notice of the happy death of twenty-six Sabbath School scholars. New Haven, Pr. by S. Babcock, for J. L. Cross, 1831. 103 p. DLC; MB; MWo. 9443

Troost, Gerard, 1776-1850.
...Address delivered before the legislature of Tennessee, at Nashville, October 19th, 1831 on the mineral resources and the utility of a geological survey of the state...By Gerard Troost, M.D.... Lexington, Ky., 1831. 491-507 p. DLC. 9444

Truair, John.
Two discourses, Aug. 21, 28, Sept. 4, 1831. Northampton, 1831. MB. 9445

---- Union among the saints of God, an indispensable duty of all who love the Lord Jesus...Two discourses...Northampton, Pr. by T. W. Shepard, 1831. 32 p. MB; MWiW; MnHi; RPB. 9446

Trueba y Cosio, Joaquin Telesforo, 1799?-1835.
The Incognito; or, Sins and peccadilloes [sic]. By the author of: "Romance of history, Spain," "The Castilian." New York, J. & J. Harper, 1831. NjHo; RLa. 9447

Trumbull, Henry.
History of the discovery of America: of the landing of our forefathers at Plymouth, and of their most remarkable engagements with the Indians in New England, from their first landing in 1620, until the final subjugation for the natives in 1679. By Henry Trumbull. Boston, George Clark, 1831. 256 p. Ct; DLC; IEN-M; MB; NN; PPHi. 9448

Trumbull, John, 1756-1843.
Catalogue of paintings by Colonel Trumbull including were subjects of the American Revolution with near 250 portraits...now exhibiting at the gallery of the Amer. academy of fine arts. New-York, Nathaniel B. Holmes, 1831. 32 p. ICHi; MH; MHi; MNF; MiDB; MiU-C; NNC; WHi. 9449

Tubal-Cain, pseud.
The mother of Masons: or sketches of the history of ancient Freemasonry, contrasted with illuminism or modern Masonry. By Tubal-Cain. Utica, Pr. by Hastings & Tracy, for the author, 1831. 14 p. MB; WHi. 9450

Tucker, Abraham, 1705-1774.
The light of nature pursued. By Abraham Tucker, Esq., from the second London ed., rev. and corr. Together with some account of the life of the author. By Sir H. P. St. John Mildmay, Bart. M. P. Cambridge, Hilliard & Brown, 1831. 4 vols. CBPac; GMM; ICT; MB; NjR; NuSchu; WM. 9451

Tucker, Henry St. George, 1780-1848.
Commentaries on the laws of Virginia, comprising the substance of a course of lectures delivered to the Winchester law school: by Henry St. George Tucker... Winchester, Pr. at the office of the Winchester Virginian for the author. 2 vols. CU; MdBB; MdBP; MiU-L; ViU; WaU. 9452

Tucker, W. C.
Predestination calmly considered from principles of reason... to which is appended the article

on divine sovereignty...by James Jamieson, D.D. Albany, B. D. Packard & Co., 1831. 252 p. IaMp; MBC; NNUT; NcCJ. 9453

Tucker, William.
The Family Dyer and Scourer: being a complete treatise on the arts of dyeing and cleaning every article of dress, bed and window furniture, silks, bonnets, feathers, etc. ... By Wm. Tucker. 2d ed., rev. and corr. Philadelphia, E. L. Carey and A. Hart, 1831. 123 p. LNT; MH; OClW; RPB; ScCMu. 9454

Tuckerman, Joseph, 1778-1840.
Ejaculatory prayer. Daily use of scripture. By Joseph Tuckerman... Boston, Gray and Bowen, 1831. 16 p. MBAU; MH-AH; MMeT-Hi; RP; RPB. 9455

---- A letter on the principles of the missionary Enterprise. 3d ed. Boston, Pr. by I. R. Butts for Gray and Bowen, 1831. 39 p. ICMe; MeBat; MH. 9456

---- Mr. Tuckerman's eighth semi-annual report of his service as a minister at large in Boston. No. 54. Pr. for The American Unitarian Association. Boston, Gray & Bowen; Dec. 1831. 48 p. ICMe; MHi; MNBedf; MeB; MeBat. 9457

---- Mr. Tuckerman's seventh semi-annual report of his service as a minister at large in Boston. Pr. for the American Unitarian Association. Boston, Gray and Bowen, 1831. 36 p. ICMe; MHi; MNF; MeB; NCH. 9458

[Tully, William], 1785-1859.
Catalogue of the phenogamous plants & the ferns, growing without cultivation, within five miles of Yale College, Ct. extracted from the appendix to Mr. E. Baldwin's History of Yale College. New Haven, H. Howe, 1831. [37] p. Ct; CtW; ICF; MH; MBHo; MSaP; NIC. 9459

Turnbull, Robert James, 1775-1833.
Speech of R. J. Turnbull, Esq., at the celebration of the state rights and free trade party of Charleston, on the fourth of July, 1831. Columbia, S.C., Pr. at the Times and Gazette office, 1831. 16 p. CSmH; NB; RPB; ScU. 9460

Turnbull, William.
A popular treatise on health ...From the last London ed. By the late Wm. Turnbull... New York, J. K. Porter, 1831. 92 p. DSG; MB; MeLewB; NPV; OCLloyd. 9461

Turner, Edward, 1797-1837.
Elements of chemistry, including the recent discoveries and doctrines of the science. By Edward Turner. 4th Amer. from the 3d London ed. with notes and emendations, by Franklin Bache. Philadelphia, Grigg & Elliott, 1831. 622 p. CtMW; Ia; KyLxT; MnU; MoSpD; OWC; PPCP; RPB; TxBrdD. 9462

Turner, Nat (1800?-1831).
The confessions of Nat Turner, the leader of the late insurrection in Southampton, Va. as fully and voluntarily made to Thomas R. Gray, in the prison where he was confined, and acknowledged by him to be such when read before the court of Southampton: with the certificate, under seal of the court convened at Jerusalem, Nov. 5, 1831, for his trial. Also an authentic account of the whole insurrection with lists of those who were murdered, and of the negroes brought before the court of Southampton, and there sentenced, &c. Baltimore, Pr. by Lucas &

Deaver, for T. R. Gray, 1831. 23 p. DLC; MB; MdBP; NcU; PHi; PPHi; ViRU; VtU; WHi. 9463

Turner, Samuel H.
The claims of the Hebrew language and literature in three lectures delivered in chapel of Columbia College, 1831. By Samuel H. Turner, D.D. ... Andover, Pr. by Flagg & Gould, 1831. 42 p. DLC; MBAt; MdBD; NNG; NjR; PPL-R. 9464

Tuttle, George, 1804-1872.
Stories about the elephant. Told by a father to his son. New Haven, S. Babcock, 1831. 109 p. CtY; MBAt; MH. 9465

[Tuttle, Sarah]
Conversations on the Mackinaw and Green-Bay Indian missions, in 2 parts, by the author of Conversations on the Sandwich Island mission, Malvina Ashton, Naval chaplain, and etc., ... rev. by the publishing committee. Boston, Pr. by T. R. Marvin, for the Massachusetts Sabbath School Union, 1831. 128 p. DLC; ICP MiD; MnHi; OMC; WStfSF. 9466

---- Letters and conversations on the Indian missions at Seneca, Tuscarora, Cattaraugus, in the state of New York, and Maumee, in the state of Ohio. In four parts. By the author of Letters and conversations on the Sandwich Islands, Bombay, Ceylon, and Indian missions... Rev. by the Publishing committee. Boston, Pr. by T. R. Marvin, for the Massachusetts Sabbath School Union, 1831. 112 p. DLC; GDecCT; ICP; NNUT; NjR; OClWHi; OHi; WHi. 9467

[----] Letters on the Chickasaw and Osage missions. By the author of Conversations on the Sandwich Islands, Bombay, and Ceylon missions, Naval chaplain &c. Revised by the publishing committee. Boston, Pr. by T. R. Marvin for the Massachusetts Sabbath School Union, 1831. 161 p. DLC; ICN; ICP; LNH; MiD; MoHi; MoKU; NHi; NN; WHi. 9468

Tweedie, Alexander, 1794-1884.
Clinical illustrations of fever comprising a report of the cases treated at the London fever hospital, 1828-1829. By Alexander Tweedie. Philadelphia, Carey & Lea, 1831. 152 p. MdBM; NBMS; NBuU-M; NhD; PP; PPCP; VtU. 9469

The two goats and the sick monkey. Concord, Fisk & Chase, 1831. 16 p. CtY. 9470

Tyler, Edward R.
The doctrine of election; a sermon by Edward R. Tyler... Middletown, Edwin Hunt; New Haven, Pr. by Baldwin and Treadway, 1831. 28 p. MA; MBNMHi; NjP; RBr. 9471

Tyler, John, President. U.S., 1790-1862.
Speech of Mr. Tyler, of Virginia, on Mr. Tazewell's motion to amend the general appropriation bill, by striking out so much thereof as went to provide for the payment of certain commissioners appointed by the president to negotiate a treaty with the Porte. In Senate, February 24, 1831. Washington, Duff Green, 1831. 16 p. DLC; MB; NcD; NcU; OClWHi; ScU; Vi; WHi. 9472

Tyng, Stephen Higginson, 1800-1885.
Lessons on the Acts of the Apostles, designed for more advanced Bible classes. By Stephen H. Tyng... Philadelphia, William Stavely, 1831. 76 p. MdBD; NjR. NNG. 9473

---- A sermon preached at the

consecration of St. Paul's church, Philadelphia, Jan. 1, 1831. By Stephen H. Tyng... Pub. by the vestry of St. Paul's church. Philadelphia, Pr. by Wm. Stavely, 1831. 27 p. CtHT; MiD-B; NjR; PHi; TJaU. 9474

Tyson, Job Roberts, 1803-1858.
Annual discourse...before the Historical Society of Pennsylvania. By Job R. Tyson... Philadelphia, Pr. by Mifflin & Parry, for E. L. Carey & A. S. Hart, 1831. 52 p. DLC; MWA; NiC; NjP; PPL; ScC; WHi. 9475

U

Union and Protection Tracts. No. 1-3. [Washington?] 1831. 32 p. NN. 9476

Union and States Rights Party.
Union and Liberty. An ode sung at the celebration of the American Independence by the Union and State Rights Party, Charleston, S.C., on the 4th July, A.D. 1831. Composed by a citizen of South Carolina...[Charleston, 1831] 3 p. MHi. 9477

Union Benevolent Association, Philadelphia.
Constitution and report explanatory of its object; also, constitution, &c. of the Ladies' assistant society. Philadelphia, Harding, 1831. 12 p. N; PHC; PPL. 9478

Union Canal Company of Pennsylvania.
Annual report of the managers of The Union Canal Co. of Pa. to the stockholders, Nov. 15, 1831. Philadelphia, Pr. by T. Desilver, Jr., 1831. 8, 8, 12 p. TU; PPi. 9479

Union Insurance Company of Philadelphia.
List of directors. Philadelphia, 1831. 1 p. PHi. 9480

Union University, Schenectady.
Catalogue of the Senior class ...1830-31. Schenectady, Pr. by S. S. Riggs, 1831. 7 p. NN; NSchU. 9481

The Unitarian Christian, no. 1 & 2. Augusta, Ga., Augusta Unitarian Association, 1831. 2 numbers. MBC; MH; MHi. 9482

Unitarian Essayist: January, 1831 to December, 1831. Meadville [Pa.] Pr. by Thomas Atkinson, 1831-2. 2 vols. DLC; IEG; MA; MHi; PHi. 9483

Unitarian monitor. v. 1-2, Apr. 29, 1831-Apr. 10, 1833. Dover, N.H., J. Mann, 1831 [-33]. 2 vols. CBPac; DLC; WHi. 9484

United States.
An act for closing certain accounts, and making appropriations for arrearages in the Indian Department. January 6, 1831. Read twice, and referred to the Committee on Indian Affairs. [Washington, 1831] 3 p. (H.R. 480). DNA. 9485

---- An act for the benefit of Percis Lovely. January 12, 1831. Read, and passed to a second reading. January 13, 1831. Read second time, and referred to Committee on Public Lands. [Washington, 1831] (H.R. 541) DNA. 9486

---- An act for the relief of James McCarty. December 30, 1831. Received [Washington, 1831] 1 p. (H.R. 6) DNA. 9487

---- An Act for the relief of the legal representatives of General Moses Hazen, deceased, February 26, 1831. Mr. Burges from the Committee on Revolutionary Claims, to which was referred the bill from the Senate entitled "An act for the relief of the legal representatives of General Moses Hazen, deceased," reported with the following amendments ... [Washington, 1831] (S. 7) DNA. 9488

---- Act act making additional appropriations for the improvement of certain harbors, and removing obstructions in the mouths of certain rivers. February 19, 1831. [Washington, 1831] (H.R. 566) DNA. 9489

---- An act making appropriations for carrying on certain roads and works of internal improvement, and providing for the surveys. February 25, 1831. Received. [Washington, 1831] 3 p. (H.R. 584) DNA. 9490

---- An act making appropriations for the completion and support of the penitentiary in the District of Columbia, and for other purposes. December 30, 1830. Received December 31, 1830. Read, and passed to a second reading, January 3, 1831, Read a second time and referred to the Committee on District of Columbia. [Washington, 1831] 2 p. (H.R. 343) DNA 9491

---- An Act making appropriations for the military service for the year (1831). February 19, 1831. Read twice, and referred to the Committee on Finance. [Washington, 1831] 5 p. (H.R. 539) DNA. 9492

---- An act making appropriations for the naval service for the year (1831). February 19, 1831. Read twice, and referred to the Committee on Finance. [Washington, 1831] 5 p. (H.R. 531) DNA. 9493

---- An act making appropriations for the support of Government for the year (1831). February 9, 1831. Engrossed. February 11, 1831. Read twice, and referred to the Committee on Finance. [Washington, 1831] 18 p. (H.R. 528) DNA. 9494

---- An act making provision for a subscription to a compilation of congressional documents. February 28, 1831. Read. [Washington, 1831] 1 p. (H.R. 652) DNA. 9495

---- An act supplementary to the "Act for the relief of certain surviving officers and soldiers of the revolution." February 18, 1831. Received. February 19, 1831. Read twice, and referred to the Committee on Pensions. [Washington, 1831] 3 p. (H.R. 567) DNA. 9496

---- An act to direct the manner of issuing patents on confirmed land claims in the territory of Florida. December 30, 1831. Received. [Washington, 1831] 1 p. (H.R. 103) DNA. 9497

---- Act to provide a national currency, secured by a pledge of United States Stocks, and to provide for the circulation and redemption thereof. Washington, 1831. 28 p. PHi. 9498

---- An act to provide for the final settlement and adjustment of the various claims preferred by James Monroe against the United States. February 7, 1821. Read, and passed to a second reading. February 8, 1831. read a second time, and referred to a select committee to consist of Messrs. Hayne, Sanford, Frelinghuysen, Bell, and Iredell, to consider and report thereon. [Washington, 1831] 1 p. (H.R. 330) DNA. 9499

---- An act to provide hereafter for the payment of six thousand dollars annually to the Seneca Indians, and for other purposes. January 3, 1831. Read and passed to a second reading. [Washington, 1831] 1 p. (H.R. 481) DNA. 9500

---- An act to regulate the foreign and coasting trade on the northern and northwestern frontiers of the United States, and for other purposes. February 24, 1831. Read twice, and referred to the Committee on Commerce. [Washington, 1831] 3 p. (H.R. 376) DNA. 9501

---- Amendment. January 4, 1831. The bill (H.R. No. 517,) to authorize the extension, construction, and use of a lateral branch of the Baltlmore and the Ohio rail road, into and within the District of Columbia, being under consideration, Mr. Semmes moved to amend the same, by adding the following new sections: [Washington, 1831] 2 p. (H.R. 517) DNA. 9502

---- Amendment. January 5, 1831. Printed by order of the House of Representatives. Mr. Vinton submitted the following as an amendment of the bill (H.R. No. 96) to graduate the price of public lands: [Washington, 1831] 1 p. DNA. (H.R. 96) 9503

---- Amendment. January 5, 1831. Read, and committed to the Committee of the Whole House to which is committed the said resolution. Mr. Tucker submitted the following as an amendment to the joint resolution reported by Mr. McDuffie on the twenty-second ultimo, in relation to the re-eligibility of the President of the United States. [Washington, 1831) 1 p. (H.R.) DNA. 9504

---- Amendment. January 13, 1831. Read, and committed to the Whole House to which the said bill is committed. Mr. Sevier submitted the following, which, when the bill (H.R. No. 513) to extend the act, entitled "An act for further extending the powers of the Judges of the Superior court of the Territory of Arkansas, under the act of the twenty-sixth day of May, one thousand eight hundred and twenty-four, and for other purposes." shall be taken up for consideration, he will move as an amendment. [Washington, 1831] 2 p. (H.R. 513) DNA. 9505

---- Amendment. January 20, 1831. [P]roposed by Mr. Smith, of Maryland, to the "Act to provide, hereafter, for the payment of the six thousand dollars annually to the Seneca Indians, and for other purposes. [Washington, 1831] 1 p. (H.R. 481) DNA. 9506

---- Amendment. January 21, 1831. Read, and committed to the Committee of the Whole House to which the said bill is committed. Mr. Williams submitted the following, which, when the bill (H.R. No. 567) supplementary to the act for the relief of certain surviving officers and soldiers of the revolution shall be taken up for consideration, he will move as an amendment. [Washington, 1831] 1 p. (H.R. 567) DNA. 9507

---- Amendment. January 25, 1831. Mr. Hemphill, from the Committee on Internal Improvements, to which was referred the bill to authorize the Territory of Florida to open a canal through the public lands between Chipola river and St. Andrew's bay, in West Florida, reported the same with an amendment. [Washington, 1831] 3 p. (S. 74) DNA. 9508

---- Amendment. January 26, 1831. Read, and committed to the committee of the Whole House to which the said bill is committed. Mr. Wickliffe submitted the following, which, when the bill (H.R. No. 440,) making further appropriations for the improvement of the navigation of the Ohio and Mississippi rivers, and their tributary streams, and for deepening the channel at the mouth of the Mississippi river, shall be taken up for consideration, he will move as an amendment: [Washington, 1831] 2 p. (H.R. 440) DNA. 9509

---- Amendment. January 31, 1831. Committed to the Committee of the Whole House to which the said bill is committed. Mr. Ramsey submitted the following, which, when the bill (H.R. No. 583,) regulating the compensation of clerks in the Post Office Department, shall be taken up for consideration, he will move as an amendment. [Washington, 1831] 1 p. (H.R. 583) DNA. 9510

---- Amendment. February 8, 1831. Mr. Ellis laid on the table the following, as an amendment to the bill to create the office of Surveyor of the public lands for the state of Louisiana. [Washington, 1831] 7 p. (S. 137) DNA. 9511

---- Amendment. February 16, 1831. Read, and referred to the Committee of the Whole House to which the said bill is committed. Mr. Duncan submitted the following, which, when the bill, (H.R. No. 581) supplementary to the act, entitled "An act to grant a certain quantity of land to the state of Indiana, for the purpose of aiding the said State in opening a canal to connect the waters of the Wabash river with those of Lake Erie," shall be taken up for consideration, he will move as an amendment. [Washington, 1831) 1 p. (H.R. 581) DNA. 9512

---- Amendment. February 19, 1831. Read, and committed to the Committee of the Whole House to which the said report is committed. Mr. Lea submitted the following resolution as an amendment to the report made by Mr. Hemphill, on the tenth instant, upon the subject of internal improvements. [Washington, 1831] 1 p. (H.R. 3) DNA. 9513

---- An amendment to strike out all after the word "repeal" in the first line, and insert "all acts imposing a duty on salt." February 4, 1831. Printed by order of the House of Representatives. Mr. Tucker submitted the following, as an amendment to the bill (H.R. No. 595) to repeal a part of an act to reduce the duty on salt: [Washington, 1831] 1 p. (H.R. 595) DNA. 9514

---- Amendment to the bill, (H.R. 602,) for the relief of Mrs Clarissa B. Harrison. February 22, 1831. Engrossed for to-morrow. Mr. Wickliffe submitted for the following amendment. [Washington, 1831] (H.R. 602) DNA. 9515

---- Amendments. January 13, 1831. Read, and committed to a Committee of the Whole House on Monday, 17th January. instant. The bill (H.R. No. 517) "to authorize the extension, construction, and use of a lateral branch of the Baltimore and Ohio rail road, into and within the District of Columbia," having been recommitted to the Committee for the District of Columbia. Mr. Doddridge, from the same committee, reported the said bill with the following: [Washington, 1831]

4 p. (H.R. 517) DNA. 9516

---- Amendments. January 25, 1831. Read and committed to a Committee of the Whole House this day. Mr. Wickliffe, from the Committee on the Public Lands, to which was referred the bill from the Senate, entitled An act supplemental to the act "granting the right of pre-emption to settlers on the public lands," approved the twenty-ninth day of May, one thousand eight hundred and thirty, reported the same with the following amendments. [Washington, 1831] (S. 64) DNA. 9517

---- Amendments. February 16, 1831. The Committee on Finance to which was referred the bill from the House of Representatives, entitled "An act making appropriations for the support of Government for the year (1831)," report the same with the following: [Washington, 1831] 2 p. (H.R. 528) DNA. 9518

---- Annual Message and Documents. President Andrew Jackson. Dec. 6, 1831. House Ex. Docs., No. 2, 22d Cong., 1st sess., Vol. I. Condition of the country; Foreign relations; internal improvements; Indian affairs; Finances; Amendment of Constitution relative to election of President and Vice-President; United States Bank; Judiciary. [Washington, 1831] 274 p. M; R. 9519

---- Army meteorological register, 1831-34. Washington, 1831-35. 2 vols. PU. 9520

---- A bill authorizing a subscription to the stock of the Monongahela Bridge Company at Brownsville, Pennsylvania. January 27, 1831. Read twice, and committed in the Committee of the Whole House, to which is committed the bill (H.R. 562,) to erect a bridge over the Ohio river at Wheeling. Mr. Letcher, from the Committee on Internal Improvements, reported the following bill. [Washington, 1831] (H.R. 579) DNA. 9521

---- A bill authorizing the construction of a road from Strong's, on the St. Francis river, in the Territory of Arkansas, to Belesville, in said Territory. January 27, 1831. Read twice, and committed to the Committee of the Whole House on the State of the Union. Mr. Letcher, from the Committee on Internal Improvements, reported the following bill. [Washington, 1831] 1 p. (H.R. 580) DNA. 9522

---- A bill authorizing the construction of naval hospitals at the Navy yards at Charlestown, Massachusetts, Brooklyn, New York, and Pensacola. February 11, 1831. Read twice, and committed to the Committee of the Whole House on the state of the Union. Mr. White, of New York, from the Committee of Naval Affairs, reported the following bill. [Washington, 1831] 1 p. (H.R. 622) DNA. 9523

---- A bill authorizing the construction of Naval Hospitals at the Navy yards at Charlestown, Massachusetts, Brooklyn, New York, and Pensacola. December 20, 1831. Read twice, and committed to a Committee of the Whole House on the state of the Union. Mr. Hoffman, from the Committee on Naval Affairs, reported the following bill: [Washington, 1831] 1 p. (H.R. 57) DNA. 9524

---- A bill authorizing the purchase from Henry Eckford of certain lands for public purposes.

January 20, 1831. Read twice, and committed to a Committee of the Whole House to-morrow. Mr. White, of New York, from the Committee on Naval Affairs, to which was referred the case of Henry Eckford, reported the following bill. [Washington, 1831] (H.R. 570) DNA. 9525

---- A bill authorizing the Register and Receiver of the St. Helena land district, in Louisiana, to receive evidence respecting the claim of Josiah Barker, assignee of Madam Hindson, to a tract of land therein mentioned. February 24, 1831. Read twice, and ordered to be engrossed, and read the third time to-morrow. Mr. Sterigere, from the Committee on Private Land Claims, reported the following bill. [Washington, 1831] (H.R. 651) DNA. 9526

---- A bill authorizing the Secretary of War to issue a warrant to Archibald Jackson for the bounty land due to James Gammens, a soldier in the late war. February 12, 1831. Read twice, and committed to a Committee of the Whole House to-morrow. Mr. Sterigere, from the Committee on Private Land Claims, reported the following bill. [Washington, 1831] 1 p. (H.R. 623) DNA. 9527

---- A bill authorizing the Secretary of War to pay to the Seneca tribe of Indians, the balance of an annuity of six thousand dollars, usually paid to said Indians, and remaining unpaid for the year one thousand eight hundred and twenty-nine. December 28, 1831. Read twice, and committed to a Committee of the Whole House to-morrow. Mr. Bell, from the Committee on Indian Affairs, reported the following bill: [Washington, 1831] 1 p. (H.R. 163) DNA. 9528

---- A bill concerning Martha Randolph, daughter and only surviving child of Thomas Jefferson, deceased. February 10, 1831. Introduced on leave by Mr. Poindexter. Bell, Webster, Tyler, and Hayne, to consider and report thereon. February 23, 1831. Reported with an amendment to wit: Strike out all after the enacting clause, and insert what follows: [Washington, 1831] (S. 154) DNA. 9529

---- A bill concerning Martha Randolph, daughter and only surviving child of Thomas Jefferson, deceased. December 22, 1831. Agreeably to notice given, Mr. Poindexter asked and obtained leave to bring in the following bill; which was read twice, and referred to a select committee to consist of Mr. Poindexter, Mr. Clay, Mr. Taylor, Mr. Hayne, and Mr. Webster. [Washington, 1831] 2 p. (S. 16) DNA. 9530

---- A bill concerning the accounts of the Treasurer of the United States. December 27, 1831. Read twice, and committed to a Committee of the Whole House to-morrow. Mr. McDuffie, from the Committee of Ways and Means, reported the following bill: [Washington, 1831] 1 p. (H.R. 145) DNA. 9531

---- A bill concerning vessels employed in the whale fishery. January 31, 1831. Agreeably to notice given, Mr. Sanford asked and obtained leave to bring in the following bill; which was read twice, and referred to the Committee on Commerce. February 1, 1831. Reported without amendment. [Washington, 1831] 1 p. (S. 131) DNA. 9532

---- A bill confirming an act of the Legislature of Virginia relating to the Chesapeake and Ohio Canal Company, passed February thirteenth, (1830). February 10, 1831. Read twice, and committed to the Committee on the Whole House on the state of the Union. Mr. Craig, from the Committee on Internal Improvements, reported the following bill. [Washington, 1831] 1 p. (H.R. 621) DNA. 9533

---- A bill confirming the claim of John B. Toulmin to a lot in the city of Mobile. February 4, 1831. Mr. Kane, from the Committee on Private Land Claims, reported the following bill; which was read, and passed to a second reading: [Washington, 1831] 1 p. (S. 144) DNA. 9534

---- A bill confirming the selections heretofore made of lands for the construction on the Michigan road, in the State of Indiana. February 9, 1831. Mr. Barton, from the Committee on Public Lands, reported the following bill, which was read, and passed to a second reading: [Washington, 1831] 1 p. (S. 152) DNA. 9535

---- A bill confirming to Joshua Kennedy, his claim to a tract of land in the City of Mobile. December 21, 1831. Mr. Kane, from the Committee on Private Land Claims, reported the following bill; which was read, and passed to a second reading. [Washington, 1831] 2 p. (S. 10) DNA. 9536

---- A bill declaratory of the law concerning contempts of court. February 10, 1831. Read twice, and committed to the Whole House on the state of the Union. Mr. Buchanan, from the Committee on the Judiciary, reported the following bill. [Washington, 1831] 1 p. (H.R. 620) DNA. 9537

---- A bill declaring the assent of Congress to an act of the General Assembly of the State of Ohio, and to authorize the States of Virginia, Pennsylvania, and Maryland, to take charge of the United States' road within their several limits. February 18, 1831. Read twice, and committed to the Committee of the Whole House on the state of the Union. Mr. Vinton, from the Committee of Internal Improvements, reported the following bill: [Washington, 1831] 10 p. (H.R. 637) DNA. 9538

---- A bill declaring the assent of Congress to an act of the General Assembly of the State of Ohio, hereinafter recited. February 18, 1831. Agreeably to notice given, Mr. Burnet asked and obtained leave to bring in the following bill; which was read twice, and referred to the Committee on Roads and Canals. February 19, 1831. Reported without amendment. [Washington, 1831] 11 p. (S. 165) DNA. 9539

A bill directing the settlement of the claim of Harris and Farrow. February 15, 1831. Read twice and ordered to be engrossed, and read the third time tomorrow. Mr. Williams, from the Committee of Claims, reported the following bill. [Washington, 1831] 1 p. (H.R. 626) DNA. 9540

---- A bill explanatory of the act entitled "An act for the relief of officers and soldiers of the Virginia line and navy, and of the continental army, during the revolutionary war," approved thirtieth of May, (1830). February 5, 1831. Read twice, and postponed until Wednesday next, 9th instant. Mr. Wickliffe, from the Committee on the Public Lands, reported the following bill. [Washington, 1831] (H.R. 600) DNA. 9541

---- A bill explanatory of the act, entitled "An act for the relief of officers and soldiers of the Virginia line and navy, and of the continental army, during the revolutionary war," approved thirtieth of May, one thousand eight hundred and thirty. December 27, 1831. Read first time--Second reading to-morrow. Mr. Wickliffe, from the Committee on the Public Lands, reported the following bill: [Washington, 1831] 1 p. (H.R. 124) DNA. 9542

---- A bill extending the right of debenture to the port of Key West, and altering the limits of the district of Key West. December 14, 1830. Agreeably to notice given, Mr. Woodbury asked and obtained leave to bring in the following bill; which was read, and passed to a second reading. December 15, 1830. Read second time, and referred to the Committee on Commerce. January 12, 1831. Reported without amendment. [Washington, 1831] (S. 5) DNA. 9543

---- A bill for an additional supplement to an act, entitled "An act for quieting possessions, enrolling conveyances, and securing the estates of purchasers." January 14, 1831. Read twice, and committed to a Committee of the Whole House on the state of the Union. Mr. Ihrie, from the Committee for the District of Columbia, reported the following bill. [Washington, 1831] (H.R. 561) DNA. 9544

---- A bill for making appropriations for the naval service for the year (1831). January 3, 1831. Read twice, and committed to the Committee of the Whole House on the state of the Union. Mr. Verplanck, from the Committee of Ways and Means, reported the following bill: [Washington, 1831] 1 p. (H.R. 531) DNA. 9545

---- A bill for the adjustment and settlement of the claims of the state of South Carolina against the United States. December 15, 1831. Read twice, and committed to a Committee of the Whole House on Wednesday, 28th instant. Mr. Drayton, from the Committee on Military Affairs, reported the following bill: [Washington, 1831] 3 p. (H.R. 4) DNA. 9546

---- A bill for the benefit of Ann Mortimer Barron. January 7, 1831. Read twice, and committed to a Committee of the Whole House to-morrow. Mr. DeWitt, from the Committee on Revolutionary Claims, reported the following bill. [Washington, 1831] 1 p. (H.R. 546) DNA. 9547

---- A bill for the benefit of Doctor Eliakim Crosby. December 23, 1831. Read twice, and committed to a Committee of the Whole house to-morrow. Mr. Cave Johnson, from the Committee on Private Land Claims, reported the following bill: [Washington, 1831] 1 p. (H.R. 106) DNA. 9548

---- A bill for the benefit of Eli Smith, a revolutionary soldier. February 4, 1831. Read twice, and committed to a Committee of the Whole House to-morrow. Mr. Chilton, from the Committee on Military Pensions reported the following bill: [Washington, 1831] 1 p. (H.R. 596) DNA. 9549

---- A bill for the benefit of

Percis Lovely. January 6, 1831. Read twice, and committed to a Committee of the Whole House on Friday, the 14th January, instant. Mr. Wickliffe, from the Committee on the Public Lands, reported the following bill. [Washington, 1831] (H.R. 541) DNA. 9550

---- A bill for the benefit of the heirs at law of William Treadwell, an officer of the revolutionary army, deceased. January 7, 1831. Read twice, and committed to a Committee of the Whole House to-morrow. Mr De Witt, from the Committee on Revolutionary Claims, reported the following bill. [Washington, 1831] 1 p. (H.R. 547) DNA. 9551

---- A bill for the better organization of the militia of the District of Columbia. January 26, 1831. Read twice, and committed to a Committee of the Whole House on Monday 31st instant. Mr. Thompson, of Georgia, from the Committee on the Militia, reported the following bill. [Washington, 1831] 48 p. (H.R. 578) DNA. 9552

---- A bill for the better organization of the militia of the District of Columbia. December 27, 1831. Read twice, and committed to a Committee of the Whole House to-morrow. Mr. Barringer, from the Committee on the Militia, reported the following bill: [Washington, 1831] 49 p. (H.R. 147) DNA. 9553

---- A bill for the continuation of the Cumberland road in the States of Ohio, Indiana, and Illinois, January 19, 1831. Mr. Hendricks, from the Committee on Roads and Canals, reported the following bill; which was read, and passed to a second reading. [Washington, 1831] (S. 100) DNA. 9554

---- A bill for the final adjustment of the claims to lands in the southeastern land district of the State of Louisiana, and for other purposes. February 5, 1831. Read twice, and postponed until Tuesday next, 8th instant. Mr. Wickliffe, from the Committee on the Public Lands, reported the following bill. [Washington, 1831] 3 p. (H.R. 601) DNA. 9555

---- A bill for the further relief of Ephraim Whitaker. January 7, 1831. Read twice, and committed to the Whole House to-morrow. Mr. Dickinson, from the Committee on Revolutionary Claims, reported the following bill. [Washington, 1831] 1 p. (H.R. 544) DNA. 9556

---- A bill for the further relief of John H. Wendell, a Captain in the revolutionary war. January 7, 1831. Read twice, and committed to the Whole House to-morrow. Mr. Dickinson, from the Committee on Revolutionary Claims, reported the following bill. [Washington, 1831] (H.R. 543) DNA. 9557

---- A bill for the further relief of John H. Wendell, a captain in the revolutionary war. December 23, 1831. Read twice, and committed to a Committee of the Whole House to-morrow. Mr. Muhlenburg, from the Committee on Revolutionary Claims, reported the following bill: [Washington, 1831] 1 p. (H.R. 108) DNA. 9558

---- A bill for the gradual increase of the Corps of Engineers. December 23, 1831. Read twice, and committed to the Committee of the Whole House on the state of the Union. Mr. Drayton, from the Committee on Military

Affairs, reported the following bill: [Washington, 1831] 2 p. (H. R. 97) DNA. 9559

---- A bill for the improvement of certain harbors, and providing for surveys. February 9, 1831. Read twice, and committed to the Committee of the Whole House on the state of the Union. Mr. Howard, from the Committee on Commerce, reported the following bill. [Washington, 1831] 5 p. (H.R. 614) DNA. 9560

---- A bill for the improvement of the mail road between Louisville and St. Louis. January 4, 1831. Agreeably to notice given, Mr. King asked and obtained leave to bring in the following bill; which was read, and passed to a second reading. January 5, 1831. Read second time, and referred to the Committee on Roads and Canals. January 29, 1831. Reported without amendment. [Washington, 1831] 1 p. (S. 57) DNA. 9561

---- A bill for the legal representatives of William Hull. December 19, 1831. Read twice, and committed to a Committee of the Whole House to-morrow. Mr. Whittlesey, from the Committee of Claims, reported the following bill: [Washington, 1831] 1 p. (H.R. 41) DNA. 9562

---- A bill for the more speedy administration of justice in the District of Columbia, and for other purposes, January 26, 1831. Read twice, and committed to a Committee of the Whole House on the State of the Union. Mr. Doddridge, from the Committee for the District of Columbia, reported the following bill. [Washington, 1831] 31 p. (H.R. 577) DNA. 9563

---- A bill for the organization of the Topographical Engineers. December 23, 1831. Read twice and committed to the Committee of the Whole House on the state of the union. Mr. Drayton, from the Committee on Military Affairs, reported the following bill: [Washington, 1831] 1 p. (H.R. 96) DNA. 9564

---- A bill for the purchase of certain books therein mentioned. February 10, 1831. Read twice, and committed to the Committee of the Whole House on the state of the Union. Mr. Everett, from the Committee on the Library, reported the following bill. [Washington, 1831] 1 p. (H.R. 618) DNA. 9565

---- A bill for the relief of Aaron Snow. December 30, 1831. Read twice, and committed to a Committee of the Whole House to-morrow. Mr. Muhlenburg, from the Committee on Revolutionary Claims, reported the following bill: [Washington, 1831] 2 p. (H.R. 170) DNA. 9566

---- A bill for the relief of Abner Slade. January 24, 1831. Mr. Foot, from the Committee on Pensions, reported the following bill; which was read, and passed to a second reading. [Washington, 1831] 1 p. (S. 114) DNA. 9567

---- A bill for the relief of Abraham Forbes. February 10, 1831. Read twice, and ordered to be engrossed, and read the third time to-morrow. Mr. Sterigere, from the Committee on Private Land Claims, reported the following bill. [Washington, 1831] 1 p. (H.R. 616) DNA. 9568

---- A bill for the relief of Adam Peck, January 10, 1831. Read twice, and committed to a

Committee of the Whole House to-morrow. Mr. Whittlesey, from the Committee of Claims, reported the following bill. [Washington, 1831] (H.R. 549) DNA. 9569

---- A bill for the relief of Adam Peck. December 19, 1831. Read twice, and committed to a Committee of the Whole House to-morrow. Mr. E. Whittlesey, from the Committee of Claims, reported the following bill: [Washington, 1831] 1 p. (H.R. 33) DNA. 9570

---- A bill for the relief of Alexander Oswald Brodie, of New York. February 15, 1831. Ordered to be engrossed for to-morrow. Mr. Cambreleng, from the Committee on Commerce, reported the following bill. [Washington, 1831] 1 p. (H.R. 628) DNA. 9571

---- A bill for the relief of Alexander Oswald Brodie, of New York. December 28, 1831. Read twice, and committed to a Committee of the Whole House to-morrow. Mr. Cambreleng, from the Committee on Commerce, reported the following bill: [Washington, 1831] 1 p. (H.R. 159) DNA. 9572

---- A bill for the relief of Allen W. Hardie. December 22, 1831. Read twice, and committed to a Committee of the Whole House to-morrow. Mr. Marshall, from the Committee on Private Land Claims, reported the following bill: [Washington, 1831] 2 p. (H.R. 76) DNA. 9573

---- A bill for the relief of Amariah Squirrel, administrator of Jacob Squirrel, deceased. January 14, 1831. Read twice, and committed to a Committee of the Whole House to-morrow. Mr. Whittlesey, from the Committee of Claims, reported the following bill. [Washington, 1831] 1 p. (H.R. 558) DNA. 9574

---- A bill for the relief of Amariah Squirrel, administrator of Jacob Squirrel, deceased. December 19, 1831. Read twice, and committed to a Committee of the Whole House to-morrow. Mr. Whittlesey, from the Committee of Claims, reported the following bill: [Washington, 1831] 1 p. (H.R. 35) DNA. 9575

---- A bill for the relief of Andrew H. Richardson, executor of Valentine Richardson. December 19, 1831. Read twice, and committed to a Committee of the Whole House tomorrow. Mr. Whittlesey, from the Committee of Claims, reported the following bill: [Washington, 1831] 1 p. (H.R. 26) DNA. 9576

---- A bill for the relief of Ann D. Baylor. December 19, 1831. Read twice, and committed to a Committee of the Whole House to-morrow. Mr. Muhlenburg, from the Committee on Revolutionary Claims, reported the following bill: [Washington, 1831] 1 p. (H.R. 154) DNA. 9577

---- A bill for the relief of Anthony Foreman, John G. Ross, Cherokee delegation. December 19, 1831. Read twice, and committed to a Committee of the Whole House to-morrow. Mr. Whittlesey, from the Committee of Claims, reported the following bill: [Washington, 1831] 1 p. (H.R. 22) DNA. 9578

---- A bill for the relief of Antoine Dequindre, and the legal representatives of Louis Dequindre, deceased. January 12, 1831.

Mr. Woodbury, from the Committee on Commerce, reported the following bill; which was read, and passed to a second reading. [Washington, 1831] 1 p. (S. 77) DNA. 9579

---- A bill for the relief of Antoine Dequindre, Richard Smith, and others, Michigan volunteers. December 19, 1831. Read twice, and committed to a Committee of the Whole House to-morrow. Mr. Whittlesey, from the Committee of Claims, reported the following bill: [Washington, 1831] 2 p. (H.R. 10) DNA. 9580

---- A bill for the relief of Ariel Ensign. December 10, 1831. Read twice, and committed to a Committee of the Whole House to-morrow. Mr. E. Whittlesey, from the Committee of Claims, reported the following bill: [Washington, 1831] 1 p. (H.R. 25) DNA. 9581

---- A bill for the relief of Arnaud Lanaux. December 22, 1831. Read twice, and committed to a Committee of the Whole House to-morrow. Mr. Cave Johnson, from the Committee on Private Land Claims, reported the following bill: [Washington, 1831] 2 p. (H.R. 75) DNA. 9582

---- A bill for the relief of Barnard Kelley. December 27, 1831. Read twice, and committed to a Committee of the Whole House to-morrow. Mr. Johnson, of Kentucky, from the Committee on the Post Office and Post Roads, reported the following bill: [Washington, 1831] 1 p. (H.R. 135) DNA. 9583

---- A bill for the relief of Benedict Joseph Flaget. December 23, 1831. Read twice, and committed to a Committee of the Whole House to-morrow. Mr. McDuffie, from the Committee of Ways and Means, reported the following bill: [Washington, 1831] 1 p. (H.R. 117) DNA. 9584

----A bill for the relief of Benedict Joseph Flaget. December 27, 1831. Agreeably to notice given Mr. Bibb asked and obtained leave to bring in the following bill; which was read, and passed to a second reading. December 28, 1831. Read a second time, and referred to the Committee on Finance. [Washington, 1831] 1 p. (S. 26) DNA. 9585

---- A bill for the relief of Benjamin Bullitt December 27, 1831. Read twice, and committed to a Committee of the Whole House to-morrow. Mr. Bullard, from the Committee on Private Land Claims, reported the following bill: [Washington, 1831] 1 p. (H.R. 140) DNA. 9586

---- A bill for the relief of Benjamin S. Smoot, of Alabama. January 18, 1831. Mr. Ruggles, from the Committee of Claims, reported the following bill; which was read, and passed to a second reading. [Washington, 1831] 1 p. (S. 91) DNA. 9587

---- A bill for the relief of Benjamin S. Smoot. January 21, 1831. Read twice, and referred to the Committee on Military Affairs. February 11, 1831. Reported without amendment. [Washington, 1831] (S. 111) DNA. 9588

---- A bill for the relief of Bernard Leonard and Jacob Black. December 27, 1831. Read twice, and committed to a Committee of the Whole House to-morrow. Mr. Bullard, from the Committee on Private Land Claims, reported the following bill: [Washington,

1831] 2 p. (H.R. 141) DNA. 9589

---- A bill for the relief of Bernard Marigny, assignee of the heirs of Antonio Bonnabel. March 1, 1831. Read twice, and committed to a Committee on the Whole House to-morrow. Mr. Sterigere, from the Committee on Private Land Claims, reported the following bill. [Washington, 1831] (H.R. 657) DNA. 9590

---- A bill for the relief of Bernard Marigny, of the State of Louisiana. December 19, 1831. Read twice, and committed to a Committee of the Whole House to-morrow. Mr. C. Johnson, from the Committee on Private Land Claims, reported the following bill: [Washington, 1831] 3 p. (H.R. 46) DNA. 9591

---- A bill for the relief of Beverly Chew, the heirs of William Emerson, deceased, and the heirs of Edwin Lorraine, deceased. December 16, 1829. Agreeably to notice given, Mr. Johnston asked and obtained leave to bring in the following bill; which was read, and passed to a second reading. December 17, 1830. Read a second time, and referred to the Committee on Finance. January 10, 1831. Committee on Finance discharged, and referred to the Committee on the Judiciary. January 27, 1831. Reported without amendment. [Washington, 1831] (S. 29) DNA. 9592

---- A bill for the relief of Brevet Major Riley, and Lieutenants Brook and Seawright. January 20, 1831. Mr. Benton, from the Committee on Military Affairs, reported the following bill; which was read, and passed to a second reading. [Washington, 1831] 1 p. (S. 102) DNA. 9593

---- A bill for the relief of Captain John Burnham. January 25, 1831. Read twice, and committed to a Committee of the Whole House to-morrow. Mr. E. Everett, from the Committee on Foreign Affairs, reported the following bill. [Washington, 1831] 1 p. (H.R. 575) DNA. 9594

---- A bill for the relief of Captain John Burnham. December 19, 1831. Read twice, and committed to a Committee of the Whole House to-morrow. Mr. Archer, from the Committee on Foreign Affairs, reported the following bill: [Washington, 1831] 1 p. (H.R. 44) DNA. 9595

---- A bill for the relief of Captain Thomas Paine. December 20, 1831. Read twice, and committed to a Committee of the Whole House to-morrow. Mr. Wilde, from the Committee of Ways and Means, reported the following bill: [Washington, 1831] 1 p. (H.R. 64) DNA. 9596

---- A bill for the relief of Celestin Chiapella. December 22, 1831. Read twice, and committed to a Committee of the Whole House to-morrow. Mr. Bullard, from the Committee on Private Land Claims, reported the following bill: [Washington, 1831] 2 p. (H.R. 78) DNA. 9597

---- A bill for the relief of certain applicants for pensions. January 31, 1831. Mr. Foot, from the Committee on Pensions, reported the following bill; which was read, and passed to a second reading. [Washington, 1831] 1 p. (S. 132) DNA. 9598

---- A bill for the relief of certain holders of certificates in lieu of lands injured by earthquakes in Missouri. January 10, 1831.

Mr. Barton, from the Committee on Public Lands, reported the following bill; which was read, and passed to a second reading. [Washington, 1831[(S. 70) DNA. 9599

---- A bill for the relief of certain importers of foreign merchandise. February 16, 1831. Read twice, and ordered to be engrossed, and read the third time on Monday next. Mr. Cambereng, from the Committee on Commerce, reported the following bill. [Washington, 1831] 1 p. (H.R. 634) DNA. 9600

---- A bill for the relief of certain importers of foreign merchandise. February 23, 1831. Read twice, and referred to the Committee on Finance. [Washington, 1831] (H.R. 634) DNA. 9601

---- A bill for the relief of Charles Cassedy. December 19, 1831. Read twice, and committed to a Committee of the Whole House to-morrow. Mr. Whittlesey, from the Committee of Claims, reported the following bill: [Washington, 1831] 1 p. (H.R. 28) DNA. 9602

---- A bill for the relief of Christopher Beehler. February 10, 1831. Read twice, and ordered to be engrossed, and read the third time to-morrow. Mr. Buchanan, from the Committee on the Judiciary reported the following bill. [Washington, 1831] 1 p. (H.R. 617) DNA. 9603

---- A bill for the relief of Cornelius Overton. In Senate of the United States. December 30, 1831 Received. [Washington, 1831] 2 p. (H.R. 150) DNA. 9604

---- A bill for the relief of Daniel Tilton. January 18, 1831. Mr. Chase, from the Committee on Pensions, reported the following bill; which was read, and passed to a second reading. [Washington, 1831] 1 p. (S. 96) DNA. 9605

---- A bill for the relief of David Banks and William Bould. December 27, 1831. Read twice, and committed to a Committee of the Whole House to-morrow. Mr. Ellsworth, from the Committee on the Judiciary, reported the following bill: [Washington, 1831] 2 p. (H.R. 131) DNA. 9606

---- A bill for the relief of David Chaplin, Israel Hale, and America Hamlin. January 31. Mr. Holmes, from the Committee on Pensions, reported the following bill; which was read, and passed to a second reading. [Washington, 1831] 1 p. (S. 130) DNA. 9607

---- A bill for the relief of David Kennard. December 20, 1831. Read twice, and committed to a Committee of the Whole House to-morrow. Mr. Hubbard, from the Committee on Revolutionary Pensions, reported the following bill: [Washington, 1831. 1 p. (H.R. 53) DNA. 9608

---- A bill for the relief of David Killbourn. December 27, 1831. Read twice, and committed to a Committee of the Whole House to-morrow. Mr. Drayton, from the Committee on Military Affairs, reported the following bill: [Washington, 1831] 1 p. (H.R. 143) DNA. 9609

---- A bill for the relief of De Gameo Jones, February 9, 1831. Read twice, and committed to a Committee of the Whole House to-morrow. Mr. Whittlesey, from the Committee on Claims, reported the following bill. [Washington, 1831] 1 p. (H.R. 612)

DNA. 9610

---- A bill for the relief of De Gameo Jones. December 19, 1831. Read twice, and committed to a Committee of the Whole House to-morrow. Mr. E. Whittlesey, from the Committee of Claims, reported the following bill: [Washington, 1831] 1 p. (H.R. 40) DNA. 9611

---- A bill for the relief of Dixon Spears. December 22, 1831. Mr. King, from the Committee on Public Lands, reported the following bill, which was read, and passed to a second reading. [Washington, 1831] 2 p. (S. 13) DNA. 9612

---- A bill for the relief of Don Carlos Dehault Delassus. December 15, 1830. Agreeably to notice given, Mr. Benton asked and obtained leave to bring in the following bill; which was read, and passed to a second reading. December 16, 1830. Read a second time, and referred to the Committee on Military Affairs. January 2, 1831. Reported with an amendment. [Washington, 1831] 1 p. (S. 10) DNA. 9613

---- A bill for the relief of Don Carlos Dehault Delassus. December 23, 1831. Agreeably to notice given, Mr. Johnston asked and obtained leave to bring in the following bill; which was read twice, and referred to the Committee of Claims. [Washington, 1831] 2 p. (S. 21) DNA. 9614

---- A bill for the relief of Dorothy Wells. December 23, 1831. Read twice, and committed to a Committe of the Whole House to-morrow. Mr. Mardis, from the Committee on Private Land Claims, reported the following bill: [Washington, 1831] 1 p. (H.R. 120) DNA. 9615

---- A bill for the relief of Duval and Carnes. January 18, 1831. Mr. Foot, from the Committee on Claims, reported the following bill; which was read, and passed to a second reading. [Washington, 1831] 1 p. (S. 93) DNA. 9616

---- A bill for the relief of Ebenezer Lobdell. January 14, 1831. Mr. Brown, from the Committee of Claims, reported the following bill; which was read, and passed to a second reading. [Washington, 1831] 1 p. (S. 86) DNA. 9617

No entry. 9618

---- A bill for the relief of Eber Hubbard. December 19, 1831. Read twice, and committed to a Committee of the Whole House to-morrow. Mr. E. Whittlesey, from the Committee of Claims reported the following bill: [Washington, 1831] 1 p. (H.R. 12) DNA. 9619

---- A bill for the relief of Edward G. Terrell. February 7, 1831. Mr. McKinley, from the Committee on Public Lands, reported the following bill; which was read, and passed to a second reading: [Washington, 1831] 1 p. (S. 148) DNA. 9620

---- A bill for the relief of Edward Lee. December 19, 1831. Read twice, and Committed to a Committee of the Whole House to-morrow. Mr. E. Whittlesey, from the Committee of Claims, reported the following bill: [Washington, 1831] 1 p. (H.R.

7) DNA. 9621

---- A bill for the relief of Edward Livingston. February 2, 1831. Read twice, and committed to a Committee of the Whole House to-morrow. Mr. Whittlesey, from the Committee of Claims, reported the following bill. [Washington, 1831] (H.R. 589) DNA. 9622

---- A bill for the relief of Edward Livingston. December 19, 1831. Read twice, and committed to a Committee of the Whole House to-morrow. Mr. E. Whittlesey, from the Committee of Claims, reported the following bill: [Washington, 1831] 1 p. (H.R. 38) DNA. 9623

---- A bill for the relief of Edward S. Meeder. February 22, 1831. Mr. Chase, from the Committee on Pensions, reported the following bill; which was read, and passed to a second reading: [Washington, 1831] 1 p. (S. 170) DNA. 9624

---- A bill for the relief of Edward S. Meeder December 22, 1831. Mr. Mangum, from the Committee on Pensions, reported the following bill; which was read, and passed to a second reading. [Washington, 1831] 1 p. (S. 15) DNA. 9625

---- A bill for the relief of Elenor Worthington, executrix, and James T. Worthington, executor of Thomas Worthington, deceased. January 5, 1831. Read twice, and committed to a Committee of the Whole House to-morrow. Mr. Foster, from the Committee on the Judiciary, reported the following bill. [Washington, 1831] 1 p. (H.R. 536) DNA. 9626

---- A bill for the relief of Elizabeth Magruder. February 24, 1831. Read twice, and committed to a Committee on the Whole House to-morrow. Mr. Young, from the Committee on Revolutionary Claims, reported the following bill. [Washington, 1831] (H.R. 650) DNA. 9627

---- A bill for the relief of Elizabeth Scott, assignee of Alexander Scott, junior. January 14, 1831. Mr. Woodbury, from the Committee on Commerce, reported the following bill; which was read, and passed to a second reading. [Washington, 1831] 1 p. (S. 85) DNA. 9628

---- A bill for the relief of Ephraim Whitaker. December 22, 1831. Read twice, and committed to a Committee on Revolutionary Pensions, reported the following bill: [Washington, 1831] 1 p. (H.R. 73) DNA. 9629

---- A bill for the relief of Eugene Borell. December 30, 1831. Read twice, and committed to a Committee of the Whole House to-morrow. Mr. Carr, from the Committee on Private Land Claims, reported the following bill: [Washington, 1831] 1 p. (H.R. 176) DNA. 9630

---- A bill for the relief of Ezekiel Canfield. January 10, 1831. Mr. Chase, from the Committee on Pensions, reported the following bill; which was read, and passed to a second reading. [Washington, 1831] 1 p. (S. 72) DNA. 9631

---- A bill for the relief of Farish Carter. February 19, 1831. Mr. Brown, from the Committee of Claims, reported to the following bill; which was read, and passed to a second reading:

---- [Washington, 1831] 1 p. (S. 167) DNA. 9632

---- A bill for the relief of Frederick Raymer. January 9, 1831. Read twice, and committed to a Committee of the Whole House to-morrow. Mr. De Witt, from the Committee on Revolutionary Claims, reported the following bill: [Washington, 1831] 1 p. (H.R. 532) DNA. 9633

---- A bill for the relief of Gabriel Godfroy and Jean Baptiste Beaugrand. January 12, 1831. Read twice, and committed to a Committee of the Whole House to-morrow. Mr. McIntire, from the Committee of Claims, reported the following bill. [Washington, 1831] 1 p. (H.R. 556) DNA. 9634

---- A bill for the relief of George B. Dameron and William Howzw, of Mississippi. January 18, 1831. Mr. Ellis, from the Committee on Public Lands, reported the following bill; which was read, and passed to a second reading. [Washington, 1831] 1 p. (S. 90) DNA. 9635

---- A bill for the relief of George Innes, of New York. December 20, 1831. Read, and committed to a Committee of the Whole House to-morrow. Mr. Cambreleng, from the Committee on Commerce, reported the following bill: [Washington, 1831] 1 p. (H.R. 60) DNA. 9636

---- A bill for the relief of George J. Knight. February 18, 1831. Read twice, and committed to a Committee of the Whole House to-morrow. Mr. Carson, from the Committee on Naval Affairs, reported the following bill. [Washington, 1831] 1 p. (H.R. 640) DNA. 9637

---- A bill for the relief of George J. Knight. December 23, 1831. Read twice, and committed to a Committee of the Whole House to-morrow. Mr. Carson, from the Committee on Naval Affairs, reported the following bill: [Washington, 1831] 1 p. (H.R. 99) DNA. 9638

---- A bill for the relief of George Johnston. December 15, 1830. Agreeably to notice, Mr. Johnston asked and obtained leave to bring in the following bill; which was read, and passed to a second reading, December 16, 1830. Read second time, and referred to the Committee on the Judiciary. January 5, 1831. Reported without amendment. [Washington, 1831] 1 p. (S. 11) DNA. 9639

---- A bill for the relief of George Nelson. February 4, 1831. Mr. Foot, from the Committee on Pensions, reported the following bill; which was read, and passed to a second reading: [Washington, 1831] 1 p. (S. 143) DNA. 9640

---- A bill for the relief of Hannah McKim. March 3, 1831. Read twice, and laid upon the table. Mr. Draper, from the Committee on Private Land Claims, reported the following bill: [Washington, 1831] (H.R. 658) DNA. 9641

---- A bill for the relief of Hannah McKim, December 27, 1831. Read twice, and committed to a Committee of the Whole House to-morrow. Mr. Marshall, from the Committee on Private Land Claims reported the following bill: [Washington, 1831] 2 p. (H.R. 137) DNA. 9642

---- A bill for the relief of Hartwell Vick, of the State of Mississippi. December 28, 1831. Mr.

Kane, from the Committee on Private Land Claims, reported the following bill; which was read, and passed to a second reading. [Washington, 1831] 1 p. (S. 27) DNA. 9643

---- A bill for the relief of Harvey Brown. December 27, 1831. Read twice, and committed to a Committee of the Whole House to-morrow. Mr. Davis, of South Carolina, from the Committee on the Judiciary, reported the following bill; [Washington, 1831] 1 p. (H.R. 142) DNA. 9644

---- A bill for the relief of Henry Chase. December 24, 1830. Agreeably to notice given, Mr. Noble asked and obtained leave to bring in the following bill; which was read twice, and referred to the Committee on Public Lands. January 19, 1831. Reported without amendment. [Washington, 1831] 1 p. (S. 36) DNA. 9645

---- A bill for the relief of Henry H. Tuckerman. December 14, 1831. Read twice, and committed to a Committee of the Whole House to-morrow. Mr. McDuffie, from the Committee of Ways and Means, reported the following bill: [Washington, 1831] 1 p. (H.R. 11) DNA. 9646

---- A bill for the relief of Henry Kilbourn. December 19, 1831. Read twice, and committed to a Committee of the Whole House to-morrow. Mr. E. Whittlesey, from the Committee of Claims, reported the following bill: [Washington, 1831] 1 p. (H.R. 18) DNA. 9647

---- A bill for the relief of Hopkins Rice. January 5, 1831. Read twice, and committed to a Committee of the Whole House to-morrow. Mr. Dudley, from the Committee on Private Land Claims, reported the following bill. [Washington, 1831] 1 p. H R. 537) DNA. 9648

---- A bill for the relief of Hopkins Rice. December 23, 1831. Read twice, and committed to a Committee of the Whole House to-morrow. Mr. Bullard, from the Committee on Private Land Claims, reported the following bill: [Washington, 1831] 1 p. (H.R. 115) DNA. 9649

---- A bill for the relief of Hugh Barnes. January 10, 1831. Mr. Chase, from the Committee on Pensions, reported the following bill; which was read, and passed to a second reading. [Washington, 1831] 1 p. (S. 73) DNA. 9650

---- A bill for the relief of Humphrey Beckett, David Smith, and Jonathan Fogg. January 28, 1831. Read twice, and committed to a Committee of the Whole House to-morrow. Mr. Trezvant, from the Committee on Military Pensions, to which had been referred the petitions of Humphrey Beckett, David Smith, and Jonathan Fogg, reported the following bill. [Washington, 1831] 1 p. (H.R. 582) DNA. 9651

---- A bill for the relief of Ichabod Ward. December 23, 1831. Read twice, and committed to a Committee of the Whole House to-morrow. Mr. Muhlenburg, from the Committee on Revolutionary Claims, reported the following bill: [Washington, 1831] 1 p. (H.R. 109) DNA. 9652

---- A bill for the relief of J. N. Cardozo. December 19, 1830. Agreeably to notice given, Mr. Hayne asked and obtained leave to bring in the following bill; which was read twice, and referred to the Committee on the Judiciary. January 13, 1831. Reported without amendment. [Washington, 1831] 1 p. (S. 49). DNA. 9653

---- A bill for the relief of J. P. and E. B. Penny. February 18, 1831. Read twice, and committed to a Committee on the Whole House to-morrow. Mr. Gilmore, from the Committee of Ways and Means, reported the following bill. [Washington, 1831] 1 p. (H.R. 636) DNA. 9654

---- A bill for the relief of J. P. and E. B. Penny. December 19, 1831. Read twice, and committed to a Committee of the Whole House to-morrow. Mr. Gilmore, from the Committee of Ways and Means, reported the following bill: [Washington, 1831] 1 p. (H.R. 49) DNA. 9655

---- A bill for the relief of Jabez Sawyer. January 18, 1831. Mr. Holmes, from the Committee on Pensions, reported the following bill; which was read, and passed to a second reading. [Washington, 1831] 1 p. (S. 92) DNA. 9656

---- A bill for the relief of James Belger. January 25, 1831. Mr. Marks, from the Committee on Pensions, reported the following bill; which was read, and passed to a second reading. [Washington, 1831] 1 p. (S. 119) DNA. 9657

---- A bill for the relief of James Hogland. January 21, 1831. Mr. Barton, from the Committee on Public Lands, reported the following bill; which was read, and passed to a second reading. [Washington, 1831] 1 p. (S. 103) DNA. 9658

---- A bill for the relief of James Lucius Sawyer. December 19, 1831. Read twice, and committed to a Committee of the Whole House to-morrow. Mr. Whittlesey, from the Committee of Claims, reported the following bill: [Washington, 1831] 1 p. (H.R. 32) DNA. 9659

---- A bill for the relief of James McCarty. December 19, 1831. Read twice, and committed to a Committee of the Whole House to-morrow. Mr. E. Whittlesey, from the Committee of Claims, reported the following bill: [Washington, 1831] 1 p. (H.R. 6) DNA. 9660

---- A bill for the relief of James Marsh. February 23, 1831. Read twice, and committed to a Committee of the Whole House to-morrow. Mr. Sutherland, from the Committee on Commerce, reported the following bill. [Washington, 1831] 1 p. (H.R. 648) DNA. 9661

---- A bill for the relief of James Soyars. December 23, 1831. Read twice, and committed to a Committee of the Whole House to-morrow. Mr. Muhlenburg, from the Committee on Revolutionary Claims, reported the following bill: [Washington, 1831] 1 p. (H.R. 129) DNA. 9662

---- A bill for the relief of James Sprague. January 13, 1831. Agreeably to notice given, Mr. Burnet asked and obtained leave to bring in the following bill; which was read twice, and referred to the Committee on Public Lands. January 19, 1831. Reported without amendment. [Washington, 1831] (S. 80) DNA. 9663

---- A bill for the relief of James Thomas, late Quartermaster General of the Army of the United States. January 4, 1831.

Mr. Ruggles, from the Committee of Claims; reported the following bill; which was read, and passed to a second reading: [Washington, 1831] 1 p. (S. 58) DNA. 9664

---- A bill for the relief of Jane Muir. December 19, 1831. Read twice, and committed to a Committee of the Whole House to-morrow. Mr. Whittlesey, from the Committee of Claims, reported the following bill: [Washington, 1831] 1 p. (H.R. 14) DNA. 9665

---- A bill for the relief of Jasiah P. Creesy and others. January 6, 1831. Read twice, and committed to a Committee of the Whole House to-morrow. Mr. Harvey, from the Committee on Commerce, reported the following bill. [Washington, 1831] 1 p. (H.R. 540) DNA. 9666

---- A bill for the relief of Jefferson College, in the State of Mississippi. February 11, 1831. Mr. Ellis, from the Committee on Public Lands, reported the following bill, which was read, and passed to a second reading: [Washington, 1831] 1 p. (S. 157) DNA. 9667

---- A bill for the relief of Jellis A. Fonda. December 22, 1831. Read twice, and committed to a Committee of the Whole House to-morrow. Mr. Pendleton, from the Committee on Revolutionary Pensions, reported the following bill: [Washington, 1831] 1 p. (H.R. 80) DNA. 9668

---- A bill for the relief of John Bosseler, his heirs or assigns. February 22, 1831. Read twice, and ordered to be engrossed, and read the third time to-morrow. Mr. Draper, from the Committee on Private Land Claims, reported the following bill. [Washington, 1831] 1 p. (H.R. 642) DNA. 9669

---- A bill for the relief of John Breckwood Taylor. December 30, 1831. Mr. Smith, from the Committee on Finance, reported the following bill; which was read, and passed to a second reading. [Washington, 1831] 1 p. (S. 32) DNA. 9670

---- A bill for the relief of John Buhler. December 28, 1831. Read twice, and committed to a Committee of the Whole House to-morrow. Mr. Mardis, from the Committee on Private Land Claims, reported the following bill: [Washington, 1831] 1 p. (H.R. 161) DNA. 9671

---- A bill for the relief of John Chandler and William Johnson. January 22, 1831. Agreeably to notice given, Mr. King asked and obtained leave to bring in the following bill; which was read twice, and referred to the Committee on the Judiciary. January 29, 1831. Reported without amendment. [Washington, 1831] 1 p. (S. 110) DNA. 9672

---- A bill for the relief of John Culbertson, and to provide an interpreter for the district court of the United States for the eastern district of Louisiana. February 1, 1831. Mr. Webster, from the Committee on the Judiciary, reported the following bill; which was read, and passed to a second reading. [Washington, 1831] (S. 136) DNA. 9673

---- A bill for the relief of John Cunningham, senior. January 21, 1831. Agreeably to notice given, Mr. Benton asked and obtained leave to bring in the following bill; which was read, and passed to a second reading. January 22,

1831. Read the second time, and referred to the Committee on Pensions. January 31, 1831. Reported without amendment. [Washington, 1831] 1 p. (S. 108) DNA. 9674

---- A bill for the relief of John Daly, late of Canada. January 11, 1831. Mr. Chase, from the Committee of Claims, reported the following bill; which was read, and passed to a second reading. [Washington, 1831] 1 p. (S. 76) DNA. 9675

---- A bill for the relief of John Gough, and other Canadian refugees. January 21, 1831. Mr. Barton, from the Committee on Public Lands, reported the following bill; which was read, and passed to a second reading. [Washington, 1831] 1 p. (S. 104) DNA. 9676

---- A bill for the relief of John H. Genter. December 23, 1831. Read twice, and committed to a Committee of the Whole House to-morrow. Mr. Hubbard, from the Committee on Revolutionary Pensions, reported the following bill: [Washington, 1831] 1 p. (H.R. 105) DNA. 9677

---- A bill for the relief of John H. Harrison. February 23, 1831. Mr. Hayne, from the Committee on the Judiciary, reported the following bill; which was read, and passed to a second reading: [Washington, 1831] 1 p. (S. 172) DNA. 9678

---- A bill for the relief of John H. Harrison. December 23, 1831. Mr. Hayne, from the Committee on the Judiciary reported the following bill; which was read, and passed to a second reading. [Washington, 1831] 1 p. (S. 17) DNA. 9679

---- A bill for the relief of John H. Thomas, claiming under Antoine Patin. December 22, 1831. Read twice, and committed to a Committee of the Whole House to-morrow. Mr. Carr, of Indiana, from the Committee on Private Land Claims, reported the following bill: [Washington, 1831] 1 p. (H.R. 82) DNA. 9680

---- A bill for the relief of John Heard, Junior, surviving assignee of Amasa Davis, Junior. December 23, 1831. Read twice, and committed to a Committee of the Whole House to-morrow. Mr. Verplanck, from the Committee of Ways and Means, reported the following bill: [Washington, 1831] 1 p. (H.R. 112) DNA. 9681

---- A bill for the relief of John J. Jacob. February 7, 1831. Mr. Bell, from the Committee of Claims, reported the following bill; which was read, and passed to a second reading: [Washington, 1831] 1 p. (S. 149) DNA. 9682

---- A bill for the relief of John J. Jacob. December 28, 1831. Agreeably to notice given, Mr. Tyler asked and obtained leave to bring in the following bill, which was read twice and referred to the Committee of Claims. [Washington, 1831] 1 p. (S. 28) DNA. 9683

---- A bill for the relief of John Knight. December 27, 1831. Read twice, and committed to a Committee of the Whole House to-morrow. Mr. Muhlenburg, from the Committee on Revolutionary Claims, reported the following bill: [Washington, 1831] 1 p. (H.R. 130) DNA. 9684

---- A bill for the relief of John McCartney. December 17, 1830. Agreeably to notice given, Mr. King asked and obtained leave to bring in the following bill; which was read, and passed to a second reading. December 20, 1830. Read a second time, and referred to the Committee of Claims. February 12, 1831. Reported without amendment. [Washington, 1831] 1 p. (S. 29) DNA. 9685

---- A bill for the relief of John McDonough. February 22, 1831. Read twice, and ordered to be engrossed, and read the third time to-morrow. Mr. Wickliffe, from the Committee on the Public Lands, reported the following bill. [Washington, 1831] (H.R. 643) DNA. 9686

---- A bill for the relief of John McDonough. December 20, 1831. Read twice, and committed to a Committee of the Whole House to-morrow. Mr. Cave Johnson, from the Committee on Private Land Claims, reported the following bill: [Washington, 1831] 2 p. (H.R. 62) DNA. 9687

---- A bill for the relief of John Menary. January 14, 1831. Read twice, and committed to a Committee of the Whole House to-morrow. Mr. Whittlesey, from the Committee of Claims, reported the following bill. [Washington, 1831] 1 p. (H.R. 557) DNA. 9688

---- A bill for the relief of John Menary. December 19, 1831. Read twice, and committed to a Committee of the Whole House to-morrow. Mr. E. Whittlesey, from the Committee of Claims, reported the following bill: [Washington, 1831] 1 p. (H.R. 34) DNA. 9689

---- A bill for the relief of John Nicks. February 1, 1831. Mr. Ruggles, from the Committee of Claims, reported the following bill; which was read, and passed to a second reading. [Washington, 1831] 1 p. (S. 135) DNA. 9690

---- A bill for the relief of John Proctor. December 22, 1831. Agreeably to notice given, Mr. King asked and obtained leave to bring in the following bill; which was read twice, and referred to the Committee on Public Lands. December 29, 1831. Reported without amendment. [Washington, 1831] 1 p. (S. 14) DNA. 9691

---- A bill for the relief of John R. Rappleye. February 4, 1831. Read twice and committed to a Committee of the Whole House to-morrow. Mr. Trezvant, from the Committee on Military Pensions, reported the following bill: [Washington, 1831] 1 p. (H.R. 597) DNA. 9692

---- A bill for the relief of John Riddle. December 28, 1830. Agreeably to notice, Mr. Chase asked and obtained leave to bring in the following bill; which was read twice, and referred to the Committee on Pensions. January 3, 1831. Reported without amendment. [Washington, 1831] 1 p. (S. 46) DNA. 9693

---- A bill for the relief of John Roberts, late Major of infantry in the war of the Revolution. December 23, 1831. Read twice, and committed to a Committee of the Whole House to-morrow. Mr. Bouldin, from the Committee on Revolutionary Claims, reported the following bill: [Washington, 1831] 1 p. (H.R. 94) DNA. 9694

---- A bill for the relief of John Rodgers. December 20, 1831. Read twice, and committed to a Committee of the Whole House to-morrow. Mr. Storrs, from the Committee on Indian

Affairs, reported the following bill: [Washington, 1831] 1 p. (H.R. 59) DNA. 9695

---- A bill for the relief of John Sapp. December 19, 1831. Read twice, and committed to a Committee of the Whole House tomorrow. Mr. E. Whittlesey, from the Committee of Claims, reported the following bill: [Washington, 1831] 1 p. (H.R. 5) DNA. 9696

---- A bill for the relief of John Teel. December 30, 1831. Read twice, and committed to a Committee of the Whole House tomorrow. Mr. Muhlenburg, from the Committee on Revolutionary Claims, reported the following bill: [Washington, 1831] 1 p. (H.R. 169) DNA. 9697

---- A bill for the relief of Jonah Garrison. February 9, 1831. Read twice, and committed to a Committee of the Whole House tomorrow. Mr. Trezyvant, from the Committee on Military Pensions, reported the following bill. [Washington, 1831] 1 p. (H.R. 611) DNA. 9698

---- A bill for the relief of Joseph Bogy. February 18, 1831. Read twice, and committed to a Committee of the Whole House tomorrow. Mr. McIntire, from the Committee of Claims, reported the following bill. [Washington, 1831] 1 p. (H.R. 635) DNA. 9699

---- A bill for the relief of Joseph Bogy. December 19, 1831. Read twice, and committed to a Committee of the Whole House to-morrow. Mr. McIntire, from the Committee of Claims, reported the following bill: [Washington, 1831] 1 p. (H.R. 48) DNA. 9700

---- A bill for the relief of Joseph Chamberlain. February 22, 1831. Mr. Chase, from the Committee on Pensions, reported the following bill; which was read, and passed to a second reading: [Washington, 1831] 1 p. (S. 169) DNA. 9701

---- A bill for the relief of Joseph Chamberlain. December 27, 1831. Mr. Foot, from the Committee on Pensions, reported the following bill; which was read, and passed to a second reading. [Washington, 1831] 1 p. (S. 24) DNA. 9702

---- A bill for the relief of Joseph E. Sprague. December 16, 1830. Agreeably to notice, Mr. Silsbee asked and obtaine leave to bring in the following bill; which was read, and passed to a second reading. December 17, 1830. Read a second time, and referred to a Committee on the Judiciary. January 4, 1831. Reported without amendment. [Washington, 1831] 1 p. (S. 19) DNA. 9703

---- A bill for the relief of Joseph Kamber. December 27, 1831. Read twice, and committed to a Committee of the Whole House tomorrow. Mr. Mardis, from the Committee on Private Land Claims, reported the following bill: [Washington, 1831] 1 p. (H. R. 138) DNA. 9704

---- A bill for the relief of Joseph S. Cannon. January 5, 1831. Mr. Hayne, from the Committee on Naval Affairs, reported the following bill; which was read, and passed to a second reading. [Washington, 1831] 1 p. (S. 66) DNA. 9705

---- A bill for the relief of Joseph Soniat Dufossat. December 22, 1831. Read twice, and committed to a Committee of the

Whole House to-morrow. Mr. Bullard, from the Committee on Private Land Claims, reported the following bill: [Washington, 1831] 1 p. (H.R. 77) DNA. 9706

---- A bill for the relief of Joseph W. Torrey. January 25, 1831. Read twice, and committed to the Whole House on the state of the Union. Mr. Daniel, from the Committee on the Judiciary, reported the following bill. [Washington, 1831] 1 p. (H.R. 574) DNA. 9707

---- A bill for the relief of Joseph W. Torrey. December 23, 1831. Read twice, and committed to a Committee of the Whole House to-morrow. Mr. Ellsworth, from the Committee on the Judiciary, reported the following bill: [Washington, 1831] 1 p. (H.R. 101) DNA. 9708

---- A bill for the relief of Josiah H. Webb. December 28, 1831. Read twice, and committed to a Committee of the Whole House to-morrow. Mr. Pearce, from the Committee on the Post Office and Post Roads, reported the following bill: [Washington, 1831] 1 p. (H.R. 153) DNA. 9709

---- A bill for the relief of Jotham Lincoln, administrator of Samuel B. Lincoln, deceased. December 19, 1831. Read twice, and committed to a Committee of the Whole House to-morrow. Mr. Whittlesey, from the Committee of Claims, reported the following bill: [Washington, 1831] 1 p. (H.R. 30) DNA. 9710

---- A bill for the relief of Judith Thomas. February 15, 1831. Read twice, and committed to a Committee of the Whole House to-morrow. Mr. Bockee, from the Committee on Military Pensions, reported the following bill. [Washington, 1831] 1 p. (H.R. 629) DNA. 9711

---- A bill for the relief of Lawrence L. Van Kleeck. February 7, 1831. Read twice, and committed to a Committee of the Whole House to-morrow. Mr. Whittlesey, from the Committee of Claims, reported the following bill. [Washington, 1831] 1 p. (H.R. 604) DNA. 9712

---- A bill for the relief of Lawrence L. Van Kleeck. December 19, 1831. Read twice, and committed to a Committee of the Whole House to-morrow. Mr. Whittlesey, from the Committee of Claims, reported the following bill: [Washington, 1831] 1 p. (H.R. 39) DNA. 9713

---- A bill for the relief of Leonard Denison and Elisha Ely. December 19, 1831. Read twice, and committed to a Committee of the Whole House to-morrow. Mr. E. Whittlesey, from the Committee of Claims, reported the following bill: [Washington, 1831] 1 p. (H.R. 17) DNA. 9714

---- A bill for the relief of Lewis Anderson, December 19, 1831. Read twice, and committed to a Committee of the Whole House to-morrow. Mr. E. Whittlesey, from the Committee of Claims, reported the following bill: [Washington, 1831] 1 p. (H.R. 31) DNA. 9715

---- A bill for the relief of Lieutenant James L. Dawson. December 28, 1831. Read twice, and committed to a Committee of the Whole House to-morrow. Mr. Drayton, from the Committee on Military Affairs, reported the following bill: [Washington, 1831] 1 p. (H.R. 152) DNA. 9716

---- A bill for the relief of Miami Exporting Company. December 19, 1831. Read twice, and committed to a Committee of the Whole House to-morrow. Mr. E. Whittlesey, from the Committee of Claims, reported the following bill: [Washington, 1831] 1 p. (H.R. 23) DNA. 9717

---- A bill for the relief of Mrs. Clarissa B. Harrison. February 5, 1831. Read twice, and postponed until Saturday next, 12th instant. Mr. Irvin, from the Committee on the Public Lands, reported the following bill. [Washington, 1831] 1 p. (H.R. 602) DNA. 9718

---- A bill for the relief of Nathaniel Blake. December 23, 1831. Read twice, and committed to a Committee of the Whole House to-morrow. Mr. McDuffie, from the Committee of Ways and Means, reported the following bill: [Washington, 1831] 1 p. (H.R. 118) DNA. 9719

---- A bill for the relief of Nathaniel Cheever and others. January 24, 1831. Mr. King, from the Committee on Finance, reported the following bill; which was read, and passed to a second reading. [Washington, 1831] (S. 116) DNA. 9720

---- A bill for the relief of Percia Tupper, executrix of Samuel Tupper, deceased. December 19, 1831. Read twice, and committed to a Committee of the Whole House to-morrow. Mr. E. Whittlesey, from the Committee of Claims, reported the following bill: [Washington, 1831] 1 p. (H.R. 16) DNA. 9721

---- A bill for the relief of Peter Cleer, of Maryland. February 14, 1831. Mr. Chambers, from the Committee on Pensions, reported the following bill; which was read, and passed to a second reading: [Washington, 1831] 1 p. (S. 160) DNA. 9722

---- A bill for the relief of Peter Peck. December 19, 1831. Read twice, and committed to a Committee of the Whole House to-morrow. Mr. E. Whittlesey, from the Committee of Claims, reported the following bill: [Washington, 1831] 1 p. (H.R. 29) DNA. 9723

---- A bill for the relief of Peters and Pond. January 11, 1831. Mr. Smith, of Maryland, from the Committee on Finance, reported the following bill; which was read, and passed to a second reading. [Washington, 1831] 1 p. (S. 75) DNA. 9724

---- A bill for the relief of Prosper Marigny. December 20, 1831. Read twice, and committed to a Committee of the Whole House to-morrow. Mr. Bullard, from the Committee on Private Land Claims, reported the following bill: [Washington, 1831] 1 p. (H.R. 61) DNA. 9725

---- A bill for the relief of Richard S. Hackley. December 19, 1831. Read twice, and committed to a Committee of the Whole House to-morrow. Mr. Archer, from the Committee on Foreign Affairs, reported the following bill: [Washington, 1831] 1 p. (H.R. 43) DNA. 9726

---- A bill for the relief of Richard W. Steele, a soldier in the late war. December 27, 1831. Read twice, and committed to a Committee of the Whole House to-morrow. Mr. Carr, from the Committee on Private Land Claims, reported the following bill: [Washington, 1831] 1 p. (H.R. 136) DNA. 9727

---- A bill for the relief of Robert A. Forsythe. December 19, 1831. Read twice, and committed to a Committee of the Whole House to-morrow. Mr. E. Whittlesey, from the Committee of Claims, reported the following bill: [Washington, 1831] 1 p. (H.R. 11) DNA. 9728

---- A bill for the relief of Robert Jones. December 19, 1831. Read twice, and committed to a Committee on the Whole House to-morrow. Mr. Clay, from the Committee on Public Lands, reported the following bill: [Washington, 1831] 2 p. (H.R. 45) DNA. 9729

---- A bill for the relief of Robert Kaine, of Buffalo, in the State of New York. December 19, 1831. Read twice, and committed to a Committee of the Whole House to-morrow. Mr. E. Whittlesey, from the Committee of Claims, reported the following bill: [Washington, 1831] 1 p. (H.R. 19) DNA. 9730

---- A bill for the relief of Robert Smart. December 19, 1831. Read twice, and committed to a Committee of the Whole House to-morrow. Mr. McIntire, from the Committee of Claims, reported the following bill: [Washington, 1831] 1 p. (H.R. 47) DNA. 9731

---- A bill for the relief of Robertson and Barnwall, December 14, 1831. Read twice, and committed to a Committee of the Whole House to-morrow. Mr. McDuffie, from the Committee of Ways and Means, reported the following bill: [Washington, 1831] 1 p. (H.R. 2) DNA. 9732

---- A bill for the relief of Samuel Coburn, of the State of Mississippi. January 10, 1831. Mr. Ellis, from the Committee on Public Lands, reported the following bill; which was read, and passed to a second reading. [Washington, 1831] (S. 69) DNA. 9733

---- A bill for the relief of Samuel Dale. February 15, 1831. Read twice, and committed to a Committee of the Whole House to-morrow. Mr. McIntire, from the Committee of Claims, reported the following bill. [Washington, 1831] 1 p. (H.R. 627) DNA. 9734

---- A bill for the relief of Samuel Dale. December 28, 1831. Read twice, and committed to a Committee of the Whole House to-morrow. Mr. McIntire, from the Committee of Claims, reported the following bill: [Washington, 1831] 1 p. (H.R. 151) DNA. 9735

---- A bill for the relief of Samuel Grice. December 23, 1831. Read twice, and committed to a Committee of the Whole House to-morrow. Mr. E. Whittlesey, from the Committee of Claims, reported the following bill: [Washington, 1831] 1 p. (H.R. 121) DNA. 9736

---- A bill for the relief of Samuel Keep. December 19, 1831. Read twice, and committed to a Committee of the Whole House to-morrow. Mr. E. Whittlesey, from the Committee of Claims, reported the following bill: [Washington, 1831] 1 p. (H.R. 21) DNA. 9737

---- A bill for the relief of Sarah Easton and Dorothy Storer. February 23, 1831. Read twice, and committed to a Committee of the Whole House to-morrow. Mr. Young, from the Committee on Revolutionary Claims, reported the following bill. [Washington, 1831] 1 p. (H.R. 646) DNA. 9738

---- A bill for the relief of Sarah Easton and Dorothy Storer. December 28, 1831. Read twice, and committed to a Committee of the Whole House to-morrow. Mr. Muhlenburg, from the Committee on Revolutionary Claims, reported the following bill: [Washington, 1831] 1 p. (H.R. 155) DNA. 9739

---- A bill for the relief of Sophia Gardner. January 21, 1831. Read twice, and referred to the Committee on Naval Affairs. February 10, 1831. Reported without amendment. [Washington, 1831] 1 p. (S. 109) DNA. 9740

---- A bill for the relief of Stephen Hook. December 19, 1831. Read twice, and committed to a Committee of the Whole House to-morrow. Mr. E. Whittlesey, from the Committee of Claims, reported the following bill: [Washington, 1831] 1 p. (H.R.S.) DNA. 9741

---- A bill for the relief of Sylvester Havens. December 19, 1831. Read twice, and committed to a Committee of the Whole House to-morrow. Mr. E. Whittlesey, from the Committee of Claims, reported the following bill: [Washington, 1831] 1 p. (H.R. 13) DNA. 9742

---- A bill for the relief of the administratrix of Captain Paschal Hickman. January 31, 1831. Mr. Benton, from the Committee on Military Affairs, reported the following bill; which was read, and passed to a second reading. [Washington, 1831] 1 p. (S. 134) DNA. 9743

---- A bill for the relief of the heirs and executors of Thomas Worthington, deceased. January 24, 1831. Mr. McKinley, from the Committee on the Judiciary, reported the following bill; which was read, and passed to a second reading. [Washington, 1831] (S. 115) DNA. 9744

---- A bill for the relief of the heirs and legal representatives of John Noble Taylor, deceased. February 4, 1831. Read twice, and committed to a Committee of the Whole House to-morrow. Mr. Brown, from the Committee on Revolutionary Claims, reported the following bill: [Washington, 1831] 1 p. (H.R. 598) DNA. 9745

---- A bill for the relief of the heirs and residuary legatees of William Carter, late of the State of Virginia, deceased. December 23, 1831. Read twice, and committed to a Committee of the Whole House to-morrow. Mr. Muhlenburg, from the Committee on Revolutionary Claims, reported the following bill: [Washington, 1831] 1 p. (H.R. 107) DNA. 9746

---- A bill for the relief of the heirs of Doctor Samuel Kennedy. December 23, 1831. Read twice, and committed to a Committee of the Whole House to-morrow. Mr. Standifer, from the Committee on Revolutionary Claims, reported the following bill: [Washington, 1831] 1 p. (H.R. 100) DNA. 9747

---- A bill for the relief of the heirs of Jean Baptiste Saucier. December 30, 1831. Read twice, and committed to a Committee of the Whole House to-morrow. Mr. Bullard, from the Committee on

Private Land Claims, reported the following bill: [Washington, 1831] 1 p. (H.R. 175) DNA. 9748

---- A bill for the relief of the heirs of Jeremiah Buckley, deceased. December 27, 1831. Read twice, and committed to a Committee of the Whole House to-morrow. Mr. Mardis, from the Committee on Private Land Claims, reported the following bill: [Washington, 1831] 2 p. (H.R. 139) DNA. 9749

---- A bill for the relief of the heirs of Joseph Noble, deceased. January 27, 1831. Mr. McKinley, from the Committee on Public Lands, reported the following bill; which was read, and passed to a second reading. [Washington, 1831] 1 p. (S. 124) DNA. 9750

---- A bill for the relief of the heirs of Nathaniel Hillen. December 28, 1831. Read twice, and committed to a Committee of the Whole House to-morrow. Mr. Cave Johnson, from the Committee on Private Land Claims, reported the following bill: [Washington, 1831] 1 p. (H.R. 149) DNA. 9751

---- A bill for the relief of the heirs of William Robertson, deceased. December 19, 1831. Read twice, and committed to a Committee of the Whole House to-morrow. Mr. Clay, from the Committee on Public Lands, reported the following bill: [Washington, 1831] 2 p. (H.R. 42) DNA. 9752

---- A bill for the relief of the heirs of William Vawters. December 23, 1831. Read twice, and committed to a Committee of the Whole House to-morrow. Mr. Bouldin, from the Committee on Revolutionary Claims, reported the following bill: [Washington, 1831] 1 p. (H.R. 93) DNA. 9753

---- A bill for the relief of the inhabitants of Terre aux Boeufs. December 27, 1831. Read twice, and committed to a Committee of the Whole House to-morrow. Mr. Cave Johnson, from the Committee on Private Land Claims, reported the following bill: [Washington, 1831] 8 p. (H.R. 125) DNA. 9754

---- A bill for the relief of the legal representatives of Antonio Bonnabel. February 19, 1831. Read twice, and ordered to be engrossed, and read the third time on Monday next. Mr. Sterigere, from the Committee on Private Land Claims, reported the following bill. [Washington, 1831] 1 p. (H.R. 641) DNA. 9755

---- A bill for the relief of the legal representatives of Christian Ish, deceased. February 2, 1831. Read twice, and committed to a Committee of the Whole House to-morrow. Mr. Crane, from the Committee on Revolutionary Claims, reported the following bill: [Washington, 1831] 1 p. (H.R. 594) DNA. 9756

---- A bill for the relief of the legal representatives of Colonel John Thornton, deceased. February 2, 1831. Read twice, and committed to a Committee of the Whole House to-morrow. Mr. Crane, from the Committee on Revolutionary Claims, reported the following bill: [Washington, 1831] 1 p. (H.R. 593) DNA. 9757

---- A bill for the relief of the legal representatives of Daniel McIntire, deceased. January 14, 1831. Agreeably to notice given, Mr. Holmes asked and obtained leave to bring in the following bill; which was read twice, and referred to the Committee on Pensions. January 18, 1831. Reported without amendment. [Washington, 1831] 1 p. (S. 84) DNA. 9758

---- A bill for the relief of the legal representatives of David Dardin, deceased. February 23, 1831. Read twice, and committed to a Committee of the Whole House to-morrow. Mr. Dickinson, from the Committee on Revolutionary Claims, reported the following bill. [Washington, 1831] 1 p. (H.R. 647) DNA. 9759

---- A bill for the relief of the legal representatives of Jacintha Vidal, Thomas Thompson, and Margaret Thompson. January 26, 1831. Mr. Poindexter, from the Committee on Private Land Claims, reported the following bill; which was read, and passed to second reading. [Washington, 1831] 3 p. (S. 122) DNA. 9760

---- A bill for the relief of the legal representatives of Job Alvord. December 30, 1831. Read twice, and committed to a Committee of the Whole House to-morrow. Mr. Bates, of Massachusetts, from the Committee on Revolutionary Claims, reported the following bill: [Washington, 1831] 1 p. (H.R. 173) DNA. 9761

---- A bill for the relief of the legal representatives of John Coleman, deceased. February 26, 1831. Read twice and committed to the Committee on the Whole House to which is committed the bill from the Senate (No. 8) for the relief of Lucien Harper. Mr. White, of New York, from the Committee on Naval Affairs, reported the following bill. [Washington, 1831] 1 p. (H.R. 655) DNA. 9762

---- A bill for the relief of the legal representatives of John McHugh. December 23, 1831. Read twice, and committed to a Committee of the Whole House to-morrow. Mr. Mardis, from the Committee on Private Land Claims, reported the following bill: [Washington, 1831] 1 p. (H.R. 119) DNA. 9763

---- A bill for the relief of the legal representatives of Palser Shilling, deceased. January 27, 1831. Mr. Poindexter, from the Committee on Private Land Claims reported the following bill; which was read, and passed a second reading. [Washington, 1831] 1 p. (S. 127) DNA. 9764

---- A bill for the relief of the legal representatives of Samuel Wagstaff. December 19, 1831. Read twice, and committed to a Committee of the Whole House to-morrow. Mr. E. Whittlesey, from the Committee of Claims, reported the following bill: [Washington, 1831] 1 p. (H.R. 27) DNA. 9765

---- A bill for the relief of the legal representatives of William Hull. February 16, 1831. Read twice, and ordered to be engrossed, and read the third time to-morrow. Mr. Whittlesey, from the Committee of Claims, reported the following bill. [Washington, 1831] 1 p. (H.R. 632) DNA. 9766

---- A bill for the relief of the mother of Fitz Henry Babbit, late a Lieutenant in the Navy of the United States. February 22, 1831. Mr. Hayne, from the Committee on Naval Affairs, reported the following bill; which was read, and passed to a second reading: [Washington, 1831] 1 p. (S. 171) DNA. 9767

---- A bill for the relief of the officers and soldiers of Fort Delaware. February 15, 1831. Agreeably to notice, Mr. Clayton asked and obtained leave to bring in the following bill; which was read twice, and referred to the Committee on Military Affairs. [Washington, 1831] 1 p. (S. 163) DNA. 9768

---- A bill for the relief of the representatives of David Dardin, deceased. December 23, 1831. Read twice, and committed to a Committee of the Whole House to-morrow. Mr. Bouldin, from the Committee on Revolutionary Claims, reported the following bill: [Washington, 1831] 1 p. (H.R. 92) DNA. 9769

---- A bill for the relief of the representatives of Doctor Hanson Catlett. January 26, 1831. Read twice, and committed to a Committee of the Whole House to-morrow. Mr. Clay, from the Committee of Claims, reported the following bill. [Washington, 1831] 1 p. (H.R. 576) DNA. 9770

---- A bill for the relief of the representatives of Doctor Hanson Catlett. December 19, 1831. Read twice, and committed to the Committee of the Whole House to-morrow. Mr. E. Whittlesey, from the Committee of Claims, reported the following bill: [Washington, 1831] 1 p. (H.R. 37) DNA. 9771

---- A bill for the relief of the sureties of Amos Edwards. December 27, 1831. Read twice, and committed to a Committee of the Whole House to-morrow. Mr. Daniel, from the Committee on the Judiciary, reported the following bill: [Washington, 1831] 1 p. (H.R. 127) DNA. 9772

---- A bill for the relief of the widow and heirs of Pedro, alias Pierre Guedry. February 1, 1831. Read twice, and committed to a Committee of the Whole House to-morrow. Mr. Draper, from the Committee on Private Land Claims, reported the following bill. [Washington, 1831] (H.R. 587) DNA. 9773

---- A bill for the relief of the widow and heirs of Pedro, alias Pierre Guedry. December 28, 1831. Mr. Carr, from the Committee on Private Land Claims, reported the following bill: [Washington, 1831] 2 p. (H.R. 162) DNA. 9774

---- A bill for the relief of Thomas Cooper, of South Carolina. December 16, 1829. Agreeably to notice given, Mr. Dickerson asked and obtained leave to bring in the following bill; which was read, and passed to a second reading. December 17, 1830. Read the second time, and referred to the Committee on the Judiciary. January 27, 1831. Reported without amendment. [Washington, 1831] (S. 23) DNA. 9775

---- A bill for the relief of Thomas Cross, Seth Dickinson and Benjamin Crofoot. December 22, 1831. Read twice, and committed to a Committee of the Whole House to-morrow. Mr. Pendleton, from the Committee on Revolutionary Pensions, reported the following bill: [Washington, 1831] 1 p. (H.R. 81) DNA. 9776

---- A bill for the relief of Thomas Hopping and Joshua P. Frothingham. December 30, 1831. Read twice, and committed to a Committee of the Whole House to-morrow. Mr. Bates, (of Mass.) from the Committee on

Revolutionary Claims, reported the following bill: [Washington, 1831] 1 p. (H.R. 171) DNA. 9777

---- A bill for the relief of Thomas Hopping and Joshua P. Frothingham, surviving heirs at law of Thomas Frothingham, late of Charlestown, in the county of Middlesex, and Commonwealth of Massachusetts, joiner, deceased. February 7, 1831. Read twice, and committed to a Committee on the Whole House to-morrow. Mr. De Witt, from the Committee on Revolutionary Claims, reported the following bill. [Washington, 1831] 1 p. (H.R. 605) DNA. 9778

---- A bill for the relief of Thomas Park. January 10, 1831. Read twice, and committed to the Committee of the Whole House to-morrow. Mr. Wingate, from the Committee on Revolutionary Claims, reported the following bill. [Washington, 1831] 1 p. (H.R. 551) DNA. 9779

---- A bill for the relief of Thomas Porter, of Indiana. January 21, 1831. Mr. Marks, from the Committee on Pensions, reported the following bill; which was read, and passed to a second time. [Washington, 1831] 1 p. (S. 107) DNA. 9780

---- A bill for the relief of Thurston Card. January 31, 1831. Mr. Holmes, from the Committee on Pensions, reported the following bill; which was read, and passed to a second reading. [Washington, 1831] 1 p. (S. 129) DNA. 9781

---- A bill for the relief of Whitford Gill. December 20, 1831. Read twice, and committed to a Committee of the Whole House to-morrow. Mr. Whittlesey, from the Committee of Claims, reported the following bill: [Washington, 1831] 1 p. (H.R. 20) DNA. 9782

---- A bill for the relief of William B. Matthews, trustee. January 13, 1831. Mr. McKinley, from the Committee on the Judiciary, reported the following bill; which was read, and passed to a second reading. [Washington, 1831] 1 p. (S. 82) DNA. 9783

---- A bill for the relief of William Bradshaw. January 10, 1831. Agreeably to notice given, Mr. Benton asked and obtained leave to bring in the following bill; which was read twice, and referred to the Committee on Public Lands. February 2, 1831. Reported without amendment. [Washington, 1831] (S. 71) DNA. 9784

---- A bill for the relief of William Burris, of Mississippi. January 12, 1831. Agreeably to notice given, Mr. Ellis asked and obtained leave to bring in the following bill; which was read, and passed to a second reading. January 13, 1831. Read second time, and referred to the Committee on Public Lands. January 18, 1831. Reported without amendment. [Washington, 1831] 1 p. (S. 79) DNA. 9785

---- A bill for the relief of William Christy. January 3, 1831. Mr. Holmes, from the Committee on Pensions, reported the following bill; which was read, and passed to a second reading. [Washington, 1831] 1 p. (S. 55) DNA. 9786

---- A bill for the relief of William D. Acker. January 25, 1831. Mr. Foot, from the Committee of Claims, reported the following bill; which was read, and passed to a second reading. [Washington, 1831] 1 p. (S. 118) DNA. 9787

---- A bill for the relief of William D. Gaines and William M. King. December 30, 1831. Read twice, and committed to a Committee of the Whole House to-morrow. Mr. Clay, from the Committee on Public Lands, reported the following bill: [Washington, 1831] 2 p. (H.R. 168) DNA. 9788

---- A bill for the relief of William D. King, James Daviess, and Garland Lincecum. December 19, 1831. Read twice, and committed to a Committee of the Whole House to-morrow. Mr. E. Whittlesey, from the Committee of Claims, reported the following bill: [Washington, 1831] 1 p. (H.R. 9) DNA. 9789

---- A bill for the relief of William Delzell, of Ohio. January 24, 1831. Mr. Marks, from the Committee on Pensions, reported the following bill; which was read, and passed to a second reading. [Washington, 1831] 1 p. (S. 117) DNA. 9790

---- A bill for the relief of William Forsythe. December 19, 1831. Read twice, and committed to a Committee of the Whole House to-morrow. Mr. E. Whittlesey, from the Committee of Claims, reported the following bill: [Washington, 1831] 1 p. (H. R. 15) DNA. 9791

---- A bill for the relief of William Hoffman, a Canadian volunteer. February 8, 1831. Read twice, and ordered to be engrossed, and read the third time to-morrow. Mr. Sterigere, from the Committee on Private Land Claims, reported the following bill. [Washington, 1831] 1 p. (H.R. 606) DNA. 9792

---- A bill for the relief of William Hoffman, a Canadian volunteer. December 29, 1831. Read twice, and committed to a Committee of the Whole House to-morrow. Mr. Carr, from the Committee on Private Land Claims, reported the following bill: [Washington, 1831] 1 p. (H.R. 167) DNA. 9793

---- A bill for the relief of William J. Quincy and Charles E. Quincy. December 14, 1831. Read twice, and committed to a Committee of the Whole House to-morrow. Mr. McDuffie, from the Committee of Ways and Means, reported the following bill: [Washington, 1831] 1 p. (H.R. 3) DNA. 9794

---- A bill for the relief of William Owens. January 24, 1831. Read twice, and committed to a Committee of the Whole House to-morrow. Mr. Whittlesey, from the Committee of Claims, reported the following bill. [Washington, 1831] 1 p. (H.R. 572) DNA. 9795

---- A bill for the relief of William Owens. December 19, 1831. Read twice, and committed to a Committee of the Whole House to-morrow. Mr. E. Whittlesey, from the Committee of Claims, reported the following bill: [Washington, 1831] 1 p. (H.R. 36) DNA. 9796

---- A bill for the relief of William Rice. February 8, 1831. Mr. McKinley, from the Committee on Public Lands, reported the following bill; which was read, and passed to a second reading: [Washington, 1831] 1 p. (S. 150) DNA. 9797

---- A bill for the relief of

William Scott, of Tennessee. January 18, 1831. Mr. Chase, from the Committee on Pensions, reported the following bill; which was read, and passed to a second reading. [Washington, 1831] 1 p. (S. 97) DNA. 9798

---- A bill for the relief of William Smith, administrator of John Taylor, deceased. January 20, 1831. Read twice, and committed to a Committee of the Whole House to-morrow. Mr. Clay, from the Committee on the Public Lands, reported the following bill: [Washington, 1831] (H.R. 569) DNA. 9799

---- A bill for the relief of William Smith, administrator of John Taylor, deceased. January 21, 1831. Mr. Barton, from the Committee of Public Lands, reported the following bill; which was read, and passed to a second reading. [Washington, 1831] (S. 105) DNA. 9800

---- A bill for the relief of William Tharp. December 19, 1831. Read twice, and committed to a Committee of the Whole House to-morrow. Mr. E. Whittlesey, from the Committee of Claims, reported the following bill: [Washington, 1831] 2 p. (H.R. 24) DNA. 9801

---- A bill for the relief of William Vance. January 18, 1831. Mr. Marks, from the Committee on Pensions, reported the following bill; which was read, and passed to a second reading. [Washington, 1831] 1 p. (S. 88) DNA. 9802

---- A bill for the relief of Woodson Wren, of Mississippi. January 4, 1831. Read, and passed a second reading. Jan'ary 5, 1831. Read second time, and referred to the Committee on Public Lands. January 10, 1831. Reported without amendment. [Washington, 1831] (S. 62) DNA. 9803

---- A bill for the sale of the lands in the State of Illinois reserved for the use of the salt springs on the Vermillion river, in that State. February 2, 1831. Read twice, and ordered to be engrossed, and read the third time to-morrow. Mr. Irvin, from the Committee on the Public Lands, reported the following bill. [Washington, 1831] 1 p. (H.R. 588). DNA. 9804

---- A bill further to provide for the relief of distressed American seamen in foreign countries. December 22, 1831. Read twice, and committed to a Committee of the Whole House on the state of the Union. Mr. Cambreleng, from the Committee on Commerce, reported the following bill: [Washington, 1831] 1 p. (H.R. 79) DNA. 9805

---- A bill granting a pension to Jared Cone. December 20, 1831. Read twice, and committed to a Committee of the Whole House to-morrow. Mr. Hubbard, from the Committee on Revolutionary Pensions, reported the following bill: [Washington, 1831] 1 p. (H.R. 50) DNA. 9806

---- A bill granting a pension to John Bradshaw, a soldier of the revolution. December 23, 1831. Read twice, and committed to a Committee of the Whole House to-morrow. Mr. Denny, from the Committee on Revolutionary Pensions, reported the following bill: [Washington, 1831] 1 p. (H.R. 110) DNA. 9807

---- A bill granting a pension to John Farrow, a soldier of the revolution. December 23, 1831.

Read twice, and committed to a Committee of the Whole House to-morrow. Mr. Denny, from the Committee on Revolutionary Pensions, reported the following bill: [Washington, 1831] 1 p. (H.R. 111) DNA. 9808

---- A bill granting a pension to Jonathan Sizer. December 22, 1831. Read twice, and committed to a Committee of the Whole House to-morrow. Mr. Hubbard, from the Committee on Revolutionary Pensions, reported the following bill: [Washington, 1831] 1 p. (H.R. 71) DNA. 9809

---- A bill granting a pension to Martin Miller. January 6, 1831. Mr. Foot, from the Committee on Pensions, reported the following bill; which was read, and passed to a second reading. [Washington, 1831] 1 p. (S. 67) DNA. 9810

---- A bill granting a pension to Robert Dunn. December 21, 1831. Read twice, and committed to a Committee of the Whole House to-morrow. Mr. Hubbard, from the Committee on Revolutionary Pensions, reported the following bill: [Washington, 1831] 1 p. (H.R. 65) DNA. 9811

---- A bill granting a pension to Samuel Patton, a revolutionary soldier. February 8, 1831. Read twice, and ordered to be engrossed, and read the third time to-morrow. Mr. Chilton, the Committee in Military Pensions, reported the following bill. [Washington, 1831] 1 p. (H.R. 607) DNA. 9812

---- A bill granting a quantity of land to the Territory of Arkansas, for the erection of a public building at the seat of Government of said Territory. January-27, 1831. Agreeably to notice, Mr. McKinley asked and obtained leave to bring in the following bill; which was read, and passed to a second reading. January 28, 1831. Read the second time, and referred to the Committee on Public Lands. February 7, 1831. Reported without amendment. [Washington, 1831] (S. 125) DNA. 9813

---- A bill granting pensions to certain persons therein named. December 21, 1831. Read twice, and committed to a Committee of the Whole House to-morrow. Mr. Hubbard, from the Committee on Revolutionary Pensions, to which had been referred the petitions of John Slaven, Abraham Parker, William Mattheny, and William Black, reported the following bill: [Washington, 1831] 1 p. (H.R. 68) DNA. 9814

---- A bill granting pensions to Elisha James, Nathaniel Standish and Eliphas Healy. December 20, 1831. Mr. Hubbard, from the Committee on Revolutionary Pensions, reported the following bill: [Washington, 1831] 1 p. (H.R. 52) DNA. 9815

---- A bill granting pensions to Enoch Hoyt and John King, soldiers of the Revolution. December 21, 1831. Read twice, and committed to a Committee of the Whole House to-morrow. Mr. Hubbard, from the Committee on Revolutionary Pensions, reported the following bill: [Washington, 1831] 1 p. (H.R. 67) DNA. 9816

---- A bill granting pensions to Henry Blankenship and Peter Buxton. December 20, 1831. Read twice, and committed to a Committee of the Whole House to-morrow. Mr. Hubbard, from the Committee on Revolutionary Pensions, reported the following bill:

[Washington, 1831] 1 p. (H.R. 51) DNA. 9817

---- A bill granting pensions to Humphrey Becket and David Smith. December 21, 1831. Read twice, and committed to a Committee of the Whole House to-morrow. Mr. Hubbard, from the Committee on Revolutionary Pensions, reported the following bill: [Washington, 1831] 1 p. (H.R. 66) DNA. 9818

---- A bill granting pensions to John Elliott and Ebenezer De Forest. December 20, 1831. Read twice, and committed to a Committee of the Whole House to-morrow. Mr. Doubleday, from the Committee on Revolutionary Pensions, reported the following bill: [Washington, 1831] 1 p. (H.R. 55) DNA. 9819

---- A bill granting pensions to John Fancher, Daniel Purdy, Roger Strong, and Isaac Dalton, December 23, 1831. Mr. Hubbard, from the Committee on Revolutionary Pensions, reported the following bill: [Washington, 1831] 1 p. (H.R. 104) DNA. 9820

---- A bill granting pensions to Jonathan Rundlet, Henry Tew, James Reynolds and Joshua Reeves, soldiers of the revolution. December 29, 1831. Read twice, and committed to a Committee of the Whole House to-morrow. Mr. Denny, from the Committee on Revolutionary Pensions, reported the following bill: [Washington, 1831] 1 p. (H.R. 166) DNA. 9821

---- A bill granting pensions to Joseph Lyon, William Grenell, and Grove Barnard. December 21, 1831. Read twice, and committed to a Committee of the Whole House to-morrow. Mr. Pendleton, from the Committee on Revolutionary Pensions, reported the following bill: [Washington, 1831] 1 p. (H.R. 69) DNA. 9822

---- A bill granting pensions to Lester Morris, John Ferguson, and William Headly. December 22, 1831. Read twice, and committed to a Committee of the Whole House to-morrow. Mr. Hubbard, from the Committee on Revolutionary Pensions, reported the following bill: [Washington, 1831] 1 p. (H.R. 70) DNA. 9823

---- A bill granting pensions to Samuel Patton and Lewis Gilbert. December 22, 1831. Read twice, and committed to a Committee of the Whole House to-morrow. Mr. Hubbard, from the Committee on Revolutionary Pensions, reported the following bill: [Washington, 1831] 1 p. (H.R. 72) DNA. 9824

---- A bill granting pensions to Stephen Dunham and Israel Beach. December 22, 1831. Read twice, and committed to a Committee of the Whole House to-morrow. Mr. Doubleday, from the Committee on Revolutionary Pensions, reported the following bill: [Washington, 1831] 1 p. (H.R. 83) DNA. 9825

---- A bill in addition to an act, entitled "An act to provide for certain persons engaged in the land and naval service of the United States in the revolutionary war," approved March eighteenth, one thousand eight hundred and eighteen. December 28, 1831. Read twice, and committed to a Committee of the Whole House to-morrow. Mr. Hubbard, from the Committee on Revolutionary Pensions, reported the following bill: [Washington, 1831] 4 p. (H.R. 157) DNA. 9826

---- A bill in addition to the act concerning the slave trade. February 21, 1831. Mr. Smith, of Maryland, from the Committee on Finance, reported the following bill; which was read, and passed to a second reading: [Washington, 1831] (S. 168) DNA. 9827

---- A bill in aid of an act entitled "An act for the relief of James Burnett." February 25, 1831. Read twice, and committed to a Committee on the Whole House to-morrow. Mr. Burges, from the Committee on Revolutionary Claims, reported the following bill. [Washington, 1831] 1 p. (H.R. 653) DNA. 9828

---- A bill increasing the pay of Captains and Masters--Commandment in the Navy of the United States, and for other purposes. February 16, 1831. Read twice, and committed to the Committee of the Whole House on the state of the Union. Mr. Dorsey, from the Committee on Naval Affairs, reported the following bill. [Washington, 1831] 1 p. (H.R. 633) DNA. 9829

---- A bill making additional appropriations for the improvement of certain harbors, and removing obstructions in the mouths of certain rivers. January 18, 1831. Read twice, and committed to the Committee on the Whole House on the state of the Union. Mr. Verplanck, from the Committee of Ways and Means, reported the following bill. [Washington, 1831] (H.R. 566) DNA. 9830

---- A bill making an appropriation for a custom-house in the city of New York. January 31, 1831. Read twice, and committed to the Committee of the Whole House on the state of the Union. Mr. Camberleng, from the Committee on Commerce, reported the following bill. [Washington, 1831] 1 p. (H.R. 585) DNA. 9831

---- A bill making an appropriation for the repairs of Fort Delaware, and for ascertaining the legal title to the Pea Patch island. February 24, 1831. Read twice, and committed to a Committee of the Whole House this day. Mr. Drayton, from the Committee on Military Affairs, reported the following bill. [Washington, 1831] 1 p. (H.R. 649) DNA. 9832

---- A bill making appropriations for building light-boats, beacons, and monuments, and placing buoys. February 8, 1831. Read twice, and committed to the Committee of the Whole House on the state of the Union. Mr. Loyall, from the Committee on Commerce, reported the following bill. [Washington, 1831] (H.R. 609) DNA. 9833

---- A bill making appropriations for carrying into effect certain Indian treaties. February 4, 1831. Mr. White, from the Committee on Indian Affairs, reported the following bill; which was read, and passed to a second reading: [Washington, 1831] (S. 145) DNA. 9834

---- A bill making appropriations for carrying on certain roads and works of internal improvement, and providing for surveys. January 28, 1831. Read twice, and committed to the Committee of the Whole House on the state of the Union. Mr. Verplanck, from the Committee of Ways and Means, reported the following bill. [Washington, 1831] (H.R. 584) DNA. 9835

---- A bill making appropriations for certain expenditures on account of the Engineer, Ordnance, and Quartermaster's Department.

January 14, 1831. Read twice, and committed to the Committee of the Whole House on the state of the Union. Mr. Drayton, from the Committee on Military Affairs, reported the following bill. [Washington, 1831] 3 p. (H.R. 559) DNA. 9836

---- A bill making appropriations for certain fortifications during the year (1831). January 7, 1831. Read twice, and committed to a Committee of the Whole House to-morrow. Mr. Verplanck, from the Committee of Ways and Means, reported the following bill. [Washington, 1831] (H.R. 545) DNA. 9837

---- A bill making appropriations for fortifications for the year one thousand eight hundred and thirty-two. December 30, 1831. Read twice, and committed to the Committee of the Whole House on the state of the Union. Mr. McDuffie, from the Committee of Ways and Means, reported the following bill: [Washington, 1831] 1 p. (H.R. 174) DNA. 9838

---- A bill making appropriations for the Indian department for the year (1831). January 14, 1831. Read twice, and committed to the Committee of the Whole House on the state of the Union. Mr. Verplanck, from the Committee of Ways and Means, reported the following bill. [Washington, 1831] (H.R. 560) DNA. 9839

---- A bill making appropriations for the Indian Department for the year one thousand eight hundred and thirty-two. December 30, 1831. Read twice, and committed to the Committee of the Whole House on the state of the Union. Mr. McDuffie, from the Committee of Ways and Means, reported the following bill: [Washington, 1831] 2 p. (H.R. 173) DNA. 9840

---- A bill making appropriations for the military service for the year (1831). January 6, 1831. Read twice, and committed to the Committee of the Whole House on the state of the Union. Mr. Verplanck, from the Committee of Ways and Means, reported the following bill. [Washington, 1831] (H.R 539) DNA. 9841

---- A bill making appropriations for the payment of revolutionary and invalid pensions. January 5, 1831. Read twice, and committed to the Committee of the Whole House on the state of the Union. Mr. Verplanck, from the Committee of Ways and Means, reported the following bill. [Washington, 1831] (H.R. 538) DNA. 9842

---- A bill making appropriations for the revolutionary and other pensioners of the United States, for the year 1832. December 27, 1831. Read twice, and committed to a Committee of the Whole House on the state of the Union. Mr. McDuffie, from the Committee of Ways and Means, reported the following bill: [Washington, 1831] 1 p. (H.R. 144) DNA. 9843

---- A bill making appropriations for the support of Government for the year one thousand eight hundred and thirty-two. December 23, 1831. Read twice, and committed to the Committee of the Whole House and the state of the Union. Mr. McDuffie, from the Committee of Ways and Means, reported the following bill: [Washington, 1831] 17 p. (H.R. 116) DNA. 9844

---- A bill making appropriations for the support of the army for the year one thousand eight hundred and thirty-two. December 28, 1831. Read twice, and committed to the Committee of the Whole House on the state of the Union. Mr. McDuffie, from the Committee of Ways and Means, reported the following bill: [Washington, 1831] 3 p. (H.R. 164) DNA. 9845

---- A bill making grants of land to the disbanded officers and others for services and sacrifices during the late war. March 1, 1831. Read twice, and laid upon the table. Mr. Duncan, from the Committee on the Public Lands, to which the subject had been referred, reported the following bill. [Washington, 1831] 1 p. (H.R. 656) DNA. 9846

---- A bill making provision for the compensation of witnesses, and payment of other expenses attending the trial of the impeachment of James H. Peck. January 12, 1831. Mr. Iredell, from the Committee on the Contingent Expenses of the Senate, reported the following bill; which was read, and passed to a second reading. [Washington, 1831] (S. 78) DNA. 9847

---- A bill providing for a grant of land to the New England Asylum for the Blind. February 5, 1831. Read twice, and committed to the Committee of the Whole House on the state of the Union. Mr. E. Everett, from the Select Committee to which the subject had been referred, reported the following bill. [Washington, 1831] (H.R 603) DNA. 9848

---- A bill providing for a grant of land to the New England Asylum for the blind, and the New York Institution for the instruction of the deaf and dumb. December 23, 1831. Read twice, and committed to a Committee of the Whole House to-morrow. Mr. E. Everett, from the Select Committee, to which the subject had been referred, reported the following bill: [Washington, 1831] 2 p. (H.R. 123) DNA. 9849

---- A bill providing for the armament of the fortifications. December 20, 1831. Agreeably to notice given, Mr. Smith asked and obtained leave to bring in the following bill; which was read, and passed to a second reading. December 21, 1831. Read a second time, and referred to Committee on Military Affairs. December 27, 1831. Reported without amendment. [Washington, 1831] 1 p. (S. 7) DNA. 9850

---- A bill providing for the final settlement of the claims of States for interest on advances to the United States, made during the last war. January 13, 1831. Agreeably to notice, Mr. Chalmers asked and obtained leave to bring in the following bill; which was read twice, and referred to the Committee on Judiciary. January 19, 1831. Reported with an amendment to wit: insert those words, "which have been or may be," in italics. [Washington, 1831] (S. 81) DNA. 9851

---- A bill providing for the final settlement of the claims of States for interest on advances to the United States, made during the last war. December 19, 1831. Agreeably to notice, Mr. Chambers asked and obtained leave to bring in the following bill; which was read twice and referred to the Committee on the Judiciary. [Washington, 1831] 2 p. (S. 5) DNA. 9852

---- A bill providing for the organization of the Ordnance

Department. December 15, 1831. Agreeably to notice given, Mr. Smith asked and obtained leave to bring in the following bill which was read twice, and referred to the Committee on Military Affairs. [Washington, 1831] 2 p. (S. 4) DNA. 9853

---- A bill providing for the organization of the Ordnance Department. December 23, 1831. Read twice, and committed to the Committee of the Whole House on the State of the Union. Mr. Drayton, from the Committee on Military Affairs, reported the following bill: [Washington, 1831] 3 p. (H.R. 95) DNA. 9854

---- A bill providing for the purchase of certain copies of the Debates on the Federal Constitution. December 30, 1831. Read twice, and committed to a Committee of the Whole House to-morrow. Mr. Everett, of Massachusetts, from the Committee on the Library, reported the following bill: [Washington, 1831] 1 p. (H.R. 178) DNA. 9855

---- A bill regulating the compensation of the clerks in the Post Office Department. January 28, 1831. Read twice, and committed to a Committee of the Whole House to-morrow. Mr. Hodges, from the Committee on the Post Office and Post Roads, reported the following bill. [Washington, 1831] 1 p. (H.R. 583) DNA. 9856

---- A bill regulating the duties, and providing for the compensation of Pursers in the Navy. December 30, 1831. Mr. Hayne from the Committee on Naval Affairs, reported the following bill; which was read, and passed to a second reading. [Washington, 1831] 4 p. (S. 33) DNA. 9857

---- A bill regulating the enlistment of seamen, ordinary seamen landsmen and boys, in the naval service of the United States. December 23, 1831. Read twice, and committed to the Committee of the Whole House on the State of the Union. Mr. Hoffman, from the Committee on Naval Affairs, reported the following bill: [Washington, 1831] 1 p. (H.R. 87) DNA. 9858

---- A bill regulating the manner of taking evidence in cases of contested elections of members of the House of Representatives. January 12, 1831. Read twice, and committed to the Committee of the Whole House on the state of the Union. Mr. Beekman, from the Committee of Elections, to which the subject had been referred, reported the following bill. [Washington, 1831] 5 p. (H.R. 555) DNA. 9859

---- A bill regulating the value of certain foreign silver coins within the United States. February 22, 1831. Read twice, and committed to the Committee of the Whole House to which is committed the bill from the Senate (No. 6) concerning the gold coins of the United States. Mr. White, of New York, from the Select Committee to which the subject had been referred, reported the following bill. [Washington, 1831] (H.R. 644) DNA. 9860

---- A bill relative to militia fines within the District of Columbia. February 16, 1831. Mr. Barnard, from the Committee on the Militia, reported the following bill; which was read, and passed to a second reading: [Washington, 1831] (S. 164) DNA. 9861

---- A bill relative to the

duties of the clerks in the Executive Departments. February 4, 1831. Read twice, and referred to the Committee on the Judiciary. February 10, 1831. Reported with an amendment, to wit: insert the words printed in italics. [Washington, 1831] 1 p. (S. 146) DNA. 9862

---- A bill respecting the city of Detroit. February 12, 1831. Read the first and second time. February 15, 1831. Committed to a Committee of the Whole House to-morrow. Mr. Strong, from the Committee on the Territories, reported the following bill. [Washington, 1831] (H.R. 624) DNA. 9863

---- A bill respecting the jurisdiction of certain district courts. February 3, 1831. Mr. Webster, from the Committee on the Judiciary, reported the following bill; which was read, and passed to a second reading: [Washington, 1831] 1 p. (S. 142) DNA. 9864

---- A bill respecting the navy pension fund, and certain persons chargeable thereon. February 18, 1831. Read twice, and ordered to be engrossed, and read the third time on Tuesday next. Mr. Hoffman, from the Committee on Naval Affairs, reported the following bill. [Washington, 1831] 5 p. (H.R. 639) DNA. 9865

---- A bill supplemental to the act "granting the right of preemption to settlers on the public lands," approved the twenty-ninth day of May, eighteen hundred and thirty. January 9, 1831. Mr. Kane, from the Committee on Public Lands, reported the following bill; which was read, and passed to a second reading. [Washington, 1831] (S. 64) DNA. 9866

---- A bill supplementary to an act to grant preemption rights to settlers on public lands. December 27, 1831. Mr. King, from the Committee on Public Lands, reported the following bill; which was read, and passed to a second reading. [Washington, 1831] 1 p. (S. 25) DNA. 9867

---- A bill supplementary to and to amend an act entitled "An act to regulate the collection of duties on imports and tonnage," approved the second day of March (1799). February 9, 1831. Read twice, and committed to the Committee of the Whole House on the state of the Union. Mr. Huntington, from the Committee on Commerce, reported the following bill. [Washington, 1831] (H.R. 610) DNA. 9868

---- A bill supplementary to the act entitled "An act to grant a certain quantity of land to the State of Indiana, for the purpose of aiding said State in opening a canal to connect the waters of the Wabash river with those of Lake Erie. January 27, 1831. Read twice, and committed to the Whole House on the state of the Union. Mr. Letcher, from the Committee on Internal Improvements, reported the following bill. [Washington, 1831] 1 p. (H.R. 581) DNA. 9869

---- A bill supplementary to the "Act for the relief of certain surviving officers and soldiers of the revolution." January 19, 1831. Read twice, and committed to the Committee of the Whole House on the State of the Union. Mr. Verplanck, from the Committee of Ways and Means, reported the following bill. [Washington, 1831] 3 p. (H.R. 567) DNA. 9870

---- A bill supplementary to the

"Act for the relief of certain surviving officers and soldiers of the revolution." December 8, 1831. Read twice, and referred to the Committee on Pensions. December 15, 1831. Reported with an amendment. [Washington, 1831] 3 p. (S. 1) DNA. 9871

---- A bill supplementary to the act to reduce the duty on salt. January 27, 1831. Mr. Silsbee, from the Committee on Finance, reported the following bill; which was read, and passed to a second reading. [Washington, 1831] 1 p. (S. 126) DNA. 9872

---- A bill supplementary to the several laws for the sale of public lands. January 3, 1831. Mr. Barton, from the Committee on Public Lands, reported the following bill; which was read, and passed to a second reading. [Washington, 1831] (S. 56) DNA. 9873

---- A bill supplementary to the several laws for the sale of public lands. December 20, 1831. Read twice, and committed to a Committee of the Whole House to-morrow. Mr. Clay, from the Committee on the Public Lands, reported the following bill: [Washington, 1831] 2 p. (H.R. 54) DNA. 9874

---- A bill supplementary to the several laws for the sale of Public Lands. December 23, 1831. Mr. King, from the Committee on Public Lands, reported the following bill; which was read, and passed to a second reading. [Washington, 1831] 2 p. (S. 22) DNA. 9875

---- A bill to abolish the duty on Alum Salt. December 19, 1831. Agreeably to notice given, Mr. Benton asked and obtained leave to bring in the following bill; which was read, and passed to a second reading. December 30, 1831. Read the second time, and referred to the Committee on Manufactures. [Washington, 1831] 1 p. (S. 31) DNA. 9876

---- A bill to adjust the Fourth Auditor's books. February 18, 1831. Read twice, and ordered to be engrossed, and read the third time to-morrow. Mr. Hoffman, from the Committee on Naval Affairs, reported the following bill. [Washington, 1831] 1 p. (H.R. 638) DNA. 9877

---- A bill to adjust the Fourth Auditor's books. December 27, 1831. Read twice, and committed to a Committee of the Whole House tomorrow. Mr. Hoffman, from the Committee on Naval Affairs, reported the following bill: [Washington, 1831] 1 p. (H.R. 132) DNA. 9878

---- A bill to allow a draw back on exported nails manufactured from imported iron. February 14, 1831. Mr. Woodbury, from the Committee on Commerce, reported the following bill; which was read, and passed to a second reading: [Washington, 1831] 3 p. (S. 162) DNA. 9879

---- A bill to alter and amend "An Act to set apart and dispose of certain public lands for the encouragement of the cultivation of the vine and olive." January 6, 1831. Agreeably to notice, Mr. King asked and obtained leave to bring in the following bill; which was read and passed to a second reading. January 7, 1831. Read second time, and referred to the Committee on Public Lands. January 19, 1831. Reported without amendment. [Washington, 1831] (S. 68) DNA. 9880

---- A bill to alter the bridge and draw over the Potomac river, in the District of Columbia. January 18, 1831. Read twice, and committed to a Committee of the Whole House to-morrow. Mr. Doddridge, from the Committee for the District of Columbia, reported the following bill. [Washington, 1831] 3 p. (H.R. 564) DNA. 9881

---- A bill to alter the bridge and draw over the Potomac river, in the District of Columbia. December 20, 1831. Mr. Chambers, from the Committee on the District of Columbia, reported the following bill; which was read, and passed to a second reading. [Washington, 1831] 3 p. (S. 8) DNA. 9882

---- A bill to alter the time of holding the spring term of the circuit court of the United States for the southern district of New York. December 23, 1831. Read twice, and ordered to be engrossed, and read the third time on Monday next. Mr. Beardsley, from the Committee on the Judiciary, reported the following bill. [Washington, 1831] 1 p. (H.R. 122) DNA. 9883

---- A bill to amend an act entitled "An act for the relief of George Johnston," passed second March, one thousand eight hundred and thirty one. December 23, 1831. Mr. March, from the Committee on the Judiciary, reported the following bill; which was read, and passed to a second reading. [Washington, 1831] 1 p. (S. 18) DNA. 9884

---- A bill to amend an act, entitled "An act to provide for paying to the State of Missouri, Mississippi, and Alabama, three per centum of the net proceeds arising from the sale of the public lands within the same." December 30, 1830. Agreeably to notice, Mr. King asked leave to bring in the following bill; which was read, and passed to a second reading. December 31, 1830. Read a second time, and referred to the Committee on Public Lands. January 3, 1831. Reported with an amendment. [Washington, 1831] 1 p. (S. 51) DNA. 9885

---- A bill to amend the act, entitled "An act for the relief of certain surviving officers and soldiers of the army of the revolution," December 28, 1831. Read twice, and committed to a Committee of the Whole House to-morrow. Mr. Hubbard, from the Committee on Revolutionary Pensions, reported the following bill: [Washington, 1831] 1 p. (H. R. 156) DNA. 9886

---- A bill to amend the act for taking the fifth census. January 4, 1831. Read twice, and ordered to be engrossed and read the third time to-morrow. Mr. Storrs, of New York, from the Select Committee to which the subject had been referred, reported the following bill. [Washington, 1831] 1 p. (H.R. 534) DNA. 9887

---- A bill to amend the act granting "certain relinquished and unappropriated lands to the State of Alabama, for the purpose of improving the navigation of the Tennessee, Coosa, Cahowba, and Blackwarrior rivers," approved the twenty-third day of May, (1828). January 18, 1831. Agreeably to notice given, Mr. McKinley asked and obtained leave to bring in the following bill; which was read twice, and referred to the Committee on

Roads and Canals. January 19, 1831. Reported without amendment. [Washington, 1831] (S. 89) DNA. 9888

---- A bill to appropriate certain lands within the State of Alabama, for the purpose of improving the navigation of the Tennessee and Coosa rivers, and connecting their waters by canal or rail road. December 30, 1831. Mr. Blair, of Tennessee, from the Committee on Internal Improvements, reported the following bill: [Washington, 1831] 3 p. (H.R. 177) DNA. 9889

---- A bill to authorize a subscription to the stock of the Alexandria Canal Company. January 31, 1831. Read twice, and committed to the Committee of the Whole House on the state of the Union. Mr. Mercer, from the Committee on Internal Improvements, reported the following bill. [Washington, 1831] 1 p. (H.R. 586) DNA. 9890

---- A bill to authorize an appropriation to turnpike the mail road between Rockville and the Monocacy bridge, in Maryland. January 20, 1831. Read twice, and committed to the Committee of the Whole House on the state of the Union, Mr. Letcher, from the Committee on Internal Improvements, reported the following bill. [Washington, 1831] 3 p. (H.R. 571) DNA. 9891

---- A bill to authorize and require the Third Auditor to examine, and report upon the claims, of Gates Hoit against the United States. December 27, 1831. Read twice, and committed to a Committee of the Whole House to-morrow. Mr. Drayton, from the Committee on Military Affairs, reported the following bill: [Washington, 1831] 1 p. (H.R. 146) DNA. 9892

---- A bill to authorize the appointment of a sub-agent to the Winnebago Indians, on Rock river. January 22, 1831. Mr. Benton, from the Committee on Indian Affairs, reported the following bill; which was read, and passed to a second reading. [Washington, 1831] 1 p. (S. 113) DNA. 9893

---- A bill to authorize the executor of Stephen Tippett to locate a tract of land in the State of Louisiana. February 11, 1831. Mr. Kane, from the Committee on Private Land Claims, reported the following bill; which was read, and passed to a second reading. [Washington, 1831] 1 p. (S. 158) DNA. 9894

---- A bill to authorize the inhabitants of the State of Louisiana to enter the back lands. December 21, 1830. Agreeably to notice, Mr. Johnston asked and obtained leave to bring in the following bill; which was read, and passed to a second reading. December 22, 1831. Read a second time, and referred to the Committee on Public Lands. January 19, 1831. Reported without amendment. [Washington, 1831] 3 p. (S. 33) DNA. 9895

---- A bill to authorize the inhabitants of the State of Louisiana to enter the back lands. December 30, 1831. Agreeably to notice given, Mr. Johnson asked and obtained leave to bring in the following bill; which was read twice, and referred to the Committee on Public Lands. [Washington, 1831] 3 p. (S. 34) DNA. 9896

---- A bill to authorize the

laying out and constructing a road from Line Creek to the Chatahooche, and for repairing the road on which the mail is now transported. February 18, 1831. Mr. Grundy, from the Committee on the Post Office and Post Roads, reported the following bill; which was read, and passed to a second reading: [Washington, 1831] (S. 166) DNA. 9897

---- A bill to authorize the laying out and constructing a road from Line Creek to the Chatahooche and for repairing the road on which the mail is now transported. December 28, 1831. Agreeably to notice given, Mr. King asked and obtained leave to bring in the following bill; which was read twice, and referred to the Committee on the Post Office and Post Roads. [Washington, 1831] 2 p. (S. 30) DNA. 9898

---- A bill to authorize the mounting and equipment of a part of the army of the United States. December 20, 1831. Agreeably to notice given, Mr. Benton asked and obtained leave to bring in the following bill; which was read, and passed to a second reading. December 21, 1831. Read a second time and referred to the Committee on Military Affairs. December 27, 1831. Reported without amendment. [Washington, 1831] 2 p. (S. 6) DNA. 9899

---- A bill to authorize the President of the United States to change the locations of the land offices in the United States. January 11, 1831. Read twice, and committed to a Committee of the Whole House on Tuesday, the 18th of January instant. Mr. Wickliffe, from the Committee on the Public Lands, reported the following bill. [Washington, 1831] 1 p. (H.R. 552) DNA. 9900

---- A bill to authorize the proper officers of the Treasury Department to credit the account of the Treasurer of the United States with the amount of unavailable funds. February 2, 1831. Read twice, and ordered to be engrossed and read a third time tomorrow. Mr. McDuffie, from the Committee of Ways and Means, reported the following bill: [Washington, 1831] 1 p. (H.R. 592) DNA. 9901

---- A bill to authorize the sale of a tract of land therein named. December 16, 1830. Agreeably to notice given, Mr. Noble asked and obtained leave to bring in the following bill; which was read twice, and referred to the Committee on Public Lands. January 10, 1831. Reported with an amendment. [Washington, 1831] (S. 17) DNA. 9902

---- A bill to authorize the sale of lands reserved from sale at Fort Jackson, in the State of Alabama. January 31, 1831. Mr. McKinley, from the Committee on Public Lands, reported the following bill; which was read, and passed to a second reading. [Washington, 1831] 1 p. (S. 133) DNA. 9903

---- A bill to authorize the Secretary of the Treasury to make compensation to the agent employed to select college lands in the Territory of Arkansas. January 19, 1831. Mr. Kane, from the Committee on Public Lands, reported the following bill; which was read, and passed to a second reading. [Washington, 1831] 1 p. (S. 98) DNA. 9904

---- A bill to authorize the Secretary of War to purchase an additional quantity of land for the fortifications at Fort

Washington, upon the river Potomac. January 11, 1831. Read, and passed to a second reading. January 12, 1831. Read second time, and referred to the Committee on Military Affairs. [Washington, 1831] (H. R. 542) DNA. 9905

---- A bill to authorize the State of Illinois to sell twenty thousand acres of the saline lands in said state. December 27, 1831. Mr. Robinson, from the Committee on Public Lands, reported the following bill; which was read, and passed to a second reading. [Washington, 1831] 1 p. (S. 23) DNA. 9906

---- A bill to authorize the State of Indiana to make a road through the public lands, and making a grant of lands to aid the State in so doing. January 27, 1831. Mr. Hendricks, from the Committee on Roads and Canals, reported the following bill; which was read, and passed to a second reading. [Washington, 1831] 1 p. (S. 123) DNA. 9907

---- A bill to authorize the States of Indiana, Illinois, and Missouri, to dispose of certain salt springs, and lands reserved for the use of the same. February 2, 1831. Mr. Kane, from the Committee on Public Lands, reported the following bill; which was read, and passed to a second reading. [Washington, 1831] 1 p. (S. 139) DNA. 9908

---- A bill to authorize the surveying and laying out a road from Detroit, westwardly, by way of Sciawassee, to the mouth of Grand River of Lake Michigan, in the Michigan Territory. December 28, 1831. Read twice, and committed to a Committee of the Whole House to-morrow. Mr. Vinton, from the Committee on Internal Improvements, reported the following bill. [Washington, 1831] 1 p. (H. R. 158) DNA. 9909

---- A bill to authorize the surveying and making of a road from La Plaisance Bay, in the territory of Michigan, to intersect the Chicago road. December 28, 1831. Read twice, and committed to a Committee of the Whole House to-morrow. Mr. Letcher, from the Committee on Internal Improvements, reported the following bill: [Washington, 1831] 2 p. (H. R. 165) DNA. 9910

---- A bill to authorize the Territory of Florida to open a canal through the public lands between Chipola river and Saint Andrew's bay, in West Florida. January 10, 1831. Mr. Hendricks, from the Committee on Roads and Canals, reported the following bill; which was read, and passed to a second reading. [Washington, 1831] (S. 74) DNA. 9911

---- A bill to carry into effect certain Indian treaties. February 22, 1831. Read twice, and committed to the Committee of the Whole House on the state of the Union. Mr. Verplanck, from the Committee of Ways and Means, reported the following bill. [Washington, 1831] 3 p. (H. R. 645) DNA. 9912

---- A bill to carry into effect the act to provide for a survey of the coast of the United States. January 11, 1831. Read twice, and committed to a Committee of the Whole House on the state of the Union. Mr. Hoffman, from the Committee on Naval Affairs, reported the following bill. [Washington, 1831] (H. R. 554) DNA. 9913

---- A bill to carry into effect

the act to provide for a survey of the coast of the United States. December 22, 1831. Read twice, and committed to the Committee of the Whole House on the state of the Union. Mr. Hoffman, from the Committee on Naval Affairs, reported the following bill: [Washington, 1831] 2 p. (H.R. 74) DNA. 9914

---- A bill to carry into full effect the fourth article of the treaty of the eighth of January, eighteen hundred and twenty-one, between the United States and the Creek nation of Indians, so far as relates to the claims of citizens of Georgia against said Indians, for injury done prior to the passage of the act of Congress regulating intercourse with Indian tribes. December 27, 1831. Read twice, and committed to a Committee of the Whole House to-morrow. Mr. Thompson, of Georgia, from the Committee on Indian Affairs, reported the following bill: [Washington, 1831] 3 p. (H.R. 128) DNA. 9915

---- A bill to change the place of holding the Circuit and District Courts of the United States from Exeter to Concord, in the State of New Hampshire. February 16, 1831. Read twice, and ordered to be engrossed, and read the third time to-morrow. Mr. Buchanan, from the Committee on the Judiciary, reported the following bill. [Washington, 1831] 1 p. (H.R. 625) DNA 9916

---- A bill to compensate Susan Decatur, widow and legal representative of Captain Stephen Decatur, deceased, and others. December 23, 1831. Read twice, and committed to a Committee of the Whole House to-morrow. Mr. Carson, from the Committee on Naval Affairs, reported the following bill: [Washington, 1831] 3 p. (H.R. 98) DNA. 9917

---- A bill to create the office of Surveyor of the public lands for the State of Louisiana. February 2, 1831. Mr. Ellis, from the Committee on Public Lands, reported the following bill; which was read, and passed to a second reading. [Washington, 1831] 3 p. (S. 137) DNA. 9918

---- A bill to direct the manner of issuing patents on confirmed land claims in the Territory of Florida. February 2, 1831. Read twice, and ordered to be engrossed, and read the third time to-morrow. Mr. Hunt, from the Committee on the Public Lands, reported the following bill: [Washington, 1831] (H.R. 591) DNA. 9919

---- A bill to enable the President to extinguish Indian title within the State of Indiana. January 4, 1831. Mr. White, from the Committee on Indian Affairs, reported the following bill; which was read, and passed to a second reading. [Washington, 1831] 1 p. (S. 59) DNA. 9920

---- A bill to enable the President to extinguish Indian title within the State of Indiana. December 21, 1831. Mr. White, from the Committee on Indian Affairs, reported the following bill; which was read, and passed to a second reading. 1 p. (S. 11) DNA. 9921

---- A bill to enable the Secretary of War to release the title of the United States to Fort Ganesvoort, in the harbor of New York. February 16, 1831. Read twice, and ordered to be engrossed, and read the third time to-morrow. Mr. Drayton, from the Committee on Military Affairs, reported the following bill. [Washington, 1831] 1 p. (H.R. 631) DNA. 9922

---- A bill to erect a bridge over the Ohio river, near Wheeling. January 14, 1831. Read twice, and committed to the Committee of the Whole House on the state of the Union. Mr. Hemphill, from the Committee on Internal Improvements, reported the following bill. [Washington, 1831] (H.R. 562) DNA. 9923

---- A bill to establish a land office in the Territory of Michigan. December 23, 1831. Read twice, and committed to a Committee of the Whole House to-morrow. Mr. Wickliffe, from the Committee on the Public Lands, reported the following bill: [Washington, 1831] 1 p. (H.R. 102) DNA. 9924

---- A bill to establish an additional land office in the State of Indiana. December 28, 1831. Mr. Hanna, from the Committee on Public Lands, reported the following bill; which was read, and passed to a second reading. [Washington, 1831] 4 p. (S. 29) DNA. 9925

---- A bill to establish a town at St. Marks, and at the mouth of Appalachicola river, in Florida. January 5, 1831. Mr. Kane, from the Committee on Public Lands, reported the following bill; which was read, and passed to a second reading. [Washington, 1831] 3 p. (S. 63) DNA. 9926

---- A bill to establish a uniform rule for computing mileage of members of Congress and Delegates of Territories. January 20, 1831. Read twice, and ordered to be engrossed, and read the third time to-morrow. Mr. Hall, from the Committee on Public Expenditures, reported the following bill. [Washington, 1831] 1 p. (H.R. 568) DNA. 9927

---- A bill to establish assay offices of the United States' Mint in the gold district of North Carolina and Georgia. February 15, 1831. Read twice, and committed to the Committee of the Whole House on the state of the Union. Mr. Verplanck from the select committee to which the subject had been referred, reported the following bill. [Washington, 1831] (H.R. 630) DNA. 9928

---- A bill to establish assay offices of the United States' Mint in the gold districts of North Carolina, South Carolina, Georgia and Virginia. December 22, 1831. Read twice, and committed to a Committee of the Whole House to-morrow. Mr. Carson from the Select Committee to which the subject had been referred, reported the following bill: [Washington, 1831] 2 p. (H.R. 84) DNA. 9929

---- A bill to establish certain post offices, and to alter and discontinue others, and for other purposes. April 14, 1830. Mr. Johnson, from the Committee on the Post Office and Post Roads, reported the following bill, which was read twice, and committed to the Committee of the Whole House on the state of the Union. December 10, 1830. Reprinted by order of the House of Representatives, with amendments. Committee of the Whole on the state of the Union discharged and committed to a Committee of the Whole House on Thursday next. February 17, 1831. Reprinted by order of the House of Representatives, with amendments. [Washington, 1831] 32 p. (H.R. 420) DNA. 9930

---- A bill to establish rope-walks for the use of the Navy of the United States. December 23, 1831. Read twice, and committed to the Committee of the Whole House on the state of the Union. Mr. Hoffman, from the Committee on Naval Affairs, reported the following bill: [Washington, 1831] 1 p. (H.R. 86) DNA. 9931

---- A bill to establish the number of clerks, and fix their compensation, in the General Land Office. January 16, 1831. Read twice, and committed to a Committee of the Whole House on the state of the Union. Mr. Ervin, from the Committee on the Public Lands, reported the following bill. [Washington, 1831] (H.R. 563) DNA. 9932

---- A bill to explain an act entitled "An act to reduce the duties on coffee, tea, and cocoa," passed the 20th May, 1830. December 20, 1831. Read twice, and committed to a Committee of the Whole House to-morrow. Mr. McDuffie, from the Committee of Ways and Means, reported the following bill: [Washington, 1831] 2 p. (H.R. 63) DNA. 9933

---- A bill to extend the limits of Georgetown, in the District of Columbia. February 8, 1831. Read twice, and committed to a Committee of the Whole House to-morrow. Mr. Washington, from the Committee for the District of Columbia, reported the following bill. [Washington, 1831] (H.R. 608) DNA. 9934

---- A bill to extend the patent of John Adamson for a further period of fourteen years. January 27, 1831. Mr. Hayne, from the Committee on the Judiciary, reported the following bill; which was read, and passed to a second reading. [Washington, 1831] 1 p. (S. 128) DNA. 9935

---- A bill to extend the patent of Samuel Browning for a further period of fourteen years. January 21, 1831. Mr. Hayne, from the Committee on the Judiciary, reported the following bill; which was read, and passed to a second reading. [Washington, 1831] 1 p. (S. 106) DNA. 9936

---- A bill to extend the time for entering certain donation claims to land in the territory of Arkansas. January 5, 1831. Read twice, and ordered to be engrossed, and read the third time to-morrow. Mr. Wickliffe, from the Committee on the Public Lands, reported the following bill. [Washington, 1831] (H.R. 533) DNA. 9937

---- A bill to extend to corps of artificers the enactments of the existing laws allowing pensions to disabled officers and soldiers who have served in the armies of the United States. January 10, 1831. Read twice, and committed to a Committee of the Whole House to-morrow. Mr. Trezvant, from the Committee on Military Pensions, reported the following bill. [Washington, 1831] 1 p. (H.R. 550) DNA. 9938

---- A bill to finish the re-building of the frigate Macedonian. December 27, 1831. Read twice, and committed to the Committee of the Whole House on the state of the Union. Mr. Hoffman, from the Committee on Naval Affairs, reported the following bill. [Washington, 1831] 1 p. (H.R. 134) DNA. 9939

---- A bill to further amend the

act entitled "An act to incorporate the inhabitants of the city of Washington," &c., passed on the fifteenth of May, (1820). February 9, 1831. Read twice, and committed to a Committee of the Whole House to-morrow. Mr. Doddridge, from the Committee for the District of Columbia, reported the following bill. [Washington, 1831] (H.R. 613) DNA. 9940

---- A bill to give the actual settlers upon the Public Lands, a right of preemption on the purchase of one quarter section, at one dollar twenty-five cents per acre. December 28, 1831. Read twice, and committed to a Committee of the Whole House to-morrow. Mr. Wickliffe, from the Committee on the Public Lands, reported the following bill: [Washington, 1831] 3 p. (H.R. 148) DNA. 9941

---- A bill to improve the condition of the non-commissioned officers and privates of the army of the United States, and to prevent desertion. December 27, 1831. Read twice, and committed to a Committee of the Whole House to-morrow. Mr. Drayton, from the Committee on Military Affairs, reported the following bill: [Washington, 1831] 2 p. (H.R. 126) DNA. 9942

---- A bill to improve the navigation of the Monongahela and Alleghany rivers. December 15, 1830. Agreeably to notice given, Mr. Marks asked and obtained leave to bring in the following bill; which was read, and passed to a second reading. December 16, 1830. Read a second time, and referred to the Committee on Roads and Canals. January 26, 1831. Committee on Roads and Canals discharged and referred to Committee on Commerce. February 1, 1831. Reported without amendment. [Washington, 1831] 1 p. (S. 12) DNA. 9943

---- A bill to incorporate Saint Vincent's Orphan Asylum, in the District of Columbia. January 5, 1831. Mr. Tyler, from the Committee on the District of Columbia, reported the following bill; which was read, and passed to a second reading. [Washington, 1831] (S. 65) DNA. 9944

---- A bill to increase the pay of Masters Commandant and First Lieutenants of the Navy. February 10, 1831. Mr. Hayne, from the Committee on Naval Affairs, reported the following bill; which was read and passed to a second reading: [Washington, 1831] 1 p. (S. 155) DNA. 9945

---- A bill to make an appropriation for the improvement of Black creek. December 31, 1830. Read second time, and referred to Committee on Commerce. January 12, 1831. Reported without amendment. [Washington, 1831] 1 p. (S. 52) DNA. 9946

---- A bill to organise and establish a uniform militia throughout the United States, and to provide for the discipline thereof. January 7, 1831. Read twice, and committed to the Committee of the Whole House on the state of the Union. Mr. Thompson of Georgia, from the Committee on the Militia, to which was recommitted the bill (H.R. No. 168) more effectually to provide for the national defence, by organising, arming, and establishing a uniform militia throughout the United States, and to provide for the discipline thereof, reported the following amendatory bill: [Washington, 1831] 13 p. (H.R. 168) DNA. 9947

---- A bill to provide for certain surveys therein specified. January 11, 1831. Read twice, and committed to the Committee of the Whole House on the state of the Union. Mr. Hoffman, from the committee on Naval Affairs, reported the following bill. [Washington, 1831] (H. R. 553) DNA. 9948

---- A bill to provide for completing the Navy Hospital at Norfolk, and the Navy Asylum at Philadelphia, and to furnish them in part. December 20, 1831. Read twice, and committed to the Committee of the Whole House on the state of the Union. Mr. Hoffman, from the Committee on Naval Affairs, reported the following bill: [Washington, 1831] 1 p. (H. R. 58) DNA. 9949

---- A bill to provide for completing the removal and erection of the Naval Monument. December 23, 1831. Read twice, and committed to the Committee of the Whole House on the state of the Union. Mr. Hoffman, from the Committee on Naval Affairs, reported the following bill: [Washington, 1831] 1 p. (H. R. 90) DNA. 9950

---- A bill to provide for constructing two steam batteries. December 23, 1831. Read twice, and committed to the Committee of the Whole House on the state of the Union. Mr. Hoffman, from the Committee on Naval Affairs, reported the following bill: [Washington, 1831] 1 p. (H. R. 89) DNA. 9951

---- A bill to provide for paying certain arrearages for surveys made by naval officers. December 23, 1831. Read twice, and committed to the Committee of the Whole House on the state of the Union. Mr. Hoffman, from the Committee on Naval Affairs, reported the following bill: [Washington, 1831] 1 p. (H. R. 91) DNA. 9952

---- A bill to provide for the advance of the travelling expences of Naval Officers, in certain cases. December 28, 1831. Read twice, and committed to a Committee of the Whole House to-morrow. Mr. Branch, from the Committee on Naval Affairs, reported the following bill: [Washington, 1831] 1 p. (H. R. 160) DNA. 9953

---- A bill to provide for the appointment of Commissioners to digest, prepare, and report to Congress, at the next session thereof, a code of statute law, civil and criminal, for the District of Columbia. January 18, 1831. Read twice, and committed to a Committee of the Whole House to-morrow. Mr. Ihrie, from the Committee for the District of Columbia, reported the following bill. [Washington, 1831] (H. R. 565) DNA. 9954

---- A bill to provide for rebuilding the frigate Java and the sloop Cyane. December 27, 1831. Read twice, and committed to the Committee of the Whole House on the state of the Union. Mr. Hoffman, from the Committee on Naval Affairs, reported the following bill: [Washington, 1831] 1 p. (H. R. 133) DNA. 9955

---- A bill to provide for the legal adjudication and settlement of the claims to land therein mentioned. December 27, 1830. Introduced by Mr. Johnston, of Louisiana, on leave, and read. December 29, 1830. Read second time, and referred to the Committee on the Judiciary.

January 13, 1830, (i.e., 1831) Reported without amendment. [Washington, 1831] 3 p. (S. 44) DNA. 9956

---- A bill to provide for the payment of arrearages in the naval service, chargeable to the enumerated contingent prior to the first day of January, 1832. December 23, 1831. Read twice, and committed to the Committee of the Whole House on the state of the Union. Mr. Hoffman, from the Committee on Naval Affairs, reported the following bill: [Washington, 1831] 1 p. (H.R. 85) DNA. 9957

---- A bill to provide for the payment of Joshua Kennedy, of Alabama, for the losses sustained by him by the destruction of his property, in the year (1813), by the hostile Creek Indians, in consequence of its having been occupied as a fort or garrison by the troops of the United States. January 4, 1831. Mr. White, from the committee on Indian Affairs, reported the following bill; which was read, and passed to a second reading. [Washington, 1831] (S. 60) DNA. 9958

---- A bill to provide for the punishment of offences committed in cutting, destroying, or removing live oak and other timber or trees reserved for naval purposes. February 26, 1831. Read twice, and ordered to be engrossed, and read the third time on Monday next. Mr. Hoffman, from the Committee on Naval Affairs, reported the following bill. [Washington, 1831] 3 p. (H.R. 654) DNA. 9959

---- A bill to provide for the removal of certain Indians from the state of Missouri. January 22, 1831. Mr. Benton, from the Committee on Indian Affairs, reported the following bill; which was read, and passed to a second reading. [Washington, 1831] 1 p. (S. 112) DNA. 9960

---- A bill to provide for the satisfaction of claims due to certain American citizens, for spoliations committed on their commerce prior to the thirtieth day of September, one thousand eight hundred. December 20, 1831. Agreeably to notice given, Mr. Wilkens asked and obtained leave to bring in the following bill; which was read twice, and referred to a select committee to consist of Mr. Wilkins, Mr. Webster, Mr. Chambers, Mr. Brown, and Mr. Dudley. [Washington, 1831] 6 p. (S. 9) DNA. 9961

---- A bill to provide for the survey and sale of certain lands in the Territory of Michigan. February 14, 1831. Introduced, on leave, by Mr. Kane; read, and passed to a second reading. February 16, 1831. Read a second time, and referred to the Committee on Public Lands. February 21, 1831. Reported without amendment. [Washington, 1831] (S. 161) DNA. 9962

---- A bill to provide iron tanks for the use of the Navy of the United States. December 23, 1831. Read twice, and committed to the Committee of the Whole House on the state of the Union. Mr. Hoffman, from the Committee on Naval Affairs, reported the following bill: [Washington, 1831] 1 p. (H.R. 88) DNA. 9963

---- A bill to reduce and fix the duties on sugars imported into the United States. February 7, 1831. Agreeably to notice given, Mr. Brown asked and obtained leave to bring in the following bill; which was read twice, and referred to the Committee on Manufactures. February 16, 1831. Reported without amendments. [Washington, 1831] 1 p. (S. 147) DNA. 9964

---- A bill to reduce the bounty on pickled fish exported. January 7, 1831. Read twice, and postponed until Monday next. Mr. McDuffie, from the Committee of Ways and Means, reported the following bill. [Washington, 1831] 1 p. (H.R. 548) DNA. 9965

---- A bill to reduce the duty on foreign books. February 11, 1831. Introduced, on leave, by Mr. Woodbury, read, and passed to a second reading. February 12, 1831. Read a second time, and referred to the Committee on the Library. February 19, 1831. Reported without amendment. [Washington, 1831] 1 p. (S. 159) DNA. 9966

---- A bill to reduce the number of the cadets at the United States' Military Academy, and for other purposes. February 4, 1831. Read twice, and committed to the Committee of the Whole House on the state of the Union. Mr. Drayton, from the Committee on Military Affairs, reported the following bill: [Washington, 1831] (H.R. 599) DNA. 9967

---- A bill to reduce the price of a portion of the public lands heretofore in market, and to grant a preference to actual settlers. January 4, 1831. Mr. Barton, from the Committee on Public Lands, reported the following bill; which was read, and passed to a second reading. [Washington, 1831] 3 p. (S. 61) DNA. 9968

---- A bill to reduce the price of a portion of the public lands heretofore in market, and to grant a preference to actual settlers. December 23, 1831. Agreeably to notice given, Mr. Benton, asked and obtained leave to bring in the following bill; which was read, and passed to a second reading. December 27, 1831. Read a second time, and referred to the Committee on the Public Lands. [Washington, 1831] 3 p. (S. 20) DNA. 9969

---- A bill to regulate the pay, emoluments, and allowances, of the officers of the Army of the United States. December 20, 1831. Read twice, and committed to a Committee of the Whole House on the state of the Union. Mr. Drayton, from the Committee on Military Affairs, reported the following bill: [Washington, 1831] 6 p. (H.R. 56) DNA. 9970

---- A bill to remit a part of the duties on a cargo imported in the brig Liberator. December 23, 1831. Read twice, and committed to a Committee of the Whole House to-morrow. Mr. Verplanck, from the Committee of Ways and Means, reported the following bill: [Washington, 1831] 1 p. (H.R. 113) DNA. 9971

---- A bill to repeal a part of "an act to reduce the duty on salt." February 3, 1931. Read the first time. Opposition being made, the question arose, Shall it be rejected? Debated. February 4, 1831. Further debated. February 5, 1831 Read a second time, and ordered to lie on the table. Mr. Mallary, from the Committee on Manufactures, reported the following bill: [Washington, 1831] 1 p. (H.R. 595) DNA. 9972

---- A bill to repeal the act to establish the district of Blakely.

February 2, 1831. Woodbury, from the Committee on Commerce, reported the following bill; which was read, and passed to a second reading: [Washington, 1831] 1 p. (S. 138) DNA. 9973

---- A bill to repeal the charges imposed on passports and clearances, and the duties on spices. January 3, 1831. Mr. Smith, of Maryland, from the Committee on Finance, reported the following bill; which was read, and passed to a second reading. [Washington, 1831] 1 p. (S. 54) DNA. 9974

---- A bill to repeal the charges imposed on passports and clearances. February 2, 1831. Read twice, and ordered to be engrossed and read a third time to-morrow. Mr. Cambreleng, from the Committee on Commerce, reported the following bill. [Washington, 1831] 1 p. (H.R. 590) DNA. 9975

---- A bill to repeal the duties on certain imported articles. January 20, 1831. Mr. Smith, of Maryland, from the Committee on Finance, reported the following bill; which was read, and passed to a second reading. [Washington, 1831] (S. 101) DNA. 9976

---- A bill to reduce the duties on Indian blankets, and certain other Indian goods not manufactured in the United States. January 18, 1831. Agreeably to notice given, Mr. Benton asked and obtained leave to bring in the following bill; which was read, and ordered to be printed. [Washington, 1831] 1 p. (S. 95) DNA. 9977

---- A bill to repeal the twenty-fifth section of an act, entitled "An act to establish the judicial courts of the United States," passed the fourth day of September (1789). January 24, 1831. Mr. Davis, of South Carolina, from the Committee on the Judiciary, reported the following bill. January 25, 1831. Printed by order of the House of Representatives. [Washington, 1831] 1 p. (H.R. 573) DNA. 9978

---- A bill to revise and amend an act entitled "An act to incorporate a company for making a certain turnpike road in the county of Washington, in the District of Columbia." February 10, 1831. Read twice, and ordered to be engrossed, and read the third time to-morrow. Mr. Taliaferro, from the Committee for the District of Columbia, reported the following bill. [Washington, 1831] (H.R. 615) DNA. 9979

---- A bill to revise and amend an act, entitled "An act to incorporate a company for making a certain turnpike road in the county of Washington, in the District of Columbia." December 23, 1831. Read twice, and committed to a Committee of the Whole House to-morrow. Mr. Washington, from the Committee for the District of Columbia, reported the following bill. [Washington, 1831] 2 p. (H.R. 114) DNA. 9980

---- A bill to revise and continue in force an act entitled "An act to provide for the Reports of the Decisions of the Supreme Court of the United States." December 23, 1831. Mr. Marcy, from the Committee on the Judiciary, reported the following bill; which was read, and passed to a second reading. [Washington, 1831] 1 p. (S. 19) DNA. 9981

---- Condensed reports of cases in the Supreme Court of the United States, containing the whole series of the decisions of the court from its organization to the commencement of Peters' reports at January term, 1827...Edited by Richard Peters...from February term 1814 to February term 1816 inclusive. Philadelphia, John Grigg, 1831. 684 p. IaUL; LNT-L; MeXR; OO. 9982

---- Constitution of the United States...Rules and Orders...in the House of Representatives. Washington, 1831. 60 p. DLC; MHi. 9983

---- Copy of instruction to Collectors. Secretary S. D. Ingham. Feb. 21, 1831. House Ex. Docs. No. 112, 21st Cong., 2d sess. Vol. IV. Copy of instructions to collectors and appraisers relative to appraisal of imported merchandise; Duties of appraisers. [Washington, 1831] 7 p. M; R. 9984

---- Correspondence on Florida Matter. A. Jackson and J. C. Calhoun. Washington, 1831. Library of B. P. Poore. On the course of Mr. Calhoun in the deliberations of the Cabinet of Mr. Monroe on the occurrences in the Seminole War. [Washington, 1831] 52 p. M; R. 9985

---- Correspondence on Weights and Measures. Sec. S. D. Ingham. April 30-June 13, 1831. Library of the Coast Survey. Letters of the Secretary of the Treasury to F. R. Hassler, Superintendent United States Standard Weights and Measures, respecting permanent standards of weights and measures for the Treasury Department, and manufacture of weights and measures for all the custom-houses in the United States, and the adoption of units of weight and capacity. [Washington, 1831] 2 p. M; R. 9986

---- Digest of Laws concerning the District of Columbia. William Cranch. 1831. Pr. by Wm. A. Davis. The Acts of Congress relating to the District of Columbia from July 16, 1790, to March 4, 1831, inclusive, and of the Legislatures of Virginia and Maryland, passed especially in regard to that District, or to persons and property within the same; With preliminary notes of the proceedings of the Congress under the Confederation, as well as under the Constitution, in regard to the permanent seat of Government of the United States. [Washington, 1831] M; R. 9987

---- Disbursements to the Indians. Letter from the Secretary of War, transmitting copies of accounts of persons charged or trusted with the disbursement of money, goods, or effects, for the benefit of the Indians, from 1st Sept. 1829, to 1st Sept. 1830, &c. &c. Feb. 15, 1831. Read and laid upon the table...[Washington, 1831] 112 p. KSalW. 9988

---- Document relating to blankets for the Indian trade; Being questions to, and answers by Adam D. Stewart, collector of the port of Mackinaw. Feb. 3, 1831. Laid on the table by Mr. Benton, and ordered to be printed. [Washington, 1831] 2 p. KSalW. 9989

---- Documents in Case of Judge James H. Peck. Jan. 7, 1831. Senate Docs. No. 27, 21st Cong., 2d sess., Vol. I. Documents relative to case of Judge James H. Peck, of the district of Missouri. [Washington, 1831] 52 p. M; R. 9990

---- Documents in Claim of Susan Decatur. Dec. 20, 1831. House Ex. Docs. No. 27, 22d.

Cong., 1st sess. Vol. II. Claim for compensation for services in the Navy of her late husband, Stephen Decatur. [Washington, 1831] 28 p. M; R. 9991

---- Documents referring to Coast Survey. Dec. 22, 1831. House Ex. Docs., No. 22, 22d Cong., 1st sess., Vol. II. Statements relative to the expediency of providing for the completion of the survey of the coasts of the United States. [Washington, 1831] 11 p. M; R. 9992

---- Documents relative to Naval Hospitals. Secretary John Branch. Feb. 4, 1831. House Ex. Docs. No. 93, 21st Cong, 2d sess. Vol. III. Relative to establishment of naval hospitals at Charlestown, Massachusetts, Brooklyn, New York, and Pensacola, Florida; Plan of hospitals; Estimated cost. [Washington, 1831] 8 p. M; R. 9993

----Documents relative to the Indian Trade. Feb. 3, 1831. Senate Docs., No. 44, 21st Cong., 2d sess., Vol. II. Statement of Aden D. Stewart, collector of the port of Mackinaw, relative blankets for the Indian trade. [Washington, 1831] 2 p. M; R. 9994

---- Estimates of Appropriations. Secretary Louis McLane. Dec. 8, 1831. House Ex. Docs., No. 10, 22d Cong., 1st sess., Vol. I. Transmitting estimates of appropriations required for the services of the year 1832. [Washington, 1831] 54 p. M; R. 9995

---- Executive Documents, printed by order of the House of Representatives, at the first Session of the 22nd Congress; begun and held at the city of Washington, December 7, 1831; and in the 56th year of the Independence of the United States. In seven vols. Washington, Pr. by Duff Green, 1831. 7 vols. CoU; M; PU; R. 9996

---- Expire to a commissioned agent of the United States at Constantinople, and submitting the same to the disposal of Congress. Have had the message under consideration and report: Washington, Pr. by Duff Green, 1831. 3 p. R. 9997

---- General statement of goods, wares, and merchandise, of the growth, produce and manufacture of foreign countries, exported from the United States, commencing on the 1st day of October, 1829, and ending on the 30th day of September, 1830. Washington, Pr. by Duff Green, 1831. R. 9998

---- House Documents, 22d Cong., 1st sess. From Dec. 6, 1831. Vol. I. Docs. Nos. 1 to 18, inclusive; Vol. II. Docs. Nos. 19 to 82, inclusive; Vol. III. Docs. Nos. 83 to 108, inclusive; Vol. IV. Docs. Nos. 104-to 185, inclusive; Vol. V. Docs. Nos. 186 to 234, inclusive; Vol. VI. Docs. 235 to 307, inclusive; Vol. VII. Docs. No. 308, Part 1, Manufactures of the United States; Vol. VIII, Docs. No. 308, Part 2, Manufactures of the United States; all printed by Duff Green. [Washington, 1831] 8 vols. M; R. 9999

---- House Journal, 22d Cong., 1st sess. Dec. 5, 1831. From December 5, 1831, to July 16, 1832. Speaker of the House, Andrew Stevenson, of Virginia, Clerk of the House, Matthew St. Clair Clarke, of Pennsylvania. Washington, Pr. by Duff Green, 1831-2. 1353 p. G; M; R. 10000

---- Indian treaties, and laws and regulations relating to Indian affairs: to which is added an appendix... [And Supplement containing additional treaties, documents, &c, relating to Indian affairs, to the end of the twenty-first Congress. Official] Washington, Pr. by Way & Giedon [1831?] 661 p. DLC; TNP. 10001

---- Information relative to Civil Officers. Secretary S. D. Ingham. March 1, 1831. House Ex. Docs. No. 126, 21st Cong., 2d sess., Vol. IV. List of officers who have been allowed other compensation than the salary fixed by law; List of persons whose salaries are fixed by executive regulation; Amount of salary and allowances. [Washington, 1831] 49 p. M; R. 10002

---- Instructions concerning Credit Land System, etc. May 27, 1831. Library of the Interior Department. Instructions to registers and receivers of the credit-system land offices, concerning lands not liable to sale under the President's late proclamation, and prescribing methods to hasten payments of small balances due the United States and the surrender of certificates for the credit. [Washington, 1831] 2 p. M; R. 10003

---- Joint resolution directing a subscription for the stereotype edition of the laws of the United States proposed to be published by Duff Green. January 25, 1831. Read twice, and committed to a Committee of the Whole House tomorrow. Mr. Wayne, from the Committee on the Library, reported the following joint resolution: [Washington, 1831] 1 p. (H.R.) DNA. 10004

---- Joint Resolution directing the Secretary of State to subscribe for seventy copies of Peters' condensed reports of decisions of the Supreme Court. February 24, 1831. Mr. Woodbury, from the Committee on the Library of Congress, reported the following resolution; which was read, and passed to a second reading. [Washington, 1831] 1 p. (S. 8) DNA. 10005

---- Joint resolution. For publishing the diplomatic correspondence of the old Confederation. February 10, 1831. Read first time. [Washington, 1831] 1 p. (H.R.) DNA. 10006

---- Joint resolution on the subject of the Cumberland road. February 11, 1831. Mr. Hendricks, from the Committee on Roads and Canals, reported the following resolution; which was read and passed to a second reading. [Washington, 1831] 1 p. (S. 3) DNA. 10007

---- Joint resolution relative to the pay of Members of Congress. January 10, 1831. Read the first time. Mr. Hall, from the Committee on Public Expenditures, reported the following joint resolution: [Washington, 1831] (H.R.) DNA. 10008

---- Land Forms and Blanks. March 9, 1831. Library of the Interior Department. Circular under act of March 31, 1830, and relating to forms and blanks to be used applicable to provisions of the act for the relief of purchasers and suppression of fraudulent practices at public sales. [Washington, 1831] 2 p. M; R. 10009

---- Land Relinquished or Reverted. April 6, 1831. Library of the Interior Department. Circular relating to lands relinquished or which have reverted to the United States and copies of proclamation of sales of said lands sent for distribution. [Washington, 1831] 1 p. M; R. 10010

---- Laws of the United States, now in force relative to commercial subjects, classed under their appropriate heads, to the close of the second session of the twenty-first Congress, ending March 3, 1831. By John Brice, of Baltimore. Baltimore, E. J. Coale and J. N. Toy & W. R. Lucas, 1831. 573 p. CtMW; MdHi; Mi-L. 10011

---- Laws of the United States. Twenty-first Congress, 2d sess. Law Library of Congress. Official edition, published under the direction of the Secretary of State. [Washington, 1831] 174 p. M; R. 10012

---- Legislation concerning District of Columbia, 1790-1831. A. Davis. Washington, 1831. Library of Congress. Acts of Congress in relation to the District of Columbia, and of the Legislatures of Virginia and Maryland in regard to that District. [Washington, 1831] 8 vols. M; R. 10013

---- Letter on Apportionment of Representatives. E. H. Cummings. Dec. 9, 1831. House Ex. Docs., No. 8, 22nd Cong., 1st sess., Vol. I. Statement showing number of Representatives to which each State would be entitled for the next ten years under various assumed ratios of representation. [Washington, 1831] 4 p. M; R. 10014

---- Letter on Contingent Fund of the Navy. Secretary L. Woodbury. Dec. 20, 1831. House Ex. Docs., No. 23, 22d Cong., 1st sess., Vol. II. Transmitted copy of proposed bill to provide for a deficiency in the contingent fund of the Navy. [Washington, 1831] 2 p. M; R. 10015

---- Letter on Fortifications. Secretary John H. Eaton. Feb. 2, 1831. House Ex. Docs., No. 81, 21st Cong., 2d sess., Vol. III. Relative to the expediency of erecting fortifications at Okracock inlet, North Carolina: Recommends that there is no immediate necessity that the inlet be fortified. [Washington, 1831] 1 p. M; R. 10016

---- Letter on Improvement of the Arkansas River. Chittenden Lyon. Jan. 26, 1831. House Ex. Docs., No. 227, 22d Cong., 1st sess. Vol. V. Transmitting information relative to plan for the improvement of the Arkansas River. [Washington, 1831] 5 p. M; R. 10017

---- Letter on Navy Appropriations. Fourth auditor Amos Kendall. Feb. 16, 1831. House Ex. Docs., No. 24, 22d Cong., 1st sess., Vol. II. Relative to transfer of appropriations on the books of the Navy. [Washington, 1831] 2 p. M; R. 10018

---- Letter on Survey of Public Lands. Gideon Fitz, surveyor. Nov. 9, 1831. Senate Docs., No. 54, 22d Cong., 1st sess., Vol. I. Relative to the survey of public lands south of Tennessee, and recommending changes in the mode of conducting the business of his office. [Washington, 1831] 7 p. M; R. 10019

---- Letter on the Contingent Fund of the Senate. Sec. Walter Lowrie. Dec. 5, 1831. Senate Docs. No. 2, 22d Cong., 1st sess., Vol. I. Transmitting statement of the expenditures from the contingent fund of the Senate during the year 1831; List of employes of the Senate; Compensation. [Washington, 1831] 4 p. M; R. 10020

---- Letter on the Growth and

Manufacture of Silk. P. S. Du Ponceau. Dec. 9, 1831. House Ex. Docs., No. 11, 22d Cong., 1st sess., Vol. I. Statement relative to cultivation of mulberry tree, raising of silk-worms, and manufacture of silk. [Washington, 1831] 4 p. M; R. 10021

---- Letter on Trade with the Indians. J. J. Astor, New York. Jan. 27, 1831. Senate Docs., No. 43, 21st Cong., 2d sess., Vol. II. Statement relative to reduction of duty on certain articles of goods furnished the Indians. [Washington, 1831] 3 p. M; R. 10022

---- Letter referring to Accounts of T. T. Tucker. Treasurer J. Campbell. March 3, 1831. House Ex. Docs., No. 133, 21st Cong. 2d sess., Vol. IV. Transmitting copies of accounts of T. T. Tucker as agent of the War and Navy Departments. [Washington, 1831] 7 p. M; R. 10023

---- Letter relative to Culture of Silk. J. D'Homergue. Feb. 23, 1831. House Ex. Docs., No. 114, 21st Cong., 2d sess., Vol. IV. Relative to growth and manufacture of silk; Number of mulberry trees to the acre; Yield of leaves; Pounds of cocoons produced. [Washington, 1831] 1 p. M; R. 10024

---- Letter relative to Internal Duties. Secretary S. D. Ingham. March 3, 1831. House Ex. Docs., No. 132, 21st Cong., 2d sess., Vol. IV. Explaining why the statement of direct taxes cannot be prepared in time to be forwarded to Congress at the present session. [Washington, 1831] 2 p. M; R. 10025

---- Letter relative to Office of Surveyor-General. Com'r of Land Office. Feb. 7, 1831. Senate Docs., No. 48, 21st Cong., 2d sess., Vol. II. Recommends creation of the office of surveyor-general of Louisiana. [Washington, 1831] 2 p. M; R. 10026

---- Letter relative to Steamboat Boilers. Secretary S. D. Ingham. March 3, 1831. House Ex. Docs., No. 131, 21st Cong., 2d sess., Vol. IV. Statement relative to guarding against dangers arising from the bursting of boilers on board of steamboats. [Washington, 1831] 4 p. M; R. 10027

---- List of Appropriations. March 3, 1831. House Ex. Docs., No. 128, 21st Cong., 2d sess. Vol. IV. Statement of appropriations made during the second session of the twenty-first Congress; Amount and object of each. [Washington, 1831] 26 p. M; R. 10028

---- Manual of Military pyrotechny, for the use of the Cadets of the U.S. military Academy West Point, 1831. (Lithographed from manuscript by I. C. Pootermans, 1831) 55 pp. ICJ; MiDT. 10029

---- Memorial and Documents. Chesapeake and Ohio Canal Company. Dec. 3, 1831. House Ex. Docs., No. 18, 22d Cong., 1st sess., Vol. I. Memorialists ask national subscription to the stock of the Chesapeake and Ohio Canal Company. [Washington, 1831] 222 p. M; R. 10030

---- Memorial Compensation as Collector. Moses Myers. Jan. 8, 1831. House Ex. Docs., No. 70, 21st Cong., 2d sess., Vol. III. Memorialist asks compensation for performing the duties of collector of the district of Norfolk and Portsmouth. [Washington, 1831] 2 p. M; R. 10031

---- Memorial for a National Road. Citizens of Virginia. Sept. 12, 1831. House Ex. Docs., No. 15, 22d Cong., 1st sess., Vol. I. Memorialists ask national aid in the construction of a road from Shelby Creek, Kentucky, to Linville Mountain, North Carolina. [Washington, 1831] 7 p. M; R. 10032

---- Memorial for Aid to New England Asylum for the Blind. The trustees. Jan. 3, 1831. House Ex. Docs., No. 20, 21st Cong., 2d sess., Vol. I. Memorialists ask national aid for the maintenance of the asylum. [Washington, 1831] 4 p. M; R. 10033

---- Memorial for an Exploring Expedition. E. Fanning and B. Pendleton. Nov. 7, 1831. House Ex. Docs., No. 61, 22d Cong., 1st sess., Vol. II. Memorialists ask that Congress make an appropriation for an exploring expedition. [Washington, 1831] 10 p. M; R. 10034

---- Memorial for Improvement of Mispillion Creek. Citizens of Delaware. Jan. 31. 1831. Senate Docs., No. 47, 21st Cong., 2d sess., Vol. II. Memorialists ask for an appropriation for improving the navigation of Mispillion Creek. [Washington, 1831] 2 p. M; R. 10035

---- Memorial for Increase of Duty on Iron. Citizens of Philadelphia. Feb. 10, 1831. House Ex. Docs., No. 100, 21st Cong., 2d sess., Vol. IV. Memorialists ask increase of duty on imported iron. [Washington, 1831] 18 p. M; R. 10036

---- Memorial for Protection of the Indians. Citizens of Massachusetts. Jan. 21, 1831. Senate Docs., No. 34, 21st Cong., 2d sess., Vol. I. Memorialists ask that the Indians may be protected in the enjoyment of their rights and the possession of their lands. [Washington, 1831] 3 p. M; R. 10037

---- Memorial for Protection of the Indians. Citizens of New Jersey. Jan. 1. 1831. Senate Docs., No. 31, 21st Cong., 2d sess., Vol. I. Memorialists ask that the Indians be protected in their rights, and that the act of Congress in relation to their removal westward be repealed. [Washington, 1831] 1 p. M; R. 10038

---- Memorial for Protection of the Indians. Citizens of Pennsylvania. Jan. 7, 1831. Senate Docs., No. 25, 21st Cong., 2d sess., Vol. I. Memorialists ask the Indians be protected in the enjoyment of their rights and the possession of their lands. [Washington, 1831] 4 p. M; R. 10039

---- Memorial for Protection of the Indians. Citizens of Pennsylvania. Jan. 19, 1831. Senate Docs., No. 33, 21st Cong., 2d sess., Vol. I. Memorialists ask that the Indians may be protected in the enjoyment of their rights and the possession of their lands. [Washington, 1831] 3 p. M; R. 10040

---- Memorial for Protection of the Indians. Citizens of Pittsburgh, Pa. Feb. 14, 1831. Senate Docs., No. 53, 21st Cong., 2d sess., Vol. II. Memorialists ask that treaties with the Indians be preserved inviolate, and that they be protected in their rights. [Washington, 1831] 5 p. M; R. 10041

---- Memorial for Removal of the Indians. Citizens of Maine. Jan. 17, 1831. House Ex. Docs., No. 89, 21st Cong., 2d sess., Vol. III. Memorialists approve of the act of Congress providing for the removal of the Indians westward. [Washington, 1831] 1 p. M; R. 10042

---- Memorial for Removal of the Indians. Citizens of Maine. Feb. 21, 1831. House Ex. Docs., No. 138, 21st Cong., 2d sess., Vol. IV. Memorialists approve the law relative to removal westward of the Southern Indians. [Washington, 1831] 2 p. M; R. 10043

---- Memorial for Removal of the Indians. Citizens of Massachusetts. Feb. 3, 1831. House Ex. Docs., No. 106, 21st Cong., 2d sess., Vol. IV. Memorialists ask for repeal of law providing for removal of Indians westward. [Washington, 1831] 5 p. M; R. 10044

---- Memorial for the Protection of the Indians. Citizens of Pennsylvania. Feb. 8, 1831. House Ex. Docs., No. 90, 21st Cong., 2d sess., Vol. III. Memorialists ask passage of law to protect Indians from intrusion on their lands. [Washington, 1831] 3 p. M; R. 10045

---- Memorial from Revolutionary Officers and Soldiers. Nov. 24, 1831. House Ex. Docs., No. 26, 22d Cong., 1st sess., Vol. II. Memorialists ask compensation for services and sacrifices in the Revolutionary army. [Washington, 1831] 2 p. M; R. 10046

---- Memorial from Revolutionary Officers and Soldiers. Dec. 20, 1831. House Ex. Docs., No. 25, 22d Cong., 1st sess., Vol. II. Memorialists ask compensation for services and sacrifices in the Revolutionary Army. [Washington, 1831] 2 p. M; R. 10047

---- Memorial from the General Assembly of the State of Missouri, that the Western Road, commonly called the Cumberland Road, may cross the Mississippi at St. Louis. February 28, 1831. Read, and ordered to be laid on the table, and printed. Washington, Pr. by Duff Green, 1831. TvFwTCU. 10048

---- Memorial of Heirs of Rambaud & Basmarien. Feb. 7, 1831. House Ex. Docs., No. 98, 21st Cong., 2d sess., Vol. III. Memorialists ask reimbursement of expenses incurred by Rambaud & Basmarien in arming and equipping American vessels during the Revolution. [Washington, 1831] 6 p. M; R. 10049

---- Memorial of Moses Myer. January 24, 1831. Washington, Pr. by Duff Green, 1831. 2 p. TxFwTCU. 10050

---- Memorial of sundry officers of the United States' Army in the late war, praying for a grant of land in consideration of their accounts. January 4, 1831. Referred to the committee on public lands. Washington, Pr. by Duff Green, 1831. R. 10051

---- Memorial of the General Assembly of the State of Missouri, that the French and Spanish Land Claims, may be speedily and equitably decided. February 28, 1831. Read, and ordered to be laid on the table, and printed. Washington, Pr. by Duff Green, 1831. R. 10052

---- Memorial of the Presidential committee of the American Board of Commissioners for Foreign Missions of Massachusetts, praying that all treaty stipulations with the Indians within the United States may be faithfully observed, &c. Feb. 9, 1831. [Washington, 1831] 10 p. KSalW. 10053

---- Memorial of the workers in iron of Philadelphia, praying that the present duty on imported iron may be repealed, etc. January 27, 1831. Read, and ordered to be printed. Ordered, that the aforesaid memorial be referred to a Select Committee, to consist of Messrs. Hayne, Dickerson, King, Bell, Tyler, to consider and report thereon. Washington, Pr. by Duff Green, 1831. R. 10054

---- Memorial of Thomas A. C. Jones. Feb. 7, 1831. House Ex. Docs., No. 87, 21st Cong., 2d sess., Vol. III. Memorialist asks passage of law allowing him Navy pension. [Washington, 1831] 4 p. M; R. 10055

---- Memorial on Dismissal from the Army. A. R. Woolley. Dec. 27, 1831. Senate Docs., No. 10, 22d Cong., 1st sess., Vol. I. Memorialist states that he has been unjustly dismissed from the military service, and prays the interposition of Congress in his behalf. [Washington, 1831] 4 p. M; R. 10056

---- Memorial on Indian Lands. The Cherokee Indians. Jan. 15, 1831. House Ex. Docs., No. 57, 21st Cong., 2d sess., Vol. III. Memorialists protest against the claim of the State of Georgia to Cherokee lands. [Washington, 1831] 9 p. M; R. 10057

---- Memorial on Northwestern Boundary of Missouri. Legislature of Mo. Jan. 17, 1831. Senate Docs., No. 71, 21st Cong., 2d sess., Vol. II. Memorialists ask for an extension of the boundary of the State, and for the grant of a mounted force to aid in the protection of the frontier. [Washington, 1831] 5 p. M; R. 10058

---- Memorial on Sunday Mail Service. Citizens of Kentucky. Jan. 31, 1831. House Ex. Docs., No. 79, 21st Cong., 2d sess., Vol. III. Memorialists remonstrate against any change in the laws which shall suspend the transportation of the mail on Sundays. [Washington, 1831] 4 p. M; R. 10059

---- Memorial on Sunday Mail Serivce. Citizens of Vermont. Jan. 12, 1831. House Ex. Docs. No. 115, 21st Cong., 2d sess., Vol. IV. Protest against the passage of any law forbidding the transportation of mail on Sunday. [Washington, 1831] 6 p. M; R. 10060

---- Memorial on Tariff. N.Y. convention of friends of domestic industry. Oct. 25, 1831. House Ex. Docs., No. 186, 22d Cong., 1st sess., Vol. V. Memorialists pray Congress to continue the import duties which were intended for the protection of American manufacturers. [Washington, 1831] 45 p M; R. 10061

---- Memorial on the Culture of Silk. Michigan Legislature. Jan. 28, 1831. House Ex. Docs., No. 95, 21st Cong., 2d sess., Vol. III. Memorialists ask for grant of land to promote the cultivation of the mulberry tree and the production of silk. [Washington, 1831] 1 p. M; R. 10062

---- Memorial on the Cumberland Road. Legislature of Missouri. Jan. 19, 1831. Senate Docs., No. 70, 21st Cong., 2d sess., Vol. II. Memorialists ask that Cumberland road may be constructed to cross the Mississippi River at St. Louis. [Washington, 1831] 2 p. M; R. 10063

---- Memorial on the Militia System. Massachusetts militia

officers. Jan. 19, 1831. Senate Docs., No. 62, 21st Cong., 2d sess., Vol. II. Memorialists ask for the adoption of a uniform system for the government of the militia of the United States. [Washington, 1831] 9 p. M; R. 10064

---- Memorial on Virginia State Claims. T. W. Gilmer, commissioner. Dec. 19, 1831. House Ex. Docs., No. 20, 22d Cong., 1st sess., Vol. II. Memorialist asks that State of Virginia be reimbursed amounts paid for maintenance of troops furnished for the common defence since passage of act of August 5, 1790. [Washington, 1831] 62 p. M; R. 10065

---- Memorial relative to Chesapeake and Ohio Canal. Citizens of Pa. April 1, 1831. Ex. Docs., No. 36, 22d Cong., 1st sess., Vol. I. Praying for a Government subscription to the stock of the company. [Washington, 1831] 2 p. M; R. 10066

---- Memorial relative to Duties on Iron. Citizens of Philadelphia. Feb. 15, 1831. Senate Docs., No. 60, 21st Cong., 2d sess., Vol. II. Memorialists ask that there be no reduction of the duties on imported iron. [Washington, 1831] 18 p. M; R. 10067

---- Memorial relative to Duty on Iron. Mechanics of Philadelphia. Jan. 14, 1831. House Ex. Docs., No. 71, 21st Cong., 2d sess., Vol. III Memorialists ask reduction of existing duties on certain grades of iron. [Washington, 1831] 14 p. M; R. 10068

---- Memorial relative to Duty on Iron. Jan. 14, 1831. Senate Docs. No. 41, 21st Cong., 2d sess., Vol. II. Memorialists ask that the present duty on iron be repealed. [Washington, 1831] 17 p. M; R. 10069

---- Memorial relative to Indian Lands. Legislature of Mississippi. Dec. 15, 1831. House Ex. Docs., No. 75, 22d Cong., 1st sess., Vol. II. Memorialists ask that lands ceded by the Choctaw Indians to the United States may be thrown open to settlers at the minimum price. [Washington, 1831] 2 p. M; R. 10070

---- Memorial relative to Land Claims. Legislature of Missouri. Jan. 15, 1831. Senate Docs., No. 69, 21st Cong., 2d sess., Vol. II. Memorialists ask that French and Spanish land claims be speedily and equitably decided. [Washington, 1831] 2 p. M; R. 10071

---- Memorial relative to Public Lands. Legislature of Alabama. Jan. 6, 1831. House Ex. Docs., No. 72, 21st Cong., 2d sess., Vol. III. Memorialists ask that further relief be granted to settlers on public lands. [Washington, 1831] 4 p. M; R. 10072

---- Memorial relative to Revolutionary Services. Officers Rev. army. Jan. 19, 1831. House Ex. Docs., No. 56, 21st Cong., 2d sess., Vol. III. Memorialists ask compensation for services, privations, and losses while in the service of the Continental Congress. [Washington, 1831] 4 p. M; R; TxFwTCU. 10073

---- Memorial relative to Services in Revolutionary War. Sept. 27, 1831. Senate Docs., No. 12, 22d Cong., 1st sess., Vol. I. New Jersey officers and soldiers ask compensation for services and sacrifices in the Revolutionary army. [Washington, 1831] 2 p. M; R. 10074

---- Memorial relative to the

Indians. American Board Foreign Missions. Jan. 26, 1831. Senate Docs., No. 50, 21st Cong., 2d sess., Vol. II. Memorialists ask that all treaty stipulations with the Indians be faithfully observed. [Washington, 1831] 10 p. M; R. 10075

---- Message on Captured Slave Vessel. President Andrew Jackson. Jan. 15, 1831. House Ex. Docs., No. 54, 21st Cong., 2d sess., Vol. III. Statement relative to Spanish slave vessel captured by United States schooner Shark. [Washington, 1831] 12 p. M; R. 10076

---- Message on Colonial Trade. President Andrew Jackson. Jan. 3, 1831. House Journal, 21st Cong., 2d sess. Communicating certain papers relating to the arrangement with Great Britain concerning trade between her colonial possessions and the United States. [Washington, 1831] 1 p. M; R. 10077

----Message on Foreign Commerce. President A. Jackson. Jan. 31, 1831. House Ex. Docs., No. 22, 21st Cong., 2d sess., Vol. I. Transmitting documents relative to trade between the United States and the British colonies. [Washington, 1831] 64 p. M; R. 10078

---- Message on Foreign Trade. President Andrew Jackson. Jan. 3, 1831. Senate Docs., No. 20, 21st Cong., 2d sess., Vol. I. Documents relating to the trade of the United States with the colonial possessions of Great Britain. [Washington, 1831] 64 p. M; R. 10079

---- Message on Impressment. President A. Jackson. Dec. 13, 1831. Senate Docs., No. 3, 22d Cong., 1st sess., Vol. I. Information relative to capture and impressment of American citizens by the authorities of New Brunswick; Measures adopted by the United States Government. [Washington, 1831] 26 p. M; R. 10080

---- Message on Indian Lands. President Andrew Jackson. Feb. 3, 1831. House Ex. Docs., No. 85, 21st Cong., 2d sess., Vol. III. Correspondence relative to location of lands ceded by the Pottawatomie Indians for the benefit of the State of Indiana. [Washington, 1831] 12 p. M; R. 10081

---- Message on Indian Treaties. President Andrew Jackson. Mar. 1, 1831. House Ex. Docs., No. 123, 21st Cong., 2d sess., Vol. IV. Copies of treaties with Cherokee Indians and with confederated tribes of Sacs and Foxes. [Washington, 1831] 20 p. M; R. 10082

---- Message on Internal Improvements. President A. Jackson. Jan. 5, 1831. House Ex. Docs., No. 30, 21st Cong., 2d sess., Vol. I. Estimates of expense of works of internal improvements for which surveys have been made; In what State; Estimated cost of each. [Washington, 1831] 20 p. M; R. 10083

---- Message on Navy Accounts. President A. Jackson. Jan. 7, 1831. House Ex. Docs., No. 33, 21st Cong., 2d sess., Vol. II. Report on accounts of the Navy in the office of the Fourth Auditor. [Washington, 1831] 96 p. M; R. 10084

---- Message on Ohio and Mississippi Rivers. President Jackson. Feb. 26, 1831. Senate Docs., No. 72, 21st Cong., 2d sess., Vol. II. Statement of application of appropriations for improvement of navigation of the Ohio and Mississippi Rivers. [Washington, 1831] 13 p. M; R. 10085

---- Message on Protection of the Western Frontiers. Pres. A. Jackson. Jan. 24, 1831. Senate Docs., No. 39, 21st Cong., 2d sess., Vol. I. Statement relative to military force for the protection of the Western frontier; Fur trade; Trade with the Mexican colonies. [Washington, 1831] 36 p. M; R. 10086

---- Message on Removal of the Indians. Pres. Jackson. Feb. 22, 1831. Senate Docs., No. 65, 21st Cong., 2d sess., Vol. II. Recommends the removal westward of the Indians, or that they be compelled to submit quietly to State laws. [Washington, 1831] 10 p. M; R. 10087

---- Message on Rescue of Crew of Vessel. Pres. A. Jackson. Dec. 13, 1831. House Ex. Docs., No. 12, 22d Cong., 1st sess., Vol. I. Recommends that compensation be made to the owners and crew of a Spanish brig for rescuing the crew of the American ship Minerva. [Washington, 1831] 5 p. M; R. 10088

---- Message on the Fifth Census. Pres. Andrew Jackson. Dec. 7, 1831. House Ex. Docs., No. 4., 22d Cong., 1st sess., Vol. I. Transmitting statement showing the number of inhabitants within the several districts of the United States. [Washington, 1831] 33 p. M; R; TxFwTCU. 10089

---- Message on the Marine Corps. Pres. A. Jackson. Jan. 25, 1831. House Ex. Docs., No. 67, 21st Cong., 2d sess., Vol. III. Recommends passage of law relative to pay and allowances of officers of the Marine Corps. [Washington, 1831] 2 p. M; R. 10090

---- Message on the Mint. Pres. Andrew Jackson. Jan. 12, 1831. House Ex. Docs., No. 46, 21st Cong., 2d sess., Vol. II. Statement of operations of the Mint during the year 1830; Coinage effected; Amount of gold derived from Mexico, South America, West Indies, and other countries. [Washington, 1831] 2 p. M; R. 10091

---- Message on the Washington Penitentiary. Pres. A. Jackson. Jan. 25, 1831. House Ex. Docs., No. 66, 21st Cong., 2d sess., Vol. III. Report of the directors of the Washington penitentiary. [Washington, 1831] 3 p. M; R. 10092

---- Message on the Washington Penitentiary. Pres. A. Jackson. Jan. 31, 1831. House Ex. Docs. No. 80, 22d Cong., 1st sess., Vol. II. Transmitting report of board of inspectors of the penitentiary for the District of Columbia. [Washington, 1831] 3 p. M; R. 10093

---- Message on Title of Fort Delaware. Pres. Andrew Jackson. Feb. 19, 1831. House Ex. Docs., No. 107, 21st Cong., 2d sess., Vol. IV. Report on title of the United States to land on which Fort Delaware is situated. [Washington, 1831] 2 p. M; R. 10094

---- Message on Tonnage Duties. Pres. A. Jackson. Dec. 21, 1831. House Ex. Docs., No. 21, 22d Cong., 1st sess., Vol. II. Transmitting information relative to tonnage duties levied at Martinique and Guadaloupe. [Washington, 1831] 10 p. M;R. 10095

---- Message on Trade with the Indians. Pres. A. Jackson. Feb. 22, 1831. Senate Journal, 21st Cong., 2d sess. Concerning trade and intercourse with the Indian tribes. [Washington, 1831] 4 p. M; R. 10096

---- Message on Treaty with Austria. Pres. Andrew Jackson. Mar. 2, 1831. House Ex. Docs., No. 129, 21st Cong., 2d sess., Vol. IV. Copy of treaty with Austria concluded March 28, 1830. [Washington, 1831] 5 p. M; R. 10097

---- Message relative to State Lines. President Jackson. Dec. 29, 1831. Ex. Docs., No. 77, 22d Cong., 1st sess., Vol. II. Transmitting communication from the Secretary of State relative to the boundary-line between Georgia and Florida. [Washington, 1831] 120 p. M; R. 10098

---- Monthly Land Abstracts. Sept. 29, 1831. Library of the Interior Department. Circular relating to monthly abstracts. [Washington, 1831] 1 p. M; R. 10099

---- Navy Register. Pub. by the Navy Department. 1831. [Washington, 1831] 73 p. M; R. 10100

---- Petition for a Land Certificate. William Smith. Jan. 20, 1831. House Ex. Docs., No. 50, 21st Cong., 2d sess., Vol. III. Petitioner asks that new land certificate be issued to him, as administrator of John Taylor, in lieu of one relinquished. [Washington, 1831] 2 p. M; R. 10101

---- Petition for a Public Hospital. Citizens of St. Louis, Missouri. Jan. 24, 1831. Senate Docs., No. 37, 21st Cong., 2d sess., Vol. I. Memorialists ask national aid in the construction of a public hospital. [Washington, 1831] 2 p. M; R. 10102

---- Petition for Aid to American Colonization Society. Citizens of Virginia. Feb. 7, 1831. House Ex. Docs., No. 88, 21st Cong., 2d sess., Vol. III. Requests national aid for the society. [Washington, 1831] 2 p. M; R. 10103

---- Petition for Claims against Denmark. Jan. 24, 1831. House Ex. Docs., No. 65, 21st Cong., 2d sess., Vol. III. Petitioners (merchants and insurance companies) ask that the sum awarded for refundment of salvage of the brig Hendrick be added to the amount to be distributed among those sharing in the benefits of the convention with Denmark. [Washington, 1831] 3 p. M; R. 10104

---- Petition for French Spoliations. George Taylor. Dec. 9, 1831. House Ex. Docs., No. 14, 22d Cong., 1st sess., Vol. I. Claims compensation for spoliations by the French on commerce. [Washington, 1831] 1 p. M; R. 10105

---- Petition for Protection of the Indians. Citizens of Massachusetts. Feb. 14, 1831. House Ex. Docs., No. 105, 21st Cong., 2d sess., Vol. IV. Petitioners ask that Congress protect the Indians in the rights guaranteed them by treaty. [Washington, 1831] 1 p. M; R. 10106

---- Petition for Protection of the Indians. Citizens of Virginia. Feb. 21, 1831. House Ex. Docs., No. 130, 21st Cong., 2d Sess., Vol. IV. Petitioners ask Congress to protect the Indians in the enjoyment of their rights. [Washington, 1831] 2 p. M; R. 10107

---- Petition of George Taylor. Dec. 15, 1831. Bound in: Executive Docs., Pr. by order of the House of Representatives, 1st sess., 22d Cong., Vol. I. Washington, Pr. by Duff Green, 1831.

1 p. TxFwTCU. 10108

---- Petition relative to Post-Office Department. Samuel Moulton. Dec. 3, 1831. House Ex. Docs., No. 19, 22d Cong., 1st sess., Vol. II. Petitioner asks that all the expenses of the postal service be paid from the general revenues of the Government, and that newspapers be transported free of postage. [Washington, 1831] 1 p. M; R. 10109

---- Post office inquiry; speech on Mr. Grundy's resolution, delivered in the Senate, U.S. Feb. 1831. Washington, 1831. 27 p. NNC. 10110

---- Proof by Land Pre-emption. Feb. 7, 1831. Library of the Interior Department. Circular in relation to proof by pre-emptors under act of May 29, 1830. [Washington, 1831] 1 p. M; R. 10111

---- Proposals for Printing Journals of the Senate. Duff Green. Dec. 27, 1831. Senate Docs., No. 9, 22d Cong., 1st sess., Vol. I. Proposals to publish stereotype reprint of the legislative journals of the Senate. [Washington, 1831] 1 p. M; R. 10112

---- Receipts and Deposits of Land Receivers. May 1, 1831. Library of the Interior Department. Circular issued by the Secretary of the Treasury and transmitted to all receivers of public moneys, relating to receipts and deposits, and modifying circular of February 22, 1826, on the same subject. [Washington, 1831] 3 p. M; R. 10113

---- A register of officers and agents, civil, military and naval, in the service of the United States, on the 30th of Sept. 1831. Together with the names, forces and conditions of all the ships and vessels belonging to the United States and when and where built. Prepared at the Department of State. In pursuance of a resolution of Congress, of the 27th of April, 1816. Washington, Pr. by Wm. A. Davis, 1831. 407 p. KyLxT. 10114

---- Regulations for Registers and Receivers. May 25, 1831. Library of the Interior Department. Prescribing rules and regulations for the government of registers and receivers in the discharge of their duties. [Washington, 1831] 7 p. M; R. 10115

---- Remarks on the Death Penalty. Senator Edward Livingston. Mar. 3, 1831. Senate Docs. No. 75, 21st Cong., 2d sess., Vol. II. Relative to the abolition of the punishment of death. [Washington, 1831] 35 p. M; R. 10116

---- Report from the Postmaster General, in compliance with a resolution of the Senate showing the Postage received at the Office in Washington City for two years ending on the 1st May, 1830. May 20, 1830. Read, Feb. 1, 1831. Ordered to be printed. Washington, Pr. by Duff Green, 1831. R. 10117

---- Report from the Secretary of the Treasury, with a statement of all lands acquired by the United States in satisfaction of debts due them, showing where those lands lie, the sums allowed for them, and their probable value; made in compliance with a resolution of the Senate. Washington, Pr. by Duff Green, 1831. R. 10118

---- Report of Assays of Foreign Coins. Secretary S. D. Ingham. Feb. 11, 1831. House Ex.

Docs., No. 99, 21st Cong., 2d sess., Vol. III. Report of assays of foreign coins made at the Mint during the year 1830. [Washington, 1831] 3 p. M; R. 10119

---- Report of the retrenchment committee to the House of Representatives of the United States, May, 1831. Washington, 1831. PPL-R. 10120

---- Report on Accounts in Suit. Solicitor of the Treasury V. Maxev. Jan. 6, 1831. House Ex. Docs., No. 32, 21st Cong., 2d sess., Vol. II. Statements of suits on Treasury transcripts pending on the 4th of July, 1830; Against whom; Cause of action; Amount involved. [Washington, 1831] 96 p. M; R. 10121

---- Report on American Seamen. Secretary Martin Van Buren. Mar. 1, 1831. House Ex. Docs., No. 127, 21st Cong., 2d sess., Vol. IV. Abstract of American seamen in the several districts of the United States; Number of passengers arriving in the United States during the year ending September 30, 1829; Occupation, age, sex. [Washington, 1831] 37 p. M; R. 10122

---- Report on Applications for Pensions. Secretary J. Branch. Jan. 28, 1831. House Ex. Docs., No. 77, 21st Cong., 2d sess., Vol. III. Statement of applications for pension made during the year 1830. [Washington, 1831] 2 p. M; R. 10123

---- Report on Army Barracks. Secretary Lewis Cass. Dec. 31, 1831. Senate Docs. No. 18, 22d Cong., 1st sess., Vol. I. Transmitting a report of the Quartermaster-General in favor of the erection of barracks at New Orleans. [Washington, 1831] 3 p. M; R. 10124

---- Report on Assay Offices. Select committee. Feb. 15, 1831. House Reports, No. 82, 21st Cong., 2d sess. Recommends the establishment of assay offices within the gold districts of North Carolina, South Carolina, and Georgia; Bill reported. [Washington, 1831] 29 p. M; R. 10125

---- Report on Assay Offices. Select committee. Dec. 22, 1831. Reports of Committees, No. 39, 22d Cong., 1st sess., Vol. I. Recommends the establishment of assay offices within the Southern gold districts; Bill reported. [Washington, 1831] 29 p. M; R. 10126

---- Report on Bank of United States. Secretary S. D. Ingham. Jan. 21, 1831. House Ex. Docs., No. 63, 21st Cong., 2d sess., Vol. III. Monthly statements of the Bank of the United States for the year 1830. [Washington, 1831] 79 p. M; R. 10127

---- Report on Bill for Relief of Mother of F. H. Babit. Naval Committee. Mar. 2, 1831. House Reports, No. 111, 21st Cong., 2d sess. Claims pay for services of Fitz Henry Babit, late lieutenant in the Navy; Committee recommends rejection of bill. [Washington, 1831] 2 p. M; R. 10128

---- Report on Bill for Relief of Sophia Gardner. Com. on Naval Affairs. Mar. 2, 1831. House Reports, No. 113, 21st Cong., 2d sess. Recommends that bill be rejected. [Washington, 1831] 1 p. M; R. 10129

---- Report on Circulation of Foreign Coins. Select committee. Feb. 22, 1831. House Reports, No. 94, 21st Cong., 2d sess. Recommends providing by law that the dollars coined by the Mexican and certain other American governments be a legal tender in payment of debts at certain specified values. [Washington, 1831] 29 p. M; R. 10130

---- Report on Claim of Aaron Snow. Committee Revolutionary Claims. Dec. 30, 1831. Reports of Committees, No. 87, 22d Cong., 1st sess., Vol. I. Recommends payment to petitioner of certificates on account of military service; Bill reported. [Washington, 1831] 1 p. M; R. 10131

---- Report on Claim of Administrator of Job Alvord. Dec. 30, 1831. Reports of Committees, No. 89, 22d Cong., 1st sess., Vol. I. Committee on Revolutionary Claims recommends issuance of land patent to petitioner on account of the military service of Job Alvord; Bill reported. [Washington, 1831] 1 p. M; R. 10132

---- Report on Claim of Amariah Squirrel, Administrator. Com. on Claims. Jan. 14, 1831. House Reports, No. 89, 21st Cong., 2d sess. Recommends allowance of claim of petitioner on account of services of Jacob Squirrel in the Army; Bill reported. [Washington, 1831] 1 p. M; R. 10133

---- Report on Claim of Ann D. Baylor. Com. on Revolutionary Claims. Dec. 28, 1831. Reports of Committees, No. 78, 22d Cong. 1st sess., Vol. I. Recommends allowance of claim of petitioner; Bill reported. [Washington, 1831] 1 p. M; R. 10134

---- Report on Claim of Ann M. Barrow. Com. on Revolutionary Claims. Jan. 7, 1831. House Reports, No. 26, 21st Cong, 2d sess. Recommends allowance of claim of petitioner for half-pay on account of services of William Barrow, late a lieutenant in the Navy; Bill reported. [Washington, 1831] 2 p. M; R. 10135

---- Report on Claim of Archbishop Jackson. Com. on Private Land Claims. Feb. 12, 1831. House Reports, No. 78, 21st Cong. 2d sess. Recommends payment to claimant of bounty land due James Gammons; Bill reported. [Washington, 1831] 2 p. M; R. 10136

---- Report on Claim of Barnet J. Staafs. Committee on Claims. Jan. 7, 1831. Senate Docs., No. 24, 21st Cong., 2d sess., Vol. I. Recommends that claim of petitioner for payment for supplies furnished the Quartermaster's Department be not allowed. [Washington, 1831] 4 p. M; R. 10137

---- Report on Claim of Benjamin Bullitt. Com. on Private Land Claims. Dec. 27, 1831. Reports of Committees, No. 72, 22d Cong., 1st sess., Vol. I. Recommends allowance of claim of petitioner to tract of land in Louisiana; Bill reported. [Washington, 1831] 1 p. M; R. 10138

---- Report on Claim of Benjamin S. Smoot. Committee on Claims. Feb. 4, 1831. House Reports, No. 61, 21st Cong., 2d sess. Bill allows compensation to claimant for destruction of property by the British; Committee recommends that bill be rejected. [Washington, 1831] 6 p. M; R. 10139

---- Report on Claim of Celestin Chiapella. Com. on Private Land Claims. Dec. 22, 1831. Reports of Committees, No. 33, 22d Cong., 1st sess., Vol. I. Recommends that petitioner be granted a patent for land claimed in Mississippi; Bill reported. [Washington, 1831]

1 p. M; R. 10140

---- Report on Claim of Clement B. Penrose. Com. on Public Lands. Jan. 6, 1831. House Reports, No. 23, 21st Cong., 2d sess. Recommends that claim of petitioner for additional compensation as commissioner to settle private land claims be not allowed. [Washington, 1831] 1 p. M; R. 10141

---- Report on Claim of D. Smith. Committee on Military Pensions. Jan. 28, 1831. House Reports, No. 48, 21st Cong., 2d sess. Recommends allowance of claim of petitioner for pension; Bill reported. [Washington, 1831] 1 p. M; R. 10142

---- Report on Claim of David Hull. Committee on Claims. Jan. 13, 1831. House Reports, No. 37, 21st Cong., 2d sess. Recommends that claim of petitioner for property destroyed by the British in 1812 be rejected. [Washington, 1831] 2 p. M; R. 10143

---- Report on Claim of De Gameo Jones. Committee on Claims. Feb. 9, 1831. House Reports, No. 76, 21st Cong., 2d sess. Recommends allowance of claim of petitioner for forage furnished the army; Bill reported. [Washington, 1831] 2 p. M; R. 10144

---- Report on Claim of Dorothy Wells, Com. on Private Land Claims. Dec. 23, 1831. Reports of Committees, No. 60, 22d Cong. 1st sess., Vol. I. Reports bill for relief of petitioner. [Washington, 1831] 1 p. M; R. 10145

---- Report on Claim of Duval Carnes. Committee on Claims. Feb. 9, 1831. House Reports, No. 74, 21st Cong., 2d sess. Recommends allowance of claim for goods seized by order of Colonel Arbuckle, of the Army; Bill reported. [Washington, 1831] 1 p. M; R. 10146

---- Report on Claim of Edward Livingston. Committee on Claims. Feb. 2, 1831. House Reports, No. 53, 21st Cong., 2d sess. Recommends allowance of claim of petitioner for timber taken by United States troops; Bill reported. [Washington, 1831] 2 p. M; R. 10147

---- Report on Claim of Edward S. Meeder. Committee on Pensions. Feb. 22, 1831. Senate Docs., No. 61, 21st Cong., 2d sess., Vol. II. Recommends allowance of claim for arrears and increase of pension; Bill reported. [Washington, 1831] 2 p. M; R. 10148

---- Report on Claim of Eliakim Crosby. Com. on Private Land Claims. Dec. 23, 1831. Reports of Committees, No. 55, 22d Cong., 1st sess., Vol. I. Recommends allowance of claim of petitioner to two sections of land; Bill reported. [Washington, 1831] 2 p. M; R. 10149

---- Report on Claim of Elizabeth Magruder. Com. on Rev. Claims. Feb. 24, 1831. House Reports, No. 101, 21st Cong., 2d sess. Recommends allowance of claim of petitioner for commutation to Lieutenant Hilary for services in the Army; Bill reported. [Washington, 1831] 1 p. M; R. 10150

---- Report on Claim of Elizabeth Owens. Committee on Claims. Jan. 24, 1831. House Reports, No. 42, 21st Cong., 2d sess. Recommends allowance of claim on account of service of William Owens in the Army; Bill reported. [Washington, 1831] 2 p. M; R. 10151

---- Report on Claim of Elizabeth Owens. Committee on Claims. Jan. 24, 1831. Senate Docs. No. 36, 21st Cong., 2d sess., Vol. I. Recommends allowance of claim of petitioner for pay and bounty land as heir of James Shirley; Bill reported. [Washington, 1831] 2 p. M; R. 10152

---- Report on Claim of Ephraim Whitaker. Com. on Revolutionary Claims. Jan. 7, 1831. House Reports, No. 25, 21st Cong., 2d sess. Recommends allowance of claim of petitioner for services in the Army; Bill reported. [Washington, 1831] 1 p. M; R. 10153

---- Report on Claim of Ephraim Whittaker. Committee on Rev. Claims. Dec. 22, 1831. Reports of Committees, No. 29, 22d Cong., 1st sess., Vol. I. Recommends allowance of claim of petitioner on account of military service; Bill reported. [Washington, 1831] 1 p. M; R. 10154

---- Report on Claim of Eugene Boreel. Com. on Private Land Claims. Dec. 30, 1831. Reports of Committees, No. 91, 22d Cong., 1st sess., Vol. I. Recommends that petitioner be confirmed in his title to land in Louisiana; Bill reported. [Washington, 1831] 2 p. M; R. 10155

---- Report on Claim of Frederick Raymer. Com. on Revolutionary Claims. Jan. 3, 1831. House Reports, No. 17, 21st Cong., 2d sess. Recommends allowance of claim of memorialist for services with team in the Army; Bill reported. [Washington, 1831] 2 p. M; R. 10156

---- Report on Claim of Gates Hoyt. Com. on Military Affairs. Dec. 27, 1831. Reports of Committees, No. 75, 22d Cong., 1st sess., Vol. I. Recommends reference of claim of petitioner for compensation for secret services to the Third Auditor for adjudication. [Washington, 1831] 1 p. M; R. 10157

---- Report on Claim of George Johnson. Committee on Claims. Feb. 18, 1831. House Reports, No. 90, 21st Cong., 2d sess. Recommends passage of bill to relieve claimant from liability as surety for purser in the Navy. [Washington, 1831] 4 p. M; R. 10158

---- Report on Claim of George K. Knight. Naval Committee. Feb. 18, 1831. House Reports, No. 80, 21st Cong., 2d sess. Recommends allowance of claim of petitioner for vessel lost in the service of the United States; Bill reported. [Washington, 1831] 4 p. M; R. 10159

---- Report on Claim of George Mayfield. Com. on Private Land Claims. Jan. 3, 1831. House Reports, No. 18, 21st Cong., 2d sess. Recommends that claim for land be disallowed. [Washington, 1831] 1 p. M; R. 10160

---- Report on Claim of Godfroy & Beaugrand. Committee on Claims. Jan. 12, 1831. House Reports, No. 35, 21st Cong. 2d sess. Recommends allowance of claim of petitioners for buildings destroyed by the British; Bill reported. [Washington, 1831] 1 p. M; R. 10161

---- Report on Claim of H. B. Livingston. Military Committee. Feb. 23, 1831. Senate Docs., No. 63, 21st Cong., 2d sess., Vol. II. Asks to be discharged from further consideration of claim of petitioner for half-pay for services during the Revolution. [Washington, 1831] 3 p. M; R. 10162

---- Reported Claim of H. Beckett. Committee on Military Pensions. Jan. 28, 1831. House Reports, No. 50, 21st Cong., 2d sess. Recommends allowance of claim of petitioner for pensions. [Washington, 1831] 1 p. M; R. 10163

---- Report on Claim of Hannah McKimm. Com. on Private Land Claims. Dec. 27, 1831. Reports of Committees, No. 69, 22d Cong., 1st sess., Vol. I. Recommends allowance of claim of petitioner to land in Louisiana; Bill reported. [Washington, 1831] 1 p. M; R. 10164

---- Report on Claim of Heirs of David Darden. Com. on Rev. Claims. Dec. 23, 1831. Reports of Committees. No. 43, 22d Cong. 1st sess., Vol. I. Recommends allowance of claim of petitioners for value of horse impressed into the Army. [Washington, 1831] 2 p. M; R. 10165

---- Report on Claim of Heirs of J. B. Sancier. Com. on Private Land Claims. Dec. 30, 1831. Reports of Committees, No. 90, 22d Cong., 1st sess., Vol. I. Recommends allowance of claim of petitioner for land in Louisiana; bill reported. [Washington, 1831] 1 p. M; R. 10166

---- Report on Claim of Heirs of J. Buckley. Com. on Private Land Claims. Dec. 27, 1831. Reports of Committes, No. 71, 22d Cong., 1st sess., Vol. I. Recommends grant of land to petitioners in compensation for timber destroyed by United States troops; Bill reported. [Washington, 1831] 2 p. M; R. 10167

---- Report on Claim of Heirs of N. Hillen. Com. on Private Land Claims. Dec. 28, 1831. Reports of Committees, No. 76, 22d Cong., 1st sess., Vol. I. Recommends allowance of claim of petitioners for land in Louisiana; Bill reported. [Washington, 1831] 1 p. M; R. 10168

---- Report on Claim of Heirs of Pedro Guedry. Feb. 1, 1831. House Reports, No. 52, 21st Cong., 2d sess. Recommends allowance of land claim of petitioners; Bill reported. [Washington, 1831] 1 p. M; R. 10169

---- Report on Claim of Heirs of Samuel Kennedy. Com. on Rev. Claims. Dec. 28, 1831. Reports of Committees, No. 48, 22d Cong., 1st sess., Vol. I. Recommends that claim of petitioner for half-pay for seven years be allowed; Bill reported. [Washington, 1831] 1 p. M; R. 10170

---- Report on Claim of Heirs of T. Frothingham. Com. on Rev. Claims. Dec. 30, 1831. Reports of Committees, No. 88, 22d Cong., 1st sess., Vol. I. Recommends allowance of claim of petitioners for destruction of buildings during the Revolution; Bill reported. [Washington, 1831] 3 p. M; R. 10171

---- Report on Claim of Heirs of William Treadwell. Com. on Rev. Claims. Jan. 7, 1831. House Reports, No. 27, 21st Cong. 2d sess. Recommends allowance of claim for reissue of land warrant; Bill reported. [Washington, 1831] 1 p. M; R. 10172

---- Report on Claim of Henry Eckford. Naval Committee. Jan. 20, 1831. House Reports, No.

41, 21st Cong., 2d sess. Recommends allowance of claim of petitioner for land occupied by the United States; Bill reported. [Washington, 1831] 4 p. M; R. 10173

---- Report on Claim of Hopkins Rice. Com. on Private Land Claims. Jan. 5, 1831. House Reports, No. 22, 21st Con., 2d sess. Recommends allowances of claim of petitioner for exchange of section of land; Bill reported. [Washington, 1831] 1 p. M; R. 10174

---- Report on Claim of J. C. Belt and G. Stockton. Com. on Claims. Jan. 3, 1831. House Reports, No. 19, 21st Cong., 2d sess. Recommends that claim of petitioners for baggage lost in the United States service be not allowed. [Washington, 1831] 2 p. M; R. 10175

---- Report on Claim of J. S. Dufossat. Com. on Private Land Claims. Dec. 22, 1831. Reports of Committees, No. 32, 22d Cong., 1st sess., Vol. I. Recommends that petitioner be granted lands in Louisiana; Bill reported. [Washington, 1831] 2 p. M; R. 10176

---- Report on Claim of J. W. Torrey. Judiciary Committee. Jan. 25, 1831. House Reports, No. 44, 21st Cong., 2d sess. Recommends allowance of claim of petitioner for services to the United States as attorney of Michigan Territory; Bill reported. [Washington, 1831] 1 p. M; R. 10177

---- Report on Claim of James L. Sawyer. Committee on Claims. Jan. 3, 1831. House Report, No. 16, 21st Cong., 2d sess. Recommends allowance of claim for services as judge-advocate on trial of Dr. Pendergrass; Bill reported. [Washington, 1831] 2 p. M; R. 10178

---- Report on Claim of James Marsh. Committee on Commerce. Feb. 23, 1831. House Reports, No. 99, 21st Cong., 2d sess. Recommends allowance of claim of petitioner for drawback on goods imported; Bill reported. [Washington, 1831] 1 p. M; R. 10179

---- Report on Claim of James S. Campbell. Com. on Revolutionary Claims. Feb. 23, 1831. House Reports, No. 96, 31st Cong., 2d sess. Recommends their claim of memorialist for losses sustained by his father, Samuel Campbell, during the Revolution be disallowed. [Washington, 1831] 1 p. M; R. 10180

---- Report on Claim of James Soyars. Com. on Revolutionary Claims. Dec. 27, 1831. Reports of Committees, No. 66, 22d Cong., 1st sess., Vol. I. Recommends allowance to petitioner of seven years' half-pay; Bill reported. [Washington, 1831] 1 p. M; R. 10181

---- Report on Claim of Jane Thornton. Committee on Rev. Claims. Feb. 2, 1831. House Reports, No. 55, 21st Cong., 2d sess. Recommends allowance of claim of petitioner for commutation of five years pay due her late husband, Colonel John Thornton. [Washington, 1831] 2 p. M; R. 10182

---- Report on Claim of John B. Taylor. Secretary S. D. Ingham. Jan. 17, 1831. House Ex. Docs., No. 83, 21st Cong., 2d sess., Vol. III. Reports that land certificate, claim for payment of which has been made by John E. Taylor, has not been paid. [Washington, 1831] 2 p. M; R. 10183

---- Report on Claim of John Buhler. Com. on Private Land Claims. Dec. 28, 1831. Reports of Committees, No. 81, 22d Cong., 1st sess., Vol. I. Recommends confirmation of land title of petitioner; Bill reported. [Washington, 1831] 2 p. M; R. 10184

---- Report on Claim of John Burnham. Committee on Foreign Affairs. Jan. 25, 1831. House Reports, No. 45, 21st Cong., 2d sess. Recommends allowance of claim of petitioner for amount paid as his ransom from slavery in Algiers; Bill reported. [Washington, 1831] 1 p. M; R. 10185

---- Report on Claim of John Daly. Committee on Claims. Jan. 11, 1831. Senate Docs., no. 30, 21st Cong., 2d sess., Vol. I. Recommends allowance of claim of petitioner for forage furnished and barn destroyed during the late war; Bill reported. [Washington, 1831] 3 p. M; R. 10186

---- Report on Claim of John H. Carter et al. Com. on Rev. Claims. Dec. 23, 1831. Reports of Committees, No. 56, 22d Cong., 1st sess., Vol. I. Recommends allowance of claim of petitioners; Bill reported. [Washington, 1831] 1 p. M; R. 10187

---- Report on Claim of John H. Thomas. Com. on Private Land Claims. Dec. 22, 1831. Reports of Committees, No. 37, 22d Cong. 1st sess., Vol. I. Recommends confirmation of land title of petitioner; Bill reported. [Washington, 1831] 1 p. M; R. 10188

---- Report on Claim of John H. Wendell. Com. on Revolutionary Claims. Dec. 21, 1831. Reports of Committees, No. 57, 22d Cong., 1st sess., Vol. I. Recommends allowance of claim of petitioner; Bill reported. [Washington, 1831] 1 p. M; R. 10189

---- Report on Claim of John McDonogh. Com. on Private Land Claims. Dec. 20, 1831. Reports of Committees, No. 13, 22d Cong. 1st sess., Vol. I. Reports bill granting claimant land in Louisiana. [Washington, 1831] 4 p. M; R. 10190

---- Report on Claim of John McKim. Naval Committee. Mar. 1, 1831. House Reports, No. 105, 21st Cong., 2d sess. Recommends that claim of memorialist for extra services in the Army be disallowed. [Washington, 1831] 3 p. M; R. 10191

---- Report on Claim of John Menary. Committee on Claims. Jan. 14, 1831. House Reports, No. 38, 21st Cong., 2d sess. Recommends allowance of claim of petitioner for horse taken by United States troops; Bill reported. [Washington, 1831] 1 p. M; R. 10192

---- Report on Claim of John R. Rappleye. Com. on Military Pensions. Feb. 4, 1831. House Reports, No. 59, 21st Cong, 2d sess. Recommends allowance of claim of petitioner for arrears of pension; Bill reported. [Washington, 1831] 1 p. M; R. 10193

---- Report on Claim of John Roberts. Committee on Rev. Claims. Dec. 23, 1831. Reports of Committees, No. 45, 22d Cong., 1st sess., Vol. I. Recommends allowance of half-pay for life to petitioner; Bill reported. [Washington, 1831] 2 p. M; R. 10194

---- Report on Claim of John Teel. Committee on Revolutionary Claims. Dec. 30, 1831.

Reports of Committees, No. 86, 22d Con., 1st sess., Vol. I. Recommends allowance of compensation to petitioner for military service; Bill reported. [Washington, 1831] 3 p. M; R. 10195

---- Report on Claim of John Watson. Naval Committee. Mar. 2, 1831. House Reports, No. 112, 21st Cong., 2d sess. Recommends that claim of petitioner for building a vessel for the United States be not allowed. [Washington, 1831] 2 p. M; R. 10196

---- Report on Claim of Jonah Garrison. Committee on Military Pensions. Feb. 9, 1831. House Reports, No. 75, 21st Cong., 2d sess. Recommends allowance of claim of petitioner for pension; Bill reported. [Washington, 1831] 1 p. M; R. 10197

---- Report on Claim of Jonathan Fogg. Committee on Military Pensions. Jan. 28, 1831. House Reports, No. 49, 21st Cong., 2d sess. Recommends allowance of claim of petitioner for pension. [Washington, 1831] 1 p. M; R. 10198

---- Report on Claim of Joseph Bogy. Committee on Claims. Feb. 18, 1831. House Reports, No. 87, 21st Cong., 2d sess. Recommends allowance of claim of petitioner for rations furnished United States troops; Bill reported. [Washington, 1831] 1 p. M; R. 10199

---- Report on Claim of Joseph Emerson. Committee on Foreign Affairs. March 2, 1831. House Reports, No. 110, 21st Cong., 2d sess. Recommends that claim of petitioner for freight on cargo of coal for French Republic be not allowed. [Washington, 1831] 1 p. M; R. 10200

---- Report on Claim of Joseph F. Cannon. Naval Committee. Feb. 8, 1831. House Reports, No. 73, 21st Cong., 2d sess. Recommends passage of bill to place claimant on the pension-list. [Washington, 1831] 1 p. M; R. 10201

---- Report on Claim of Joshua Shaw. Military Committee. Jan. 7, 1831. House Reports, No. 22, 21st Cong., 2d sess. Petitioner asks that the United States purchase his patent right for improvement in discharging cannon; Committee recommends that petitioner have leave to withdraw his papers. [Washington, 1831] 1 p. M; R. 10202

---- Report on Claim of Judith Thomas. Committee on Military Pensions. Feb. 15, 1831. House Reports, No. 80, 21st Cong., 2d sess. Recommends allowance of claim of petitioner for five years' half-pay on account of services of John Thomas in the Army. [Washington, 1831] 1 p. M; R. 10203

---- Report on Claim of Lawrence L. Van Kleeck. Committee on Claims. Feb. 7, 1831. House Reports, No. 67, 21st Cong., 2d sess. Recommends claim of petitioner for compensation as collector of internal revenue; Bill reported. [Washington, 1831] 2 p. M; R. 10204

---- Report on Claim of Leonard & Black, Com. on Private Land Claims. Dec. 27, 1831. Reports of Committees, No. 72, 22d Cong. 1st sess., Vol. I. Recommends allowance of claim of petitioners to lands in Louisiana; Bill reported. [Washington, 1831] 1 p. M; R. 10205

---- Report on Claim of Martha Bailey, Adm'x. Committee on Claims. Feb. 2, 1831. House Reports, No. 57, 21st Cong., 2d sess. Recommends that claim of petitioner for payment for rations furnished the Army by Theodorus Bailey be rejected. [Washington, 1831] 13 p. M; R. 10206

---- Report on Claim of Minerva Catlett. Committee on Claims. Jan. 20, 1831. House Reports, No. 47, 21st Cong., 2d sess. Recommends allowance of claim of petitioner for services of Hanson Catlett in the Army; Bill reported. [Washington, 1831] 1 p. M; R. 10207

---- Report on Claim of Nancy B. Hickman. Committee on Claims. Feb. 16, 1831. House Reports, No. 84, 21st Cong., 2d sess. Recommends allowance of claim of petitioner for salary of William Hull, late Governor of Michigan; Bill reported. [Washington, 1831] 1 p. M; R. 10208

---- Report on Claim of Peters & Pond. Committee on Finance. Jan. 11, 1831. Senate Docs., No. 29, 21st Cong., 2d sess., Vol. I. Recommends that claim of petitioners for refundment of money paid him into the Treasury on account of violation of the revenue laws be allowed; Bill reported. [Washington, 1831] 10 p. M; R. 10209

---- Report on Claim of Representatives of D. Darden. Feb. 23, 1831. House Reports, No. 98, 21st Cong., 2d sess. Recommends allowance of claim for horse impressed into the Revolutionary service; Bill reported. [Washington, 1831] 1 p. M; R. 10210

---- Report on Claim of S. Eaton and D. Storer. Feb. 23, 1831. House Reports, No. 116, 21st Cong., 2d sess. Recommends allowance of claim of petitioners for commutation of half-pay due their late father, Robert H. Harrison, as colonel in the Revolutionary army; Bill reported. [Washington, 1831] 3 p. M; R. 10211

---- Report on Claim of S. Eastman and D. Storer. Com. on Rev. Claims. Dec. 28, 1831. Reports of Committees, No. 79, 22d Cong., 1st sess., Vol. I. Concurs in report made on this case at the second session of the twenty-first Congress and reports bill for relief of petitioners. [Washington, 1831] 1 p. M; R. 10212

---- Report on Claim of Samuel Caldwell. Committee on Commerce. Mar. 2, 1831. House Reports, No. 114, 21st Cong., 2d sess. Recommends that claim for services as brigadier-general be rejected. [Washington, 1831] 2 p. M; R. 10213

---- Report on Claim of Samuel Dale. Committee on Claims. Feb. 15, 1831. House Reports, No. 79, 21st Cong., 2d sess. Reports bill for adjustment of claim of petitioner for rations and forage furnished the Army. [Washington, 1831] 2 p. M; R. 10214

---- Report on Claim of Samuel Grice. Committee on Claims. Dec. 23, 1831. Reports of Committees, No. 61, 22d Cong., 1st sess., Vol. I. Recommends refundment of petitioner of amount deducted for failure to fulfil literally terms of contract for furnishing live-oak; Bill reported. [Washington, 1831] 2 p. M; R. 10215

---- Report on Claim of Sterling Johnson. Committee on Claims. Feb. 15, 1831. House Reports, No. 81, 21st Cong., 2d sess. Recommends that claim of petitioner for damages caused by the grading of Cumberland road be rejected. [Washington, 1831] 1 p. M; R. 10216

---- Report on Claim of Susan McHugh. Com. on Private Land Claims. Dec. 23, 1831. Reports of Committees, No. 59, 22d Cong., 1st sess., Vol. I. Reports bill for relief of petitioner. [Washington, 1831] 1 p. M; R. 10217

---- Report on Claim of T. Paine. Committee on Ways and Means. Dec. 20, 1831. Reports of Committees, No. 14, 22d Cong., 1st sess., Vol. I. Reports bill allowing petitioner compensation for provisions lost on vessel destroyed. [Washington, 1831] M; R. 10218

---- Report on Claim of Thomas A. C. Jones. Naval Committee. Mar. 1, 1831. House Reports. No. 104, 21st Cong., 2d sess. Recommends that claim of memorialist for pension be disallowed. [Washington, 1831] 3 p. M; R. 10219

---- Report on Claim of Thomas Belden. Committee on Claims. Feb. 18, 1831. House Reports, No. 92, 21st Cong., 2d sess. Report states that claimant is not entitled to alleged balance due on sale of brigs to the United States. [Washington, 1831] 2 p. M; R. 10220

---- Report on Claim of W. Hoffman. Committee on Private Land Claims. Dec. 29, 1831. Reports of Committees, No. 84, 22d Cong., 1st sess., Vol. I. Recommends granting bounty land to petitioner for military services; Bill reported. [Washington, 1831] 1 p. M; R. 10221

No entry. 10222

---- Report on Claim of W. Lomis and A. Gray. Committee on Claims. Jan. 7, 1831. House Reports, No. 28, 21st Cong., 2d sess. Recommends that claim of petitioners for work done on Cumberland road be not allowed. [Washington, 1831] 1 p. M; R. 10223

---- Report on Claim of William A. Tennille. Judiciary Committee. Feb. 8, 1831. House Reports No. 72, 21st Cong., 2d sess. Recommends that claim of memorialist be disallowed. [Washington, 1831] M; R. 10224

---- Report on Claim of William B. Matthews. Committee on Claims. Feb. 7, 1831. House Reports, No. 69, 21st Cong., 2d sess. Recommends passage of bill granting claimant compensation for slaves taken by the British. [Washington, 1831] 2 p. M; R. 10225

---- Report on Claim of William Vawters. Committee on Rev. Claims. Dec. 23, 1831. Reports of Committees; No. 44, 22d Cong., 1st sess., Vol. I. Recommends allowance to petitioner of half-pay for life; Bill reported. [Washington, 1831] 1 p. M; R. 10226

---- Report on Clerks in Post-Office Department. P. M. General Barry. Feb. 7, 1831. House Ex. Docs., No. 97, 21st Cong., 2d sess., Vol. III. List of clerks employed in the Post-Office Department, during the year 1830; Compensation. [Washington, 1831] 3 p. M; R. 10227

---- Report on Clerks in the Navy Department. Sec. John Branch. Jan. 7, 1831. House Ex. Docs., No. 38, 21st Cong., 2d sess., Vol. II. List of clerks employed in the Navy Department during the year 1830; Times employed; Compensation. [Washington, 1831] 3 p. M; R. 10228

---- Report on Clerks in the State Department. Sec. Martin

Van Buren. Jan. 13, 1831. House Ex. Docs., No. 51, 21st Cong., 2d sess., Vol. III. List of clerks employed in the State Department during the year 1830; Time employed; Compensation. [Washington, 1831] 2 p. M; R. 10229

---- Report on Clerks in the Treasury Department. Sec. S. D. Ingham. Jan. 10, 1831. House Ex. Docs., No. 39, 21st Cong., 2d sess., Vol. II. List of clerks employed in the Treasury Department during the year 1830; Time employed; Compensation. [Washington, 1831] 8 p. M; R. 10230

---- Report on Clerks in the War Department. Secretary J. H. Eaton. Jan. 12, 1831. House Ex. Docs., No. 45, 21st Cong., 2d sess., Vol. II. List of clerks employed in the War Department during the year 1830; Time employed; Compensation. [Washington, 1831] 2 p. M; R. 10231

---- Report on Commerce and Navigation. Secretary S. D. Ingham. March 1, 1831. House Ex. Docs., No. 124, 21st Cong., 2d sess., Vol. IV. Explaining why the report on commerce and navigation for the past year cannot be laid before Congress at the present session. [Washington, 1831] 1 p. M; R. 10232

---- Report on Commerce with Island of St. Croix. Com. on Commerce. Mar. 2, 1831. House Reports, No. 117, 21st Cong., 2d sess. Recommends that the committee be discharged from further consideration of the matter. [Washington, 1831] 2 p. M; R. 10233

---- Report on Compensation for Rescue of Seamen. Com. on Commerce. Dec. 22, 1831. Reports of Committees, No. 34, 22d Cong. 1st sess., Vol. I. Recommends that the crew of the Spanish brig Leon be compensated out of the fund for the relief of American seamen for exertions in saving the passengers and crew of the American ship Minerva; Bill reported. [Washington, 1831] 1 p. M; R. 10234

---- Report on Compensation of Members of Congress. Jan. 10, 1831. House Reports, No. 84, 21st Cong., 2d sess. The Committee on Expenditures recommends passage of accompanying joint resolution deducting the pay of members of Congress for time absent, unless by order of the House or in consequence of sickness. [Washington, 1831] 1 p. M; R. 10235

---- Report on Construction of Navy Hospitals. Secretary John Branch. Feb. 4, 1831. House Ex. Docs., No. 16, 22d Cong., 1st sess., Vol. I. Transmitting statements relative to construction of naval hospital at Charlestown, Massachusetts. [Washington, 1831] 8 p. M; R. 10236

---- Report on Construction of Road. Jan. 27, 1831. Senate Docs., No. 42, 21st Cong., 2d sess., Vol. II. Recommends donation of land for construction of road from Lawrenceburgh to southern bend of the St. Joseph's River; Bill reported. [Washington, 1831] 5 p. M; R. 10237

---- Report on Contingent Expenses of Navy. Com. on Naval Expenditures. Feb. 22, 1831. House Reports, No. 93, 21st Cong. 2d sess. Recommended that in future money drawn from the Treasury be applied to the precise object of the appropriation. [Washington, 1831] 4 p. M; R. 10238

---- Report on Contingent Expenses of Post-Office Department. Mar. 3, 1831. House Reports, No. 118, 21st Cong., 2d sess. Committee on Expenditures report that accounts have been examined and found correct. [Washington, 1831] 7 p. M; R. 10239

---- Report on Contingent Expenses of the House. Clerk M. St. Clair Clarke. Dec. 5, 1831. House Ex. Docs., No. 7, 22d Cong., 1st sess., Vol. I. Appropriation and expenditures of the contingent fund of the House of Representatives for the year 1831. [Washington, 1831] 4 p. M; R. 10240

---- Report on Contingent Expenses of the Navy. Sec. John Branch. Jan. 4, 1831. House Ex. Docs., No. 28, 21st Cong., 2d sess., Vol. I. Statement of disbursements on account of the contingent expenses of the Navy for the year ending September 30, 1830. [Washington, 1831] 21 p. M; R. 10241

---- Report on Cumberland Road. Sec. John H. Eaton. Jan. 8, 1831. House Ex. Docs., No. 86, 21st Cong., 2d sess., Vol. II. Statement relative to expenditures on Cumberland road; Amount of work done; Appropriation necessary to complete road. [Washington, 1831] 1 p. M; R. 10242

---- Report on Customs Affairs. Sec. S. D. Ingham. Feb. 28, 1831. House Ex. Docs., No. 122, 21st Cong., 2d sess., Vol. IV. Abstract of official emoluments of officers of the customs; Salaries and fees of collectors, naval officers, and surveyors. [Washington, 1831] 13 p. M; R. 10243

---- Report on Danish Brig Henrick. Committee on Foreign Affairs. Feb. 23, 1831. House Reports, No. 100, 21st Cong., 2d sess. Memorialists claim reimbursement of salvage allowed for recapture of brig; Committee recommends that prayer of memorialists be not granted. [Washington, 1831] 5 p. M; R. 10244

---- Report on Desertions in the Army. Committee on Military Affairs. Dec. 27, 1831. Reports of Committees, No. 63, 22d Cong. 1st sess., Vol. I. Recommends reduction of length of term of enlistment from five to three years. [Washington, 1831] 5 p. M; R. 10245

---- Report on Dike at Bonnet Carré Point. Com. Internal Improvements. Feb. 5, 1831. House Reports, No. 63, 21st Cong., 2d sess. Recommends that an examination be made and estimate of cost furnished for building a dike at Bonnet Carré Point, on the Mississippi. [Washington, 1831] 1 p. M; R. 10246

---- Report on Distribution of Surplus Funds in Treasury. Select committee. Jan. 28, 1831. House Reports, No. 51, 21st Cong., 2d sess. Recommends the subject to the further consideration of the House. [Washington, 1831] 14 p. M; R. 10247

---- Report on Duties and Drawbacks. Sec. Louis McLane. Dec. 13, 1831. House Ex. Docs., No. 13, 22d Cong., 1st sess., Vol. I. Transmitting statement of duties and drawbacks of articles imported into the United States and re-exported during the years 1828, 1829, 1830. [Washington, 1831] 8 p. M; R. 10248

Report on Duties and Drawbacks. Sec. S. D. Ingham. Feb. 12, 1831. House Ex. Docs., No. 108, 21st Cong., 2d sess., Vol. III. Statement of amount of duties and drawbacks on articles imported into the United States and re-exported during the years 1827, 1828, and 1829. [Washington, 1831] 8 p. M; R. 10249

---- Report on Duties on Sugar. Committee on Manufactures. Feb. 16, 1831. Senate Docs., No. 56, 21st Cong., 2d sess., Vol. II. Reports bill without amendment. [Washington, 1831] 3 p. M; R. 10250

---- Report on Duty on Salt. Committee on Manufactures. Feb. 3, 1831. House Reports, No. 70, 21st Cong., 2d sess. Recommends repeal of law passed at last session relative to duty on salt. [Washington, 1831] 40 p. M; R. 10251

---- Report on Erection of a Hospital. Committee on Commerce. Feb. 4, 1831. Senate Docs., No. 46, 21st Cong., 2d sess., Vol. II. Recommends that prayer of memorialists for the erection of a hospital on the Western waters for seamen be not granted. [Washington, 1831] 2 p. M; R. 10252

---- Report on Expenditures in Treasury Department. Mar. 1, 1831. House Reports, No. 108, 21st Cong., 2d sess. Committee on Expenditures reports that it has examined the contingent accounts of the Treasury Departments and finds them correct. [Washington, 1831] 36 p. M; R. 10253

---- Report on Exported Nails. Committee on Commerce. Feb. 14, 1831. Senate Docs., No. 52, 21st Cong., 2d sess., Vol. II. Recommends drawback on exported nails made from foreign iron. [Washington, 1831] 4 p. M; R. 10254

---- Report on Foreign commerce. Sec. S. D. Ingham. Apr. 28, 1831. Senate Docs., No. 76, 21st Cong. 2d sess., Vol. II. Statement respecting commerce between the United States and Foreign countries during the year ending September 30, 1830; Tonnage of the United States for the Year 1829; Total amount of goods on which duties were collected. [Washington, 1831] 302 p. M; R. 10255

---- Report on Gold and Silver Coins. Select committee. Feb. 22, 1831. House Reports, No. 95, 21st Cong., 2d sess. Recommends passage of bill regulating the relative value of gold and silver. [Washington, 1831] 27 p. M; R. 10256

---- Report on Imported Sugars. Sec. S. D. Ingham. House Ex. Docs., No. 55, 21st Cong., 2d sess., Vol. III. Statement of quantity and value of sugars imported from October 1, 1820, to September 30, 1829; Whence imported. [Washington, 1831] 11 p. M; R. 10257

---- Report on Improvement of the Ohio. Com. Internal Improvements. Feb. 23, 1831. House Reports, No. 97, 21st Cong., 2d sess. Recommends appropriation for improving the navigation of the Ohio River. [Washington, 1831] 1 p. M; R. 10258

---- Report on Improvement of the Ohio River. Sec. John H. Eaton. Jan. 4, 1831. House Ex. Docs., No. 29, 21st Cong., 2d sess., Vol. I. Report on improvement of the Ohio River at the falls of Louisville. [Washington, 1831] 6 p. M; R. 10259

---- Report on Improvement of the Savannah River. Sec. S. D. Ingham. Feb. 16, 1831. House Ex. Docs., No. 104, 21st Cong., 2d sess., Vol. III. Statement of appropriations and expenditures for removing obstruction from the Savannah River, Georgia. [Washington, 1831] 58 p. M; R. 10260

---- Report on Indian Accounts. Sec. John H. Eaton. Feb. 9, 1831. House Ex. Docs., No. 101, 21st Cong., 2d sess., Vol. III. Copies of accounts of persons who have disbursed money or goods for the benefit of the Indians for the year ending August 31, 1830. [Washington, 1831] 112 p. M; R. 10261

---- Report on Indian Annuities. Sec. John H. Eaton. Feb. 8, 1831. House Ex. Docs., No. 102, 21st Cong., 2d sess., Vol. III. Statement relative to annuities paid to Cherokee Indians. [Washington, 1831] 2 p. M; R. 10262

---- Report on Indian Depredation Claims. Auditor Peter Hagner. Feb. 28, 1831. House Ex. Docs., No. 38, 22d Cong., 1st sess., Vol. II. Statement of claims of persons who have lost property by Indian depredations. [Washington, 1831] 117 p. M; R. 10263

---- Report on Indian Depredation Claims. Auditor Peter Hagner. Feb. 28, 1831. Ex. Docs., No. 26, 21st Cong., 1st sess., Vol. I. Statement relative to claims of certain citizens of the United States for property lost by Indian depredations. [Washington, 1831] 117 p. M; R. 10264

---- Report on Indian Depredation Claims. Com. on Indian Affairs. Dec. 27, 1831. Reports of Committees, No. 65, 22d Cong., 1st sess., Vol. I. Recommends that claims of citizens of Georgia on account of depredations by the Creek Indians be paid; Bill reported. [Washington, 1831] 4 p. M; R. 10265

---- Report on Indian Trade Licenses. Sec. John H. Eaton. Jan. 7, 1831. House Ex. Docs., No. 41, 21st Cong., 2d sess., Vol. II. List of licenses granted to trade with the Indians in the year ending September 30, 1830; Date of license; To whom granted; Term of License; Amount of trade; Capital employed. [Washington, 1831] 9 p. M; R. 10266

---- Report on Infantry Tactics. Sec. John H. Eaton. Jan. 12, 1831. House Ex. Docs., No. 47, 21st Cong., 2d sess., Vol. II. Statement relative to apportionment and distribution of copies of Infantry tactics. [Washington, 1831] 2 p. M; R. 10267

---- Report on Internal Improvements. Com. on Internal Improvements. Feb. 10, 1831. House Reports, No. 77, 21st Cong., 2d sess. Report states that it is inexpedient to prosecute internal improvements by direct appropriations of money. [Washington, 1831] 67 p. M; R. 10268

---- Report on Invalid Pensioners. Sec. John H. Eaton. Feb. 7, 1831. House Ex. Docs., No. 86, 21st Cong., 2d sess., Vol. III. Satement giving the names of invalid pensioners and the dates they were inscribed on the pension-rolls. [Washington, 1831] 30 p. M; R. 10269

---- Report on Land Claims. Commissioner Elijah Hayward. Jan. 3, 1831. House Ex. Docs., No. 23, 21st Cong., 2d sess., Vol. I. Report of register and receiver of the Saint Helena land district upon land claims in Louisiana. [Washington, 1831] 4 p. M; R. 10270

---- Report on Land Claims. Commissioner Elijah Hayward.

Dec. 31, 1831. Senate Docs., No. 14, 22d Cong., 1st sess., Vol. I. Statement relative to unconfirmed land claims in Missouri; Claims which have not been presented; Claims not prosecuted to final decision. [Washington, 1831] 7 p. M; R. 10271

---- Report on Land Claims. Committee on Private Land Claims. Dec. 28, 1831. Reports of Committees, No. 82, 22d Cong., 1st sess., Vol. I. Recommends that Pedro Guedry and Francis Daigre be allowed land claimed; Bill reported. [Washington, 1831] 1 p. M; R. 10272

---- Report on Live-Oak Timber Land. Naval Committee. Feb. 26, 1831. House Reports, No. 102, 21st Cong., 2d sess. Recommends that certain live-oak timber lands belonging to the United States be reserved from sale. [Washington, 1831] 80 p. M; R. 10273

---- Report on Map of Public Lands. Secretary S. D. Ingham. Mar. 3, 1831. House Ex. Docs., No. 130, 21st Cong., 2d sess. Vol. IV. Explaining why map of public lands surveyed has not been prepared. [Washington, 1831] 2 p. M; R. 10274

---- Report on Mediterranean Passports. Sec. S. D. Ingham. Jan. 4, 1831. House Ex. Docs. No. 26, 21st Cong., 2d sess., Vol. I. Statement of amount of payments made for the years 1826 to 1829, inclusive, for papers called "Mediterranean passports." [Washington, 1831] 2 p. M; R. 10275

---- Report on Memorial of Citizens of Detroit. Com. on Territories. Feb. 12, 1831. House Reports, No. 83, 21st Cong., 2d sess. Recommends that the law granting to the Governor and judges of Michigan authority to lay out the burnt portion of the town of Detroit be repealed, and that the matter be left to the town itself; Bill reported. [Washington, 1831] 14 p. M; R. 10276

---- Report on Memorial of Creek Indians. Indian Committee. Mar. 2, 1831. House Reports. No. 109, 21st Cong., 2d sess. Reports it inexpedient to notice claim of memorialists for indemnification for property alleged to have been taken by citizens of Georgia. [Washington, 1831] 3 p. M; R. 10277

---- Report on Memorial of Legislature of Illinois. Com. on Public Lands. Feb. 2, 1831. House Reports, No. 54, 21st Cong., 2d sess. Recommends that the State of Illinois be authorized to sell lands reserved to salt springs; Bill reported. [Washington, 1831] 3 p. M; R. 10278

---- Report on Memorial of Legislature of Indiana. Indian Committee. Jan. 4, 1831. Senate Docs., No. 22, 21st Cong., 2d sess., Vol. I. Recommends extinguishment of Indian title to certain lands in Indiana; Bill reported. [Washington, 1831] 4 p. M; R. 10279

---- Report on Memorial of Merchants of Philadelphia. Com. on Commerce. Mar. 2, 1831. House Reports, No. 115, 21st Cong., 2d sess. Recommends that committee be discharged from further consideration of memorials relative to tonnage levied upon United States commerce in the island of Cuba. [Washington, 1831] 1 p. M; R. 10280

---- Report on Memorial of S. W. Meeteer. Com. on Contingent Fund. Feb. 15, 1831. Senate Docs., No. 55, 21st Cong., 2d sess., Vol. II. Recommends that prayer of memorialist for an alteration in the mode of procuring paper for the public printing be not granted. [Washington, 1831] 1 p. M; R. 10281

---- Report on Memorial of State of South Carolina. Com. Military Affairs. Dec. 15, 1831. Reports of Committees, No. 1, 22d Cong. 1st sess., Vol. I. Reports bill reimbursing to the State of South Carolina amount of money expended in maintaining militia during the war of 1812. [Washington, 1831] 71 p. M; R. 10282

---- Report on Memorial of T. Hopping and J. P. Frothingham. Feb. 7, 1831. House Reports, No. 68, 21st Cong., 2d sess. Committee on Revolutionary Claims recommends claim of memorialists for value of building burned by order of an officer in the Continental service; Bill reported. [Washington, 1831] 3 p. M; R. 10283

---- Report on Memorials of Army Officers. Committee on Public Lands. Mar. 1, 1831. House Reports, No. 103, 21st Cong. 2d sess. Recommends provision granting public land to such officers as were disbanded in the consolidation of regiments during the war; Bill reported. [Washington, 1831] 8 p. M; R. 10284

---- Report on Memorials of Dealers in Teas. Committee on Finance. Dec. 19, 1831. Senate Docs. No. 4, 22d Cong., 1st sess., Vol. I. Reports that it is inexpedient to make any change in the present rates of duty on teas. [Washington, 1831] 4 p. M; R. 10285

---- Report on Mileage of Members of Congress. Com. on Expenditures. Jan. 7. 1831. House Reports, No. 30, 21st Cong., 2d sess. Committee is unable to devise any plan relative to a uniform role for estimating mileage to members of Congress. [Washington, 1831] 2 p. M; R. 10286

---- Report on Military Roads. Sec. John H. Eaton. Jan. 11, 1831. House Ex. Docs., No. 48, 21st Cong., 2d sess. Vol. II. Statement of roads constructed by the Army; Location; Extent; Period of construction; Cost. [Washington, 1831] 10 p. M; R. 10287

---- Report on National Armories. Sec. John H. Eaton. Mar. 2, 1831. House Ex. Docs., No. 125, 21st Cong., 2d sess. Vol. IV. Statement of expenditures at United States armories and of arms manufactured during the year 1830. [Washington, 1831] 5 p. M; R. 10288

---- Report on Naval Appropriations. Sec. John Branch. Feb. 14, 1831. House Ex. Docs., No. 100, 21st Cong., 2d sess., Vol. III. Report on condition of appropriations for the naval service for the year 1830. [Washington, 1831] 13 p. M; R. 10289

---- Report on Naval Pensions. Naval Committee. Feb. 18, 1831. House Reports, No. 86, 21st Cong. 2d sess. Recommends granting arrearages of pensions; Bill reported. [Washington, 1831] 8 p. M; R. 10290

---- Report on Navy Pension Fund. The Commissioners. Jan. 27, 1831. House Ex. Docs., No. 75, 21st Cong. 2d sess., Vol. III. Statement of amount paid into the Treasury to the credit of the Navy pension fund during the year 1830; Payments made from the Treasury on account of said fund; List of pensioners. [Washington, 1831] 31 p. M; R. 10291

---- Report on New England Asylum for the Blind. Feb. 5, 1831. House Reports, No. 66, 21st Cong., 2d sess. Recommends granting national aid to said asylum; Bill reported. [Washington, 1831] 2 p. M; R. 10292

---- Report on Okracock Inlet. Sec. John H. Eaton. Jan. 7, 1831. House Ex. Docs., No. 40, 21st Cong., 2d sess., Vol. II. Statement of operations at Ocracock Inlet, North Carolina; Estimate of amount required for the year 1831 for Improving the navigation of inlet. [Washington, 1831] 5 p. M; R. 10293

---- Report on Patents. Sec. Martin Van Buren. John 1, 1831. House Ex. Docs., No. 49, 21st Cong., 2d sess., Vol. II. List of patents granted during the year 1830; Name of inventor; Date of issue of patent. [Washington, 1831] 57 p. M; R. 10294

---- Report on Patents. Sec. Martin Van Buren. Jan. 11, 1831. House Ex. Docs., No. 50, 21st Cong., 2d sess. Vol. II. List of all patents granted by the United States; Acts of Congress relating to patents; Decisions of United States courts on the subject of patents. [Washington, 1831] 504 p. M; R. 10295

---- Report on Pay in the Navy. Committee on Naval Affairs. Feb. 16, 1831. House Reports, No. 85, 21st Cong., 2d sess. Recommends increase of pay of captains and masters commandant; Bill reported. [Washington, 1831] 16 p. M; R. 10296

---- Report on Pay of Army Officers. Committee on Military Affairs. Dec. 20, 1831. Reports of Committees, No. 9, 22d Cong., 1st sess., Vol. I. Recommends changes in law regulating the pay emoluments of officers of the Army. [Washington, 1831] 6 p. M; R. 10297

---- Report on Pay of Member of Congress. Judiciary Committee. Feb. 4, 1831. Senate Docs., No. 45, 21st Cong., 2d sess., Vol. II. Recommends that House resolution relative to pay of members of Congress be rejected. [Washington, 1831] 1 p. M; R. 10298

---- Report on Pay of the Army. Sec. John H. Eaton. Feb. 21, 1831. House Ex. Docs., No. 111, 21st Cong., 2d sess., Vol. IV. Statement of sums paid to officers of the Army on account of extra compensation for the year 1829; Name and rank; Pay and emoluments; Nature of extra services. [Washington, 1831] 16 p. M; R. 10299

---- Report on Petition of A. Lanaux. Com. on Private Land Claims. Dec. 22, 1831. Reports of Committees, No. 30, 22d Cong., 1st sess., Vol. I. Recommends that title of petitioner to land be confirmed; Bill reported. [Washington, 1831] 1 p. M; R. 10300

---- Report on Petition of A. Parker. Com. on Revolutionary Pensions. Dec. 21, 1831. Reports bill allowing pension to petitioner. [Washington, 1831] 1 p. M; R. 10301

---- Report on Petition of Adam Peck. Committee on Claims. Jan. 10, 1831. House Reports, No. 32, 21st Cong., 2d sess.

Rcommends that accounting officers be authorized to settle petitioner's accounts as recruiting officer upon the principles of justice and equity; Bill reported. [Washington, 1831] 1 p. M; R. 10302

---- Report on Petition of Allen W. Hardie. Com. on Private Land Claims. Dec. 22, 1831. Reports of Committees, No. 31, 22d Cong., 1st sess., Vol. I. Recommends that petitioner be allowed to complete payments and receive patent for land located; Bill reported. [Washington, 1831] 1 p. M; R. 10303

---- Report on Petition of B. Kelley. Com. on Post-Office and Post-Roads. Dec. 27, 1831. Reports of Committees, No. 67, 22d Cong., 1st sess., Vol. I. Recommends that petitioner be allowed credit in his accounts as postmaster for value of stamps, etc., destroyed by fire. [Washington, 1831] 3 p. M; R. 10304

---- Report on Petition of B. Marigny. Committee on Private Land Claims. Dec. 19, 1831. Reports of Committees, No. 3, 22d Congress, 1st sess., Vol. I. Reports bill confirming title of petitioner to land. [Washington, 1831] 1 p. M; R. 10305

---- Report on Petition of Benjamin Crofoot. Committee on Rev. Pensions. Dec. 22, 1831. Reports of Committees, No. 36, 22d Cong., 1st sess., Vol. I. Recommends allowance of pension to petitioner; Bill reported. [Washington, 1831] 1 p. M; R. 10306

---- Report on Petition of Bernard Marigny. Mar. 1, 1831. House Reports, No. 106, 21st Cong., 2d sess. Committee on Private Land Claims recommends that petitioner be confirmed in his title to two tracts of land in Louisiana; Bill reported. [Washington, 1831] 1 p. M; R. 10307

---- Report on Petition of Charles Drish. Com. on Revolutionary Claims. Feb. 2, 1831. House Reports, No. 56, 21st Cong., 2d sess. Recommends payment to petitioner of certificates erroneously issued to Christian Ish for services during the Revolution; Bill reported. [Washington, 1831] 1 p. M; R. 10308

---- Report on Petition of Clarissa B. Harrison. Com. on Public Lands. Feb. 5, 1831. House Reports, No. 65, 21st Cong., 2d sess. Recommends that petitioner be relieved from the liability incurred by her late husband, J. C. S. Harrison, while reciver of the land office; Bill reported. [Washington, 1831] 5 p. M; R. 10309

---- Report on Petition of Daniel Purdy. Committee on Rev. Pensions. Dec. 23, 1831. Reports of Committees, No. 51, 22d Cong., 1st sess., Vol. I. Recommends allowance of pension to petitioner; Bill reported. [Washington, 1831] 1 p. M; R. 10310

---- Report on Petition of Daniel Reddington. Committee on Pensions. Dec. 22, 1831. Senate Docs. No. 7, 22d Cong., 1st sess., Vol. I. Recommends that prayer of petitioner to be placed on the pension-rolls be not granted. [Washington, 1831] 1 p. M; R. 10311

---- Report on Petition of David Brooks. Com. on Military Pensions. Jan. 18, 1831. House Reports, No. 31, 21st Cong., 2d sess. Recommends that prayer of petitioner for arrears of pension be not granted. [Washington,

1831] 1 p. M; R. 10312

---- Report on Petition of E. Healy. Com. on Revolutionary Pensions. Dec. 20, 1831. Reports of Committees. No. 15, 22d Cong., 1st sess., Vol. I. [Washington, 1831] 1 p. M. 10313

---- Report on Petition of E. Marin and J. Wogin. Dec. 27, 1831. Reports of Committees, No. 62, 22d Cong., 1st sess., Vol. I. Committee on Private Land Claims recommends that title of petitioners to land in Louisiana be confirmed; Bill reported. [Washington, 1831] 3 p. M; R. 10314

---- Report on Petition of Ebenezer De Forrest. Com. On Rev. Pensions. Dec. 20, 1831. Reports of Committees, no. 8, 22d Cong., 1st sess., Vol. I. Reports bill allowing pension to petitioner. [Washington, 1831] 1 p. M; R. 10315

---- Report on Petition of Eli Smith. Committee on Pensions. Feb. 4, 1831. House Reports, No. 58, 21st Cong., 2d sess. Report states that petitioner is entitled to pension. [Washington, 1831] 2 p. M; R. 10316

---- Report on Petition of Executors of T. Worthington. Com. on Judiciary. Jan. 24, 1831. Senate Docs., No. 38, 21st Cong., 2d sess., Vol. I. Recommends that petitioners be released from payments of judgment obtained against Thomas Worthington, deceased, as surety for Samuel Finley, receiver of public moneys; Bill reported. [Washington, 1831] 2 p. M; R. 10317

---- Report on Petition of Executors of T. Worthington. Judiciary Com. Jan. 5, 1831. House Reports, No. 21, 21st Cong., 2d sess. Recommends that petitioners be relieved from payment of judgment obtained against Thomas Worthington as surety for Samuel Finley, collector of public moneys; Bill reported. [Washington, 1831] 3 p. M; R. 10318

---- Report on Petition of George Innes. Committee on Commerce. Dec. 15, 1831. Reports of Committees, No. 11, 22d Cong., 1st sess., Vol. I. Reports bill allowing compensation to petitioner for services in custom-house. [Washington, 1831] 3 p. M; R. 10319

---- Report on Petition of George J. Knight. Com. on Naval Affairs. Dec. 23, 1831. Reports of Committees, No. 47, 22d Cong., 1st sess., Vol. I. Recommends compensation to petitioner for loss of schooner while in the service of the United States; Bill reported. [Washington, 1831] 4 p. M; R. 10320

---- Report on Petition of George N. Johnson. Judiciary Committee. Jan. 5, 1831. Senate Docs., No. 23, 21st Cong., 2d sess., Vol. I. Recommends that petitioner be relieved from liability as surety of B. F. Bourne, purser in the Navy; Bill reported. [Washington, 1831] 12 p. M; R. 10321

---- Report on Petition of H. Blankenship. Com. on Rev. Pensions. Dec. 20, 1831. Reports of Committees, No. 46, 22d Cong., 1st sess., Vol. I. Recommends allowance of pension to petitioner; Bill reported. [Washington, 1831] 1 p. M; R. 10322

---- Report on Petition of Harvey Brown. Committee on the Judiciary. Dec. 27, 1831. Reports of Committees, No. 74,

22d Cong., 1st sess., Vol. I. Recommends payment by the United States of judgment obtained in suit against petitioner as assistant quartermaster; Bill reported. [Washington, 1831] 2 p. M; R. 10323

---- Report on Petition of Henry Alexander. Judiciary Committee. Dec. 28, 1831. Senate Docs., No. 11, 22d Cong., 1st sess., Vol. I. Recommends that prayer of petitioner for extension of patents for improvement in the manufacture of mineral paints, in the cleansing of wool, and for other inventions be not granted. [Washington, 1831] 3 p. M; R. 10324

---- Report on Petition of Henry Fried. Com. on Revolutionary Claims. Jan. 12, 1831. House Reports, No. 62, 21st Cong., 2d sess. Recommends that prayer of petitioner for redemption of Continental money in his possession be not granted. [Washington, 1831] 1 p. M; R. 10325

---- Report on Petition of Isaac Dalton. Committee on Rev. Pensions. Dec. 23, 1831. Reports of Committees, No. 52, 22d Cong. 1st sess., Vol. I. Recommends allowance of pension to petitioner; Bill reported. [Washington, 1831] 1 p. M; R. 10326

---- Report on Petition of Israel Beach. Committee on Rev. Pensions. Dec. 22, 1831. Reports of Committees, No. 38, 22d Cong., 1st sess., Vol. I. Recommends that petitioner be allowed pension. [Washington, 1831] 1 p. M; R. 10327

---- Report on Petition of J. Elliott. Com. on Revolutionary Pensions. Dec. 20, 1831. Reports of Committees, No. 7, 22d Cong., 1st sess., Vol. I. Reports bill allowing pension to petitioner. [Washington, 1831] 1 p. M; R. 10328

---- Report on Petition of J. Kambler. Com. on Private Land Claims. Dec. 27, 1831. Reports of Committees, No. 70, 22d Cong., 1st sess., Vol. I. Recommends that request of petitioner for exchange of land title be granted; Bill reported. [Washinggon, 1831] 1 p. M; R. 10329

---- Report on Petition of J. P. & E. B. Pinney. Com. on Ways and Means. Feb. 18, 1831. House Reports, No. 88, 21st Cong., 2d sess. Recommends remission to petitioners of penalty exacted on goods imported; Bill reported. [Washington, 1831] 1 p. M; R. 10330

---- Report on Petition of J. P. & E. P. Penney. Com. on Ways and Means. Dec. 10, 1831. Reports of Committees, No. 4, 22d Cong., 1st sess., Vol. I. Reports bill refunding to petitioners excess of duties paid. [Washington, 1831] 1 p. M; R. 10331

---- Report on Petition of J. Rodgers. Committee on Indian Affairs. Dec. 20, 1831. Reports of Committees, No. 10, 22d Cong., 1st sess., Vol. I. Reports bill confirming land title of petitioner. [Washington, 1831] 1 p. M; R. 10332

---- Report on Petition of J. Vidal. Committee on Private Land Claims. Jan. 26, 1831. Senate Docs. No. 40, 21st Cong., 2d sess. Vol. I. Recommends that the legal representatives of Jacintha Vidal be allowed tract of land in Louisiana; Bill reported. [Washington, 1831] 3 p. M; R. 10333

---- Report on Petition of Jared

Cone. Com. on Revolutionary Pensions. Dec. 20, 1831. Reports of Committees, No. 5, 22d Cong., 1st sess., Vol. I. Reports bill allowing pension to petitioner. [Washington, 1831] 1 p. M; R. 10334

---- Report on Petition of Jellis A. Fonda. Committee on Rev. Pensions. Dec. 22, 1831. Reports of Committees, No. 35, 22d Cong., 1st sess., Vol. I. Recommends granting pension to petitioner; Bill reported. [Washington, 1831] 1 p. M; R. 10335

---- Report on Petition of John Fancher. Com. on Rev. Pensions. Dec. 23, 1831. Reports of Committees, No. 50, 22d Cong., 1st sess., Vol. I. Recommends allowance of pension to petitioner; Bill reported. [Washington, 1831] 1 p. M; R. 10336

---- Report on Petition of John Ferguson. Com. on Rev. Pensions. Dec. 22, 1831. Reports of Committees, No. 24, 22d Cong., 1st sess., Vol. I. Recommends allowance of pension to petitioner; Bill reported. [Washington, 1831] 1 p. M; R. 10337

---- Report on Petition of John H. Genther. Com. on Rev. Pensions. Dec. 23, 1831. Reports of Committees. No. 54, 22d Cong., 1st sess., Vol. I. States that petitioner furnishes sufficient evidence to prove his military service. [Washington, 1831] 1 p. M; R. 10338

---- Report on Petition of John H. Harrison. Judiciary Committee. Feb. 23, 1831. Senate Docs., No. 64, 21st Cong., 2d sess., Vol. II. Recommends that prayer of petitioner to be released from liability as surety of Francis Adams, collector of internal revenue, be granted; Bill for relief reported. [Washington, 1831] 2 p. M; R. 10339

---- Report on Petition of John H. Harrison. Judiciary Committee. Dec. 23, 1831. Senate Docs., No. 8, 22d Cong., 1st sess., Vol. I. Recommends that petitioner be relieved from judgment obtained against him as surety of Francis Adams, late collector of internal revenue; Bill reported. [Washington, 1831] 2 p. M; R. 10340

---- Report on Petition of John Heard. Committee on Ways and Means. Dec. 23, 1831. Reports of Committees, No. 58, 22d Cong., 1st sess., Vol. I. Recommends repayment to petitioner, as assignee of Amasa Davis, of moiety of penalty for violation of slave-trade laws. [Washington, 1831] 2 p. M; R. 10341

---- Report on Petition of John Slavens. Committee on Rev. Pensions. Dec. 21, 1831. Reports of Committees, No. 20, 22d Cong., 1st sess., Vol. I. Reports bill allowing pension to petitioner. [Washington, 1831] 1 p. M; R. 10342

---- Report on Petition of Jonathan Sizer. Com. on Rev. Pensions. Dec. 22, 1831. Reports of Committees, No. 26, 22d Cong., 1st sess., Vol. I. Recommends allowance of pension to petitioner; Bill reported. [Washington, 1831] 1 p. M; R. 10343

---- Report on Petition of Joseph Lyon. Committee on Rev. Pensions. Dec. 21, 1831. Reports of Committees, No. 17, 22d Cong. 1st sess., Vol. I. Reports bill allowing pension to petitioner. [Washington, 1831] 1 p. M; R. 10344

---- Report on Petition of Josiah H. Webb. Post-Office Committee. Dec. 28, 1831. Reports of Committees No. 77, 22d Cong., 1st sess., Vol. I. Recommends allowance of pension to petitioner on account of injuries received in carrying the mail; Bill reported. [Washington, 1831] 1 p. M; R. 10345

---- Report on Petition of Lester Morris. Com. on Revolutionary Pensions. Dec. 22, 1831. Reports of Committees, No. 23, 22d Cong., 1st sess., Vol. I. Recommends that name of petitioner be restored to pension roll; Bill reported. [Washington, 1831] 1 p. M; R. 10346

---- Report on Petition of Lewis Gilbert. Committee on Rev. Pensions. Dec. 22, 1831. Reports of Committees, No. 28, 22d Cong. 1st sess., Vol. I. Recommends allowance of pension to petitioner; Bill reported. [Washington, 1831] 1 p. M; R. 10347

---- Report on Petition of Lewis Marks. Committee on Commerce. Dec. 28, 1831. Reports of Committees, No. 80, 22d Cong., 1st sess., Vol. I. Recommends reimbursement to petitioner of portion of duty paid on books; Bill reported. [Washington, 1831] 1 p. M; R. 10348

---- Report on Petition of Martha Bailey. Committee on Claims. Feb. 18, 1831. House Reports, No. 91, 21st Cong., 2d sess. Supplemental report correcting certain errors in Report No. 87 on the same case. [Washington, 1831] 1 p. M; R. 10349

---- Report on Petition of Mechanics of Philadelphia. Select committee. Feb. 28, 1831. Senate Docs., No. 67, 21st Cong., 2d sess., Vol. II. Committee agrees with the general views of the petitioners respecting the rate of duties on iron, but is not inclined at present to do more than recommend the whole subject to the consideration of the next Congress. [Washington, 1831] 61 p. M; R. 10350

---- Report on Petition of P. Marigny. Com. on Private Land Claims. Dec. 20, 1831. Reports of Committees, No. 12, 22d Cong., 1st sess., Vol. I. Reports bill for confirmation of land title to petitioner. [Washington, 1831] 1 p. M; R. 10351

---- Report on Petition of Peter Buxton. Com. on Revolutionary Pensions. Dec. 20, 1831. Reports of Committees, No. 6, 22d Cong., 1st sess., Vol. I. Reports bill allowing pension to petitioner. [Washington, 1831] 1 p. M; R. 10352

---- Report on Petition of R. W. Steele. Com. on Private Land Claims. Dec. 27, 1831. Reports of Committees, No. 68, 22d Cong., 1st sess., Vol. I. Recommends that petitioner be granted bounty land; Bill reported. [Washington, 1831] 1 p. M; R. 10353

---- Report on Petition of Robert Dunn. Committee on Rev. Pensions. Dec. 21, 1831. Reports of Committees, No. 16, 22d Cong., 1st sess., Vol. I. Reports bill allowing pension to petitioner. [Washington, 1831] 1 p. M; R. 10354

---- Report on Petition of Roger Strong. Com. on Rev. Pensions. Dec. 28, 1831. Reports of Committees, No. 53, 22d Cong., 1st sess., Vol. I. Recommends allowance of pension to petitioner; Bill reported. [Washington,

1831] 1 p. M; R. 10355

---- Report on Petition of Samuel Patton. Committee on Rev. Pensions. Dec. 22, 1831. Reports of Committees, No. 27, 22d Cong., 1st sess., Vol. I. Recommends allowance of pension to petitioner. [Washington, 1831] 1 p. M; R. 10356

---- Report on Petition of Seth Dickinson. Committee on Rev. Pensions. Dec. 22, 1831. Reports of Committees, No. 42, 22d Cong., 1st sess., Vol. I. Recommends allowance of pension to petitioner; Bill reported. [Washington, 1831] 1 p. M; R. 10357

---- Report on Petition of Stephen Dunham. Committee on Rev. Pensions. Dec. 22, 1831. Reports of Committees, No. 41, 22d Cong., 1st sess., Vol. I. Recommends allowance of pension to petitioner; Bill reported. [Washington, 1831] 1 p. M; R. 10358

---- Report on Petition of Sureties of Amos Edwards. Judiciary Com. Dec. 27, 1831. Reports of Committees, No. 64, 22d Cong., 1st sess., Vol. I. Recommends partial release of petitioners from liability as sureties of Amos Edwards, collector of internal revenue; Bill reported. [Washington, 1831] 3 p. M; R. 10359

---- Report on Petition of Thomas Cross. Committee on Rev. Pensions. Dec. 22, 1831. Reports of Committees, No. 40, 22d Cong., 1st sess., Vol. I. Recommends allowance of pension to petitioner; Bill reported. [Washington, 1831] 1 p. M; R. 10360

---- Report on Petition of Thomas Park. Com. on Revolutionary Claims. Jan. 10, 1831. House Reports, No. 33, 21st Cong., 2d sess. Recommends compensation of petitioner for property taken by the British; Bill reported. [Washington, 1831] 2 p. M; R. 10361

---- Report on Petition of William Black. Com. on Revolutionary Pensions. Dec. 21, 1831. Reports of Committees, No. 22, 22d Cong., 1st sess., Vol. I. Recommends allowance of pension to petitioner; Bill reported. [Washington, 1831] 1 p. M; R. 10362

---- Report on Petition of William Grennell. Committee on Rev. Pensions. Dec. 21, 1831. Reports of Committees, No. 18, 22d Cong., 1st sess., Vol. I. Reports bill granting pension to petitioner. [Washington, 1831] 1 p. M; R. 10363

---- Report on Petion of William Headley. Com. on Rev. Pensions. Dec. 22, 1831. Reports of Committees, No. 25, 22d Cong., 1st sess., Vol. I. Recommends allowance of pension to petitioner; Bill reported. [Washington, 1831] 1 p. M; R. 10364

---- Report on Petition of William M. King. Committee on Public Lands. Dec. 30, 1831. Reports of Committees, No. 85, 22d Cong., 1st sess., Vol. I. Recommends that title of petitioner to land in Alabama be confirmed; Bill reported. [Washington, 1831] 2 p. M; R. 10365

---- Report on Petition of William Matheny. Committee on Rev. Pensions. Dec. 21, 1831. Reports of Committees, No. 19, 22d Cong., 1st sess., Vol. I. Reports bill allowing pension to petitioner. [Washington, 1831] 1 p. M; R. 10366

---- Report on Post-Office

Contracts. Postmaster-General W. T. Barry. Feb. 24, 1831. House Ex. Docs., No. 117, 21st Cong., 2d sess., Vol. IV. Statement of contracts made by the Post-Office Department during the year 1830 for transportation of the mail; Name of contractor; Route; Mode of conveyance; Price per annum. [Washington, 1831] 14 p. M; R. 10367

---- Report on Post-Office Department. Select committee. Mar. 3, 1831. Senate Docs., No. 73, 21st Cong., 2d sess., Vol. II. Statement relative to the distribution of labor; Clerks employed; Number of agents; Compensation of contractors; Incidental expenses of the Department for the four years ending June 30, 1830. [Washington, 1831] 95 p. M; R. 10368

---- Report on Present from Sultan of Turkey. Com. on Foreign Affairs. Mar. 1, 1831. House Reports, No. 107, 21st Cong., 2d sess. Recommends that the committee be discharged from the further consideration of the subject of the presentation of Arabian horses to the commissioned agent of the United States at Constantinople. [Washington, 1831] 3 p. M; R. 10369

---- Report on Printing the Laws and Treaties. Library Committee. Jan. 25, 1831. House Reports, No. 46, 21st Cong., 2d sess., Recommends adoption of resolution for printing a stereotype edition of the laws and treaties of the United States. [Washington, 1831] 2 p. M; R. 10370

---- Report on Production of Sugar. Sec. S. D. Ingham. Mar. 2, 1831. House Ex. Docs., No. 134, 21st Cong., 2d sess., Vol. IV. Statement of quantity of sugar manufactured in the United States, in the State of Louisiana; Average quantity of sugar produced to the acre; Quantity of land in Louisiana adapted to the cultivation of sugar. [Washington, 1831] 7 p. M; R. 10371

---- Report on Proposed National Road. Lieutenant-Colonel S. H. Long. Sept. 16, 1831. Ex. Docs., No. 169, 22d Cong., 1st sess., Vol. IV. Reconnaissance and survey of route for a national road from Portsmouth, Ohio, to Linville Mountain, North Carolina. [Washington, 1831] 32 p. M; R. 10372

---- Report on Public Documents. Sec. of Senate and Clerk of House. Dec. 29, 1831. House Ex. Docs., No. 35, 22nd Cong., 1st sess., Vol. II. Statement of proceedings under the act providing for the republication of public documents. [Washington, 1831] 5 p. M; R. 10373

---- Report on Public Lands. Commissioner Elijah Hayward. Feb. 8, 1831. Senate Docs., No. 51, 21st Cong., 2d sess., Vol. II. Estimates of quantity of surveyed public lands; Revenues derived from sale of public lands from the earliest period to June 30, 1830. [Washington, 1831] 3 p. M; R. 10374

---- Report on Public Lands. Sec. S. D. Ingham. Feb. 14, 1831. Senate Docs., No. 54, 21st Cong., 2d sess., Vol. II. Statement of lands acquired by the United States in satisfaction of debts; Location; Names of debtors; Sums allowed; Probable value of lands; Where situated. [Washington, 1831] 28 p. M; R. 10375

---- Report on Receipts and Expenditures. Sec. Louis McLane.

Dec. 7, 1831. House Ex. Docs. No. 3, 22d Cong., 1st sess., Vol. I. Statement of public revenues and expenditures; Public debt; Estimate of revenues and expenditures for the year 1832; Amount of American and foreign tonnage employed in foreign commerce of the United States. [Washington, 1831] 72 p. M; R. 10376

---- Report on Reduction of the Army. Secretary John H. Eaton. Jan. 11, 1831. House Ex. Docs. No. 61, 21st Cong., 2d sess. Vol. III. Relative to reduction of the number of officers in the Army; Reports that no necessity exists for any reduction or reorganization of officers of the line; Recommends reform in the Pay Department; That the office of surgeon-general be abolished; That the number of inspectors-general be reduced to one. [Washington, 1831] 63 p. M; R. 10377

---- Report on Rejected Pension Claims. Sec. John H. Eaton. Jan. 5, 1831. House Ex. Docs. No. 31, 21st Cong., 2d sess. Vol. II. Report on rejected applications for pension; Names, residences, and rank of persons whose claims have been rejected; Reasons for rejection; List of Revolutionary pensioners whose names have been stricken from the pension-list. [Washington, 1831] 84 p. M; R. 10378

---- Report on Relief of Francis Larche. Committee on Claims. Jan. 19, 1831. House Reports. No. 40, 21st Cong., 2d sess. Recommends that bill be rejected. [Washington, 1831] 1 p. M; R. 10379

---- Report on Relief of Garrison at Fort Delaware. Com. Military Affairs. Feb. 19, 1831. Senate Docs., No. 58, 21st Cong. 2d sess., Vol. II. Recommends that bill lie on the table. [Washington, 1831] 1 p. M; R. 10380

---- Report on Relief of Virginia Troops. Committee on Public Lands. Mar. 3, 1831. Reports of Committees, No. 2, 22d Cong., 1st sess., Vol. I. Adverse to passage of bill granting lands to troops of the Virginia State line for services in the Revolution. [Washington, 1831] 2 p. M; R. 10381

---- Report on Repairs to Fort Delaware. Secretary John H. Eaton. Feb. 21, 1831. House Ex. Docs. No. 110, 21st Cont., 2d sess., Vol. IV. Recommends appropriations for repairs of Fort Delaware. [Washington, 1831] 1 p. M; R. 10382

---- Report on River Improvements. Secretary J. H. Eaton. Feb. 23, 1831. House Ex. Docs. No. 118, 21st Cong., 2d sess. Vol. IV. Relative to reappropriation of balance of funds for improving the Pascagonia, Red, and Kennebec Rivers. [Washington, 1831] 1 p. M; R. 10383

---- Report on Sale of Public Lands. Sec. S. D. Ingham. Feb. 22, 1831. House Ex. Docs., No. 113, 21st Cong., 2d sess., Vol. IV. Transmitting copies of correspondence relative to sale of lands at New Orleans. [Washington, 1831] 9 p. M; R. 10384

---- Report on Steam Carriages. Printed by order of the House. Oct. 12, 1831. House Ex. Docs., No. 101, 22d Cong., 1st sess. Vol. III. Report on steam carriages by a select committee of the House of Commons, with the minutes of evidence and appendix. [Washington, 1831] 346 p. M; R. 10385

---- Report on Survey of

Connecticut River. Sec. J. H. Eaton. Feb. 28, 1831. House Ex. Docs., No. 121, 21st Cong., 2d sess., Vol. IV. Report of survey of the Connecticut River; Estimate of annual expense for continuing improvement; Expense of constructing canal from Hartford to Dodge Falls. [Washington, 1831] 39 p. M; R. 10386

---- Report on Survey of Wabash River. Sec. John H. Eaton. Feb. 2, 1831. House Ex. Docs., No. 82, 21st Cong., 2d sess., Vol. III. States that the report will be forwarded to the House as soon as practicable. [Washington, 1831] 1 p. M; R. 10387

---- Report on Survey of Wabash River. Sec. Lewis Cass. Dec. 15, 1831. Senate Docs., No. 21, 22d Cong., 1st sess., Vol. I. Report of surveys of Wabash River; Estimated expense of removal of obstructions to navigation. [Washington, 1831] 17 p. M; R. 10388

---- Report on Tennessee and Holston Rivers. Com. Internal Improvements. Feb. 5, 1831. House Reports, No. 64, 21st Cong., 2d sess. Recommends that a survey and estimates be made for the improvement of the navigation of said rivers. [Washington, 1831] 2 p. M; R. 10389

---- Report on the Alexandria Canal Company. Com. on Int. Improvements. Jan. 31, 1831. House Reports, No. 71, 21st Cong. 2d sess. Recommends national aid for construction of Alexandria Canal; Bill reported. [Washington, 1831] 22 p. M; R. 10390

---- Report on the Army. Secretary John H. Eaton. Feb. 7, 1831. House Ex. Docs., No. 92, 21st Cong., 2d sess., Vol. III. Statement showing number and rank of field and company officers of the Army now on duty; Number on furlough; Length of furlough. [Washington, 1831] 5 p. M; R. 10391

---- Report on the Army and Military Academy. Military Committee. Feb. 4, 1831. House Reports, No. 60, 21st Cong., 2d sess. Recommends that commissions in the Army be given to meritorious non-commissioned officers; Also a reduction of the number of cadets in the Military Academy; Bill reported. [Washington, 1831] 2 p. M; R. 10392

---- Report on the Consular System. Committee on Commerce. Feb. 16, 1831. Senate Docs., No. 57, 21st Cong., 2d sess., Vol. II. Recommends postponement of the subject until the next Congress. [Washington, 1831] 13 p. M; R. 10393

---- Report on the Corps of Engineers. Sec. John H. Eaton. Jan. 13, 1831. House Ex. Docs., No. 52, 21st Cong., 2d sess., Vol. III. Relative to the necessity for increasing the number of officers of the Corps of Military and Topographical Engineers. [Washington, 1831] 2 p. M; R. 10394

---- Report on the Corps of Engineers. Sec. J. H. Eaton. Jan. 20, 1831. House Ex. Docs., No. 60, 21st Cong., 2d sess., Vol. III. Recommends increase and reorganization of Topographical Engineer Corps. [Washington, 1831] 2 p. M; R. 10395

---- Report on the Eastern Mail. Postmaster-General W. T. Barry. Feb. 10, 1831. House Ex. Docs., No. 96, 21st Cong., 2d sess., Vol. III. Statement relative to causes of the irregularity in the arrival of the Eastern mail. [Washington, 1831] 1 p. M; R. 10396

---- Report on the Judicial System. Judiciary Committee. Jan. 24, 1831. House Reports, No. 43, 21st Cong., 2d sess. Recommended repeal of the twenty-fifth section of the act of September 4, 1789. [Washington, 1831] 20 p. M; R. 10397

---- Report on the Marine Corps. Sec. John Branch. Feb. 5, 1831. House Ex. Docs., No. 120, 21st Cong., 2d sess., Vol. IV. Statement giving the pay, rations, and emoluments of officers of the Marine Corps. [Washington, 1831] 4 p. M; R. 10398

---- Report on the Military Academy. Sec. John H. Eaton. Jan. 4, 1831. House Ex. Docs., No. 27, 21st Cong., 2d sess. Vol. I. Statement of the expenditures of the contingent fund of the Military Academy for the year 1830. [Washington, 1831] 5 p. M; R. 10399

---- Report on the Military Academy. Sec. J. H. Eaton. Jan. 28, 1831. House Ex. Docs., No. 76, 21st Cong., 2d sess., Vol. III. Statement showing number of officers and teachers at the Military Academy; Pay and emoluments of each. [Washington, 1831] 9 p. M; R. 10400

---- Report on the Mint. Sec. S. D. Ingham. Mar. 3, 1831. House Ex. Docs., No. 135, 21st Cong., 2d sess., Vol. IV. Balance of gold and silver in the Mint December 31, 1829; Amount deposited during the year 1830; Species of coin minted and paid out on account of deposits; Amount of copper purchased from the establishment of the Mint to December 31, 1830. [Washington, 1831] 7 p. M; R. 10401

---- Report on the Navy Pension Fund. Commissioners of the fund. Dec. 8, 1831. House Ex. Docs. No. 5, 22d Cong., 1st sess., Vol. I. Accounts of Navy hospital fund from February 26, 1811, to November 18, 1831; Accounts of Navy pension fund for the year 1831. [Washington, 1831] 14 p. M; R. 10402

---- Report on the Relief of Jonathan Crocker. Jan. 4, 1831. House Reports, No. 20, 21st Cong. 2d sess. Recommends passage of Senate bill allowing pension to Jonathan Crocker. [Washington, 1831] 1 p. M; R. 10403

---- Report on the Sinking Fund. The Commissioners. Feb. 7, 1831. House Ex. Docs., No. 91, 21st Cong., 2d sess., Vol. III. Statement of funds received and applied during the year 1830; Payment of interest and principal of public debt. [Washington, 1831] 8 p. M; R. 10404

---- Report on the Sugar-Cane. Sec. S. D. Ingham. Jan. 19, 1831. House Ex. Docs., No. 62, 21st Cong., 2d sess., Vol. III. Varieties of sugar-cane; Temperature in which seed is produced; Cultivation of sugar-cane and manufacture of sugar; Methods of refining sugar; average quantity of sugar raised from an acre. [Washington, 1831] 68 p. M; R. 10405

---- Report on the Tariff. Committee on Manufactures. Jan. 13, 1831. House Reports, No. 36, 21st Cong., 2d sess. Recommends that there be no change made in the present tariff. [Washington, 1831] 12 p. M; R. 10406

---- Report on Treasury Balances. Comptroller Joseph Anderson. Feb. 17, 1831. House Ex. Docs. No. 108, 21st Cong., 2d sess. Vol. IV. List of balances on the books of the revenue which have been due more than three years prior to September 30, 1830; Receivers of public lands; Collectors of internal revenue and direct taxes. [Washington, 1831] 17 p. M; R. 10407

---- Report on Treasury Balances. Comptroller Joseph Anderson. Dec. 7, 1831. House Ex. Docs., No. 6, 22d Cong., 1st sess., Vol. I. List of balances on books of the Treasury which have remained unsettled for more than three years prior to September 30, 1831. [Washington, 1831] 17 p. M; R. 10408

---- Report on Treasury Balances. Comptroller Joseph Anderson. Dec. 10, 1831. House Ex. Docs. No. 9, 22d Cong., 1st sess., Vol. I. Statement of balances unaccounted for on the books of the Third Auditor of the Treasury. [Washington, 1831] 98 p. M; R. 10409

---- Report on Unproductive Post-Routes. P. M. Gen. W. T. Barry. Feb. 24, 1831. House Ex. Docs., No. 116, 21st Cong., 2d sess., Vol. IV. List of unproductive post-routes; Amount paid for transportation of mail. [Washington, 1831] 12 p. M; R. 10410

---- Report on War Department Contracts. Secretary J. H. Eaton. Jan. 24, 1831. House Ex. Docs., No. 73, 21st Cong., 2d sess., Vol. III. Statement of contracts made by the War Department during the year 1830. [Washington, 1831] 66 p. M; R. 10411

---- Report on Weights and Measures. Secretary S. D. Ingham. Mar. 3, 1831. Senate Docs. No. 74, 21st Cong., 2d sess., Vol. II. Relative to comparison of weights and measures used in custom-houses. [Washington, 1831] 2 p. M; R. 10412

---- Reports of cases argued and determined in the Circuit court of the United States for the first circuit. Vol. V. 1831. Containing the cases determined in the districts of New Hampshire, Rhode Island, Massachusetts, and Maine, from the New Hampshire October term, 1827, to the Massachusetts October term, 1830. Both inclusive. Boston, Hilliard, Gray, Little & Wilkins, 1831. 597 p. KyLxT; L; M; MdUL; Nc-S; ODaL. 10413

---- Reports of committees of the House of Representatives, at the first session of the twenty-second congress, begun and held at the city of Washington, Dec. 9, 1831 and in the fifty-sixth year of the independence of the United States, in five vols. Washington, Pr. by Duff Green, 1831. 5 vols. G; O; PScr. 10414

---- Resolution concerning Duties on Imports. Senator Poindexter. Dec. 22, 1831. Senate Docs., No. 6, 22d Cong., 1st sess., Vol. I. That the Committee on Finance be instructed to inquire into the expediency of altering and fixing the rate of duties on imports; That the committee inquire into the expediency of giving effect to said system of duties June 30, 1832. [Washington, 1831] 1 p. M; R. 10415

---- Resolution disposing of certain copies of the Journal of the Convention for forming the present Constitution. Feb. 21, 1831. Mr. Robbins, from the Joint Committee on the Library of Congress, reported the following resolution; which was read and passed to a second reading. [Washington, 1831] 1 p. (S. 6) DNA. 10416

---- Resolution disposing of certain public documents printed by Congress. Feb. 21, 1831. Mr. Robbins, from the Joint Committee on the Library of Congress, reported the following resolution; which was read, and passed to a second reading. [Washington, 1831] 1 p. (S. 4) DNA. 10417

---- A resolution distributing certain copies of the secret journals of the old Congress. Feb. 21, 1831. Mr. Robbins, from the Joint Committee on the Library of Congress, reported the following resolution; which was read, and passed to a second reading. [Washington, 1831] 1 p. (S. 5) DNA. 10418

---- Resolution for Distribution of Surplus Revenue. Rep. Martin. Jan. 20, 1831. House Reports, Resolution No. 2, 21st Cong., 2d sess. That the distribution of the surplus revenue of the United States among the several States would be unjust and unconstitutional. [Washington, 1831] 1 p. M; R. 10419

---- Resolution for Printing Copies of Infantry Tactics. Rep. Thompson. Jan. 10, 1831. House Reports, Resolution No. 1, 21st Cong., 2d sess. That the Secretary of War be instructed to report what measures have been taken to carry into effect the act providing for printing and binding copies of infantry tactics. [Washington, 1831] 1 p. M; R. 10420

---- Resolution for Repair of Cumberland Road. Citizens of Pennsylvania. Jan. 24, 1831. House Ex. Docs., No. 78, 21st Cong., 2d sess., Vol. III. Asking Congress to appropriate a sufficient sum to put the Cumberland road in a state of complete repair. [Washington, 1831] 1 p. M; R. 10421

---- A resolution in relation to certain evidences to be admitted by the several Executive Departments, in the adjudication of all claims under any act of Congress of the United States. Jan. 21, 1831. Mr. Foot, from the Committee on Pensions, reported the following resolution; which was read, and passed to a second reading. [Washington, 1831] 1 p. (S. 2) DNA. 10422

---- Resolution relative to Manufactures. Mr. Baldwin. Dec. 22, 1831. Reports of Committees, Resolution No. 1, 22d Cong., 1st sess., Vol. V. That the Committee on Manufactures investigate and report on the comparative cost of production of iron, salt, woollen goods, etc., in the United States, and in foreign countries. [Washington, 1831] 1 p. M; R. 10423

---- Resolution relative to Roanoke Inlet. Legislature of North Carolina. Jan. 11, 1831. House Ex. Docs., No. 64, 21st Cong. 2d sess., Vol. III. That the Roanoke Inlet should be reopened by the General Government. [Washington, 1831] 1 p. M; R. 10424

---- Resolutions of the Legislature of the State of Delaware, approving the tariff of 1828; and that the construction of works of internal improvements by Congress is Constitutional and expedient. Feb. 28, 1831. Read, and laid upon the table. Washington, Pr. by Duff Green, 1831. R. 10425

---- Resolutions on Duties on Imports. Senator Benton. Feb. 26, 1831. Senate Docs., No. 66, 21st Cong., 2d sess., Vol. II. That Congress designate at the next session articles on which duties whall be abolished, and further regulate the collection of duties on imports. [Washington, 1831] 3 p. M; R. 10426

---- Resolutions on the Northeastern Boundary. Legislature of Maine. Portland, 1831. Library of Congress. Respecting the advice of the King of the Netherlands on the northeastern boundary. [Washington, 1831] M; R. 10427

---- Resolutions relative to Commerce. Senator Holmes. Dec. 20, 1831. Senate Docs., No. 5, 22d Cong., 1st sess., Vol. I. That the President communicate to the Senate a statement showing the number of vessels, cargoes, and the tonnage which have cleared from United States ports since October 5, 1830, and amount of American and foreign tonnage cleared for and entered from the Swedish and Danish West Indies since October 5, 1830. [Washington, 1831] 1 p. M; R. 10428

---- Resolutions relative to the Cumberland Road. Citizens of Pennsylvania. Jan. 5, 1831. House Ex. Docs., No. 44, 21st Cong., 2d sess., Vol. II. That State representation in Congress be requested to use their endeavors to procure an appropriation for construction and repair of Cumberland road and an appropriation for the western section of the Chesapeake and Ohio Canal. [Washington, 1831] 2 p. M; R. 10429

---- Resolutions relative to the Tariff. Legislature of Delaware. Feb. 21, 1831. House Ex. Docs., No. 137, 21st Cong., 2d sess., Vol. IV. That the tariff law of 1828 and the laws relating to internal improvements are constitutional and for the best interests of the country. [Washington, 1831] 2 p. M; R. 10430

---- Returns of Banks in the District of Columbia. Sec. S. D. Ingham. Feb. 3, 1831. House Ex. Docs., No. 84, 21st Cong., 2d sess., Vol. III. Copies of returns made by banks of the District of Columbia for the year 1830. Capital stock; Notes in circulation; Deposits. [Washington, 1831] 10 p. M; R. 10431

---- Revenue Laws. John Brice. Law Library of Congress. Laws of the United States relative to commercial subjects, brought down to March 3, 1831. [Washington, 1831] M; R. 10432

---- Rules...for the first circuit in and for the Rhode Island district both in law and equity... with a list of the officers and... attornies. Providence, 1831. 23 p. RHi; RPB; RPL. 10433

---- Sale of lands in the first district of Louisiana. Correspondence. Letter from the Secretary of the Treasury... Feb. 23, 1831. [Washington, 1831] 9 p. P. 10434

---- Senate Documents, Twenty-second Congress. First session. From Dec. 6, 1831. Vol. I. Docs, Nos. 2 to 55, incl.; Vol. II, Docs. Nos. 56 to 110, incl.; Vol. III, Docs. Nos. 111 to 182, incl. [Washington] Pr. by Duff Green, [1831-2] 3 vols. M; R. 10435

---- Senate Journal, Twenty-second Congress, First Session. Dec. 5, 1831. From December 5, 1831, to July 16, 1832. Vice-President, John C. Calhoun of South Carolina; President of the Senate pro tempore, Littleton W. Tazewell, of Virginia, elected July 9, 1832; Secretary of the Senate, Walter Lowrie, of Pennsylvania. Washington, Pr. by Duff Green, 1831. 697 p. M; R. 10436

---- A statement exhibiting the quantity of American and foreign tonnage entered into and departing from each district, during the year ending on the 30th September, 1830. Washington, Pr. by Duff Green, 1831. R. 10437

---- Statement of Contracts. Sec. S. D. Ingham. Feb. 9, 1831. House Ex. Docs., No. 94, 21st Cong., 2d sess., Vol. III. Contracts authorized by the Secretary of the Treasury during the year 1830; Light-houses; Marine hospitals; Miscellaneous. [Washington, 1831] 11 p. M; R. 10438

---- Statement of Drawback on Sugar. Sec. S. D. Ingham. Feb. 18, 1831. Senate Docs., No. 59, 21st Cong., 2d sess., Vol. II. Statement showing amount of drawback paid on refined sugar for the years 1825 to 1829, inclusive, and estimated amounts for the year 1830. [Washington, 1831] 3 p. M; R. 10439

---- Statement of Internal Duties. Sec. S. D. Ingham. Jan. 17, 1831. House Ex. Docs., No. 35, 21st Cong., 2d sess., Vol. II. Amount of internal duties which accrued during the years 1814 to 1817, inclusive; Amount paid by each State; Statement of direct taxes from 1814 to 1816, inclusive. [Washington, 1831] M; R. 10440

---- Statement of Navy Contracts. Sec. John Branch. Jan. 8, 1831. House Ex. Docs., No. 42, 21st Cong., 2d sess., Vol. II. Statement of contracts and purchases made by the Commissioners of the Navy during the year 1830. [Washington, 1831] 23 p. M; R. 10441

---- Statement of Post-Office Receipts. P. M. Gen. W. T. Barry. Feb. 26, 1831. House Ex. Docs. No. 119, 21st Cong., 2d sess., Vol.. IV. Statement of net amount of postage accruing at each post-office in the United States for the year ending March 31, 1830. [Washington, 1831] 88 p. M; R. 10442

---- Statement of the Commerce of each State and Territory, commencing 1st Oct., 1829, and ending 30th September, 1830. Washington, Pr. by Duff Green, 1831. R. 10443

---- Statement of War Department Appropriations. Sec. J. H. Eaton. Mar. 3, 1831. House Ex. Docs., No. 136, 21st Cong., 2d sess., Vol. IV. Appropriation for the War Department for the year 1830; Amount expended; Balance on hand December 31, 1830. [Washington, 1831] 16 p. M; R. 10444

---- Statements exhibiting the amount of internal duties which accrued in the United States in 1814-'15-'16-'17, prepared in obedience to a resolution of the House of Representatives of the 29th May, 1830. Washington, Pr. by Duff Green, 1831. MH; R. 10445

---- Statistical view of the Commerce of the United States, exhibiting the value of every description of imports from, and the value of every description of exports to each foreign country; also, the tonnage of American and foreign vessels, arriving from, and departing to, each foreign country, during the year ending on the 30th day of September, 1830. Washington, Pr. by Duff Green, 1831. R. 10446

---- Supplement to the Catalogue of the Library of Congress. December, 1831. [Washington, Pr. by Duff Green, 1831] 320 p. DLC; MH-L; MHi; ScU; WaU. 10447

---- Table of the post offices in

the United States, arranged by states and counties; as they were October 1, 1830; with a supplement, stating the offices established between the 1st October, 1830, and the first of April, 1831. Also, an index to the whole. By direction of the postmaster general. Washington, Pr. by D. Green, 1831. 359 p. MH; MiD; NcU; NjP; OCHP; PU; RPA. 10448

---- Transportation of Public Moneys. May 28, 1831. Library of the Interior Department. Circular in relation to inadequacy of allowance for transporting public moneys. [Washington, 1831] M; R. 10449

---- Treaty of amity, commerce, and navigation, between the United States of America and the United Mexican states. Concluded on the 5th of April, 1831. [Washington, 1831] 26 p. TxU. 10450

The United States' spelling book, with appropriate reading lessons: being a easy standard for spelling, reading and pronouncing the English language, according to the rules established by John Walker, in his critical and pronouncing dictionary. By sundry experienced teachers. Improved stereotyped ed. Pittsburgh, Luke Loomis [1831] 156 p. CoU. 10451

United States Temperance Almanac for 1832. New York, Van Valkenburgh & Crosley [1831] MWA; NN. 10452

The United States working man's almanack and farmer's and mechanick's every day book, 1831. Boston, 1831. RPB. 10453

The Universal comic songster;... containing all the popular songs of Barnes, Jefferson, Dibdin, Coleman, G. Dixon, Sloman and other eminent vocalists...New York, J. Lomax, 1831. 144 p. DLC; MH. 10454

Universal Letter Writer, and complete correspondent. Baltimore, Pr. by R. J. Matchett, 1831. PPeSchw. 10455

The Universalist expositor. Vol. I. H. Ballow, and H. Ballow, 2d. editors. Boston, Waitt & Dow, 1831. 2 vols. NCaS; Od. 10456

Universalists. General Convention.

Report of the committee to publish the constitution of the general convention of Universalists. Boston, Pr. at the Office of the Expositor, 1831. 12 p. MMeT; MMeT-Hi. 10457

Upham, Charles Wentworth, 1802-1875.

History of witchcraft in Salem, in 1692. Boston, 1831. MBL. 10458

---- Lectures on witchcraft, comprising a history of the delusion in Salem, in 1692. By Charles W. Upham... Boston, Carter, Hendee and Babcock, 1831. 280 p. CSt; CU; ICP; MA; P. 10459

Upham, Thomas Cogswell, 1799-1872.

Elements of mental philosophy, by Thomas C. Upham... Portland, S. Colman; Boston, Hilliard, Gray & Co., [etc.] 1831. 2 vols. DLC; Ia; In; MBC; MBL; MWiW; MiD; Nj. 10460

Upham, Timothy, 1783-1855, plaintiff.

Report of the trial, Timothy Upham vs. Hill & Barton, for an alleged libel, at the court of common pleas. Rockingham Co., Oct. term, 1830, Comp. from notes taken at the trial and the original papers in the case to which is added an appendix, containing the evidence ruled out by the court, and many interesting original papers not before published, Concord, Hill & Barton, 1831. 96, 24 p. DLC; KyDC; MH-L; NIC; Nh. 10461

Useful, Philip, (pseud.)
Philip Useful's Natural history of birds for amusement and instruction. Baltimore, Pub. by George McDowell and Son [1831?] 8 p. MB; MdHi. 10462

Utica, New York.
To the citizens of the village of Utica. Utica, Pr. by E. A. Maynard, 1831. 29 p. NN; Nut. 10463

Utica Gymnasium, Utica, N.Y.
Catalogue of the Utica Gymnasium. [Utica? Pr. by Hastings & Tracy, 1831?] 11 p. MB; MH. 10464

V

Vacations at home; In two parts. New Haven, Jeremy L. Cross, General agent of the Connecticut Sabbath School Union [Pr. by S. Babcock] 1831. 2 vols. MPeHi; NjR. 10465

Valpy, Francis Edward J.
Greek exercises;...the elements of grammar to the higher parts of syntax;...to which specimens of the Greek dialects, and the critical canons of Dawes and Porson are added. By Rev. F. E. J. Valpy, M.A. Rev. and rearr. from the Last London ed. by J. M. Cairns, M. A., ... New-York, G. & C. & H. Carvill, 1831. 236 p. DLC; NjP; OO; PV; ScNC. 10466

[Valpy, Richard], 1754-1836.
Delectus sententiarum graecarum, ad usum tironum accommodatus; cum notulis et lexico. Ed. americana 3. Prioribus emendatior. Bostoniae, sumptibus Hilliard, Gray, Little et Wilkins, 1831. 103 p. ICU; MB; MBAt; MH; OO; PPL. 10467

---- The elements of Greek grammar. By R. Valpy. 5th ed. New York, Collins & Co., 1831. 322 p. GMiluC; PReaA. 10468

---- ---- 7th American ed. Boston, Hilliard, Gray, Little & Wilkins, 1831. 270 p. ArCH; ICU; MoFloSS; OCl; PMA. 10469

[Vandewater, Robert J.]
The tourist, or Pocket manual for travellers on the Hudson River, the western canal, and stage road, to Niagara Falls. Comprising also the routes to Lebanon, Ballston, and Saratoga Springs. 2d ed., enl. and imp. New York, Ludwig & Tolefree, prs., 1831. 69 p. CU; DeWi; MnSM; NBu; NjR; OClWHi. 10470

[Varle, Charles]
Moral encyclopaedia, or Varle's self instructor, No. 3 - in literature, duties of life, and rules of good breeding. Interspersed with popular quotations, mottoes, maxims and adages in Latin and other languages, also with the French words generally met with in newspapers, and works of taste and fancy faithfully translated. New York, McElrath & Bangs, 1831. 301 p. CtMW; MNS; MdBS-P; NbU; ViAl. 10471

Vassalborough, Maine.
Memorial of inhabitants of Vassalborough, Maine. Jan. 3, 1831. [1831] 4 p. TxFwTCU. 10472

Velpeau, Alfred Armand Louis Marie, 1795-1867.
An elementary treatise on midwifery; or, Principles of tokology

and embryology; by Alfred A. L. M. Velpeau. Trans. from the French by Charles D. Meigs. Philadelphia, John Grigg, 1831. 584 p. ICJ; MdBJ; MeB; PU; RPM; TNV; VtU. 10473

---- Midwifery. Philadelphia, Pr. by James Kay, Jun. & co., 1831. 585 p. PPiAM. 10474

Vergilius Maro, Publius.
Bucolica, Georgica, et aeneis, accedunt clavis, metrica, notulae anglicae, et questiones. Boston, Hilliard, Gray, Little, 1831. 490 p. CtHT; NcW; PL. 10475

---- Publu Virgilu Maronis opera; or, the works of Virgil. With copious notes...3d Stereotyped ed. New York, White, Gallaher & White, 1831. 615 p. IAIS; IQC; MWA; MdCatS; NCatS. 10476

Virginia and North Carolina Almanack for 1832. By David Richardson. Richmond, Va., John Warrock [1831] MWA. 10477

Vermont.
Acts passed by the Legislature of the State of Vermont, at their October session, 1831. Pub. by authority. Middlebury, Pr. for the state by A. Colton, 1831. 126 p. Ia; Ky; MdBB; Mi-L; NNLI; Nb; Nj; Nv; R; TxU-L; W; CU-Law. 10478

---- Exposition of the system of instruction and discipline pursued in the University of Vermont. By the Faculty. [Drawn by Prof. Geo. W. Benedict] 2d ed. Burlington, Chauncey Goodrich, 1831. 32 p. CSmH; DLC; ICU; MHi; NNUT. 10479

---- Governor's speech. Gentlemen of the Council and Gentlemen of the House of Representatives no choice of a chief magistrate having been made by the people... Montpelier, Oct. 18, 1831. Tuttle. 10480

---- Journal of the General Assembly of the State of Vermont, at their session begun and holden at Montpelier, Washington County, on the 13th day of October, A.D. 1831. Woodstock, Pr. by Rufus Colton [1831] 215 p. Mi. 10481

---- University of Vermont.
Commencement. Order of exercises. [Burlington] Pr. by C. Goodrich, [1831] Broadside. VtU. 10482

Verplanck, Gulian Crommelin, 1786-1870.
A letter to Col. William Drayton, of South-Carolina, in assertion of the constitutional power of Congress to impose protecting duties. By Gulian C. Verplanck... New York, Pr. for E. Bliss, 1831. 31 p. Ct; DLC; MB; MHi; NjR; PHi; Vi. 10483

Verren, A.
Prieres publiques. By A. Verren. New York, T. & J. Swords, 1831. 464 p. GMilvC. 10484

Vesey, Francis.
English Chancery, reports, temp. Hardwicke, 1746-56. 1st Amer. from the last London ed. by Robt. Belt. Philadelphia, 1831. 2 vols. PPB. 10485

Vethake, Henry, 1792-1866.
An introductory lecture on political economy; delivered at Nassau-hall, January 31, 1831. By Prof. Vethake...Princeton, Pr. by W. D'Hart, 1831. 27 p. CtY; ICU; N; NN; NjP; P. 10486

Views in theology... New York, John P. Haven, American tract societies house, 1831. CSansS; IAIS; MPiB; NjR. 10487

The village pastor; or, The origin and progress of the American Bible Society. By the author of conversations and letters on the Sandwich Islands...Rev. by the publishing committee. Boston, T. B. Marvin for the Massachusetts Sabbath School Union, 1831. 124 p. DLC; ICP; MB; MH-AH; NNMr; OMC. 10488

The Vine-Stalk: and the history of Benjamin the Gardener. Providence, 1831. 16 p. RHI. 10489

Virginia.

Acts passed at a General Assembly of the Commonwealth of Virginia, begun and held at the capitol, in the city of Richmond, on Monday, the sixth day of December, in the year of our Lord one thousand eight hundred and thirty, and of the commonwealth the fifty-fifth. To which are prefixed the Declaration of Rights and the Constitution of Virginia. Richmond, Pr. by Thomas Ritchie, pr. to the Commonwealth, 1831. 358 p. IaU-L; Ky; MdHi; Mi-L; NNLI; Nj; Nv; W; WvW-L. 10490

---- Enactments relating to the constitution and government of the University of Virginia. ... Charlottesville, Pr. by Cary, Watson & co., 1831. 69 p. DLC; MH; PHi; ViU. 10491

---- Journal of the House of Delegates of the Commonwealth of Virginia... Richmond, Pr. by Thomas Ritchie, 1831. Ct; Vi. 10492

---- A list of lands and lots returned as delinquent in Frederick County, for the non-payment of taxes for 1820, and prior thereto, and which are redeemable on or before the 1st day of January, 1832... [Richmond, 1831] 1 p. WHi. 10493

---- A list of lands and lots returned as delinquent in Jefferson County, for the non-payment of taxes, for 1820, and prior thereto, and which are redeemable on or before the 1st day of January, 1832... [Richmond, 1831] [5] p. WHi. 10494

---- A list of lands and lots returned as delinquent, in Lee county, Va. Pr. by Samuel Shepherd and Co., Oct. 1831. 10 p. IaHi. 10495

---- A list of lands and lots returned as delinquent, in Monongahela County, Va., for the non-payment of taxes, for 1820, and prior thereto, and which are redeemable on or before the 1st day of January, 1832... [Richmond, 1831] WHi. 10496

---- A list of lands and lots returned as delinquent in Morgan County, for the non-payment of taxes for the year 1820, and which are redeemable on or before the 1st day of January, 1832 ... [Richmond, 1831] [4] p. WHi. 10497

---- A list of lands and lots returned as delinquent, in Rockbridge County, Va. for non-payment of taxes due for the year 1820, and prior thereto, and which are redeemable on or before the 1st day of January, 1832... [Richmond, 1831] WHi. 10498

---- Reports of cases (Leigh's) argued and determined in the court of appeals, and in the general court. Richmond, 1831 [-1854] vols. 1-12. IaDaGL. 10499

---- To the Senate and House of Representatives, in Congress, the memorial of the undersigned Colliers, in the county of Chesterfield, Virginia... [Richmond, S. Shepard & Co., 1831] 10 p. MH-BA. 10500

Virginia Society for the Promotion of Temperance.
Fourth annual meeting... with the amendment Constitution and annual report. Richmond, Off. of Religious Herald, 1831. PPPrHi. 10501

A vision, exhibiting the arraigning, trying and condemning of an unfaithful shepherd, before a spiritual court... By an acute observer. Chillicothe, J. Hough, 1831. 35 p. OClWHi. 10502

Volksfreund und Hagerstauner Calender auf des Jahr 1832. Hagerstown, Johann Gruber [1831?] 15 l. MWA; MdH; PHi. 10503

Volney, Constantin Françoise Charreboeuf, comte de, 1757-1820.
Ruins, or meditation on the revolution of empires. Trans. under the immediate inspection of the author from the 6th Paris ed. To which is added The law of nature, and a short biographical notice by Count Daru, also The controversy between Dr. Priestly and Volney. Boston, C. Gaylord, 1831. 216 p. MH; MSte; OMC; RPE. 10504

Voltaire, Francois Marie Arouet de, 1694-1778.
Historie de Charles XII, Roi De Suede. Par Voltaire. D'une Ed. Stereotype de Paris. New York, Collins & Co., 1831. 287 p. MB; MiU; NPla; OCl. 10505

---- The History of Charles the Twelfth, King of Sweden. A new trans., from the last Paris ed. Hartford, Silas Andrus, 1831. 276 p. IAIS; NLitf; NN; WvU. 10506

Vose, Richard Hampton, 1803-1864.
A poem delivered on the anniversary of the literary fraternity of Waterville College, July 26, 1831. Augusta, Eaton and Severance, 1831. 16 p. CSmH; DLC; MWA; MnH; PHi. 10507

W

Wade, John, 1788-1875.
Select proverbs of all nations: with notes and comments. A summary of ancient pastimes, holidays and customs; with an analysis of the ancients, and of the Fathers of the Church. The whole arranged on a new plan. Baltimore, B. Cram, 1831. 280 p. KyLo; MdBD; MdBP; MdHi; ViRut. 10508

Walker, George, 1772-1847.
The three Spaniards. A romance... New York, 1831. 2 vols. RPB. 10509

Walker, James, 1781-1861.
Report to the directors of the Liverpool and Manchester railway, on the comparative merits of locomotive and fixed engines, as a moving power. By James Walker... Observations on the comparative merits of locomotive and fixed engines, as applied to railways. By Robert Stephenson and Joseph Locke... An account of the Liverpool and Manchester railways. By Henry Booth... Philadelphia, Carey & Lea, 1831. 206 p. DLC; IC; LNL; MdBP; NjR; ViU. 10510

[Walker, James] 1794-1874.
Causes of the progress of liberal Christianity in New England. 3d ed. Boston, Gray & Bowen, 1831. 16 p. CBPac; ICMe; MB; MB-HP; MB-FA; MMeT; MWA. 10511

Walker, John, 1732-1807.
A critical pronouncing dictionary, and expositor of the English language. To which is annexed a

Key to the classical pronunciation of Greek, Latin, and Scripture proper names, &c. New-York, Collins and Hannay, 1831. FWpR; MH; NR; NSyHi; PPL. 10512

---- A Key to the classical pronunciation of Greek, Latin, and scripture proper names in which the words are accented and divided into syllables exactly as they ought to be pronounced, according to rules drawn from analogy and the best usage to which are added terminational vocabularies of Hebrew, Greek, and Latin proper names. By John Walker. Stereotyped by B. & J. Collins, New York. New York, Collins & Hannay, 1831. 103 p. MNBedf. 10513

Walker, Joseph.
A friendly letter to the Reverend Adam Wilson on the mode of baptism. By the author of the examination, etc. Norway [Me.] W. E. Goodnow, 1831. 36 p. MH; PPPrHi. 10514

Walker, Timothy, 1802-1856.
Elements of Geometry, with Practical applications for the use of schools. By T. Walker. 3d ed. imp. Boston, Richardson, Lord & Holbrook, 1831. 129 p. KWiU; MB; MH; OCHP; TxD-W; VtNofN. 10515

Walsh, Michael.
The mercantile arithmetic, adapted to the commerce of the United States, in its domestic and foreign relations: with an appendix, containing practical systems of mensuration, gauging and book-keeping. A new ed., stereotyped, rev., and enl. By Michael Walsh, A.M. Boston, Richardson, Lord & Holbrook, 1831. 336 p. LNH; MH; MeAu; NNC; NcU. 10516

Walsh, Robert, 1772-1852.
Notices of Brazil in 1828 and 1829... Boston, Richardson, Lord & Holbrook; New York, G. & C. & H. Carvill [etc., etc.] 1831. 2 vols. CSt; IaK; MDeeP; OCHP; TxU. 10517

Walton's Vermont register and farmer's almanac, for the year of our Lord, 1832. Astronomical calculations by Zadock Thompson, A.M. No. XV. Montpelier, Pr. by E. P. Walton, for J. S. Walton, [1831] 144 p. Ct; DLC; MHi; MWA; NhHi; OO. 10518

Wanostrocht, Nicholas, 1745-1812.
A grammar of the French language, with practical exercises. By N. Wanostrocht...11th Amer. from the last London ed. To which is added, a very comprehensive table of contents, and an alphabetical arrangement of the irregular verbs, with reference to the places where they are conjugated, with alterations, additions, and improvements; and a scheme for parsing. Also, a treatise on French versification, by M. De Wailly... Boston, Richardson, Lord & Holbrook, 1831. 447 p. TxU-T. 10519

---- Recueil choisi de traits historiques et de contes moraux: avec la signification des mots en anglois au bas de chaque page ...Par N. Wanostrocht...New York, Collins, 1831. 299 p. CtMW; KyBvu; MH; MdBM; MiDSH. 10520

Wansley, Thomas J., d. 1831, defendant.
Trial and sentence, of Thomas J. Wansley and Charles Gibbs, for murder and piracy on board the brig Vineyard. New York, Pr. by C. Brown, 1831. MHi. 10521

Wanzer, Ira.

A new and easy introduction to the mathematics: containing a system of theoretical and practical arithmetic... Designed for the use of schools, academies, and private learners. By Ira Wanzer. Danbury, Conn., W. & M. Yale, 1831. 396 p. LNH; NIC-A; NNC; OO. 10522

The Warbler, containing a collection of modern and popular songs. ...By an amateur. 3d ed. Baltimore, Pr. by Sands & Neilson, 1831. 224 p. MNF; RPB. 10523

Ward, Malthus A.
An address pronounced before the Massachusetts horiticultural society, in commemoration of its third annual festival, Sept. 21, 1831. [and proceedings of the society] By Malthus A. Ward... Boston, Pr. by J. T. & E. Buckingham, 1831. 56 p. CU; M; MHi; MWA; MW; PPL. 10524

Ward, Robert Plumer, 1765-1846.
De Vere or the Man of Independence. By the author of "Tremains." New York, J. & J. Harper, 1831. 2 vols. MB; MH; NjR; PU. 10525

[Warden, David Baillie] 1778-1845.
Bibliotheca Americana, being a choice collection of books relating to North and South America and the West Indies... Philadelphia, 1831. PPM. 10526

Ware, Henry, Jr., 1794-1843.
The duty of improvement. A new years' sermon. [Boston, 1831] 18 p. MH; MH-AH. 10527

---- Hints on extemporaneous preaching, by Henry Ware, jr., professor of pulpit eloquence and the pastoral care of Harvard College, 3d ed. Boston, [Pr. by James Loring] for Hilliard, Gray, Little & Wilkins, 1831. 98 p. CSansS; DLC; IAlS; LNH; MA; MWA; OMC; PPLT. 10528

---- On the formation of the Christian character. Addressed to those who are seeking to lead a religious life. Cambridge, Hilliard & Brown; Boston, Gray & Brown, 1831. 175 p. CtHC; IaU; MBC; MBevHi; RPB; Vt. 10529

---- ---- 2d ed. Cambridge, Hilliard & Brown [etc.] 1831. 176 p. GHi; McNc; MH; RPB. 10530

---- ---- 3d ed. Cambridge, Hilliard & Brown, booksellers to the University, 1831. 176 p. Ct; IaJ; KWiU; MB; MBedf; MH; MB-FA; OO; PMA; WHi. 10530

---- ---- 4th ed. Cambridge, 1831. MB. 10531

---- Three important questions answered relating to the Christian name... 6th ed. Boston, 1831. MB. 10532

Ware, John, 1795-1864.
Remarks on the History and Treatment of Delirium Tremens... By John Ware, M.D... Boston, Pr. by W. L. Lewis on N. Hale's Steam Power Press, 1831. 61 p. CSt-L; ICJ; MBAt; MH-AH; MH-M; MeB. 10533

Ware, William, 1797-1852.
The Antiquity and Revival of Unitarian Christianity. By Wm. Ware. No. 47. Pr. for The American Unitarian Association. Boston, Gray & Bowen; Boston, Pr. by I. R. Butts, 1831. 28 p. ICME; MB; MH; MHi; MNF; MN; MeB; N; PPAmP; RP. 10534

---- The Danger of Delay. 2d ed. 1st ser. No. 31. Pr. for the American Unitarian Association. Boston, Gray & Bowen, 1831. 28 p. CBPac; ICMe; MB-FA;

MB-HP; MH; MMeT-Hi; MeB; NUT. 10535

[Warner, Samuel]
Authentic and impartial narrative of the tragical scene which was witnessed in Southampton County (Virginia) on Monday the 22d of August last, when fifty-five of its inhabitants (mostly women and children) were unhumanly massacred by the blacks! Communicated by those who were eye witnesses of the bloody scene, and confirmed by the confessions of several of the blacks while under sentence of death. [New York Warner & West, 1831. 38 p. DLC; MB; NN; TxU; Vi. 10536

Warnes, Jose Quintana.
El Maestro de si mismo, o guia analitica para el estudio y facil comprension dela lengua inglesa compuesta de una selecta variedad de lecciones traducidas primeramente palabra por palabra al espanol, oespuis de la voz inglesa, y en seguida, la traduccion libre en ambos idiomas. Esta obra es la primera y unica en su especie. Philadelphia, T. T. Ash, 1831. 291 p. DLC; MiU. 10537

---- The Spanish expositor; or, An analytical guide to the study of the Spanish language; consisting of exercises of select and varied passages... By Jose Quintana Warnes... Philadelphia, T. T. Ash, 1831. 291 p. DLC; MAm; MPiB. 10538

---- Tratado sobre las Enfermedades que producen las lombrices en el cuerpo Humano y su método curativo. Obra interesente para los Hacendados y agricultores de las Islas de Cuba y Puerto Rico, y para los habitantes de la America setentrional y meridional. Trans. by John H. Coffin of Boston. Impreso, por Adam Waldie, cuidad de Philadelphia, Estado de Pensylvania, Ano de 1831. 190 p. MdBD; OClCF. 10539

Warrell's Gallery, Boston.
Catalogue of...Paintings, June 6, 1831. Boston [1831?] 16 p. MHi. 10540

[Warren, Samuel] 1807-1877.
...Affecting scenes; being passages from the diary of a physician... New York, J. & J. Harper, 1831. 2 vols. CtMW; FH; LU; MB; Vi. 10541

Warren's Northern Almanack. Ballston Spa., N.Y., A. & C. A. Warren, 1831. MWA. 10542

Washburn, Emory, 1800-1887.
A lecture, read before the Worcester lyceum, March 30th, 1831... Worcester [Mass.] Dorr & Howland, 1831. 22 p. Ct; M; MdBJ; MiD-B; NN; OClWHi; PHi. 10543

[Washington, George] pres., U.S., 1732-1799.
Washington's legacy: published for the Union and state rights party. Charleston, July 5, 1831. 15 p. MHi; ScCC; ScU. 10544

Washington, D.C.
Law of the corporation of the city of Washington; passed by the twenty-eighth council. Pr. by order of the council. Washington, Pr. by Way & Gideon, 1831. 66 p. In-SC; MdBB. 10545

Washington County Advocate. (James J. Brenton), Editor and proprietor. Vol. 1. Wickford, R.I., 1831. DNA-SD. 10546

[Waterbury, Jared Bell]
Advice to a young Christian on the importance of aiming at an elevated standard of piety.

By a village pastor. With an introductory essay by Rev. Dr. Alexander. 4th ed., rev. and corr. New York, G. & H. Carvill, 1831. 196 p. MH; OO; OSW; RNR. 10547

Waterhouse, Benjamin, 1754-1846.
An essay on Junius and his letters; embracing a sketch of the life and character of William Pitt, Earl of Chatham...By Benjamin Waterhouse... Boston, Gray & Bowen, 1831. 449 p. CU; ICN; MB; MH; PPA. 10548

Waterman, Thomas Glasby, 1788-1862.
The justice's manual: or, A summary of the powers and duties of justices of the peace, in the state of New York; containing a variety of practical forms, adapted to cases civil and criminal. 3d ed. Albany, 1831. 296 p. WHi. 10549

Watkins, Oliver.
A sketch of the life, trial, and execution of Oliver Watkins, who was hung at Brooklyn, (Conn.) on the 2d day of August 1831, for the murder of his wife... Norwich, 1831. 42 p. CtHT-W; MH-L; RPB. 10550

Watson, Richard, 1781-1833.
The life of the Rev. John Wesley, A.M., with notes and translations. Albany, W. Disturnell, 1831. 328 p. NFrf; WM. 10551

---- ---- 1st Amer. official ed. with translations and notes, by John Emory. New York, for the Methodist Episcopal Church, 1831. J. Emory and B. Waugh. 323 p. Ct; MdBE; NcU; OHi; OO; RPA; VtCoU. 10552

---- ---- ---- New York, Nelson & Phillips [1831] CLSU; GEU-T; IaLamG; KBB; NySU. 10553

---- Theological institutes; or a view of the evidences, doctrines, morals and institutions of Christianity. By Richard Watson. Stereotype ed., comp. in 1 vol. New York, Emory & B. Waugh for the Methodist Episcopal Church atthe Conference Office, Pr. by J. Collard, 1831. 454 p. ArBaA; IEG; LNB; NcD; TNP; ViU. 10554

[Watts, Isaac], 1674-1748
Aids to devotion, in three parts. Including Watts' Guide to prayer. Boston, Lincoln & Edmands; New York, J. Leavitt; Utica, Bennett & Bright; Philadelphia, Key & Meilke; Baltimore, Cushing & sons, 1831. 288 p. CtY; MBC; MH; NIC; PU. 10555

---- Divine songs, attempted in easy language, for the use of children. By I. Watts, D.D. ... Utica, William Williams, 1831. (72) p. PP. 10556

---- Hymns and spiritual songs. In three books. 1. Collected from the scriptures, 2. Composed on divine subjects. 3. Prepared for the Lord's supper... New York, White, Gallaher & White, 1831. DLC. 10557

---- The psalms and hymns of Dr. Watts, arranged by Dr. Rippon; with Dr. Rippon's selection, in one vol., with enl. and imp. indexes. Stereotyped by L. Johnson, Philadelphia. Philadelphia, David Clark, 1831. 906 p. ICBB; ICU; LNStM; NNUT; PCA; ScSpW. 10558

---- Psalms carefully suited to the Christian Worship in the United States of America. By Watts... New York, White, Gallaher and White, 1831. 583 p. MWHi; TxShA. 10559

---- The psalms of David, imitated in the language of the New Testament and applied to the Christian state and worship. By Isaac Watts, D.D. Albany, J. G. Shaw, 1831. 604 p. MB; Nil. 10560

---- ---- Boston, Charles Gaylord, 1831. 282 p. MNS. 10561

---- A rational defence of the Gospel. By Isaac Watts, D.D. With a preface by A. Alexander, D.D. New York, Jonathan Leavitt; Boston, Crocker & Brewster, 1831. 150 p. CtHC; MB; NCH; OBerB; PPL. 10562

---- A short view of the whole Scripture history with a continuation of the Jewish affairs from the Old Testament till the time of Christ... By Isaac Watts, D.D. Rev. and enl. and adapted to modern usage... A comparison of Scripture types and Anti-types; Prophecies and their Accomplishments [etc.] 1st Amer. from a new London ed. rev. and corr. New York, H. C. Sleight; Boston, Pierce & Parker; Philadelphia, Towar & Hogan, 1831. 506 p. CtMW; CU; MdBJ; MiU; NjR. 10563

Wayland, Francis, 1796-1865.
An address, delivered before the Providence Association for the promotion of temperance, Oct. 20, 1831. Also the First report of the State Temperance Society. Providence, Weeden & Knowles, 1831. 10, 20 p. CtHC; MB; MH; MH-AH; PPPrHi; RPB; WHi. 10564

---- ---- 2d ed. Providence, Weeden & Knowles, 1831. 16 p. MBC; MH; RPB; WHi. 10565

---- A Discourse on the philosophy of analogy, delivered before the Phi Beta Kappa Society of Rhode Island, September 7, 1831. By Francis Wayland, D.D. ...Boston, Hilliard, Gray, Little and Wilkins [Freeman & Bolles, prs.] 1831. 32 p. ICU; MAnP; MBAt; MBC; MH; MHi; MW; MeB; PCA. 10566

---- The moral efficacy of the doctrine of the atonement. A sermon, delivered on the evening of February 3, 1831, in the First Baptist Meeting House in Boston, at the installation of the Rev. William Hague. Boston, Pr. at the office of the New England Baptist Register, by True & Greene, [1831] 36 p. MA; MB; MBC; MH; MW; NHCS; PCC; RHi; RPB. 10567

---- The philosophy of analogy. Discourse deliv'd Sept. 7, 1831. Boston, Hilliard, Gray, Little & Wilkins, 1831. 32 p. CtHC. 10568

Wayne County, Michigan (Territory).
To the Republican citizens of Detroit, and of the county of Wayne. Whereas... Detroit, Jan. 28, 1831. [Detroit, 1831] Broadside. MiD-B. 10569

Webb, George James.
"Homeward bound!" A ballad composed for the piano forte by Geo. J. Webb. Boston 6. Bradlee [c 1831] 2 p. ViU. 10570

---- It is not that my lot is low. Boston, 1831. MB. 10571

---- Soft Glides the Sea, Bounding and Free. Cavatina. Words by Mrs Eliza Walker. Music by Geo. Jas. Webb. Boston, C. Bradlee [c 1831] 5 p. MBNEC. 10572

---- Star of the east, a sacred trio. By Geo. J. Webb. Words written by Bishop Heber. Boston, C. Bradlee [c 1831] 4 p.

MNF. 10573

---- Weep not for me! A sacred song. Words by Dale, Music by G. J. Webb. Boston, Bradlee, 1831. 2 p. MB; MH. 10574

Webb, Herbert Laws.
Practical guide to the testing of insulated wires and cables. New York, Van Nostrand, 1831. 118 p. PPFrankI. 10575

Webber, C. M. F.
The Sicillian knight. New York, 1831. MB. 10576

Webster, Benjamin Nottingham, 1797-1882.
...Highways & by-ways; a farce, in two acts... New York, Samuel French & son [etc.], [1831?] 35 p. OCl. 10577

Webster, Daniel.
Speeches of Chancellor Kent and... see Kent, James.

Webster, Noah, 1758-1843.
An American dictionary of the English language; exhibiting the origin, orthography, pronunciation, and definitions of words, by Noah Webster, LL.D. Abridged from the quarto edition of the author; to which are added, a synopsis of words differently pronounced by different orthoëpists; and Walker's Key to the classical pronuncation of Greek, Latin, and Scripture proper names. (7th ed.) New York, S. Converse [1831] 1011 p. CoD; InCW; MShM; OMC; WLAL. 10578

---- The American Spelling book, for the use of Schools in the United States. Rev. and imp. Cincinnati, N. & G. Guilford, Morgan & Sanxay and O. Farnsworth, 1831. 144 p. IaLau. 10579

---- ---- The rev. impression with the latest corr. Philadelphia, Kimber & Sharpless [1831?] ICP; MH. 10580

---- A dictionary of the English language: abridged from the American dictionary, for the use of primary schools and the counting house. By Noah Webster, LL.D. New York, White Gallaher & White, 1831. 532 p. CL; MStoc; ViLRM. 10581

---- The Elementary Primer, or First Lessons for children; being an introduction to the Elementary Spelling Book. [New York] M'Elrath & Bangs, 1831. DLC. 10582

---- The elementary spelling book; being an improvement on The American spelling book... Baltimore, Cushing and sons, 1831. 168 p. MdHi. 10583

---- ---- Boston, Richardson, Lord & Holbrook, 1831. OMC. 10584

---- ---- Burlington, Vt., Chauncey Goodrich; Wells River, White & Wilcox, 1831. 168 p. MH; VtMidSM. 10585

---- ---- New Haven, Durrie and Peck, 1831. 168 p. CtHT-W. 10586

---- An improved grammar of the English language. New Haven, H. Howe, 1831. 180 p. ICU; LLP; LHN; MA; MMS; MiU; WU. 10587

---- Rudiments of English grammar; being an abridgment of the improved grammar of the English language. By Noah Webster, LL.D. New-Haven, Durrie & Peck, 1831. 87 p. MH; NNC. 10588

Websters Calendar see Albany Almanack for 1832.

Weckliffe, pseud.
Peoples right defended see Winchester, Samuel Grover, 1805-1841.

Weems, Mason Locke, 1759-1825.
The life of Gen. Francis Marion, a celebrated partisan officer in the Revolutionary War, against the British and Tories in South Carolina and Georgia. M. L. Weems... Philadelphia, Joseph Allen, 1831. 252 p. OCl; PHi; PScrHi; PU. 10589

---- The life of George Washington; with curious anecdotes, equally honourable to himself, and exemplary to his young countrymen...embellished with six engravings. By M. L. Weems. Philadelphia, J. Allen, 1831. 228 p. ArSeH; MB; MdHi; PHi; TxU. 10590

The well-timed dream...by C. [J. A.] New York, 1831. 108 p. NN. 10591

Wells, J. H.
An essay, to defend and establish some of the principal points of the good old scripture doctrine, now almost universally suffering perversion, from the general prevalence of imperfect men's philosophy and vain deceit, after the tradition of men, after the rudiments of the world, and not after Christ. By J. H. Wells. Tuscaloosa, Pr. by Wiley, M'Guire & Henry, 1831. 32 p. AU. 10592

Wells, Seth Youngs.
A Brief illustration of the principles of war and peace see Ladd, William, 1778-1841.

Wells' annual register and almanac, for 1832. Calculated for the meridian of Detroit... Detroit, Pr. at the office of the Courier for S. Wells [1831] 36 p. MiD-B. 10593

Wesley, John, 1703-1791.
A collection of hymns, for the use of the Methodist Episcopal Church, principally from the collection of the Rev. John Wesley, M. A. ...Rev. and corr., with the titles of appropriate tunes, and the corresponding page of the Harmonists, prefixed to each hymn. New York, Pr. by James Collard, for J. Emory and B. Waugh and the Methodist Episcopal Church, at the Conference Office, 1831. 543 p. MMhHi; MsJMC; NCD; NNMHi; NjMD; PAnL. 10594

---- ---- 19th ed. New York, S. Hoyt & Co., for the use of the Methodist Episcopal Church in the U. S., 1831. 546 p. VtMiDSM. 10595

---- Explanatory notes upon the New Testament by John Wesley. 11th ed. New York, Carlton [1831] InGrD. 10596

---- Sermons on several occasions, by the Rev. John Wesley. New York, J. Emory & B. Waugh, 1831-1834. 2 vols. GMWa; InNomanC; OHi; PU; TxU. 10597

---- The works of the Rev. John Wesley, A. M...1st Amer. complete and standard ed., from the latest London ed., with the last corr. of the author...by John Emory. In 7 vols. New York, Pr. by J. Collard, for J. Emory and B. Waugh and the Methodist Episcopal Church, 1831. 7 vols. NcD; PLT; ViRu. 10598

West [George Montgomery]
Mr. W.'s claim to the Episcopate. From the Protestant

Episcopalian for March 1831. Philadelphia? 1831? OClWHi; PPL. 10599

West, John.
Sermon, preached at Salem, Mass., before the annual convention of the Protestant Episcopal church, in the Eastern Diocese. Sept. 28, 1831. By the Rev. John West... Windsor, Vt., Pr. by Simeon Ide, 1831. 21 p. MBD; MHi; MiD-B; N; RPB. 10600

West Boston Bridge
An act to incorporate the proprietors of West Boston Bridge with the subsequent acts relative to that institution and the bye-laws as amended, July 19, 1831. Boston, S. N. Dickinson, 1831. 32 p. MB; MH. 10601

West Chester Rail Road Company.
Act of incorporation. 1831. 8 p. PHi. 10602

The Western almanac for 1832... Batavia, N.Y., Sherman, Parker & Co. [1831] 12 l. CSmH. 10603

The Western farmer's almanac for the year of our Lord 1832: being bissextile, or leap year, and after the fourth of July, the 57th year of American independence. Calculated by the Rev. John Taylor. Pittsburgh, H. Holdship & Son, [1831] 36 p. MWA; PPi. 10604

Western Reserve University. Cleveland, Ohio.
Catalogue...Hudson, Cleveland, 1831-1856. Catalogues for 1830/31-1881/82 are the catalogues of Western Reserve college, the predecessor of Adelbert college. No catalogues were issued for the years 1852/53 and 1853/54. ICHi; MHi; OClW. 10605

---- Notes on the Library rules and regulations of Western Reserve college [1831-1850] 5 p. Typewritten extracts from the Laws of the Western Reserve college, 1833, 1838, 1845 and from the Catalogue of the Library, 1850, and from the rules of the Adelphic Society, 1831, arranged by G. F. Strong. OClW. 10606

Western Theological Seminary. Allegheny, Pa.
An appeal in behalf of the Western Theological Seminary, 1831. Pittsburgh, Stewart, 1831. PPPrHi. 6 p. 10607

Westwood, John see Rennie, James, 1787-1867.

Weyer, A.
The family physician, or Poor man's friend, and married lady's companion: containing a great variety of valuable medical recipes, designed to assist heads of families, travellers, and seafaring people in curing diseases ...by A. Weyer. St. Clairsville, O., Pr. by H. J. Howard, for the author, 1831. 216 p. DLC; IEN-M; In; OMC. 10608

Whately, Richard, Abp. of Dublin, 1787-1863.
Essays on some of the difficulties in the writings of Paul, and in other parts of the New Testament. By Richard Whately. 1st Amer. ed. New York, Pr. at the Protestant Episcopal Press, 1831. 204 p. CtMW; ICU; MdBD; NcU; PPLT; ScCMu. 10609

Wheaton, Henry, 1785-1848.
An abridgment of the law of nisi prius. With notes and references to the decisions of the courts of this country. 4th American ed., from the 7th London ed. New Haven, E. F. Backhus, 1831. 2 vols. Ky; MD; MSU;

MWC; PPR. 10610

---- History of the Northmen, or Danes and Normans, from the earliest times to the Conquest of England by William of Normandy. By Henry Wheaton. Philadelphia, Carey & Lea, 1831. 367 p. GEU; MW; NbU; OCY; RNR; ScU; VtU; WHi. 10611

Wheeler, Daniel.
Address to professing Christians. York [Pa.] 1831. PSC-Hi. 10612

Wheeler, Ulysses M.
A discourse delivered before the annual convention, of the Protestant Episcopal Church in the Diocese of Mississippi, on the fourth day of May 1831, in Trinity Church, Natchez: By the Rev. U. M. Wheeler, A. B. Pub. by request of the convention. Pr. by Andrew Marschalk, 1831. 14 p. MB; Ms-Ar. 10613

Whelphley, Samuel, 1766-1817.
A compend of history, from the earliest times; comprehending a general view of the present state of the world with respect to civilization, religion, and government; and a brief dissertation on the importance of historical knowledge. By Samuel Whelpley... 10th ed., with corr. and important additions and imp. By Rev. Joseph Emerson. Boston, Richardson & Lord, 1831. 2 vols. in 1. MB; MH; NBU; NjR; OC; OClW. 10614

Whig against Tory: or, The military adventures of a shoemaker. A tale of the revolution. For children. New Haven, A. H. Maltby, 1831. 104 p. DLC; MNF; MiD-B; MiK; NN. 10615

Whitcomb, Samuel, 1793-1879.
An address before the working men's society of Dedham... September 7, 1831. By Samuel Whitcomb, Jr... Dedham, Mass., L. Powers, 1831. 24 p. ICN; MH; MHi; MeHi; N; PHi. 10616

White, Edward Douglas, 1795-1847.
Speech of E. D. White, of Louisiana, delivered in the House of Representatives, of the United States, February 1831, on a resolution proposing the reduction of the duty on sugar. Washington, National journal, 1831. 24 p. ICU; MH; NjR; OClWHi; PHi; ScCC; TxU; WHi. 10617

White, [E(lihu)?]
Specimen of modern and light face printing types and ornaments, cast at the Thames-Street Letter Foundry of E. White. New York, 1831. NN. 10618

White, Henry Kirke, 1785-1806.
The complete works of Henry Kirke White, of Nottingham... With an account of his life. By Robert Southey... Boston, N. H. Whitaker, 1831. ICU; MH; Nh; OCl; RPB. 10619

White, Joseph M., 1781-1839, supposed author.
The Presidency. Political essays subscribed to An Old Man; directed against the re-election of General Jackson. By J. M. White? [Baltimore? 1831] 45 p. MB; MBAt; MdHi; DLC; NcU. 10620

---- Substance of an Argument, in the Supreme Court of the United States, in the Cases of Colin Mitchell and others versus the United States and F. M. Arredondo and others versus the same. By one of the Counsel for the Petitioners. Washington, Duff Green, 1831. 75 p. 10621

White, William, 1748-1836.

An Episcopal charge, on the sustaining of the unity of the church, in contrariety to disorder, disunion, and division. By the Rev. William White, D.D. Philadelphia, Jesper Harding, 1831. 20 p. MBD; MHi; MdBD; NGH; NjR; PHi. 10622

---- A sermon for the settling of faith, for the sustaining of hope, and for the excitement of charity... New York, Protestant Episcopal press, 1831. 23 p. CtHT; InID; MdB; NjR; PHi; RPB. 10623

Whitecross, John

The pleasing expositor; or, anecdotes illustrative of select passages of the New Testament. By John Whitecross. New-York, Jonathan Leavitt; Boston, Crocker & Brewater [Pr. by John T. West & co.] 1831. 288 p. CtHC; GMM; IEG; MBev; MiU. 10624

Whitehead, John Crawford.

Five pieces, viz. Modern mythology; or The gods universally worshipped in the present day. On the condition of mankind in the world, and the spiritual birth. On the state of truth in the world. Terrible mistakes in religion. What is it to be a servant of Christ? or What is natural and heathenish religion? Charleston, S.C., 1831. 32 p. N. 10625

Whitehouse, Henry John.

An address delivered before the Englossian and Alpha Phi Delta Societies of Geneva College, at the annual commencement of that institution, August 3, 1831. By Henry John Whitehouse, A.M. Rector of St. Luke's Church, Rochester. Rochester, Pr. by Hoyt, Poster & Co., 1831. 32 p. CSmH; MH; NCanHi; NGH; NN; PPL. 10626

Whiting, Henry, 1788-1851.

An address to the public, on the Importance of Restoring Health to the Sick, by H. Whiting. New York, D. Murphy, 1831. 14 p. NN. 10627

---- A discourse on the anniversary of the Historical Society of Michigan, June, 1831. Detroit, 1831. 40 p. DLC; OClWHi; PHi. 10628

---- Sannillac, a poem by Henry Whiting. With notes, by Lewis Cass and Henry R. Schoolcraft, esqs. Boston, Carter & Babcock, 1831. 155 p. DLC; ICN; MB; NN; WHi. 10629

Whiting, Isaac N.

A catalogue of valuable books, for sale by Isaac N. Whiting, at his new book store...Columbus. Columbus, E. Glover, 1831. 40 p. OClWHi. 10630

Whitman, Bernard, 1796-1834.

An answer to Eliphalet Pearson's letter to The Candid: by Bernard Whitman. Boston, Christian Register Office, 1831. 32 p. MB; MBAU; MBC; MWA. 10631

---- A letter to an orthodox minister, on revivals of religion. By Bernard Whitman. Boston, Gray & Bowen, 1831. 64 p. M; MB; MBAU; MBAt; MBC; MH-AH; MNF; MWA; NNUT; NjR; OO; PPAmP; PPPrHi. 10632

---- On Christian Salvation. 1st Series. No. 33. 3d ed. American Unitarian Association. Boston, Gray & Bowen, 1831. 44 p. CBPSR; MB-HP; MH; MMeT-Hi; MeB; MeBat. 10633

---- A Reply to the Review of Whitman's Letters to Professor Stuart, in the "Spirit of the Pilgrims," for March 1831. By Bernard Whitman. Boston, Gray and

Bowen, 1831. 84 p. M; MA; MHi; MeBat; NjR; OO; PHi. 10634

---- Two Letters to the Rev. Moses Stuart on the subject of religious liberty... Bernard Whitman. 2d ed. Boston, Gray & Bowen, 1831. 162 p. Ct; MHi; Nh; NjR; OClW; PPM. 10635

Whittemore, Benjamin.
Review of Rev. J. H. Fairchild's sermon on the deity of Jesus Christ. By Benjamin Whittemore... Boston, B. B. Mussey and Waitt & Dow, 1831. 32 p. MBUPH; MMeT; MMeT-Hi. 10636

Whittemore, Thomas, 1800-1861.
100 arguments in favor of Universalism. By Thomas Whittemore. Boston, Pub. at the Trumpet Office, 1831. 17 p. MMeT-Hi; MWA. 10637

---- A sermon, on the parable of the rich man and Lazarus, by Thomas Whittemore. 4th ed. Boston, Pr. by G. W. Bazin, Trumpet office, 1831. 20 p. MH; MMeT; MMeT-Hi; MWA; NNG; PPPrHi. 10638

---- A sermon, on the parable of the sheep and goats. By Thomas Whittemore. 2d ed. Boston, Pr. by G. W. Bazin, Trumpet Office, 1831. 20 p. MB; MMeT; MMeT-Hi; MWA; PPPrHi. 10639

Whittier, John Greenleaf, 1807-1892.
Legends of New-England... Hartford, Hanmer & Phelps, etc. 1831. 142 p. CSt; ICU; MH; MNB; NBu; NN; RNHi; ViU. 10640

Whittingham, W. R.
Standard works adapted to the use of the Protestant Episcopal Church in the United States. New York, New York Protestant Episcopal Press at their bldgs, 1831. 5 vols. InID; KyLoP; MnHi; MdBD; NNS. 10641

Whittlesey, Frederick.
An oration delivered in Venice, the 4th of July, 1831; it being the fifty-fifth anniversary of the independence of the United States. By Frederick Whittlesey. Auburn, Pr. by T. M. Skinner, 1831. 16 p. NN. 10642

[Whitty, (Mrs.) E.]
A mother's journal, during the last illness of her daughter, Sarah Chrisman. Revised by the committee of publication of the American Sunday School Union. Philadelphia, American Sunday School Union, 1831. 156 p. NBatHL. 10643

Wickliffe, Robert, 1775-1859.
Speech of Robert Wickliffe, in the Senate of Kentucky, on a bill to repeal an act of the General Assembly of the state of Kentucky, entitled: "An act to regulate civil proceedings against certain communities having property in common." [Lebanon, Ohio, 1831] (16) p. CSmH; NN; OCHP; OClWHi. 10644

Wilberforce, William, 1759-1833.
A practical view of the prevailing religious system of professed Christians, in the higher and middle classes, contrasted with real Christianity, By Wm. Wilberforce, esq. From a late London ed. New York, American Tract Society [183-?] 10645

Wilbur, Hervey, 1787-1852.
Elements of astronomy, descriptive and physical; in which the general phenomena of the heavenly bodies and the theory of the tides are familiarly explained... The work is designed to facilitate the study of a science peculiarly useful, interest-

ing, and sublime...2d ed., with an appendix of problems on the globes and useful tables. New-Haven, Durrie & Peck, 1831. 144 p. Ct; MB; MBC; MeBat; NNT-C. 10646

Wilkins, John H.
Elements of astronomy, illustrated with plates for the use of schools and academies, with questions. By John H. Wilkins, A.M. Stereotype ed. Boston, Hilliard, Gray, Little & Wilkins, 1831 [c1832] 152 p. CtHWatk; ICU; MH; NbOM; NjR; PPM. 10647

Wilkins, William, 1779-1865.
An oration, by the Hon. William Wilkins, delivered before the Jackson Republican citizens of Allegheny county, assembled at Stewart's island, on the 4th of July, 1831, the 55th anniversary of American independence... [Pittsburgh] L. S. Johns [1831] 12 p. DLC. 10648

Wilks, Mark.
Memoir of Clementine Cuvier, daughter of Baron Cuvier, with reflections, by Rev. John Angell James... New York, The American Tract Society, [183-?] 10649

Willard, Mrs. Emma (Hart), 1787-1870.
Abridgement of the history of the United States; or, republic of America. Accompanied with maps. By Emma Willard... New York, White, Gallaher, and White, 1831. 360 p. DLC; MB; NN; OClWHi. 10650

---- Ancient geography, as connected with chronology, and preparatory to the study of ancient history; accompanied with an atlas. By Emma Willard.... Compiled chiefly from D'Anville, Adam, Lavoisne, Malte Brun, and other standard works. To which are added problems on the globes, and rules for the construction of maps. To accompany the modern geography by William C. Woodbridge. 4th ed., imp. Hartford, O. D. Cooke & co., 1831. 96 p. CU; IHi; TxU. 10651

---- The fulfillment of a promise; by which poems, by Emma Willard are published, and affectionately inscribed to her past and present pupils. New York, White, Gallaher & White, 1831. 124 p. MH; NBu; NN; NTEW; TxU. 10652

---- Geography for beginners... Hartford, O. D. Cooke & Co., 1831. 123 p. ScU. 10653

---- History of the United States, or Republic of America: exhibited in connexion with its chronology and progressive geography, by means of a series of maps: the first of which shows the country as inhabited by various tribes of Indians at the time of its discovery; and the remainder, its state at different subsequent epochs; so arranged as to associate the principal events of the history and their dates with the places in which they occurred; arranged on the plan of teaching history adopted in Troy Female Seminary, designed for schools and private libraries. 4th ed., rev. and corr. By Emma Willard, principal of Troy Female Seminary. New-York, White, Gallaher, & White, 1831. 424 p. CtMW; FU; GEU; ICN; MBAt; MoSW; NjR; OCl; ScDue. 10654

---- Poems. 1st ed. New York, 1831. 124 p. MB. 10655

Willard, Samuel, 1776-1859.
Rhetoric or the principles of elocution. Boston, 1831. MB. 10656

---- Secondary lessons and the improved reader; intended as a sequel to the Franklin primer. By a friend of youth. 15th ed. 1831. 186 p. MH; MPiB. 10657

---- ---- 16th ed. Worcester, Dork & Howland, 1831. 186 p. CSt; MDeeP; MH; NNT-C. 10658

---- Valedictory discourse, preached to the First Church and Society in Deerfield, Mass. By Samuel Willard. 2d ed. Boston, Leonard C. Bowles, 1831. 23 p. Ct; ICN; ICU; MBAt; MHi; MWA; NNG; RPB; WHi. 10659

Willem II, King of the Netherlands.

Decision in regard to the disputed point of boundry between the United States and Great Britain. Dated at the Hague, January 10, 1831. With the protest of the American minister. [Washington, 1831?] 16 p. MB; MH; MoS; NN; RPB. 10660

Willett, Wm. Marinus, 1803-1895.

A narrative of the military actions of Colonel Marinus Willett, taken chiefly from his own manuscript. Prepared by his son William M. Willett. New-York, G. & C. & H. Carvill, 1831. 162 p. ICU; MDeeP; MiD-B; NjP; OCl; OFH; PHi; ViU. 10661

Willetts, Jacob, 1785-1860.

Easy grammar of geography. By Jacob Willetts. 13th ed. Poughkeepsie, Paraclete Potter, 1831. 197 p. MH; NP. 10662

---- Scholar's arithmetic. By Jacob Willetts. 4th ed. Poughkeepsie, Paraclete Potter, 1831. 191 p. NP. 10663

William, Ara.

A universal vocabulary of proper names, ancient and modern; together with classes of people, religious, national and philosophical; and titles ecclesiastical and civil among Christians, Jews, Mohametans and Pagans. By Ara Williams. Cincinnati, E. Denning, 1831. 536 p. IC; KyLxT; LNH; MoS; OC; WHi. 10664

Williams, Edwin.

The New-York annual register for the year of our Lord 1831... by Edwin Williams. New-York, Pr. by J. Seymour, for Jonathan Leavitt and Collins & Hannay, 1831. 356, 14 p. MoU; NNMuCN; NSY. 10665

Williams, John, 1792-1858.

The life and actions of Alexander the Great. New York, Harper, 1831. 351 p. ICEM; MH; OM; PP; ViL. 10666

Williams, Samuel, 1743-1817.

A history of the American revolution. Intended as a reading book for schools. 12th stereotyped ed. New Haven, W. Storer, 1831. 204 p. MH. 10667

---- ---- 13th ed. New Haven, W. Storer, jun., 1831. 204 p. Ct; ICU; MH; MiD-B; NGlf. 10668

Williams, William R.

Lectures on the Lord's Prayer. By Wm. R. Williams. New York, Anson D. F. Randolph & Co., [1831] 241 p. PLT. 10669

Williams College.

Alumni register. 1831-. Williamstown, Mass., [1831] PU. 10670

Willis, Nathaniel Parker, 1806-1867.

Poem delivered before the society of United Brothers, at Brown University on the day preceding commencement, September 6, 1831. With other poems. By N. P. Willis. New York, J. & J. Harper, 1831. DLC; GEU; ICU;

MB; NBuG; PU; TxU; WMa. 10671

Willis, William, 1794-1870.
Collections of the Maine Historical Society. Vol. 1. Portland, Day, Frazer & Co, 1831. 566 p. NSy. 10672

---- The history of Portland, from its first settlement, with notices of the neighboring towns and of changes of government in Maine. In two parts. From 1700-1833, Part 1. Portland, Day, Frazer & Co., 1831. 243 p. ICU; KHi; MdBP; OFH; PHi; RP. 10673

Willison, John, 1680-1750.
The young communicants catechism. With questions and answers for young converts by Rev. Ashbel Green, 1831. 72 p. PPPrHi; RPB. 10674

Willson [Estevan Julian].
Documents relating to Grants of Lands, made to Don Estevan Julian Wilson, and Don Richard Exter, in Texas. New-York, Pr. by Ludwig & Tolefree, 1831. 48 p. NN. 10675

Willson, James Renwick, 1780-1853.
The vow: a sermon, preached in Newburgh, April 10, 1831, on the evening after the dispensation of the Lord's Supper. By James R. Willson, D.D. pastor of the Reformed Presbyterian church, Albany. Pub. by request. Newburgh, Pr. by Charles U. Cushman, office of the Telegraph, 1831. 39 p. N; PPPrHi. 10676

Wilson, Alexander, 1766-1813.
American Ornithology; or, The natural history of the birds of the United States. Illustrated ... By Alexander Wilson and Charles Lucion Bonaparte. Popular ed. Philadelphia, Porter and Oates, 1831. 2 vols. MsSC 10677

Wilson, Daniel, 1778-1858.
Analysis of Religion Criticism of Butler. Boston, J. Loring, 1831. KyDC. 10678

---- The divine authority and perpetual obligation of the Lord's day, asserted in seven sermons, delivered at the parish church of St. Mary. Islington... 1st Amer. ed. with a recommendatory preface by Rev. L. Woods... Boston, Crocker & Brewster; New York, J. Leavitt, 1831. 212 p. ICP; MB; MoS; OMC; PU; RP. 10679

[Wilson, John] 1785-1854.
The notes Ambrosianae of "Blackwood." 1831? 4 vols. 10680

Wilson, [Joseph].
The Devil Turned Doctor. A poem. By Joseph Wilson. New-York, Pr. by Robert Nesbit, 1831. 12 p. MB; NN. 10681

Wilson, Joshua Lacy, 1774-1846.
Four propositions sustained against the claims of the American home missionary society... Cincinnati, Pr. by Robinson & Fairbank, for the author, 1831. 19 p. CSmH; GDecCT; MH; NCH; PLT; WHi. 10682

---- ---- New York, 1831. 14 p. ICU; MBC; NjR; PPPrHi. 10683

---- ---- Philadelphia, Pr. by Russell & Martien, for Wm. Moorhead, 1831. 16 p. NNUT; PHi; PPM; PPPrHi; RPB; TxH. 10684

Wilson, Thomas.
A brief and plain introduction for the better understanding of the Lord's Supper, with the necessary preparation; for the benefit of young communicants, and of such as have not well considered this holy ordinance. By the late Right Rev. Thomas Wilson, D.D., bishop of Sodor and Man. Auburn,

(N.Y.), Pr. at the C.K. Society's Press, by Philo B. Barnum, 1831. 56 p. NAuCM; NAuHi; NGH. 10685

Winchester, Elhanan, 1751-1797.
The Universal Restoration exhibited in Four Dialogues between a Minister and his Friend...by Elhanan Winchester. Boston, Benjamin B. Muzzey, 1831. 301 p. ICP; IaMP; MeBat; NhPet; ViSwc. 10686

Winchester, Samuel Gover, 1805-1841.
An examination of the Romish principle of withholding the Scriptures from the laity, together with a discussion of some other points in the Romis controversy. By Rev. S. G. Winchester...To which is appended A discourse on transubstantiation, by...John Tillotson...Philadelphia, Wm. F. Geddes, 1831. 228 p. NNUT; PWW. 10687

---- (Pseud. Weckliffe).
Peoples right defended, being an examination of the Romish principles of withholding the Scriptures from the laity, together with a discussion of some other points in the Romish controversy to which is appended a Discourse on transubstantiation, by John Tillotson... Philadelphia, W. F. Geddes, 1831. 228 p. ICP; MB; NjP; ScU; ViRut. 10688

Windship, Martha.
Thoughts on Teaching. By M. Windship. Boston, Pr. by J. Howe for, Merchants Row 1831. 16 p. MH; MWA. 10689

Wirt, Elizabeth Washington Gamble.
Flora's dictionary. By Mrs. Elizabeth Washington Gamble Wirt... Baltimore, Fielding Lucas, jun; [1831] 280 p. LNH; NjN; NjR; PP. 10690

Wirt, William, 1772-1834.
Anti-Masonic pamphlets No. 7 Hon. William Wirt's letter accepting the Anti-Masonic nomination for President of the United States. Baltimore, 28th September, 1831 [Baltimore, 1831] 80 p. PPFM. 10691

---- The letters of the British spy. 9th ed. with the last corr. of the author. Baltimore, F. Lucas, jun. [1831] 224 p. MB-FA; MH; MoSW; TNP; ViU. 10692

---- Life of Patrick Henry. By William Wirt. 4th ed., corr. by the author. New York, M'Elrath & Bangs, 1831. 443 p. ArVb; Ct; MdBJ; PP; TNP. 10693

---- Sketches of the life and character of Patrick Henry. By William Wirt. 5th ed., corr. by the author. New York, McElrath & Bangs, 1831. 443 p. MBC; WvC. 10694

Wiseman, N.
Letters to John Poynder upon his work entitled "Popery in alliance with heathenism." Philadelphia, 1831. PPL. 10695

Wisner, Benjamin B[lydenburg], 1794-1835.
Influence of religion on liberty. A discourse in commemoration of the landing of the Pilgrims, delivered at Plymouth, December 22, 1830. Boston, Perkins & Marvin, 1831. 36 p. CtHT; DLC; MBC; RPB; WHi. 10696

Witherell, George.
An impartial statement of the facts in the case of Rev. George Witherell, pastor of the Baptist Church in the Town of Hartford, Washington County, New York in relation to the outrage committed on his family... Boston, Pub. at the office of the Boston Press,

1831. 24 p. DLC; MB; MBC; MBNEH; MH. 10697

Withers, Alexander Scott, 1792-1865.
Chronicles of border warfare, or A history of the settlement by the whites, or northwestern Virginia: and of the Indian wars and massacres, in that section of the state; with reflections, anecdotes, &c. By Alexander S. Withers. Clarksburg, Va., J. Israel, 1831. 319 (2) p. GEU; InHi; MH; OFH; ViU. 10698

Withington, Leonard, 1789-1885.
A Sermon preached at the annual election, May 25, 1831, before His Excellency Levi Lincoln, Governor, His Honor Thomas L. Winthrop, Lieutenant Governor, The Honorable Council, and the Legislature of Massachusetts, by Leonard Withington. Boston, Dutton & Wentworth, prs. to the state, 1831. 48 p. CSmH; IU; NjR; PHi; WHi. 10699

The wonders of the universe; or, Curiosities of nature and art; including memoirs and anecdotes of wonderful and eccentric characters of every age and nation from the earliest period to the present time. New York, Solomon King, 1831. 439 p. MB; NIC-M; Nj; RLa; TNV. 10700

Wood, Benjamin, 1772-1849.
A review of Dr. Wood's letters to Dr. Taylor on the permission of sin. Together with remarks on Dr. Billamy's treatise on the same subject. 50 p. Ct; IaDU; MB; NjP; VTU. 10701

Wood, Samuel R.
Letter from Samuel R. Wood, to Thomas Kittera, esq., chairman of a Joint committee of councils, on the subject of the sale of the Walnut-street prison: with some observations on the necessity of a new system of police for the city and county of Philadelphia. Philadelphia, J. W. Allen, 1831. 13 p. MHi; NjR; PHi; WHi. 10702

Wood, Thomas.
The mosaic history of the creation of the world. Illustrated by discoveries and experiments derived from the present enlightened state of science... Rev. and imp. by the Rev. J. P. Durbin. 1st Amer., from the 2d London ed. New York, M'Elrath & Bangs, 1831. 409 p. IHi; KyLx; NNUT; PU; WHi. 10703

Woodbridge, William Channing, 1794-1845.
A lecture on vocal music as a branch of common education... By Wm. Channing Woodbridge. Boston, Hilliard, Gray, Little and Wilkins, 1831. 25 p. DLC; NjN. 10704

---- ...Modern Atlas, on a new plan; to accompany the system of Universal geography; a new ed., imp. by Wm. Channing Woodbridge...exhibiting, in connection with the outlines of countries, the prevailing religions, forms of government, and degrees of civilization...4th ed. Hartford, Oliver D. Cooke, 1831. MH; TxUT. 10705

---- Preparatory lessons for beginners: or, First steps to geography, by W. C. Woodbridge. [1831] 36 p. DLC. 10706

---- Remarks on vocal music, as a branch of common education ... Boston, 1831. PPL. 10707

---- School Atlas... Hartford, J. Beach, 1831. 7 p. MiU. 10708

---- Rudiments of geography... By Wm. C. Woodbridge, A.M.

...15th ed., rev. and imp. Hartford, Oliver D. Cooke & co., 1831. 208 p. MH; NNC. 10709

---- A system of universal geography, on the principles of comparison and classification. By William Channing Woodbridge ... 4th ed., illus. with maps and engravings; and accompanied by an atlas. ...Hartford, O. D. Cooke & co., 1831. 336 p. CU; FTU; ICBB; MB; NjR. 10710

Woodhouselee, Alexander Fraser Tyler, lord, 1747-1813.
Elements of general history, ancient and modern. By Alexander Fraser Tyler, F.R.S.E. ... With a continuation, terminating at the demise of King George III, 1820. By Rev. Edward Nares, D.D. ...To which are added a succinct history of the United States; with additions and alterations by an American gentleman. ...With an improved table of chronology; a comparative view of ancient and modern geography; and questions on each section. Adapted for the use of schools and academies by an experienced teacher. Stereotyped by T. H. Carter & Co., Boston. Concord, N.H., Horatio Hill & Co., 1831. 527, 44 p. NAnge; OOxM; TxH; UPB; ViU. 10711

Woodruff, Samuel.
Journal of a tour to Malta, Greece, Asia Minor, Carthage, Algiers, Port Mahon, and Spain, in 1828... To which is appended, an account of the distribution of the cargo of provisions and clothing to the suffering Greeks, by the agents of the Greek committee of the city of New York, sent in the brig Herald, May 1828. Hartford, Cooke & co., 1831. 283 p. CtHT; KHi; NNA; OC; RPA. 10712

Woods, Alva, 1794-1887.
Inauguration as President of the University of Alabama, Tuscaloosa, April 12, 1831. [Tuscaloosa? 1831] 4 p. AU. 10713

---- Introductory address, delivered before the Lyceum of Tuscaloosa, Alabama, June 11, 1831. [Tuscaloosa? 1831] 20 p. AU. 10714

Woods, Leonard, 1774-1854.
The Great encouragement to ministerial effort. A sermon delivered at the installation of the Rev. Thomas Mather Smith as pastor of the Presbyterian Church, Catskill, N.Y. By Leonard Woods, D.D., Professor of Christian Theology in the Theological Seminary, Andover. Andover, Pr. by Flagg & Gould, 1831. 21 p. CoU; ICN; NjR; PPPrHi; RPB. 10715

---- Hinderance to the Spread of the Gospel. A sermon delivered at the annual meeting of the American Board of Commissioners for Foreign Missions. New Haven, Conn. October 5, 1831. By Leonard Woods, D.D....Andover, Pr. by Flagg & Gould, 1831. 19 p. MBC; NcMHi; PPPrHi; RPB; VtMidSM. 10716

---- Importance of a Minister's Reputation. A sermon delivered at the installation of the Rev. Nathaniel Hewit, D.D. as Pastor of the Second Congregational Church of Christ, in Bridgeport, Conn., Dec. 1, 1830. By Leonard Woods, D.D., Professor of Christian Theology in the Theological Seminary, Andover. Andover, Pr. by Flagg & Gould, 1831. 22 p. CoU; ICN; MH; PPPrHi; RPB. 10717

---- A sermon on the death of Jeremiah Euarts, Esq., corresponding Secretary of A.B.C.F. M., delivered in Andover, July 31, 1831, by appointment of the Prudential Committee. By Leonard Woods, D.D....Andover (Mass.), Pr. by Flagg & Gould, 1831. 27 p. GDecCT; MB; PHi; RPB; WHi. 10718

Wood's almanac for the year 1832. ...Calculated for the latitude and meridian of New York, by Joshua Sharp. New York, Samuel Wood & sons [1831] (35) p. MWA; NNA. 10719

Woodward, E.

A brief view of Methodist Episcopacy, in which their arbitrary and unscriptural form of government as laid down in the discipline of 1828, is clearly brought to light. Lexington, Pr. by Herndon & Savary, 1831. 40 p. ChU. 10720

Woodworth, Samuel, 1785-1842.

American festivals, games, and amusements... New York, 1831. MDeeP. 10721

---- Melodies, duets, trios, songs, and ballads, pastoral, amatory, sentimental, patriotic, religious, and miscellaneous. Together with metrical epistles, tales and recitations. 3d ed. New York, for the author by Elliot & Palmer, 1831. MB; MH; NBuG; OUrC; TxU. 10722

Worcester, Joseph Emerson, 1784-1865.

A comprehensive pronouncing and explanatory dictionary of the English language, with pronouncing vocabularies of classical and scripture proper names. By J. E. Worcester. Boston, Hilliard, Gray, Little, and Wilkins, 1831. 400 p. CSt; CtHT; LShU; MH. 10723

---- ---- Burlington Vt., O. Goodrich, 1831. MH; NR; VtHi; VtU. 10724

---- ---- 2d ed. New York, Collins & Hannay; 1831. 400 p. MBAt; MNowdHi; NcAS; Nh-Hi. 10725

---- Elements of Geography, ancient and modern with an atlas. By J. E. Worcester. A new ed. Boston, Hilliard, Gray, Little, and Wilkins, 1831. 324 p. CSt; DLC; KAStB; MiD-B; TNP. 10726

---- Elements of history, ancient and modern: with a chart and tables of history included within the volume. By J. E. Worcester ... Boston, Hilliard, Gray, and company, 1831. 403 p. CSt; CLU; MdW; OMC; P; VtBrt. 10727

---- Epitome of history. 3d ed. Cambridge, Hilliard & Brown, 1831. MH. 10728

---- Historical atlas accompanying Epitome of history. 3d ed. Cambridge, Hilliard & Brown, 1831. MH; NjR; PNAZmHi. 10729

---- Outlines of scripture geography. Boston, 1831. MB; PPL. 10730

---- Worcester's modern atlas. Boston, Hilliard, Gray, Little & Wilkins [1831] MH. 10731

Worcester, Noah, 1758-1837.

Causes and evils of contentions unveiled in letters to Christians, by Noah Worcester. Boston, Gray & Bowen, 1831. 120 p. CBPSR; IEG; MBC; Nh-Hi; NhPet; PMA. 10732

---- The doctrine of pronouns applied to Christ's testimony of himself. 2d ed., 1st Ser. No. 15. Pr. for the American Unitarian Association. Boston, Gray & Bowen, 1831. 24 p. MB-FA; MB-HP; MMeT-Hi; MeBat; MNF. 10733

Worcester, Samuel, 1793-1844.

A first book of geography, by

Samuel Worcester...2d ed, with imp. Boston, Crocker & Brewster; New York, Jonathan Leavitt, 1831. 80 p. CtHWatk; DLC; MH; NNC; TxU-T. 10734

---- A second book for reading and spelling. By Samuel Worcester. New ed. Boston, Richardson, Lord & Holbrook, 1831. 144 p. DLC. 10735

---- The Young Astronomer, designed for common schools. Illustrated by cuts. By Samuel Worcester. Author of several popular school books. Boston, Richardson, Lord & Holbrook, 1831. 80 p. DLC; MH; NcHiC; PHi. 10736

Worcester, Samuel Thomas, 1804-1882.

Worcester's spelling book. A spelling book for the United States of America by Samuel Worcester. Boston Crocker & Brewster and Carter, Hendee, and Babcock, 1831. 168 p. CtHWatk; MWbor; OMC; RP. 10737

---- Sequel to the spelling book. By S. T. Worcester. Boston, Hilliard, Gray, Little, and Co., 1831. 128 p. DLC; MB; MWey. 10738

Worcester Historical Society. Incorporated, Feb. 19, 1831. Worcester, 1831. MWHi. 10739

Worthington, Ohio. Reformed Medical College.

The reformed practice of medicine as taught at the reformed medical colleges... By professors and members of the reformed medical colleges in New York and Worthington, Ohio. Boston, 1831. 2 vols. in 1. MH; NBMS; NRU-M; RPM; WU-M. 10740

Wrentham, Mass., Church in the North Parish.

Report of a committee of the church on the reply of the Rev. Moses Thacher to their request to administer to them the Lord's Supper, as published in the Boston Telegraph of Feb. 9, 1831. Boston, Peirce & Parker, 1831. 21 p. MB; MH. 10741

[Wright, Alfred], 1788-1853.

Chahta ikhananchi, or the Choctaw instructor: containing a brief summary of Old Testament history and biography; with practical reflections, in the Choctaw language. By a missionary. Utica, Press of William Williams, 1831. 157 p. MBAt; NN; OMC. 10742

---- Chahta vba istl taloa holisso, or Choctaw hymn-book. Utica, Wm. Williams, 1831. Boston, 1833 (Pilling, Muskhogean Languages, p. 99) is named "second edition." 10743

Wright, E.

A review of the most important events relating to the rise and progress of the United Society... See McNemar, Richard, 1770-1839.

Wright, Frances.

Course of popular lectures as delivered by Frances Wright. With three addresses. 4th ed. New York, Pub. at the office of the Free Enquirer, Hall of Science, 1831. 239 p. ICP; PPM. 10744

---- Supplement course of lectures, containing the last four lectures delivered in the United States, by Frances Wright. New York, Wright & Owen, 1831. 21 p. ICP; NBQ; NN; PPM. 10745

Wyatt, William Edward, 1789-1864.

The Christian Altar or Offices of Devotion for the use of

persons using the Lord's Supper together with a treatise relating to that Sacrament & directions for the Communicants daily walk with God by Wm. E. Wyatt, D.D., Baltimore, E. J. Coale, 1831. 200 p. GDecCT; MdBS; MdHi; ScCMu. 10746

Wyatt, Rev. Dr.
Morning visits to the rector's study; or, conversations between a clergyman, and a parishioner with his friend, on the subject of baptism. By Rev. Dr. Wyatt. Pr. by John D. Toy, 1831. 36 p. MdBD. 10747

Wylie, Andrew, 1789-1851.
A discourse delivered before the Indiana Historical Society in the Hall of the House of Representatives at its annual meeting on Saturday, 11th Dec. 1831. By Andrew Wylie, D.D. Indianapolis, Pr. by A. F. Morrison, 1831. 26 p. In; InHi; MiU; OCHP; WHi. 10748

X Y Z

Xenophon.
The Cryopaedia; translated by the Hon. Maurice Ashley Cooper, in two volumes. New York, J. & J. Harper, 1831. 2 vols. CtHTW; MoSpD; NN; TxH. 10749

---- Xenophon. "in 2 volumes." Vol. 1. The anabasis; tr. by Edwards Spelman: Vol. 2. The Cyroaedia; tr. by Maurice Ashley Cooper. New York, J. & J. Harper, 1831. 2 vols. CSdl; IU; ICU; MNawd; MB; NL; NN; PPA; WHi. 10750

Yale University.
Catalogue of books belonging to the Calliopean Society. Yale College, June, 1831. New Haven, Pr. by H. Howe [1831] 38 p. Ct; CtY. 10751

---- Catalogue of books belonging to the Linonian Society. Yale college, October, 1831. New Haven, Pr. by Baldwin & Treadway, 1831. 40 p. CtY. 10752

---- Commencement, Order of exercises, September 1831. New Haven, H. Howe [1831] 4 p. CtY. 10753

---- Meeting of the class of 1821 on the annual commencement of the college, September 14, 1831. New Haven, H. Howe, 1831. 7 p. M; MHi. 10754

---- Orations before the Phi Beta Kappa Society, 1831. New Haven, H. Howe, 1831. PPL. 10755

Yandell, Lunsford Pitts.
An introductory lecture on the advantages and pleasures of the study of chemistry, delivered in the chemical laboratory of Transylvania University on the 11th Nov. 1831, and pub. at the request of the class. By Lunsford P. Yandell, M.D. Lexington, Pr. by N. L. Finnell & J. F. Herendon, 1831. 26 p. KyDC; KyU; MiD-B; OC; TxU. 10756

...The Yankee. The farmer's almanack for the year of our Lord 1832...By Thomas Spofford ...Boston, Willard Felt & Co., [1831] 36 p. MWA; PPL; VtMidbC; WHi; WaSp. 10757

Yates, William.
Memoirs of the early life of John Chamberlain, late missionary in India; with his diary of religious exercises...Abr. from Calcutta ed. Boston, J. Loring, 1831. 204 p. GDecCT; MB; NNMr; NcU; OClW. 10758

York Manufacturing Company.

By-laws. Boston, 1831. MH. 10759

Young, James Hamilton.
Map of the U.S. Philadelphia, S. Augustus Mitchell, 1831. ICHi; PHi. 10759a

---- The tourist's pocket map of Pennsylvania, exhibiting its internal improvements, roads, distances &c. Philadelphia, 1831- 2 p. NIC; PHi. 10760

Young, John Clarke, 1803-1857.
An address to the senior class, delivered at the commencement in Centre College, September 22d, 1831... Danville, Ky., Pr. at J. J. Polk's office, 1831. 15 p. DLC; KyDC; MH-AH; NjR; PPPrHi. 10761

---- Redemption by the blood of Christ; a sermon preached ... 1831. Lexington, Pr. by T. T. Skillman, 1831. 16 p. KyDC; PPM; PPPrHi. 10762

Young, Richard.
Remarks on the contemplated communication between the Atlantic ocean and the waters of the river Ohio. By Richard Young. Richmond, Pr. by T. W. White, 1831. 16 p. Vi. 10763

The young communicant's assistant, or 100 questions and answers suitable for young persons about to commune at the Lord's table for the first time. By a member of the Associate Reformed Church... Pittsburgh, Johnston & Stockton, 1831. 18, 35, 62 p. ICP. 10764

The young gardeners; to which is added The heedless girl. New Haven, S. Babcock, Sidney's press [1831?] 23 p. CtY. 10765

Young, James, comp.
A history of the most interesting events in the rise and progress of Methodism, in Europe and America. Compiled by James Youngs, A. M.... 2d ed. with additions and alterations. New Haven, Daniel McLeod, 1831. 468 p. GEU-T; IEG; MB; OClWHi; PPLT; TNMPH; ViRU. 10766

The Youth's instructer and Sabbath School and Bible class assistant... New York, Emory, 1831. 3 vols. CtMW. 10767

Youth's Keepsake; A Christmas and New Year's gift for young people. ... Boston, Carter & Hendee, 1831. 216 p. ArL; CtHWatk; ICU; NjR; PHi. 10768

Zane, Sarah.
On the will of Sarah Zane. Philadelphia, 1831. PSC-Hi. 10769

Zavala D. Lorenzo de, 1788-1836.
Ensayo historico de las revoluciones de Magico deode 1808 hasta 1830. Lord Lorenzo de Zavala. Paris, Imp. de P. Dupont et G. Laguienie [etc.] 1831-1832. 2 vols. in 1. DLC; OCHP. 10770

Zeuner, Charles H.
Church music, consisting of new original anthems, motets and chants, for public worship. By C. H. Zeuner. Boston, Richardson, Lord & Holbrook, 1831. 151 p. ICN; MB; MCon; MFai; MeLewB; MH. 10771

---- The evening gun. Words by Thomas Moore, adapted to a favorite melody. Arranged for the pianoforte by Ch. Zeuner. Boston, C. Bradlee, 3 p. MB; MNF. 10772

---- Otis's quick step. Boston, 1831. 1 p. MB; MH-Mus. 10773

The Zion Songster: a collection of Hymns and Spiritual Songs... Compiled by Peter D. Myers. (5 lines quote) New York, M'-Elrath & Bangs, 1831. 352 p. NNUT; Nh; OrSaw. 10774

Zumpt, Carl Gottlob.
A grammar of the Latin language...By C. G. Zumpt. 2d American from the latest German ed. New York, G. & C. & H. Carvill, 1831. xi, 242 p. ICU; KWiU; MH; OMC; PU. 10775